I0896935

Craftsmen and Jewelers in the Middle and Lower Danube Region (6th to 7th Centuries)

East Central and Eastern Europe in the Middle Ages, 450–1450

General Editors

Florin Curta and Dušan Zupka

VOLUME 67

The titles published in this series are listed at *brill.com/ecee*

Craftsmen and Jewelers in the Middle and Lower Danube Region (6th to 7th Centuries)

By

Daniela Tănase

BRILL

LEIDEN | BOSTON

This volume is a revised and enlarged English version of the book *Prelucrarea metalelor în lumea barbară la Dunărea Mijlocie și Inferioară în sec. VI–VII* (Timișoara: Excelsior Art, 2010).

Cover illustration: stone mold for casting Maltese crosses discovered in the settlement from Botoșana, Suceava County, Romania (second half of the 6th century–first half of the 7th century). Museum of the History of Moldova Iași. Photo by Ionuț Ionescu.

Library of Congress Cataloging-in-Publication Data

Names: Tănase, Daniela, author. | Tănase, Daniela. Prelucrarea metalelor în lumea barbară la Dunărea Mijlocie și Inferioară în secolele VI–VII.
Title: Craftsmen and jewelers in the Middle and Lower Danube region (6th to 7th centuries) / by Daniela Tănase.
Other titles: Prelucrarea metalelor în lumea barbară la Dunărea Mijlocie și Inferioară în secolele VI–VII. English
Description: Leiden ; Boston : Brill, [2021] | Series: East Central and Eastern Europe in the Middle Ages, 1450–1450, 1872–8103 ; volume 67 | Revised and enlarged, English version of the book published ten years ago in Romanian as Prelucrarea metalelor în lumea barbară la Dunărea Mijlocie și Inferioară în sec. VI–VII. | Includes bibliographical references.
Identifiers: LCCN 2020040606 (print) | LCCN 2020040607 (ebook) | ISBN 9789004380370 (hardback) | ISBN 9789004436930 (ebook)
Subjects: LCSH: Metal trade—Romania—History—To 1500. | Metal trade—Europe—History—To 1500. | Metal-work, Medieval—Romania. |Metal-work, Medieval—Europe. | Archaeology, Medieval—Romania. | Archaeology, Medieval—Europe. | Romania—Antiquities. | Europe—Antiquities.
Classification: LCC HD9506.R72 T3613 2021 (print) | LCC HD9506.R72 (ebook) | DDC 338.4/767109398809021—dc23
LC record available at https://lccn.loc.gov/2020040606
LC ebook record available at https://lccn.loc.gov/2020040607

Typeface for the Latin, Greek, and Cyrillic scripts: "Brill". See and download: brill.com/brill-typeface.

ISSN 1872-8103
ISBN 978-90-04-38037-0 (hardback)
ISBN 978-90-04-43693-0 (e-book)

Copyright 2021 by Daniela Tănase. Published by Koninklijke Brill NV, Leiden, The Netherlands.
Koninklijke Brill NV incorporates the imprints Brill, Brill Hes & De Graaf, Brill Nijhoff, Brill Rodopi, Brill Sense, Hotei Publishing, mentis Verlag, Verlag Ferdinand Schöningh and Wilhelm Fink Verlag.
Koninklijke Brill NV reserves the right to protect this publication against unauthorized use. Requests for re-use and/or translations must be addressed to Koninklijke Brill NV via brill.com or copyright.com.

This book is printed on acid-free paper and produced in a sustainable manner.

Contents

Acknowledgements

This volume represents the revised and enlarged, English version of the book I have published ten years ago in Romanian as *Prelucrarea metalelor în lumea barbară la Dunărea Mijlocie și Inferioară în sec.* VI–VII (Timișoara: Excelsior Art, 2010). To a great extent, that book was based on the doctoral dissertation that I have defended in November 2006 at the "Vasile Pârvan" Institute of Archeology in Bucharest, having as adviser Dr. Radu Harhoiu, whom I also thank for this collaboration.

Special thanks to Professor Florin Curta (University of Florida, USA) for offering the possibility of publishing the English version, as well as for suggestions and bibliographic material made available.

Sincere thanks to my colleagues who helped me with suggestions, information and bibliographic material: Szabolcs Nagy (National Museum of History of Transylvania, Cluj-Napoca), Rodica Oanţă Marghitu, Silviu Oţa (National History Museum of Romania, Bucharest), Monica Dejan (Bucovina Museum Suceava), Andrei Măgureanu, Erwin Gáll, Daniel Spânu ("Vasile Pârvan" Institute of Archeology, Bucharest), Niculina Dinu ("Carol I" Museum, Brăila), Florin Mărginean (Arad County Museum Complex, Arad), Senica Ţurcanu (Museum of the History of Moldova, Iași).

My thanks go also to Coralia Costaș ("Moldova" National Museum Complex, Iași) for the contribution to the translation of the text into English.

Special thanks also to all those who contributed to the illustration: Silviu Saftu (Banat National Museum, Timișoara) and Márton Ferenczi (SC Transarcheo SRL, Cluj-Napoca) for the drawing of objects; Sergiu Odenie (National Museum of History of Transylvania, Cluj-Napoca), Marius Amarie (National History Museum of Romania, Bucharest), Milan Șepeţan (Banat National Museum, Timișoara), Nelu Scripciuc (Arad County Museum Complex, Arad), Ionuţ Ionescu (Museum of the History of Moldova, Iași) for artifact photographs; Daniel Spânu ("Vasile Pârvan" Institute of Archeology, Bucharest) for the maps layout.

Daniela Tănase

Figures

Introduction

In Europe, in general, as well as in Romania, in particular, metalworking and of craftsmen practicing ironmongery and goldsmithing in the early Middle Ages have preoccupied scholars especially during the second half of the 20th century. This was largely the result, after World War II, of archaeological excavations on a large scale, which in turn led to the accumulation of a very large quantity of artifacts pertaining to the whole set of daily activities. Equally important in this respect was the systematic application of archaeometrical approaches, particularly metallographic and physico-chemical analyses.

The first remains related to metalworking that have been found on the present territory of Romania are the molds discovered in Felnac (Arad County) in the late 19th century. The most notable discovery, however, is the grave with tools from the cemetery excavated in the early 20th century in Band, tomb no. 10 (Mureș County). In the lands to the south and to east from the Carpathian Mountains, the first archaeological discoveries pertaining to metalworking were made between the two world wars – molds, tools, smelting furnaces, and wasters. Those were either settlement or isolated (stray) finds. At the current stage of research, when mapping all known discoveries of this type from Romania it becomes clear that one deals with different cultural areas, and different populations inhabiting those territories. However, irrespective of the cultural area, there is a clear Byzantine influence on local metalworking.

Despite such early beginnings, in Romania the early medieval metalworking has not so far been the subject of systematic research in Romania, especially not within a narrowly defined chronological span and with a detailed approach to the problems raised by metalworking practices. That is why I chose to study the 6th and 7th centuries, a period of important political, military, demographic, and cultural changes in both the Middle and the Lower Danube regions, which historians tend to regard as marking the beginning of the Middle Ages in those parts of the European continent. Between 500 and 700, a number of Germanic kingdoms disappeared (Herules, Lombards, Gepids), and new power structures emerged which are associated to steppe nomads (Avars and Bulgars). Those steppe nomads posed a greater and much more serious threat to the Byzantine Empire than any of the Germanic peoples that had for decades been under its influence. All those changes significantly altered the cultural relations between the Byzantines and the populations in the lands to the north from the Danube River. My goal is to identify the differences and

© DANIELA TĂNASE, 2021 | DOI:10.1163/9789004436930_002

similarities between the archaeological evidence of different populations in the Middle and Lower Danube regions, with a special emphasis on metalworking and burial practices.

I chose to look at both the Carpathian Basin (the Middle Danube region) and the territory outside the Carpathian Mountains (Lower Danube region) because of the extraordinary abundance of archaeological evidence, and the great potential for comparative analysis. Several settlements have been excavated in Moldavia (eastern Romania, where excavations were carried out by Dan Gh. Teodor and Ioan Mitrea) or Walachia (southern Romania, where excavations were carried out by Suzana Dolinescu-Ferche, Victor Teodorescu, and Margareta Constantiniu), and numerous tools as well as wasters discovered in each one of them bespeak the development of local crafts. My approach is different from that of most other Romanian scholars, who have examined the topic, in that all of them chose a very broad chronological span (between the 4th and the 11th century), with in-depth analysis of either the metalworking techniques or the changes in the social conditions of production. Since the last significant studies devoted to this subject have been published in 1997 by Dan Gh. Teodor and Ştefan Olteanu, the number of finds has increased considerably. Time is ripe not only for an update, but for an entirely new perspective, which will take into consideration not just the technological aspects of ironworking and goldsmithing, but also the specific economic and social circumstances and implications.

The catalog in the second part of this book includes not only finds from Romania, but also from the neighboring territories in Hungary, Serbia, the Republic of Moldova, Bulgaria, and Ukraine. In doing so, my goal was to offer a solid base for comparison of technologies employed in producing dress accessories, the most expressive and innovative domain of the metalworking during the 6th and 7th centuries. I paid particular attention to all other details of the archaeological evidence that could in one way or another relate to the production of dress accessories. I treated separately tools from settlements and graves, and I advanced a new tool typology. On that basis, I attempted to reconstruct the production process and the main techniques employed by craftsmen to decorate dress accessories, a topic that shifted the emphasis to cultural influences from several directions – the Byzantine Empire, the steppe world and the Merovingian environment of Central Europe.

The lands on either side of the Carpathian Mountains formed an area of cultural interaction during the early Middle Ages, with different technological options in the west and in the east, respectively. A careful study of the archaeological evidence will answer the fundamental question of why rudimentary melting techniques and mold casting were preferred in the regions outside the

Carpathian Basin. Conversely, such a study will explain why in the Carpathian Basin, most dress accessories were produced by pressing. Although several scholars have already noted such technological choices, there has been no attempt to study the evidence of Central and Eastern Europe comparatively. My goal is therefore to point out those cultural practices that would resonate with technological choices made both inside and outside the Avar Qaganate. Of great importance in this respect are the numerous metallographic analyses of both tools and products, which have been found on several sites of Central and Eastern Europe. On the other hand, the use of chemical analyses raised the thorny question of the origin and supply of raw materials, as well as the equally difficult question of alloying recipes, both topics discussed in this book.

Another important category of archaeological sources is that of burial assemblages with tools. My goal is to compare tools found in graves to those found in settlements, in order to understand why such implements were deposited in the 6th and 7th centuries in graves, such as those found at Band, Felnac (Arad County) and Sărata Monteoru (Buzău County). I will demonstrate that the symbolism of those tools is directly related to the various metalworking techniques that the craftsmen were supposed and expected to master. In fact, tools found in graves cover the entire range of metalworking techniques: blacksmithing, bronze casting, plating, and gilding. Craftsmen produced not only jewelry and weapons, but also tools and household utensils. A few crafts are more important than others in terms of tools deposited in graves, as well as of industrial activities documented for settlements – blacksmithing, silversmithing, and goldsmithing. Evidence suggests that the distinction between these specialties, especially between blacksmithing and goldsmithing, was quite fluid, which means that blacksmiths could produce jewels, and jewelers were able to produce tools and weapons. Although the structure of the toolkit mainly indicates blacksmithing activities, there are also tools that could be used to create ornaments.

The deposition of tools in graves was certainly symbolic, but that symbolism was undoubtedly related to the status of the craftsman and to his social role in the community. In other words, the ritual must have brought to mind a series of cultural practices without which it would have made no sense. The fact that only the graves of a small number of individuals were equipped with tools is a clear indication not only of their high rank, but most likely, of certain occupations that were assigned to them, whether or not they had practiced them during lifetime. In short, the archaeological evidence highlights the economic and military role of craftsmen. In this book, I shall discuss the significance of the deposition of tools along with such objects as the helmet from Band or the pieces of armor from Kölked-Feketekapu B and from Kunszentmárton.

Another interesting area of current research is the study of matches between ornaments for certain types of dress accessories or parts thereof, many of which were cast in molds found at considerable distance from each other. This indicates the existence of regional decorative styles. In the light of archaeological sources, several regions with increased activity in terms of metalworking can be identified, which suggests a concentration of demand, and therefore of social and political entities: the sub-Carpathian region of Moldavia, the south-eastern part of Walachia, and central Transylvania. In this respect, I shall also address the issue of large-scale imitation of Byzantine dress accessories, both in the Carpathian Basin (where mainly pressing on dies was used for producing imitations) and in the extra-Carpathian area of Romania and the neighboring regions to the east (where imitations were produced primarily by casting in molds). In both cultural areas, Byzantine products were adapted and modified according to different sets of rules as well as technological constraints.

CHAPTER 1

History of the Research

1 Discovery of the First Tombs with Tools

The bronze dies discovered at Adony (Fejér County, Hungary) – the first items that could be linked to the local production of jewels in the Middle Danube region – entered the collections of the Hungarian National Museum in Budapest, in 1876.[1] In respect to the present-day territory of Romania, however, the first items that could be connected to metal processing in the 6th and 7th centuries were discovered in 1899 in the village of Felnac (Arad County), at a short distance from the Mureș River. In 1900, the Hungarian archaeologist József Hampel (1849–1913) published 26 dies from Felnac, which he knew as having been accidentally discovered during land draining works.[2] One year later, László Dömötör, a teacher from Arad, published new information about the Felnac find together with another 17 dies, which had been brought to the Kölcsey Society in Arad.[3] Among the details that Dömötör brought to light, particularly important is the fact that, according to him, the dies had been found together with human and horse bones.[4] The Felnac find were then republished fully by Hampel in his important work on antiquities in Hungary.[5]

In the early 20th century, during the excavations carried out at Gátér (Bács-Kiskun County, Hungary), another grave with tools was discovered. Beside dress accessories, the associated assemblage included eight dies similar to those found in Felnac.[6]

In 1913, István Kovács (1880–1955), at that time a professor at the Reformed Theological College in Cluj, published the results of his 1906 and 1907

1 Zsófia Rácz, *Die Goldschmiedegräber der Awarenzeit* (Mainz: Verlag des Römisch-Germanischen Zentralmuseums, 2014), 5.

2 József Hampel, "Emlékek és leletek. Újabb haza leletek az avar uralom korából [Relics and artifacts. Recent findings from the period of the avars's domination]," *Archaeologiai Értesitő* 20 (1900), 117–123.

3 László Dömötör, "Ujabb lemezsajtoló bronzmintár Fönlakról [Newer bronze dies from Fónlak]," *Archaeologiai Értesitő* 21 (1901), 63. The Kölcsey Society was a cultural association established in 1882 and dedicated to local history.

4 Dömötör, "Ujabb lemezsajtoló bronzmintár Fönlakról," 66.

5 Hampel, *Altertümer des frühen Mittelalters in Ungarn*, 3 vols (Braunschweig: Verlag Friedrich Vieweg und Sohn, 1905), 2: 392–396; 3: 747–751.

6 Elek Kada, "Gátéri (Kun-Kisszállási) temető a régibb középkorból [Gátér (Kun-Kisszállás) cemetery from the early Middle Ages]," *Archaeologiai Értesitö* 25 (1905), 368–370.

© DANIELA TĂNASE, 2021 | DOI:10.1163/9789004436930_003

excavations of an inhumation cemetery in Band (Mureș County). Most graves had been robbed in the early Middle Ages, but one of them still had a helmet and a toolbox containing pliers, hammers, anvils, drills (including mechanically driven drills), fragments of bronze sheet and slag.[7] Kovács described the grave goods in great detail and rightly assumed that it was the grave of a blacksmith.[8]

2 The History of Research regarding Burials with Tools (First Half of the 20th Century)

Nándor Fettich (1900–1971), a Hungarian goldsmith turned archaeologist, first dealt with the dies discovered in Felnac, as well as with a gold ring decorated in Animal Style II with a dentil ornament, that Kovács found in another grave of the Band cemetery, in a paper discussing the ornamental styles of the Avar age. He compared the Band ring with another from Keszthely (Zala County, Hungary),[9] and drew important chronological conclusions from that in terms of dating the Band cemetery (including the grave of the craftsman). In a note, Fettich mentioned that some of the Felnac dies had been brought to the Hungarian National Museum in Budapest, while others were in the local museum in Arad. In 1925, when he undertook a study trip to Romania, he also visited Arad, and noted that seven of the items said to have been in the local museum had meanwhile been lost.[10] Fettich's information was later confirmed by the archaeological gazetteer of the Arad County.[11]

Fettich's lifetime goal was the analysis of the ornamental styles in the Carpathian Basin, and he distinguished between Byzantine, Germanic and Avar influences, as well as their different combinations. At the same time, he emphasized the importance of the steppe culture and claimed that when the Avars settled in the Carpathian Basin new artistic forms, new technologies and new fashions appeared, with the belt becoming the most important

7 István Kovács, "A mezőbándi ásatások. Őskori telepnyomok és temető, La-Tène ízlésű temetkezés, népvándorláskori temető. [The excavations in Mezőband. Traces of settlements and cemeteries dated to the Bronze Age, a Latène burial, and a Great Migration-age cemetery]," *Dolgozatok Cluj* 4 (1913), 398–403.

8 Kovács, "A mezőbándi ásatások," 428.

9 Nándor Fettich, *Das awarenzeitliche Kunstgewerbe in Ungarn* (Archaeologia Hungarica, 1) (Budapest, 1926), 47–48.

10 Fettich, *Das awarenzeitliche Kunstgewerbe*, 49.

11 *Repertoriul arheologic al Mureșului Inferior. Județul Arad* [The archaeological repertoire of the Lower Mureș. Arad County] (Timișoara: Editura Orizonturi Universitare, 1999), 68.

part of the dress.[12] Since the belt was typically decorated with mounts, Fettich used his goldsmithing expertise to describe in detail how such mounts were produced by means of pressing with dies such as those discovered in Felnac and Gátér, and he stressed the importance of Byzantine influences on Avar art and craftsmanship.[13]

Meanwhile, two more graves with a rich array of tools were found in Hungary. One of them was discovered in 1928 in Kunszentmárton (Jász-Nagykun-Szolnok County). Many of the tools and dies among the grave goods have good analogies in Felnac and Band.[14] The other grave was found during Gyula Rhé's excavation of a large inhumation cemetery in Jutas (now included into Veszprém).[15] The Jutas cemetery was among the first to produce skeletal material that was examined by professional anthropologists. On the basis of its skull, the skeleton in the jeweler's grave was therefore classified as of Mongoloid type.[16]

Shortly afterwards, a number of Merovingian graves with tools were found in Germany, and scholars began to pay attention to the sociological dimension of the burial, particularly to social status. Instrumental in this shift was the 1931 discovery of a grave with tools in Wallerstädten (near Darmstadt, in Germany).[17] The excavator believed that to have been the grave of an individual of a high social rank.[18] Conversely, the grave with tools found in Neuwied (near Koblenz, Germany) also produced weapons. Some interpreted that as an indication that the goldsmith buried there had been a free man, although the excavator did not exclude the possibility of a bondman.[19] The German archaeologist Kurt Böhner (1914–2007), who published the Neuwied grave, first discussed the legal status of goldsmiths in the Merovingian era. Relying on German folk tales, as well as on the story of Wayland the Smith (first attested in the Lay of Völund, the tenth poem in the Poetic Edda, dated to the 9th century at the earliest), Böhner claimed that in Germanic societies, the craftsmen were free.

12 Fettich, *Das awarenzeitliche Kunstgewerbe*, 58.

13 Fettich, *Das awarenzeitliche Kunstgewerbe*, 62.

14 Dezső Csallány, *A Kunszentmártoni avarkori ötvösir* (*Goldschmiedgrab aus der Awarenzeit von Kunszentmárton Ungarn*) [The grave of a goldsmith from the avars time at Kunszentmárton] (Szentes 1933), 49–53.

15 Gyula Rhé, Nándor Fettich, *Jutas und Öskü* (Prag: Seminarium Kondakovianum 1931), 32.

16 Rhé, Fettich, *Jutas und Öskü*, 57–58.

17 Werner Schnellenkamp, "Ein Grabhügel bei Wallerstädten in Hessen-Starkenburg mit Bestattungen der Hallstatt-, Latène- und Merowingerzeit," *Mainzer Zeitschrift* 27 (1932), 63–70. The grave goods are illustrated on page 65, fig. 5.

18 Schnellenkamp, "Ein Grabhügel," 70.

19 Kurt Böhner, "Ein fränkisches Goldschmiedegrab aus dem Neuwieder Becken," *Reinische Vorzeit in Wort und Bild* 2 (1939), 113–119.

3 The Status of Early Medieval Craftsmen in European Historiography

After World War II, the focus of discussion shifted again with the German archaeologist Joachim Werner (1909–1994), who brought the discussion about metalworking in relation to coin minting. Werner first pointed to the presence of coins and scales in Merovingian graves, and in that context drew on the evidence from the Avar-age graves in Jutas and Kunszentmárton. He also mentioned the grave in Band, which he (wrongly) dated to the 6th century and attributed to the Gepids, but had nothing to say either about Felnac or about Gátér.[20]

In 1970, Werner returned to the question with a study entirely dedicated to the craftsmen of the Merovingian era. Like Böhner, Werner believed that goldsmiths were legally free, itinerant craftsmen, who owned their tools, and worked upon commission.[21] However, Werner also explained the distribution of certain types of artifacts as the result either of trade or of long-distance, matrimonial alliances. He believed that on the basis of a particular type of ornament, the area of a particular tribe, and therefore the area of a craftsman's activity could be determined. According to Werner, dies for dress accessories spread around by means of trade.[22]

At about the same time, two other German scholars, Hans Torsten Capelle (1939–2014) and Hayo Vierck (1939–1989) drew comparisons between the molds and the dies of the Merovingian and those of the Viking age. Unlike Werner, they were interested in technology, as well as in the genesis of some regional, specifically Scandinavian and Anglo-Saxon ornamental styles.[23] They brought to the fore an interesting assemblage, a grave with tools (mold, balance, and weights) found at Burton-upon-Humber (North Lincolnshire, UK), which unlike all other graves of craftsmen known until then, contained a female, not a male skeleton. However, Capelle and Vierck did not believe that the woman in question could have been involved in the jewelry production.[24] Vierck, on the other hand, has the merit of bringing the life and work of a

---

20 Joachim Werner, "Waage und Geld in der Merowingerzeit," *Sitzungsberichte der Bayerischen Akademie der Wissenschaften. Philosophisch-historische Klasse* 1 (1954), 25–26; 39–40.

21 Joachim Werner, "Zur Verbreitung frühgeschichtlicher Metallarbeiten (Werkstatt-Wanderhandwerk-Handel-Familienverbindung)," *Antikvarist arkiv* 38 (1970), 68–70.

22 Werner, "Zur Verbreitung," 73–78.

23 Torsten Capelle, Hayo Vierck, "Modeln der Merowinger- und Wikingerzeit," *Frühmittelalterliche Studien* 5 (1971), 43–90.

24 Capelle, Vierck, "Modeln," 71–73 and 77.

Merovingian goldsmith to scholarly attention. Eligius, Bishop of Noyon, was the goldsmith and the minter of the Frankish kings Chlothar II (584–629) and Dagobert I (623–638). He is credited for a number of liturgical utensils, which Vierck analyzed from the point of view of technique and ornamental style.[25] Vierck's study for the first time put together the archaeological and the *contemporaneous* written sources, in an attempt to draw general conclusions about craftsmanship in the 7th century. In doing so, he effectively demonstrated that craftsmen could be, and in this particular case certainly were, members of the elite.

In the 1970s, Viking-age blacksmithing was also a popular topic of research. Michael Müller-Wille studied tools found in Viking-age burial assemblages in Scandinavia. He drew attention to a mechanical drill found in a grave in Vestly (Rogaland, Norway), the only parallel for which is that found in Band.[26] On the basis of the grave goods with which the drill in Vestly was associated (weapons and horse harness), Müller-Wille concluded that in Viking-age societies, blacksmiths had an elevated status; they must have been members of the elite.[27] When publishing the grave of a blacksmith from Hovgärdsberg Vendel (Uppland, Sweden), the Swedish archaeologist Birgit Arrhenius reached a similar conclusion, even though she also claimed that the blacksmith in question was a traveling craftsman, who owned his tools, a reminiscence of Werner's ideas.[28]

Werner's ideas were also echoed by the Slovak archaeologist Vladimír Turčan. According to him, despite the lack of excavated workshops in the 6th- to 7th-century Carpathian Basin, graves of goldsmiths were the only evidence that, given that tools were associated with weapons, those craftsmen were socially free. Like Werner, Turčan believed those craftsmen to have been itinerant, semi-finished products from the Byzantine Empire, which they then finished according to their customers' desire and taste. According to Turčan, the raw material for golden or gilded artifacts came from molten Byzantine *solidi*, which had entered the Carpathian Basin as subsidies paid to the barbarians,

25 Hayo Vierck, "Werke des Eligius," in *Festschrift für Joachim Werner*, 2 vols, ed. Georg Kossack and Ulbert Günter (Munich: C. H. Beck, 1974), 2: p. 309–378.

26 Michael Müller-Wille, "Der frühmittelalterliche Schmied im Spiegel skandinavischer Grabfund," *Frühmittelalterliche Studien* 11 (1977), 159.

27 Müller-Wille, "Der frühmittelalterliche Schmied," 193.

28 Birgit Arrhenius, "Ein Goldschmiedgrab von Hovgardsberg Vendel, Uppland, Schweden," *Frühmittelalterliche Studien* 13 (1979), 393–414.

even though he did not exclude the possibility that gold was mined from the Kremnica Mountains in Slovakia or the Apuseni Mountains in Romania.[29]

Perhaps the most important study regarding the long tradition of graves with tools in Europe was published in the early 1990s by the German archaeologist Joachim Henning. He focused on the late Iron Age (La Tène) as well as the Roman period and included Band in his gazetteer of finds.[30] However, he ignored both Felnac and other similar finds (such as Aradac, Central Banat, Serbia) that had been published in the meantime.

The value of Henning's study rests primarily on his observations about the structure of the grave goods, particularly the idea that the types of tools chosen for deposition were deliberately selected. According to him, the tools available to Merovingian craftsmen were the result of the blending of Roman and Germanic-Celtic traditions of tool making. In that respect, Henning believed that the mechanical drill from Band was a unicum in the Germanic world.[31] Henning also argued that without the legal freedom of the early medieval blacksmiths, the structures of economic life in the later medieval cities in Western Europe could not have come into being.[32]

The legal and social status of craftsmen in Late Antiquity was also the subject of an interesting study by Claus von Carnap-Bornheim. According to the German archaeologist, the social position of Germanic goldsmiths during the first half of the first millennium AD was defined by personal mobility, economic independence, as well as political and military power.[33] The archaeological correlate of the mobility of the craftsmen was represented by artifacts made with the same technology and the same combination of decorative patterns, even though one had to account for the regional preference for certain decorative objects and details. Because they were free to move as they wished, craftsmen could buy their own materials, especially those active in areas close to

29 Vladimir Turčan, "Hroby zlatníkov v 6.–7. storočí v Karpatskej Kotline [Burials of Goldsmith of the 6th–7th centuries AD in the Carpathian Basin]," *Archeologické rozhledy* 36 (1984), 481–489. No evidence exists that gold was mined in either region during the early Middle Ages. The Roman mines in the Apuseni Mountains were not reopened until the Late Middle Ages or the early modern era. Gold washing is a theoretical alternative, but no metallographic analysis has so far been done to prove or disprove that possibility.

30 Joachim Henning, "Schmiedegräber nördlich der Alpen. Germanisches Handwerk zwischen keltischer Tradition und römischen Einfluß," *Saalburg Jahrbuch* 46 (1991), 80.

31 Henning, "Schmiedegräber," 70–73.

32 Henning, "Schmiedegräber," 77.

33 Claus von Carnap-Bornheim, "The Social Position of the Germanic Goldsmith A.D. 0–500," in *Roman Gold and the Development of the Early Germanic Kingdom. Kungliga Vitterhets Historie och Antikvitets Akademien (KVHAA) Konferenser 51*, ed. Bente Magnus (Stockholm: Almqvist & Wiksell International, 2001), p. 263.

the Roman frontier. It was from Roman markets that they thus procured not only their models, but also their tools.[34] The transfer of technology (but also of tools and raw materials) from the Romans to the barbarians thus becomes an argument in favor of the great mobility of the Germanic goldsmiths, which in turn is regarded as an indication of their elevated social status.[35] A similar line of arguments have been put to use in order to prove the great mobility of the Avar-age goldsmiths in the Carpathian Basin, a conclusion drawn on the basis of a careful analysis of the distribution of certain decorative patterns, especially the so-called "dot-comma" motif believed to be of Byzantine origin. That pattern appears repeatedly on several dies from Felnac (hence its other name common among Hungarian archaeologists – the "Felnac type"), but also on dies and belt fittings from sites on the southern shore of Lake Balaton in southern Hungary, as well as in the southern parts of the Tisza Plain, especially in the region of the confluence of the Mureș and Tisza rivers.[36]

However, not everybody agreed with Werner's idea that craftsmen in the early Middle Ages were legally free. In the early 1970s, the German archaeologist Jürgen Driehaus (1927–1986) argued instead that goldsmiths were legally dependent, as indicated in the so-called barbarian lawcodes, such as the Visigothic Code, the Burgundian Laws, *Lex Alamannorum*, as well as the Ripurian and the Salian Laws. In each one of them, the *wergild* for the murder of a goldsmith was different from that for the murder of a free person.[37] According to Driehaus, the tools found in graves must be interpreted in the same manner, especially when not associated with weapons. The Merovingian *aurifex* was an unfree and immobile craftsman, who could be loaned, sold or gifted by his owner.[38] It is important to note that Driehaus's views were adopted by Hans Torsten Capelle for the interpretation of a grave with tools found in Beckum (North Rhine-Westphalia, Germany).[39]

The first monograph on early medieval crafts was published in 1986 by another German archaeologist, Helmut Roth (1941–2003). His book dealt extensively with metalworking, and relied on written sources of the Merovingian era

34 von Carnap-Bornheim, "The Social Position," 265–267.

35 von Carnap-Bornheim, "The Social Position," 276.

36 Éva Garam, *Funde bizantinischer Herkunft in der Awarenzeit vom Ende des 6. bis zum Ende des 7. Jahrhunderts*, (Monumenta Avarorum) 5, (Budapest: Magyar Nemzeti Múzeum, 2001), 116–119.

37 Jürgen Driehaus, "Zum Problem merowingerzeitlicher Goldschmiede," *Nachrichten der Akademie der Wissenschaften in Göttingen phil.-hist. Klasse* 7 (1972), 400–402.

38 Driehaus, "Zum Problem," 403–404.

39 Torsten Capelle, *Das Gräberfeld Beckum I* (Münster-Westfalen: Aschendorff, 1979), 31–32, 49–50; pl. 27.

for the discussion of workshops and craftsmen.[40] Like Driehaus, Roth believed that the Merovingian craftsmen were unfree, and worked as *servi* for kings, noblemen and churchmen.[41]

From an archaeological point of view, it is important to note that recently the discussion has shifted again to the results of archaeometric studies attempting to establish to what extent tools found in graves have been used by the persons with which they were buried. Traseological approaches borrowed from forensic anthropology are now used to identify the degree of wear on tools deposited in graves, often in combination with metallographic analysis, as in the case of the tools in two 6th-century graves from Poysdorf (northeastern Austria) and Brno (Czech Republic).[42]

This is also the approach adopted by the Austrian-Hungarian archaeologist Bendeguz Tobias in his 2008 Ph.D. dissertation from the University of Vienna. Tobias insists the deposition of a toolbox in a grave is first and foremost a demonstration of skill, and a sign of practicing the craft(s). Although, some craftsmen were members of the elite, very rarely were tools used to mark only social rank.[43]

4 Graves with Tools in Early Medieval Europe. The Case of the Avar Qaganate

The number of known graves with tools increased dramatically during the second half of the 20th century, no doubt as a result of the scholarly interest

40 Helmut Roth, *Kunst und Handwerk im frühen Mittelalter* (Stuttgart: Konrad Theiss, 1986), 40–65.

41 Roth, *Kunst und Handwerk*, 128–130.

42 Falko Daim, Mathias Mehofer, Bendeguz Tobias, "Die langobardischen Schmiedegräber aus Poysdorf und Brno. Fragen, Methoden, erste Ergebnisse," in *Die Langobarden. Herrschaft und Identität, Forschungen zur Geschichte des Mittelalters*, eds. Falko Daim and Peter Erhart (Wien: Verlag der Österreichischen Akademie der Wissenschaften, 2005), pp. 201–224.

43 Bendeguz Tobias, "Eliten und Schmiedegräber – Untersuchungen zu frühmittelalterlichen Gräbern mit Schmiedewerkzeugen im Rahmen des Eliteprojektes," in *Aufstieg und Untergang: Zwischenbilanz des Forschungsschwerpunktes "Studien zu Genese und Struktur von Eliten in vor-und frühgeschichtlichen Gesellschaften"*, ed. Markus Egg and Dieter Quast (Mainz: Verlag des Römisch-Germanischen Zentralmuseums, 2009), pp. 143–151; Bendeguz Tobias, *Frühmittelalterliche Gräber mit Beigabe von Schmiede-werkzeugen. Einleitung*. PhD dissertation: Wien 2008, 7–9 (see https://www.academia.edu/24313533/B._Tobias_Frühmittelalterliche_Gräber_mit_Beigabe_von_Schmiedewerkzeugen_Diss._Universität_Wien_2008. Accessed November 11, 2017). Tobias's unpublished dissertation is copiously cited by Zsófia Rácz in her 2014 book on graves of craftsmen in the Avar age.

developing at that same time. Two graves with tools – one with blacksmithing tools, the other with a bronze model (or die) – were found in the early 1950s during the excavation of a large, Early Avar-age cemetery Aradac (near Zrenjanin, in Vojvodina, Serbia).[44] In 1966, the graves with tools from Poysdorf (Austria) and Vestly (Norway) were published.[45] Only five years later, another grave with many tools was published together with the other burial assemblages from the Merovingian cemetery excavated in Hérouvillette (Calvados, France).[46] That is probably the closest analogy to the grave with tools from Band, and the excavator's comments about the sociological interpretation of the Hérouvillette finds may also apply to assemblage from Transylvania.[47]

The number of finds has increased considerably in recent times, particularly in Western and Northern Europe, but the finds have not been always properly published. Most tools have been published separately, usually in studies dedicated to the problem of the deposition of tools in graves. On the other hand, such studies have the tendency to lump together examples from different periods, from the Iron to the Viking Age.[48] The situation is radically different in Central Europe, first and foremost because recent finds of 6th- to 7th-century graves with tools have been properly published in great detail.

The largest number of graves with tools, and some of the most interesting assemblages at that, have been found in Hungary and are dated to the Avar age.[49] A female grave from the cemetery excavated in the early 1970s in Vác

---

44 Sandor Nagy, "Nekropola kod Aradaca iz ranog srednjeg veka [The early medieval cemetery near Aradac]" *Rad Vojvodjanskih Muzeja* 8 (1959), 57 and 62–63; 71 pl. IV. 7–21; 72 pl. V. 1–6; 92 pl. XXV.9–17; 93 pl. XXVI.1–6.

45 Eduard Beninger, "Der Langobardenfriedhof von Poysdorf, Niederösterreich," *Archaeologia Austriaca* 40 (1966), 177–178, 179, 186, fig. 5; 187, fig. 6; Bente Magnus, Odmund Mollerop, Thorleif Sjovold, "Migration Period Graves," in *Inventaria Archaeologica. Norway*, ed. Per Fett, 1 set. N 1. N 3. (Bonn: Rudolf Habelt Verlag, 1966), N 3. 5 (1–4).

46 Jean Decaens et al., *Un nouveau cimetière du haut Moyen Age en Normandie: Hérouvillette* (Caen: Centre de Recherches Archéologiques Médiévales, 1971), 12–17.

47 Decaens et al., *Un nouveau cimetière*, 82–90.

48 Typical in that respect are Michael Müller-Wille and Joachim Henning's studies, as well as Bendeguz Tobias, a small portion of which has been made available online at academia.edu. See Müller-Wille, "Der frühmittelalterliche Schmied," 127–201; Michael Müller-Wille, "Der Schmied im Spiegel archäologischer Quellen. Zur Aussage von Schmiedegräbern der Wikingerzeit," in *Das Handwerk in vor- und frühgeschichtlicher Zeit. Bericht über die Kolloquien der Kommission für die Altertumskunde Mittel- u. Nordeuropas in den Jahren 1977–1980*, vol. 2 (Archäologische und Philologische Beiträge), eds. Herbert Jankuhn, Walter Janssen, Ruth Schmidt-Wiegand and Heinrich Tiefenbach (Göttingen: Vandenhoeck & Ruprecht, 1983), pp. 216–60; Henning, "Schmiedegräber," 77–81; Tobias, *Frühmittelalterliche Gräber*, 7–9.

49 It is worth mentioning at this point the research undertaken by Polish and Czech scholars on casting in East Central Europe between the 6th and the 8th centuries: Dagmar Jelinková,

(Pest County) contained a mold,[50] while a pair of tongs was found in a male grave of the Late Avar cemetery excavated in 1973 in Kiskundorozsma (near Szeged, Csongrád County).[51] Equally impressive are the graves with tools from the very large cemetery excavated in the 1980s and early 1990s in Zamárdi (Somogy County).[52] A grave with many tools, dress accessories, and weapons was discovered in a cemetery excavated by Attila Kiss between 1972 and 1993 in Kölked (Baranya County).[53] The excavator did not comment on this particular grave, but simply attributed it to a blacksmith and dated it to the 6th and 7th centuries.[54]

Meanwhile, a number of graves with tools came to light in eastern parts of the Great Hungarian Plain. For example, Csilla Balogh published a grave from the Klárafalva (Csongrád County, near the Romanian-Hungarian border, less than 25 miles to the west from Felnac). In addition to tools, the burial assemblage also included silver and bronze belt fittings, as well as weapons.[55] Equally significant in this respect are three graves from the Early Avar-age

---

Vladimír Šrein, Martin Šťastný, "Doklady slévačství neželezných kovů v kultuře s keramikou pražského typu na Moravě [Evidence of non-ferrous metal foundry in the culture with Prague-type pottery of Moravia]," in *Mezi raným a vrcholným středověkem. Pavlu Kouřilovi k šedesátým narozeninám přátelé, kolegové a žáci*, ed. Jiří Doležel and Martin Wihoda, pp. 69–90. Brno: Archeologický ústav Akademie věd České Republiky, 2012; Bartłomiej Sz. Szmoniewski, "Production of early medieval ornaments made of non-ferrous metals. Dies from archaeological finds in north-east Romania," *ActaArchCarpathica* 37 (2002), 111–135; Bartłomiej Sz. Szmoniewski, "The production of objects from non-ferrous metals in the area of Central and Eastern Europe, in the initial phases of the Early Middle Ages," *Revista Română de Studii Eurasiatice* 1 (2005) no. 1, 107–120; Bartłomiej Sz. Szmoniewski, "Two worlds, one hoard: what do metal finds from the forest-steppe belt speak about?" in *The Other Europe in the Middle Ages. Avars, Bulgars, Khazars and Cumans. East Central and Eastern Europe in the Middle Ages, 450–1450*, ed. Florin Curta and Roman Kovalev, vol. 2, pp. 263–296 (Leiden-Boston: Brill, 2008); Bartłomiej Sz. Szmoniewski, "Byzantium and the Slavs in the Light of Goldsmiths' Production," in *Intelligible Beauty. Recent Research into Byzantine Jewellery*, eds. Chris Entwistle, Nöel Adams, pp. 161–172. London: British Museum Press, 2010.

50 Sarolta Tettamanti, *Das awarenzeitliche Gräberfeld in Vác-Kavicshánya* (Budapest: Magyar Nemzeti Múzeum, 2000), 32–33; 133, pl. 5; 167, pl. 39.

51 Katalin Vályi, "Das Detail eines spätawarenzeitlichen Gräberfeldes in Szeged-Kiskundorozsma-Hármashatár," *A Móra Ferenc Múzeum Évkönyve, Studia Archaeologica* IX (2003), 223, 226, fig. 3. 10.

52 Edith Bárdos, Éva Garam, *Das awarenzeitliche Gräberfeld in Zamárdi-Rétiföldek* (Budapest: Magyar Nemzeti Múzeum, 2009), 1: 43, pl. 31; 84, pl. 73, 1; 95, pl. 84, 11; 114, pl. 100, 2.

53 Attila Kiss, *Das awarenzeitliche Gräberfeld in Kölked-Feketekapu B*, 2 vols. (Budapest: Magyar Nemzeti Múzeum, 2001), 1: 24, fig. 7; 25–26; 2: 38–41, pl. 24–27.

54 Kiss, *Das awarenzeitliche Gräberfeld*, 1: 332–333.

55 Csilla Balogh, "Martinovka-Típusú övgarnitúra kecelről. A Kárpát-medencei maszkos veretek tipokronológiája [Martinovka-type belt set from Kecel. Tipo-chronology of the

cemetery that Balogh excavated on the nearby site at Makó (Csongrád County, less than 2 miles to the east from Klárafalva).[56] Grave 61 in that cemetery is of a craftsman specializing in bone and antler processing, judging from the half-manufactured products and the composite bow reinforcement plates found in the grave. That craftsman, however, also engaged in metalworking.[57] This discovery is remarkable, as it proves beyond doubt that craftsmen in the early Middle Ages specialized in multiple areas of industrial activity.

The most important, recent contribution to the study of Avar-age graves with tools is the monography of Zsófia Rácz. The book includes a complete catalog of all known assemblages, some of them unpublished.[58] Rácz discussed the chronology and distribution of certain categories of tools, as well as the social status of craftsmen in the Avar age.[59]

5 Tools in Assemblages of the Forest-Steppe Belt of Eastern Europe

The forest-steppe belt north of the Black Sea covers much of the territory of the present-day Republic of Moldova and Ukraine. In this area, most tool finds or artifacts related to metalworking come from settlement sites or stray finds. No burial assemblages with tools are so far known from this region.

---

mask-shaped belt fittings in the Carpathian Basin]," *A Móra Ferenc Múzeum Évkönyve* x (2004), 266–267; 291–294, fig. 15–18.

56 Rácz, *Die Goldschmiedegräber*, 191.

57 Csilla Balogh, "Karpat havzası'nda bir avar yay ustasının mezar kalıntalırı eski türklerde bileşik (kompozit) yay yapımına ilişkin arkeolojik bulgular [The Grave of an Avar Bowyer in the Carpathian Basin]," *Art Sanat* 6 (2016), 109–120.

58 Rácz, *Die Goldschmiedegräber*, 143–200. For earlier publications, see János Gábor Ódor, Zsófia Rácz, "Szerszámmellékletes sír a Szekszárd-Tószegi-dűlőiavar temetőből [Tomb with tools from the Avar cemetery in Szekszárd-Tószegi-dűlő]," *A Móra Ferenc Múzeum Évkönyve, Studia Archaeologica* 12 (2011), 245–255; Zsófia Rácz, "Emberalakos kistárgyak az avar korból [Miniature human figures from the Avar era]," in *Thesaurus Avarorum. Régészeti tanulmányok Garam Éva tiszteletére* [Archaeological Studies in Honour of Éva Garam], ed. Tivadar Vida (Budapest, 2012), pp. 409–436.

59 Zsófia Rácz, "Avar kori ötvös-és kovácsszerszámok [Avar-age goldsmiths and blacksmiths]," in *A vasművesség évezredei a Kárpátmedencébeni*, eds. János Gömöri, János Szulovszky and Zoltán Nagy (Szombathely, 2009), 67–95; Zsófia Rácz, "Sind Goldschmiede in den „Goldschmiedegräber" der Awarenzeit bestattet?" in *Macht des Goldes, Gold der Macht. Herrschafts- und Jenseitsrepräsentation zwischen Antike und Frühmittelalter im mittleren Donauraum*, eds. Matthias Hardt and Orsolya Heinrich-Tamáska, (Weinstadt: Bernhard A. Greiner Verlag, 2013), pp. 361–379.

Stone and clay molds for casting small items have been found during the excavation of the settlements of Dănceni (Ialoveni district)[60] and Selişte (Orhei district),[61] both in the Republic of Moldova. The same site also produced other categories of evidence of casting, in the form of ladles and crucibles. Such artifacts are also known from sites in the Upper Dniester region of what is now Ukraine.[62] One of the most interesting discoveries, however, is a workshop in a settlement excavated in 1990 in Bernashivka (Vinnitsa region, Ukraine), on the left bank of the river Dniester. The workshop was a sunken-floored building in which archaeologists found a ladle and no less than 64 stone molds for the casting of a wide variety of dress accessories (bow fibulae, buckles, pendants) and ornament parts. That the workshop was also a dwelling results not only from the existence of a fireplace, but also from the abundant ceramic material – hand- and wheel-made pottery. The excavator has initially dated the assemblage between the late 5th and the first half of the 6th century, and interpreted the settlement feature as the workshop of a jeweler working in a goldsmithing center on the border between the tribal lands of the Antes and those of the Sclavenes.[63] However, on the basis of the associated small finds, the workshop has been recently re-dated between the late 6th and the mid-7th century.[64]

The stone and bone molds, discovered in Moldavia, Moldova, and Ukraine, have been the subject of several studies of the Polish archaeologist Bartłomiej Szymon Szmoniewski, who pointed out to the important of the casting

60 Dergacev, Larina, and Postică, "Raskopki 1980 g. na mnogosloinom poselenii Dancheny I," 128, fig. 8.9.

61 Isaak A. Rafalovich, "K voprosu o vremeni poiavleniia pervykh politicheskikh obrazovaniĭ romanizirovannogo naseleniia na zemliakh k severu ot Dunaia [To the question of the time of the first political entities romanized population on earth north of the Danube]." In *Iugo-Vostochnaia Evropa v epokhu feodalizma (Reziume dokladov Kishinevskogo simpoziuma 1973 g.)* (Kishinev: Shtiintsa, 1973), pp. 140–141, fig. 3.2.

62 Igor Corman, *Contribuţii la istoria spaţiului pruto-nistrian în epoca evului mediu timpuriu (sec. V–VII d. Chr.)* [Contributions to the history of the Pruto-Dniester area in the Early Middle Ages (5th–7th century AD)] (Chişinău: Cartdidact, 1998), 57–59.

63 Ion S. Vynokur, "Ein Goldschmiede-Fundkomplex frühmittelalterlicher Slawen," *Archaeoslavica* 3 (1998), 226.

64 Olga A. Shcheglova, "K voprosu o meste i vremeni formirovaniia traditsii izgotovleniia svintsovo-olovyannykh ukrahseniĭ v formochkakh "tipa Kamno-Ryuge" [Where and when did appear the tradition of producing tin-lead-alloy accessories in molds of the "Kamno-Ryuge" type?]," in *Migratsii i osedlost' ot Dunaia do Ladogi v I tysiacheletii khristianskoĭ éry: pamiatnye chteniia pamiati Anny Machinskoĭ. Staraia Ladoga, 21–22 dekabria 2000. Materialy k chteniiam*, eds. Dmitrii A. Machinskii and A. A. Selin (St. Petersburg: Staroladozhskoi istoriko-arkhitekturnyi i arkheologicheskii muzei-zapovednik, 2001), p. 52, with bibliography.

technology for the production of dress accessories in the region, and sought possible connections between several cultural areas in Eastern Europe. Szmoniewski also made a number of assumptions about the ethnic and social identity of the craftsmen.[65] In addition, he dealt with lead processing in the early Middle Ages in Central and Eastern Europe.[66]

In a study dedicated to fibulae of Werner's class I D that appear in north-eastern Poland, the Middle Dnieper region, Crimea, and the Lower Danube region, Florin Curta has advanced a number of ideas pertaining to the technology of their production. He notes that clay, stone, and metal molds, as well as ladles employed in casting (some of which were used with the "lost wax" technique) appear in the regions mentioned above, sometimes on one and the same site, or even assemblage. Most exemplary in this respect is the discovery of a "workshop" in Bernashivka. The distribution of those tools suggests not that the same technology was in use, but also a certain degree of communication between elites located at long distances from each other. The dress accessories produced by local craftsmen in similar, if not identical manners carried a certain social symbolism for those who commissioned such work.[67] In other words, Curta attributed the distribution of certain dress accessories from the forest-steppe region of Eastern Europe to the Lower Danube not to migratory movements (specifically, of the Slavs, as Joachim Werner believed), but to

65 Szmoniewski, "Production," 111–135; Bartłomiej Sz. Szmoniewski, "Anthropozoomorfic brooches of the Dnepr Type in initial phases of the Early Middle Ages. The migration of a style-idea-object," in *Wedrówká rzeczy i jdei w średniowieczu, špotkania bytomskie, v. V*, ed. Sławomir Moździoch, pp. 111–137. Wroclaw 2004; Szmoniewski, "The production," 107–120; Szmoniewski, "Two worlds," 263–296; Szmoniewski, "Byzantium and the Slavs," 161–172.

66 Dariusz Rozmus, Bartlomiej Sz. Szmoniewski, "Early medieval lead processing in the slavic territories and the possible mention of trade in lead by Ibrāhīm Ibn Ya'qūb," *Peuce* 6 (2008), 323–330.

67 Florin Curta, "*Slavic* bow fibulae? Werner's class I D revisited," *Acta Archaeologica Hungarica* 57 (2006), 446–460. In that study, Curta builds upon ideas already advanced in an earlier study of another group of Werner's "Slavic" bow fibulae (Florin Curta, "Werner's class I H of "Slavic" bow fibulae revisited," *Archaeologia Bulgarica* 8, no. 1 (2004), 59–78). Those ideas were then developed in other late studies by Florin Curta, "A contribution to the study of bow fibulae of Werner's class I G," *Arheologia Moldovei* 29 (2006), 93–124; Florin Curta, "Some remarks on bow fibulae of Werner's class I C," *Slavia Antiqua* 49 (2008), 45–98; Florin Curta, "Neither Gothic, nor Slavic: bow fibulae of Werner's class II B," *Archaeologia Austriaca* 93 (2009), 45–77; Florin Curta, "Werner's Class I C: Erratum Corrigendum Cum Commentarii," *Ephemeris Napocensis* XXI (2011), 63–110; Florin Curta, "'Slavic' Bow Fibulae: Twenty Years of Research," *Bericht der Römisch-Germanischen Komission* 93 (2012), 1–108).

long-distance inter-elite contacts. In other words, he interpreted the archaeological finds from a sociological and anthropological perspective.

Even though the geographical focus of this book is limited to the east by the river Dniester, it is worth mentioning that a number of important discoveries have been made farther to the east, particularly in the Middle Dnieper region, which pertain to the casting technique with molds.[68] No graves of craftsmen are known from the entire area of the forest-steppe belt in Moldova and Ukraine. In order to find any parallels to burial assemblages with tools in the Carpathian Basin, one has to move much farther to the northeast, in the forest zone between the Vetluga and the Viatka rivers (particularly the territory of the present-day Mari El Republic). That is the area in which ladles, crucibles, and semi-finished products related to casting were systematically deposited in female graves dated between the 6th and the 8th centuries.[69] Russian scholars have advanced an interesting argument, according to which women played a great role in the production of jewelry among populations presumably speaking Finno-Ugrian languages in the northern and eastern parts of European Russia. Such ideas were first formulated in the first half of the

68 Ekaterina A. Shablavina, "Vizual'no opredelyaemye osobennosti lit'ia metallcheskikh ukrasheniĭ po voskovoĭ modeli Dneprovskogo Levoberezh'ia VII v. n. é. [The visual assessment of the technological details employed for the casting of metal artifacts in the lost-wax technique from the Dnieper Left Bank in the 7th century AD]," in *Drevnie remeslenniki Priural'ia. Materialy Vserossiiskoi nauchnoi konferencii, Izhevsk, 21–23 noiabria 2000 g.*, ed. V. I. Zav'ialov (Izhevsk: Udmurtskii institut istorii, iazyka i literatury Ural'skogo Otdeleniia RAN, 2001), pp. 308–321; R. S. Minasian, "Osobennosti ranneslavianskogo liteĭnogo i iuvelirnogo proizvodstva [Characteristics of the Slavic casting technology and jewelry production]," in *Drevnosti Podvin'ia: istoricheskiĭ aspekt. Po materialam kruglogo stola, posviashchennogo pamiati A. M. Mikliaeva (6–8 oktiabria 1999)*, eds. G. V. Vilinbakhov, B. S. Korotkevich, A. N. Mazurkevich and Iu. Piotrovskii (Sankt Petersburg: Izdatel'stvo Gosudarstvennogo Ermitazha, 2003), pp. 206–211; Olga A. Shcheglova, "Kompleks iuvelira iz Bernshevki na Dnestre i "antskie" klady Dneprovskogo Levoberezh'ia [The workshop of Bernashivka on the Dniester and the "Antian" hoards in Left-Bank Ukraine]," in *Vostochnoslavianskiĭ mir Dnepro-Donskogo mezhdurech'ia i kochevniki iuzhno-russkikh stepeĭ v épokhu rannego srednevekov'ia Materia-ly nauchnogo konferencii*, ed. A. Z. Vinnikov (Voronezh: Istoki, 2008), pp. 35–40; Ya. V. Volodarets-Urbanovich, "Livarni formochki slov'ian rann'ogo seredn'ovichchia reinterpretatsiia znakhidok [Casting molds of the early medieval Slavs: a reinterpretation of finds]," *Arkheologiia i Davnia istoriia Ukraini* 22 (1) (2017), 331–346.

69 Tatiana B. Nikitina, Diana Yu. Efremova, "Pogrebal'nyĭ obriad kompleksov s liteĭnymi prinadlezhnostiami iz srednevekovykh mogil'nikov IX–XII vv. Vetluzhsko-Viatskogome zhdurech'ia [The funeral rite of complexes with molded tools from medieval sepulchers of IX–XII centuries of the Vetluga-Vyatka Interfluve]," *Povolzhskaia Arkheologiia* 2 (2012), 149.

20th century by Vasilii Gorodcov and Boris Rybakov,[70] but its main advocates were three remarkable women archaeologists – Leonilla Golubeva, Tatiana Nikitina, and Diana Efremova. All three pointed to the relevance of burial assemblages. No less than 16 such assemblages dated between the late 5th and the 8th century, and containing skeletons of women or children (presumably girls), produced tool kits employed in casting and jewelry production, as well as half-manufactured products. The relative richness of the other grave goods and the very fact of the deposition of such tools in their graves bespeak the elevated social status of those female smelters.[71] While the beginnings of this phenomenon are in the early Middle Ages, its "golden age" spanned the 9th to the 13th centuries, a period to which over 100 burials of females with tools may be dated.[72] More recently, the interpretation of this phenomenon has shifted from the technology and casting (i.e., from taking the deposition of tools as direct evidence that some women practiced such crafts) to symbolism attached to particular rituals for the protection of the house and of the family.[73] Such assumptions have also triggered debates between Golubeva (who believes that little girls learned as apprentices the craft of casting), on one hand,[74] and, on the other hand, Nikitina and Efremova, who claim that only mature, married women were involved in jewelry production.[75]

Even though the predominant technique in the forest-steppe zone of Eastern Europe during the early Middle Ages seems to have been casting in stone or clay molds, there is also sufficient evident of the pressing technique in the form of metal dies, particularly in the Middle Dnieper region. Recent finds from that region are similar in some respects with the Felnac dies.[76] Such dies seem to point to contact with workshops in Byzantine Crimea.[77]

70 Leonilla Anatol'evna Golubeva, "Devochki-Liteĭshchitsy [Young females as casters]," in *Drevnosti Slavyan i Rusi*, ed. Boris A. Timoshchuk (Moskva: Nauka, 1988), 31.

71 Leonilla Anatol'evna Golubeva, "Zhenshchiny-liteĭshchitsy (k istorii zhenskogo remeslennogo lit'ia u finno-ugrov) [Female casters (on the history of female craft casting and Finno-Ugric peoples)]," *Sovetskaia Arkheologiia* 4 (1988), 75–79; Golubeva, "Devochki-Liteĭshchitsy," 31–32.

72 Golubeva, "Zhenshchiny-liteĭshchitsy," 79–88; Golubeva, "Devochki-Liteĭshchitsy," 32–33.

73 Nikitina, Efremova, "Pogrebal'nyĭ obriad," 160–162.

74 Golubeva, "Devochki-Liteĭshchitsy," 33.

75 Nikitina, Efremova, "Pogrebal'nyĭ obriad," 153–154.

76 Zsófia Rácz, "Ein frühmittelalterlicher Pressmodelfund aus dem Mittleren Dnjepr-Gebiet," in *Between Byzantium and the Steppe. Archaeological and Historical Studies in Honour of Csanád Bálint on the Occasion of his 70th Birthday*, eds. Ádám Bollók, Gergely Csiky and Tivadar Vida (Budapest: Institute of Archaeology, Research Centre for the Humanities, Hungarian Academy of Sciences, 2016), pp. 175–178.

77 Rácz, "Ein frühmittelalterlicher Pressmodelfund," p. 179.

6 Early Medieval Metalworking in the Literature Published in Romania after World War II

Following World War II and the establishment of the Communist regime, there was a remarkable development in Romania of medieval archaeology, in general, and of research on 6th- and 7th-century settlement sites. Those were the circumstances in which much evidence pertaining to metalworking was discovered. Since the research at that time, as well as later, took on a regional character, I will divide the following discussion of the history of research by the historical provinces of Romania, in order to facilitate the presentation of the research directions (Fig. 1).

Only few works dealt with the entirety of the Romanian territory. Prominent among them is the book of the Romanian archaeologist Ligia Bârzu (1930–2003) on the continuity of material and spiritual culture of the Romanian people on the territory of the former province of Dacia. In that book, she also referred to the material culture of the 6th and 7th centuries, and viewed the adoption of such techniques as the casting as proof of the integration of the Lower Danube region into the economic (especially commercial) space of Byzantium.[78] Bârzu also stressed low level of material culture of the Slavs, who supposedly lacked any metallurgical traditions.[79] By contrast, she saw plenty of evidence of Roman and early Byzantine traditions in the pottery making and goldsmithing of communities of the so-called Ipotești-Cândești-Ciurel culture of southern Romania. She identified those traditions in other cultural areas on the territory of Romania, albeit to a lesser extent – Bratei 2 in Transylvania, and Suceava-Botoșana II in Moldavia.[80] In a book published 16 years later, Dan Gh. Teodor tackled the problem of iron ore extraction and ingots between the 4th and the 11th centuries. On the basis of his own excavations at Lozna (Botoșani County, Romania), Teodor believed that unlike all migratory populations that have crossed the territory of present-day Romania, only the native population knew where to find iron ores.[81] Nonetheless, like Bârzu, he emphasized the Byzantine influence on production techniques, and attributed to that influence the supposedly high quality of the agricultural implements and craft tools

78 Ligia Bârzu, *La continuité de la création matérielle et spirituelle du peuple roumain sur le territoire de l'ancienne Dacie* (Bucharest: Editura Academiei Republicii Socialiste România, 1980), 63, fig. 14. 1–3; 68, fig. 16.4–5; 80.

79 Bârzu, *La continuité*, 81.

80 Bârzu, *La continuité*, 84.

81 Dan Gh. Teodor, *Meșteșugurile la nordul Dunării de Jos în secolele IV–XI* [Crafts in the region to the north of the Lower Danube, 4th–11th centuries] (Iași: Editura Helios, 1996), 12–23.

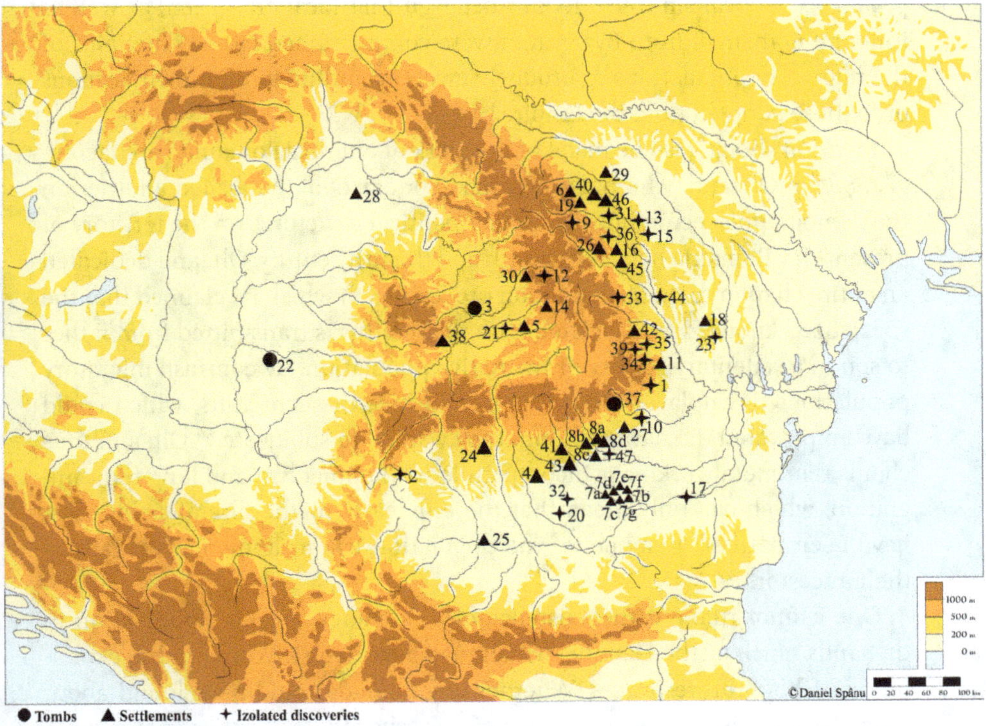

FIGURE 1 **Metalworking tools discovered on the territory of Romania.** 1. Aldeni (Buzău co.); 2. Banat (Danube Gorges area); 3. Band (Mureș co.); 4. Băleni-Români (Dâmbovița co.); 5. Bratei (Sibiu co.); 6. Botoșana (Suceava co.); 7. Bucharest (Bucharest); 7a. Băneasa; 7b. Casa Armatei; 7c. Dămăroaia; 7d. str. Soldat Ghivan no. 10; 7e. Străulești-Lunca; 7f. Străulești-Măicănești; 7g. Tei; 8. Budureasca (Vadu Săpat village, Fântânele commune, Prahova co.); 8a. Budureasca 3; 8b. Budureasca 4; 8c. Budureasca 5; 8d. Budureasca 9; 9. Cacica (Suceava co.); 10. Cândești (Buzău co.); 11. Coroteni (Slobozia Bradului commune, Vrancea co.); 12. Corund (Harghita co.); 13. Costești (Iași co.); 14. Cristuru Secuiesc (Harghita co.); 15. Cucuteni (Iași co.); 16. Davideni (Neamț co.); 17. Dichiseni (Călărași co.); 18. Dodești (Vaslui co.); 19. Dolheștii Mari (Suceava co.); 20. Dulceanca (Teleorman co.); 21. Dumbrăveni (Sibiu co.); 22. Felnac (Arad co.); 23. Giurcani (Vaslui co.); 24. Govora (Mihăiești commune, Vâlcea co.); 25. Gropșani (Olt co.); 26. Izvoare-Bahna (Neamț co.); 27. Izvorul Dulce (Merei commune, Buzău co.); 28. Lazuri (Satu Mare co.); 29. Lozna (Dersca commune, Botoșani co.); 30. Morești (Ungheni commune, Mureș co.); 31. Moțca (Iași co.); 32. Olteni (Dobrogostea village, Olteni commune, Teleorman co.); 33. Onești (Bacău co.); 34. Poienița (Vrancea co.); 35. Răcoasa (Vrancea co.); 36. Răden (Păstrăveni commune, Neamț co.); 37. Sărata Monteoru (Buzău co.); 38. Sânmiclăuș (Șona commune, Alba co.); 39. Soveja (Vrancea co.); 40. Suceava-Șipot (Suceava co.); 41. Șirna (Prahova co.); 42. Ștefan cel Mare (Gutinaș village, Ștefan cel Mare commune, Bacău co.); 43. Târgșor (Prahova co.); 44. Traian (Bacău co.); 45. Traian (Neamț co.); 46. Udești (Suceava co.); 47. Vadu Săpat (Prahova co.)

produced by local smiths.[82] Teodor believed that local craftsmen, as well as itinerant craftsmen from Byzantium were commissioned by the chieftains of the migratory populations to produce jewels according to their own fashions or to those adopted from the Empire.[83]

Mention should also be made of the work of another Romanian archaeologist, Ștefan Olteanu, who one year after Teodor's book published another on the demographic, economic, and social-political structures on the territory of present-day Romania between the 4th and the 11th century. Olteanu dedicated an entire chapter to metal extraction processing, in which he claimed that the specialized knowledge associated with that craft was transmitted from father to son in a sedentary society of the native population. By contrast, migratory populations downplayed the social significance of such crafts, which could have empowered the natives whom they wanted to subjugate.[84] Olteanu thus claims that metalworking is incompatible with nomadism and long-term migration, which can only mean that the only early medieval craftsmen must have been natives, members of the population whom Romanians regard as their ancestors.[85]

One cannot rule out the existence of a Romance-speaking population in the lands north of the Danube, which may have been involved in the exploitation of bog iron resources. Whether any nomads could have found about such resources is of course a matter of pure speculation. However, it is quite clear that the early Slavs in the region outside the Carpathian Mountains knew how to extract metal from bog iron, as indicated by finds from Ukraine and Slovakia.[86] Similarly, the Gepids who lived in Transylvania together with the Romance-speaking population,[87] knew how to extract and process iron. The existence of Germanic traditions in ironworking is beyond any doubt.[88]

82 Teodor, *Meșteșugurile*, 25.

83 Teodor, *Meșteșugurile*, 26; 30–33.

84 Ștefan Olteanu, *Societatea carpato-danubiano-pontică în secolele IV–XI. Structuri demo-economice și social*-politice [The Carpathian-Danubian-Pontic society in the 4th–11th centuries. Demo-economic and social-political structures] (Bucharest: Editura Didactică și pedagogică R.A., 1997), 106; 109 and confer note 176 with the bibliography.

85 Olteanu, *Societatea*, 111.

86 Dmitrij Nedopako, "Development of Iron-working in the Ukraine in the 1st Millennium AD," in *Traditions and Innovations in the Early Medieval Iron Production*, ed. János Gömöri (Sopron-Somogyfajsz: Dunaferr, 1999), pp. 77–81; Alena Pribulová, Ljubomir Mihok, Marta Mácelová, "Forschung über die Herstellung und Verarbeitung von Eisen in der slawische Siedlung Sliač-Horné Zeme," in *Traditions and Innovations in the Early Medieval Iron Production*, ed. János Gömöri, pp. 94–103. Sopron-Somogyfajsz: Dunaferr, 1999.

87 The presence during the early Middle Ages of a Romance-speaking population in the lands north of the Lower Danube, in general, but especially in Transylvania, remains a

matter of controversy to this day. Most scholars in Central Europe are skeptical. Their main arguments are linguistic, and the most recent presentation of those arguments is in Gottfried Schramm, *Ein Damm bricht. Die römische Donaugrenze und die Invasionen des 5.–7. Jahrhunderts im Lichte von Namen und Wörtern* (München: R. Oldenbourg Verlag, 1997), pp. 275–368. Romanian scholars, on the other hand, as well as a few non-Romanian linguists, argue that linguistic and place names clearly attest the existence of a Romance-speaking population in Transylvania throughout the Middle Ages. See Nicolae Saramandu, "À propos de l'origine du roumain (à partir de quelques ouvrages récentes)," *Revue des Études Sud-Est Européennes* 47, no. 1–4 (1999), 315–321; Giuliano Bonfante, *Studii Române* [Romanian Studies], translated by Mariana Adameşteanu (Bucharest: Saeculum I. O., 2001), pp. 46–69; Nicolae Saramandu, "Originea românei şi a dialectelor sale (observaţii critice pe marginea unor lucrări recente) [The origin of Romanian and its dialects (critical observations on recent works)]," *Philologica Jassyensia* 4, no. 2 (2008), 159–164; Dragoş Moldovanu, "Toponime de origine romană în Transilvania şi în sud-vestul Moldovei [Toponyms of Roman origin in Transylvania and southwestern Moldavia]," *Anuar de Lingvistică şi Istorie Literară* 49, no. 1 (2009–2010), 17–95; Nicolae Saramandu, "În legătură cu teritoriul de formare a limbii române (perspectivă istorică) [In connection with the territory of the formation of the Romanian language (historical perspective)]," in *Lucrările celui de-al XIV-lea Simpozion Internaţional de Dialectologie*, eds. Nicolae Mocanu, Dumitru Loşonţi and Eugen Beltechi (Cluj-Napoca: Argonaut Scriptor, 2012), pp. 355–368; Dan Ungureanu, "*Româna şi dialectele italiene* [Romanian and the Italian Dialects]" (Bucharest: Editura Academiei Române, 2016), 9–64; Nicolae Saramandu, "Teritoriul şi perioada de formare a limbii române. Originea dialectelor româneşti [The territory and the period of formation of the Romanian language. The origin of the Romanian dialects]," *Fonetică şi Dialectologie* 35 (2016), 5–25.

A key role in the debate is the critical approach to a few written sources, often read or interpreted in the light of the linguistic evidence. See Rudolf Windisch, "Die frühesten Erwähnugen der Rumänen und ihrer Vorfahren in den antiken, bzyantinischen, mittelalterlichen und neuren Quellen," *Buletinul Bibliotecii Române: studii şi documente româneşti* 8 (12) (1980–1981), 153–192; Rudolf Windisch, "Teza lui Robert Rösler – O sută de ani mai târziu [Robert Rösler's thesis – One hundred years later]," in *Logos Semantikos. Studia linguistica in honorem Eugenio Coseriu*, ed. Jürgen Trabant, volume 1, (Madrid/Berlin/New York: Walter de Gruyter Berlin-New York, Editorial Gredos Madrid, 1981), pp. 405–415; Rudolf Windisch, "Die Herkunft der Rumänen im Lichte der deutschen Forschung," *Vox Romanica* 41 (1982), 46–72; Nicolae Saramandu, "Despre coborârea aromânilor în sudul Peninsulei Balcanice. "Mărturia lui Kekaumenos" [On the migration of the Vlachs to the southern Balkans. The "testimony" of Kekaumenos]," *Studii şi Cercetări Lingvistice* 48, no. 1–4 (1997), 407–417; Nicolae Saramandu, "Atestări istorice ale continuităţii (secolele IV–VII) [Historical attestations of continuity (4th–7th centuries)]," *Studii şi Cercetări Lingvistice* 59, no. 1 (2008), 219–227.

The two most important sources are both late, the *Russian Primary Chronicle* (early 12th century) and the *Gesta Hungarorum* of an unknown author writing, most likely, in the early 13th century. Both sources mention Vlachs (presumably speaking a Romance language) in the lands north of the river Danube, which is why they were both dismissed as either too late or untrustworthy. See Windisch, "Die Herkunft der Rumänen im Lichte der deutschen Forschung," 50–55; Sorin Paliga, "Etnicitatea mileniului I: studii de caz în drumul spre o analiză globală [Ethnicity in the 1st millennium CE: case studies towards a global analysis]," in *Arheologia mileniului I p. Chr.* 5, ed. Bogdan Ciupercă (Brăila: Muzeul

Brăilei "Carol I", Editura Istros 2016), pp. 309–320; Sorin Paliga, "Terram uero, que est a fluuio morus usque ad Castrum Vrscia (Anonymus, Gesta Hungarorum, VI)," in *Arheovest IV/2. Interdisciplinaritate în Arheologie și Istorie. In honorem Adrian Bejan*, eds. Dorel Micle, Andrei Stavilă, Cristian Oprean and Sorin Forțiu (Szeged: JatePress Kiadó, 2016), pp. 861–872.

Archaeologists have not engaged in the debate as much as linguists and historians. Despite the perennial problem of "reading" ethnicity in the archaeological record, there are categories of evidence pointing to the presence in the lands north of the Danube of populations other than those mentioned in the sources (such as Goths, Gepids, Avars, Slavs etc.). Of particular interest in this respect is the cluster of artifacts manufactured by means of a particular technique, which bespeaks a certain craft tradition. The attempt to use the concept of chaîne opératoire in this particular debate is quite recent. For example, there is clear and by now abundant evidence of wheel-made coarse pottery oxidizing fired produced during the early Middle Ages in Transylvania, but neither in Hungary, nor in Bulgaria. See Ioan Stanciu, "Despre ceramica medievală de uz comun, lucrată la roata rapidă, în așezările de pe teritoriul României (secolele VIII–X) [About the medieval ceramics of common use, worked on the fast wheel, in the settlements on the territory of Romania (8th–10th centuries)]," *Arheologia Medievală* 3 (2000), 143, 145). No such pottery has been recorded on sites attributed either to Germanic, or to Slavic populations, and its absence from sites in the interior of the Carpathian Basin makes any connection with the Avars dubious. The conclusion has therefore been drawn that, since the pottery in question clearly employs techniques of Roman tradition, this may well be the marker of a Romance-speaking population surviving under Gepid and, later, Avar rule. See Dan Băcueț-Crișan, "Despre cuptorul de olar din perioada medievală timpurie descoperit la Sighișoara "Dealul Viilor"-sector Necropolă (jud. Mureș). Observații privind tehnica de modelare a ceramicii și cronologia. Comparații cu olăria medievală timpurie modelată la roata rapidă din spațiul nord-vestic al României [About the early medieval pottery kiln discovered in Sighișoara "Dealul Viilor"-Necropolă Sector (Mureș County). Observations on chronology and the pottery modelling technology. Comparisons with the early medieval pottery made on the fast turning potters' wheel in the north-western part of Romania]," in *Locuirea medievală timpurie din Transilvania și vecinătăți, Orbis mediaevalis 1*, eds. Florin Mărginean, Ioan Stanciu, Dan Băcueț-Crișan (Cluj-Napoca: Editura Mega, 2017), pp. 205–206. Of exceptional significance in this respect is the relatively recent discovery of a kiln in Sighișoara-Dealul Viilor, which produced wheel-made pottery. See Daniel Spânu and Erwin Gáll, "Cuptorul de olar din secolul al VIII-lea p. Chr. de la Sighișoara-Dealul Viilor [The pottery oven of the 8th century AD from Sighișoara-Dealul Viilor]," *Materiale și Cercetări Arheologice* 12 (2016), 177–185. It is important to note, on the other hand, that the continuity of the late antique traditions of pottery making in Pannonia has been also attributed to the survival of a Romance-speaking population. See Dan Băcueț-Crișan, "Despre cuptorul de olar din perioada medievală timpurie," 206; Vida, Tivadar. "Conflict and coexistence: the local population of the Carpathian Basin under Avar rule (sixth to seventh century)," in *The Other Europe in the Middle Ages. Avars, Bulgars, Khazars and Cumans*, ed. Florin Curta (Leiden-Boston: Brill, 2008), pp. 36–38. The weak link in this line of thinking is the direct association between wheel-made pottery and a Romance-speaking population. However, the recent discovery at Jucu de Sus (Cluj County), in the valley of the Someșul Mic river, of wheel-made pottery with striation on the interior surface of the pot has added fuel to the debate. The pottery in question comes from a late 8th to early 9th-century settlement, but its only analogies

6.1 *Finds from Walachia*

There is a remarkable concentration of finds in southern area of Romania, particularly on the territory of the city of Bucharest, in Teleorman Plain, as well as in the hills of the Prahova, Buzău and Dâmbovița counties. Such a distribution may well be a reflection of the current state of research, but it is worth mentioning that those areas seem to be those most intensely inhabited during the early Middle Ages.

Archaeological excavations in Bucharest started in earnest in the 1950s, first at Curtea Veche (the Old Royal Palace) and then in the Dămăroaia suburb.[89] Much credit for the excavations done in the 1960s and 1970s goes to two female archaeologists – Margareta Constantiniu[90] and Suzana

---

are those from the southeastern and central parts of the Alps, in present-day Austria and Slovenia. Those analogies are all dated to the 4th to 6th centuries and have been attributed to a Romance-speaking population. See Ioan Stanciu *Așezarea de la Lazuri-Lubi Tag (jud. Satu Mare). Aspecte ale locuirii medievale timpurii în nord-vestul României* [The settlement in Lazuri-Lubi Tag (Satu Mare County). Aspects of early medieval habitation in north-west Romania] (Cluj-Napoca: Editura Mega, 2019), pp. 264–265. Therefore, such parallels could be interpreted not necessarily as proof of the survival in Transylvania of a Romance-speaking population, but as evidence of migration from the southeastern Alps to the Transylvania, possibly linked to transhumance. Two categories of pottery exist in Transylvania that cannot possibly be associated with the Gepids, the Avars, and the Slavs. This seems to be sufficient reason to reopen the question of the early medieval cemetiers in Transylvania in the light of the possible coexistence in the region of different ethnic groups, which may not have marked their boundaries as sharply as initially thought. Equally promising, particularly for the discussion of possible (short- or long-distance) migrations, are the strontium isotope analyses, as well as multiple radiocarbon dates. At any rate, leaving aside the extreme politicization of the issue, the question of the Romance-speaking population in the lands north of the Danube remains without a definitive answer. Besides evidence, archaeology can bring an entirely new point of view, provided that the interpretation moves away from the 19th-century obsession with ethnic attribution.

88 Confer the already quoted works signed by K. Horedt, J. Henning, M. Müller-Wille, J. Werner etc.

89 L. Lăzărescu-Ionescu et al., "Săpăturile arheologice din sectorul Curtea Veche [The archaeological excavations in the Curtea Veche sector]," in *Bucharest. Rezultatele săpăturilor arheologice și ale cercetărilor istorice din anul 1953* (Bucharest: Editura Academiei Republicii Populare Române 1954), pp. 259–260; p. 231, fig. 40.8; Sebastian Morintz, Dinu V. Rosetti, "Din cele mai vechi timpuri și până la formarea Bucureștiului [From the earliest times to the formation of Bucharest]," in *Bucureștii de odinioară* (Bucharest: Editura Științifică, 1959), pp. 11–47.

90 Margareta Constantiniu, "Elemente romano-bizantine în cultura materială a populației autohtone din partea centrală a Munteniei în secolele VI–VII e.n. [Romano-Byzantine elements in the material culture of the native population from the central part of Muntenia in the 6th–7th centuries]," *Studii și Cercetări de Istorie Veche* 17, no. 4 (1966), 673–674; 674,

Dolinescu-Ferche,[91] who made important discoveries at Băneasa, Străulești-Lunca, Străulești-Măicănești, and on the Soldat Nicolae Ghivan Street. The mold for crosses found at Străulești-Lunca was put forward as an argument in support of the idea that the settlements discovered on the territory of Bucharest were inhabited by the a population of Dacian and Roman ancestry, while the Christian character of the find was interpreted as a sign of the ties between the native population and the Empire during Justinian's reign.[92] Constantiniu and Dolinescu-Ferche believed that the material culture of the Bucharest settlements had much in common with that from other parts of Walachia, from Moldavia and southeastern Transylvania, and attributed it to the Romance-speaking population.[93]

However, the first study of all finds pertaining to metalworking between the 5th and the 7th centuries was published by Victor Teodorescu (1932–2004).[94] The author believed that there were several industrial centers on the territory of Bucharest, which produced jewelry that was then distributed not only to all regions of the Ipotești-Cândești culture, but also to the entire area under Avar rule during the 6th–7th centuries.[95] Like Olteanu, Teodorescu believed that the Avars, being nomads, had no traditions of metalworking, so their dress accessories must have been produced by the native (specifically Romance-speaking) population. In doing so, Teodorescu not only engaged in gross exaggeration, but deliberately ignored finds from Hungary, which clearly demonstrated that metalworking was practiced by the Avars in the Tisza Plain, as well as by Slavs in the forest-steppe region of Russia and Ukraine. Since Teodorescu first introduced the concept of the Ipotești-Cândești culture into (Romanian) archaeology, his may well have been a plea *pro domo*.[96] It is nonetheless clear that he

---

fig. 5.1 – the crucible of Băneasa, fig. 5.2 – mould of Soldat N. Ghivan str., fig. 5.3 – mold of Străulești-Lunca.

91 Suzana Dolinescu-Ferche, Margareta Constantiniu, "Un établissement du VIe siècle à Bucarest. Découvertes de la rue Soldat Ghivan N.," *Dacia* 25 (1981), 293–324; 321, fig. 17.16; 323, fig. 19.1.

92 Constantiniu, "Elemente," 675.

93 Dolinescu-Ferche, Constantiniu, "Un établissement," 329–330.

94 Victor Teodorescu, "Centre meșteșugărești din sec. V/VI–VII. e. n. în București [Craft centers from the 5/6th–7th century AD in Bucharest]," *Materiale de Istorie și Muzeografie* 9 (1972), 73–99.

95 Teodorescu, "Centre meșteșugărești," 79–88, 92.

96 Victor Teodorescu, "Despre cultura Ipotești-Cîndești în lumina cercetărilor arheologice din nordul-estul Munteniei (regiunea Ploiești) [About the Ipotești-Cîndești culture in the light of archaeological researches in the north-east of Muntenia (Ploiești region)]," *Studii și Cercetări de Istorie Veche* 15, no. 4 (1964), 485–503; Victor Teodorescu, "La civilisation Ipotești-Cîndești (V–VII-e s.)," in *Actes du VII-e Congrès international des sciences préhistoriques et protohistoriques, Prague 21–27 août 1966*, ed. Jan Filip, vol. 2 (Prague: Academia,

missed an excellent (and early) opportunity to engage in comparative work over a large area extending beyond the political borders of Romania.

Finds pertaining to metalworking are also known from several sites in the Teleorman County, and they were published by Constantin Preda[97] and Suzana Dolinescu-Ferche. The latter excavated several settlement sites at Dulceanca (near Roşiorii de Vede), and brought to light clear evidence of iron smelting and smithing at sites I,[98] II,[99] and IV.[100] She believed that to be a craft practiced exclusively by the native, Romance-speaking population, since bog iron deposits must have remained unknown to all newly arrived, migratory populations. The knowledge involved in that craft was transmitted from generation to generation only within the local population, whose ancestors had lived on those lands since times immemorial.[101] Dolinescu-Ferche also claimed that the community in Dulceanca IV maintained strong ties with the early Byzantine Empire, from which new techniques of smelting and metalworking must have been brought.[102] To be sure, chemical analyses of some of the metal artifacts found in the region have indeed revealed that they were made of bog iron from local sedimentary-alluvial formations.

Meanwhile, similar claims were made by Ştefan Olteanu in his interpretation of the site he has excavated at Şirna (Prahova County). Short, preliminary

---

1971), pp. 1041–1044; Victor Teodorescu, "O nouă cultură arheologică recent precizată în ţara noastră, cultura Ipoteşti-Cîndeşti (sec. V–VII) [A new archeological culture recently specified in our country, the Ipoteşti-Cîndeşti culture (5th–7th centuries)]," in *Sesiunea de comunicări ştiinţifice a muzeelor de istorie, dec. 1964*, vol. 2, 104–130. Bucharest, 1971.

97 Constantin Preda, "Tipar pentru bijutierii din secolul al VI-lea e. n., descoperit la Olteni (r. Videle, reg. Bucureşti) [Pattern for jewelers from the 6th century AD discovered in Olteni (Videle district, Bucharest region)]," *Studii şi Cercetări de Istorie Veche* 18, no. 3 (1967), 513–516.

98 Suzana Dolinescu-Ferche, *Aşezări din secolele III şi VI e. n. în sud-vestul Munteniei. Cercetările de la Dulceanca (jud. Teleorman)* [Settlements from the 3rd and 6th centuries AD in the southwest of Muntenia. Researches from Dulceanca (Teleorman county)] (Bucharest: Editura Academiei Republicii Socialiste România, 1974), 83; 87, fig. 5; 87; 90; 96, fig. 106, 4, 8.

99 Suzana Dolinescu-Ferche, "Contributions archéologique sur la continuité daco-romaine. Dulceanca, deuxiéme habitat de VIe siècle de n.è.," *Dacia Nouvelle Série* 30, no. 1–2 (1986), 153.

100 Suzana Dolinescu-Ferche, "Habitats des VIe et VIIe siècle de notre ère à Dulceanca IV," *Dacia* 36 (1992), 153; 157; 171, fig. 35.24; 29; 172; 167, fig. 31.8; 168, fig. 32.27; 169, fig. 33.13; 31.

101 Dolinescu-Ferche, *Aşezări*, 129.

102 Dolinescu-Ferche, "Habitats," 174–175.

reports of the 1979[103] and 1980[104] excavations were followed by the publication of the site monograph, with detailed descriptions of the many settlement features and phases of occupation between the 2nd and the 10th century. During the phase dated between the 5th and the first half of the 6th century, iron smelting on the site is illustrated by furnaces, a large amount of iron slag, and casting tools.[105] Like Dolinescu-Ferche, Olteanu believed that only the native, Romance-speaking population (the ancestors of the Romanians) could have been involved in such activities, with knowledge passed from one generation to another within the local community.[106] The finds from Șirna became the basis for a study on ironworking during the 1st millennium AD. The authors argued that newly arrived populations (different groups of barbarians) did not destroy the structures they found on local (native) sites, did not prevent the transmission of knowledge from one generation to the other, and thus contributed, if only indirectly, to the continuity of technological progress from Antiquity to the Middle Ages.[107] Migratory populations may have regarded crafts as degrading work, and therefore used the local population for that purpose. Itinerant craftsmen could only be locals or sedentized members of migratory communities.[108]

In parallel to Olteanu' excavations in Șirna, Victor Teodorescu excavated a number of settlements in the hills of the eastern parts of the Prahova County, at Budureasca. A great number of important finds were made here in the 1960s, but only a few have been published – black- and goldsmith tools.[109] Teodorescu

---

103 Ștefan Olteanu, Victor Teodorescu, Nina Neagu, "Rezultatul cercetărilor arheologice de la Șirna, cu privire la secolele III–XI [The result of the archaeological researches from Șirna regarding the 3rd–11th centuries]," *Materiale și Cercetări Arheologice* 14 (1980), 417–419.

104 Ștefan Olteanu, Nina Neagu, "Rezultatele cercetărilor de la Șirna-Prahova [Results of research from Șirna-Prahova]," *Materiale și Cercetări Arheologice* 15 (1983), 385–386.

105 Ștefan Olteanu, Nina Grigore, Victor Nicolae, *Comunitatea sătească de la Șirna, județul Prahova (secolele II–X d. H.) în lumina izvoarelor arheologice* [The village community from Șirna, Prahova county (2nd–10th centuries AD) in the light of archaeological sources] (Bucharest: Editura Mașina de scris, 2007), 42–43; 47–50; 176, fig. 23. 4–5; 187, fig. 34. 1; 50; 103–104.

106 Olteanu, Grigore, Nicolae, *Comunitatea sătească*, 111.

107 Ștefan Olteanu, Nina Neagu, Doina Șeclăman, "Tehnologia obținerii fierului din minereu și problema continuității istorice pe teritoriul României în mileniul I e. n. [The technology of obtaining iron from the ore and the problem of historical continuity on the territory of Romania in the 1st millennium AD]," *Studii și Comunicări de Istorie Veche și Arheologie* 32, no. 2 (1981), 218–219.

108 Olteanu, Neagu, Șeclăman, "Tehnologia," 226.

109 Ion Miclea, Radu Florescu, *Strămoșii românilor. Vestigii milenare de cultură și artă. Daco-romanii* [The ancestors of the Romanians. Millennial vestiges of culture and art. Daco-Romans]. vol. 2 (Bucharest: Editura Meridiane, 1980), fig. 818, fig. 820–822; 212.

published a number of studies that referred, if only tangentially, to such finds, together with Marinela Peneş[110] and others.[111] Those studies repeated Teodorescu's earlier claims that the craftsmen in Budureasca were ancient Romanians,[112] and the technological secrets involved in casting or forging were known only to the natives, as they were based on rich traditions of Dacian and Roman origin.[113]

By contrast, the historian Alexandru Madgearu believed that earrings with star-shaped pendant and their derivatives must have been produced by craftsmen in the early Byzantine hillforts south of the river Danube or by itinerant craftsmen coming from that same region.[114]

After Teodorescu's death, the task of publishing the enormous material resulting from excavations in Budureasca fell upon Bogdan Ciupercă, who, together with Andrei Măgureanu, published a number of molds while paying special attention to the information about the archaeological context in which they have been found. Măgureanu and Ciupercă linked the molds to local workshops, but did not eliminate the idea of itinerant craftsmen. They pointed out to remarkable links with other cultural areas from the Great Hungarian Plain to the Middle Dnieper region in Ukraine.[115] In another article, Ciupercă and Măgureanu claimed that at least some of the 6th- to 8th-century molds found in southern and eastern Romania may have been brought from the Empire or made by craftsmen who were not native. Since the technique of mold making is Byzantine, they advanced the idea that such molds must have

---

110 Victor Teodorescu, Marinela Peneş, "Matricea de incidenţă a siturilor arheologice de la Budureasca (Budureasca 1–31) [The incidence matrix of the archaeological sites from Budureasca (Budureasca 1–31)]," *Anuarul Prahova* 1 (1984), 18; 44, fig. 19; 46, fig. 2.

111 Victor Teodorescu, Vasile Dupoi, Marinela Peneş, Dan Lichiardopol, Gheorghe Panait, "Staţiunea arheologică Budureasca, jud. Prahova. Complexe daco-romane şi străromâneşti [Budureasca archeological station, Prahova county. Daco-Roman and Old Romanian assemblages]," *Materiale şi Cercetări Arheologice* 17 (1993), 373–374.

112 Teodorescu, Peneş, "Matricea de incidenţă," 18; 44, fig. 19; 46, fig. 2.

113 Teodorescu, Dupoi, Peneş, Lichiardopol, Panait, "Staţiunea arheologică Budureasca," 384; Victor Teodorescu, Vasile Dupoi, Marinela Peneş, Gheorghe Panait, "Budureasca, străveche şi statornică vatră de civilizaţie la originile poporului român (Cercetările arheologice din anul 1983 privind complexele străromâneşti de tip Ipoteşti-Cândeşti, sec. V–VII e. n.) [Budureasca, ancient and steadfast hearth of civilization at the origins of the Romanian people (The archaeological researches from 1983 regarding the Old Romanian assemblages of type Ipoteşti-Cândeşti, 6th–7th centuries AD)]," *Mousaios* 5 (1999), 93–96.

114 Alexandru Madgearu, *Continuitate şi discontinuitate culturală la Dunărea de Jos în secolele VII–VIII* [Cultural continuity and discontinuity at the Lower Danube in the 7th–8th centuries], Bucharest: Editura Universităţii din Bucureşti, 1997, 67.

115 Andrei Măgureanu, Bogdan Ciupercă, "The 6th–8th Centuries Metallurgical Activity from Budureasca Valley. The Molds," *ActaMN* 41–42/I, 2004–2005 (2007), 301.

been made by specialized craftsmen from the Empire, who arrived in the lands north of the Danube either as prisoners of war or as defectors.[116] On the basis of a typological analysis of molds, Măgureanu discussed the influence of the Byzantine and Avar cultures upon the styles and technologies employed by local craftsmen.[117]

6.2 *Finds from Transylvania and Banat*

Nothing compares with the significance of the earlier finds from Felnac (Banat) and Band (Transylvania), but more recent finds illustrate various metalworking practices. For example, Kurt Horedt wrote about the dies from Corund (Harghita County) and Dumbrăveni (Sibiu County),[118] as well as about the finds from Moreşti (Mureş County).[119] Eugenia Zaharia brought to the fore the finds from another settlement site excavated at Bratei (Sibiu County).[120] A stone mold for casting dress accessory discovered at Cristuru Secuiesc (Harghita County) offered the possibility to Zoltán Székely to argue that the influence of the Byzantine culture reached deep into the southeastern corner of Transylvania.[121] He also linked that find to those in the area of the so-called Ipoteşti-Cândeşti culture, which, according to him, maintained permanent ties with the Roman-Byzantine world.[122]

Much like Ştefan Olteanu, the Romanian archaeologist Mircea Rusu (1928–1999) dealt with the question of metal extraction and processing during the 6th to 9th centuries. He claimed, however, that many of the metal pieces discovered in Transylvania, Banat, and Hungary originally came from Byzantine workshops

116 Bogdan Ciupercă, Andrei Măgureanu, "Unele observaţii asupra problemei tiparelor din secolele V–VII descoperite în spaţiul extra-carpatic [Regarding the problem of the 6th–7th century mould finds in the extra-Carpathian area]," *Buletinul Muzeului Judeţean Teleorman. Seria Arheologie* 1 (2009), 152–153.

117 Andrei Măgureanu, "Observaţii privind semnificaţia unor descoperiri din spaţiul extra-carpatic (sec. VI–VII p. Chr.) [Remarks on the significance of some findings from the extra-Carpathian space (6th–7th AD)]," *Mousaios* 13 (2008), 173–190.

118 Kurt Horedt, *Contribuţii la istoria Transilvaniei, sec. IV–XIII* [Contributions to the history of Transylvania, 4th–13th centuries] (Bucharest: Editura Academiei Republicii Populare Romîne, 1958), 69–70; 75. 5–7; 88; 95.

119 Kurt Horedt, *Moreşti, Grabungen in einer vor- und frügeschichtlichen Siedlung in Siebenbürgen* (Bucharest: Kriterion Verlag, 1979), 150; pl. 43.1.

120 Eugenia Zaharia, "La station nº 2 de Bratei, Dép. de Sibiu (VIe - VIIIe siècles)," *Dacia Nouvelle Série* 38–39 (1994–1995), 301, 328–329, 356, fig. 20.8.

121 Zoltán Székely, "Săpăturile executate de Muzeul Sfântu Gheorghe [The excavations performed by the Sfântu Gheorghe Museum]," *Materiale şi Cercetări Arheologice* 10 (1970), 222.

122 Zoltán Székely, "Eléments byzantins dans la civilization matérielle des VIe - VIIIe siècles dans la Sud-Est de la Transylvanie," *Dacia Nouvelle Série* 15 (1971), 357–358.

along the Danube, or from the former province of Pannonia. He noted, however, that settled or itinerant craftsmen were documented archeologically.[123] Like Olteanu, Rusu believed that mining was practiced by the natives, who relied upon Roman knowledge and experience. The large number of gold objects in hoards discovered in Transylvania proves, therefore, that the natives engaged in gold mining in the Apuseni Mountains.[124] Like Teodorescu, Rusu seems to have deliberately ignored the absence of any evidence that the Roman mines were still in operation during the early Middle Ages. Nor is there any evidence that the gold of the artifacts found in Transylvania was mined, and not the raw material provided by melting early Byzantine *solidi*.

More than half-a-century after the publication of Rusu's study, there is still no metallographic analysis of any artifact that could decide what exactly was used for raw material. At any rate, no evidence exists that the gold mines in Transylvania were in use during the second half of the 1st millennium. Much, if not all gold processed into jewelry must have come from subsidies.[125]

The finds in Felnac were again brought to the fore, a little short of a century after their discovery, by the Romanian archaeologist Liviu Mărghitan. His book on the archaeology of the Banat contains, however, a number of inaccuracies regarding the number of dies, the material out of which they were made, and the number of craftsman who may have employed them.[126] This is probably the result of Mărghitan's cavalier treatment, if not neglect of the Hungarian literature of the early 20th century, which gives details about the circumstance and nature of the finds.[127] Such a conclusion is substantiated by Mărghitan's preposterous claim that Felnac is the only hoard of dies known from the entire European continent, for, according to him, no other find is known with such a large and varied set of dies.[128] He must have deliberately ignored the finds from Kunszentmárton, particularly the larger number of dies (41) found in that assemblage together tools, weapons and horse bones[129] Mărghitan believed that

---

123 Mircea Rusu, "Transilvania și Banatul în secolele VI–IX [Transylvania and Banat in the 6th–9th centuries]," *Banatica* 4 (1976), 191–192.

124 Rusu, "Transilvania și Banatul," 192; 207–210 – the list of gold ores and washing spots; 210 – list of iron and copper ores.

125 Michaela Aufleger, "Metallarbeiten und Metallverarbeitung," in *Die Franken wegbereiter Europas. Vor 1500 Jahren: König Chlodwig und seine Erben* [*Ausstellungskatalog*] (Mainz: Verlag Philipp von Zabern, 1996), 618.

126 Liviu Mărghitan, *Banatul în lumina arheologiei* [The Banat in the light of archeology], vol. 3 (Timișoara: Facla, 1985), 3: 43–44.

127 Hampel, "Emlékek és leletek," 117; Hampel, *Altertümer*, 2: 392; 3: 747; see also above, notes 2–5.

128 Mărghitan, *Banatul*, 44.

129 Csallány, *A Kunszentmártoni avarkori ötvösir.*

Felnac proved the existence of local craftsmen working on commission for the chiefs of migratory populations (such as the Avars). Such craftsmen maintained many and permanent ties to Byzantium, for pressing with dies such as those found in Felnac was a Byzantine technique.[130] Because of ignoring the information of the earliest archaeological reports, Mărghitan thus wrongly interpreted Felnac as a hoard of dies, and not as a grave with tools. That explains why he believed the assemblage to indicate a local, not an itinerant (Avar) craftsman.[131]

The only contribution regarding metalworking in northwestern Transylvania is that of Ioan Stanciu, which is based on his excavations at Lazuri (Satu Mare County). In that settlement, Stanciu identified several traces of metalworking, such as a ladle, a clay mold, a small fragment of iron ingots, and slag. He believed that the craftsmen at Lazuri were Slavs.[132] Stanciu also noted that metal artifacts were rare, if not altogether absent on settlement sites in Lazuri and Zalău (Sălaj County), which can only indicate that such artifacts were of high value (and recycled) and therefore not discarded in abandoned settlements.[133]

6.3 *Finds from Moldavia*

The first studies dedicated to metalworking during the 6th to 8th centuries in Moldavia belong to Dan Gh. Teodor.[134] His early remarks may be found in studies of the history and archaeology of the lands between the Carpathian Mountains and the Dniester River between the 5th to 9th, the 6th to 10th, or even the 4th to 13th centuries. In those studies he tackled the problem of tools, smelting furnaces, and the archaeological contexts in which they were

130 Mărghitan, *Banatul*, 59–60.

131 Daniela Tănase, "Câteva observații cu privire la mormântul de orfevru din epoca avară descoperit la Felnac (jud. Arad) [Some observations on the Avar-age goldsmith grave discovered in Felnac (Arad county)]," *Analele Banatului Serie Nouă* 12–13 (2004–2005), 245–249.

132 Ioan Stanciu, "Așezarea slavă timpurie de la Lazuri [Early Slavic settlement from Lazuri]," *Satu Mare. Studii și comunicări* 15–16 (1998–1999), 156–157; 172, 216, pl. V.8, 226, pl. XIV.5; Ioan Stanciu, *Locuirea teritoriului nord-vestic al României între antichitatea târzie și perioada de început a epocii medievale timpurii (mijlocul sec. V–sec. VII timpuriu)* [The habitation of the north-western territory of Romania between the Late Antiquity and the beginning period of the Early Middle Ages (the middle of the 5th century–early 7th century)] (Cluj-Napoca: Editura Academia Română. Centrul de Studii Transilvane. Editura Mega, 2011), 279–280.

133 Stanciu, *Locuirea*, 280.

134 Dan Gh. Teodor, "Unele probleme privind evoluția culturii materiale din Moldova în secolele VI–X [Some problems regarding the evolution of material culture in Moldova in the 6th–10th centuries]," *Carpica* 2 (1969), 269, fig. 10; 270, fig. 11; 271, fig. 12; 272, fig. 13; the marl mold from Lozna-Dorohoi is mentioned on page 271.

found.[135] Ghenuță Coman[136] and Victor Bobi[137] followed in Teodor's footsteps. In their work on the discoveries in the counties of Vaslui and Vrancea, respectively, they were preoccupied with proving the continuity of the ancient Romanian population. Similarly, Ioan Mitrea (1937–2017) compared finds from 6th- to 9th-century sites in Moldavia to those pertaining to metalworking and found within the area of the Ipotești-Cândești culture.[138] Mitrea believed that casting in stone molds was a Byzantine technique or the result of the Byzantine influence upon local centers of production.[139] In a discussion of the specialization of craftsmen, Mitrea advanced the idea that both the ore extraction and the processing of the metal were performed by one and the same craftsman.[140] Finds dated to the 6th and 7th centuries come from systematically excavated settlement sites, such as Lozna,[141] Botoșana (Suceava County),[142] Dodești

135 Dan Gh. Teodor, *Teritoriul est-carpatic în veacurile V–XI e. n., contribuții arheologice și istorice la problema formării poporului român* [The East-Carpathian territory in the 5th–11th centuries AD, archaeological and historical contributions to the problem of the formation of the Romanian people] (Iași: Editura Junimea, 1978), 18; 30–31; 161, fig. 2/2; 166, fig. 7/1.

136 Ghenuță Coman, "Contribuții la cunoașterea fondului etnic al civilizației secolelor V–XII în jumătatea sudică a Moldovei [Contributions to the knowledge of the ethnic background of the civilization of the 5th–12th centuries in the southern half of Moldavia]," *Carpica* 11 (1979), 187.

137 Victor Bobi, "Contribuții la repertoriul arheologic al județului Vrancea (Dovezi ale continuității de locuire, sec. II–VII e.n.) [Contributions to the archaeological repertoire of Vrancea county (Proofs of continuity of habitation, 2nd–7th centuries AD)]." *Vrancea. Studii și comunicări* 4 (1981), 107, 111–113; 138, fig. 25.6.

138 Ion Mitrea, "Regiunea centrală a Moldovei dintre Carpați și Siret în secolele VI–IX [The central region of Moldavia between the Carpathians and Siret in the 6th–9th centuries]," *Carpica* 12 (1980), 71, 90; 188, pl. XLVIII.4,5,8; pl. XLVIII.3; 184, pl. XLIV.7; 188, pl. XLVIII.10.

139 Mitrea, "Regiunea centrală," 92; Ion Mitrea, "Dovezi arheologice privind prelucrarea metalelor în secolele VI–IX, în regiunea subcarpatică a Moldovei [Archaeological evidence on the processing of metals in the 6th–9th centuries, in the sub-Carpathian region of Moldavia]," *Studii și Comunicări de Istorie a Civilizației Populare din România* 2 (1981), 14;17, fig. 3; 18.

140 Mitrea, "Dovezi," 13.

141 Dan Gh. Teodor, "Cercetări în așezarea din secolele VII–VIII de la Lozna-Strâteni, Jud. Botoșani [Research in the settlement of the 7th–8th centuries from Lozna-Strâteni, Botoșani County]," *Materiale și Cercetări Arheologice* 14 (1980), 456–459; Dan Gh. Teodor, "Principalele rezultate ale cercetărilor arheologice de la Lozna-Strâteni, jud. Botoșani [The main results of the archaeological researches from Lozna-Strâteni, Botoșani county]." *Materiale și Cercetări Arheologice* 15 (1983), 452–454; Dan Gh. Teodor, "Tipare din secolele VI–XI d. Hr. în regiunile carpato-nistriene [Patterns from the 6th–11th centuries AD in the Carpathian-Dniestrian regions]," *Arheologia Moldovei* 28 (2005), 159–174.

142 Dan Gh. Teodor, *Civilizația romanică la est de Carpați în sec. V–VII e. n. Așezarea de la Botoșana-Suceava* [Romance civilization east of the Carpathians in the 5th–7th centuries AD. The settlement from Botoșana-Suceava] (Bucharest: Editura Academiei Republicii Socialiste România, 1984), 36–37; 46–48; 56–57; 89, fig. 10.a; 99, fig. 20. 1–6; 100, fig. 21.1–2.

(Vaslui County),[143] all investigated by Dan Gh. Teodor, as well as Davideni (Neamţ County),[144] Izvoare-Bahna (Neamţ County),[145] and Ştefan cel Mare-Gutinaş (Bacău County),[146] which were explored Ioan Mitrea.

According to Mitrea, the 5th- to 7th-century inhabitants of the settlement in Davideni were of native origin and spoke a Romance language.[147] The site monograph includes a description of the settlement features with tools.[148] To judge by such finds (so Mitrea), the territory of present-day Moldavia must have been not only under a strong Roman-Byzantine influence, but even a Roman-Byzantine cultural province.[149]

Similarly, Dan Gh. Teodor argued that the casting mold found in Botoşana have analogies in Walachia, and represent the archaeological remains of a native population speaking a Romance language.[150] A specialized workshop was in operation at Dodeşti, which produced dress accessories, pointing to the development and social and economic stage of the native communities in Moldavia.[151]

Both Teodor and Mitrea repeatedly dealt with the question of the Byzantine influence upon the material culture in Moldavia. Teodor attributed to that

---

143 Dan Gh. Teodor, *Continuitatea populaţiei autohtone la est de Carpaţi în secolele VI–XI e. n. Aşezările din secolele VI–XI e.n. de la Dodeşti-Vaslui* [Continuity of the autochthonous population to the east of the Carpathians in the 6th–11th centuries AD Settlements of the 6th–11th centuries from Dodeşti-Vaslui] (Iaşi: Editura Junimea, 1984), 25; 29, fig. 6.1, 3, 11; 30, fig. 7.1–3; 31, fig. 8.6–7.

144 Ion Mitrea, "Principalele rezultate ale cercetărilor arheologice din aşezarea de la Davideni (sec. V–VII) [The main results of the archaeological researches from the Davideni settlement (5th–7th centuries)]," *MemAntiq* 6–8 (1974–1976) (1981), 70–72; 82–84; Ion Mitrea, "Aşezarea din secolele V–VII de la Davideni – Neamţ. Cercetările arheologice din anii 1988–1991 [The settlement from the 5th–7th centuries from Davideni – Neamţ. Archaeological researches from 1988 to 1991]," *Memoria Antiquitatis* 19 (1994), 393.

145 Ion Mitrea, "Aşezarea prefeudală de la Izvoare-Bahna, contribuţii la arheologia epocii de formare a poporului român [Pre-feudal settlement from Izvoare-Bahna, contributions to the archeology of the epoch of formation of the Romanian people]," *Carpica* 10 (1978), 215; 230, fig. 10.10; 230, fig. 10. 9–12.

146 Ion Mitrea, Constantin Eminovici, Vasile Momanu, "Aşezarea din secolele V–VII de la Ştefan cel Mare, judeţul Bacău [The settlement from the 5th–7th centuries from Ştefan cel Mare, Bacău County]," *Carpica* 18–19 (1986-1987), 224–225.

147 Mitrea, "Principalele rezultate," 88–89.

148 (L= dwelling), Ion Mitrea, *Aşezarea de la Davideni din secolele V–VIII* [The settlement from Davideni from the 5th–8th centuries] (Piatra Neamţ: Editura Constantin Matasă, 2001), L. 5, 42; L. 17, 55, (fig. 63/6); L. 33, 63, (fig. 94/5, 98/2); L. 36, 71–72, (fig. 103/5, fig. 61/5, fig. 65/5); L. 39, 80, (fig. 61/3); L. 42, 85, (fig. 60/8–9); L. 46, 88, fig. l; 112, 113, fig. 60/1; 133.

149 Mitrea, *Aşezarea de la Davideni*, 193–194; 203.

150 Teodor, *Civilizaţia romanică*, 57.

151 Teodor, *Continuitatea*, 35.

influence the finds of stone and bone molds.[152] Their users must have been either Byzantine or local craftsmen, much like those buried in Felnac and Band.[153] The Byzantine influence, according to Teodor, was also particularly strong on the production techniques and the decorative styles. On the basis of mold finds, Teodor advanced the idea of workshops in Walachia, Moldavia, and Transylvania, in which Byzantine craftsmen or local craftsmen trained by the Byzantines exercised their trade.[154] The techniques employed for the production of dress accessories thus became a proof of specialized, workshop-based production based on local craftsmen or traveling craftsmen coming from Byzantium.[155] Like Teodor, Mitrea pointed out similarities between stone molds from Moldavia, Walachia, and southeastern Transylvania.[156] He also endorsed Teodor's idea of a widespread Byzantine influence moving across Moldavia along the Siret and its main tributaries, the Trotuș, the Bistrița and the Moldova. To him, that was sufficient proof that Moldavia belonged to the Byzantine civilization and that the region was inhabited by a native, Romance-speaking population.[157]

Echoing earlier ideas put forward by Olteanu and Teodorescu, Dumitru Boghian recently published a stone mold from Cucuteni (Iași County) and claimed on that basis that the jewelry used by the elites of the nomadic populations was produced by native craftsmen, as the native population was forced into paying tribute to the nomads. This, according to him, results clearly from rectangular belt mounts found in Avar graves in Hungary, which may have been produced with stone molds like that from Cucuteni.[158] However, there is no attempt at studying more closely analogies between the mold and the said belt mounts, while the idea that the native population paid tribute in jewelry needs

152 Dan Gh. Teodor, "Elemente și influențe bizantine în Moldova în secolele V–XI [Byzantine elements and influences in Moldavia in the 5th–11th centuries]," *Studii și Cercetări de Istorie Veche* 21, no. 1 (1970), 97–128, 101–102; 106; 107, fig. 6/12.

153 Teodor, "Elemente și influențe bizantine," 106.

154 Dan Gh. Teodor, *Romanitatea carpato-dunăreană și Bizanțul în veacurile V–XI* [Carpathian-Danube Romanity and Byzantium in the 5th–11th centuries] (Iași: Editura Junimea, 1981), 31–33. Molds are also illustrated: 103, fig. 11: Costești Iași; 105, fig. 13: 1. Botoșana, 2. Dumbrăveni, 3. Bucharest-Străulești, 4. Olteni, 5. Traian, 6. Poienița, 7. Cristuru Secuiesc.

155 Teodor, "Tipare," 159–174.

156 Ion Mitrea, "Influențe bizantine în cultura materială și spirituală din regiunea sub-carpatică a Moldovei în secolele VI–IX [Byzantine influences in the material and spiritual culture of the sub-Carpathian region of Moldova in the 6th–9th centuries]," *Studii și Cercetări de Istorie Veche* 30, no. 2 (1979), 145–149; 151–152; 153, Fig. 4.

157 Mitrea, "Influențe bizantine," 159.

158 Dumitru Boghian, "Un moule en pierre des VIe - VIIe siècles découvert á Cucuteni (dép. de Iași)." *Studia Antiqua et Archaeologica* 6 (1999), 119.

demonstration. At any rate, there is nothing in, the written sources to support that idea. Nonetheless, Boghian correctly noticed that dress accessories of the same type have been found in the lands to the east and to the southeast from the Eastern Carpathians.[159]

Some of the most important finds pertaining to metalworking have been recently published in monographs dedicated to the settlement sites excavated in Lozna, Suceava, and Ştefan cel Mare-Gutinaş. An industrial center was discovered at Lozna, which is dated between the late 7th and the late 8th century.[160] Iron was extracted from nearby deposits of limonite, and both smelting furnaces and casting tools (molds, crucibles, and ladles) have been found on the site. Besides local craftsmen, traveling (Byzantine) craftsmen supposedly worked here for the production of metal objects.[161] The 6th- to 7th-century in Suceava-Şipot is believed to have been inhabited by the native, Romance-speaking population and by groups of Slavs and Antes.[162] The production of dress accessories is documented by finds of copper and bronze waste, as well as a stone mold and several clay crucibles.[163]

A smelting furnace and several tools, including a stone mold have been found in Ştefan cel Mare-Gutinaş, a settlement dated between the 5th and the 7th century.[164] However, the excavator does not consider the possibility of specialized craftsmen operating on site.

It is worth noting that the three monographs highlighted the strong influence of Roman-Byzantine and of the Byzantine civilizations on the local population, which coexisted with the Slavs and the Antes.

159 Boghian, "Un moule," 118–119.

160 Dan Gh. Teodor, *Un centru meşteşugăresc din evul mediu timpuriu. Cercetările arheologice de la Lozna-Botoşani* [A craft center from the Early Middle Ages. The archaeological research from Lozna-Botoşani] (Brăila: Editura Istros a Muzeului Brăilei, 2011), 9–13.

161 Teodor, *Un centru*, 45.

162 Dan Gh. Teodor, *Aşezarea medievală timpurie de la Suceava-Şipot* [Early medieval settlement from Suceava-Şipot] (Iaşi: Casa Editorială Demiurg Plus, 2013), 8, 41–43, 51–52.

163 Teodor, *Aşezarea medievală timpurie*, 51.

164 Ion Mitrea, *Aşezarea medievală timpurie de la Ştefan Cel Mare-Gutinaş, judeţul Bacău* [Early medieval settlement from Ştefan Cel Mare-Gutinaş, Bacău county] (Oneşti: Magic Print, 2015), 19, 45–46, 77–78, 92–93.

CHAPTER 2

The Archaeology of Metalworking

The archaeological evidence from settlements confirms the conclusions drawn on the basis of graves with tools.

Two categories of evidence are known from settlement sites: smelting furnaces and specific tools found in features that may be interpreted as workshops. While the former are easily recognizable, especially when associated with such finds as blooms, slag, and tools, the latter pose a much more difficult problem of interpretation, even though the presence of tools and slag definitely constitute the main arguments in that interpretation.

1 Workshops

1.1 *Transylvania*

Only a few remains of metalworking are known from sites in Transylvania that have been so far published. At Morești-Podei (Mureș County) (Fig. 2.1), a pair of pliers was accidentally found by a local. Kurt Horedt, who has excavated the nearby settlement, believed that the pliers are somehow associated with the 6th-century site, and insisted upon numerous for analogies graves with tools across in Europe. He pointed out that the pliers found in Aradac (Serbia), Poysdorf (Austria) and Schönebeck (Germany) are almost the same size as those found in Morești (30.5 cm). The Aradac pliers are 27 cm, the Poysdorf pliers 32.5 cm, and the Schönebeck pliers 32.7 cm long. As such they could be just as good for work in a smithy as for a jeweler. Nonetheless, Horedt opted for interpreting the Morești pliers as the tool of a blacksmith. Horedt concluded that a smithy must have been in existence in the settlement, but there is actually no evidence for that. To be sure, slag was found inside the settlement in area LIII (thus outside any settlement feature), but cannot be stratigraphically correlated and therefore dated. Horedt's claim that smelting, not blacksmithing may have been the activity performed on the site is dubious.[1] Be as it may, both the pliers – which have indeed good analogies in the 6th century – and the slag are clear indications of some kind of metalworking. A smithy, however, is nowhere to be found among the 37 settlement features (primarily dwellings) that Horedt has excavated on the site.

1 Horedt, *Morești*, 150; plate 43.1.

© DANIELA TĂNASE, 2021 | DOI:10.1163/9789004436930_004

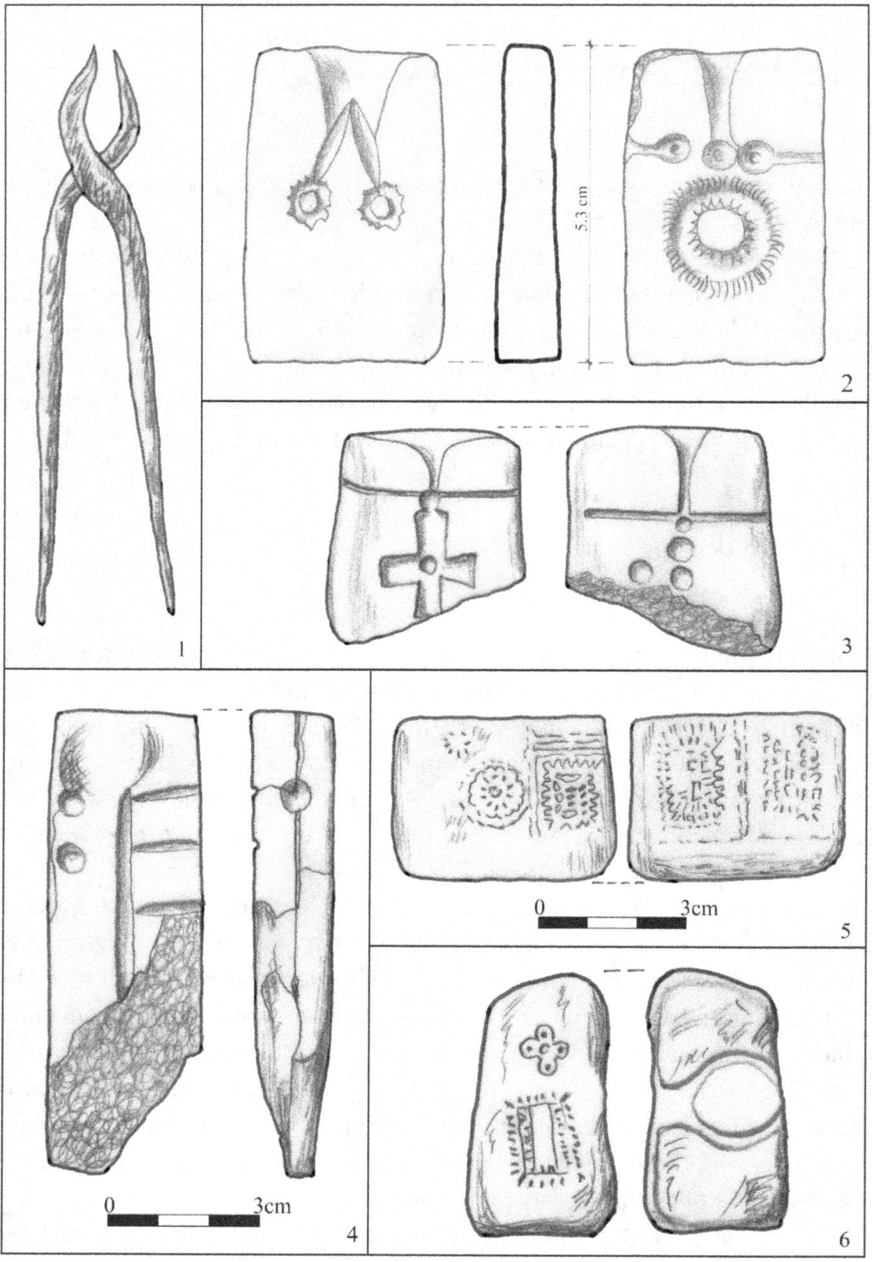

FIGURE 2 **1. Morești** (Mureș co.): pliers – **2. Moțca** (Iași co.): stone mold – **3. Olteni** (Teleorman co.): stone mold – **4. Onești** (Bacău co.): stone mold – **5. Poienița** (Vrancea co.) – stone mold – **6. Răcoasa** (Vrancea co.): stone mold. 1, 3, 6 without scale

The second occupation phase at Bratei 1 (phase "b") was dated to the 5th and first half of the 6th century. That phase produced evidence of smelting, such as the bloom from house 20 and slag from houses 33 and 45.[2] There were also ladles in houses 30 and 78, as well as oven 2, but no illustration of any of them has been published. It is difficult therefore to establish what kind of ladles those were, but it is quite possible that those were casting tools.[3] One of the sunken-floored houses excavated in Bratei 2 (Sibiu County), in hut no. 1, which is dated to the 6th and 7th centuries, a ladle was found along with ceramic remains (Fig. 3).[4] Metalworking on that site is also documented by finds of iron slag in the filling of most 7th- to 8th-century settlement features, particularly in that of sunken-floored building 16.[5] Another ladle is known from the 7th-century settlement excavated in Lazuri-Lubi tag (Satu Mare County). The ladle came from the filling of one of the sunken-floored buildings found on the site, while a bloom was retrieved from the filling of another settlement feature. A clay mold was found inside the clay oven of another sunken-floored building from that same settlement site, along with clay rolls and lumps (Fig. 4.1).[6]

However, no traces of metalworking are known from other 6th-century settlements excavated in Transylvania, such as Porumbenii Mici (Harghita County),[7] Soporu de Câmpie (Cluj County),[8] and Țaga.[9] Among artifacts found in the assemblage associated with one of the sunken-floored buildings in the 7th- to 8th-century settlement excavated in Cristuru Secuiesc – "Valea Pârâului Cetății", there was half of two-part, gritstone mold for casting dress accessories (Fig. 5.1).[10]

To be sure, contemporaneous settlements dated to the 7th and 8th centuries, are also known from the nearby sites at Bezid and Sălașuri (Mureș County),[11]

2 Ligia Bârzu, "La station n° 1 de Bratei, dép. De Sibiu (IVe - VIIe siècles)," *Dacia Nouvelle Série* 38–39 (1994–1995), 241–242, 261, 264–265.

3 Bârzu, "La station n° 1 de Bratei," 265, 268.

4 Zaharia, "La station n° 2 de Bratei," 301–302, 356, fig. 20.8.

5 Zaharia, "La station n° 2 de Bratei," 327.

6 Stanciu, *Locuirea*, 279; 631, pl. 22/8, 8a.

7 Zoltán Székely, "Săpăturile arheologice de la Porumbenii Mici [Archaeological excavations from Porumbenii Mici]," *Materiale și Cercetări Arheologice* 6 (1959), 523–530.

8 Dumitru Protase, Ioan Țigărea, "Șantierul arheologic Soporul de Câmpie [The Soporul de Câmpie archaeological site]," *Materiale și Cercetări Arheologice* 6 (1959), 383-395.

9 Dumitru Protase, *Țaga. Două așezări din perioada finală a etnogenezei românilor* (*sec. IV–VI și sec. VII–VIII*) [Țaga. Two settlements from the final period of Romanians' ethnogenesis (4th–6th centuries and 7th–8th centuries)] (Cluj-Napoca: Nereamia Napocae, 2003).

10 Székely, "Săpăturile executate de Muzeul Sfântu Gheorghe," 222; 223, fig. 3.4; Székely, "Eléments byzantins dans la civilization matérielle," 354, fig. 1.3; 357.

11 Zoltán Székely, "Contribuții la cultura slavă în sec. VII–VIII în sud-estul Transilvaniei [Contributions to the Slavic culture in the 7th–8th centuries in southeastern Transylvania],"

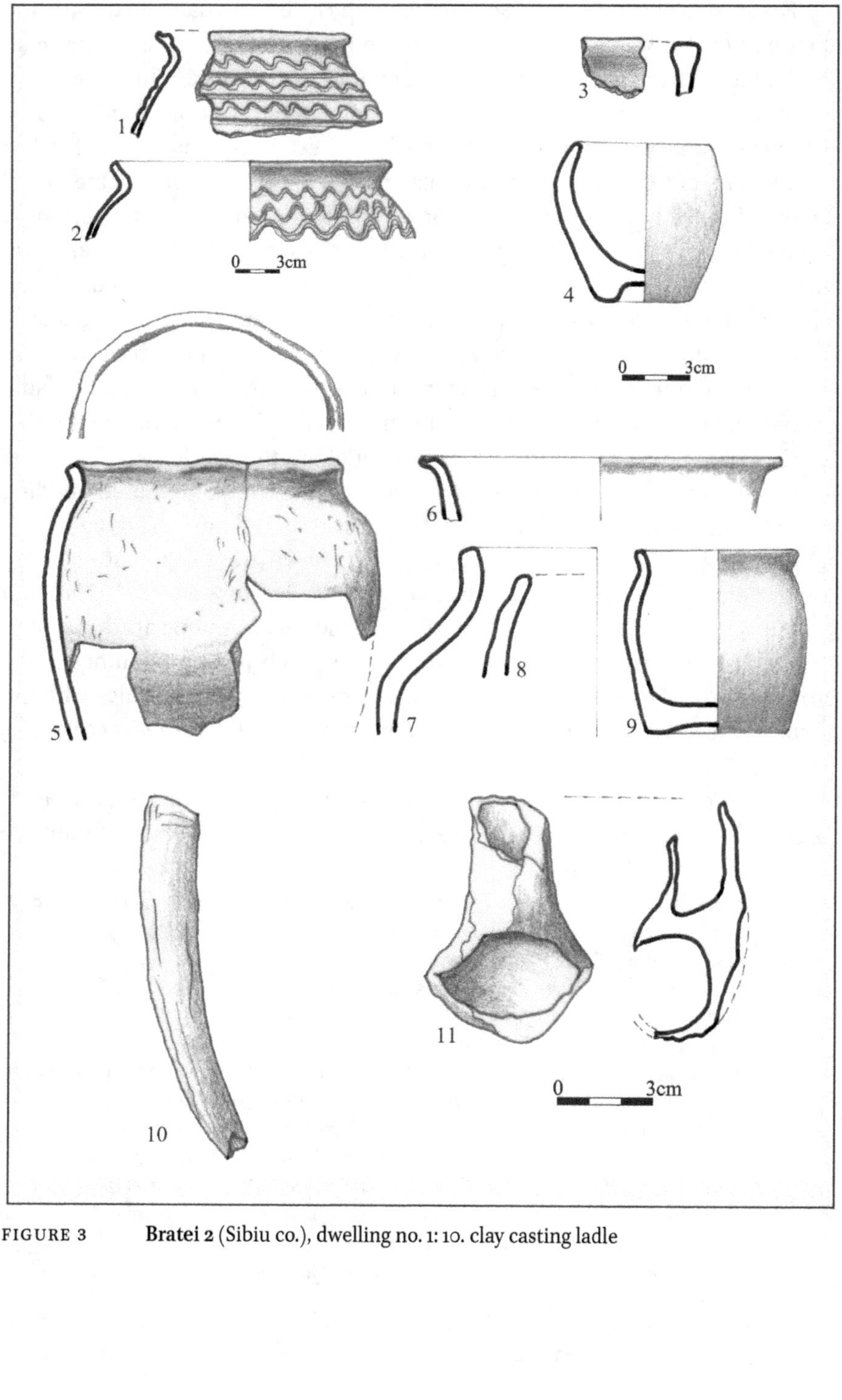

FIGURE 3 **Bratei 2** (Sibiu co.), dwelling no. 1: 10. clay casting ladle

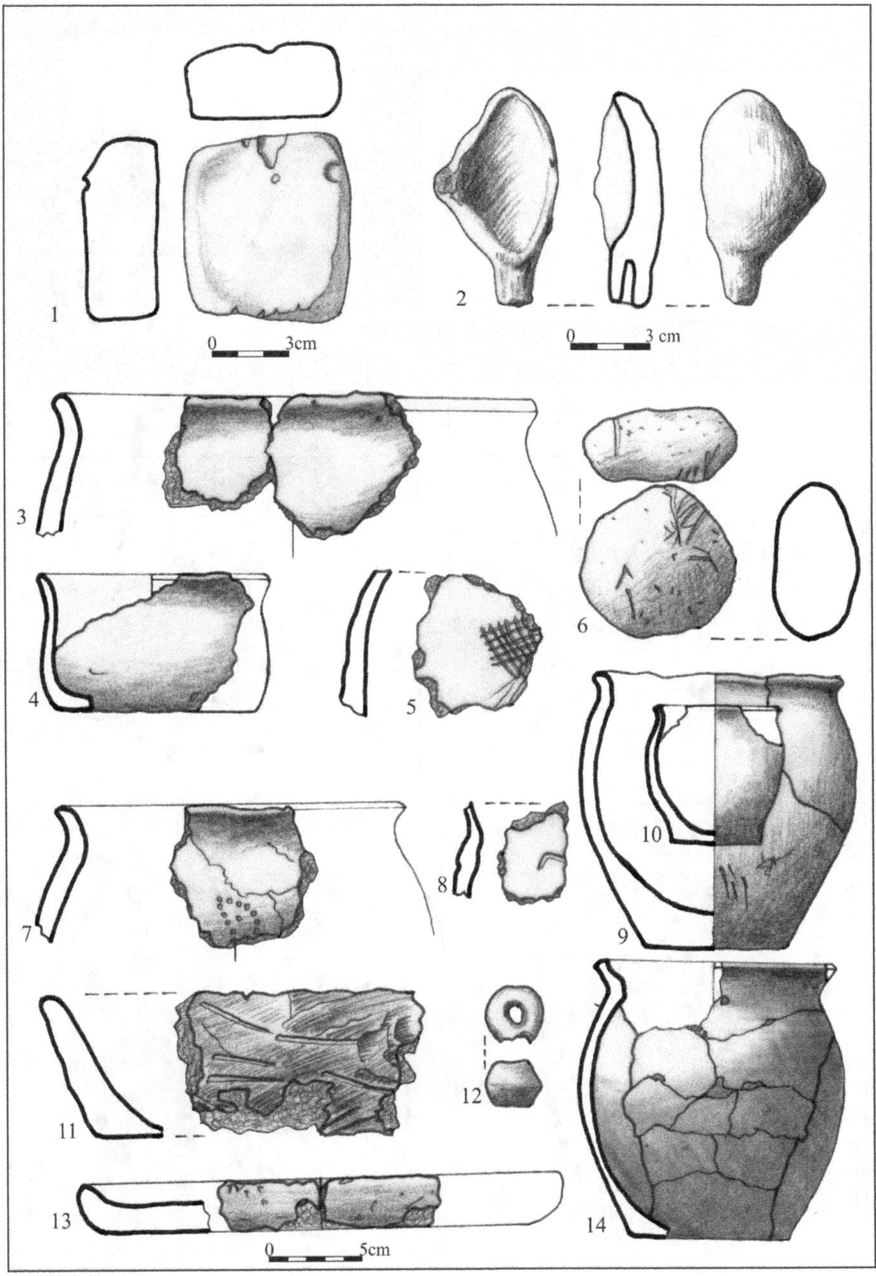

FIGURE 4 **Lazuri** (Satu Mare co.), dwelling no. 1: 1. clay mold; 2. clay casting ladle

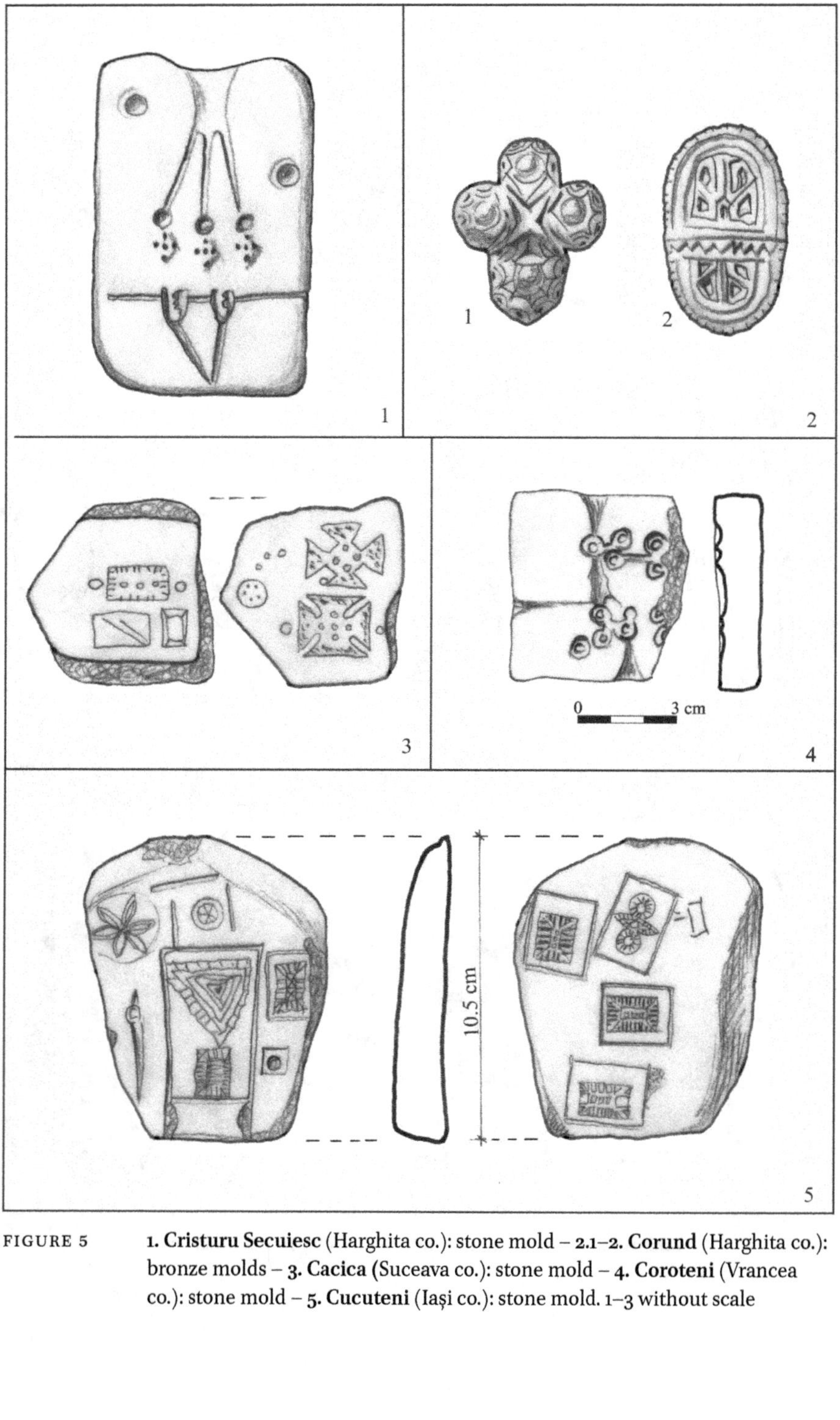

FIGURE 5 **1. Cristuru Secuiesc** (Harghita co.): stone mold – **2.1–2. Corund** (Harghita co.): bronze molds – **3. Cacica** (Suceava co.): stone mold – **4. Coroteni** (Vrancea co.): stone mold – **5. Cucuteni** (Iași co.): stone mold. 1–3 without scale

but no remains of metalworking have been found in any of them. The only tool is a wimble from one of the sunken-floored buildings excavated in Bezid-Fâneaţa Mare,[12] but that may well be a carpenter, not a blacksmith's tool.

The information about the tools found on the 6th-century settlement site excavated in Sânmiclăuş (Alba County) are contradictory. A clay mold for casting crosses, earrings, and buckles is said to have been found, perhaps accidentally, in 1975 (Fig. 6.2). According to some, the mold was found on the floor of a sunken-featured building, the associated assemblage of which also included a coin struck for the Hungarian king Stephen III (1162–1172). In reality, the coin struck for King Stephen IV (1162–1163) was found in trench 3 (1974), and the excavators make no mention of the mold, which in any case was definitely not found together with the coin.[13] However, that report seems to be confused, and the fact that the mold served for casting so-called Maltese crosses suggests rather a 6th-century date.[14] Later reports claim that no less than three molds have been found in 1974 on the settlement site at Sânmiclăuş-Răstoci – a mold for crosses, a stone mold, and a clay mold.[15] However, none has so far been properly published.

1.2 *Walachia and Oltenia*

No 6th- to 7th-century settlements have so far been excavated in Little Walachia (Oltenia), except Gropşani (Dolj County). There were in fact two settlements on that site, one at "Gura Gurgotei," the other at "Ovrei". In a sunken-floored

Studii şi Cercetări de Istorie Veche 13, no. 1 (1962), 47–58.

12 Székely, "Contribuţii la cultura slavă în sec. VII–VIII," 48.

13 Gheorghe Anghel, Mihai Blăjan, "Săpăturile arheologice de la Sânmiclăuş (com Şona, jud. Alba-1974) [The archaeological excavations from Sânmiclăuş (comm. Şona, Alba county-1974)]," *Apulum* 15 (1977), 286.

14 Nicolae Dănilă, "Consideraţii asupra noilor materiale arheologice paleocreştine din Transilvania [Considerations on the new paleo-Christian archaeological materials from Transylvania]," *Biserica Ortodoxă Română* 100, no. 7–8 (1982), 735–736; Nicolae Dănilă, "Tipare pentru turnat cruci, din secolele IV–VI, descoperite pe teritoriul României [Patterns for the casting of crosses, from the 4th–6th centuries, discovered on the territory of Romania]," *Biserica Ortodoxă Română* 101, no. 7–8 (1983), 560.

15 Ana-Maria Velter, *Transilvania în secolele V–XII. Interpretări istorico-politice şi economice pe baza descoperirilor monetare din bazinul carpatic, secolele V–XII* [Transylvania in the 5th–12th centuries. Historical-political and economic interpretations based on the monetary discoveries in the Carpathian Basin, 5th–12th centuries] (Bucharest: Paideia, 2002), 458. The stone mold is also mentioned in Gabriel T. Rustoiu, "Habitatul în Transilvania în a doua jumătate a secolului al V-lea şi prima jumătate a secolului al VI-lea [The Habitat in Transylvania in the second half of the 5th century and the first half of the 6th century]," in *Relaţii interetnice în Transilvania (secolele VI–XIII)*, eds. Zeno Karl Pinter, Ioan Marian Ţiplic and Maria Emilia Ţiplic (Bucharest: Editura Economică, 2005), p. 63.

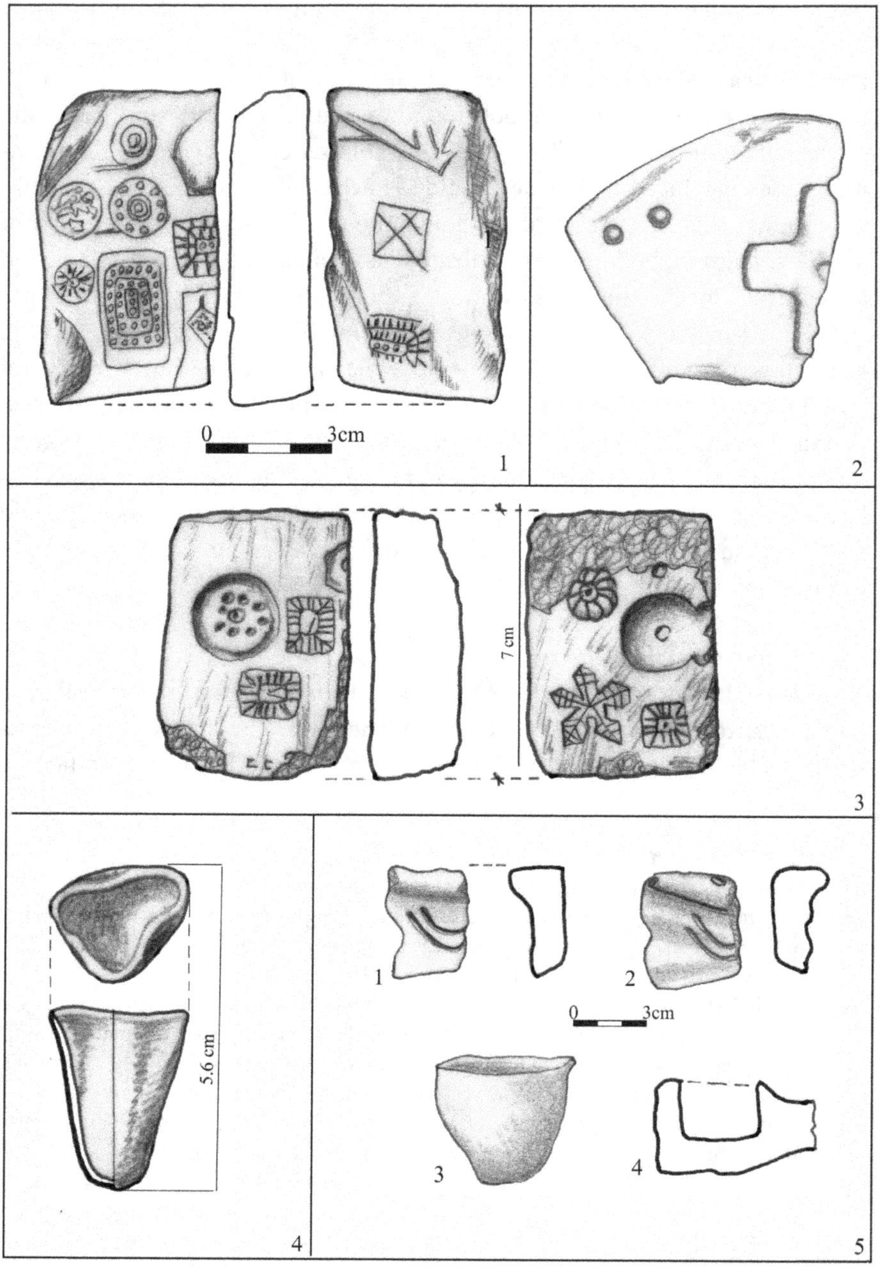

FIGURE 6 **1. Rădeni** (Neamț co.): stone mold – **2. Sânmiclăuș** (Alba co.): clay mold – **3. Soveja** (Vrancea co.): stone mold – **4. Sărata Monteoru** (Buzău co.): clay crucible – **5. Șirna** (Prahova co.): 5.1–2. stone mold; 5.3. clay crucible; 5.4. clay casting ladle. 2, 5.3–4 without scale

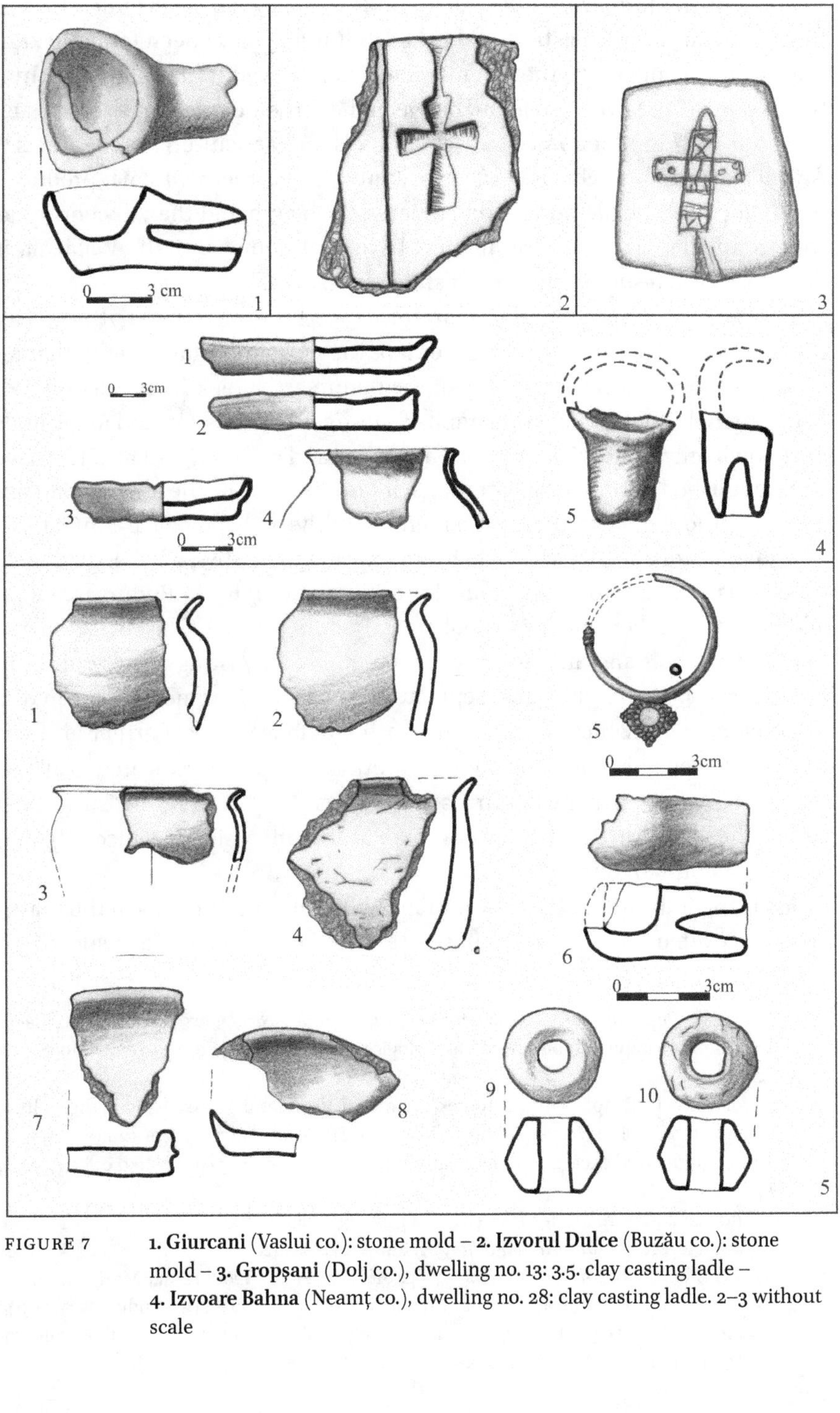

FIGURE 7 **1. Giurcani** (Vaslui co.): stone mold – **2. Izvorul Dulce** (Buzău co.): stone mold – **3. Gropșani** (Dolj co.), dwelling no. 13: 3.5. clay casting ladle – **4. Izvoare Bahna** (Neamț co.), dwelling no. 28: clay casting ladle. 2–3 without scale

building of the former, a ladle was found (Fig. 7.4.5). No clear indications as to its exact location have been published, but it may have been found next to the clay oven, much like the ceramic remains retrieved from that house. Iron billets are said to have been found between the settlement features, which suggests the local production of household tools and agricultural implements.[16] A trial excavation at Govora (Vâlcea County), in northern Oltenia, produced hand- and wheelmade pottery dated between the 5th and the 7th century, as well as a ladle. That few casting tools have been found in Little Walachia is most likely the result of the current state of research.[17]

In Walachia proper, there is more evidence both for 6th- to 7th-century settlements and for metalworking. Perhaps the most important sites in that respect are those excavated in valley of the Budureasca creek (Prahova County). Unfortunately, there is no monograph of those settlement sites, and many finds are known only from brief mentions in articles and reports. Most artifacts have been published with poor illustrations, if any. Because of the antiquarian approach to those objects, there is no mention of the archaeological context. For example, Victor Teodorescu published engraving tools, dies, a ladle, fragments of lead, as well as two stone molds for casting jewelry from Budureasca 4, in addition to another engraving tool from Budureasca 3.[18] Chisels, engraving tools, pins, a bolt and another three stone molds for casting jewelry, all from Budureasca 4,[19] were published separately, along with hammers discovered at Budureasca 9, for which, however, no further details exist.[20] Further artifacts were published later with very poor illustrations in a paper dedicated to all settlements discovered in the Budureasca Valley – site 3 ("La Greci" or "La Stupina CAP Vadu"), site 4 ("Puțul Tătarului" or "Puțul Mare"), site 5 ("Oncești"), and site 9 ("La Puțul lui Burciu").

Again, no indication exists of the archaeological context of any of those artifacts, not even on which one of those sites they have been found, respectively.

16 Gheorghe Popilian, Marin Nica, *Gropșani. Monografie arheologică* [Gropșani. Archaeological monograph], (Bibliotheca Thracologica) 24 (Bucharest: Editura Semne, 1998), 28; 124; 272, fig. 20.5.

17 Carol Terteci, "Despre cultura Ipotești-Cândești în județul Vâlcea [About the culture Ipotești-Cândești in Vâlcea county]," *Buridava. Studii și Materiale* VIII (2010), 103–109. Although the trial excavation took place in 1984, its results were published only 26 years later.

18 Teodorescu, "Centre meșteșugărești," 85, fig. 6. 1–3, 5–13.

19 Miclea, Florescu, *Strămoșii românilor*, fig. 819, 820–822; 212.

20 Miclea, Florescu, *Strămoșii românilor*, fig. 818, 212; Victor Teodorescu, Marinela Peneș, "Matricea de incidență a siturilor arheologice de la Budureasca (Budureasca 1–31)," *Anuarul Prahova* 1 (1984), 21; 46, fig. 21.22: the only additional information is that concerning the year of the discovery (1963).

One can sort out the finds on the basis of information published elsewhere. For examples, engraving tools, punches, and fragments of metal sheet were found at Budureasca 3.[21] From Budureasca 4, further items are known: engraving tools, punches, a mandrel, a hammer, pliers, clay crucibles, as well as lead and bronze ingots (Fig. 8–9).[22]

A mandrel and a stone mold are known from Budureasca 5 (Fig. 10.1), while crucibles and hammers have been found in Budureasca 9 (Fig. 10.2).[23]

Only one artifact has been published with its archaeological context – a stone mold found in a sunken-featured building from Budureasca 4.[24] Although the mold is said to have been found together with two belt buckles, ceramic remains, and a fragment of a scythe, it is not illustrated at all, which makes it impossible to establish for what exactly it was used. According to the excavator, slag and even iron ore were found elsewhere at Budureasca 4, while at Budureasca 5 a smithy is said to have been found, complete with smelting furnaces and weapons produced by the local blacksmith.[25] More recently, several assemblages have been published from the Budureasca Valley, some of them with stone molds. Three of them come from a sunken-floored building excavated in Budureasca 3 (Fig. 11.1).[26]

Four stone molds have been found in a refuse pit on site 4 (at "Puțul Tătarului"), but only two of them have been published (Fig. 9). A clay mold is said to be from Budureasca 4, but with no information about the archaeological context.[27] One stone mold for casting files was found in a sunken-floored building excavated on site 5 ("La Oncești") together with a fibula with bent stem and ring with a bezel decorated with a cross, as well as an engraving tool and slag fragments (Fig. 10.1.1).[28] The archaeological context, particularly the fibula, strongly suggests a 6th-century date.

---

21 Teodorescu, Peneș, "Matricea de incidență," 46, fig. 21.2, 16.

22 Teodorescu, Peneș, "Matricea de incidență," 45, fig. 30.6 (item that is also described in Teodorescu, "Centre meșteșugărești," Miclea, Florescu, *Strămoșii românilor*, 46, fig. 21. 1, 3–5, 7–14, 17–19, 21, 23–24).

23 Teodorescu, Peneș, "Matricea de incidență," 46, fig. 21. 20, 22.

24 Teodorescu, Dupoi, Peneș, Panait, "Budureasca," 93.

25 Maria Comșa, "Socio-economic organization of the Daco-Romanic and Slav populations on the Lower Danube during the 6th–8th centuries," in *Relations between the autochthonous population and the migratory populations on the territory of Romania*, eds. Miron Constantinescu, Ștefan Pascu and Petre Diaconu (Bucharest: Editura Academiei Republicii Socialiste România, 1975), p. 183.

26 Măgureanu, Ciupercă, "The 6th–8th Centuries Metallurgical Activity," 293.

27 Măgureanu, Ciupercă, "The 6th–8th Centuries Metallurgical Activity," 293–294.

28 Măgureanu, Ciupercă, "The 6th–8th Centuries Metallurgical Activity," 294, 303.

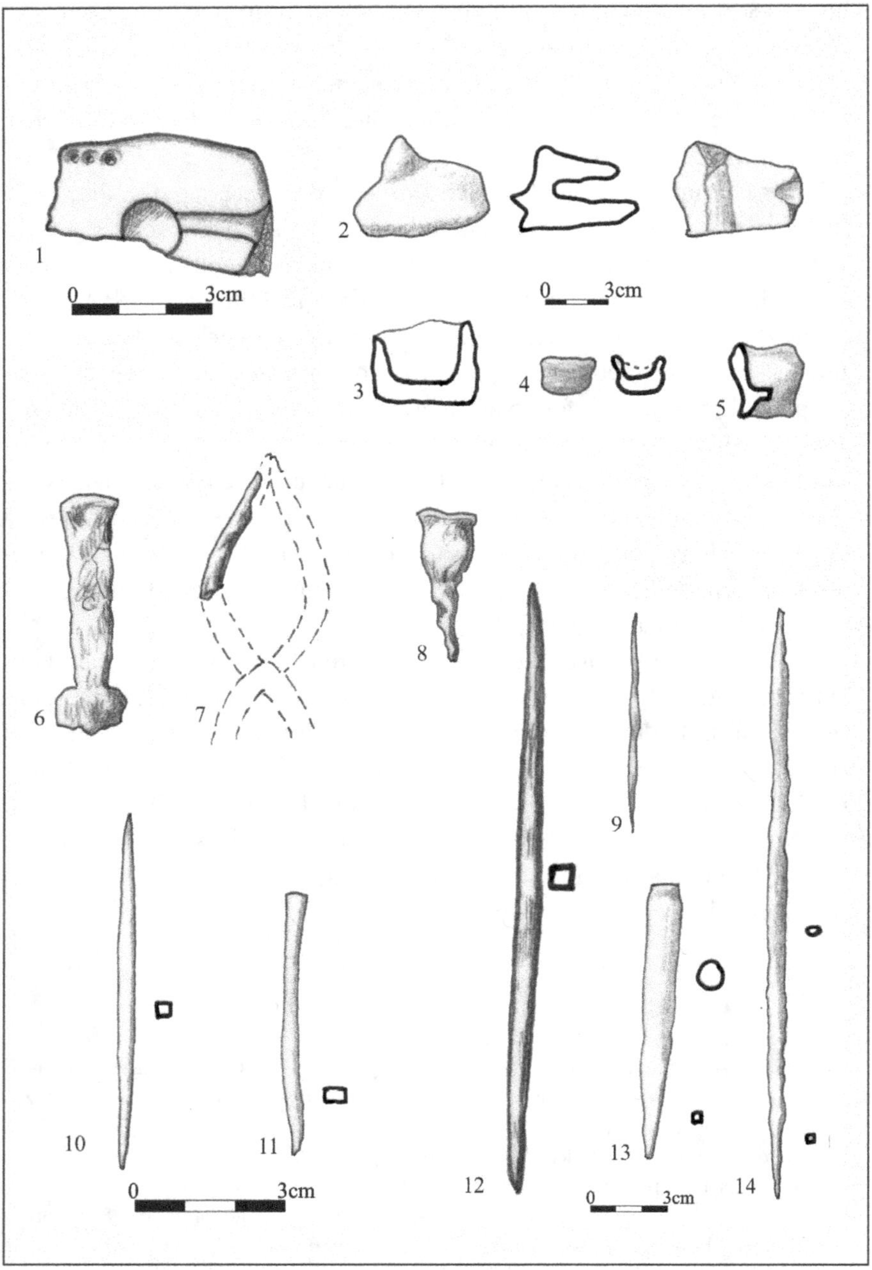

FIGURE 8 **Budureasca 4** (Prahova co.): 1. stone mold; 2. clay casting ladle; 3–5. clay crucibles; 6, 13. mandrels/punches; 7. jewelry pliers; 8. anvil; 9, 11, 14. gravers; 10. small knife for engraving. 6–8 without scale

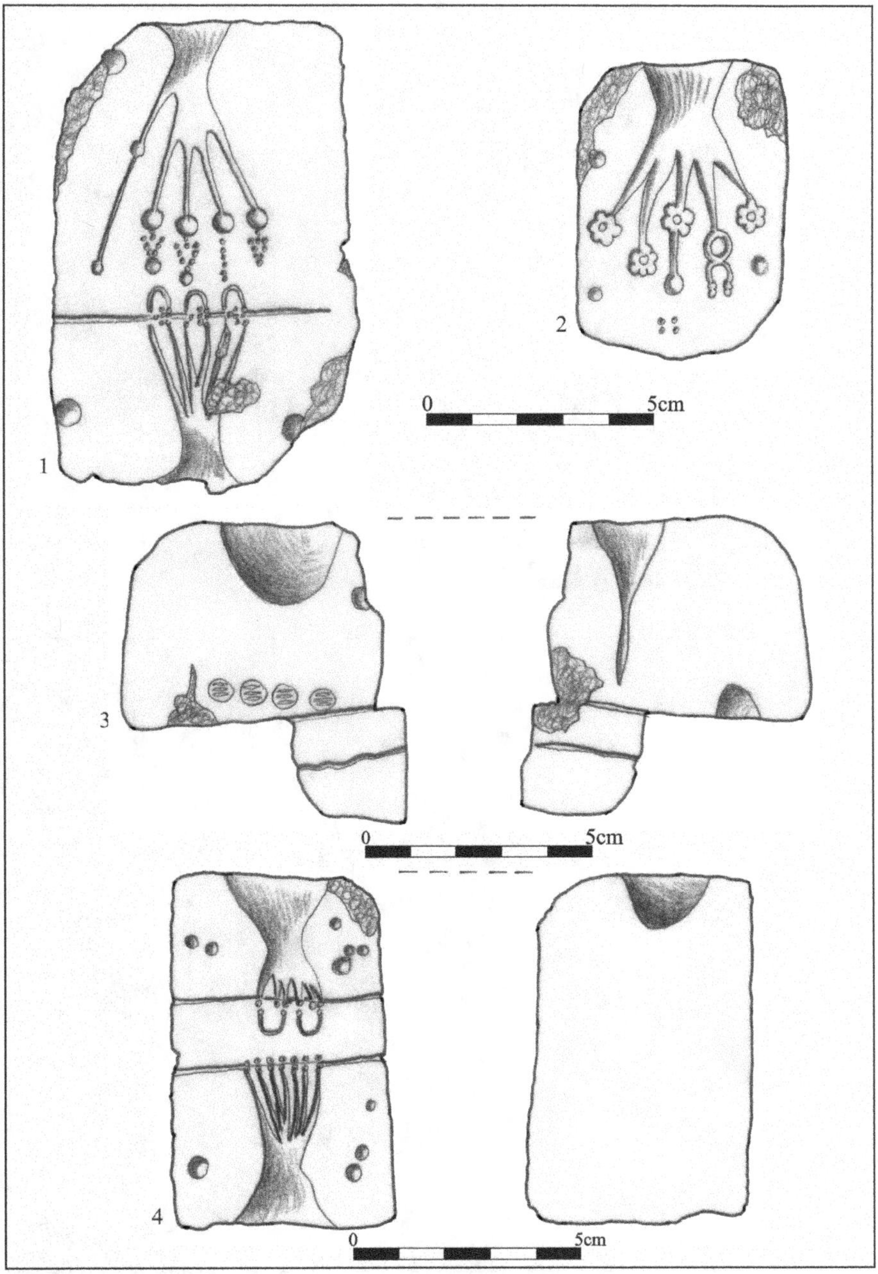

FIGURE 9 **Budureasca 4**, pit A/1965 (1–2), pit G. T./1967 (3–4): stone molds

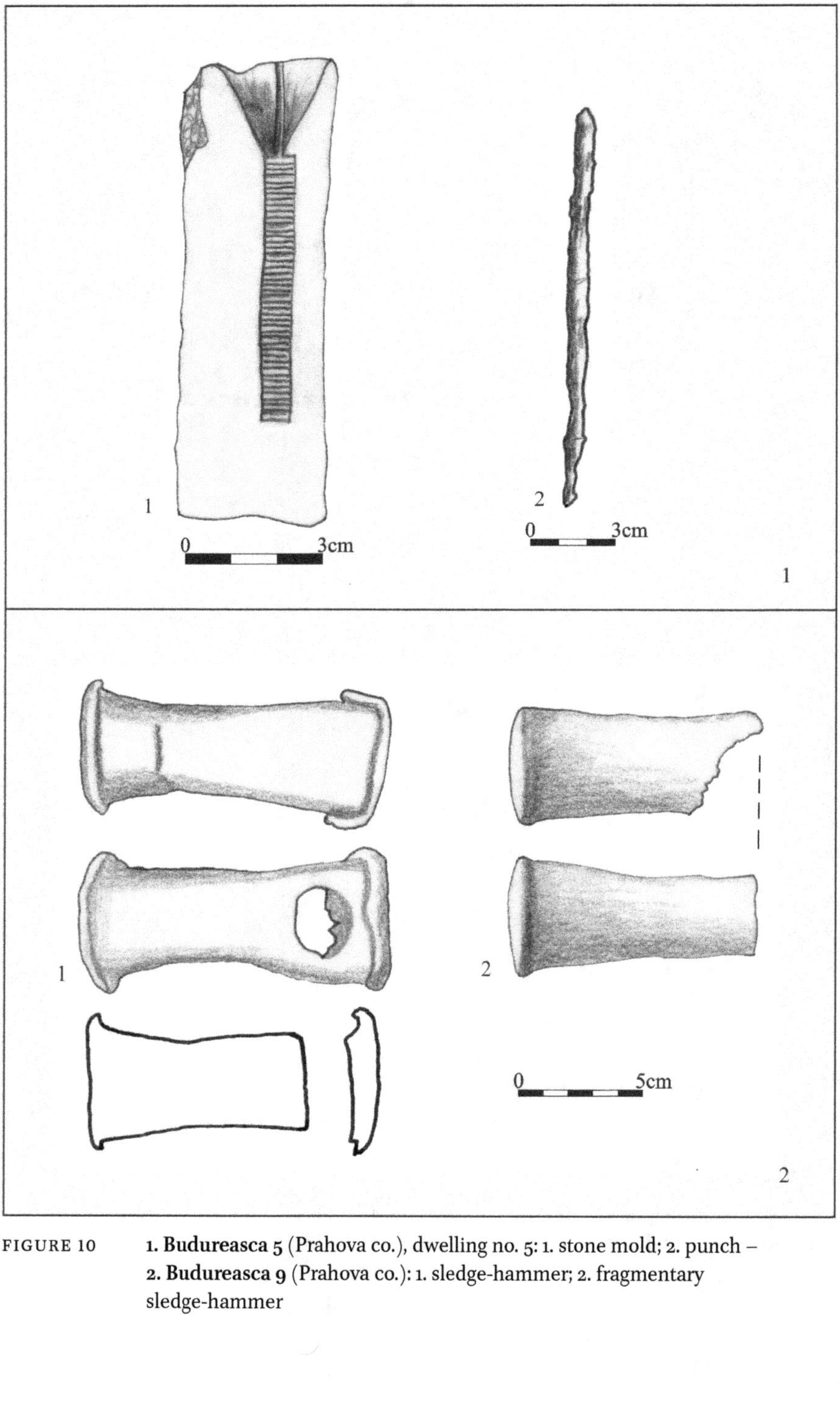

FIGURE 10 1. **Budureasca 5** (Prahova co.), dwelling no. 5: 1. stone mold; 2. punch – 2. **Budureasca 9** (Prahova co.): 1. sledge-hammer; 2. fragmentary sledge-hammer

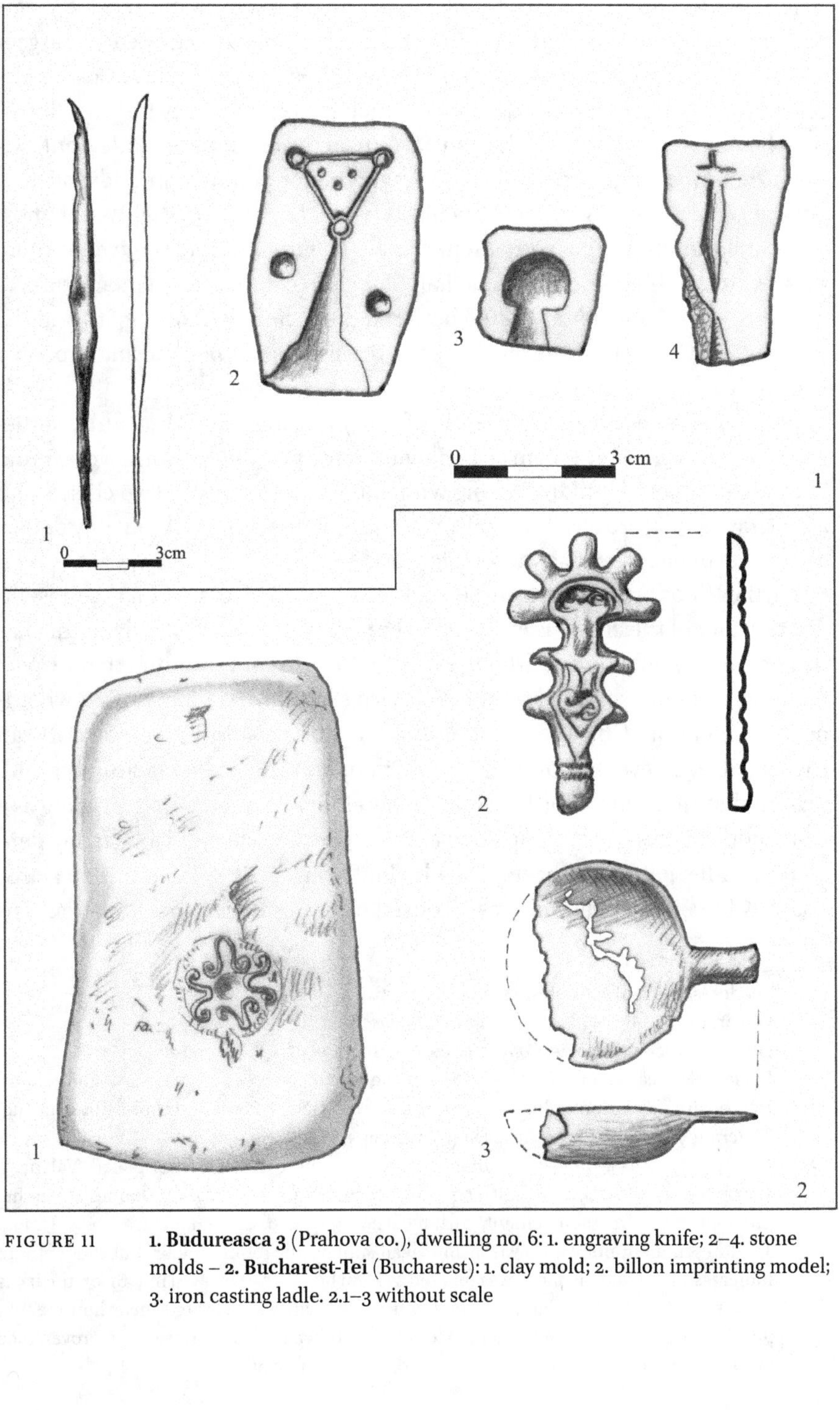

FIGURE 11 **1. Budureasca 3** (Prahova co.), dwelling no. 6: 1. engraving knife; 2–4. stone molds – **2. Bucharest-Tei** (Bucharest): 1. clay mold; 2. billon imprinting model; 3. iron casting ladle. 2.1–3 without scale

A tongue-shaped, iron tool with traces of lead was published by Victor Teodorescu as from the 6th- to 7th-century settlement excavated in Târgșor (Prahova County), about 25 miles to the southeast from Budureasca, as the crow flies. No information exists for the archaeological context of this find.[29] Another six miles to the south from Târgșor, at Șirna, another settlement was excavated, from which several mold fragments are known, in addition to a crucible, a ladle, and fragments of chisels (Fig. 6.5.1–4). Nonetheless, the most spectacular finds on that settlement site are smelting furnaces – two of them dated between the 5th and the first half of the 6th century (settlement features 12 and 17)[30] and seven more dated between the second half of the 6th and the 7th century. Out of those seven furnaces, three were in open air, and probably used only intermittently.[31]

About ten miles farther to the west from Șirna, another 6th-century settlement was excavated at Băleni (Dâmbovița County). Two crucibles were found in a sunken-floored building, along with handmade pottery.[32] Two chisels and an engraving tool are also known from that settlement, but without any details about the archaeological context (Fig. 12.1).[33]

Further finds are known from several settlements excavated on the present-day territory of the city of Bucharest. To be sure, evidence of metalworking has been found on only some of them. Perhaps the most important in that respect is the settlement excavated on the southern shore of Lake Fundeni in what is now the Doamna Ghica residential quarter, along the former Soldat Ghivan Nicolae Street. Several tools were found in one of the sunken-featured buildings on that site, and Victor Teodorescu therefore interpreted that building as a workshop. The assemblage included a single-piece, stone mold for earring pendants, a ladle, pair of tweezers and a billknife (Fig. 13.6).[34] In addition, a large quantity of ceramic material was retrieved from this house, including remains

29 Teodorescu, "Centre meșteșugărești," 85, fig. 6.4.

30 Olteanu, Grigore, Nicolae, *Comunitatea sătească*, 42–43.

31 Olteanu, Grigore, Nicolae, *Comunitatea sătească*, 47–50.

32 Luciana Muscă, Tiberiu I. Muscă, "Săpăturile arheologice de la Băleni-Români, județul Dâmbovița [The archaeological excavations from Băleni-Români, Dâmbovița county]," *Materiale și Cercetări Arheologice* 14 (1980), 426–427; 428, fig. 8.

33 Miclea, Florescu, *Strămoșii românilor*, fig. 840, 213, where the site is misspelled "Văleni".

34 Victor Teodorescu, "Centre meșteșugărești," 77; 81, fig. 3, 1–5; 83, fig. 5.1; Dolinescu-Ferche, Constantiniu, "Un établissement," 292, fig. 1; 293, 307, 309, 320, 321, fig. 17.18, 323, fig. 19.1. Teodorescu mentioned an "Avar" arrow head supposedly found in 1962, but the footnote indicates that while the piece was marked as from house 10 excavated in 1961, on the basis of its record in the museum register it came from trench 2 excavated (near house 2?) in 1961. Teodorescu therefore decided to leave the artifact aside as of unsecured provenance (Victor Teodorescu, "Centre meșteșugărești," 76 with note 21).

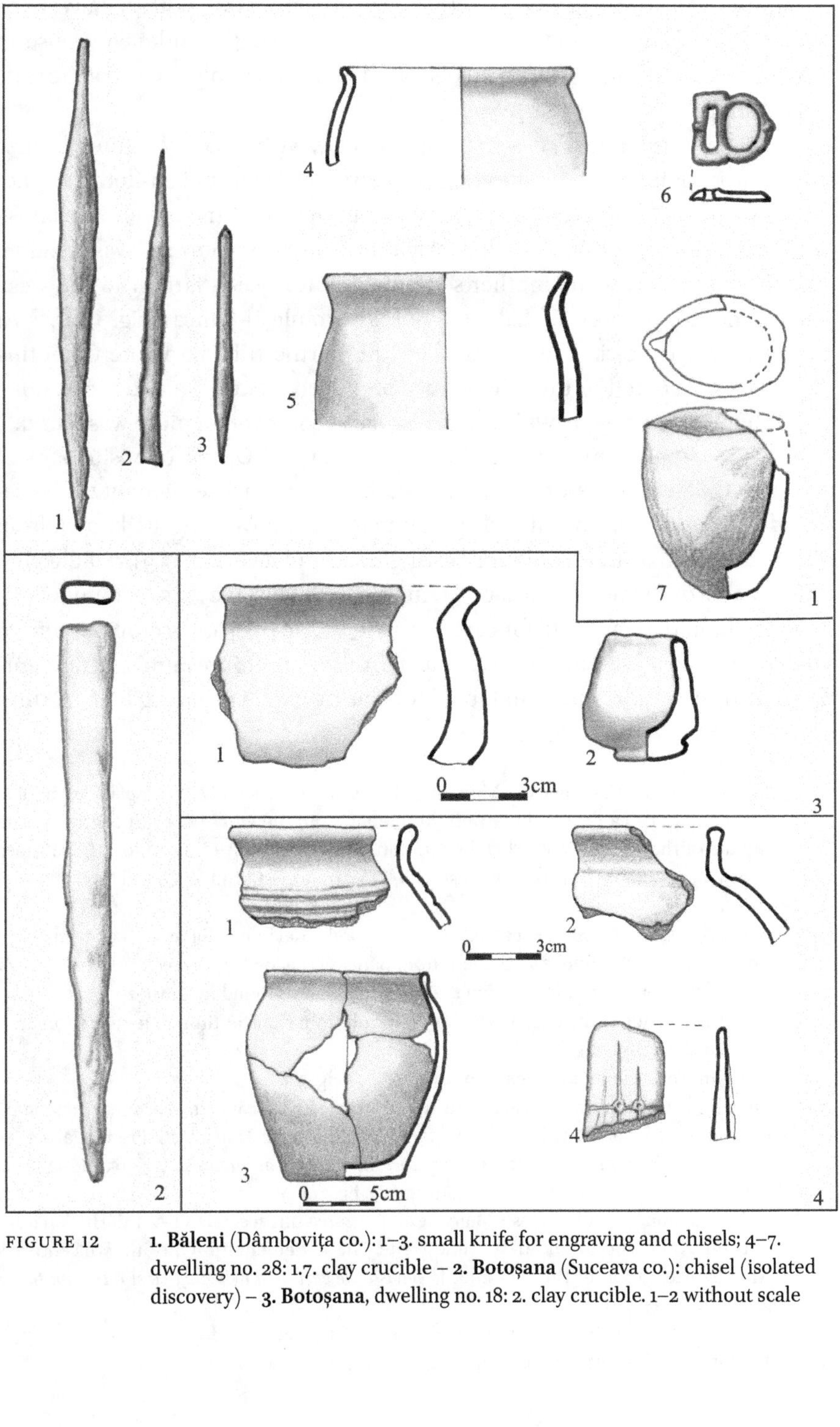

FIGURE 12 **1. Băleni** (Dâmbovița co.): 1–3. small knife for engraving and chisels; 4–7. dwelling no. 28: 1.7. clay crucible – **2. Botoșana** (Suceava co.): chisel (isolated discovery) – **3. Botoșana**, dwelling no. 18: 2. clay crucible. 1–2 without scale

of amphoras. Given that no less than 1124 fragments of pottery have been found, some have advanced the idea that, after being abandoned, house 10 served as a refuse pit.[35] If so, the tools found in the assemblage cannot indicate a workshop.

A 3.5 cm-long trilobate crucible made of clay, with traces of molten bronze inside, was found together with handmade pottery in a sunken-floored building of the settlement excavated on the northern side of the city of Bucharest, at Băneasa-La Stejar (Fig. 13.1).[36] A clay mold for casting crosses was accidentally found in or next to another settlement, a few yards farther to the west, on the northern shore of Lake Grivița, at Străulești-Lunca (Fig. 13.4).[37] At Străulești-Măicănești, a site located on the northern bank of the Colentina River, a house dated to the 4th century produced a part of a two-piece stone mold, but it is not clear in which archaeological context that piece was found.[38] A crucible was also found in the filling of house 150.[39] On the opposite bank of the river Colentina, a few miles to the southeast, another settlement was excavated at Dămăroaia. Several finds pertaining to metalworking are known from this settlement: a stone mold for casting buckle plates (Fig. 13.3), a ladle, and the remains of a smelting furnace.[40] An iron ladle (Fig. 11.2), a silver model of a bow fibula, and a clay mold for casting earring pendants, and a crucible similar to that from Băneasa-La Stejar are known from another (presumed settlement) farther to the east on the same bank of the river Colentina, at Tei.[41] A third

35 Eugen S. Teodor, Ceramica din Muntenia, de la sfârșitul veacului al v-lea până la mijlocul veacului al VII-lea [The pottery from Muntenia, from the end of the 5th century to the middle of the 7th century]. PhD dissertation, Universitatea "Alexandru Ioan Cuza" (Iași, 2001), 115. (available at http://www.esteo.ro/TTW/index_est.html. Accessed November 20, 2016).

36 Margareta Constantiniu, "Așezarea autohtonă prefeudală de la Băneasa (La Stejar) [The Pre-feudal autochthonous settlement from Băneasa (La Stejar)]," *Cercetări Arheologice în București* 2 (1965), 95 only mention that the crucible was found in house 20. That it came from the interior of the oven in that house result from Constantiniu, "Elemente romano-bizantine," 673; 674, fig. 5.1.

37 Constantiniu, "Elemente romano-bizantine," 674, fig. 5.3.

38 Margareta Constantiniu, "Săpăturile de la Străulești-Măicănești. Așezarea prefeudală I. Așezarea prefeudală II [The excavations from Străulești-Măicănești. Pre-feudal settlement I. Pre-feudal settlement II]," *Cercetări Arheologice în București* 2 (1965), 161, fig. 72; Victor Teodorescu, "Centre meșteșugărești," 83, fig. 5/4, 95.

39 Vasilica Sandu, "Situl Străulești-Măicănești. Așezarea din secolele VI–VII d. Hr. Săpătura din anul 2000 [The Străulești-Măicănești site. The settlement from the 6th–7th centuries AD The excavation of the year 2000]," *Revista de cercetări arheologice și numismatice* 2 (2016), 168, 183, pl. II.7.

40 Lăzărescu-Ionescu et al., "Săpăturile arheologice," 259–260; 231, fig. 40.8.

41 Teodorescu, "Centre meșteșugărești," 82, fig. 4.1, 4–5; 95–96.

crucible was accidentally found in downtown Bucharest on the northern side of the Carol I Boulevard, next to the Casa Armatei/Military Club (Fig. 13.2).[42] Victor Teodorescu draws analogies between that crucible and those found in Târgșor and Budureasca 9.[43] Only his claim regarding the latter site can be verified.[44] Besides the smelting furnaces from Dămăroaia and Lunca Bârzești 1,[45] more evidence of ironworking comes in the form of slag from Curtea Veche,[46] Ciurel (on the northwestern side of Bucharest), Străulești-Lunca[47] Lunca-Bîrzești,[48] and Militari.[49] Blooms have also been found in the filling of the oven in house 4 of the settlement site excavated in Lunca-Bîrzești 1, and on the hearth of the oven in house 5 in Lunca-Bîrzești.[50]

The abundant evidence of metalworking on the territory of the present-day city of Bucharest, and the many parallels between finds from different sites raises interesting questions about the relations between the communities inhabiting those settlements.

No less than four different settlements have been excavated on different sites near the village of Dulceanca (Teleorman County), in southern Walachia, some 20 miles to the north from the river Danube. A bronze chisel was found together with ceramic remains, bronze and iron artifacts, as well as a whetstone in one of the sunken-floored buildings excavated on site 1.[51] Three more whetstones were associated with a stone mold in the filling of another house

---

42 Morintz, Rosetti, "Din cele mai vechi timpuri," pl. XXXI, 11–12.

43 Teodorescu, "Centre meșteșugărești," 75, note 11.

44 Teodorescu, Peneș, "Matricea de incidență," 46, fig. 21.20.

45 Vasilica Sandu, "Cercetări arheologice în zona Lunca-Bârzești [Archaeological research in the Lunca-Bârzești area]," *Cercetări Arheologice în Bucharest* 4 (1992), 188, fig. 2; 189.

46 Panait I. Panait, Aristide Ștefănescu, *Muzeul Curtea Veche. Palatul Voievodal* [The Curtea Veche Museum. Voivodal Palace] (Bucharest: Muzeul de Istorie a Municipiului Bucharest, 1973),14.

47 Maria Comșa, "Quelques données concernant les rapports des territoires nord-danubiens avec Byzance aux VIe - VIIIe siècles (Pendants d'oreille en forme d'étoile)." *Revue des Études Sud-Est Européennes* 9, no. 3 (1971), 183; Ștefan Olteanu, "Vechi preocupări de reducere a minereului de fier pe teritoriul orașului București [Old preoccupations about the reduction of iron ore in the territory of Bucharest]," *București* 9 (1972), 111; Suzana Dolinescu-Ferche, "Ciurel, habitat des VIe - VIIe siècles de notre ère," *Dacia* 23 (1979), 179–230.

48 Sandu, "Cercetări arheologice," 186, 188–189, 190–191.

49 Mircea Negru, Alexandru Bădescu, Vasilica Cuculea-Sandu, *Militari-Câmpul Boja, an Archaeological Site on the Territory of Bucharest (Archaeological Investigations since 1958 up to 2005). VI. Settlements Dating from the 5th–7th Centuries* (Bucharest: Minerva Expres, 2009), 16.

50 Sandu, "Cercetări arheologice," 188, 190.

51 Dolinescu-Ferche, *Așezări*, 81, 83, 86, fig. 91.4; 87, fig. 92.5.

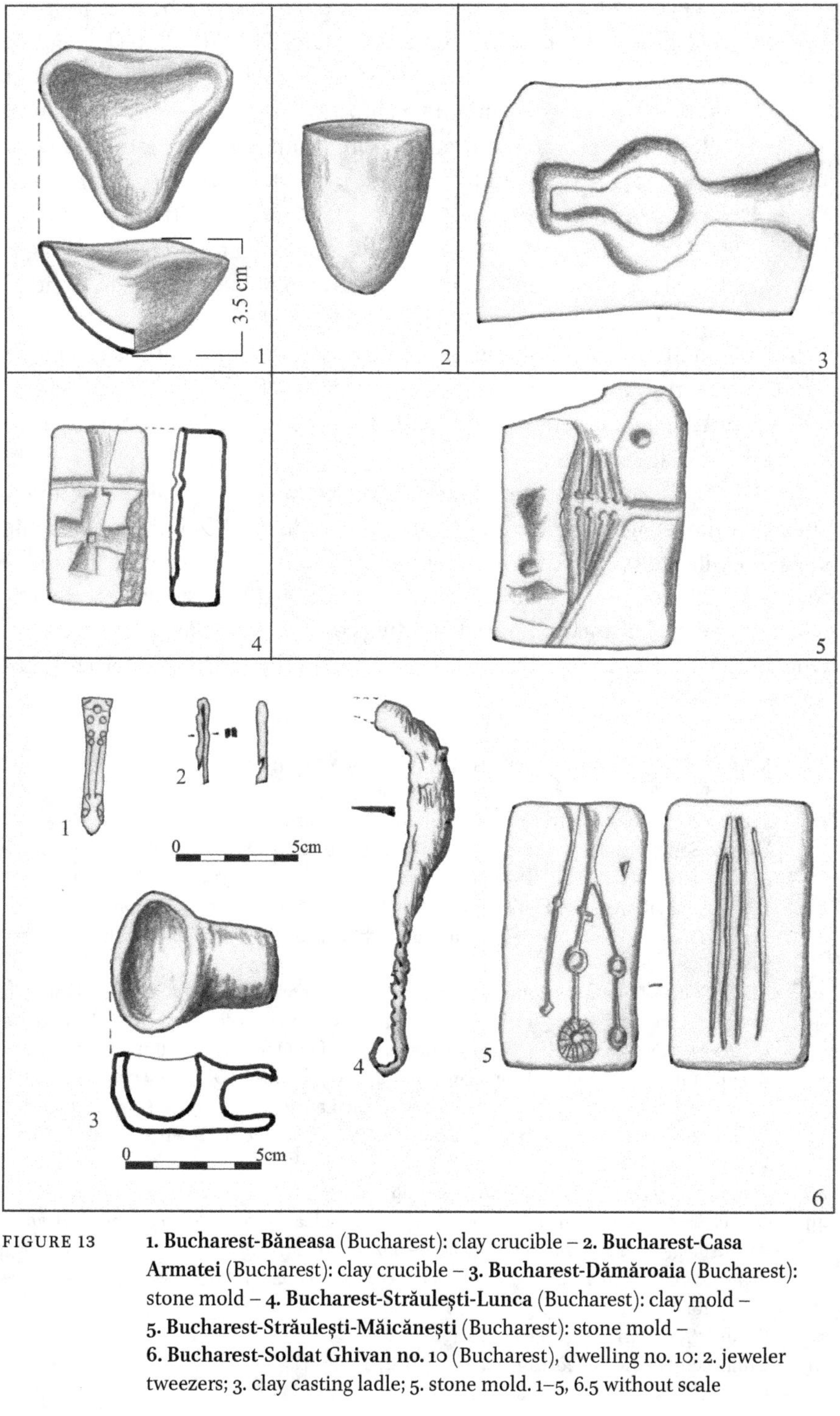

FIGURE 13 **1. Bucharest-Băneasa** (Bucharest): clay crucible – **2. Bucharest-Casa Armatei** (Bucharest): clay crucible – **3. Bucharest-Dămăroaia** (Bucharest): stone mold – **4. Bucharest-Străulești-Lunca** (Bucharest): clay mold – **5. Bucharest-Străulești-Măicănești** (Bucharest): stone mold – **6. Bucharest-Soldat Ghivan no. 10** (Bucharest), dwelling no. 10: 2. jeweler tweezers; 3. clay casting ladle; 5. stone mold. 1–5, 6.5 without scale

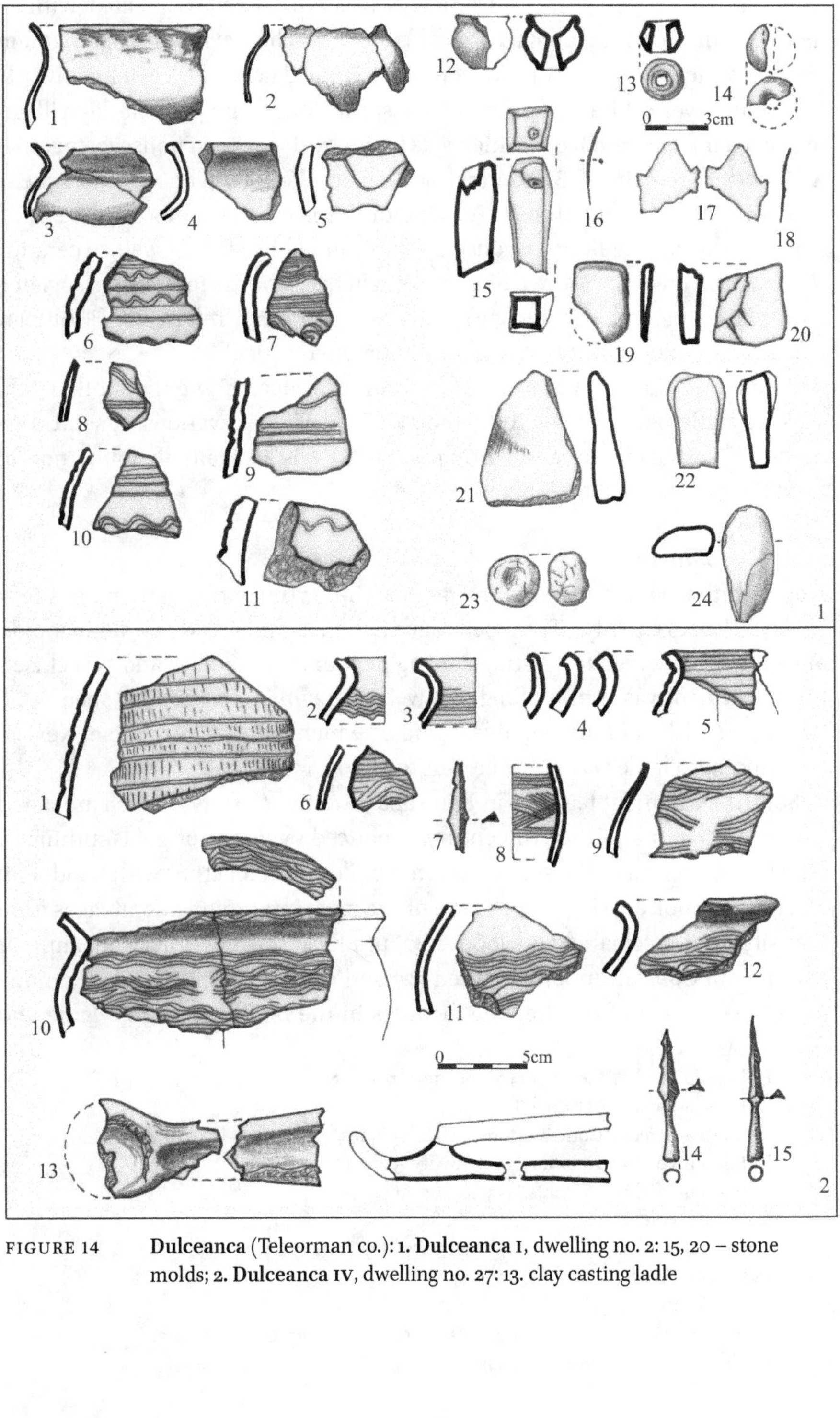

FIGURE 14 **Dulceanca** (Teleorman co.): **1. Dulceanca I**, dwelling no. 2: 15, 20 – stone molds; **2. Dulceanca IV**, dwelling no. 27: 13. clay casting ladle

from the same site (Fig. 14.1).[52] Iron slag is also mentioned in the area, with no information about the archaeological context.[53] The neighboring settlement at site 2, which is dated to the 6th century produced no evidence of metalworking whatsoever.[54] Site 3, on the northeastern side of the present-day village, produced only an iron ladle, which was found by the oven in house 17, together with pottery remains.[55] By contrast, several clay ladles are known from site 4, which is dated to the 7th century. One of them was found in a refuse pit.[56] Another was on the floor of house 23, surrounded by slag, as well as ceramic remains and knives.[57] More ladles are known from the assemblages associated with houses 26 and 27 (Fig. 14.2), and from two other refuse pits.[58] All clay ladles from Dulceanca bear traces of molten metal (slag).[59]

Some ten miles to the northeast from Dulceanca, at Olteni, another 6th-century settlement was found by means of salvage excavations. A sandstone mold for casting crosses and earring pendants was accidentally found not far from the excavation site (Fig. 2.3).[60]

1.3 *Moldavia*

A goldsmith's workshop was found on the 6th- to 7th-century settlement site at Dodești (Vaslui County). The assemblage in house 4 included two stone molds, once of which served for casting earring pendants, a mandrel and two chisels (one of which was in the filling), as well as fragments of copper sheet – all associated with ceramic remains, some of which were of amphorae. Next to the building, a ladle was discovered as well (Fig. 15–16).[61]

Several settlement features in Botoșana (Suceava County), which are dated between the 5th and the 7th century, produced evidence of goldsmithing. A crucible was found in the sunken-floored building 18, together with hand- and wheel-made pottery (Fig. 12.3).[62] One of the most important assemblages from that site, that associated with house 20, produced a coin struck for Emperor Justinian in Constantinople between 527 and 538. The coin was found among the stones of one of two heating facilities in the building, while a ladle and

52 Dolinescu-Ferche, *Așezări*, 86, 87, 96, fig. 106.4, 6–8.
53 Dolinescu-Ferche, *Așezări*, 98.
54 Dolinescu-Ferche, "Contributions archéologiques," 121–154.
55 Dolinescu-Ferche, "Habitats," 133; 146, fig. 15.20.
56 Dolinescu-Ferche, "Habitats," 155; 167, fig. 31.7.
57 Dolinescu-Ferche, "Habitats," 157; 167, fig. 31. 35.
58 Dolinescu-Ferche, "Habitats," 168, fig. 32.27; 169, fig. 33.7, 13, 31.
59 Dolinescu-Ferche, "Habitats," 1992, 172.
60 Preda, "Tipar," 513–516.
61 Teodor, *Continuitatea*, 24–25, 27, fig. 5.d, 29, fig. 6.1–3, 10–11, 30, fig. 71–3.
62 Teodor, *Civilizația romanică*, 35, 99, fig. 20.6.

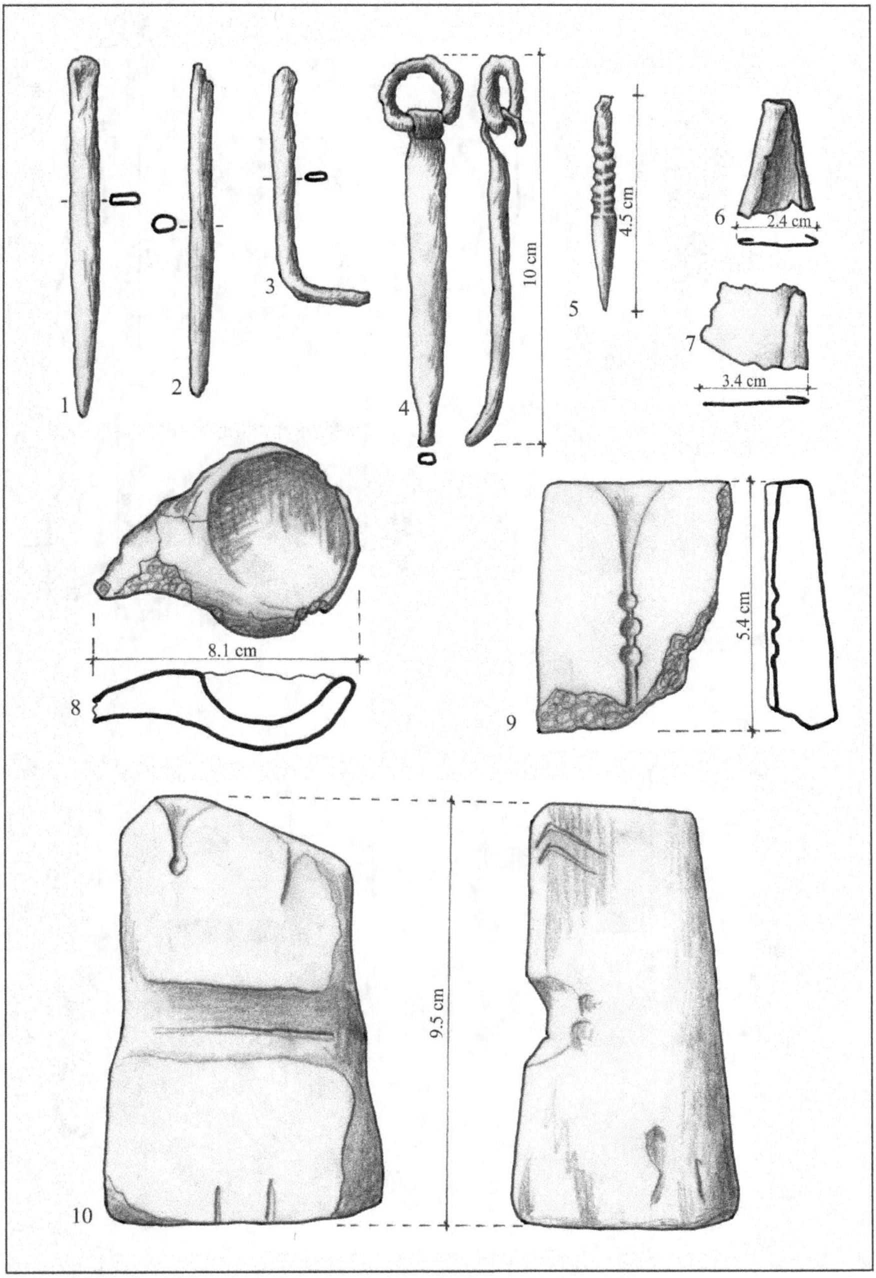

FIGURE 15 **Dodești** (Vaslui co.), dwelling no. 4: 1. chisel; 2. graver?; 5. drill-file; 8. clay casting ladle; 9–10. stone molds. 1–3 without dimensions

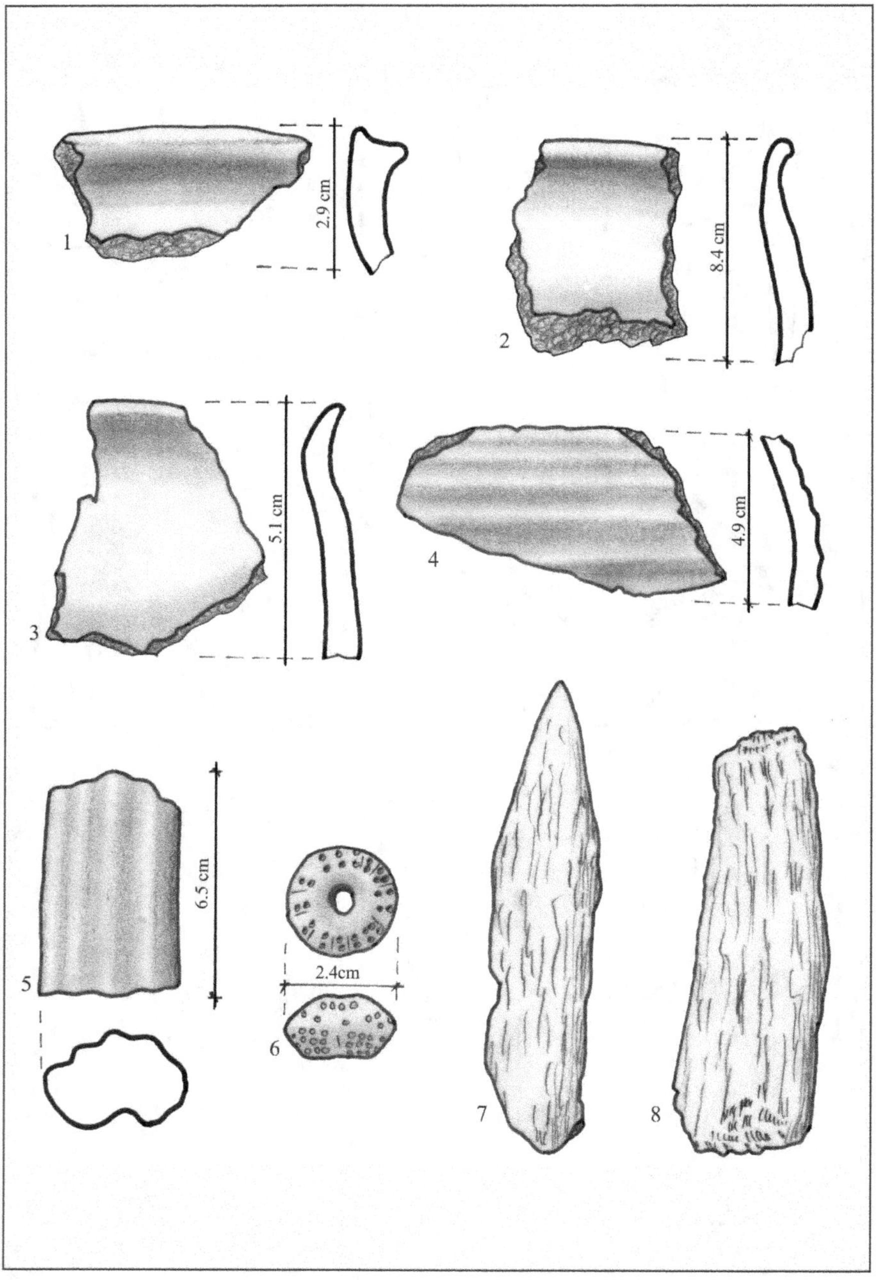

FIGURE 16 **Dodești** (Vaslui co.), dwelling no. 4. 7–8 without dimensions

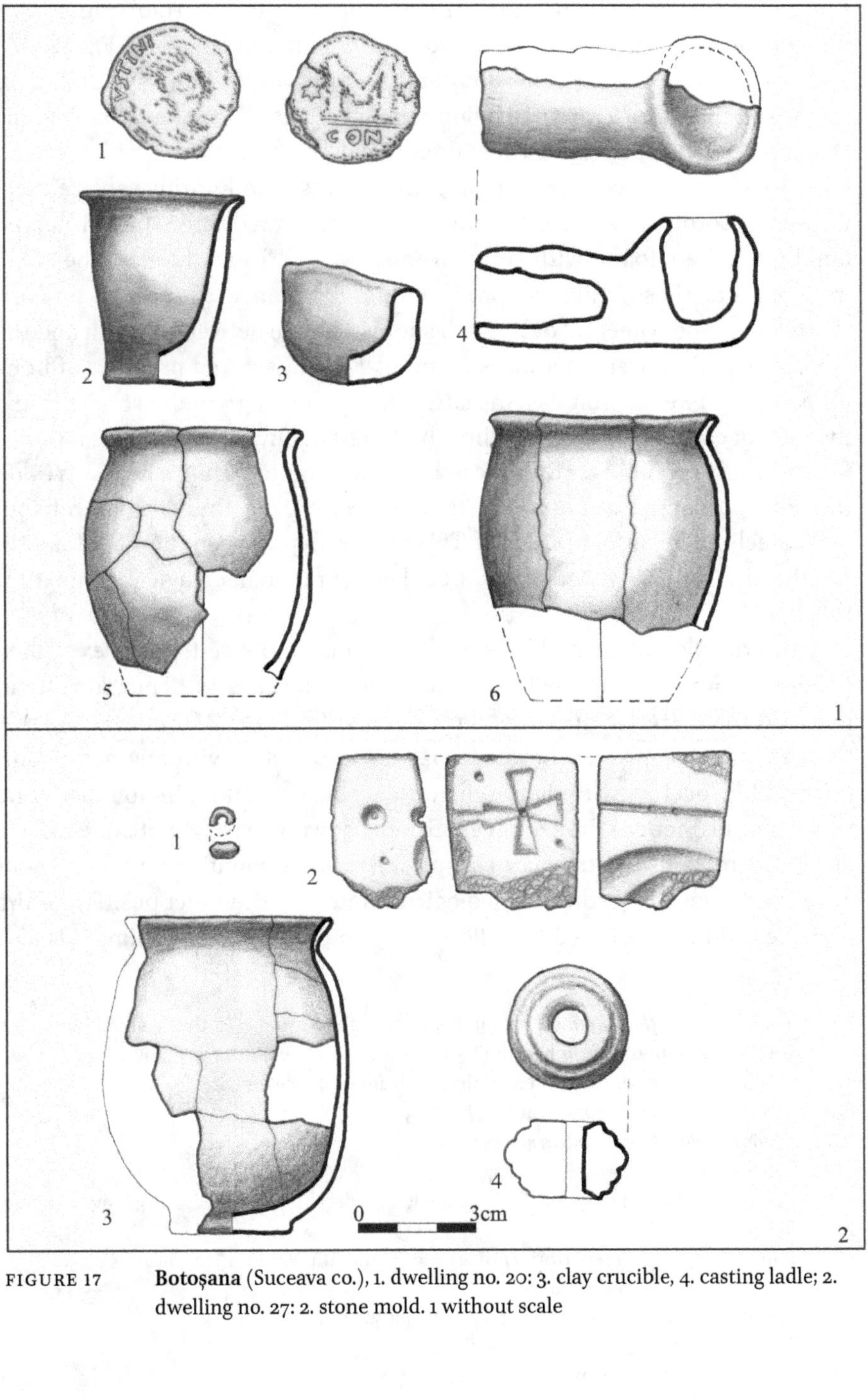

FIGURE 17 **Botoşana** (Suceava co.), 1. dwelling no. 20: 3. clay crucible, 4. casting ladle; 2. dwelling no. 27: 2. stone mold. 1 without scale

a crucible were found on a hearth in its northeastern corner (Fig. 17.1).[63] A stone mold for casting dress accessories was found in house 25 (Fig. 12.4).[64] The other stone mold from Botoşana was retrieved from the filling of house 27 (Fig. 17.2).[65] Two small blooms are said to have been found next to the house 20 and inside house 12 (near the stone oven).[66]

A stone mold for casting dress accessories was found during salvage excavations in Coroteni (Vrancea County), which uncovered three sunken-floored buildings, all equipped with stone ovens (Fig. 5.4). In addition to the stone mold, two of those buildings produced an abundance of ceramic remains (both hand- and wheel-made), which suggests a date between the 6th and the 7th century. Moreover, excavators found half-manufactured products of bone processing, as well as iron slag, the latter clearly showing a metalworking activity. It is not clear in which of the three buildings (if any), the mold was found.[67] Similarly, a stone mold for dress accessories was found during a field survey on the neighboring site at Răcoasa (Vrancea County), together with both hand- and wheel-made pottery (Fig. 2.6). This may well have been the site of another 6th- to 7th-century settlement, but there is no archaeological context for the mold.[68]

Four crucibles and a mold are also known from the settlement excavated in Suceava-Şipot, and to the late 6th and early 7th century.[69] The crucibles in houses 8 and 19 were found together with knives and awls (Fig. 18.1; Fig. 19.1).[70] The crucible in house 16, however, was not associated with any other tools (Fig. 19.2).[71] Together with that from house 15, the excavator also found a stone mold and fragment of bronze sheet, as well as two knives (Fig. 18.2).[72] Bronze and brass remains, particularly casting wasters, are mentioned, but without any information about the archaeological context.[73] The exact position of the crucibles and the mold – on the floor of the building or in its filling – is also

63 Teodor, *Civilizaţia romanică*, 37, 99, fig. 20.2, 5. Teodor believes that a small bowl with everted rim found next to hearth (Teodor, *Civilizaţia romanică*, 37, 99, fig. 20.4) was also used in metalworking, but there is absolutely no evidence for that.

64 Teodor, *Civilizaţia romanică*, 40, 99, fig. 20.3.

65 Teodor, *Civilizaţia romanică*, 41, 99, fig. 20.1.

66 Teodor, *Civilizaţia romanică*, 56–57.

67 Bobi, "Contribuţii la repertoriul arheologic al judeţului Vrancea," 107, 138, fig. 25.6; 140, fig. 27. 6–7.

68 Bobi, "Contribuţii la repertoriul arheologic al judeţului Vrancea," 107, 140, fig. 27.5.

69 Teodor, *Aşezarea medievală*, 7.

70 Teodor, *Aşezarea medievală*, 17 and 22; 124, fig. 32/4–6.

71 Teodor, *Aşezarea medievală*, 21; 124, fig. 32/2.

72 Teodor, *Aşezarea medievală*, 20; 124, fig. 32/7–8.

73 Teodor, *Aşezarea medievală*, 29 and 51.

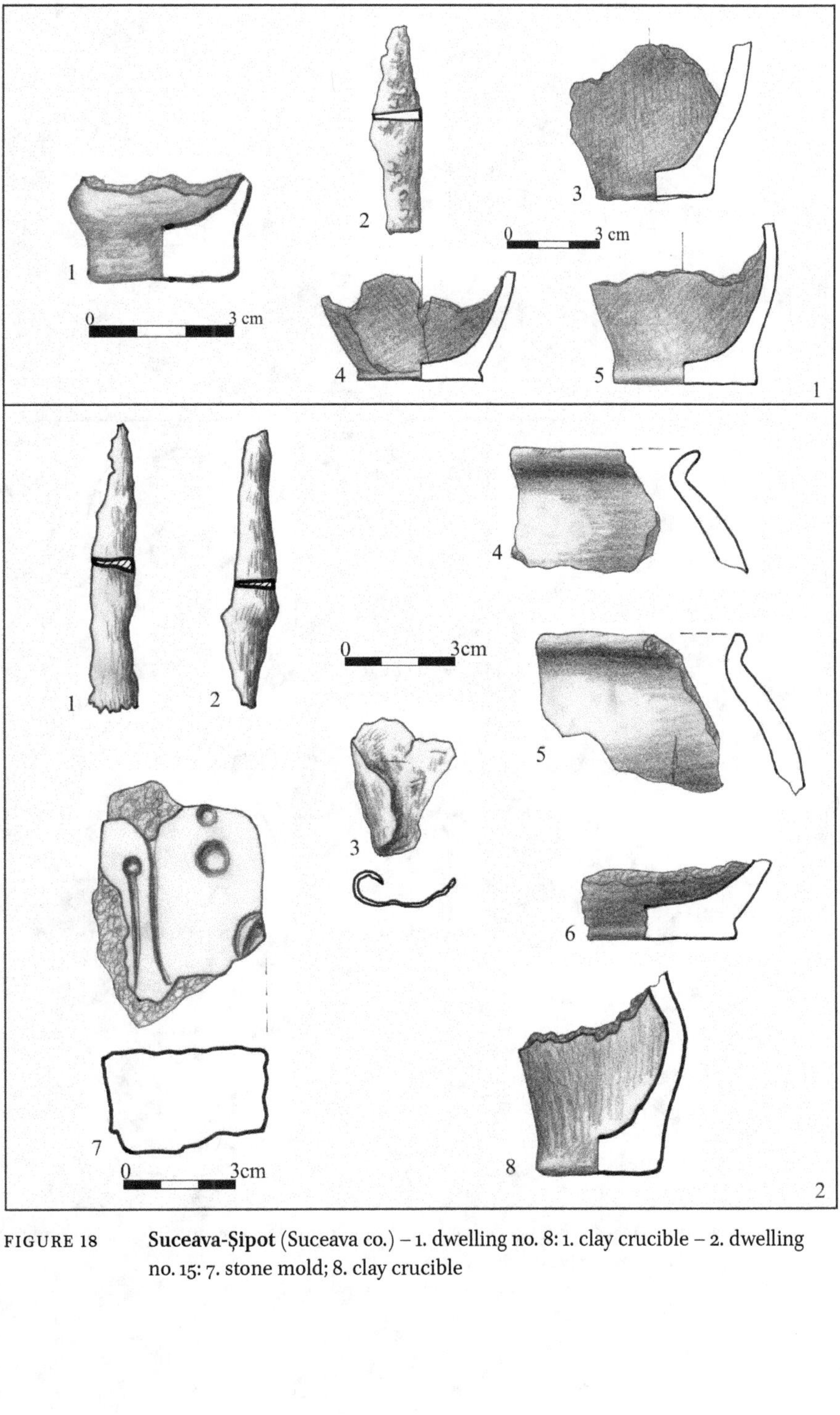

FIGURE 18 **Suceava-Șipot** (Suceava co.) – 1. dwelling no. 8: 1. clay crucible – 2. dwelling no. 15: 7. stone mold; 8. clay crucible

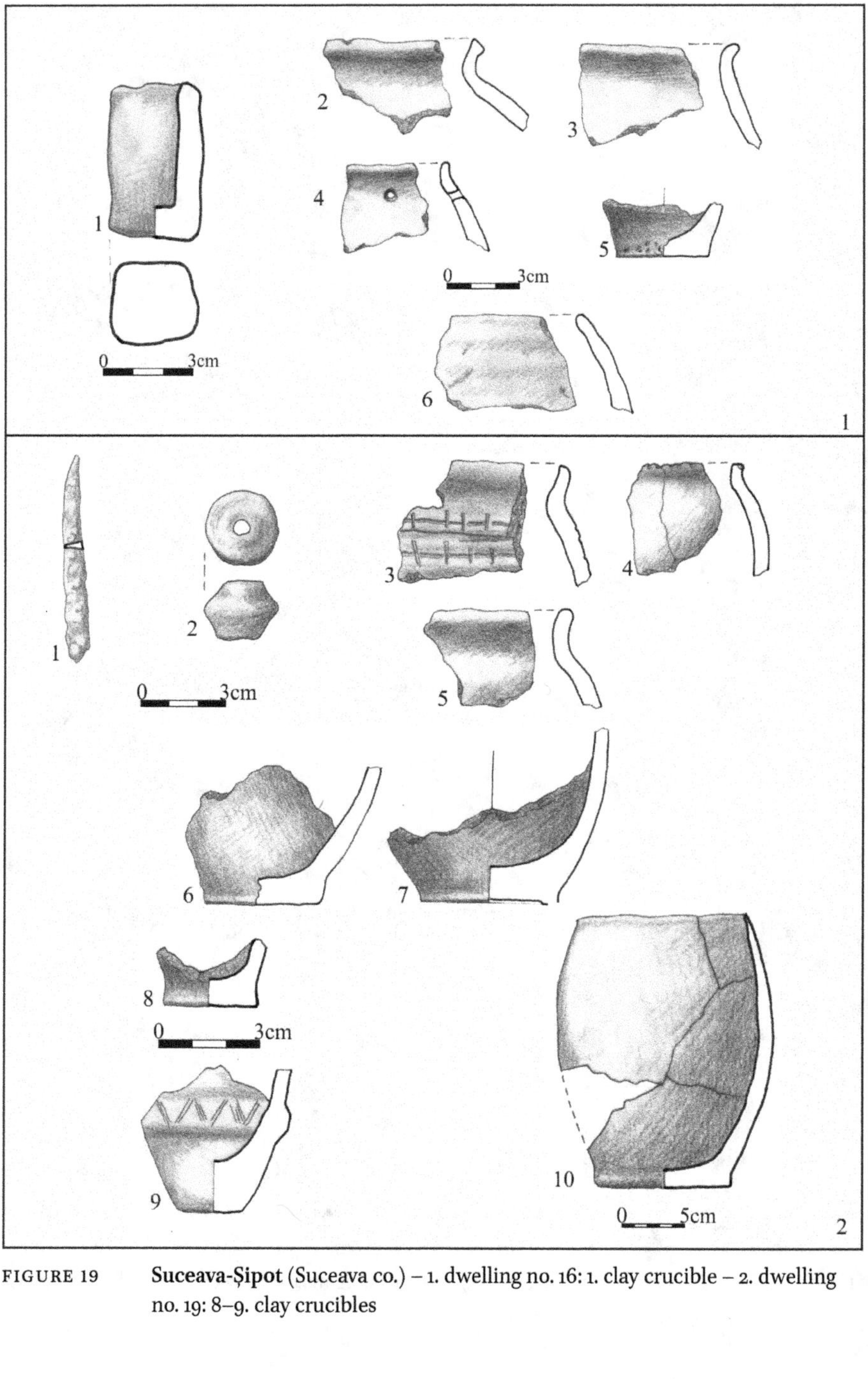

FIGURE 19 **Suceava-Șipot** (Suceava co.) – 1. dwelling no. 16: 1. clay crucible – 2. dwelling no. 19: 8–9. clay crucibles

unknown. It is not even sure that all small ceramic vessels interpreted as crucibles were truly used in metalworking, since none had traces of molten metal.

Metalworking, however, was most certainly practiced on the settlement site excavated in Davideni (Neamţ County).[74] That much results from the discovery of a chisel inside the clay oven in house 5.[75] The same is true for numerous finds of engraving tools. Such tools are known from several, well-dated assemblages, e.g., houses 6 and 72, the associated assemblages of which included iron fibulae with bent stem dated to the 6th century.[76] Another was found in house 17 together with knives, a buckle, and a hook.[77] In the filling of house 33, which also produced an engraving tool, the excavator found a stone mold for casting dress accessories (Fig. 20.10). The ceramic assemblage in that feature included a tumbler, which the excavator took for a crucible.[78] The engraving tool from house 35 was associated with two mandrels, one found in the building, the other in the filling.[79] A mandrel and an engraving tool were found together with a stone mold and a crucible in house 36 (Fig. 21.11–13).[80] This may well have been the dwelling (and/or workshop) of a goldsmith. The association of an engraving tool with a crucible is also documented in the case of house 39, the associated assemblage of which also included a knife and a flint-steel.[81] The engraving tool from house 74 was found in the filling, like the knife and the fragment of a sickle.[82] A knife and an engraving tool were found together with a needle and two bone awls in house 69.[83] Only the engraving tools in houses 37 and 46 were found alone, with no other tools or implements.[84] A bronze fibula with bent stem, which is also dated to the 6th century, was found in house 75 together with a ladle and remains of amphorae (Fig. 22.2).[85] Another such fibula comes from a trench dug out in 1970, in which a stone mold for casting dress accessories was also discovered.[86] A small wimble, a mandrel, and another engraving tool have also been found outside any settlement features (Fig. 22.1).[87]

---

74 Mitrea, *Aşezarea de la Davideni*, 10.
75 Mitrea, *Aşezarea de la Davideni*, 42.
76 Mitrea, *Aşezarea de la Davideni*, 54 and 117–119, 321, fig. 61.4.
77 Mitrea, *Aşezarea de la Davideni*, 55.
78 Mitrea, *Aşezarea de la Davideni*, 71–72, 321, fig. 61.5; 325, fig. 65.5; 364, fig. 103.5.
79 Mitrea, *Aşezarea de la Davideni*, 73–75, 320, fig. 2.
80 Mitrea, *Aşezarea de la Davideni*, 75–76, 321, fig. 61, 9–10; 325, fig. 65.4; 370, fig. 109.4.
81 Mitrea, *Aşezarea de la Davideni*, 79–80, 323, fig. 51.3.
82 Mitrea, *Aşezarea de la Davideni*, 120–121, 321, fig. 61.6.
83 Mitrea, *Aşezarea de la Davideni*, 112–113, fig. 320, fig. 60.1.
84 Mitrea, *Aşezarea de la Davideni*, 77–78 and 87–88, 320, fig. 60.4.
85 Mitrea, *Aşezarea de la Davideni*, 121–122, 326, fig. 56.6, 335, fig. 74.5.
86 Mitrea, *Aşezarea de la Davideni*, 128.
87 Mitrea, *Aşezarea de la Davideni*, 129 and 130, 320, fig. 60.3, 321, fig. 61.8, 323, fig. 63.4.

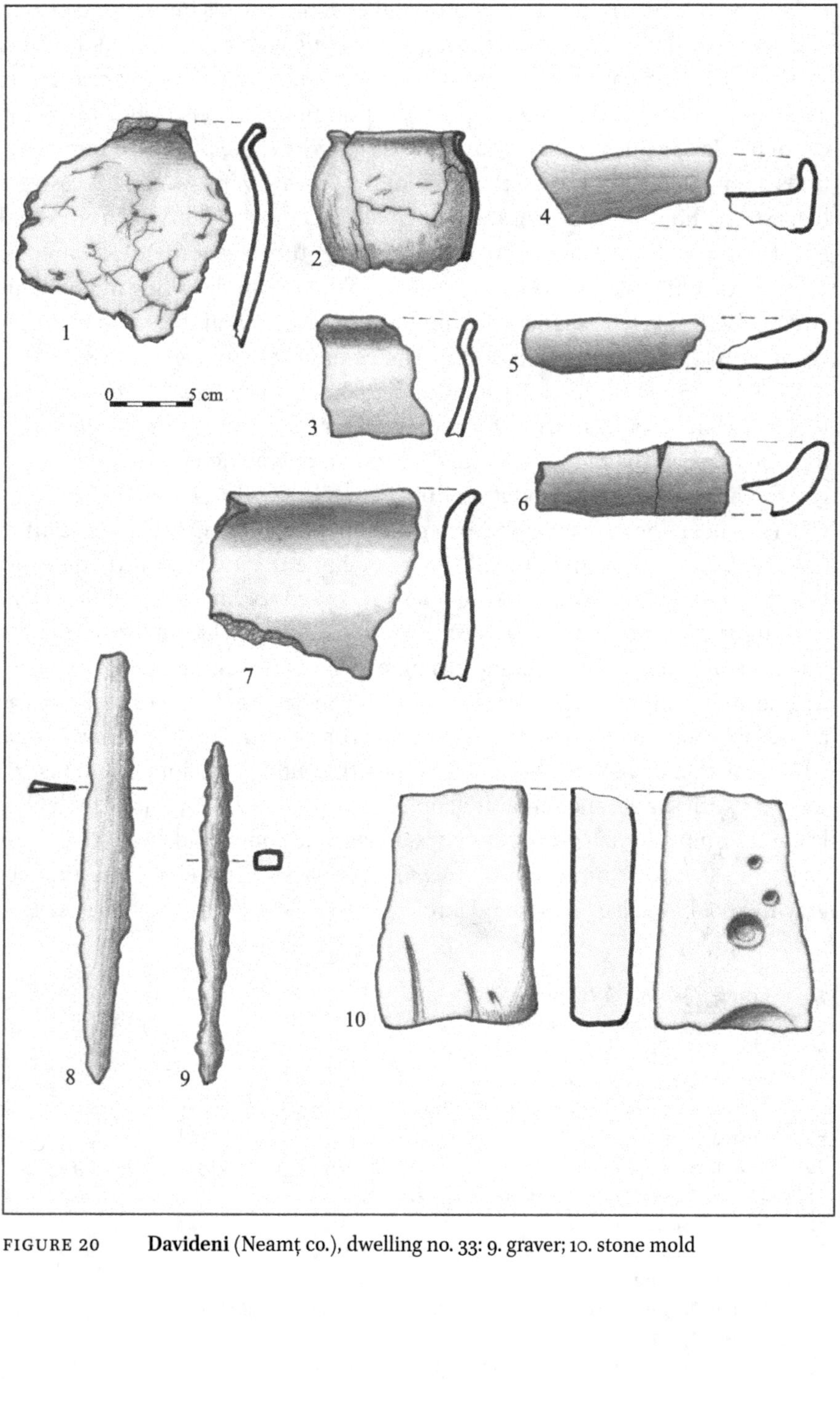

FIGURE 20 **Davideni** (Neamţ co.), dwelling no. 33: 9. graver; 10. stone mold

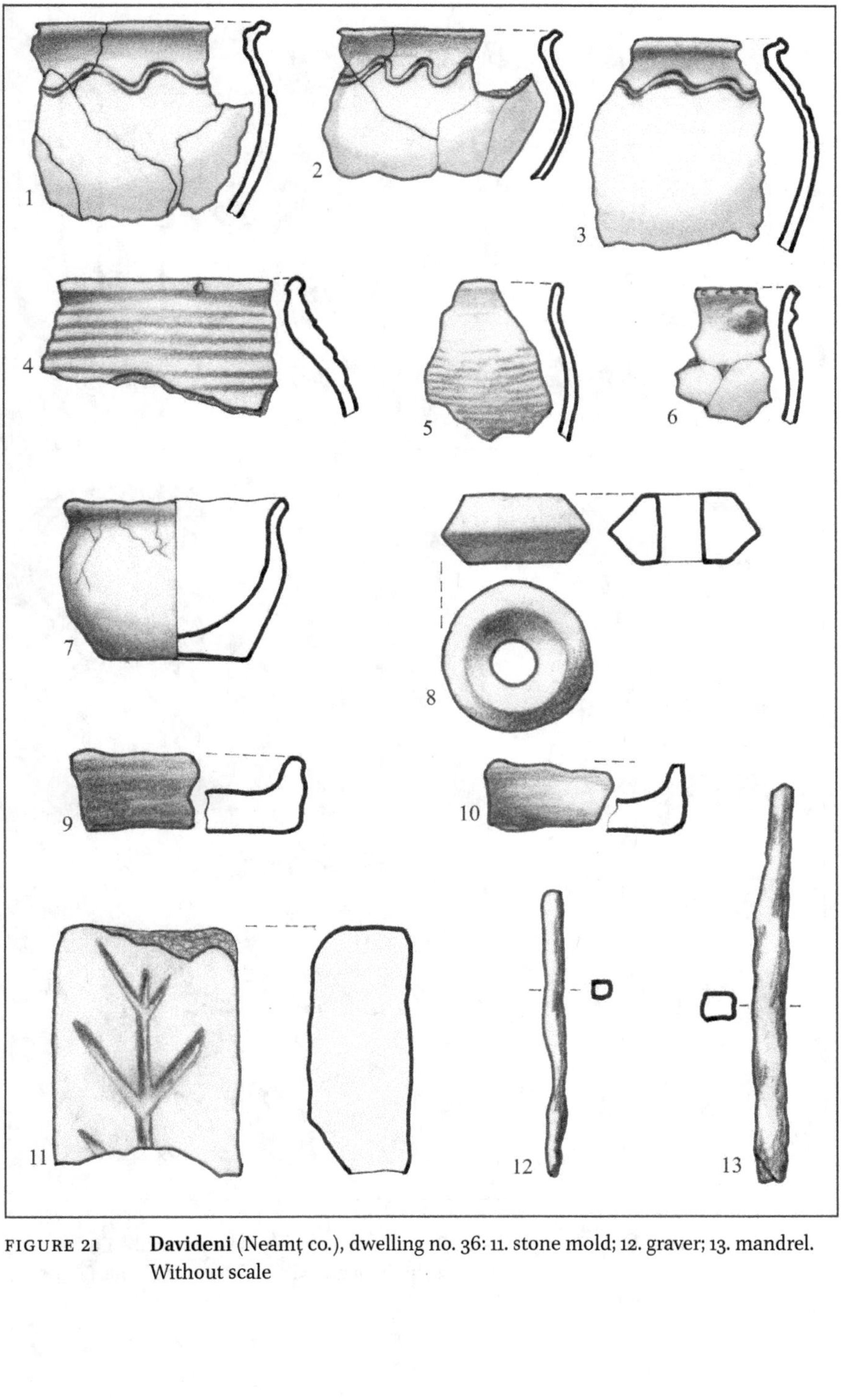

FIGURE 21 **Davideni** (Neamț co.), dwelling no. 36: 11. stone mold; 12. graver; 13. mandrel. Without scale

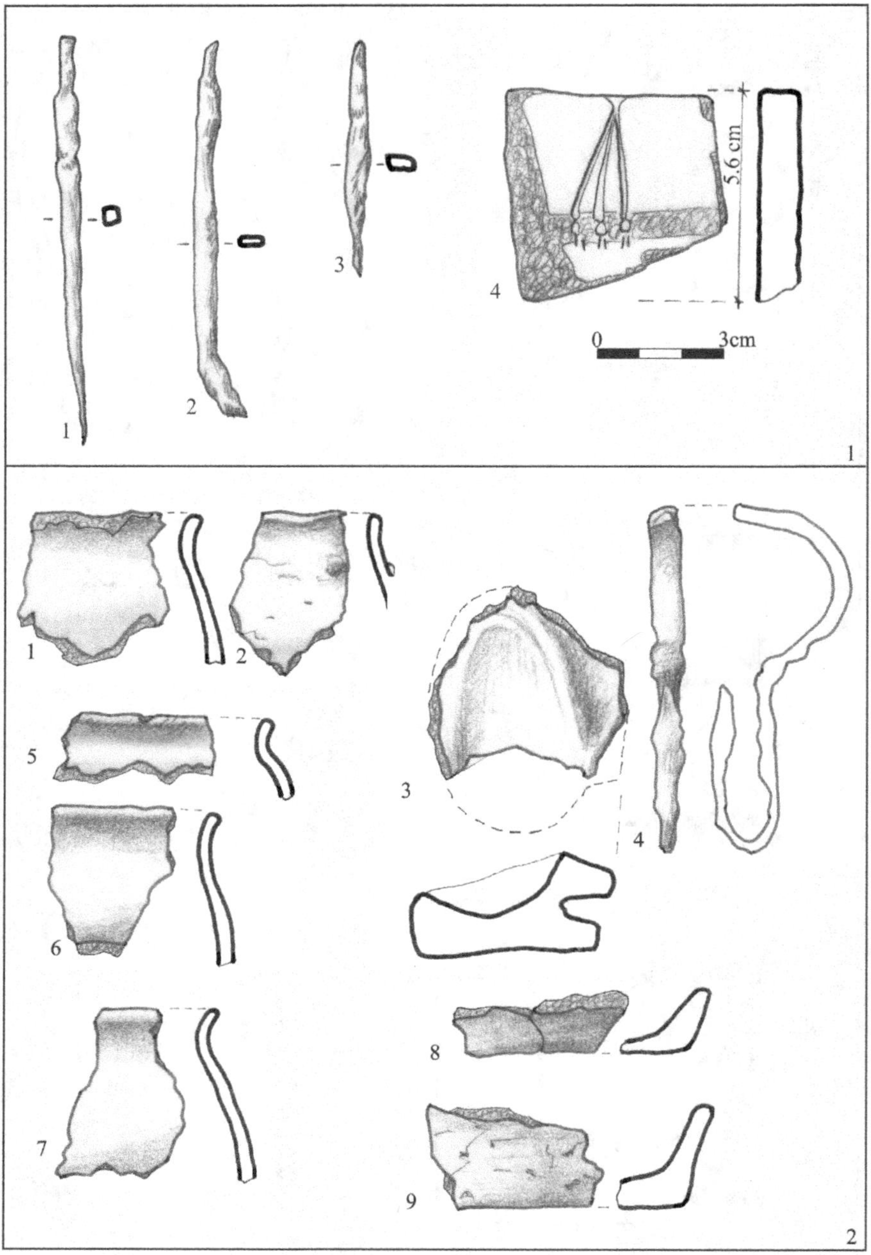

FIGURE 22 **Davideni** (Neamț co.) – 1.1. S LVIII: engraver – 1.2. S XXX: punch – 1.3. S LIV: drill – 1.4. S I: stone mold – 2. dwelling no. 75: 2.9. clay casting ladle. 1.1–3, 2 without scale

A clay mold for casting earring pendants is also known from a 6th- to 7th-century settlement excavated at Traian-Săbăoani (Neamţ County). The sunken-floored building in which the mold was found has been interpreted as a workshop (Fig. 23.2).[88] A stone mold for casting dress accessories is also known from a sunken-floored building of the settlement excavated in Ştefan cel Mare-Gutinaş-La Selişte (Bacău County) (Fig. 23.1.2).[89] Fragments of copper sheet with traces of cutting, no doubt for processing, were found in another feature, together with a fragment of an amphora and a knife.[90] House 5 had two ovens, one of clay, and another of stone, with a strongly burnt clay crust on the hearth (presumably from some kind of metalworking activity). The associated assemblage included an engraving tool, found right by the stone oven (Fig. 23.1.1).[91] Another engraving tool was discovered by the oven in the sunken-floored building 18.[92] A chisel was also found in the filling of house 8 (Fig. 23.1.3).[93]

A chisel was found in Izvoare-Bahna (Neamţ County), a settlement dated to the 6th and 7th centuries, but outside any of the excavated features. Another instrument, probably a chisel as well, is illustrated, but with no information about the whereabouts of its finding.[94] Engraving tools have also been found in houses 17 and 30 together with slag and blooms. There was a smelting furnace in house 30, inside which there was a bloom. Both houses, however, are dated to the second occupation phase on the site, which is dated between the 8th and the 9th century.[95] There is evidence of ironworking, in the form of slag and

88 George Dan Hânceanu, "Două piese din secolele VI–VII p. Chr. descoperite la Traian (jud. Neamţ) [Two pieces from the 6th–7th centuries AD discovered at Traian (Neamţ County)]," *Mousaios* XX (2015), 123–124.

89 Mitrea, "Regiunea centrală a Moldovei," 108; pl. XLVI/1: Mitrea, *Aşezarea medievală timpurie de la Ştefan Cel Mare-Gutinaş*, 77; 169, fig. 48.2; 170, fig. 49.2.

90 Mitrea, Eminovici, Momanu, "Aşezarea din secolele V–VII de la Ştefan cel Mare," 224, 250, fig. 17.1; Mitrea, *Aşezarea medievală*, 45; 171, fig. 50/1.

91 Mitrea, Eminovici, Momanu, "Aşezarea din secolele V–VII de la Ştefan cel Mare," 224–225, 250, fig. 17.2; Mitrea, *Aşezarea medievală*, 46.

92 Mitrea, *Aşezarea medievală*, 63.

93 Mitrea, *Aşezarea medievală*, 51; 171, fig. 50/7.

94 Mitrea, "Aşezarea prefeudală," 215, 240, fig. 10.10; 239, fig. 9.11. Several other instruments, possibly chisels, are said to have been found in sections 7 and 44 (Ion Mitrea, *Aşezarea din secolele VI–IX de la Izvoare Bahna* [The 6th- to 9th-century settlement from Izvoare Bahna] (Piatra Neamţ: Editura Nona, 1998), 171, fig. 55. 10–12; 172, fig. 56. 11, 13).

95 Mitrea, *Aşezarea din secolele VI–IX*, 24–26, 61–62, 69–70.

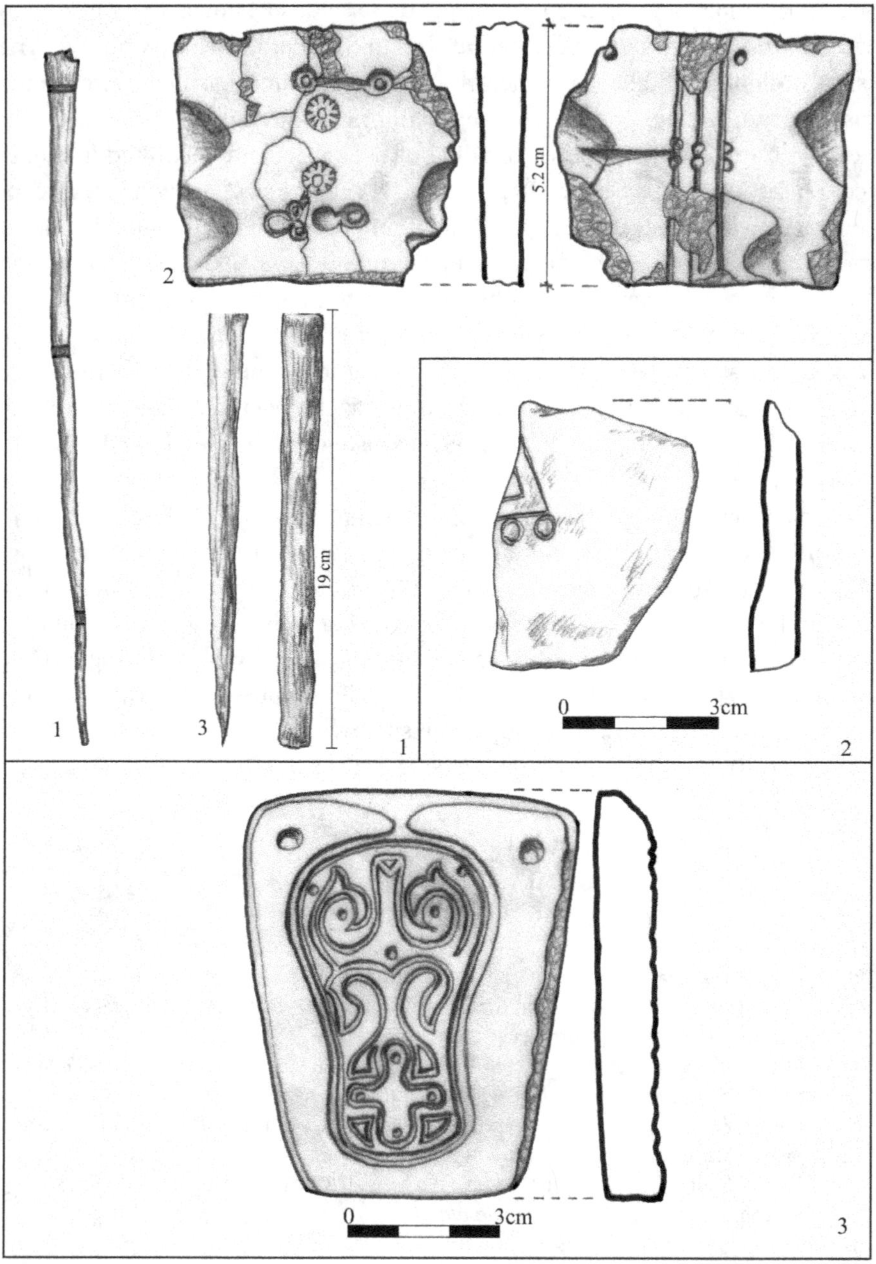

FIGURE 23 **1. Ştefan cel Mare** (Bacău co.), dwelling no. 2: 1.2. stone mold, dwelling no. 5: 1.1. engraving needle, dwelling no. 8; 1.3 – chisel; **2. Traian-Săbăoani** (Neamţ co.): clay mold; **3. Traian** (Bacău co.) – stone mold. 1.1, 1.3 without scale

blooms from house 17.[96] A ladle was found in house 28 together with remains of its wooden handle, and was most likely used by a goldsmith (Fig. 7.4).[97]

Although its chronology covers mainly the 8th century (as well as the first decades of the 9th century, as the excavator believes), the occupation of the settlement site excavated between 1963 and 1989 at Lozna-Strătenì (Botoșani County) began in the 7th century.[98] This is perhaps the most important site in terms of metalworking, specifically smelting of the iron ore extracted from bog iron (limonite) in the peat bog at Dersca.[99] A conical bowl with an opening at the bottom was found in one of the sunken-floored buildings; it is believed to have been used in smelting.[100] Another sunken-floored building may have been a workshop, judging by the hand-made pots and thick-walled bowls with traces of partially slagged iron oxides. Several blooms were found in the filling of the feature, with a total weight of 50 to 60 kilograms (110 to 132 lbs.), in addition to a small mandrel, several fragmentary clay crucibles, and a clay nozzle for hand bellows (Fig. 24.3–4).[101] Two ovens were found inside another workshop, the associated assemblage of which included several blooms weighing over 50 kilograms (over 110 lbs.). The assemblage also contained a chisel, a mandrel, several clay crucibles, a ladle, and a fragment of a clay mold (Fig. 25.10–11). Iron artifacts – a hook, a ring, and four knives – have also been found inside the feature.[102] Fragments of clay crucibles have also been found on the hearth of the clay oven in the neighboring feature, the sunken-floored building 8 (Fig. 26.1.10–11). The associated assemblage included many iron artifacts (a knife, an engraving tool, a buckle, a hook, and a fragment of a chain). However, because of many half-manufactured antler products, and no less than 12 bone awls, the building was interpreted as a bone-processing workshop.[103]

96 Mitrea, *Așezarea din secolele VI–IX*, 61. More slag was found in houses 10 and 29 (Mitrea, *Așezarea din secolele VI–IX*, 53 and 69).

97 Mitrea, *Așezarea din secolele VI–IX*, 37–38, 141, fig. 25.7.

98 Teodor, *Un centru*, 9.

99 Teodor, "Unele probleme privind evoluția culturii materiale," 268; Teodor, "Principalele rezultate," 452; Teodor, *Un centru*, 9–12.

100 Teodor, *Un centru*, 16; 160, fig. 77.3.

101 Teodor, *Un centru*, 17–18; 116, fig. 33/6; 125, fig. 42/8. The reference to the illustration of a crucible in dwelling no. 6 is a mistake, as fig. 42/2 shows a metal ladle, found in dwelling no. 7; the crucible might be the one of fig. 42/4. At any rate, no mention is made of a metal ladle in dwelling no. 6.

102 Teodor, "Tipare," 164, 172, fig. 7. 6; Teodor, *Un centru*, 18; 118, fig. 35/11, 15; 123, fig. 40/1; 124, fig. 41/2; 125, fig. 42/2. There is no reference in the text to plates related to the discovered crucibles, therefore we consider that fig. 42/4 comes from dwelling no. 6.

103 Teodor, "Tipare," 164, 172, fig. 7. 1; Teodor, *Un centru*, 18–19; 123, fig. 40/3; 124, fig. 41/8; 125, fig. 42/1. To be sure, the assemblage in the sunken-floored building 8 also included a

A fourth settlement feature (sunken-floored building 10) was also interpreted as workshop, primarily on the basis of the clay mold and the two fragmentary clay crucibles in the associated assemblage (Fig. 26.2.13–14). There was also found a fragment of a large handmade pot with thick walls, with an opening at the bottom, which is believed to have been used in smelting.[104] A crucible was also found in the filling of the sunken-floored building 12, together with three knives and two belt buckles, along with six bone awls (Fig. 27.1).[105] A similar combination is known from house 17, which, in addition, also produced a mandrel, an axe blade, a buckle, a spear and arrow head, as well as bone awls and other artifacts, including half-manufactured antler products (Fig. 27.2).[106] Two more crucibles were found together with another arrow head, knives, and an iron plate, as well as awls and half-manufactured antler products on the floor of house 21 (Fig. 28.1).[107] By contrast, the two crucibles from house 27 were associated with a ladle, while the filling of the feature contained slag and fragments of bronze artifacts (Fig. 28.2).[108] Another pair of crucibles was found together with a fragment of a clay mold in house 28 (Fig. 27.3).[109] Four molds, all fragmentary, are known from house 37, in which they were associated with a ladle, as well as three crucibles (Fig. 29.1).[110] Finally, a large, circular pit was interpreted as workshop, because iron and brass slag was found on its bottom, in addition to a crucible.[111] The only stone mold found on the site is from one three features, that were perhaps smelting furnaces (Fig. 29.2).[112]

Much of the evidence of smelting and ironworking from Lozna seem to pertain to the 8th century. However, some of the molds for dress accessories

---

fragment of a glass tumbler, as well as four spindle whorls, all of which have nothing to do either with bone- or with ironworking.

104 Teodor, *Un centru*, 19–20; 123, fig. 40/5, 11; 124, fig. 41/3; 125, fig. 42/6. In addition, the features produced several iron artifacts (four knives, a pair of tweezers, axe blades, and a flint steel), spindle whorls, and awls.

105 Teodor, *Un centru*, 21; 125, fig. 42/13.

106 Teodor, *Un centru*, 23; 118, fig. 35/4; 125, fig. 42/9.

107 Teodor, *Un centru*, 25–26; 123, fig. 40/10; 125, fig. 42/3, 10.

108 Teodor, *Un centru*, 28–29; 123, fig. 40/12; 125, fig. 42/5, 7, 14. Because of the presence of slag in the filling, the excavator interpreted house 27 as a workshop.

109 Teodor, "Tipare," 172, fig. 7. 7; Teodor, *Un centru*, 29; 124, fig. 41/4.

110 Teodor, "Tipare," 164, 172, fig. 7. 2; Teodor, *Un centru*, 33–34; 123, fig. 40/2, 4, 7, 9; 124, fig. 41/1, 5, 7, 9; 125, fig. 42/11–12.

111 Teodor, *Un centru*, 35–36.

112 Dan Gh. Teodor, Ioan Mitrea, "Cercetări arheologice în așezarea prefeudală de la Lozna-Dorohoi [Archaeological research in the pre-feudal settlement of Lozna-Dorohoi]," *Arheologia Moldovei* 4 (1966), 288, fig. 8.13; Teodor, *Un centru*, 36; 124, fig. 41/6. The reference to fig. 40/6 is wrong, as it shows a round shape, probably of clay, whose purpose, (crucible?) cannot be specified due to the poor quality of the photograph.

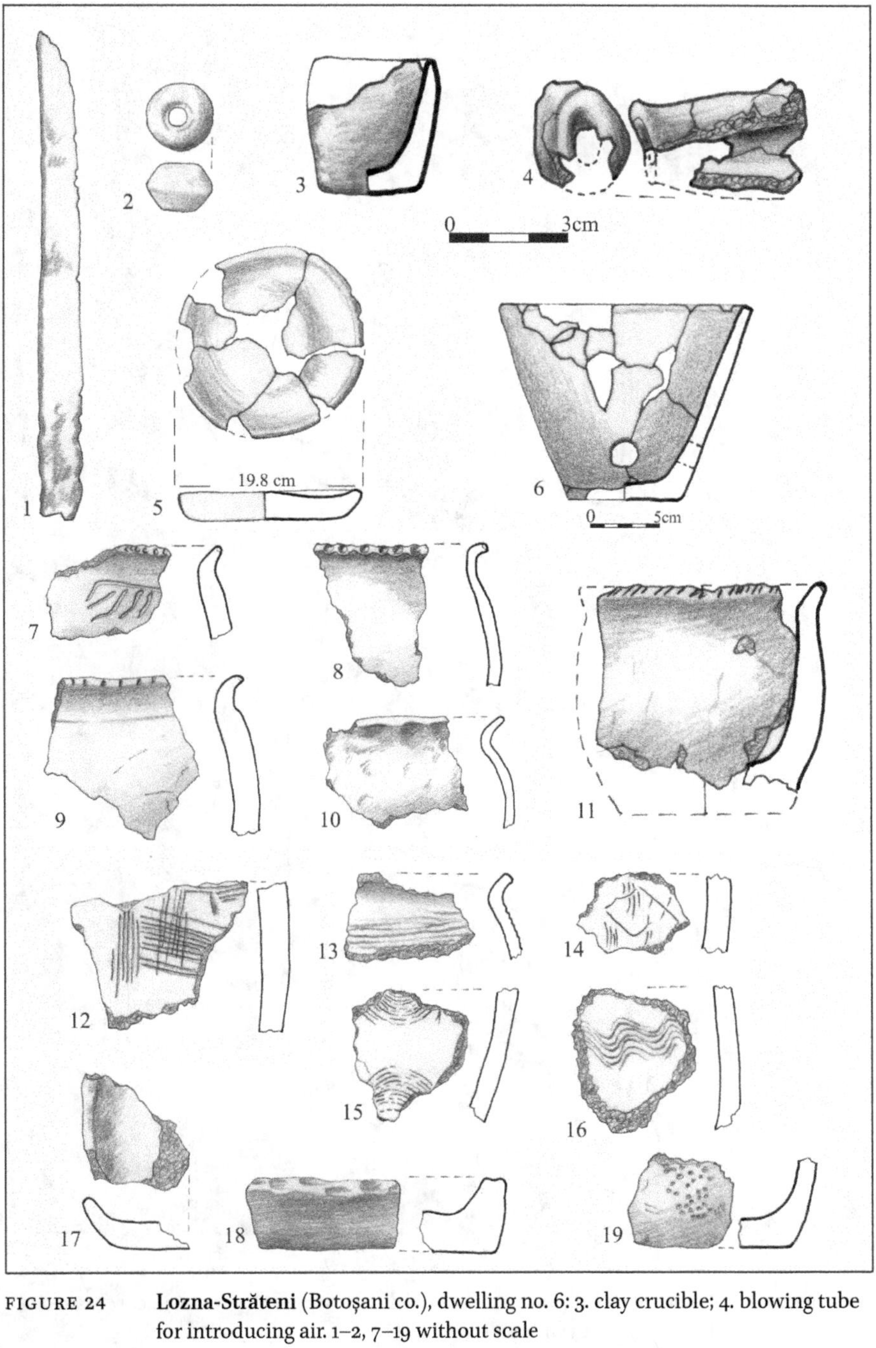

FIGURE 24 **Lozna-Străteni** (Botoșani co.), dwelling no. 6: 3. clay crucible; 4. blowing tube for introducing air. 1–2, 7–19 without scale

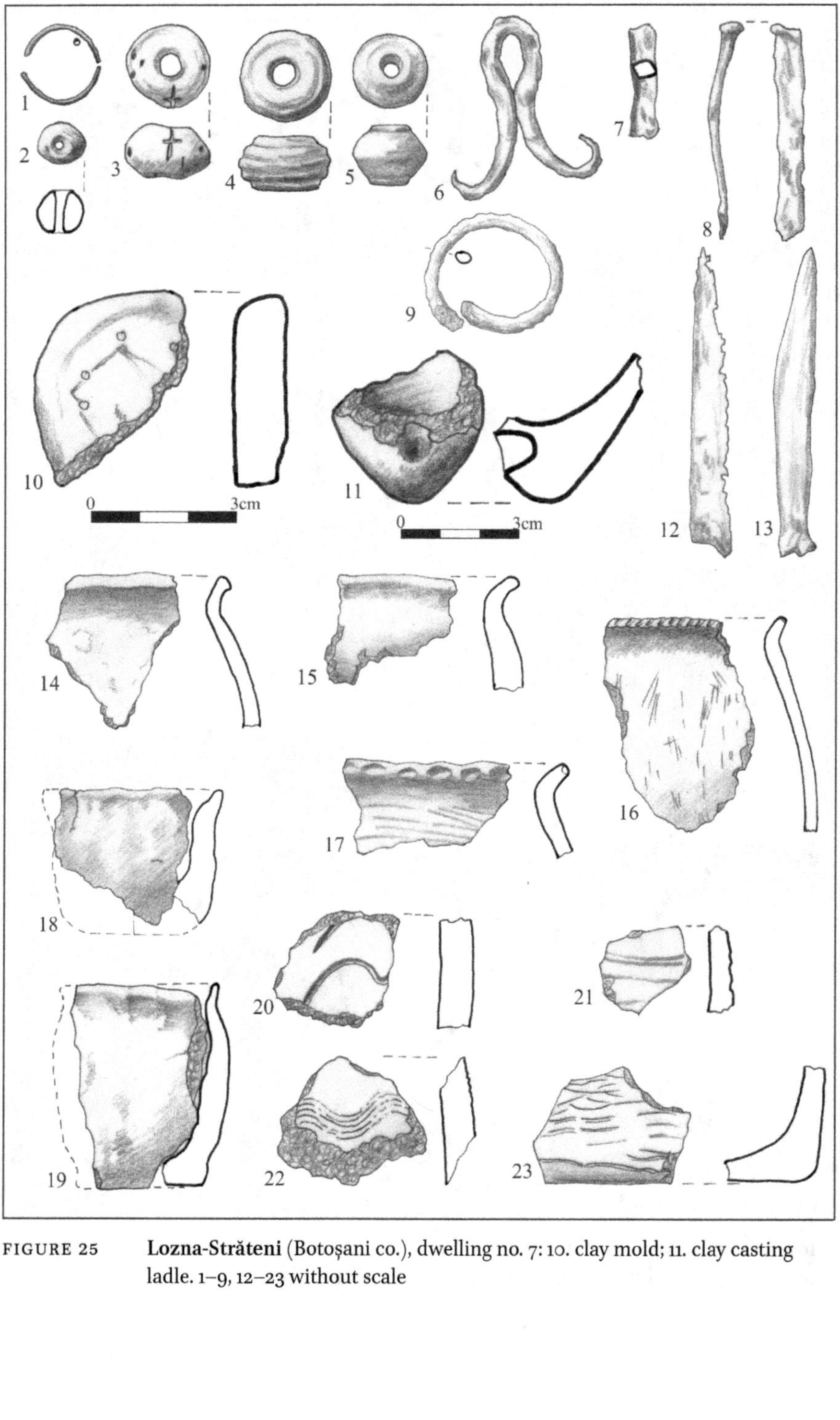

FIGURE 25 **Lozna-Strâteni** (Botoșani co.), dwelling no. 7: 10. clay mold; 11. clay casting ladle. 1–9, 12–23 without scale

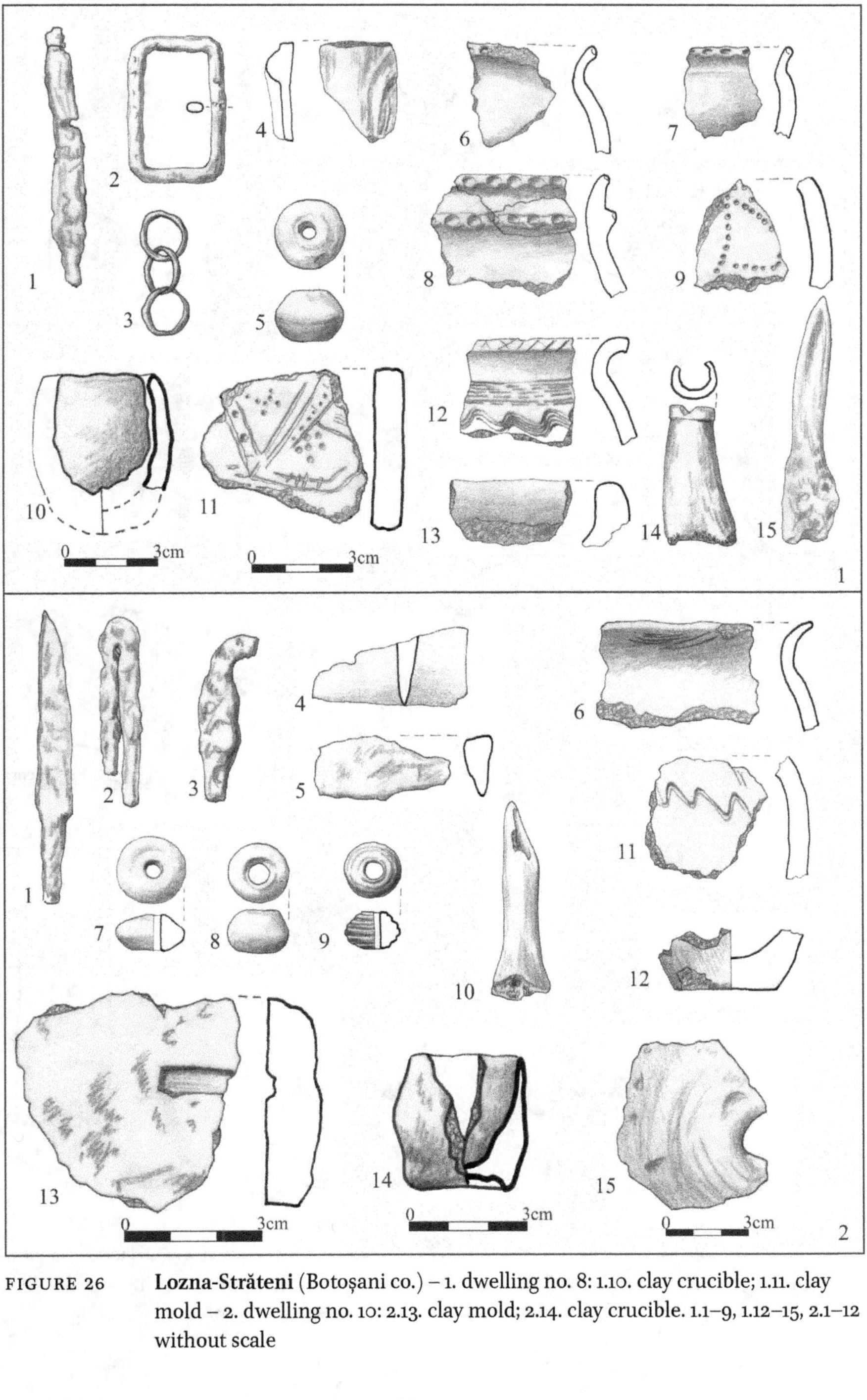

FIGURE 26 **Lozna-Străteni** (Botoșani co.) – 1. dwelling no. 8: 1.10. clay crucible; 1.11. clay mold – 2. dwelling no. 10: 2.13. clay mold; 2.14. clay crucible. 1.1–9, 1.12–15, 2.1–12 without scale

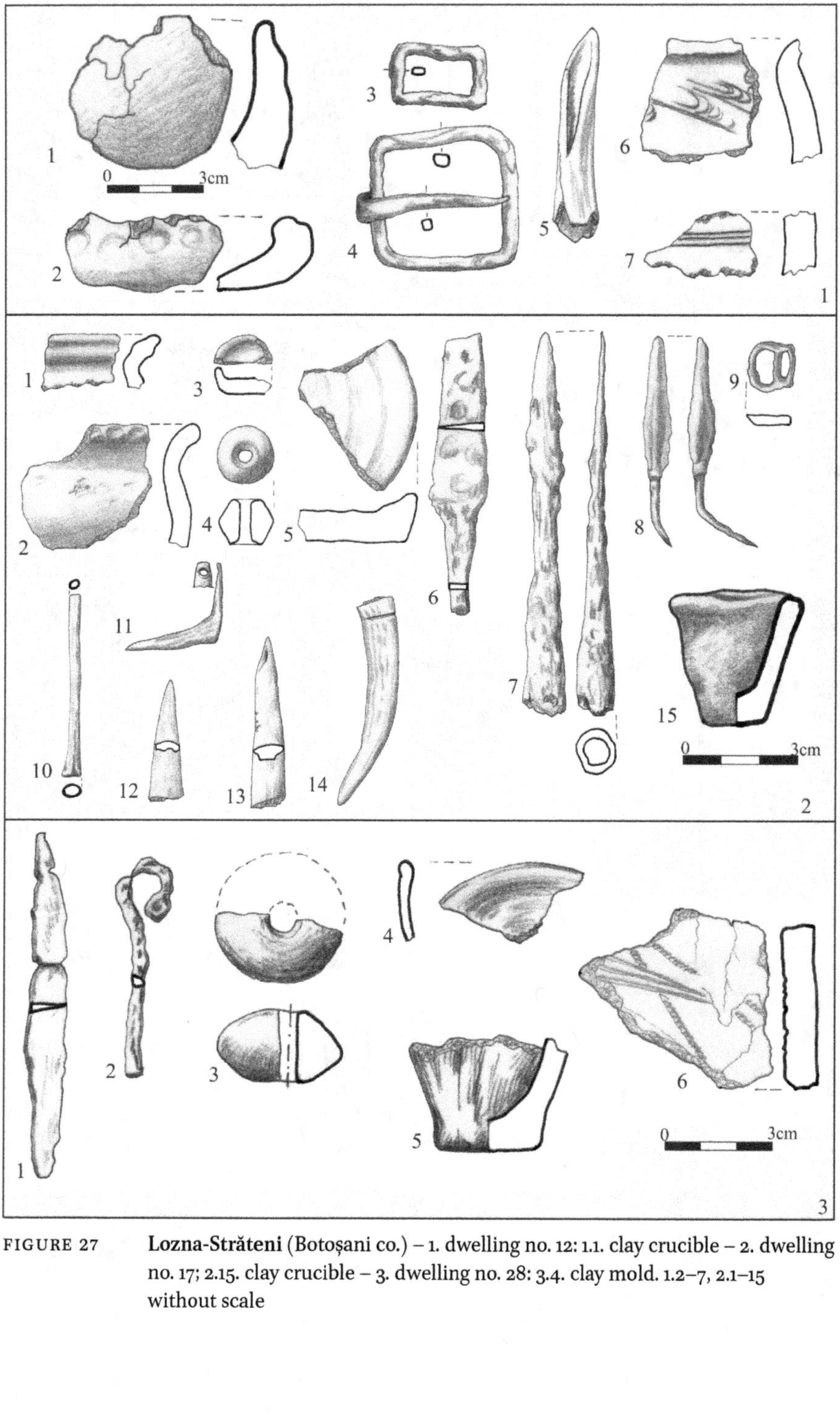

FIGURE 27 **Lozna-Străteni** (Botoșani co.) – 1. dwelling no. 12: 1.1. clay crucible – 2. dwelling no. 17; 2.15. clay crucible – 3. dwelling no. 28: 3.4. clay mold. 1.2–7, 2.1–15 without scale

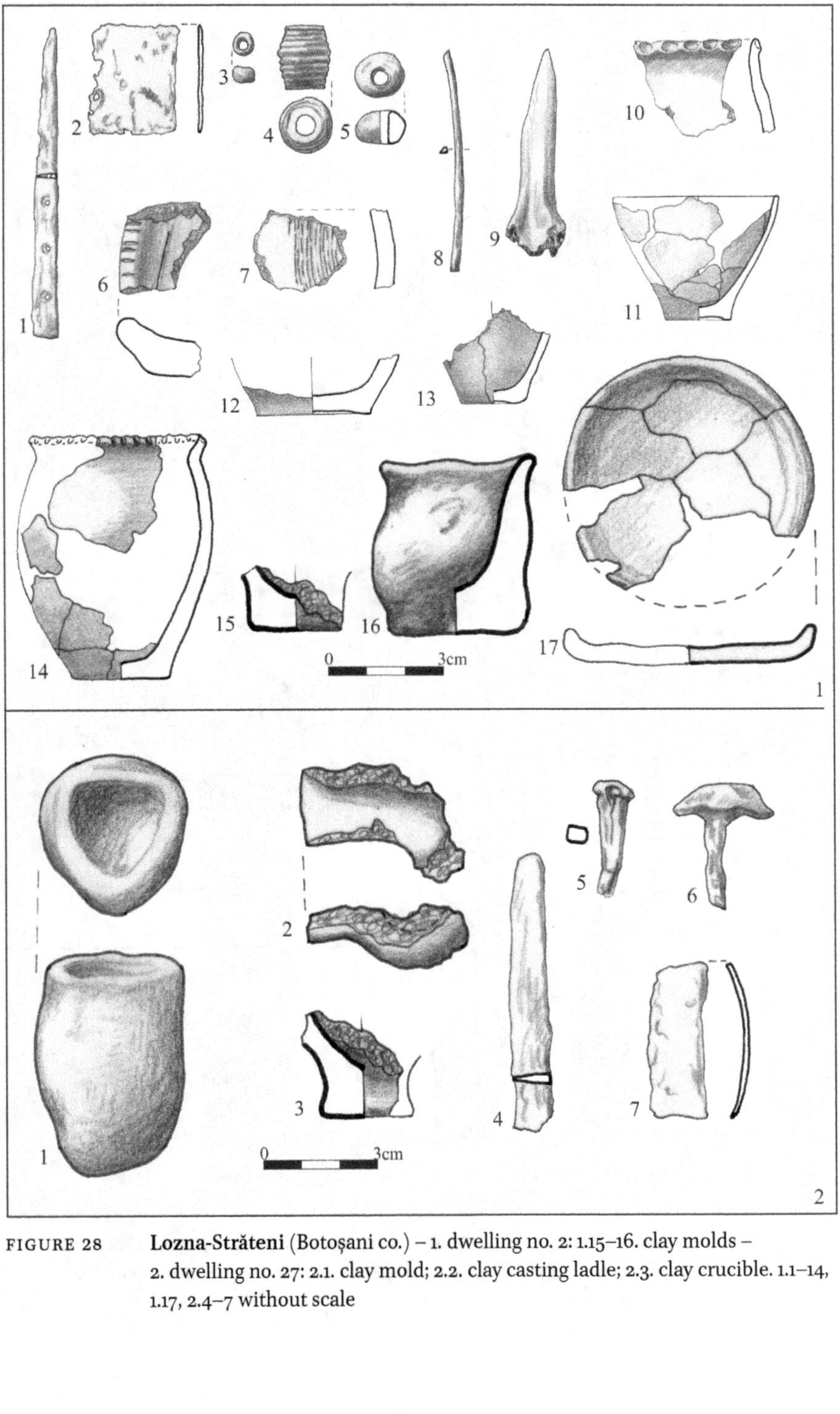

FIGURE 28 **Lozna-Strâteni** (Botoșani co.) – 1. dwelling no. 2: 1.15–16. clay molds – 2. dwelling no. 27: 2.1. clay mold; 2.2. clay casting ladle; 2.3. clay crucible. 1.1–14, 1.17, 2.4–7 without scale

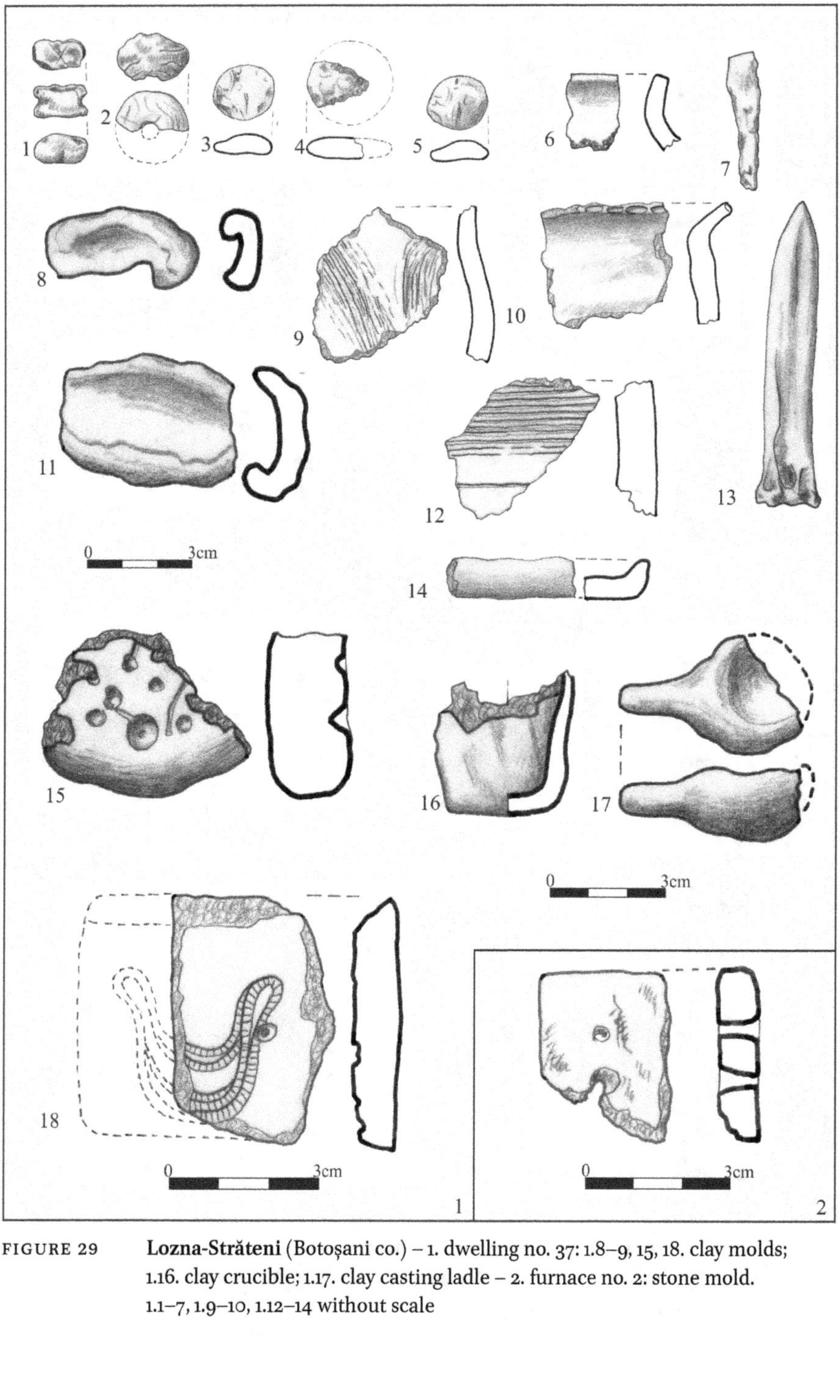

FIGURE 29 **Lozna-Străteni** (Botoșani co.) – 1. dwelling no. 37: 1.8–9, 15, 18. clay molds; 1.16. clay crucible; 1.17. clay casting ladle – 2. furnace no. 2: stone mold. 1.1–7, 1.9–10, 1.12–14 without scale

may be also be dated earlier, to the 7th century. At any rate, if they are of an 8th-century date, that actually proves the continuity of the casting technology from the earlier period. The most important innovation documented in Lozna, however, is the method of obtaining iron blooms inside ceramic pots with very thick walls.

2 Graves

The deposition of tools in graves, a phenomenon known since prehistory, is well documented for the barbarian world both during the Roman period[113] and the early Middle Ages as well. Although graves with tools are known from different parts of Europe, from Transylvania to Norway, most finds of the Avar age cluster in the Tisza Plain. They were typically found next to rivers or old Roman roads, crossroads, or central places in the region network of settlements.[114] In this respect, the finds in the Carpathian Basin are different from those in the regions outside the Carpathian Mountains to the east and to the south, in which most finds are from settlements typically located along rivers. No evidence exists in those regions outside the Carpathian Mountains of any roads, even though river valleys most certainly facilitated communication. It is important to note the absence of any graves with tools from those regions outside the Carpathian Mountains, the only exception being grave 14 in Sărata Monteoru (Buzău County), which may be interpreted as the grave of a goldsmith, judging from the eight crucibles found there.[115]

Some seventy years ago, only a few graves with tools were known from the Carpathian Basin.[116] The number of such finds increased dramatically during the last few decades of the 20th century. By 1991, 28 graves with tools were known.[117] Even more finds were added to the list during the last decades, primarily because of the archaeological research in Hungary (see chapter XII.2). The number of graves with tools remains nonetheless small when compared with the sheer number of burial assemblages known from 6th- and 7th-century

113 Henning, "Schmiedegräber," 66.

114 Gyula László, *Steppenvölker und Germanen: Kunst der Völkerwanderungszeit* (Vienna-Munich: Anton Schroll, 1970), 79.

115 Ion Nestor et al., "Şantierul Sărata-Monteoru [The Sărata-Monteoru site]," *Studii şi Cercetări de Istorie Veche* 4, no. 1–2 (1953), 85, fig. 16.

116 Joachim Werner, "Waage und Geld," 39–40 and Joachim Werner, *Die Langobarden in Pannonien. Beiträge zur Kenntniss der langobardischen Bodenfunde vor 568* (Munich: Verlag der Bayerischen Akademie der Wissenschaften, 1962), 308, knew only seven.

117 Henning, "Schmiedegräber," 80–81. Henning ignores both Felnac and Aradac.

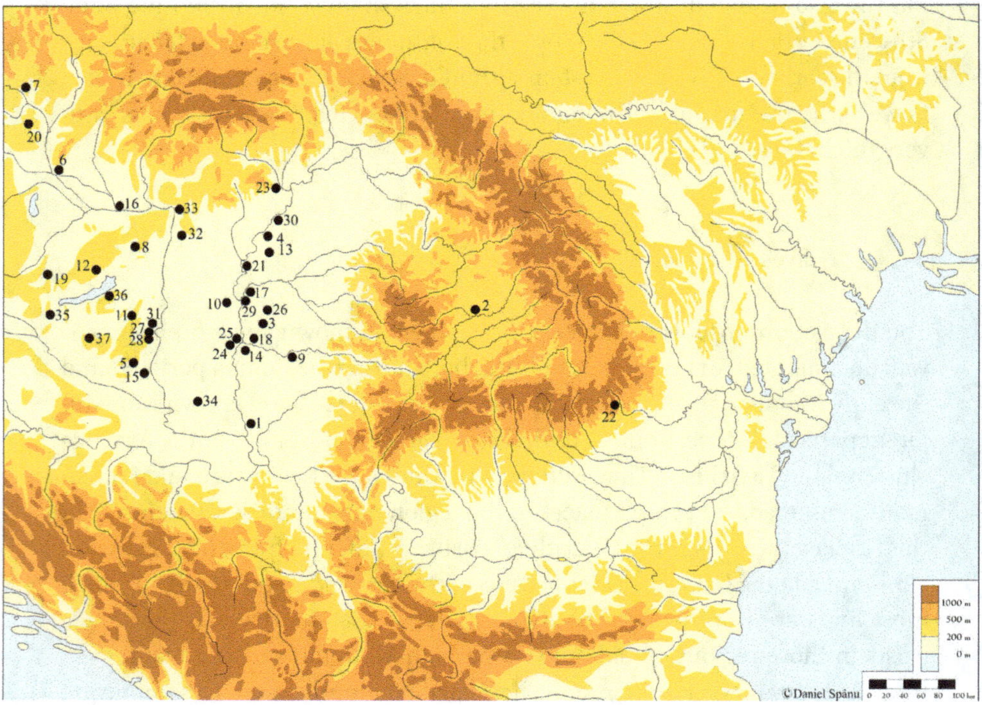

FIGURE 30 **Tombs with tools at the Middle and Lower Danube, 6th–7th centuries:** 1. Aradac (Serbia); 2. Band (Romania); 3. Békéssámson (Hungary); 4. Berekfürdő (Hungary); 5. Bóly (Hungary); 6. Bratislava (Slovakia); 7. Brno (Czech Republic); 8. Csákbereny-Orondpuszta (Hungary); 9. Felnac (Romania); 10. Gátér (Hungary); 11. Gyönk (Hungary); 12. Jutas (Hungary); 13. Kisújszállás (Hungary); 14. Klárafalva B (Hungary); 15. Kölked-Feketekapu B (Hungary); 16. Komárno (Slovakia); 17. Kunszentmárton (Hungary); 18. Makó (Hungary); 19. Pókaszepetk (Hungary); 20. Poysdorf (Austria); 21. Rákóczifalva-Kastélydomb (Hungary); 22. Sărata Monteoru (Romania); 23. Sajópetri (Hungary); 24. Szeged-Bilisics (Hungary); 25. Szeged-Kiskundorozsma (Hungary); 26. Székkutas (Hungary); 27. Szekszárd-Palánk (Hungary); 28. Szekszárd-Tószegi-dűlő (Hungary); 29. Szentes-Kaján (Hungary); 30. Tiszafüred-Majoros (Hungary); 31. Tolna (Hungary); 32. Üllő (Hungary); 33. Vác-Kavicsbánya (Hungary); 34. Vrbas (Hungary); 35. Zalakomár (Hungary); 36. Zamárdi (Hungary); 37. Zselickislak (Hungary)

cemetery sites. However, it is likely that not all goldsmiths or blacksmiths were buried with their own tools. To date, 45 such assemblages are known from 39 sites in Central Europe (Fig. 30), and the number is likely to increase in the nearest future.

Central Europe is therefore directly comparable with such other areas of the continent as Scandinavia, where hundreds of tools were deposited in graves, from the Iron to the Viking age.[118] In both regions of Europe, the graves with tools have constituted the basis for the discussion of crafts, the social position of craftsmen in society, and the role of burial customs in understanding the economic practices revealed by such assemblages. As no deposition of tools is known from burial assemblages of the steppe belt of Eastern Europe in the 6th and 7th centuries, the practice seems to have been specific to the population inhabiting the Carpathian Basin. My own focus is on graves with tools found on the territory of Romania – Band (Fig. 31–36), Felnac (Fig. 37.2–41), and Sărata Monteoru (Fig. 6.4) – as well as related assemblages in Hungary and Serbia (see Chapter XII.2).

Scholars distinguish between "Germanic"[119] graves in which tools were deposited along with personal belongings, weapons, and sometimes pots with food offerings, and "Avar"[120] graves in the Tisza Plain.[121] The latter are different from the former group because they typically include horse bones, such as found in Kunszentmárton (Hungary) and Felnac. Even though such graves are called "Avar" and are thus attributed to a population of the nomadic origin presumably coming from the steppe lands north of the Black Sea, no such burial assemblages with tools are known so far from that region. In addition, a few cremation burials are known, the associated assemblages of which suggest goldsmithing activities, as in Pókaszepetk (Hungary)[122] and Sărata Monteoru (Buzău County).

Two categories of tools are particularly common in all those assemblages – hammers and pliers. Those are typically small tools, with the notable exception of the pliers found in Band (Fig. 35.1, Fig. 36.1). Along with hammers and pliers, other tools were also deposited in graves – anvils, files, punches,

118 Müller-Wille, "Der Schmied im Spiegel archäologischer Quellen," 247 – mentions about 600 tombs dated to the Iron Age until the Vikings' period; Tobias, *Frühmittelalterliche Gräber*, 8 – mentions more than 400 tombs with implements dated to the early Middle Ages and the Vikings' period only in Norway.

119 For example the Band grave was attributed to a Gepid smith by Kovács, "A mezőbándi ásatások," 429; Joachim Werner, "Waage und Geld," 40; Rácz, *Die Goldschmiedegräber*, 137.

120 The Felnac assemblage was attributed to an Avar goldsmith by Kurt Horedt, "Das Awarenproblem in Rumänien," *Študijné Zvesti* 16 (1968), 104 and 116; Tănase, "Câteva observații," 245–246. For graves attributed to Avar goldsmiths, in general, see also László, *Steppenvölker*, 75; Garam, *Funde*, 163.

121 For a recent discussion of ethnicity (-ies) in the Carpathian Basin during the Avar age, see Tivadar Vida, "Conflict and coexistence: the local population of the Carpathian Basin under Avar rule (sixth to seventh century)," in: *The Other Europe in the Middle Ages: Avars, Bulgars, Khazars and Cumans. East Central and Eastern Europe in the Middle Ages, 450–1450*, 2, ed. Florin Curta (Leiden-Boston: Brill, 2008), pp. 13–46.

122 Ágnes Cs. Sós, "Frühmittelalterliche Brandbestattung mit Feinwaage in Pókaszepetk," *Slovenská Archeológia* 26, no. 2 (1978), 424, fig. 1; 426, fig. 3.

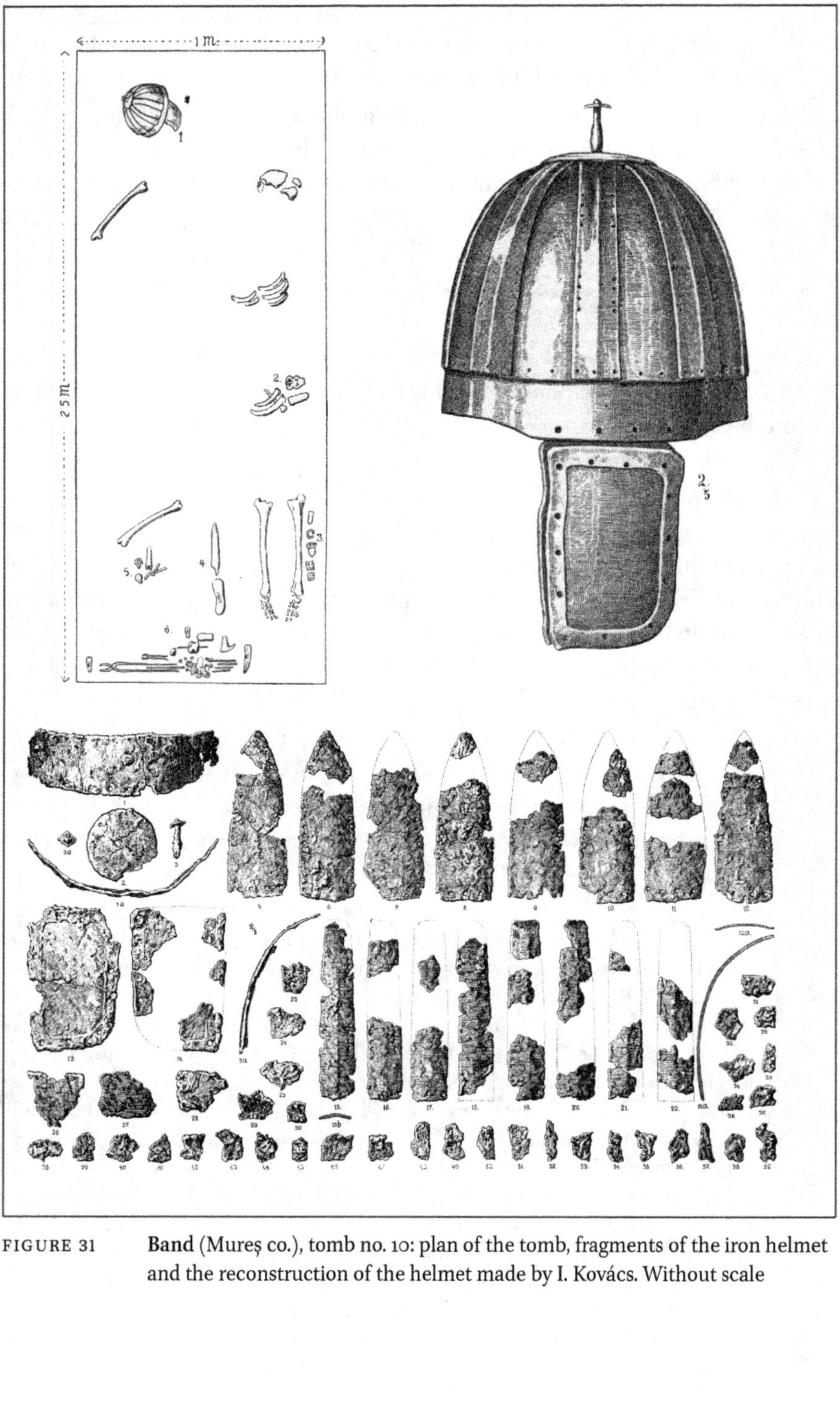

FIGURE 31 **Band** (Mureș co.), tomb no. 10: plan of the tomb, fragments of the iron helmet and the reconstruction of the helmet made by I. Kovács. Without scale

FIGURE 32 **Band** (Mureș co.), tomb no. 10: fragments of iron and bronze clothing items, tools made of iron, clay and stone, fragments a wooden box, fragments of silver mirror, bronze rivets. Without scale

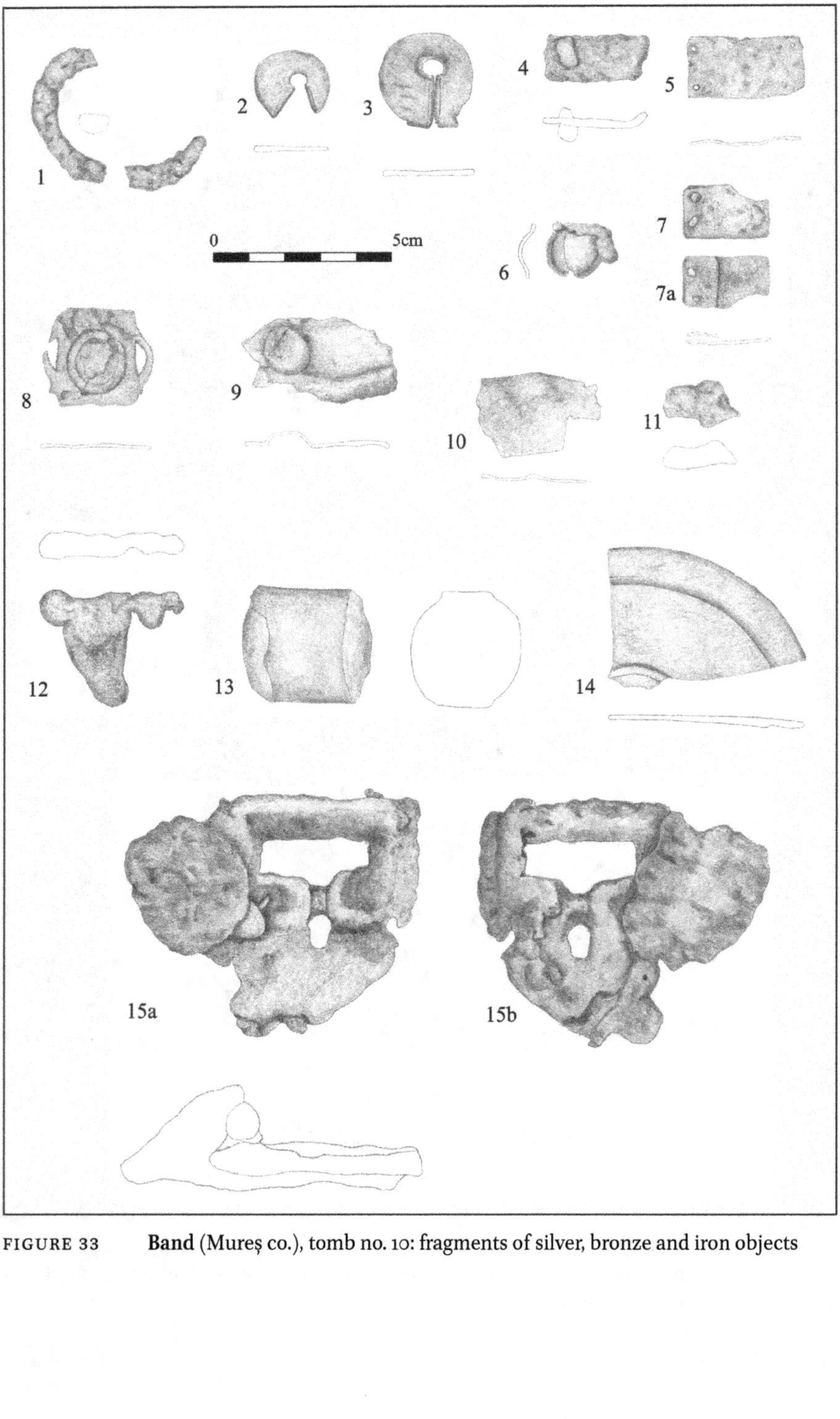

FIGURE 33 **Band** (Mureș co.), tomb no. 10: fragments of silver, bronze and iron objects

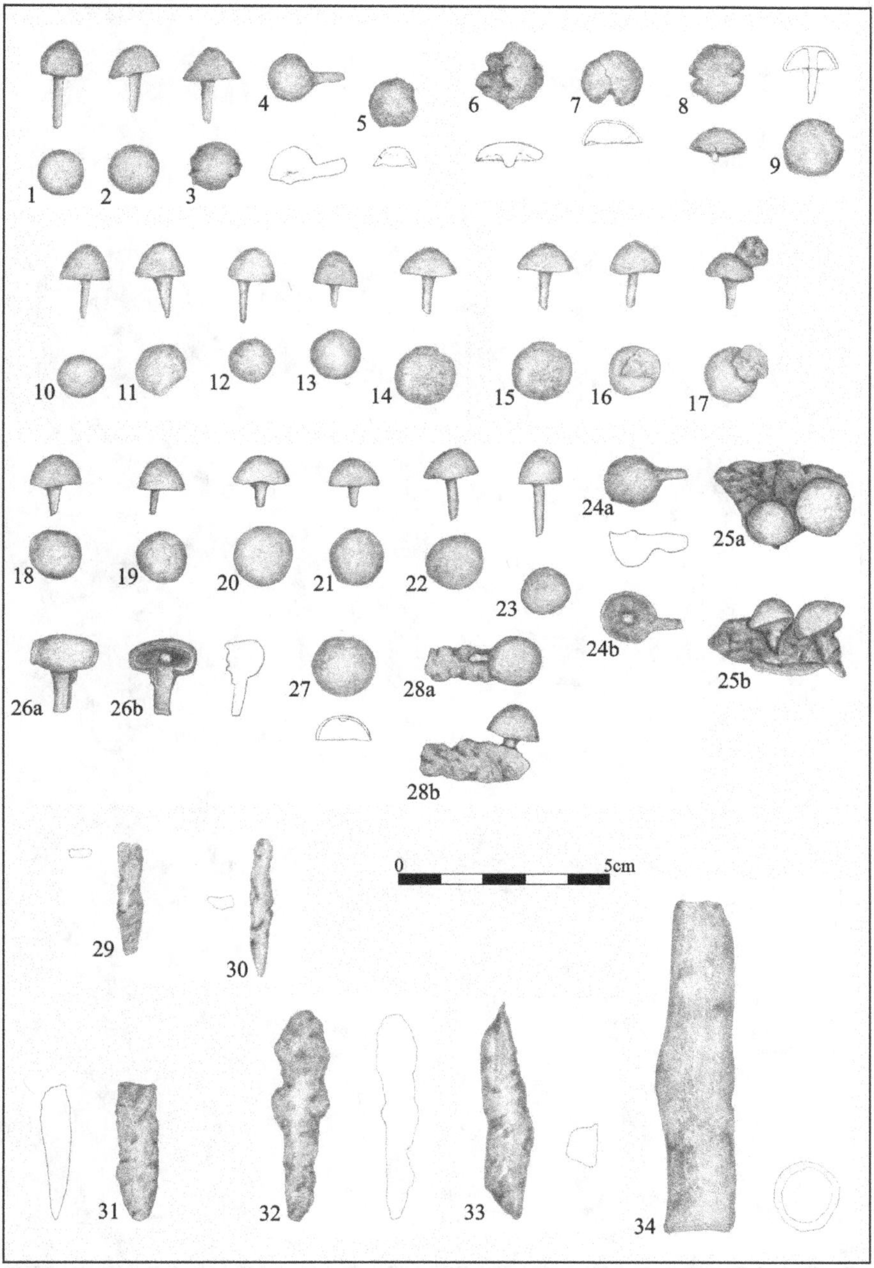

FIGURE 34 **Band** (Mureș co.), tomb no. 10: bronze rivets, fragments of iron objects and tools

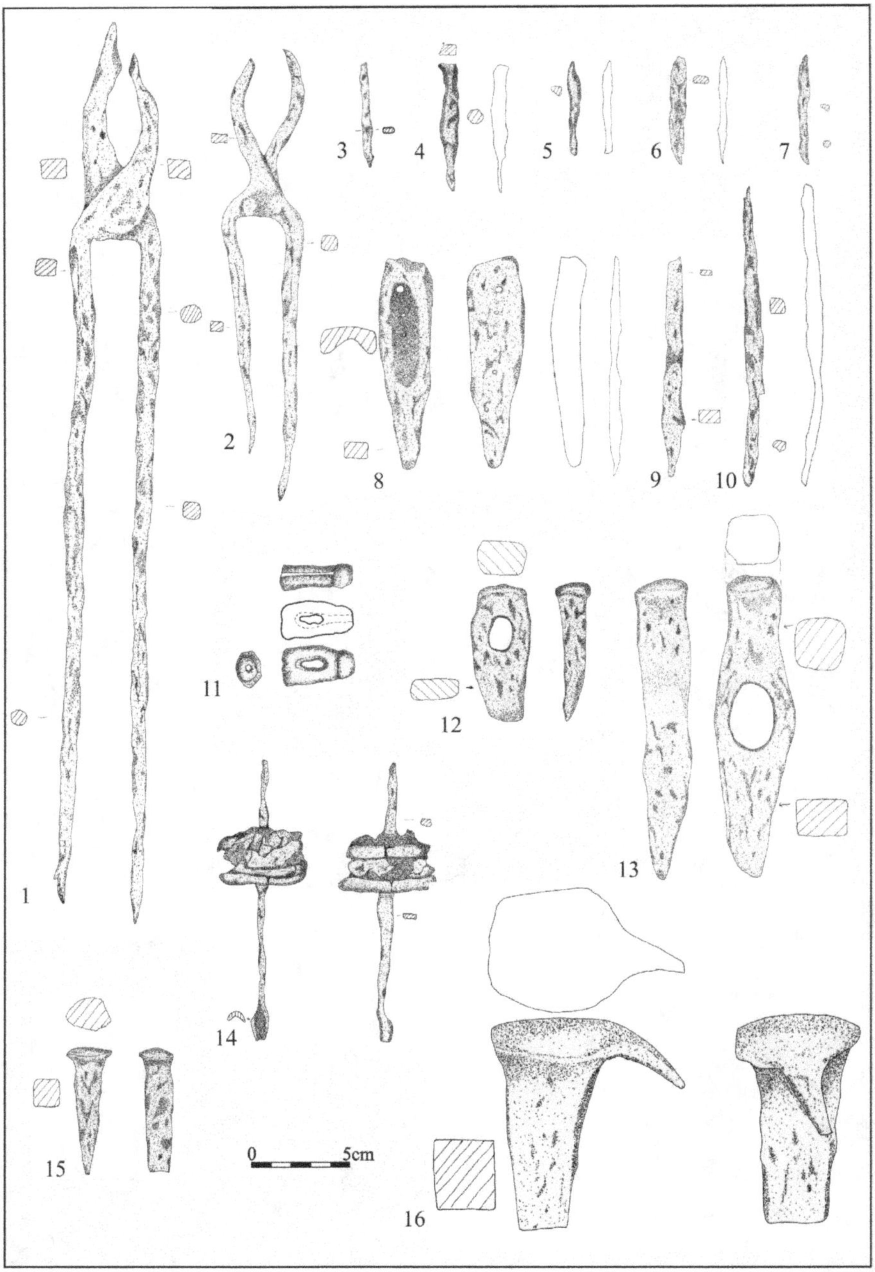

FIGURE 35 **Band** (Mureș co.), tomb no. 10, drawings of tools: 1. pliers; 2. jewelry pliers; 3–7. drills; 8. wire drawing plate/nail crafting tool; 9–10. chisel; 11. nail and rivet tool; 12. jeweler's hammer; 13. hammer; 14. mechanical drill; 15. anvil/chisel/(?); 16. anvil

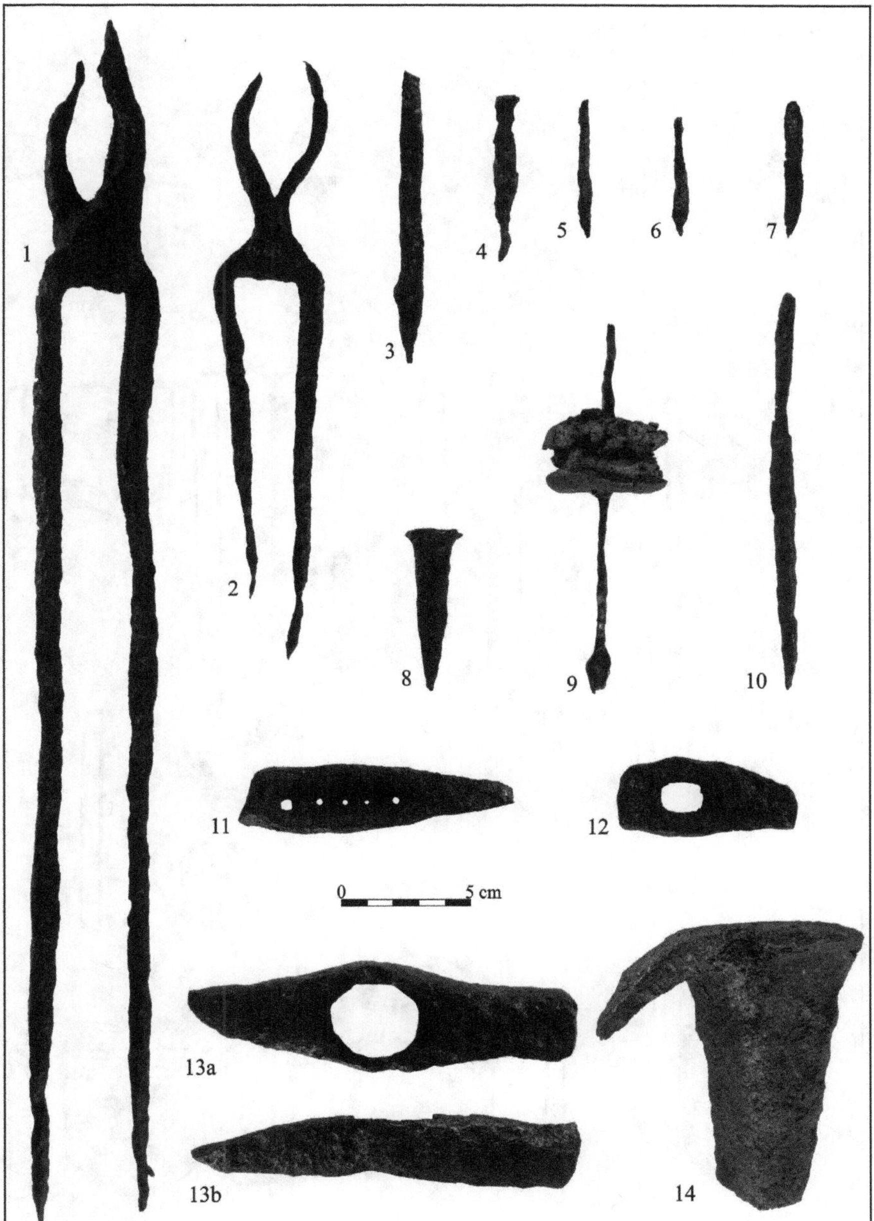

FIGURE 36 **Band** (Mureș co.), tomb no. 10, photos of tools: 1. pliers; 2. jewelry pliers; 3–7. drills; 8. wire drawing plate/nail crafting tool; 9–10. chisel, 11. nail and rivet tool; 12. jeweler's hammer; 13. hammer; 14. mechanical drill; 15. anvil/chisel/(?); 16. anvil

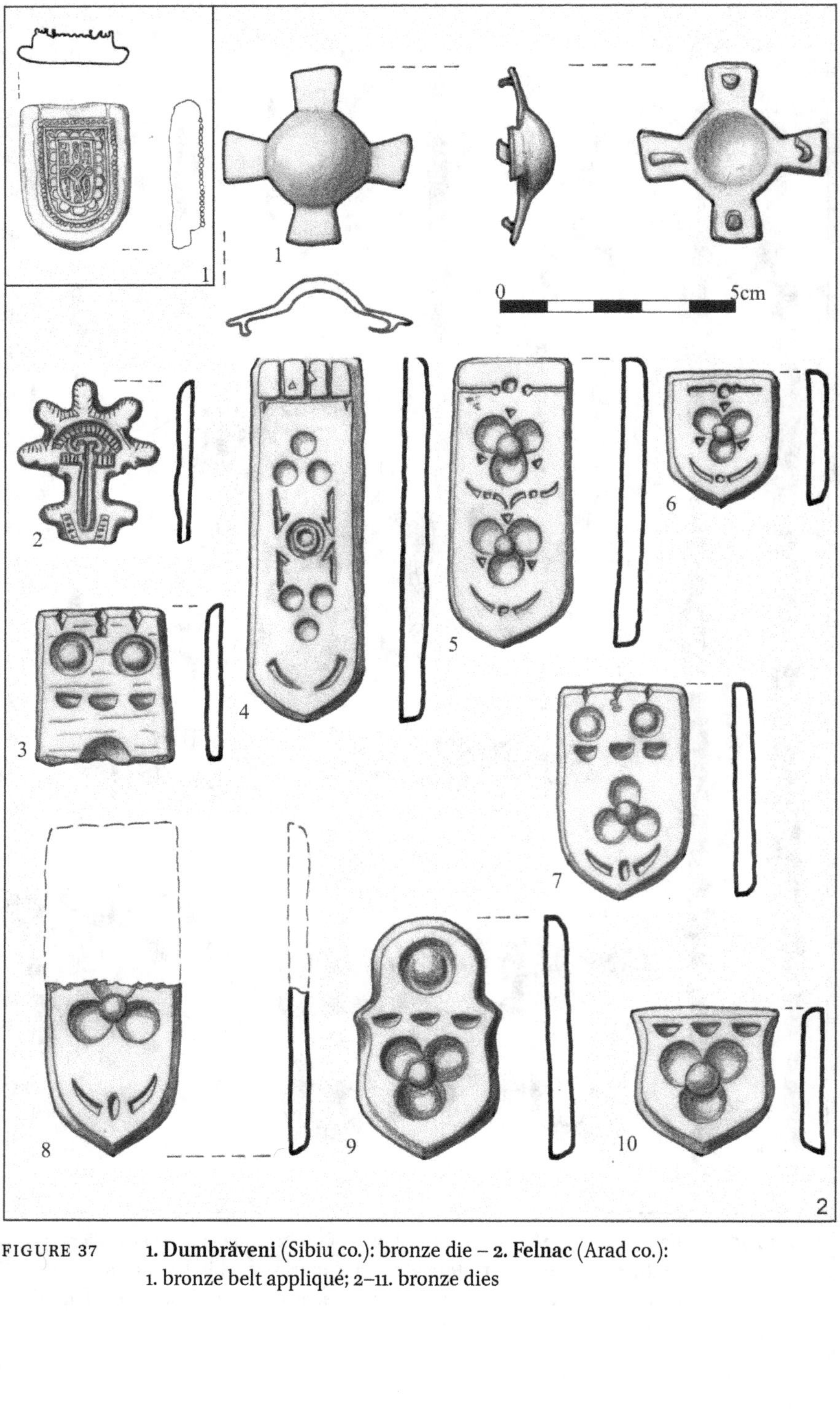

FIGURE 37 **1. Dumbrăveni** (Sibiu co.): bronze die – **2. Felnac** (Arad co.): 1. bronze belt appliqué; 2–11. bronze dies

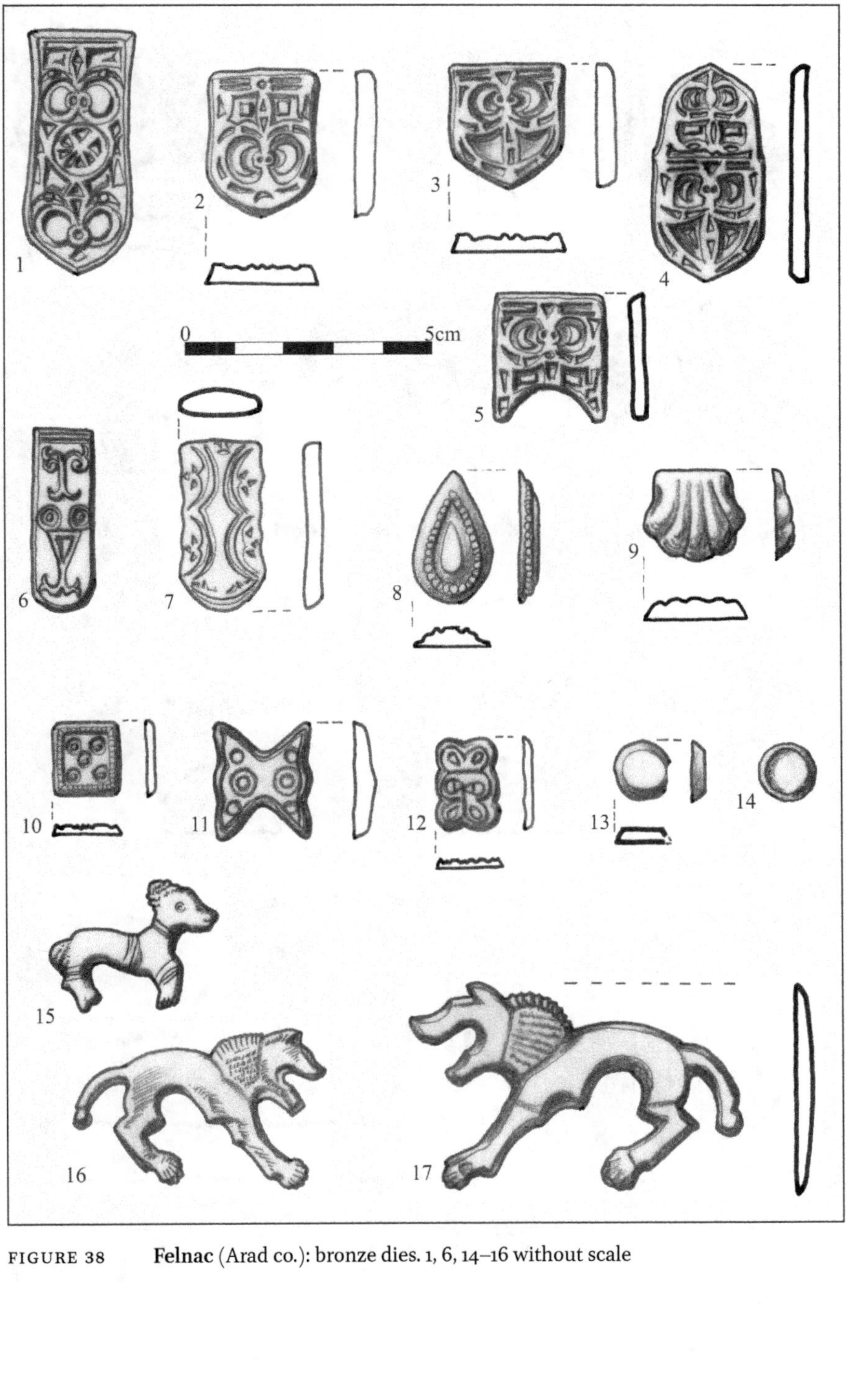

FIGURE 38 **Felnac** (Arad co.): bronze dies. 1, 6, 14–16 without scale

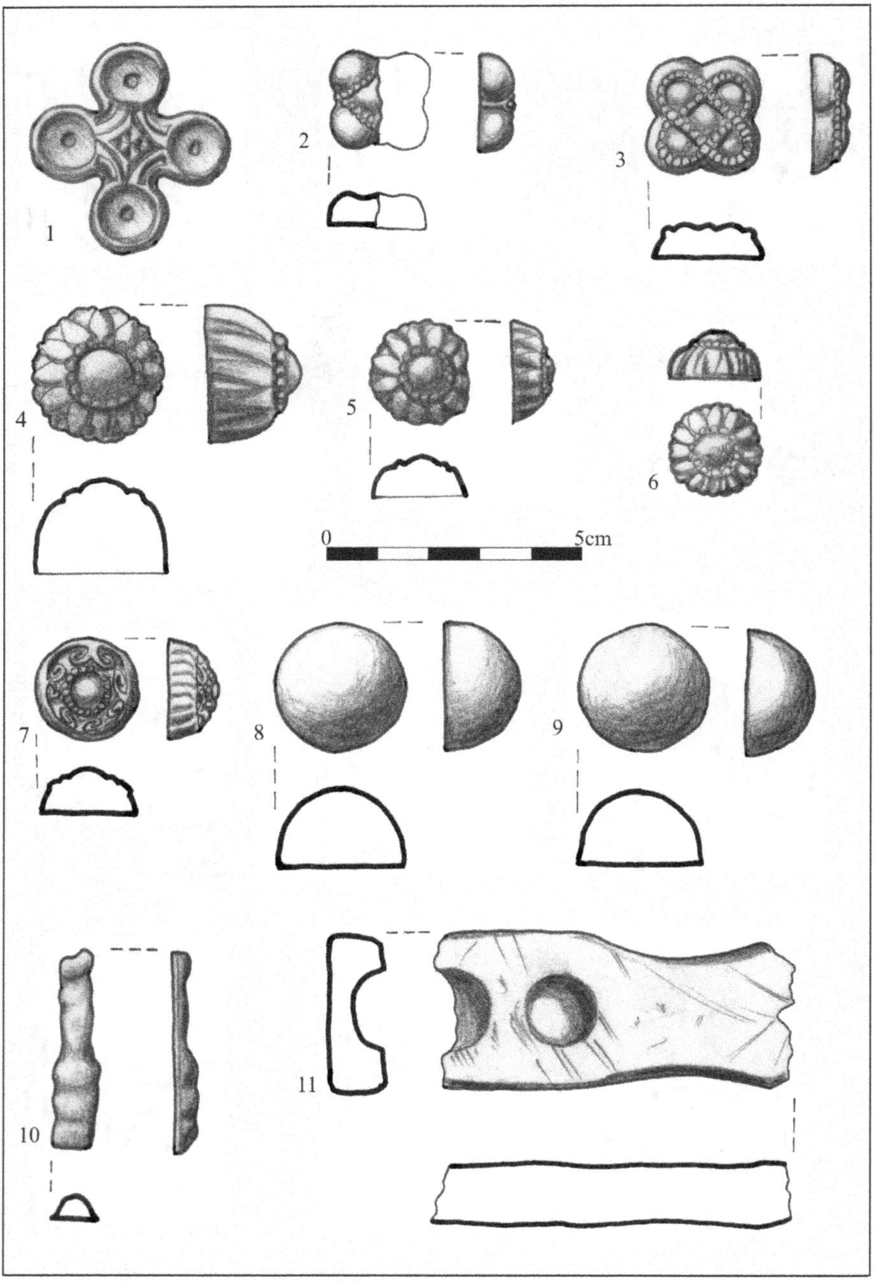

FIGURE 39 **Felnac** (Arad co.): bronze dies. 1, 6 without scale

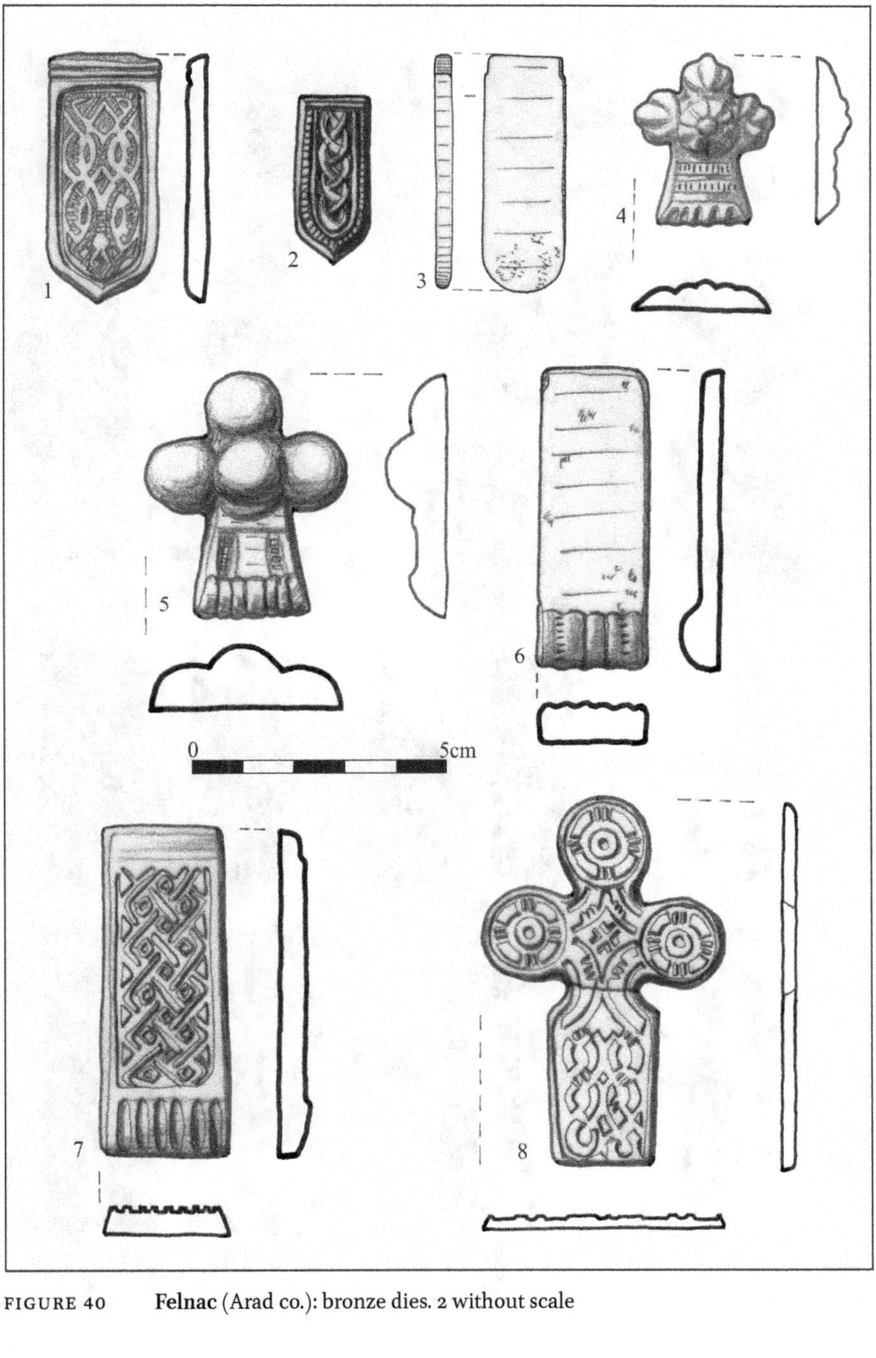

FIGURE 40 **Felnac** (Arad co.): bronze dies. 2 without scale

FIGURE 41 **Felnac** (Arad co.): bronze dies: 1–5, 7–10. 6 without scale

engravers, chisels, shears, and wimbles – as well as scales and weights. One is left with a strong impression that what was meant to be deposited in the grave was a tool kit, not individual implements. Judging from those kits, some graves were not of blacksmiths, but of craftsmen, who besides ironworking, were also involved in goldsmithing, as indicated, for example, by the presence of scales and weights, molds, punchers, and engravers.

In only two years (1906–1907), István Kovács brought to light 186 graves in the 5th- to 7th-century cemetery in Band (Mureș County). Almost all of them were robbed or disturbed.[123] The individual buried in grave 10, on the southern side of the cemetery, was apparently laid in the grave pit together with a tool box placed between his legs. Despite being robbed, this was one of the richest assemblages in the cemetery (Fig. 31–36). Next to it, grave 32 contained only horse bones, and a few human remains. It has recently been suggested that grave 32 may have also been that of a craftsmen.[124] However, there is no way to prove the point, especially since in the absence of any datable artifacts, it is not even certain that this was an early medieval assemblage; it may well have been a prehistoric grave.[125] Fragments of a human skull were found in grave 10 together with the remains of an iron helmet. Judging from the thigh bone found on the southern part of the pit, and the leg bones found in place on the right side of the grave, this was an adult buried in supine position. Most parts of the skeleton, however, are simply missing.

In the pelvic area, an iron belt buckle was discovered and next to it, an iron strap end. Next to the left calf was another iron buckle, and fragments from an iron and a bronze strap end. Next to the left leg, there was a knife with iron sheath, and large whetstone, a fragment of a spear head, a hook (which was more likely the fragment of a flint steel), and several cylindrical and prismatic fragments of iron (most likely fragments of tools or implements). Most tools were on the eastern side of the grave pit, in the region of the feet, and may have initially been placed in a wooden box, of which there were several fragments.

In the box, there was a whole set of goldsmithing tools: long and short pliers, short-arm pliers, wimbles, a mechanically driven drilling tool, a chisel, a hammer-shaped cat's paw and a similar tool to pull wire, which might have also been used for making nails, a large and a small hammer, a large and a small anvil, a small whetstone, four prismatic bronze rods, 22 bronze rivets, as well

123 Kovács, "A mezőbándi ásatások," 396–429.

124 Kovács, "A mezőbándi ásatások," 407, 423–424.

125 Kovács, "A mezőbándi ásatások," 407, 423–424. For Bronze-Age and Latène assemblages in Band, see Kovács, "A mezőbándi ásatások," 268–279.

as scrap metal (in the form of a fragment of silver mirror, bronze wasters, and small fragments of iron), as well as a piece of tar.[126]

The richness and variety of the grave goods give sufficient reasons to assume that there were also artifacts of precious metal in the grave, even, perhaps, coins that the robbers may have taken. That, at least, is the case with several other graves with tools that have been found in Europe. In fact, Band may be compared, in terms of abundance and variety of tools with the grave found in Hérouvillette, in northern France, which contained a gold coin struck in Reims between 534 and 537, and 27 silver coins struck in Ostrogothic Italy and Frankish Gaul in the mid-6th century. There were also weapons in the assemblage – a lance head, a sword in its sheath, a scramasax, and an axe – as well as a tool box, which contained pliers, hammers, chisels, files, borers, punches, shears, and metal sheet knives. There was also scrap metal in the form of Roman bronze coins, as well as bronze wasters. The only thing missing to complete the comparison with Band is an anvil. In addition, the grave with tools in Hérouvillette produced a scale and glass weights.[127]

Several graves with tools are known from Central Europe. None has a tool kit as complete as that in Band, but they included pliers, hammers, anvils, and files. Such graves are known from Aradac-Mečka (Serbia),[128] Brno (Czech Republic),[129] Poysdorf (Austria),[130] and Kölked-Feketekapu B (Hungary)[131] (see Fig. 2 – the map of graves with tools, Chapter XIV.2.2).

A good comparison may be drawn with a later grave from Vestly (Norway).[132] The Viking-age assemblage included a glass beaker repaired with a thin gold-plated stripe ornamented in Animal Style I, a golden finger ring, as well as weapons – sword, shield, spear, lance, arrowhead. In addition there were utensils of everyday use (tweezers, scissors, knives, whet- and flintstones), vessels (a bronze vessel, a ceramic pot, and a bucket with iron hoops). Tools were deposited by the feet – a hammer, an anvil, pliers, a borer, a chisel, scissors, a punch, and whetstones. The most remarkable analogy is a mechanically driven drill very similar to that from Band. In addition, both assemblages contained lances.

At the eastern end of the grave pit in Band, the excavator found a spindle whorl. Its deposition may have been symbolical, as a way to convey the idea

126 Kovács, "A mezőbándi ásatások," 398–403.

127 Decaens et al., *Un nouveau cimetière*, 84.

128 Nagy, "Nekropola kod Aradaca," 57; 71, pl. IV, 7–21; 72, pl. V, 1–6.

129 Werner, "Waage und Geld," 23; 24, fig. 7;25.

130 Beninger, "Der Langobardenfriedhof," 177.

131 Kiss, *Das awarenzeitliche Gräberfeld in Kölked-Feketekapu B*, 1: 24, fig. 7; 24–25; 2: 38–41: pl. 24–27.

132 Magnus, Mollerop, Sjovold, "Migration Period Graves," N 3, 5 (1–5).

that the man buried there mastered various crafts, including spinning. Some of the tools in the kit, on the other hand, were used in woodworking, much like some of those found in Hérouvillette and Vestly.[133] The fact that (some) goldsmiths were also carpenters is in fact confirmed by the written sources.[134] However, spindle whirls have not been found in any other grave with tools. The only known association of a spindle whorl with tools is that from a cremation grave excavated in Bratei 1, not far from Band. The 5th-century assemblage in that grave included a pair of blacksmith pliers.[135] Whether that refers to a conceptual association of trades that was specific to the region remains a matter for future research.

Unlike Band, the grave in Felnac was not found through excavations, but accidentally, after the high waters of the Mureș River withdrew from a gravel quarry in 1899. The find was next to a small mound with a ditch and traces of buildings.[136] The dies were mixed with human and horse bones, which led to the conclusion that the assemblage was associated with the grave of an itinerant craftsman. No less than 44 bronze dies have been recovered, each used for producing dress accessories, belt and harness fittings. In addition, there was a bronze belt mount in the shape of a Maltese cross (Fig. 37.2.1).[137] Another 7th-century inhumation tomb was later found in Felnac,[138] but the archaeological gazetteer of the Arad County mentions two graves dated to the same period.[139] No association may be established between those graves and the one discovered in 1899.

There are good analogies to the Felnac grave, in terms of burial customs and grave goods. Grave 1 in Kunszentmárton, a site on the banks of the river Criș/Körös in Hungary, contained the skeletons of a man and of a horse. Next to them was a set of weapons (sword, lance- and arrowheads, breastplate), and wooden box with bronze and silver mounts, in which there was a scale, as well as bronze and glass, Byzantine weights. In addition to bronze and iron belt

133 Decaens et al., *Un nouveau cimetière*, 15–16; Rácz, *Die Goldschmiedegräber*, 137.

134 Roth, *Kunst*, 41.

135 Ligia Bârzu, *Continuitatea populației autohtone în Transilvania în secolele IV–V (Cimitirul 1 de la Bratei)* [Continuity of the native population in Transylvania in the 4th–5th centuries (Cemetery 1 from Bratei)], (Bucharest: Editura Academiei Republicii Socialiste România, 1973), 224.

136 Dömötör, "Újabb lemezsajtoló bronzmintár Fönlakról," 65.

137 Hampel, "Emlékek és leletek," 117–123; Dömötör, "Újabb lemezsajtoló bronzmintár Fönlakról," 62–65; Hampel, *Altertümer des frühen Mittelalters*, 2: 392–396; 3: 747–749.

138 Mircea Zdroba, Mircea Barbu, "Săpăturile arheologice de la Felnac și Vladimirescu (rapoarte preliminare) [The archaeological excavations from Felnac and Vladimirescu (preliminary reports)]," *Ziridava* 6 (1976), 49.

139 *Repertoriul arheologic al Mureșului Inferior*, 68.

fittings, the burial assemblage included 41 dies (40 of bronze and one of lead), a bronze ladle, a hammer, pliers, an anvil, two pairs of shears, slitting and engraving tools, a cat's paw, and scrap metal in the form of silver, brass, copper and bronze sheet and wasters.[140] A bronze die for belt mounts was found in a male burial of the 7th-century cemetery in Aradac-Mečka (Serbia), on the left bank of the Tisza River, only about 25 miles to the southwest from Felnac. The burial assemblage included also scrap metal, in the form of fragments of a bronze jug.[141] Eight dies for belt and harness fittings have also been found in grave 11 of the Avar-age cemetery excavated in Gátér (Hungary), in association with two silver earrings, bronze buckles, and silver belt mounts. Two half-manufactured products – a belt mount and an earring – were also deposited in the grave, along with a hammer and a bronze object interpreted as crucible, as well as scrap metal in the form of a fragment of bronze sheet.[142] When considered against the background of other graves with dies, Felnac seems to fit very well in the group of Avar-age burials with horses and tools. There can be no doubt therefore that Felnac is a grave assemblage, not a hoard or a workshop.

Much more difficult is the interpretation of the cremation grave 14, which was discovered in 1952 in Sărata Monteoru (Buzău County). Together with the cremated remains, the excavators found eight conical, poorly fired beakers, each with a trilobed mouth (Fig. 6.4). Some of them were upside down, but none contained cremated bones, and, except fragments of a knife, there were no other grave goods.[143] Similar beakers have been found in Bucharest-Băneasa and interpreted as crucibles.[144] The specimen from Bucharest-Băneasa is shorter, while those from Sărata Monteoru are slender. At any rate, the analogy encouraged scholars to draw the conclusion that grave 14 in Sărata Monteoru was that of a craftsman, possibly a goldsmith.[145] Even though no traces of molten metal have been found on any of the eight beakers, crucibles deposited in female graves in central Russia are also devoid of any traces of metalworking.[146] Clay crucibles have also been deposited in inhumation graves discovered in Germany in Schönebeck, Wallerstädten, and Neuwied. The only other cremation burial for which a similar interpretation has been advanced is an extraordinary burial assemblage in Pókaszepetk (Hungary), which produced a scale

140 Csallány, *A Kunszentmártoni avarkori ötvösir*, 3; 49–51; Rácz, *Die Goldschmiedegräber*, 171–181.
141 Nagy, "Nekropola kol Aradaca," 93, pl. XXVI.1–16.
142 Kada, "Gátéri (Kun-Kisszállási) temető," 368–370.
143 Nestor et al., "Șantierul Sărata-Monteoru," 84–85.
144 Constantiniu, "Elemente romano-bizantine," 673.
145 Comșa, "Socio-economic organization," 186, 188.
146 Capelle and Vierck, "Modeln," 77.

and weights. This has promptly been interpreted as the grave of a merchant.[147] Others, however, claim that it was the grave of a goldsmith.[148] The latter interpretation seems more plausible in view of the fact that the burial assemblage also included scrap metal in the form of first- to fourth-century Roman coins, some pierced. Moreover, the deposition of a belt buckle with opposing, rampant animals and of a lance head are directly comparable to the graves in Aradac and Band, respectively. Both crucibles and scales with weights are typically found in graves of craftsmen (see chapter XII.2).

3 Hoards

Hoards are generally understood as deposits of valuables, but when such collections are meant to be abandoned (i.e., never to be retrieved), archaeologists employ the phrase "deposits."[149] Most famous are deposits in or next to water.[150] The key element in the archaeological definition of "deposits," however, is the existence of a sufficiently large number of items found together, in the same context, which can be asserted with certainty as not being part of a settlement feature or of a grave.[151] If so, then the complete absence of tool deposits dated to the 6th and 7th centuries is puzzling, the more so that deposits of tools and implements are known from both earlier (4th to 5th century, e.g., Tattabánya, Hungary[152]), and later periods (8th to 9th centuries).[153]

Kurt Horedt first used the term "deposit" in reference to the Felnac assemblage.[154] Others followed suit, completely disregarding the clear evidence of

147 Sós, "Frühmittelalterliche Brandbestattung," 424, fig. 1, 426, fig. 3.

148 Garam, *Funde*, 163.

149 Florin Curta, "Blacksmiths, Warriors and Tournaments of Value: Dating and Interpreting Early Medieval Hoards of Iron Implements in Eastern Europe," *Ephemeris Napocensis* 7 (1997), 214.

150 Radu Harhoiu, "Semnificația tezaurelor din secolul al v-lea de pe teritoriul României [The significance of the hoards from the 5th century on the territory of Romania]," *Studii și Cercetări de Istorie Veche și Arheologie* 43, no. 4 (1992), 426; Michael Schmauder, *Oberschichtgräber und Verwahrfunde in Südosteuropa im 4. und 5. Jahrhundert*, (Archaeologia Romanica 3) 2 vols. (Bucharest: Editura Academiei Române, 2002), 36–37.

151 Adrian Canache, Florin Curta, "Depozite de unelte și arme medievale timpurii de pe teritoriul României [Deposits of early medieval tools and weapons on the territory of Romania]," *Mousaios* 4/1 (1994), 182.

152 János László, "Ein Eisengerätfund vom Fundort Tatabánya-24," *A Móra Ferenc Múzeum Évkönyvei: Studia Archaeologica* 9 (2003), 168.

153 Curta, "Blacksmiths," see the catalog.

154 Horedt, *Contribuții*, 70.

a burial assemblage.[155] Such finds as the dies from Adony (Hungary)[156] and Biskupija (Croatia),[157] for which no information exists on the archaeological context, may also be regarded as burial assemblages, not tool deposits. A change in burial customs is clearly visible in the 5th century in such assemblages as grave B in Bratei[158] or two graves in Csongrád-Kenderfőldek (Hungary) (each with a set of pliers, hammer, and wimble).[159] In the former case, along with pliers, no less than five sickles, the sleeve and the axle of a cart were deposited in the grave, perhaps as an indication of the variety of objects that the craftsman was capable of producing. It is also possible that the deposition of agricultural tools was meant to signal a farmer who was also a craftsman. Similarly, 8th- to 9th-century deposits of tools have been interpreted as an expression of craft appreciation, and also as defining social status or social aspirations.[160]

That deposits of tools are absent in the 6th and 7th century may be explained in terms of the great importance given to burial rituals, which provided sufficient opportunities for the expression of the concepts and ideas conveyed by deposits in earlier and later periods. Such burial rituals were clearly rooted in the pre-Avar culture of the Germanic populations in the Carpathian Basin. This may explain why graves with tools, which remained numerically important during the Early Avar age, disappear after ca. 700 (i.e., during the Late Avar age). The profound economic and social changes taking place in Avar society at that time made it necessary to express wealth and social difference by other means.

Hoards represent collections of valuable goods, which are often at the same time prestige items, owned by high-ranking individuals. The accumulation in the hoard has not only an intrinsic value, but also a social one,[161] which is usually on display in various ceremonies. Scholars, however, maintain that hoards were buried during the Migration period on the territory of present-day Romania because of political or military troubles, with no concern for socially

155 Mărghitan, *Banatul*, 44; Olteanu, *Societatea*, 130.

156 Fettich, *Das awarenzeitliche Kunstgewerbe*, pl. VI.1–13.

157 Zdenko Vinski, "O nalazima 6. i 7. stoleća u jugoslaviji s posebnim obzirom na arheološku ostavštinu iz vremena prvog avarskoga kaganata [On the findings of the 6th and 7th centuries in Yugoslavia with special reference to the archeological heritage from the time of the first Avar kaganate]," *Opuscula Archaeologica/Radovi Arheološkog zavoda* 3 (1958), 27–30; pl. XVI.

158 Bârzu, *Continuitatea*, 224; 302, pl. XXI.

159 Mihály Párducz, "Archäologische Beiträge zur Geschichte der Hunnenzeit in Ungarn," *Acta Archaeologica Academiae Scientiarum Hungaricae* 11 (1959), 310; pl. I.3; 317; pl. I.1–2.

160 Curta, "Blacksmiths," 248.

161 Schmauder, *Oberschichtgräber*, 37–38.

important or sacred occasions.[162] Unlike hoards of gold or silver, those of bronze may truly be associated with commercial relations with the Empire, because their small value makes it unlikely that such collections of radiate were obtained either as booty or as gifts.[163]

Two hoards are particularly important in this respect to my discussion of metalworking during the 6th and 7th centuries. One of them was found in Priseaca (Olt County). It consisted of a ceramic pot, which contained 141 silver coins [eight struck for Emperor Constans II (641–668) and 133 for Emperor Constantine IV (668–685)], as well as two silver earrings.[164] Two interpretations have been put forward in relation to this particular hoard. According to one of them, this was a collection of a Byzantine craftsman, who had brought the coins from the Empire in order to use them as scrap metal for jewelry produced on commission from local rulers, as silver was not readily available in the lands north of the Danube River.[165] According to others, this was in fact a collection of a local leader, who had once been employed in the Byzantine army and had therefore been paid in Byzantine silver.[166] Some have advanced the idea that this hoard was in fact a bribe or a gift from the Byzantine emperor to some local chieftain, aimed at obtaining a political alliance.[167] Exactly who were the people over whom that chieftain may have exercised authority has been the subject of some debate – Bulgars[168] or Slavs.[169] However, the close analysis of the coins strongly suggests that this was a person's wealth at a particular moment, not the result of accumulation over time.[170] Given the date of

162 Harhoiu, "Semnificația tezaurelor," 426.

163 Florin Curta, "Invasion or inflation? Sixth- to seventh-century Byzantine coin hoards in Eastern and Southeastern Europe," *Annali dell'Istituto Italiano di Numismatica* 43 (1996), 95–97, 106–107.

164 Mihai Butoi, "Un tezaur de monede și obiecte de podoabă din secolul al VII-lea descoperit în comuna Priseaca-Slatina [A treasure of coins and jewelry from the 7th century discovered in the village of Priseaca-Slatina]." *Studii și comunicări. Istorie-Științele Naturii – Muzeul din Pitești* 1 (1968), 98–101.

165 Butoi, "Un tezaur de monede și obiecte de podoabă din secolul al VII-lea," 102; Bucur Mitrea, "Date noi cu privire la secolul al VII-lea. Tezaurul de hexagrame bizantine de la Priseaca (jud. Olt) [New data on the seventh century. The Byzantine Hexagram Treasure from Priseaca (Olt County)]," *Studii și Cercetări de Numismatică* 6 (1975), 125.

166 Butoi, "Un tezaur," 103.

167 Curta, "Invasion or inflation?" 112–116; Péter Somogyi, "New remarks on the flow of Byzantine coins in Avaria and Walachia during the second half of the seventh century," in *The Other Europe in the Middle Ages. Avars, Bulgars, Khazars, and Cumans*, ed. Florin Curta (Leiden-Boston: Brill, 2008), pp. 130, 133–135.

168 Curta, "Invasion or inflation?" 114.

169 Somogyi, "New remarks," 133, 145.

170 Mitrea, "Date noi," 117.

the last coin, most scholars have explained the hoard in relation to the migration of the Bulgars to the northern Balkans.[171] Most 7th-century coins found in the lands north of the Danube are of silver (*hexagrams*), and it is quite possible that hoards such as Priseaca represent gifts or bribes sent from Constantinople to the Bulgars on Lower Danube, either in order to ensure good relations with them, or to buy their military alliance.[172]

A hoard of similar content – silver coins and jewels – was also found on the opposite bank of the Danube, at Silistra (Bulgaria). Along with 21 earrings and two finger-rings, there were three coins, one of which was struck for Emperor Justin II (565–578).[173] While initially the burial of the hoard was placed in the 7th century, that moment was most likely at some point during the last two or three decades of the 6th century. At any rate, it is unlikely that the hoard was a collection of bullion, as initially thought. Nor can the owner have been a Byzantine goldsmith working during the 7th century in Durostorum, for an ethnically heterogeneous population.[174] Despite or, perhaps, because of the structural similarity to the Priseaca hoard, this was a combination of coins and jewelry that could hardly be interpreted as bullion for a goldsmith, whether Byzantine or of any other origin. Several 6th- to 7th-century hoards of gold, silver, or even bronze include both coins and dress accessories. This strongly suggests that such collections of metal had nothing to do jewelry production.[175] It would of course be important to test the coins and the earrings from Priseaca, as well as the earrings and the finger-rings from Silistra, for the purity of the silver, but such an analysis has not so far been carried out on any of those two assemblages. No hypothesis could therefore be verified in terms of the origin of the metal that went into the production of jewelry. It is unlikely that hoards of silver so far found on the territory of Romania represent anything like collections of bullion, since no traces of scrap metal have been found in any of them. On the contrary, the fact that artifacts seem to have been carefully selected

171 Butoi, "Un tezaur," 103; Mitrea, "Date noi," 117.

172 Curta, "Invasion or inflation?" 114; Florin Curta, "Byzantium in Dark-Age Greece (the numismatic evidence in its Balkan context)," *Byzantine and Modern Greek Studies* 29, no. 2 (2005), 118.

173 Stefka Angelova and Vladimir Penčev, "Un trésor d'argent de Silistra," *Archaeologiia* 31, no. 2 (1990), 38–41. The authors mistook two coins without legends as struck for Emperor Constantine IV. For the correct identification of the coins, see Cécile Morrison, Vladislav Popović, and Vujadin Ivanišević, *Les trésors monétaires byzantins des Balkans et d'Asie Mineure (491–713)* (Paris: Lethielleux, 2006), 155; Florin Curta and Andrei Gândilă, "Hoards and hoarding patterns in the early Byzantine Balkans," *Dumbarton Oaks Papers* 65–66 (2011–2012), 101.

174 Angelova and Penčev, "Un trésor d'argent," 43.

175 Curta and Gândilă, "Hoards," 54, 56–58, and 94–95.

for hoarding, often in pairs, suggests ostentatious consumption and "destruction," of a kind recently associated with potlatch-like ceremonies performed at moments of social and political tension, in which such ceremonies marked a rite of passage or access to power, at the same time reflecting the privileges of aristocratic groups.[176] The interpretation of the Priseaca hoard, therefore, may definitely be associated to a high-ranking person in the local society, but has nothing to do with metalworking and the position of craftsmen in that society.

Only the hoard found in Horgești (Bacău County), in which the coins were found deposited inside a copper-alloy pitcher, may be related to a craftsman's activity, as besides coins, the collection also included a bronze chain with S-shaped rings, as well as pieces of scrap metal (two pieces actually showing traces of metalworking similar to those on the pitcher). The coins were collected over a relatively short period of time, the last third of the 6th and the early 7th century.[177] It is likely that the chain, the pieces of scrap metal, and, perhaps, the pitcher itself were supposed to serve as raw material for the craftsman.[178]

4 Isolated (Stray) Finds

In addition to "closed finds" such as burials, several artifacts pertaining to metalworking are known from accidental discoveries. Such finds have no archaeological context and may therefore be treated separately, as "isolated" or "stray." Two bronze dies for harness fittings are known from Corund (Harghita County; Fig. 27.2). They were found apparently on a sand dune before World War II, shipped to Hungary, and subsequently lost.[179] Another bronze dies was found under unknown circumstances in Dumbrăveni (Sibiu County), and is now in the collection of the Hungarian National Museum in Budapest (Fig. 37.1).[180] According to Kurt Horedt, it is likely that those dies were from graves disturbed in one way or another. They definitely fit into the picture of Early Avar-age graves (presumably of goldsmiths) with dies.[181] A pewter model for casting

176 Florin Curta, *The Making of the Slavs. History and Archaeology of the Lower Danube Region, c. 500–700* (Cambridge: Cambridge University Press, 2001), 224–225.

177 Viorel Căpitanu, "Tezaurul de monede bizantine descoperit la Horgești (jud. Bacău) [The Byzantine coin hoard discovered in Horgești (Bacău county)]," *Carpica* 4 (1971), 253–259.

178 Sergiu Musteață, "Unele concretizări privind vasul de metal din tezaurul monetar de la Horgești, jud. Bacău, România [Some remarks regarding the metal vessel from the coin hoard found in Horgești, Bacău County, Romania]," in *Arheologia între știință, politică și economia de piață*, ed. Sergiu Musteață (Chișinău: Pontos, 2010), p. 103.

179 Rácz, *Die Goldschmiedegräber*, 149.

180 Rácz, *Die Goldschmiedegräber*, 152.

181 Horedt, *Contribuții*, 69–70, 75, fig. 13.6–8, 95.

bow fibulae is also known from an unknown location in the region of the Iron Gates. The artifact is now in the collection of the Banat National Museum in Timişoara. As the artifact was part of a late 19th-century, private collection based on finds from the territory of what is now northeastern Serbia, the exact location of the find is impossible to establish. The model initially had an appendix in the form of a human mask, as indicated on the collector's drawing (Fig. 42.2a–c).[182] At some point before its first publication, however, the model broke, and the appendix got lost.[183] It is possible that the model came from a disturbed grave, like the model for a bow fibula found in Felnac.

While stray finds of dies and models are known from inside the Carpathian Basin, most prominent among isolated finds from the lands outside are stone molds for casting dress accessories. One of them was found in Olteni (Teleorman County), during a trial excavation to the west from the road linking Alexandria and Piteşti (Fig. 2.3). While the mold is most likely of a 6th-century date, it was actually found on the territory of a 9th- to 10th-century settlement, which most likely superposed another of an earlier date.[184] A limestone mold for crosses and earring pendants is known from Izvorul Dulce (Buzău County; Fig. 7.3).[185] Another stone mold for dress accessory details is a stray find from Vadu Săpat (Prahova County; Fig. 43.2).[186] Two other stray finds of molds are known from Poieniţa (Vrancea County; Fig. 2.5) and Aldeni (Buzău County; Fig. 42.1).[187] Another stone mold for casting small crosses and lunula-pendants was accidentally found in Dichiseni (Călăraşi County), about 12 miles to the northeast from Silistra, across the river Danube (Fig. 44.2).[188]

182 Daniela Tănase, Mircea Mare, "Piese de port şi de podoabă din secolele III–VII în colecţia Pongrácz. Catalog [Costume and adornment pieces from the 3rd–7th centuries in the Pongrácz collection. Catalog]," *Analele Banatului Serie Nouă* 9 (2001), 206. The collector was Imre Pongrácz, who had been the commander of the Honvéd garrison in the port Orşova during the last third of the 19th century.

183 Ion Nestor, Constantin Nicolăescu-Plopşor, "Die völkerwanderungszeitlichen Schatz Negrescu," *Germania* 22 (1938), plate 9.2; Dan Gh. Teodor, "Fibules byzantines des Ve - VIIe siècles dans l'espace carpato-danubiano-pontique," *Études byzantines et post-byzantines* 3 (1997), 88, fig. 8.3.

184 Preda, "Tipar," 513, 512, fig. 1; 515.

185 Miclea, Florescu, *Strămoşii românilor*, 209 and fig. 760.

186 Măgureanu, Ciupercă, "The 6th–8th Centuries Metallurgical Activity," 301–302.

187 Victor Teodorescu, "Centre meşteşugăreşti,", 86, fig. 7.1- Poieniţa, fig. 7.3- Aldeni; 91, note 47.

188 *Două milenii de creştinism/Deux millénaires de christianisme* (Exhibition catalog), ed. Mircea Mamalaucă (Bârlad: Muzeul Vasile Pârvan, 2000), 34, fig. 33.

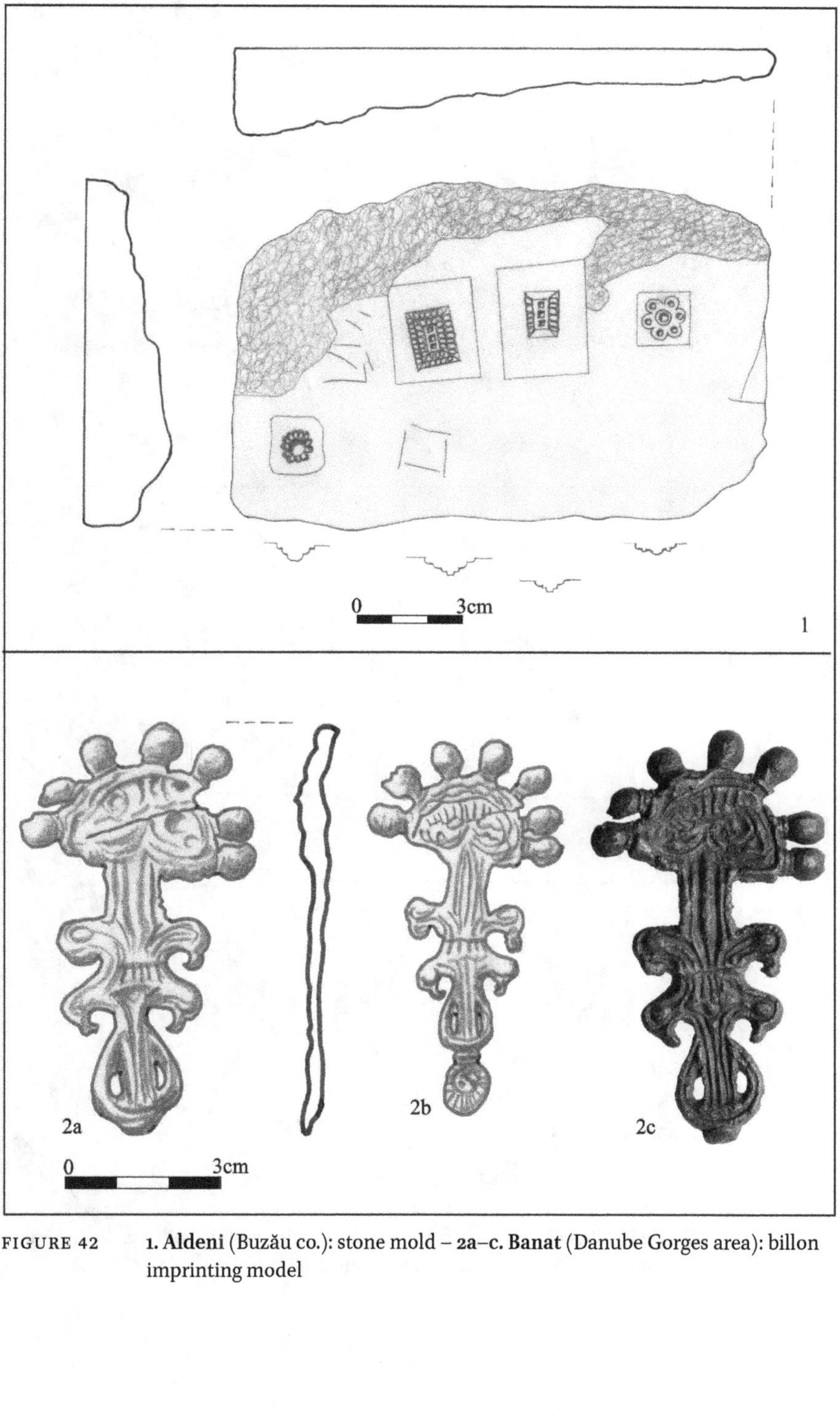

FIGURE 42 **1. Aldeni** (Buzău co.): stone mold – **2a–c. Banat** (Danube Gorges area): billon imprinting model

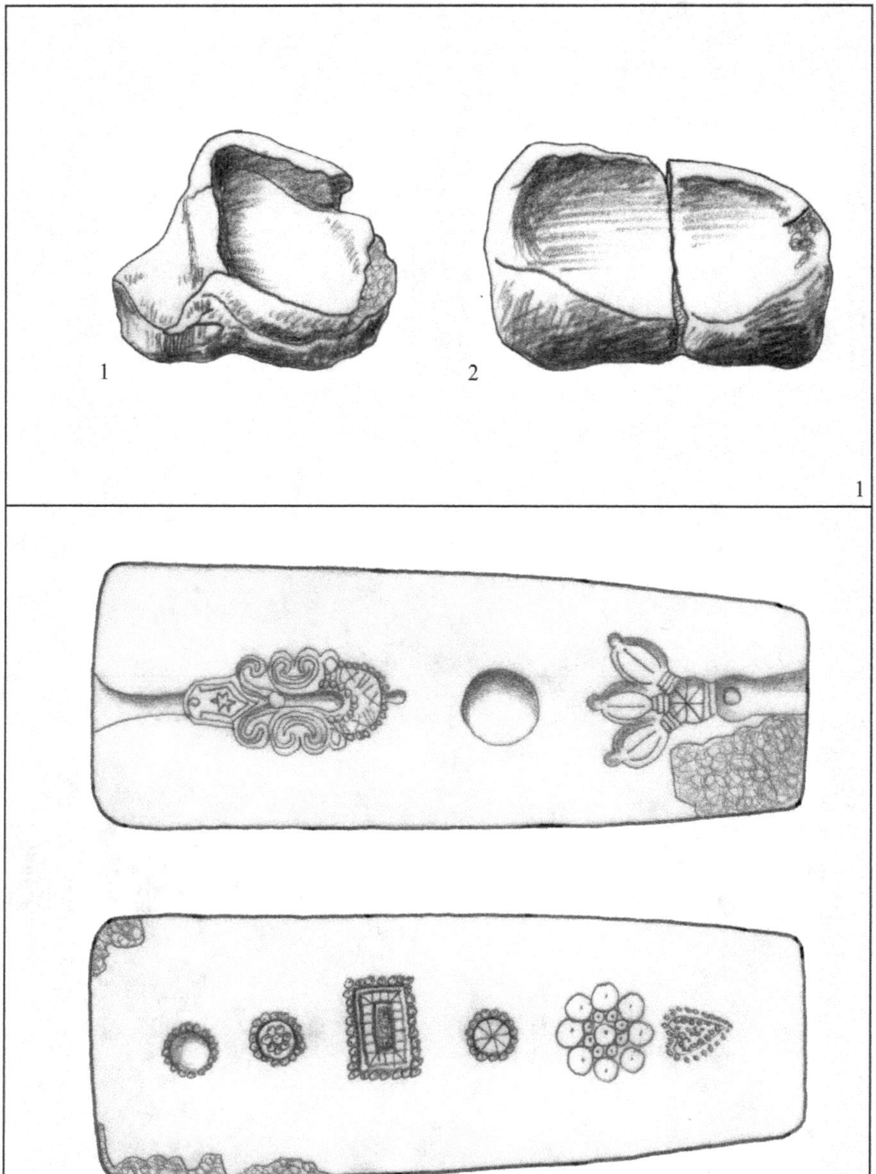

FIGURE 43 **1. Udești** (Suceava co.): 1.1. clay crucible; 1.2. clay casting ladle – **2. Vadu Săpat** (Prahova co.): stone mold. 1.1–2 without scale

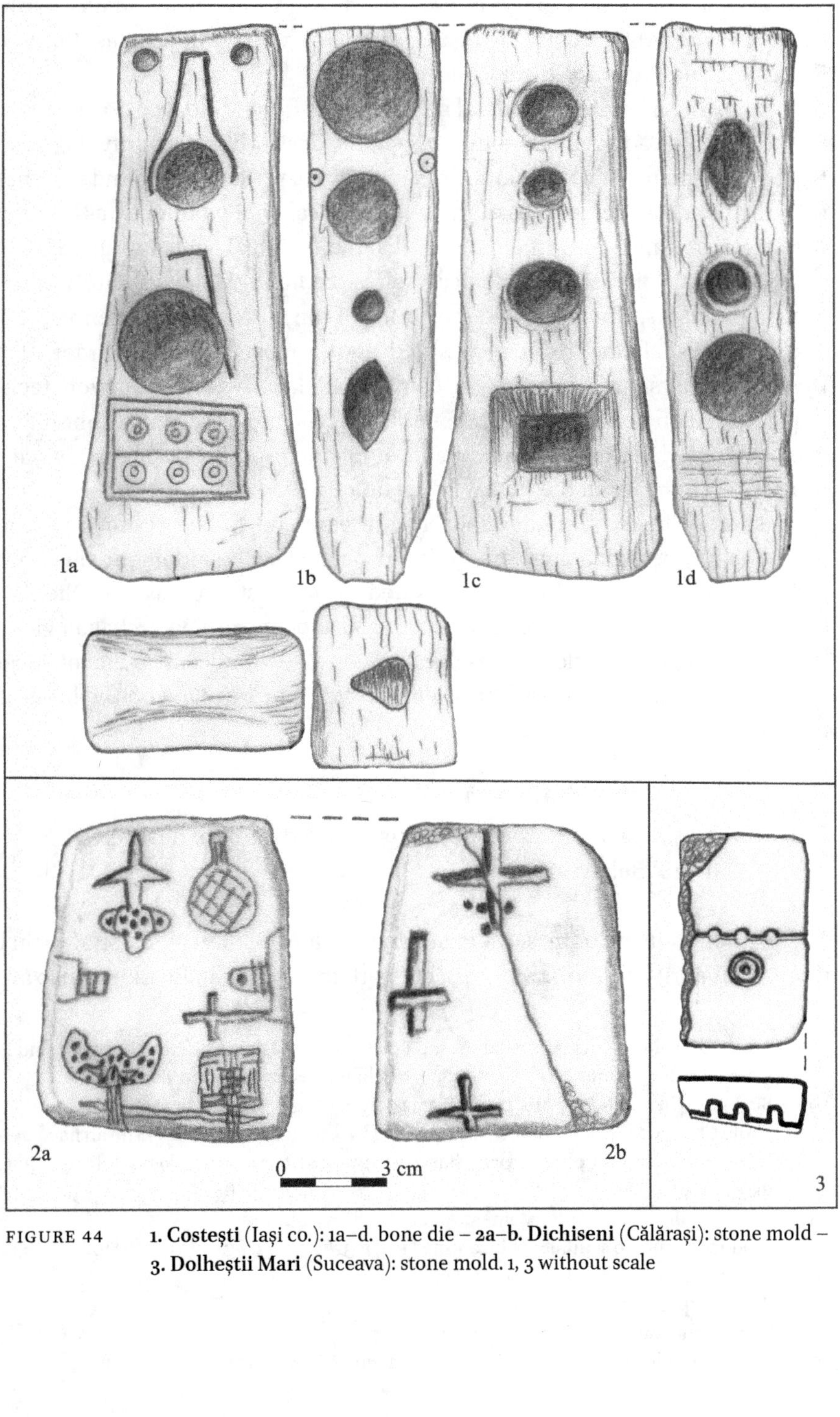

FIGURE 44 **1. Costești** (Iași co.): 1a–d. bone die – **2a–b. Dichiseni** (Călărași): stone mold – **3. Dolheștii Mari** (Suceava): stone mold. 1, 3 without scale

Stray finds of stone mold are also known from Moldavia: Traian (Bacău County; Fig. 23.3),[189] Cucuteni (Iași County; Fig. 5.5),[190] Moțca (Iași County; Fig. 2.2),[191] and Rădeni (Neamț County, Fig. 6.1).[192]

Perhaps the most remarkable of all stray finds from Moldavia, however, are the bone molds accidentally found in 1960 in Costești (Iași County; Fig. 44.1, Fig. 45). Fragments of copper and silver sheet were presumably found together with the molds, which bespeaks an archaeological context directly associated with metalworking.[193] The molds are a clear indication of goldsmithing, as they were essential for casting dress accessories, including earrings with lunula-shaped pendants, which allowed the dating of the finds to the 7th century.

The Costești finds are now regarded as the most important proof of a Byzantine craftsman operating in central Moldavia with production techniques based on bone molds. It is possible that the molds served for obtaining wax models, which in turn could be used for the production of earring with star-shaped pendant in the "lost wax" technique.[194]

Most stray finds from the lands to the east and to the south from the Carpathian Mountains are likely to be associated with settlement sites that have not yet been identified or excavated. In at least two cases – Olteni[195] and Coroteni[196] – such an assumption has also been verified archaeologically, even though the molds themselves remained without any archaeological context. Elsewhere, the case for settlement sites may be made on the basis of field surveys.[197]

5 Workshops or Funerary Contexts – an Indicator of a Different Cultural Behavior

The examination of both settlement and isolated (stray) finds shows that the vast majority of tools and artifacts pertaining to metalworking that are

189 Teodor, "Unele probleme privind evoluția culturii materiale", 272. Sometimes the find is referred as being from Parincea or Prăjești – old names for the same village.

190 Boghian, "Un moule," 115–116, 122, fig. 2.1; 124, fig. 4.

191 Vasile Chirică, Marcel Tanasachi, *Repertoriul arheologic al Județului Iași* [The archaeological repertoire of Iași County], 2 vols. (Iași: Institutul de Istorie și Arheologie "A. D. Xenopol", 1985), 1: 255, fig. 12.12.

192 Mitrea, "Influențe bizantine," 151–52 and note 48; 153 fig. 4/3.

193 Teodor, "Elemente și influențe bizantine," 102, 103, fig. 3; 104, fig. 4; 105, fig. 5; 106.

194 Szmoniewski, "Production," 113, 121–122.

195 Preda, "Tipar," 513, 512, fig. 1; 515.

196 Bobi, "Contribuții," 107, 138, fig. 25.6; 140, fig. 27. 6–7.

197 Teodor, "Unele probleme," 272; Boghian, "Un moule," 115–116, 122, fig. 2.1; 124, fig. 4.

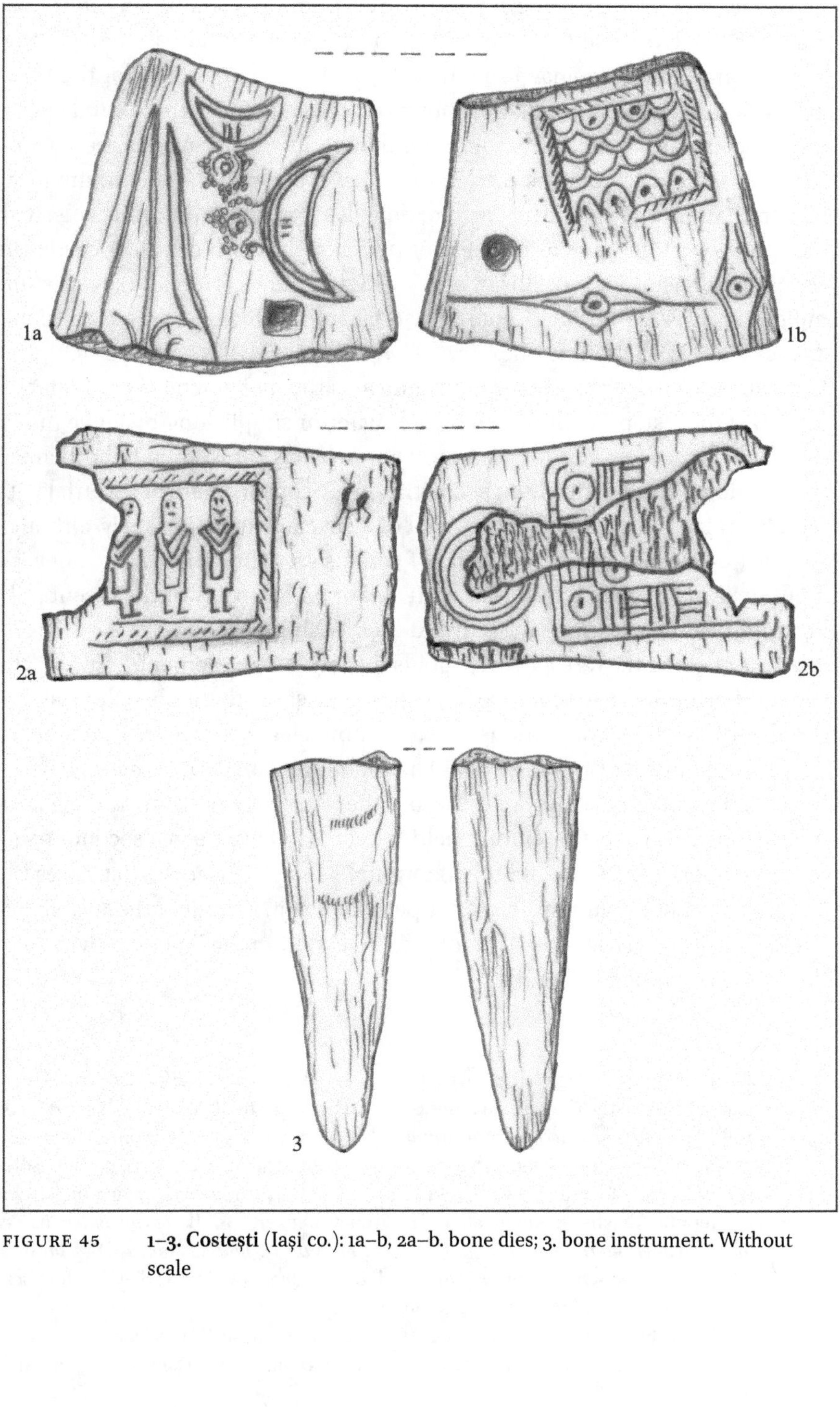

FIGURE 45 1–3. **Costești** (Iași co.): 1a–b, 2a–b. bone dies; 3. bone instrument. Without scale

known from the lands to the south and east from the Carpathian Mountains are associated with settlements. Only one possible burial assemblage, that from Sărata Monteoru, may bring into discussion the possibility of the ritual deposition tools for a population practicing cremation, with cultural ties to northeastern and eastern Europe, even though in all those areas metalworking tools (molds, crucibles, and ladles) have been found in inhumation, not cremation graves, particularly of females.[198] Female inhumations with tools, however, are known from a later period (7th to 8th century) inside the Carpathian Basin: Szeged-Bilisics and Vác-Kavicsbánya (Hungary), with stone molds; Gyönk-Vásártéri út, Komárno IV – J. Váradiho Street, Szekszárd-Palánk, Zselickislak, with bronze dies (see Chapter XII.2 with the bibliography). Whether such a distribution of finds indicates the movement of a population from east to west, perhaps driven by the Avars, or simply long-distance matrimonial alliances remains for the moment unclear. That women in both areas, at a considerable distance from each other, were socially marked in burial with metalworking tools is a subject in need of a special study. Curiously, although gender has recently become a topic of serious study in Avar archaeology, no mention is made of female burials with dies or molds in any of the recent publications dealing with Avar women and their position in society.[199]

As for metallurgy, especially goldsmithing in settlements inside the Carpathian Basin, it is remarkable how inconsistent the archaeological evidence is basically, only mentions of slag without clear archaeological contexts. Slag appears in Moreşti, Bratei, and Lazuri, but no smelting furnaces have so far been documented on any of those, or other sites in the region. Judging from the existing evidence, therefore, smelting seems to have been a secondary activity, or at least one that left little, if any archaeological traces. That raises the possibility that populations in the Carpathian Basin, including the Avars, procured their iron (in the form of blooms or billets) from the Balkan provinces of the early Byzantine Empire.[200]

198 Nikitina, Efremova, "Pogrebal'nyĭ obriad," 149. No such grave is so far known from the entire area between the Carpathian Mountains and the Dniester River covered in this book.

199 Anton Distelberger, *Österreichs Awarinnen. Frauen aus Gräbern des 7. und 8. Jahrhunderts* (St. Pölten: Niederösterreichischer Institut für Landeskunde, 2004), 7–59; Orsolya Heinrich-Tamáska, "Frühe 'Awarinnen' und späte "Germaninnen"? Bemerkungen zur Interpretation reicher Frauengräber der Frühawarenzeit," in *Weibliche Eliten in der Frühgeschichte. Internationale Tagung vom 13. bis zum 14. Juni 2008 im RGZM im Rahmen des Forschungschwerpunktes "Eliten"*, ed. Dieter Quast (Mainz: Verlag des Römisch-Germanischen Zentralmuseums, 2011), pp. 89–110.

200 Rusu, "Transilvania şi Banatul," 190–192. As an alternative, Rusu, "Transilvania şi Banatul," 190 with n. 45 suggests that iron may have also been brought from Central Asia (the Altai

A completely different picture emerges for the lands outside the Carpathian Mountains, to the east and to the south. There, one can find clear evidence of smelting, even though the archaeological contexts in which tools have been found do no justify entirely the use of the term "workshop." A very important aspect of the discussion about workshops is the stratigraphic position of the tool finds – whether on the floor of the settlement feature, or in its filling. Tools found in the filling were likely to have been discarded there, as if in dumping place, and cannot be used as evidence of any metalworking activities taking place in that settlement feature. Be as it may, there can be no doubt about the metalworking activity on many settlement sites, and the possibility (if not likelihood) that workshops were in operation in at least some of them. First to come to mind in that respect are the sunken-floored building 10 in the settlement excavated on the Soldat Ghivan Nicolae Street in Bucharest, or the many discoveries in the Budureasca Valley. On sites excavated in Moldavia, such as Davideni, Suceava-Șipot, or Dodești, tools have been found in several features of one and the same settlement, suggests that metal casting and the making of ornaments was done not by one, but by many craftsmen at the same time. In other words, several people within one and the same community had the necessary skills to engage in metalworking. This was definitely the case of the community of specialized craftsmen in Lozna, where clear evidence has been found of smelting and forging. A case can also be made for Șirna that at least some of its inhabitants were specialist smelters. Conversely, the many ladles found in Dulceanca IV, which had traces of molten metal, suggest that casting was not an activity restricted to a small group of specialists. Important goldsmithing centres existed in Walachia in the Budureasca Valley, as well as on the territory of the present-day city of Bucharest. By contrast, the archaeological evidence from Moldavia suggests that in the absence of any center (with the exception of Lozna), casting and jewelry making were activities performed on several sites simultaneously.

Such evidence of intense metalworking in Walachia and Moldavia also suggests that the populations in those lands, unlike those in the Carpathian Basin, did not rely on Byzantium for procuring good-quality iron, as they were perfectly capable of exploiting the local resources. Given that such resources were mostly of bog iron, many of the iron artifacts found in 6th- to 7th-century settlements are of a rather poor quality.

Within the Carpathian Basin, much evidence of metalworking derives from burial, not settlement assemblages. Judging from the tools deposited in

---

region). As high-quality steel is known only from the Early Avar period, ties with Central Asia may have broken after ca. 650.

graves, craftsmen were both blacksmiths and goldsmiths at the same time. Nonetheless, those who buried the two men in Band and Kölked Feketekapu B wanted to emphasize goldsmithing, particularly the making of fine jewelry. Moreover, some tools suggest that goldsmiths were also skilled carpenters (Band) or artisans working with bone and antler (Makó). The excellent quality of the associated iron artifacts suggests that the raw material, at least, originated in the Empire, which could explain why blacksmithing was not a prominent concern for those burying their dead in the Carpathian Basin. Unlike the lands outside the Carpathian Mountains, there is in fact no evidence that local ore sources, such as bog iron, were exploited in the Carpathian Basin. In the absence of a comparable number of settlement sites, it would be a mistake to push that argument too far. A few Avar-age settlement sites identified in recent years seem to indicate ironworking, but the chronology needs serious refinement. Large-scale, salvage archaeological excavations were undertaken recently in Hungary as a consequence of the building of highways. Among the most spectacular finds, an ironworking center was discovered in southwestern Hungary, which could be dated between the 7th and the 9th century. Smelting sites have been discovered in Kaposvár and Zamárdi, which processed the nearby limonite ores. Roasting pits, smelting furnaces, smithies, blooms, and a very large quantity of slag testify to a relatively low quality iron obtained on those sites.[201] There are striking similarities between the ironworking sites in southwestern Hungary and Lozna-Străteni, which raise interesting questions

201 Zsolt Gallina, Péter Hornok, "Avar kori vaskohászati centrum Zamárdiban (Magyarország, Somogy megye) [An Avar-age Ironworking Center in Zamárdi (Hungary, Somogy County)]," in *Bányászati, kohászati és földtani konferencia. Sepsiszentgyörgy, 2006, április 6–9.* (Cluj-Napoca: Erdélyi Magyar Múszaki Tudományos Társaság, 2006), pp. 161–170; Zsolt Gallina, Péter Hornok, "Vorbericht über die archäologische Untersuchung eines awarischen Eisenverhüttungszentrums in der Gemeinde Zamárdi, Komitat Somogy (Ungarn)," in *Arts and Crafts in Medieval Rural Environment: 22nd–29th September 2005*, eds. Jan Klápště and Petr Sommer (Turnhout: Brepols, 2007), pp. 71–81; Zsolt Gallina, "Avar kori vaskohászati és települési centrum Zamárdiban [An Avar-age Ironworking and settlement Center in Zamárdi]," in *A Barbaricum ösvényein ... A 2005-ben Kecskeméten tartott tudományos konferencia előadásai*, eds. Agnés Somogyvári, György V. Székely and Valéria Kulcsár (Kecskemét: Bács-Kiskun Megyei Önkormányzat Katona József Múzeum, 2011), pp. 179–198; János Gömöri, "The legacy of 9th century craftsmen in the Carpathian Basin," in *The History of Handcraft in Hungary*, ed. János Szulovszky (Budapest: Hungarian Chamber of Commerce and Industry, 2012), pp. 15–22; Béla Török, Árpád Kovács, Zsolt Gallina, "Iron metallurgy of the Pannonian Avars of the 7th–9th century based on excavations and material examinations," in *Archaeometallurgy in Europe III. Proceedings of the 3rd International Conference, Deutsches Bergbau-Museum, Bochum, June 29–July 1, 2011*, eds. Andreas Hauptmann and Diana Modarressi-Tehrani (Bochum: Deutsches Bergbau-Museum, 2015), pp. 229–238.

about the nature of those communities of metalworkers, their similar technologies and possible contacts between them.

The deposition of tools in graves is also an indication of a different type of society, much more stratified, with a clearly defined elite that appreciated craftsmen capable of producing tools, weapons, and dress accessories upon commission. Very large quantities of precious metals entered the Carpathian Basin during the late 6th and first half of the 7th century, as indicated both by archaeological (primarily from graves) and written sources (such as Theophylact Simocatta's *History*, mentioning the large subsidies paid to the Avars by the early Byzantine emperors).

The custom of depositing tools in graves, which pre-dates the arrival of the Avars and was specific to the Central Europe, shows that despite the establishment of the Avar Qaganate, social structures of the previous period survived, in one form or the other, at least as far as burial customs show. Such practices are not known from the lands to the east and to the south from the Carpathian Basin, with the only possible exception of the grave with crucibles (if that is what they are) from Sărata Monteoru. To be sure, comparatively fewer burial assemblages are known from the area outside the Carpathian Mountains, and tool deposition has not so far been documented in any of them. To the south and to the east from the Carpathian Mountains, local communities had a different understanding of social hierarchies, especially of the role of craftsmen in society. Theirs was a material culture capitalizing on resources readily available in the immediate vicinity, with little, if any mobility, and no need of raw materials from the Byzantine Empire.

CHAPTER 3

Sources of Raw Materials

Unlike stone or bone, there are various working options for metals: cold or hot processing, in soft, liquid state, or alloy state. There is also the possibility to (re)use scrap metal. In ancient times, only eight of the 75 metals used today were known: gold, silver, copper, tin, zinc, iron, lead, and mercury.[1]

1 Extraction and Reduction of Iron Ore

There is clear evidence of iron ore processing on 4th-century settlement sites excavated in Romania. Particularly important in this respect are the smelting furnaces and large quantities of slag discovered on such settlement sites as Fizeș (Caraș-Severin County),[2] Sfântu Gheorghe-Chilieni (Covasna County),[3] and on sites in Walachia.[4] Most significant among the latter is Șirna (Prahova County), where smelting furnaces appeared in the 4th- to 5th-century occupation phase.[5] Missing, however, is any evidence of such processing of the iron in the intervening period until the (late) 6th century, and even the 7th century, when the archaeological evidence of smelting could be dated on sites in the lands outside the Carpathian Mountains to the east and to the south, but also in Transylvania.

1.1 *Exploitation of Iron Deposits*

Some Romanian archaeologists maintain that the old mines of the Roman times still operated after the withdrawal of the Roman administration from the former province of Dacia, and that they remained in use throughout the early Middle Ages.[6] There is however no clear evidence to support such claims:

1 Aufleger, "Metallarbeiten," 618.

2 Eugen Iaroslavschi, Richard Petrovszky, "Cuptoarele de redus minereul de fier de la Fizeș, jud. Caraș-Severin [Furnaces for the reduction of iron ore from Fizeș, Caraș-Severin county]," *Tibiscus* 3 (1974), 147–155.

3 Zoltán Székely, "Vestigiile unui cuptor de topit minereu de fier din secolul al IV-lea d. Ch. de la Sfântu-Gheorghe-Chilieni [The remains of an iron ore smelting furnace from the 4th century AD from Sfântu-Gheorghe-Chilieni]," *Acta Musei Napocensis* 31 (1994), 299–304.

4 Olteanu, *Societatea*, 111.

5 Olteanu and Neagu, "Rezultatele," 385; Olteanu, Grigore, and Nicolae, *Comunitatea sătească*, 29–41.

6 Teodor, *Meșteșugurile*, 12.

© DANIELA TĂNASE, 2021 | DOI:10.1163/9789004436930_005

no traces of exploitation that could be dated to the early Middle Ages, no tools or artefacts that could be associated to miners or blacksmiths, and no settlements next to the old mines. Others have claimed that the exploitation of iron deposits on the territory of the former province of Dacia continued throughout the 4th to 7th century, as well as later, within the same settlements on which it was documented archaeologically for earlier periods. This is further used as an argument for settlement continuity in about 20 cases.[7] However, at a closer examination, most such settlements may be dated to the 2nd and 3rd centuries, a few to the 4th century and some others to the 6th and 7th centuries. One of the latter is the settlement site Şirna,[8] where six smelting furnaces have been found and associated with the 6th- to 7th-century occupation phase on the site. There is, in fact, no example of straight continuity from Roman times to the 7th century. Instead, several sites were occupied at different moments in time, but with chronological gaps between those occupation phases (Fig. 46).

Mircea Rusu drew a list of copper (39 sites) and iron deposits (49 sites) and plotted them on a map, to show where the two metals were exploited and processed for the production of tools, weapons, and jewelry.[9] Many settlements in Transylvania and Banat that are on that list,[10] were taken over from the *Tabula Imperii Romani*, and as such must be regarded as sites where ore mining was practiced in the Roman era. However, the list has absolutely no bearing on what was going on in the same areas during the 6th and 7th centuries. Moreover, it is likely that during the early medieval period, local sedimentary minerals were targeted for surface exploitation, with smelting taking place in nearby settlements.[11] The metallographic analysis of some metal finds from two settlements in Dulceanca (II and IV) shows the presence of aluminum in relatively large quantity (9 percent), as well as a strong presence of silicon dioxide (66 percent), both indicating that the source of iron in those cases were siliceous schists, which contain mineralizations of neoformation iron oxides.[12] Furthermore, the analysis of slag from 2nd- to 4th-, as well as 9th- to 12th-century sites in Transylvania and the Banat, and from 7th- to 10th-century sites Walachia has indicated two sources of iron ore: sedimentary limonite and alluvial magnetite from "deep" iron deposit areas. Smelting was done at high

7 Olteanu, Neagu, and Şeclăman, "Tehnologia," 226, 231, fig. 3 – Map of sites within the territory of Romania, where iron deposit processing vestiges were found.

8 Olteanu, Grigore, and Nicolae, *Comunitatea sătească*, 47–50.

9 Rusu, "Transilvania şi Banatul," 192.

10 Rusu, "Transilvania şi Banatul," 210, where E. Stoicovici is mentioned as the source of information, but with no bibliographic reference.

11 Olteanu, Neagu, and Şeclăman, "Tehnologia," 220.

12 Olteanu, Neagu, and Şeclăman, "Tehnologia," 230.

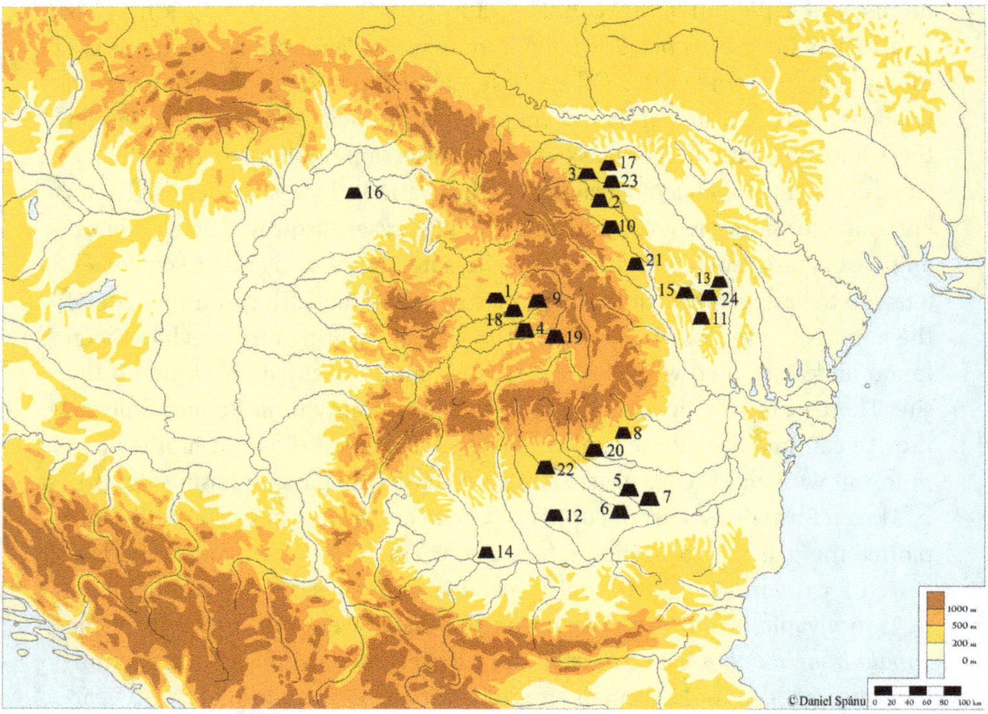

FIGURE 46 **Reduction of iron ore.** 1. Bezid (Mureş co.); 2. Borniş (Neamţ co.); 3. Botoşana (Suceava co.); 4. Bratei (Sibiu co.); 5. Bucharest-Ciurel; 6. Bucharest-Dămăroaia; 7. Bucharest Străuleşti; 8. Budureasca (Prahova co.); 9. Cristuru Secuiesc (Hargita co.); 10. Davideni (Neamţ co.); 11. Dodeşti (Vaslui co.); 12. Dulceanca (Teleorman co.); 13. Epureni (Vaslui co.); 14. Gropşani (Dolj co.); 15. Horga (Vaslui co.); 16. Lazuri (Satu Mare co.); 17. Lozna-Străteni (Botoşani co.); 18. Moreşti (Mureş co.); 19. Poian (Covasna co.); 20. Şirna (Prahova co.); 21. Ştefan cel Mare (Bacău co.); 22. Târgovişte (Dâmboviţa co.); 23. Udeşti (Suceava co.); 24. Valea Mare (Vaslui co.)

temperature reduction with a reducing flux applied to an ore batch, and charcoal added after that.[13] By processing the iron-carbon alloy, the following types were obtained: steel, soft (forgeable) iron, as well as white or black cast iron. The metallurgical procedure is the same as that known since Antiquity and was based on the idea of separate fusible silicates at relatively low temperatures (1200°C), and to extract iron from the bloom. This method remained in use until the 12th century.[14] The fluxes that the early medieval smelters used were limestone and chalk, as evidenced by analyses of 6th-century artifacts

13 Eugen Stoicovici, "Unele caracteristici ale zgurilor din atelierele metalurgice daco-romane şi prefeudale," *Banatica* 7 (1983), 240–241.

14 Stoicovici, "Unele caracteristici," 245–246.

from Ciurel and Târgoviște.[15] The use of limestone as flux was also documented for Șirna.[16]

No evidence exists so far that iron ore was mined during the early Middle Ages, particularly during the 6th–7th centuries. It seems more likely that the main source of iron were alluvial sediments, as indicated by metallographic analyses of slag from Morești, Bratei, and Lazuri. Such analyses, as well as those of various iron artifacts from 6th- to 7th-century settlements show that they were made of poor-quality iron, which would be expected if smelting was done in rudimentary furnaces, most of them inside dwellings, and not in furnaces especially designed for that purpose. The only settlements so far on which smelting has been documented archaeologically are Șirna, Budureasca 5 and Lozna-Străteni. One cannot exclude the possibility that iron may have been obtained by means of trade from outside the region, especially where there were no surface deposits. However, a definite answer in such cases may be given only by metallographic analyses of artifacts found in the region.

How exactly iron was procured in the early Middle Ages is mentioned in some written sources pertaining to Central Europe. According to a charter of 788, the Abbey of Lorsch received 66 lbs. (30 kilograms) of iron every year from the village of Weilnau, while a donation of an unspecified amount of iron is mentioned in 912 for the Abbey of Fulda.[17]

1.2 *Smelting in Furnaces*

The discovery of smelting furnaces and smithies is the most important evidence for the significance of ironworking for early medieval populations. Blacksmiths produced most agricultural tools, as well as most weapons for hunting and for war. Several villages could be served by one and the same blacksmith, often based at favorable locations, next to sources of iron.[18] Early medieval smelting is documented archaeologically in Romania by furnaces found either inside or outside dwellings. However, iron was also smelted in pits and in ceramic vessels. Whatever the method, the rock (limonite or magnetite) had

15 Olteanu, Neagu, and Șeclăman, "Tehnologia," 229.

16 Olteanu, Grigore, and Nicolae, *Comunitatea sătească*, 77.

17 Vasco La Salvia, "Notes on early Medieval Ironmaking in Italy," in *Traditions and Innovations in the Early Medieval Iron Production*, ed. János Gömöri (Sopron-Somogyfajsz: Dunaferr, 1999), p. 85.

18 The same is true for the later Middle Ages. In southern Belarus, for example, during the 9th and 10th centuries there was a blacksmith working for all communities within a five to fifteen square km territory (Joachim Werner, "Fernhandel und Naturwirtschaft im östlichen Merowingerreich nach archäologischen Zeugnissen." *Bericht der Reinisch-Germanischen Komission* 42 (1962), 309).

to be cleaned with water and then dried. The furnace was made of stone, sand, and clay, and heated with charcoal up to a temperature of between 1200 and 1300 centigrades. To reach that high temperature, air was continually driven into the furnace by means of bellows, whose tip was inserted into an opening in the wall of the furnace.[19] In the process, pieces of metal got were separated from molten slag, and periodically removed through an opening. The iron obtained by such means was not liquid, but soft and mixed with coal. Pieces of iron remained on the hearth of the furnace, mixed with slag, but they were retrieved after cooling. Those pieces had to be cleaned by hammering, heated, and then hammered again, in order to remove the slag residues.[20] In order to reach the high temperature necessary for smelting to take place, furnaces were typically short, and their lower part could even be sunken into the soil.[21]

Such furnaces have been found in Fizeș (Caraș-Severin County), and dated to the 4th century. They were round, about 30 inches (75 cm) in diameter at the exterior base and a little more than 15 inches (40 cm) inside. None of them was taller than 33 inches (85 cm). Archaeologists found fragments of clay tuyeres, slag, and charcoal. There was chalk inside the furnace, which was meant to act as flux. The temperature necessary for smelting must have required the use of bellows, but no openings have been found on the walls of the furnace. Instead, the tuyere went through the semicircular gate of the furnace.[22] Tuyeres very similar to those from Fizeș have been discovered on the 7th- to 8th-century site at Lozna-Străteni.[23] This strongly suggests that the smelting procedure was also similar. However, in both Moldavia and Walachia, smelting furnaces were typically found inside dwellings, and were used for one or more batches of ore.

The limonite at Lozna-Străteni, in the form of a red-orange powder, came from bog iron located near the settlement, where several alluvial mineralization patches have been identified. Moreover, there was bog iron along the banks of the Bahna creek originating from the bog and flowing by the settlement.[24] For every 100 grams of bog iron there are 41.92 grams of iron dioxide, with a

19 Heidi Amrein, Eugen Binder, "Mit Hammer und Zange an Esse und Amboss: Metallgewinnung und Schmiedekunst im frühen Mittelalter," in *Die Alamannen*, ed. Karlheinz Fuchs (Stuttgart: Theiss, 1997), 359.

20 Amrein, Binder, "Mit Hammer und Zange," 359–360.

21 Curta, "Blacksmiths," 246.

22 Iaroslavschi, Petrovszky, "Cuptoarele," 148–149; 150, fig. 36.

23 Teodor, *Un centru*, 47; 125, fig. 42/8.

24 That bog iron was also used in the early Middle Ages inside the Carpathian Basin results from macroscopic observations, as well as the chemical analysis of both slag and artifacts from the 7th- to 9th-century settlement site in Sliač-Zorné (Slovakia: Pribulová, Mihok, Mácelová, "Forschung," 102–103).

concentration of iron at 29.93 percent.[25] The raw material was introduced into furnace, which must have been no taller than 15 to 23 inches (40 to 60 cm). The charcoal was made of beech or oak, and when placed inside the furnace, it was mixed with fragments of animal bones, which acted as flux. By means of bellows, the temperature was raised to about 800 to 1000 centigrades, which was sufficient to separate a good quantity of iron from the ore. A spongy bloom was thus obtained, which had then to be forged.[26] The ultimate proof that smelting did indeed happen in those settlement features is the occasional finds of blooms, each weighing between 110 and 132 lbs. (50 to 60 kg).[27] At Lozna, all smelting furnaces were inside the dwellings.[28]

The slag found by the oven carved into the southwestern wall of the sunken-floored building 19 discovered in Davideni (Neamţ County) was sufficient for the excavator to conclude that some metalworking activity must have taken place inside the building. To be sure, although there were no tools in that house, the oven was not its only heating facility, as a stone oven was also found in the center of the northwestern wall of the house pit. If the clay oven was used for metalworking, it is unlikely that it served as a smelting furnace.[29]

True smelting furnaces have been found, however, on 6th-century sites in Walachia, at Budureasca, and Şirna (Prahova County), while the large quantity of slag from Dulceanca 4 (Teleorman County) indirectly points to their existence, despite the absence of any such finds. No less than five such furnaces are known from Budureasca. One of them had a lateral opening for the removal of the bloom, and may have been used more than one time.[30] Nine furnaces – two dated between the 5th and the 6th centuries, and seven dated between the 6th and the 7th centuries – are also known from Şirna. They have all been found inside sunken-floored buildings, as that in Davideni, but their hearths were covered with a thick crust rich in iron oxides. There were also fragments of blooms and slag inside each one of those furnaces.[31] Smelting is also documented archaeologically, if only indirectly, in Dulceanca IV. Although no furnaces have been found on the site, large amounts of slag have been retrieved

25 Teodor, *Un centru*, 47.

26 Teodor, *Meşteşugurile*, 17–18; Teodor, *Un centru*, 47.

27 Teodor, *Un centru*, 17–18.

28 Teodor, *Un centru*, 17–18, 28–29.

29 Mitrea, "Principalele rezultate," 70; Mitrea, *Aşezarea de la Davideni*, 56; 287, fig. 27/3.

30 Teodorescu, Dupoi, Peneş, Lichiardopol, Panait, "Staţiunea arheologică Budureasca," 373–374.

31 Olteanu, Teodorescu, Neagu, "Rezultatul cercetărilor," 417–419; Olteanu, Neagu, "Rezultatele cercetărilor de la Şirna-Prahova," 385–386; Olteanu, Grigore, Nicolae, *Comunitatea sătească*, 79–80.

from all sunken-floored buildings and refuse pits. Metallographic and chemical analyses revealed three categories of slag. One of them is rich in iron (72.1 percent), but has also calcium and silicon dioxide. A second category has more glass (60 percent) with crystals of quartz and other elements, which suggest failed smelting. The glass content, however, suggests that the ore came from sedimentary-alluvial formations in the area, most likely from the hills along the river Vedea and the Burdea creek.[32]

One of the sunken-floored buildings discovered during salvage excavations on the southeastern side of the present-day city of Bucharest, to the west from the Vitan-Bârzești ring-road, had a clay oven. The existence of an opening in the side wall, as well as the large quantity of blooms and slag inside the oven bespeak the use of his installation as a smelting furnace.[33] Moreover, the opening suggests that the furnace was used for more than one smelting of ore extracted from the banks of the nearby river Dâmbovița.[34] In house 5, pieces of iron ore and of slag have been found inside the oven, which may indicate smelting.[35]

The smelting furnaces found on the territory of present-day Romania have many analogies in central and western Europe. Particularly relevant in that respect are the many bloomeries found in Zamárdi, Tarjánpuszta and Kaposvár, which are, however, of a slightly later date (7th–8th centuries), and thus coincide in time with the furnaces in Lozna.[36]

1.3 *Ore Reduction in Clay Vessels*

Lozna produced evidence of an alternative smelting method. Fragments of thick-walled ceramic pots with traces of strong firing were found together with

32 Dolinescu-Ferche, "Habitats," 174–176.

33 Sandu, "Cercetări arheologice," 186, 188, fig. 2.

34 Sandu, "Cercetări arheologice," 189.

35 Sandu, "Cercetări arheologice," 190.

36 Török, Kovács, Gallina, "Iron metallurgy," pp. 235–236; János Gömöri, "Frühmittelalterliche Eisen-schmelzofen von Tarjanpuszta und Nemeskér," *Acta Archaeologica Academiae Scientiarum Hungaricae* 32 (1980), 317–343; János Gömöri, "Az avar kori és X–XI. századi vaskohaszát régészeti emlékei Somogy megyében [The archaeometallurgical sites of county Somogy in the Avar and early Árpád-period]," *Somogyi Múzeumok Közleményei* 14 (2000), 163–217. Very similar bloomeries activated by bellows are also known from the 6th- to 7th-century sites at Boécourt Switzerland), as well Nonnenweier and Kippenheim (Germany), which have been attributed to the Alamans (Amrein, Binder, "Mit Hammer und Zange an Esse und Amboss," pp. 359–360). Another smelting furnace, which was radiocarbon-dated to 590–680, has been found in the Gabbia valley of northern Italy. A later, 7th- to 8th-century bloomer is known from Misobolo (Piedmont), located near iron mines. The furnace was short and rebuilt after each smelting (La Salvia, "Notes on early Medieval Ironmaking in Italy," pp. 84–85).

blooms and iron oxides in the sunken-floored house 7.[37] In house 6, a bowl was found with an opening on the side, supposedly for a tuyere. A fragment of a hand-made pot with a similar opening was found in house 10.[38] The evidence from Lozna suggests that smelting of ore from alluvial sediments could be performed in ceramic, large crucible of the size of pots made of clay mixed with silica. Such vessels had 2- to 4-cm-thick walls and an opening close to the bottom, about 2 cm in diameter. The ore was mixed with charcoal and fragments of limestone, as well as crushed animal bones, all covered with a stone. The vessel was then placed in a simple oven, and heated. At the same time, the charcoal was ignited, and by means of bellows, the nozzle of which was introduced into the side opening, the temperature was raised to 800–900°C, which was sufficient for a smelting reaction, without melting the iron. The result was a spongy bloom on the bottom of the vessel. The bloom was still rich in gangue, chunks of charcoal and limestone, and therefore needed forging. The percentage of carbon in the bloom was relatively small, and the iron needed further work to harden. Smelting in pots has also been documented on other sites in Moldavia, at Valea Mare (Vaslui County), Borniș (Neamț County), and Udești (Suceava County),[39] as well as in sub-Carpathian Ukraine and in Moldova.[40]

1.4 *Ore Reduction in Pits*

Another method archaeologically documented in Romania is smelting in so-called "wolf mouths," namely special pits filled with charcoal, a certain amount of ore, and limestone as flux. Such pits have been found in Horga (Vaslui County) and Petruha (Republic of Moldova).[41] A similar pit was found in the center of the sunken-floored building 28, and another "wolf mouth" was found on the southern side of the settlement at Lozna ("Gr. A"). Unlike smelting furnaces and crucible-pots, this seems to have been a highly inefficient method.[42] To be sure, smelting in furnaces located inside or outside dwellings is documented archaeologically in other parts of Europe as well, but alternative methods, such as "wolf mouths" may have been simply an adaptation to

37 Teodor, *Un centru*, 18.

38 Teodor, "Principalele rezultate," 452–454; Teodor, *Un centru*, 17–18, 20. The excavator mentions a smelting bowl found in house 3, but the corresponding illustration is of a crucible otherwise said to have been found in house 6 (Teodor, *Un centru*, 16, 18).

39 Ștefan Olteanu, "Quelques remarques sur les activités industrielles pratiquées dans le territoire de la Roumanie aux IVe - XIe siècles," *Slovenska Archeologia* 26 (1978), 46–47; Teodor, *Meșteșugurile*, 20.

40 Teodor, *Meșteșugurile*, 19–20; Teodor, *Un centru*, 48.

41 Teodor, *Meșteșugurile*, 21; 34, notes 54–56.

42 Teodor, *Un centru*, 48.

an environment otherwise rich in surface deposits. The settlement in Lozna raises the question of skilled craftsmen living together, which further brings to the fore issues of social hierarchy, for which there is however no discussion at the current stage of research in Romania. Many of the similar discoveries have remained unpublished, but the analysis of the finds in the aggregate may shed a new light on the social value of iron production and the accumulation of prestige goods. Comparisons between settlements with or without traces of metalworking activity could also open new avenues of research in the social archaeology of the early Middle Ages in Romania.

2 Alloys

The main alloys used in the early Middle Ages were bronze (copper, tin and lead) and brass (copper, zinc, tin and lead). The ancient bronze alloy contained about 90 percent copper and 10 percent of a tin and lead mix. The same proportion appears in the early Middle Ages, when copper appears allied in both bronze and brass, an indication that craftsmen used scrap metal as raw material.[43] For example, the bronze bowls with pearl-like rim decoration that are known from Merovingian, 5th- to 6th-century finds, have considerably different alloy compositions, because the metal sheet of which they were made came from ancient bronze artifacts of different origins.[44]

The reuse of ancient material from ancient constructions is mentioned by Gregory of Tours. In the *Gesta Dagoberti*, the extraction of lead from Melle is reported in the context of the repair of a church roof in southern France during the time of King Dagobert I (629–638). At Melle, metals have been extracted ever since the Roman era, but according to *Gesta Dagoberti*, the old galleries must have remained in use well into the 7th century. The natural association of lead and silver ore leads to the conclusion that silver was also exploited on that site.[45]

This is one of the rare pieces of information regarding the exploitation of ancient Roman mines in early medieval Europe. As with the iron mines, copper, tin, or lead ore mining is not documented on the territory of Romania for the early Middle Ages. One would have expected an abundance of byproducts, such as ingots of alloyed material, had that been the case. Instead, all bronze and brass artifacts known from 6th- and 7th-century sites in Romania are made

43 Aufleger, "Metallarbeiten," 618.
44 Werner, *Die Langobarden*, 312.
45 Aufleger, "Metallarbeiten," 618.

of scrap metal, recycled from older and discarded objects. That some of those bronze and brass artifacts may not even have been manufactured on the territory of Romania, but have been brought there from the Empire results from the analysis of a few belt buckles, some of the Sucidava-type and others with cross-shaped plate. The analysis revealed the provincial Byzantine style, the rather low quality of casting, and the use of a similar technology of production.[46] Similarly, dress accessories found in graves were manufactured from recycled Roman artifacts – coins, other dress accessories, fragments of bronze vessels or statues.[47] The use of older coins as raw material is documented archaeologically in Hérouvillette. Grave 10 in that cemetery included a small bronze ingot, fragments of a bronze vessel, Roman bronze (the earliest struck for Vespasian in 77/78, the latest for Antoninus Pius in 158/159), as well as copper coins (the oldest struck for Claudius II, ca. 270, the most recent for Theodosius I between 388 and 392).[48] In the toolkit found in Kölked-Feketekapu B-Grave 80 also produced fragments of Roman bronze statues and vessels, as well as Roman coins.[49] Scrap metal (silver, bronze, lead, and copper) has also been found in the craftsman grave in Kunszentmárton.

There was an ingot-like piece of bronze in grave 18 of the cemetery excavated in Aradac-Mečka, which was probably produced by melting scrap metal.[50] Such pieces of copper-alloy have also been found in a grave in Kisújszállás-Nagykert and in grave 60 of the Klárafalva-B cemetery, both in Hungary.[51] The Roman fibula and the bronze chain in a grave from another Avar-age cemetery in Tiszafüred-Majoros may have also been scrap metal,[52] much like the fragments of bronze and iron objects from two graves with tools in Zamárdi-Rétiföldek-dűlő cemetery (Hungary).[53] Fragments of iron objects, bronze discs and plates found in grave 10 in Band have been interpreted as wasters, but may just as well represent scrap metal. That much results from the presence of a bronze buckle and of fragments of a mirror made of poor-quality silver.[54]

46 Alexandru Barnea, Sorin Bercea, "Neuf bronzes paléochrétiens," in *The Antique Bronzes: Typology, Chronology, Authenticity. The Acta of the 16th International Congress of Antiqua Bronzes Bucharest May 26th–31h 2003*, ed. Crișan Mușețeanu (Bucharest: Editura Cetatea de Scaun 2004), pp. 45–47.

47 Werner, *Die Langobarden*, 309, 314.

48 Decaens et al., *Un nouveau cimetière*, 84.

49 Kiss, *Das awarenzeitliche Gräberfeld*, vol. 1, 26; vol. 2, 38, pl. 24. 36, 42, 44–46.

50 Nagy, "Nekropola kol Aradaca," 57, 71, pl. IV.18.

51 Rácz, *Die Goldschmiedegräber*, 163; Balogh, "Martinovka-típusú övgarnitúra," 267.

52 Rácz, *Die Goldschmiedegräber*, 196.

53 Rácz, *Die Goldschmiedegräber*, 197–198.

54 Kovács, "A mezőbándi ásatások," 402.

Bronze and lead ingots, as well as scrap pieces of copper and bronze, some with cuts, are known from such settlements as Budureasca 3 and 4,[55] Dodești,[56] and Davideni.[57] A piece of copper sheet with traces of cuts was found in house 4 of the settlement in Ștefan cel Mare-Gutinaș.[58]

At Lozna-Străteni, small beads of copper and copper alloy were found in the so-called workshop pit A, as well in furnace no. 2. Furthermore, there was a small bronze ingot in house 37.[59] Although no metallographic analyses have so far been carried out, it is therefore likely that, much like in contemporaneous, Merovingian Gaul, and in Left-Bank Ukraine, most dress accessories were made of scrap metal, often with various parts from different batches.[60]

An interesting case in that respect is a coin hoard found in Horgești hoard (Bacău County).[61] The collection consists of a copper-alloy pitcher, inside which was bronze chain (perhaps from a chandelier), 13 pieces of copper sheet, most likely from discarded vessels, and 57 bronze coins struck for the emperors Justin II, Tiberius II and Maurice, the latest in 597/598.[62] The pitcher was made in the Empire at some point during the third quarter of the 6th century, and like the artifacts deposited inside it, it had intrinsic value as bullion.[63] Metallographic analyses of such vessels known to have been made in Byzantium in Late Antiquity or the early Middle Ages have shown that all of them are made of copper alloy with 98 to 99 percent copper. Such a large copper component was undoubtedly meant to make the alloy more malleable and therefore easy to bend into the desire shapes.[64]

Both bronze coins and bronze accessories are known from a hoard found in the Gymnasium of Corinth.[65] James Dengate believed that the collector of the hoard was a "scavenger at Corinth collecting what metal he could find."[66] Such an interpretation could hardly apply to a hoard found in *barbaricum*. Exactly how could the Horgești hoard reach the lands north of the Lower Danube

55 Victor Teodorescu, "Centre meșteșugărești," 85, fig. 6. 11–12; Teodorescu, Peneș, "Matricea de incidență," 46, fig. 21. 16, 23–24.
56 Teodor, *Continuitatea*, 25, 31, fig. 8. 6–7.
57 Mitrea, *Așezarea de la Davideni*, 85, 166.
58 Mitrea, *Așezarea medievală*, 45.
59 Teodor, *Un centru*, 36, 45.
60 Curta, *The Making of the Slavs*, 271.
61 Căpitanu, "Tezaurul de monede," 253–255.
62 Curta, Gândilă, "Hoards," 105.
63 Musteață, "Unele concretizări," 103.
64 Musteață, "Unele concretizări," 100.
65 James A. Dengate, "Coin hoards from the Gymnasium area at Corinth," *Hesperia* 50 (1981), 153–175.
66 Dengate, "Coin hoards," 157.

remains unknown. At any rate, the collection was definitely not obtained as booty, given its relatively low value. Much more likely is the possibility that the collection was formed somewhere in the Balkans and moved as such to the lands on the other side of the Danube by some itinerant craftsman.

Metal sheet was clearly available to craftsmen in 6th-century Moldavia, as indicated by the fragment of a metal vessel from a sunken-floored building to the settlement excavated in Coroiești (Vaslui County).[67] Fragments of copper or bronze sheet have also been found in Davideni (some with traces of processing)[68] and Dodești.[69] Similar finds are also known from Dulceanca I,[70] Gropșani,[71] Budureasca 3 and Budureasca 4,[72] Bucharest-Militari.[73]

Some of the ovens found on sites excavated in Moldavia and Walachia have vitrified hearths, which suggest very high temperatures such as associated with metalworking. In Botoșana, a few ovens found inside settlement features may be interpreted in relation to metalworking. There was no slag in any of them, only two small blooms, one of which was in the filling of a sunken-floored feature. The oven in house 20 was paved sandstone slabs, but remains of the clay superstructure show signs of vitrification due to intense heat. House 28 had two ovens – one inside, the other outside the building. The latter was also paved with sandstone slabs, while the hearth of the former was vitrified.

A similar situation may be found in house 5 of the settlement site excavated in Ștefan cel Mare-Gutinaș (Bacău County). The building had two ovens, one of which had been carved into the southwestern wall of the feature pit. Its hearth was almost round (about 20 inches in diameter), covered with a slaggy crust because of being strongly fired. The presence of an engraving tool by the oven suggests that some kind of ironworking activity took place inside that building.[74]

---

67 Teodor, "Fibules," 71.

68 Mitrea, *Așezarea de la Davideni*, 85.

69 Teodor, *Continuitatea*, 25.

70 Dolinescu-Ferche, *Așezări*, 90, 96, fig. 106.5.

71 Popilian, Nica, *Gropșani*, 15, 22.

72 Teodorescu, Peneș, "Matricea de incidență," 46, fig. 21.12, 16.

73 Negru, Bădescu, Cuculea-Sandu, *Militari-Câmpul Boja*, 21.

74 Mitrea, Eminovici, Momanu, "Așezarea," 225, 239, fig. 6; Mitrea, *Așezarea medievală*, 46. Iron ores have been found in the alluvial deposits on the banks of the river Trotuș, as well as along its tributaries.

3 Precious Metals

With the withdrawal of the Roman power from Dacia, the mining of gold Transylvania stopped. So far, no evidence exists that mining of gold continued in the old Roman galleries, despite extensive archaeological research at Alburnus Maior (now Roșia Montană). Nonetheless, some still claim that at least part of the gold going into the manufacturing of Avar-age dress accessories came from the Carpathian Mountains in Slovakia (Kremnica and Štiavnica) or in Transylvania.[75] The archaeological research on the mining sites in the Apuseni Mountains have demonstrated that after a 2nd- to 3rd-century occupation,[76] mining resumed only in the 11th to 13th centuries,[77]

---

75 Turčan, "Hroby," 489.

76 Horia Ciugudean, Vasile Moga, Radu Ciobanu, Matei Drîmbărean, Aurel Dragotă, Adrian Gligor, Constantin Inel, Béatrice Cauuet, Christian Rico, Bruno Ancel, "Roșia Montană, jud. Alba (Alburnus Maior) [Roșia Montană, Alba County (Alburnus Maior)]," in *Cronica cercetărilor arheologice din România (campania 2000)*, eds. Mircea Victor Angelescu, Corina Borș and Irina Oberländer-Târnoveanu (Bucharest: cIMeC Institutul de Memorie Culturală, 2001), 209–213); Cristan-Aurel Roman, Adela Paki, Viorica Rusu-Bolindeț, Adriana Isacu, Emilian Bota, Monica Bodea, Felix Marcu, Tiberiu Tecar, "Roșia Montană, jud. Alba (Alburnus Maior) [Roșia Montană, Alba County (Alburnus Maior)]," in *Cronica cercetărilor arheologice din România (campania 2001)*, eds. Mircea Victor Angelescu, Corina Borș and Irina Oberländer-Târnoveanu (Bucharest: cIMeC Institutul de Memorie Culturală, 2002), 257–261; Valentin Voișian, Ovidiu Țentea, Béatrice Cauuet et al., "Roșia Montană, jud. Alba (Alburnus Maior). Punct: Cârnic [Roșia Montană, Alba County (Alburnus Maior). Point: Cârnic]," in *Cronica cercetărilor arheologice din România (campania 2003)*, eds. Mircea Victor Angelescu, Irina Oberländer-Târnoveanu, Florela Vasilescu, Carmen Bem, Paula Jercan and Irina Nicolae (Bucharest: cIMeC Institutul de Memorie Culturală, 2004), 283–288; Paul Damian et al., "Roșia Montană, jud. Alba (Alburnus Maior) [Roșia Montană, Alba County (Alburnus Maior)]," in *Cronica cercetărilor arheologice din România (campania 2003)*, eds. Mircea Victor Angelescu, Irina Oberländer-Târnoveanu, Florela Vasilescu, Carmen Bem, Paula Jercan and Irina Nicolae (Bucharest: cIMeC Institutul de Memorie Culturală, 2004), 262–280; Paul Damian et al., "Roșia Montană, jud. Alba (Alburnus Maior) [Roșia Montană, Alba County (Alburnus Maior)]," in *Cronica cercetărilor arheologice din România (campania 2004)*, eds. Mircea Victor Angelescu, Irina Oberländer-Târnoveanu and Florela Vasilescu (Bucharest: cIMeC Institutul de Memorie Culturală, 2005), 297–316; P. Damian et al., "Roșia Montană, jud. Alba (Alburnus Maior) [Roșia Montană, Alba County (Alburnus Maior)]," in *Cronica cercetărilor arheologice din România (campania 2005)*, eds. Mircea Victor Angelescu and Florela Vasilescu (Bucharest: cIMeC Institutul de Memorie Culturală, 2006), 292–301.

77 Cristina Crăciun, "Roșia Montană, jud. Alba (Alburnus Maior) [Roșia Montană, Alba County (Alburnus Maior)]," in *Cronica cercetărilor arheologice din România (campania 2000)*, eds. Mircea Victor Angelescu, Corina Borș and Irina Oberländer-Târnoveanu (Bucharest: cIMeC Institutul de Memorie Culturală, 2001), 214.

if not even later, in the 16th and 17th centuries.[78] The main source of raw material for goldsmiths operating in the lands north of the river Danube was coined gold, which was made available by substantial subsidies paid by the imperial government to Germanic kings, to the Huns and to the Avars.

According to Mircea Rusu, it cannot be denied that gold was washed in the valleys of the rivers originating in the Apuseni Mountains. That, and not the coined gold from subsidies, was the source of raw material for the barbarian goldsmiths.[79] But without any metallographic analysis, Rusu's claim cannot be substantiated. Indeed, the idea that gold was mined or washed in Transylvania could be confirmed only when metallographic analyses of the gold artifacts discovered in the Carpathian Basin (as well as in the lands outside the Carpathian Mountains) could prove the origin of the gold. Until then, however, it remains a supposition, with no basis in the existing evidence, despite being embraced by some scholars in Central and Eastern Europe. Instead, one needs to entertain the idea that recycling old gold may have also been an option. In the 5th and 6th centuries, golden rings were made in Norway out of late antique *solidi*.[80] In Scandinavia, at least, metallographic analyses have demonstrated that the material used to make jewelry was refined, which strongly suggests that it came from the Empire, since no evidence of gold mining in Scandinavia at that time has so far been discovered.[81]

The idea that late Roman and early Byzantine gold coins were the main source of raw material for barbarian goldsmiths is substantiated by finds from craftsman graves such as Kunszentmárton, Jutas, Kölked Feketekapu A, and Pókaszepetk. In all those cases, even though no gold coins have actually been found, the assemblages include weighing scales that were typically employed for weighing (and therefore testing the purity of the) gold. In the Empire, gold of different degrees of purity was struck into coins, which therefore had different weight values. Although a few gold coins have been found inside the Carpathian Basin and in the lands outside the Carpathian Mountains, there is no evidence that they were used there for monetary exchanges. In other words, they were appreciated for their intrinsic value.

By contrast, silver in the barbarian world seems to have been mined, and not just procured from coins. Silver mines were active in the 6th and 7th centuries in the Harz region of Germany, in the valleys of the rivers Angren in

78 Paul Damian et al., "Roșia Montană, jud. Alba (Alburnus Maior)," in *Cronica cercetărilor arheologice din România* (*campania 2003*): 263, 278–279.

79 Rusu, "Transilvania și Banatul," 192.

80 Werner, "Waage," 21.

81 Roth, *Kunst*, 65–66.

Afghanistan and Talas in Kyrgyzstan, as well as in the Karamazar Mountains of present-day Uzbekistan and the Pamir range in Tajikistan. The metallographic analysis of silver artifacts from hoards found in the forest-steppe belt of Eastern Europe has indicated a significant percentage of zinc, which is apparently a specific signature of the silver ore in Uzbekistan. It is therefore possible that those artifacts were made of silver ultimately originating in Central Asia.[82]

3.1 *Byzantine Gold and Silver North of the Danube*

The flow of gold coin from the Empire to the lands north of the Danube River continued, albeit at a reduced scale, even after the fall of the Hunnic Empire. Following the battle on the Nedao (454), Emperor Marcian recognized the power of the king of the Gepids, Ardarich, whom he turned into a client by agreeing to pay annual subsidies. The amount paid to Ardarich (about 100 lbs. of gold) was only a fraction of what the Empire had previously paid to the Huns.[83] However, the subsidies were paid regularly until the reign of Justinian, who first stopped the payments in retaliation for the Gepids occupying the city of Sirmium. Nonetheless, the payments briefly resumed a few years later, before ending for good in the circumstances of the Gepid-Lombard wars.[84] Ever since their first envoys to Constantinople in 558, the Avars received from the Byzantines many gifts, "golden chains, beds, silk garments, and many other things capable of softening hearts full of pride."[85] John of Ephes claims that the envoys of the qagan to Constantinople received gold and silver from Justinian, golden belts and harnesses, while the Suda lexicon explains that all that the Avars wanted was gold, silver, and precious stones.[86] To be sure, rich "princely graves" dated to the 7th century and found in Hungary, such as Igar[87] and Kunbábony,[88] bear witness to the wealth of the Avar elites.

Byzantine writers mention that the Avars received stipends from Constantinople, but also that they bought commodities from Byzantium. They also procured gold and silver by extortion. For example, according to Menander the Guardsman, during the siege of Sirmium in 568, the qagan Bayan promised

82 Szmoniewski, "Two worlds," 278–280.

83 István Bóna, *Der Anbruch des Mittelalters. Gepiden und Longobarden im Karpatenbecken* (Budapest: Corvina Verlag, 1976), 16.

84 Procopius of Caesarea, *Wars* VII 33. 8–9, ed. Jakob Haury (Indianapolis/Cambridge, 2014).

85 Menander the Guardsman, *History*, frg. 5, ed. R. C. Blockley (Liverpool, 1985).

86 Walter Pohl, *Die Awaren. Ein Steppenvolk im Mitteleuropa 567–822 n. Chr.* (München: Verlag C. H. Beck, 1988), 180.

87 Gyula Fülöp, "Die awarenzeitliche Fürstenfunde von Igar," *Acta Archaeologica Academiae Scientiarum Hungaricae* 40 (1988), 151–190.

88 Elvira H. Tóth, Attila Horváth, *Kunbábony. Das Grab eines Awarenkhagans* (Kecskemét 1992), 25–52, 54–56; fig. 1–16.

to lift the siege if paid a silver disk, some gold, and a silk robe.[89] After securing a raise of the annual stipends to 80,000 gold coins, Targitios, the skillful envoy of the qagan, returned home not only with the gold, but also with goods purchased in Byzantium.[90] That the Avars were paid at one time no less than 80,000 *solidi* (over 800 lbs. of gold) is also confirmed by Theophylact Simocatta, who, writing in the early 7th century, knew that the amount of the stipends eventually went up to 100,000 *solidi.*[91] Moreover, at the siege of Singidunum in 592, the qagan extorted from the besieged 2,000 gold coins, a table plated in gold, and sumptuous piece of clothing, most likely made of silk.[92] The annual stipends must have been at the origin of the enormous hoard of the qagan which the Franks reputedly captured during Charlemagne's wars against the Avars: "but now so much gold and silver were found in the palace, so precious spoils were seized by them in their battles, that it might fairly be held that the Franks had righteously taken from the Huns what they unrighteously had taken from other nations."[93] Large quantities of gold, either coined or in the form of jewelry, existed among the Sclavenes as well, since, as qagan Bayan prepared to attack those living in the lands north of the Lower Danube, he became "convinced that he would find many fortunes in their country, because the lands of the Romans had been plundered many times by the Sclavenians, while their land had never been transgressed by other peoples."[94]

Silver, on the other hand, appears in coined form in 7th-century hoards found in southern Romania, in Priseaca (Olt County), Vârtop (Dolj County) and Drăgășani (Vâlcea County). Silver dress accessories – bow fibulae, earrings, and a torc – have also been found in that same region of Romania, at Coșovenii de Jos (Dolj County).[95] Unfortunately, no analysis has so far been carried out to test the quality of the metal. It is therefore not possible to test the idea that those dress accessories were made of recycled silver from coins. In the absence of any substantial silver ore sources in the region outside the Carpathian Mountains, as well as of any evidence that silver from Central Asia ever reached that far to the west, it is likely nonetheless that the dress accessories found in 7th-century Walachia were made out of coined silver. Both gold and silver, therefore, had no monetary value in the lands north of the river

89 Menander the Guardsman, *History*, frg. 27.
90 Menander the Guardsman, *History*, frg. 63.
91 Theophylact Simocatta, *History* I 3 and 6, ed. Carl de Boor and Peter Wirth (Stuttgart, 1972).
92 Theophylact Simocatta, *History* VI 4.
93 Eginhard, *The Life of Charlemagne*, 13, ed. Arthur James Grant (Cambridge/Ontario, 1999).
94 Menander the Guardsman, *History*, frg. 48.
95 Nestor, Nicolăescu-Plopșor, "Die völkerwanderungszeitlichen Schatz," 33–35.

Danube, even though they were hoarded as symbols of social status and, probably, as raw material for the production of jewelry.[96] Furthermore, precious metals deposited in graves could also become a source of raw material. That is most likely the reason behind the widespread grave robbing which is so conspicuous in 7th-century cemeteries in Merovingian Gaul, but also in contemporaneous cemeteries in Transylvania.[97] However, this phenomenon cannot possibly be linked to a crisis of gold. Unlike the Merovingian world, Byzantine gold in various forms continued to enter the Carpathian Basin, as well as the adjacent regions to the southeast and east during the 7th century.

4 Trade as a Possible Source of Raw Material

Trade between the Romans and the barbarians across the river Danube is specifically documented for the 4th century in the stipulations of the treaty of Noviodunum, which restricted all commercial transactions to two frontier forts.[98] Romans continued to be interested in buying slaves and various goods from the barbarians, as mentioned by Priscus in his account of the embassy to Attila. According to Priscus, the envoys were prohibited from buying slaves, horses, or any other commodities, except food for themselves.[99] Commercial exchanges were now restricted to markets in cities south of the river Danube, such as Naissus (present-day Niš, in central Serbia).[100] Under Emperor Leo I (457–474), Attila's sons demanded a market closer to the Danube, but their request was denied.[101] Meanwhile, the traditional restrictions on trade with the barbarians were repeated in the Theodosian Code, as well as in that of Justinian. Emperor Marcian (454–457) even forbade anyone to sell weapons of any kind, or even a piece of iron (worked or not yet worked) to barbarians coming to Constantinople or to any other place in the Empire. Any violators were treated as traitors, their property confiscated, and they could face capital punishment.[102] That such a law was necessary at all suggests that barbarians had no problems buying iron from the Empire. That the law had little, if any

96 Madgearu, *Continuitate*, 89; Radu Harhoiu, *Die frühe Völkerwanderungszeit in Rumänien* (Bucharest: Editura Enciclopedică, 1998), 143–147; pl. CXXII–CXXVII, pl. CXXX.

97 Kurt Horedt, "Die östliche Reihengräberkreis in Siebenbürgen," *Dacia* 21 (1977), 267–268.

98 Themistios, *Orations* 10. 133–140, ed. Heinrich Schenkl and Glanville Downey (Leipzig, 1965–1974).

99 Priscus of Panion, frg. 129, ed. Roger C. Blockely (Liverpool, 1983).

100 Priscus of Panion, frg. 579.5.

101 Priscus of Panion, frg. 587.18, 588.

102 *Codex Iustinianus* IV. 41. 2, ed. Paul Krüger (Berlin, 1892).

effect, also results from the fact that it was later incorporated into the legislation adopted under Leo VI between 887 and 893.[103]

On the other hand, there is clear evidence that the law was enforced, whenever possible. According to Menander the Guardman, the envoys of the Avars coming to Constantinople in 562, received from the emperor gifts of garments and weapons. The latter, however, were confiscated at the emperor's order, before the Avar envoys left the Empire.[104] Theoretically, at least, there is a possibility that barbarians purchased metal from the Byzantine Empire, in the form of ingots. Nor can the possibility be excluded that iron from the Empire reached the area north of the Lower Danube, even though metallographic analyses so far performed on artifacts from settlements in Walachia and Moldavia indicate that the metal came from iron ore in local surface deposits.

The treaties between the Avars and Byzantium stipulated that the annual stipends were to be paid "in the form of a commodity trade." Besides coined gold, the Avars received gold and silver objects, especially jewelry, as well as glassware, silk garments, spices, and wine. There were definitely relations with Lombard Italy and the Merovingian world, but it is not clear whether such relations were commercial.[105] What exactly did the Avars trade in exchange for those goods remains unknown. War captives may have been sold as slaves played, but cattle and hides may have been significant in this respect. That much results from sources pertaining to cattle, horses and hides in commercial exchanges between the Onogurs and Byzantium in the 6th century, or to horses that the Chinese bought from the steppe peoples at the same time.[106]

In the context of trade relations, barbarian craftsmen may have obtained certain types of tools or even half-manufactured products from the Empire. The bronze dies found in graves with tools discovered in the Carpathian Basin had different designs and were clearly produced by different craftsmen – the simplest by local artisans, perhaps. However, most dies came from the Byzantine

103 Canache, Curta, "Depozite," 195.

104 Menander the Guardsman, *History*, frg. 9.

105 Pohl, *Die Awaren*, 195–196. Walter Pohl believes that amphorae are an indication of trade between the Avars and the Empire, but such an interpretation is not supported by the existing archaeological evidence. For amphorae in the Avar milieu, see Florin Curta, "Amphorae and seals: the 'sub-Byzantine' Avars and the *quaestura exercitus*," in *Zwischen Byzanz und der Steppe. Archäologische und historische Studien. Festschrift für Csanád Bálint zum 70. Geburtstag*, eds. Ádám Bollók, Gergely Csiky and Tivadar Vida (Budapest: Institute of Archaeology, Research Centre for the Humanities, Hungarian Academy of Sciences, 2016), pp. 307–334.

106 Pohl, *Die Awaren*, 196–197.

Empire.[107] Trade, therefore, implied not only finished products, but also tools and weighing scales, such as used at that same time in the Empire.[108] The decoration of the dies found in Felnac is certainly of Byzantine origin – "dot-comma" motifs, scrollwork, drops.[109] It is also important to note that all weights so far known from Avar-age graves in the Carpathian Basin (especially those of Kunszentmárton, Jutas, and Pókaszepetk) are Byzantine.[110]

Trade implies transportation and roads. Gregory of Tours mentions roads, bridges, and toll booths in Merovingian Gaul, many of which have been built in Antiquity.[111] It is possible that the Roman system of roads north of the Danube was still in use in the 6th century. This may explain the presence of a lead seal of the Gepid king Cunimund (550–567) at Tomis (now Constanța, on the Black Sea coast), although the letter may have just as well traveled from Sirmium (on the Sava River) to the Black Sea coast on Roman roads south of the river Danube.[112] Roads may have existed along the valleys of the main, northern tributaries of the Danube, as indicated by archaeological and numismatic finds along the rivers Olt, Vedea, Argeș, Ialomița, Siret, and Prut.[113] Inside the Carpathian Basin, graves with tools typically appear next to rivers or old Roman roads, even though that cannot be interpreted as an indication of where workshops were located in relation to the road network.[114]

Plotting on a map finds of molds and dress accessories produced by such means suggests strong connections between communities inside and outside

---

107 Bronze dies may have been produced in Constantinople or in some other city in the Balkan Peninsula, Crimea, or in Italy. They could have easily moved into the lands of barbarians by means of Byzantine craftsmen, who worked outside the Empire, and not just of Byzantine merchants. For a detailed discussion of the origin of dies with typically Byzantine ornamentation that have been found inside the Avar Qaganate, as well as of their imitation, see Rácz, *Die Goldschmiedegräber*, 94–95.

108 Werner, "Zur Verbreitung," 72–73.

109 Garam, *Funde*, 335, pl. 84; 341, pl. 90.7; 351, pl. 100.5; 356, pl. 105.8.

110 For a detailed analysis of the Byzantine bronze and glass weights found in Kunszentmárton, and their analogies in Central and Southeastern Europe, see Chris Entwistle, "The Early Byzantine weights from Kunszentmárton, Hungary," *Acta Archaeologica Academiae Scientiarum Hungaricae* 67 (2016), 287–300.

111 Joachim Henning, "Handel, Verkehrswege und Beförderungsmittel im Merowingerreich," in *Die Franken wegbereiter Europas. Vor 1500 Jahren: König Chlodwig und seine Erben [Ausstellungskatalog]* (Mainz: Verlag Philipp von Zabern 1996), 792–793.

112 For the idea that the letter traveled from Transylvania (or the central parts of the Carpathian Basin) across the territories north of the Lower Danube, see Alexandru Barnea, "Voies de communication au Bas-Danube aux IVe - VIe s. ap. J. C.," *Études Byzantines et post-byzantines* 3 (1997), 30.

113 Barnea, "Voies de communication," 39.

114 László, *Steppenvölker*, 79.

the Carpathian Mountains.[115] Others point to contacts between the lands north of the river Danube and the Empire. For example, molds for granular crosses and grains, such as found in Cristuru Secuiesc, Budureasca 4, Străulești-Măicănești and Argamum/Jurilovca (Tulcea County) are linked to each other, which implies contacts between the Roman fort at Argamum (on what was then the Black Sea shore), to communities in central and northern Walachia, across the Danube, or even in eastern Transylvania (across the Carpathian Mountains). Such contacts must have been along routes crossing the river at important fords and the mountains through main passes.[116]

Bronze coins most certainly used as coins (not as bullion) appear in great numbers in the lands north of the Lower Danube, albeit with considerable fluctuations between the age of Justinian and that of Heraclius (the latest coins struck for that emperor dated between 613 and 625). There is therefore no serious reason to doubt that the region in question was part of the Byzantine economic system, and that traffic of personnel and goods took place across the Danube.[117] Most coins found in the lands north of the Lower Danube have been minted in Constantinople. When the number of coins dwindled, that was largely the consequence of the fluctuating minting activity in Constantinople, and not of the invasion of the Slavs. There is in fact a strong correlation between coin finds north and south of the river Danube.[118] Nonetheless, the population of the lands north of the Lower Danube clearly preferred the heavy bronze coins, in other words the coins with the greatest intrinsic value (and weight).[119]

---

115 Măgureanu, "Observații," 181.

116 Rodica Oanță-Marghitu, "Argamum între Imperiul Roman târziu și „barbari". Obiectele mărunte ca ipostaze ale comunicării [Argamum between the late Roman Empire and "barbarians". Small objects as hypostases of communication]," in *Orgame/Argamum. Supplementa 1. A la recherché d'une colonie. Actes du Colloque International 40 ans de recherche archéologique à Orgamè/Argamum, Bucarest-Tulcea-Jurilovca, 3–5 octobre 2005*, ed. Mihaela Mănucu-Adameșteanu (Bucharest: Edition Agir, 2006), p. 361.

117 Ernest Oberländer-Târnoveanu, "La monnaie byzantine des VIe - VIIIe siècles au-delà de la frontière du Bas-Danube. Entre politique, économie et diffusion culturelle." *Histoire & Mesure* 17, (2002), 5–6; 8–11; Andrei Gândilă, "Face value or bullion value? Early Byzantine coins beyond the Lower Danube border," in *Byzantine Coins in Central Europe Between the 5th and 10th Century. Proceedings from the Conference Organized by the Polish Academy of Arts and Sciences and the Institute of Archaeology of the University of Rzeszów under the Patronage of Union Académique International (Programme No. 57 Moravia Magna), Kraków, 23–26 IV 2007*, ed. Marcin Wołoszyn (Cracow: Institute of Archaeology University of Rzeszów, 2009), p. 459.

118 Gândilă, "Face value or bullion value?" p. 454, p. 456.

119 Oberländer-Târnoveanu, "La monnaie byzantine," 16–17; Gândilă, "Face value or bullion value?" pp. 451–452, pp. 458–459.

Judging from the distribution of finds, more early Byzantine coins crossing the Danube in the 6th century did so in the direction of Little Walachia (Oltenia), Walachia, and southern Moldavia, than in any other direction. In other words, the farther one is from the line of the Danube, the fewer the coin finds.[120] Moreover, plotting so-called "Slavic" bow fibulae on the map, it becomes apparent that a great number of finds appear in the same region in which 6th-century bronze coin finds cluster. This may well be an indication of a regional center of power, which, given the presence of valuable goods, was in existence during the last third of the 6th century.[121] On the other hand, that was also the region with two early Byzantine bridgeheads, one at Drobeta (Drobeta-Turnu Severin, Mehedinți County) and the other at Sucidava (Celei, Olt County). That the proximity of Roman settlements played a key role in such a distribution results from the fact that after the abandonment of the Balkan provinces of the Empire after ca. 620, bronze coins appear only sporadically in the lands north of the river Danube: the coin struck for Constans II found in Novaci (Ilfov County) 646–659,[122] or the coin hoard from Obârșeni (Vaslui County) with the latest coin struck for the same emperor between 655 and 658.[123] One of the reasons for abrupt interruption of the influx of Byzantine bronze coins into the area north the Danube after ca. 620 was the complete abandonment of settlements – towns and forts – in the northern Balkans.[124] In the absence of towns and markets, the bronze coins lost their value as a means of exchange. Even the Obârșeni hoard may in fact be a collection of cash from the Empire, not formed locally.[125] If so, it may well have been the hoard of a traveling craftsman. Similarly, only a few 7th-century coins are known from Banat and Transylvania: a coin struck for Heraclius and found in Sânnicolau Mare (Timiș County)[126] and the coins struck for Tiberius III Apsimar and

120 Madgearu, *Continuitate*, 74–75.

121 Madgearu, *Continuitate*, 72.

122 Madgearu, *Continuitate*, 85.

123 Viorel M. Butnariu, "Răspândirea monedelor bizantine din secolele VI–VII în teritoriile carpato-dunărene [The spread of Byzantine coins from the 6th–7th centuries in the Carpathian-Danube territories]." *Buletinul Societății Numismatice Române* 78–79 (1983–1985) (1986), 212.

124 Butnariu, "Răspândirea," 216.

125 Butnariu, "Răspândirea," 212.

126 Butnariu, "Răspândirea," 222.

found in la Mediaş (Mureş County).[127] Most other coins found in the Lower Mureş area, in the Banat, are either gold or silver.[128]

Bronze coins are important because they are related to the presence of the Byzantine military, and they signal low-value transactions, most likely with food, on local markets.[129] In my opinion, this is at least in part true for the bronze coins found north of the river Danube, which show ties with the early Byzantine bridgeheads. If find spots are any indication at all, they seem to show that the bronze coins spread northwards from the line of the Danube, which in turn suggests the directions to which trade transactions moved. Did Byzantine merchants visit the lands north of the river Danube? If they did, they were most likely looking for slaves, cattle, hides, or perhaps even salt from Transylvania or northeastern Walachia.[130] They brought in exchange jewelry, metal and ceramic vessels, fabrics, and spices. This hypothesis should not be neglected, as the barbarians' preference for luxury goods from the Empire results indirectly from the written sources.[131]

To be sure, the archaeological evidence of Byzantine artifacts is quite solid: a gilded silver strap end decorated with a cross and found in Noşlac (Alba County),[132] buckles of the Sucidava, Salona-Histria, and Syracuse type, or with cross-shaped plate, which were discovered on many sites in Romania.[133] Such pieces were then imitated by local craftsmen, and that is how the buckles of the Pápa type appeared, for they derive from the Salona-Histria type.[134] Imitations of the Sucidava type were also found in the Tisza Plain at Szelevény

127 Constantin Preda, "Circulaţia monedelor bizantine în regiunea carpato-dunăreană [The circulation of Byzantine coins in the Carpathian-Danube region]," *Studii şi Cercetări de Istorie Veche* 23, no. 3 (1972), 403.

128 Butnariu, "Răspândirea monedelor bizantine," 213, pl. VII.

129 Curta, "Byzantium," 121–124; Florin Curta, "Coins, Forts and Commercial Exchanges in the Sixth and Early Seventh-Century Balkans," *Oxford Journal of Archaeology* 36 (2017), 448–450.

130 Kurt Horedt, *Siebenbürgen in spätrömischer Zeit* (Bucharest: Kriterion Verlag, 1982), 16–18; Oberländer-Târnoveanu, "La monnaie byzantine," 5, 16–17.

131 Menander the Guardsman, *History*, frg. 63.

132 Mircea Rusu, "The Prefeudal Cemetery of Noşlac (VI–VII centuries)," *Dacia* 6 (1962), 272, fig. 2.17.

133 Dan Gh. Teodor, *Creştinismul la est de Carpaţi, de la origini până în secolul al XIV-lea* [Christianity at east of the Carpathians, from its origins to the fourteenth century] (Iaşi: Editura Mitropoliei Moldovei şi Bucovinei, 1991), 130–131; 132, fig. 1; 133, fig. 2; 134, fig. 3; 135, fig. 4; 136, fig. 5; 137, fig. 6; 138, Map of the spreading of costume items of Byzantine origin.

134 Alexandru Madgearu, "Despre cataramele de tip „Pápa" şi unele probleme ale secolului al VII-lea [About "Pápa" type buckles and some problems of the 7th century]," *Studii şi Cercetări de Istorie Veche şi Arheologie* 44, no. 2 (1993), 174–176.

(Hungary).[135] Similarly, an iron buckle found in a sunken-floored building of the settlement excavated in Budureasca 3, was an imitation of cast Byzantine buckles.[136] Early Byzantine fibulae with bent stem were also imitated in the lands north of the river Danube, as demonstrated by such finds as Bârlălești and Hansca.[137]

Of equally Byzantine origin were some of the tools involved in the making of jewelry. For example, the molds for making triangular pendants from Budureasca 3 (Prahova County) and Bernashivka (Ukraine) (Fig. 47.7, 8), have good analogies at Oescus (now Gigen, near Pleven Bulgaria)[138] (Fig. 48.2.3) and Tropaeum Traiani (now Adamclisi, near Medgidia)[139] (Fig. 49.5). Such analogies strongly suggest that the fashion epitomized by such ornaments originated in the Empire, and with it the production technology as well.

135 Vladimir Varsik, "Byzantinische Gürtelschnallen im mittleren und unteren Donauraum im 6. und 7. Jahrhundert," *Slovenská Archeológia* 11, no. 1 (1992), 99, plate 1.4.

136 Măgureanu, Ciupercă, "The 6th–8th Centuries Metallurgical Activity," 293.

137 Curta, *The Making of the Slavs*, 245.

138 Metodi Daskalov, Dimitar J. Dimitrov, "On a Production in the 6th–7th Centuries in the Bulgarian Lands," *Arheologiia* 42, no. 3–4 (2001), 69, fig. 1.1.

139 Ion Barnea et al., *Tropaeum Traiani. Cetatea* [Tropaeum Traiani. Fortress], vol. 1, (Bucharest: Editura Academiei Republicii Socialiste România, 1979), 191, no. 10.14, fig. 169.

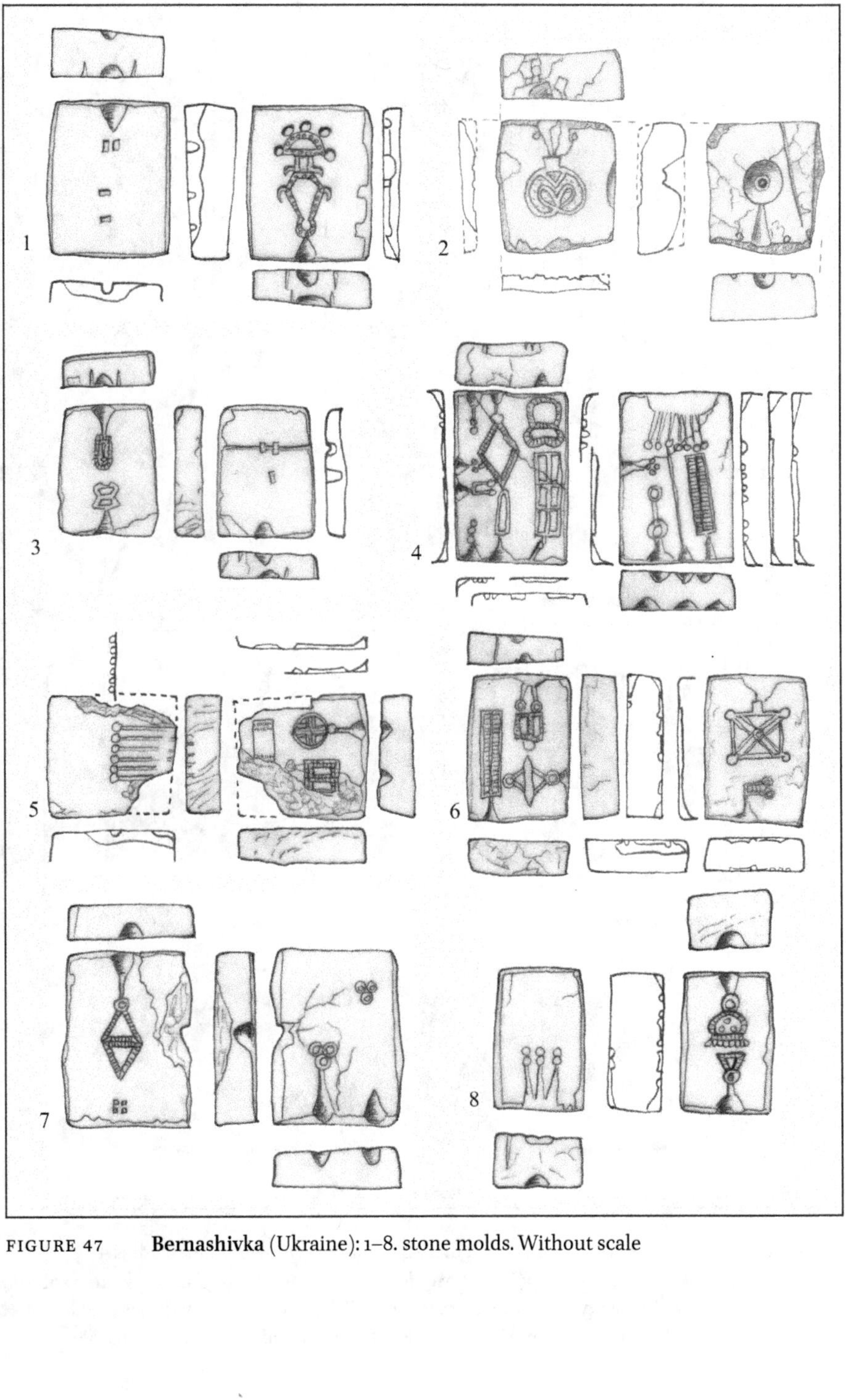

FIGURE 47 **Bernashivka** (Ukraine): 1–8. stone molds. Without scale

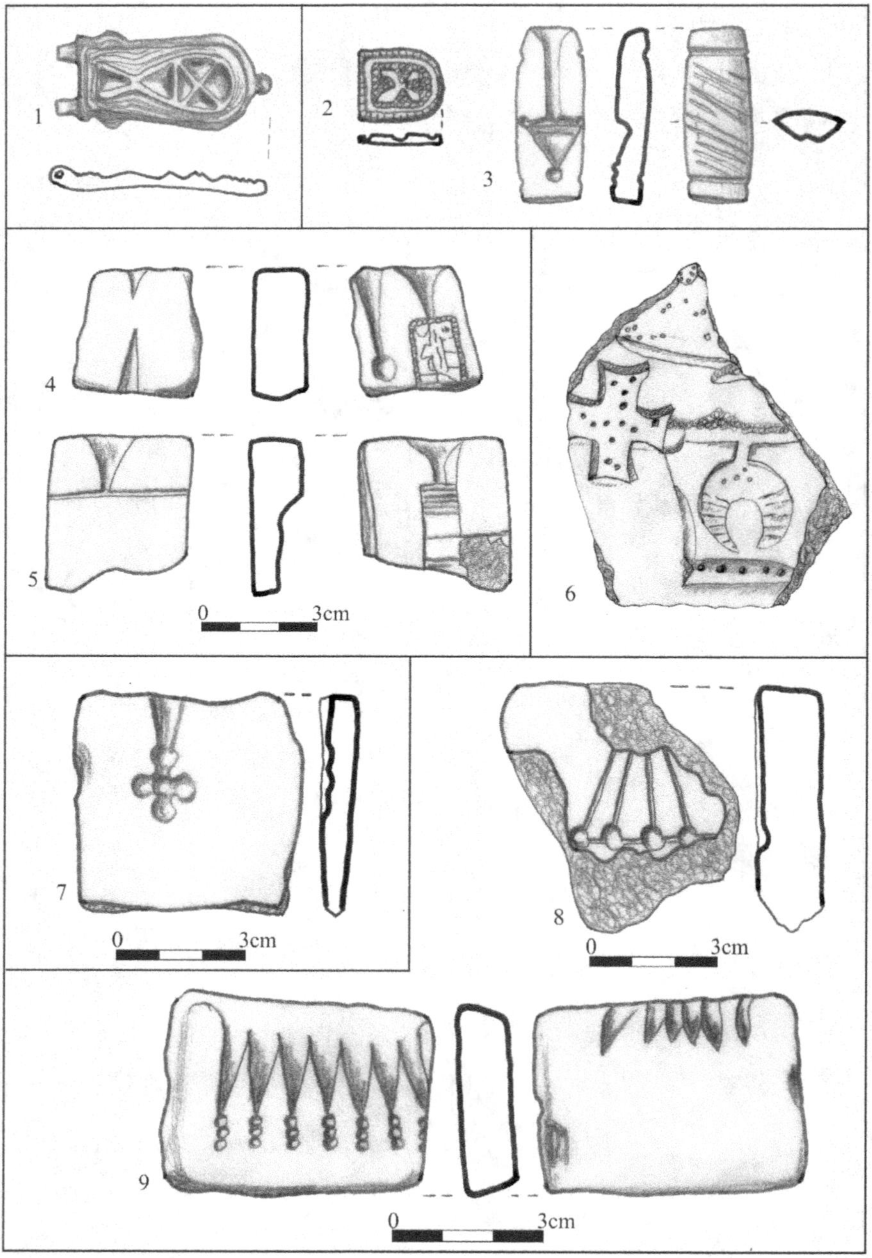

FIGURE 48 **1. Vratsa** (Bulgaria): metal die – **2–3. Oescus** (Bulgaria): metal dies – **4–5. Dănceni** (Republic of Moldova): stone molds – **6. Jász-Nagykun-Szolnok co.** (Hungary): clay mold – **7. Hansca** (Republic of Moldova): clay mold; **8–9. Seliște-Orhei** (Republic of Moldova): stone molds. 1–3, 6 without scale

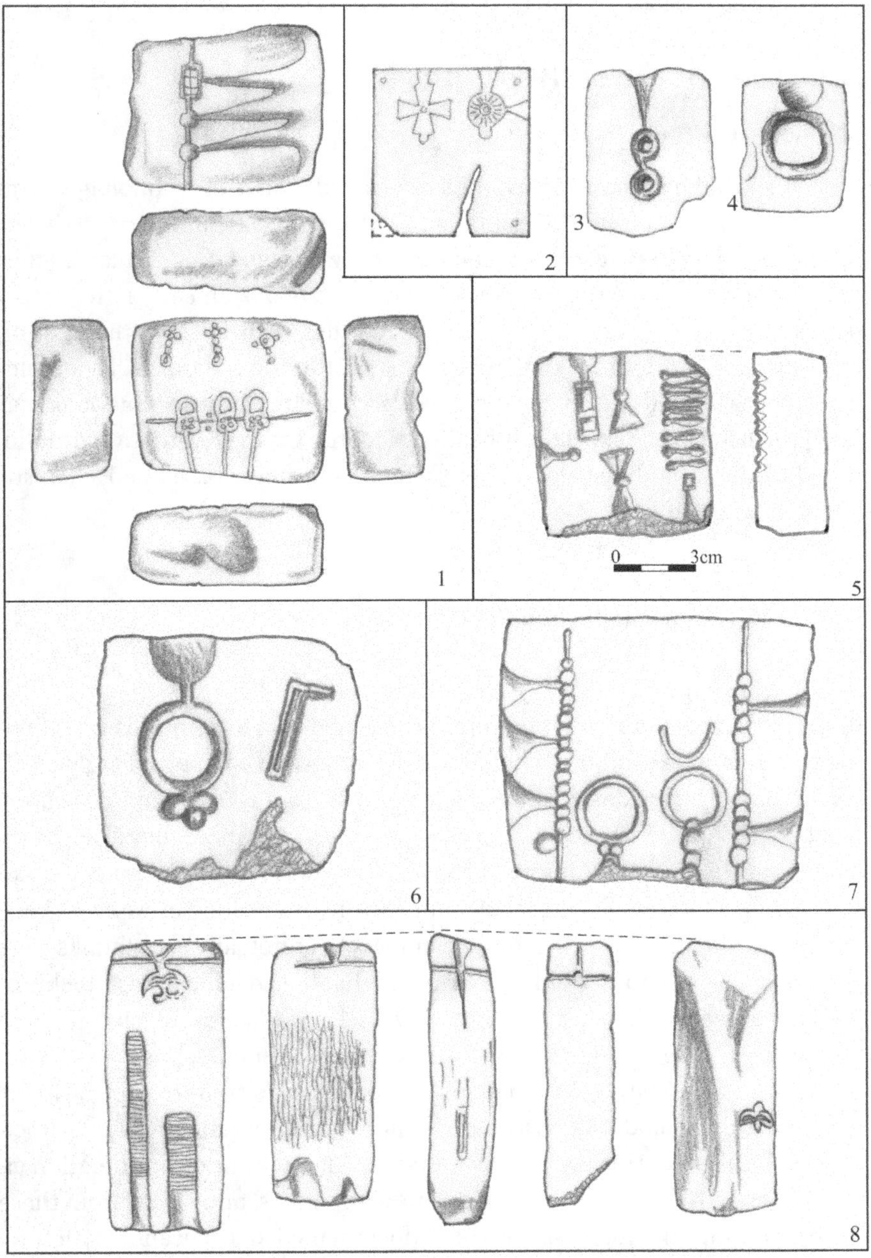

FIGURE 49 **1. Argamum** (Tulcea co.): stone mold – **2. Golemanovo Kale** (Bulgaria): stone mold – **3–4. Capidava** (Constanța co.): stone molds – **5. Tropaeum Traiani** (Constanța co.): stone mold – **6. Aegyssus** (Tulcea co.): stone mold – **7. Szeged-Bilisics** (Hungary): stone mold – **8. Vác-Kavicsbánya** (Hungary): stone mold. 1–4, 6–8 without scale

CHAPTER 4

Metallurgical Technologies

Early medieval black- and goldsmiths used a wide range of technologies. This results clearly both from the examination of the objects that they produced, and from written sources pertaining to metalworking. Of particular interest in this respect is *On Various Crafts* (*De Diversis Artibus*), an early 12th-century detailed description of metalworking techniques, as well as methods of ornamentation and tool making, which was written by a monk – Theophilus Presbyter.[1] The goldsmithing techniques described in this true handbook may have well been in use since the 6th and 7th century, as they were strongly influenced by the Byzantine goldsmithing, which in turn was based on Hellenistic and Roman traditions.

1 Metalworking Techniques

1.1 *Forging*

Blacksmithing was an important craft. Early medieval blacksmiths used forging for agricultural and household tools, as well as for weapons. Forging is in fact a form of plastic deformation, hot or cold, by means of a hammer. Beating was a method used to obtain the desired shape of the piece, but also the intended finish. Blacksmithing required auxiliary tools, as the metal could not stay hot for too long. Forging thus required the use of long-arm pliers, large hammers, and anvils. Forging tongs, hammers, cast iron and slag chunks were discovered in grave 10 in Band, an indication that the craftsman was capable of producing weapons and ordinary implements. Large blacksmith hammers and tongs have also been found in settlements 4 and 9 at Budureasca.

So far, the metallographic analyses carried out on slag from Bratei, Ciurel, Dulceanca, Şirna, and Târgovişte have demonstrated that the iron was extracted from local ores.[2] However, such analyses did not take into consideration either all iron artifacts found on those same settlements, or artifacts from those settlements on which smelting has been documented. In Dulceanca IV, despite

1 Theophilus Presbyter's work was translated into German and commented by Erhard Brepohl, *Theophilus Presbyter und die mittelalterliche Goldschmiedekunst* (Vienna/Cologne/Graz: Böhlau, 1987).

2 Olteanu, *Societatea*, 112, 118.

© DANIELA TĂNASE, 2021 | DOI:10.1163/9789004436930_006

the presence of metalworking remains (in the form of slag) in the filling of almost every sunken-floored building and refuse pit, the quality of the iron artifacts found on the site was not very good. At a closer look, iron knives, as well as the other objects, showed forging imperfections, hammering marks, in addition to a rough appearance, often with large rust marks.[3] One can of course not generalize from finds from a single site, but it is worth noting that iron artifacts are not particularly common on 6th- and 7th-century settlement sites. Those that have been found are often in a poor state of preservation, primarily because of poor raw materials and technical procedures.

Elsewhere in the barbarian world, iron artifacts have been found that are clearly superior to those found Romania, in terms of quality. For example, at Pastyrs'ke (in the region of Cherkasy, on the right bank of the river Dnieper, in Ukraine), 60 percent of the 7th- to 8th-century tools found on the site were of pure iron, and 30 percent of steel. Blacksmiths in Pastyrs'ke knew also how to weld iron to steel, as shown by the examination of an axe blade that has been hardened without quenching, as it had been made of steel welded to an iron core. The same technology was used for 16 percent of all artifacts found on the site.[4]

Forging and quenching, especially for tools, are described as follows by Theophilus Presbyter: "large and medium-size files were made of massive steel, and were square, triangular and round. There were also others, which had inside a soft iron core, while the outside was covered in steel. The steel coating is as thick as the blacksmith wants, then he polishes the item all around with a whetstone, and then he makes the tip using a hammer. Others were made using a chisel, as I said before. These (files) will be used for polishing worked surfaces. When all the parts have edges, the hardening is done as follows: an ox horn, turned red in the fire, is raked and two thirds of the raked horn powder is mixed with one third of salt and the whole is totally crushed. Then the file is put in the fire and when it gets red, the mixture is spread on all sides and burning coals are placed all around, then one blows strongly all over, still taking care that the hardening mixture does not fall off, and after it is taken out of the hearth is immediately put into the water and then slightly dried on the fire. This is how all files made of steel are reinforced."[5] In the same work, the author describes how to make grooves on the iron files (see Chapter VI.7).

Most common iron objects obtained by forging and found on settlement sites are the knives, rarely weapons. In cemeteries, knives, cramps (from

3 Dolinescu-Ferche, "Habitats," 153.
4 Nedopako, "Development," 80–81.
5 Brepohl, *Theophilus*, 78.

coffins), and weapons have been found. For example, a blade and fragments of blades have been found together with cramps in Bratei (Sibiu County).[6] Knife blades, knives and spear heads are known from Bistriţa (Bistriţa-Năsăud County).[7] Both knives and cramps have been found in the 7th-century cemetery in Iclod (Cluj County).[8] Many more iron objects have been retrieved from other cemetery sites in Transylvania, such as Band, Moreşti, Noşlac, Târgu Mureş, Unirea (Vereşmort), or Valea Largă. Wrought iron is known from such settlement sites as Moreşti,[9] Bratei 2,[10] Aiton (Cluj County), Alba Iulia, Blăjenii de Sus (Bistriţa-Năsăud County),[11] Poian (Covasna County),[12] Porumbenii Mici (Harghita County),[13] Sânmiclăuş (Alba County),[14] and Şirioara (Bistriţa-Năsăud County).[15] Iron artifacts are conspicuously lacking from settlements excavated in northwestern Romania, at Lazuri-Lubi Tag (Satu Mare County) and Zalău-Bul. Mihai Viteazul (Sălaj County). One possible explanation is that on those sites, iron was used for a long time, before being recycled as scrap metal, and not abandoned deserted homes or discarded in dumping grounds.[16]

A large variety of artifacts is known from sites to the south and to the east from the Carpathian Mountains: plowshares, sickles, billknives, flint steels, rings, cramps, fishing hooks, strap ends and buckles, needles, three-edged or

---

6 Ligia Bârzu, "Gepidische Funde von Bratei," *Dacia* 36 (1992), 213, fig. 4.2, 6.

7 Corneliu Gaiu, "Le cimetière gépide de Bistriţa," *Dacia* 36 (1992), 117, fig. 2.6, 12–14, 16–17, 24; 119, fig. 3, 2–9, 11, 14–15, 17.

8 Ioana Hica-Cîmpeanu, "Un grup de morminte din secolul al VII-lea e.n. la Iclod (jud. Cluj) [A group of tombs from the 7th century AD at Iclod (Cluj County)]," *Acta Musei Napocensis* 15 (1978), 287–295; 289, fig. 2.2.5–7.

9 Horedt, *Moreşti*, 149, fig. 70.1–19.

10 Zaharia, "La station n° 2 de Bratei," 327, 347, fig. 11.14–15, 19–23.

11 Rustoiu, "Habitatul," 54–61.

12 Zoltán Székely, "Aşezări din sec. VI.–IX p. Ch. în bazinul Oltului Superior [Settlements from the 6th–11th centuries AD in the Upper Olt basin]," *Studii şi Cercetări de Istorie Veche şi Arheologie* 43, no. 3 (1992), 246–279.

13 Kurt Horedt, Zoltán Székely, Ştefan Molnár, "Săpăturile de la Porumbenii Mici (r. Odorhei) [The excavations from the Porumbenii Mici (Odorhei district)]," *Materiale şi Cercetări Arheologice* 8 (1962), 633–636.

14 Anghel, Blăjan, "Săpăturile arheologice," 285–297; Gheorghe Anghel, Mihai Blăjan, "Săpăturile arheologice de la Sînmiclăuş-'Gruişor', comuna Şona, judeţul Alba, 1978 [The archaeological excavations from Sînmiclăuş-'Gruişor', Şona commune, Alba county, 1978]," *Materiale şi Cercetări Arheologice* 13 (1979), 282–283; Velter, *Transilvania în secolele V–XII*, 458; Rustoiu, "Habitatul," 63.

15 Corneliu Gaiu, "Aşezarea prefeudală de la Şirioara, com. Şieu-Odorhei, jud. Bistriţa Năsăud [Pre-feudal settlement from Şirioara, Şieu-Odorhei commune, Bistriţa Năsăud county]," *Marisia* 13–14 (1983–1984), 59–61.

16 Stanciu, *Locuirea*, 280.

diamond-shaped arrow heads lance and spear heads, engraving tools.[17] Two small billets have been found in two houses of the settlement excavated in Botoșana (20 and 42), but no analysis of the iron has been carried out. At any rate, several tools are known from the same occupation phase: whole or fragmentary knife blades, hooks, flint steels. Numerous whetstone indirectly point to the common presence of iron artifacts on the site.[18] Knife blades, hooks and arrow heads, metalworking (such as engraving tools and chisels), as well as small finds, such as flint steels, rings, and buckles – have all been discovered in the settlement at Davideni.[19] Such artifacts are also known from other settlements in Moldavia: Izvoare-Bahna,[20] Dodești (Vaslui County),[21] Ștefan cel Mare-Gutinaș,[22] Suceava-Șipot,[23] and Lozna-Strătenii.[24] The same is true for settlements from Walachia: Dulceanca,[25] Budureasca,[26] Bucharest-Ciurel[27] and Soldat-Ghivan Street,[28] as well as Gropșani-Gura Gurgotei.[29]

1.2 *Slitting, Piercing, Riveting*

In the early Middle Ages several surface processing and mounting techniques were used, such as riveting, treading, and punching. Slitting involves pulling and twisting. The pearl wire could be obtained by wrapping or, as Theophilus Presbyter put it, by means of a rotating die, an *organarium*.[30] To make the wire, the soft metal was pulled through a plate with holes of decreasing diameter, to obtain various degrees of thickness and various cross-sections (round, square, or triangular). A tool with five holes, that was used for slitting, but also employed making nails, was found in grave 10 in Band (Fig. 17.8). There are good

17 Dan Gh. Teodor, "Slavii la nordul Dunării de Jos în secolele VI–VII d. Hr. [The Slavs north of the Lower Danube in the 6th–7th centuries AD]," *Arheologia Moldovei* 17 (1994), 231–232.

18 Teodor, *Civilizația romanică*, 56–57.

19 Mitrea, *Așezarea de la Davideni*, 320, fig. 60.1–7; 421, fig. 61.1–10; 322, fig. 62. 1–16; 323, fig. 63.1–8; 324, fig. 64. 4–11.

20 Mitrea, *Așezarea din secolele VI–IX*, 141, fig. 25.2–3, 5–6; 142, fig. 26.3–5, 9–10, 12.

21 Teodor, *Continuitatea*, 32, 35.

22 Mitrea, *Așezarea medievală*, 77; 171, 1–2, 4–7.

23 Teodor, *Așezarea medievală*, 25; 116, fig. 24.1–12; 117, fig. 25.1–3, 5, 8–14.

24 Teodor, Mitrea, "Cercetări arheologice," 287, 288, fig. 8.1–2; Teodor, *Un centru*, 41–44; 112–120, fig. 29–fig. 37.

25 Suzana Dolinescu-Ferche, *Așezări*, 87, fig. 92.1–3, 5–7; Dolinescu-Ferche, "Habitats," 138, fig. 7–9–10; 139, fig. 8.5, 22; 162, fig. 26.2, 5, 17, 20; 163, fig. 27.24–25; 165, fig. 29.2,7; 167, fig. 31.9, 16, 34; 169, fig. 33.7, 14–15, 33; 170, fig. 34.8, 20; 171, fig. 35.2, 24.

26 Teodorescu, Peneș, "Matricea de incidență," 44, fig. 19.1, 3–11; 45, fig. 20. 2, 4–9, 11–12.

27 Dolinescu-Ferche, "Ciurel," 205, fig. 22.3, 15.

28 Dolinescu-Ferche, Constantiniu, "Un établissement," 322, fig. 18, 7–10, 14–23.

29 Popilian, Nica, *Gropșani*, 172, fig. 20.8; 174, fig. 21.12; 175, fig. 23.4–5.

30 Brepohl, *Theophilus*, 69.

analogies for this tool among the goods from 80 in Kölked-Feketekapu B,[31] as well as among 8th-century grave finds from Bygaland (Norway)[32] and hoard finds from Staraia Ladoga (Russia).[33] Wire, however, could also be obtained with pulling through special tools. Ever since prehistory, craftsmen employed instead molded sticks or strips of sheet that were beaten on the anvil, deformed and smoothed. It was also customary for the raw material to be placed in the recessed areas of the anvil and processed until the desired diameter was obtained. Twisting of the four-edged threads was done by forging or cutting the sheet to obtain strips of rectangular or square section and with sharp edges that twisted around the length of their axis, and then were smoothed by spinning.[34]

Well into the modern age (18th century), metal sheets of various thickness were made according to the same basic technique.[35] The sheet was cut with special shears that had one straight and one bent (L-shaped) arm. Such shears have been found in graves with tools discovered in Aradac-Mečka, Klárafalva-B, and Jutas, as well as in Hérouvillette.[36]

Various artifacts, from armor plates to garment items had to be punched in order to be assembled. Drills were used for drilling, some of them provided with leaded disks to render greater force and a faster movement. Such drills are known from Band (Fig. 35.14) and Vestly.[37] A leaded disk for mechanical drilling was also found in the grave with tools from Brno.[38] Moreover, a third example of mechanical drill (besides Band and Vestly) is known from a 6th-century burial assemblage from Anrås (Sweden).[39]

Riveting is a non-reversible operation to join components of an item by means of rivets. Early medieval craftsmen employed only cold riveting. As a rule, the head of the rivet was formed by hammer and dolly, or with a notched punch.[40] Rivet or nail heads could also be made by passing a rod through the

---

31 Kiss, *Das awarenzeitliche Gräberfeld*, vol. 2, 39, pl. 25.11.

32 Müller-Wille, "Der Schmied," 258, fig. 23.9.

33 Jochem Wolters, "Goldschmied, Goldschmiedekunst," in *Reallexicon der germanischen Altertumskunde*, vol. 12, eds. Heinrich Beck, Heiko Steuer and Dieter Timpe (Berlin-New York: Walter de Gruyter, 1998), 370, fig. 60.39.

34 Wolters, "Goldschmied," 378–379.

35 Wolters, "Goldschmied," 378.

36 Nagy, "Nekropola kol Aradaca," 72, pl. V.6; Balogh, "Martinovka-típusú övgarnitúra," 294, fig. 18.7; Rhé, Fettich, *Jutas und Öskü*, pl. IV.14; Decaens et al., *Un nouveau cimetière*, 115, fig. 19.3.

37 Magnus, Mollerop, Sjovold, "Migration Period Graves," pl. 5 (4).19.

38 Daim, Mehofer, Tobias, "Die langobardischen Schmiedegräber," 206; 219, fig. 5.15.

39 Wolters, "Goldschmied," 375.

40 Wolters, "Goldschmied," 380.

hole of a tool specially made for that purpose and then hammering its end into the intended shape (semi-globular or flat). Such a special tool for making rivets with semi-globular heads was also found in grave 10 of the Band cemetery (Fig. 35.11), together with rivets with heads matching the shape of the tool. Iron rivets were employed also for the helmet found in that same burial assemblage, but were more commonly used to assemble combs, such as found in Sighișoara,[41] Bratei,[42] Bistrița,[43] Morești,[44] and Bratei 3.[45]

2 Techniques of Non-Ferrous Metallurgy

2.1 *Hammering, Chiseling and Polishing*

By hammering, partial shaping or striking was done, embossed or deeply engraved, on the face or on the back of the metal plate. This method was used to process both the outer and the inner part of the object, but it was necessary to reheat it several times to avoid breakage. The tools used for the purpose were hammers of various sizes, and punches. In the case of metal hammers, soft supports were used – leather, resin, tar, or lead – while in the case of wood or antler hammers, hard supports were preferred.[46]

The modeling of ornaments in relief on the back of the plate was done with the bent end of the punch, in order to obtain vaulted surfaces, and with a small, globular hammer for globular ornaments. This technique is also called *au repoussé*. In this manner trapezoidal pendants were made of bronze and silver, which were employed in the Carpathian Basin as braid ornaments for women.[47]

---

41 Ioana Hica-Câmpeanu, Alexe Mureșan, "Un mormânt din secolul al VI-lea e.n. la Sighișoara [A tomb from the 6th century AD in Sighișoara]," *Marisia* 8 (1978), 761.

42 Bârzu, "Gepidische Funde," fig. 3.3–4, fig. 5.3, fig. 6.1–2.

43 Gaiu, "Le cimetière gépide," 117, fig. 2.3.

44 Horedt, *Morești*, 155, fig. 71.5; 157, fig. 72.2; 163, fig. 78.6; 166, fig. 81.10; 167, fig. 82.1; 176, fig. 91.9.

45 Ligia Bârzu, *Ein gepidisches Denkmal aus Siebenbürgen. Das Gräberfeld Nr. 3 von Bratei*, ed. Radu Harhoiu, with contributions from Eugenia Zaharia and Radu Harhoiu (Archaeologia Romanica) 4 (Cluj-Napoca: Editura Accent, 2010), 288, pl. 10, G.51.2; 289, pl. 11, G.57.5; 290, pl. 12, G.60.2; 303, pl. 25, G.155.1; 315, pl. 37, G.223.5; 325, pl. 47, G.275.1.

46 Radu Harhoiu, Daniel Gora, *Aurul migrațiilor. Das Gold der Völkerwanderungszeit* (Bucharest: Editura Enciclopedică, 2000), 67.

47 Maria Comșa, "Bemerkungen über die Beziehungen zwischen den Awaren und Slawen im 6.–7. Jahrhundert," in *Interaktionen der mitteleuropäischen Slawen und anderen Ethnika im 6.–10. Jahrhundert. Symposium Nove Vozokany 3.–7. Oktober 1983*, ed. Bohuslav Chropovský (Nitra, 1984), p. 67, fig. 4. 1–23.

Chiseling is a finishing technique without loss of material, using a hammer and a punch on surfaces of objects made by casting or hammering, placed on a soft support of lead, resin, pitch, wax, or leather. This involved operations such as scraping, shaping and cutting. The scraping was used to model the linear ornaments, for straight lines the straight end of the punch was used, and for the curved lines the curved end. The lines obtained by such means are rounder, edges have a less sharp profile than the engraved lines.[48] In the chiseling phase, the decorated surfaces were plastically shaped (chiseling by pushing) or the cast items were again processed (casting). In the already modelled surface, putty was applied and, on a soft support, the item was processed again, using various punches and chiseling hammers.[49] The chiseling of the ornaments made by casting or hammering could also be done with the chisel or by polishing with fine sands or pieces of sandstone.[50]

Polishing was done with steel and stone tools. The smoothing was done with the help of hammers with slightly arched edges to minimize any traces of hammering. Also, when smoothing the metal surface and the sharp edges, files were used.[51]

On the current territory of Romania, tools have been found that were employed in those techniques: the hammer discovered in Band in grave 10 (Fig. 35.12) with a bent blade and a rounded end, the punches found at Davideni, Budureasca 4, Budureasca 5 (Fig. 10.2), or the file at Dodești (Fig. 15.5). However, no pieces of precious metal that would have been decorated through those techniques have been found, except the hoard of Sânnicolau Mare (Timiș County), with its 23 gold objects surviving, some of which may be dated to the 7th century: the drinking horn, two cups, and two pitchers with horizontally grooved neck.[52] Precious metal containers were also discovered in the Carpathian Basin in 7th-century princely tombs: a silver tumbler and a jug in Kunágota (the first third of the 7th century); a silver pitcher, a chalice and a gold horn for drinking in Bócsa (the first half of the 7th century); a silver chalice and a pitcher in Ozora (last third of the 7th century); a gold drinking horn and a pitcher in Kunbábony (middle of the 7th century); silver pitchers in

48 Birgit Bühler, "Untersuchungen zu Guß, Oberflächenbearbeitung und Vergoldung an frühmittelalterlichen Bunt- und Edelmetallgegenständen," *Archaeologia Austriaca* 82–83 (1998–1999), 431.

49 Wolters, "Goldschmied," 378.

50 Harhoiu, Gora, *Aurul*, 67.

51 Bühler, "Untersuchungen," 437.

52 Csanád Bálint, "Über den Schatz von Nagyszentmiklós – kurze Übersicht," in *Gold der Awaren. Der Goldschatz von Nagyszentmiklós*, eds. Tibor Kovács and Éva Garam (Budapest: Magyar Nemzeti Múzeum. Helikon kiadó, 2002), pp. 75–76.

Kiskőrös-Vágóhid and Budapest-Rákos (the last third of the 7th century); and as two silver chalices in Szeged-Fehértó (the last third of the 7th century).[53]

Inside the Carpathian Basin, several copper-alloy vessels have been found, particularly in the western parts (Budakalász, Kölked-Feketekapu B, Várpalota, Zamárdi), as well as in the valley of the Tisza (Tiszagyenda), always in high-status burials. Those vessels have been most clearly manufactured in the Empire, either in Italy or in the eastern Mediterranean region, and reached Avaria through commercial transactions, as gifts, or as booty.[54]

2.2 *Engraving, Punching, Stamping*

For transforming metal, the preferred procedures were engraving, punching, and stamping. Engraving is a decorative technique involving the use of sharp tools, engraving implements, engraving needles or chisels; to remove certain portions from the surface of the metal, ditches or notches were created, forming geometric or vegetal motifs, sometimes in relief. Also, the ornamental details of items already cast or processed by hammering were often completed by means of engraving.[55]

Theophilus Presbyter describes punching as an operation taking place after gilding copper plates, as opposed to engraving, which was performed before gilding: "The copper plate is again taken and the decorative pattern with figures, flowers and animals is engraved and the composition is so oriented that small fields remain between them. Then the plate was cleaned with sand and polished, gilded and polished again. Then the plate was punched. The tool (the punch) was made out of steel, no bigger than one finger, with one thin end, and the other thick. Using the thin end of this fine tool, and a small hammer, a small hole is made and around it with the file the item is processed until the edge has equally sharp edges and a whole circle results. (…) You gently tap the punch with a small hammer and fill the field entirely with small circles and tie them as tightly as you want them to each other. If you fill all the fields in this way, place the plate on the burning coals until each notch gets a yellow color. (…) Repeat the same copper plate, but thicker as before, on which you

53 Éva Garam, "Die Verbindung awarenzeitlicher Fürsten- und Gemeinvolk- Grabfunde mit dem Schatz von Nagyszentmiklós," in *Gold der Awaren. Der Goldschatz von Nagyszentmiklós*, eds. Tibor Kovács and Éva Garam (Budapest: Magyar Nemzeti Múzeum. Helikon kiadó, 2002), 83, fig. 1; 84, fig. 4; 86, fig. 8; 88, fig. 10; 91, fig. 13; 97, fig. 22.5. Many of the sites mentioned here are located in the eastern part of the Tisza Plain.

54 Tivadar Vida, *Die frühbyzantinische Messingkanne mit Jagdszenen von Budakalász (Ungarn)* (Budapest: Institut für Archaeologie. Forschungzentrum für Humanwissenschaften Ungarische Akademie der Wissenschaften, 2017), 179–184.

55 Harhoiu, Gora, *Aurul*, 68.

draw the desired motifs and grave them as before. Then take a thin and wide tool, according to the size of the field, at a smooth and sharp end at the other end. Place the plate on the anvil and emboss the fields between the motifs using the tool mentioned above which you tap with the hammer. When all the fields have been embossed, smooth all around the engraved drawings with a small file. Once it's ready, gild and polish the plate."[56]

Engraving tools were discovered more in settlements from the lands to the south and to the east of the Carpathian Mountains (see Chapter XI) than in those from Transylvania.

The ornamenting items and the vessels were further decorated by stamping and punching. The stamp had a mirrored ornamentation and it was hammered onto the metal object. While stamping was somehow connected to the minting of coins, punching is a decorative technique just like chiseling, in which reliefs were obtained without losing material.[57] With the sharp point of the punch, dot-shaped ornaments were made.[58] Punches were found in tombs in the Carpathian Basin – at Kölked-Feketekapu B, Kunszentmárton, Jutas – in France at Hérouvillette, in Germany at Neuwied,[59] and in Norway at Vestly.[60] The presence of punches was also documented in settlements in Moldavia (Davideni) and in Walachia (Budureasca 4 and 5). Punched belt fittings are known from Noșlac[61] and from Band.[62]

56 Brepohl, *Theophilus*, 223.
57 Aufleger, "Metallarbeiten," 622.
58 Harhoiu, Gora, *Aurul*, 69.
59 Böhner, "Ein fränkisches Goldschmiedegrab," 114.
60 Magnus, Mollerop, Sjovold, "Migration Period Graves," N3.5 (4).20(28).
61 Rusu, "The Prefeudal cemetery," 272, fig. 2. 39.
62 Kovács, "A mezőbándi ásatások," 309, fig. 30. 3–4, 7–9.

CHAPTER 5

Special Technological Methods for the Manufacture of Clothing and Harness Accessories Made of Non-Ferrous Metals

In what follows, I will discuss a number of techniques employed in the production and decoration of dress accessories and jewelry, as well as mounts for the horse tack. Those are the commonest and, at the same time, the most representative artifacts now available, which illustrate the craft activity of the 6th and 7th centuries, and distinguish it from the earlier period, particularly in what concerns the production of new types (e.g., belt fittings) and the introduction of new techniques. Many of the techniques mentioned in the previous chapter (4.2.1 and 4.2.2) were also in use, but the most representative are discussed below. Several have been documented archaeologically not only by means of the final products, but also through finds of tools (the most significant are dies and molds, see Fig. 50–51).

1 Pressing on Dies

Pressing was done on dies made of bronze, stone, or wood, with embossed or hollowed decoration. Between the die and the bronze, silver, or gold sheet to be processed an additional protective sheet, commonly of lead, was placed before the object was hammered onto the die. The pressing could also be done without a protective plate, in which case a metal pin was used, with edges further processed later, to remove excess material.[1] Using this manual technique, it was possible to produce quickly and easily dress accessories made of metal sheet, often no more than 1 mm thick.[2]

Here is how Theophilus Presbyter describes the technique: "The iron plate, 1 finger thick and 3 to 4 fingers wide, 1 foot long, must be in good condition on the outside, so that the top does not have any defects or tear. In these narrow and wide stripes of ornaments, resembling a seal, flowers, animals, and birds or dragons with their twisted necks and queues are engraved. They do not have to be too deep, but should have the due depth and should be precisely

1 Amrein, Binder, "Mit Hammer und Zange," 365–366.
2 Roth, *Kunst*, 52.

© DANIELA TĂNASE, 2021 | DOI:10.1163/9789004436930_007

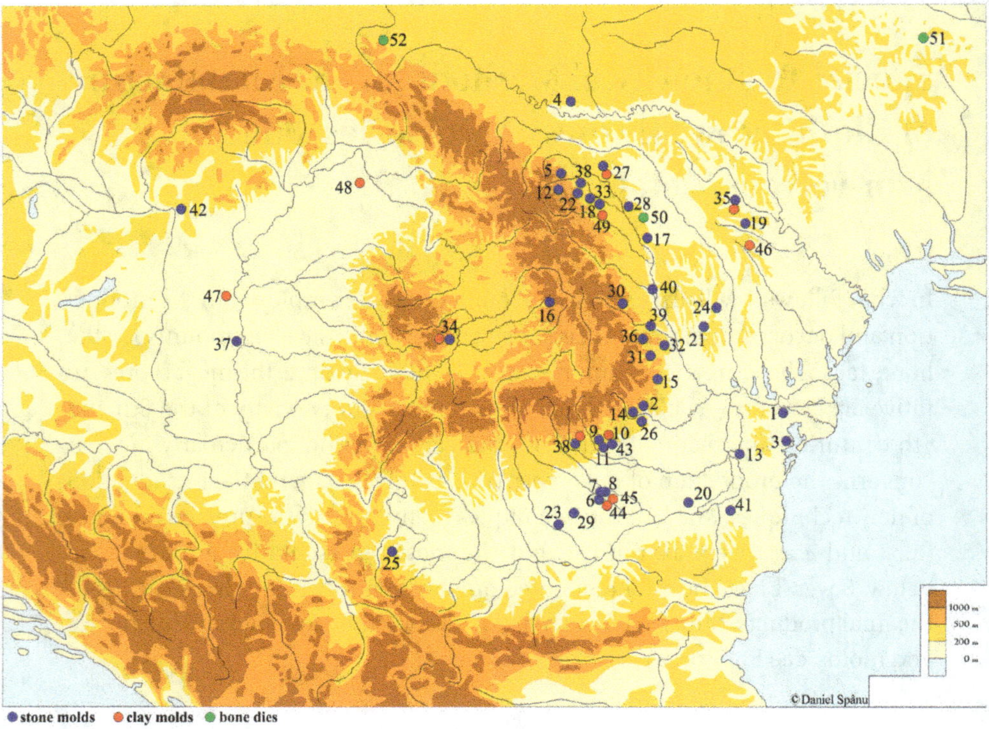

FIGURE 50 **Stone and clay molds and bone dies: the Carpathian Basin and the Dniestrian-Danube area – a. stone molds:** 1. Aegyssus (Tulcea, Tulcea co.); 2. Aldeni (Buzău co.); 3. Argamum (Jurilovca, Tulcea co.); 4. Bernashivka (Ukraine); 5. Botoșana (Suceava co.); 6. Bucharest-Dămăroaia (Bucharest); 7. Bucharest-str. Soldat Ghivan no. 10 (Bucharest); 8. Bucharest-Străulești-Măicănești (Bucharest); 9. Budureasca 3 (Prahova co.); 10. Budureasca 4 (Prahova co.); 11. Budureasca 5 (Prahova co.); 12. Cacica (Suceava co.); 13. Capidava (Constanța co.); 14. Cândești (Buzău co.); 15. Coroteni (Slobozia Bradului commune, Vrancea co.); 16. Cristuru Secuiesc (Harghita co.); 17. Cucuteni (Iași co.); 18. Davideni (Neamț co.); 19. Dănceni (Republic of Moldova); 20. Dichiseni (Călărași co.); 21. Dodești (Vaslui co.); 22. Dolheștii Mari (Suceava); 23. Dulceanca (Teleorman co.); 24. Giurcani (Vaslui co.); 25. Golemanovo Kale (Bulgaria); 26. Izvorul Dulce (Merei commune, Buzău co.); 27. Lozna (Dersca commune, Botoșani co.); 28. Moțca (Iași co.); 29. Olteni (Dobrogostea village, Olteni commune, Teleorman co.); 30. Onești (Bacău co.); 31. Poienița (Vrancea); 32. Răcoasa (Vrancea co.); 33. Rădeni (Păstrăveni commune, Neamț co.); 34. Sânmiclăuș (Șona commune, Alba co.); 35. Seliște (Republic of Moldova); 36. Soveja (Vrancea co.); 37. Szeged-Bilisics (Hungary); 38. Șirna (Prahova co.); 39. Ștefan cel Mare (Gutinaș village, Ștefan cel Mare commune, Bacău co.); 40. Traian = Parincea (Bacău co.); 41. Tropaeum Traiani (Adamclisi, Constanța co.); 42. Vác-Kavicsbánya (Hungary); 43. Vadu Săpat (Prahova co.) – **b. clay molds:** 44. Bucharest-Străulești-Lunca (Bucharest); 45. Bucharest-Tei (Bucharest); 10. Budureasca 4 (Prahova co.); 46. Hansca (Republic of Moldova); 47. Jász-Nagykun-Szolnok co. (Hungary); 48. Lazuri (Satu Mare co.); 28. Lozna (Botoșani co.); 34. Sânmiclăuș (Alba co.); 35. Seliște-Orhei (Orhei co., Republic of Moldova); 38. Șirna (Prahova co.); 49. Traian (Neamț co.) – **c. bone dies:** 50. Costești (Iași co.); 51. Pastyrs'ke (Ukraine); 52. Zimne (Ukraine)

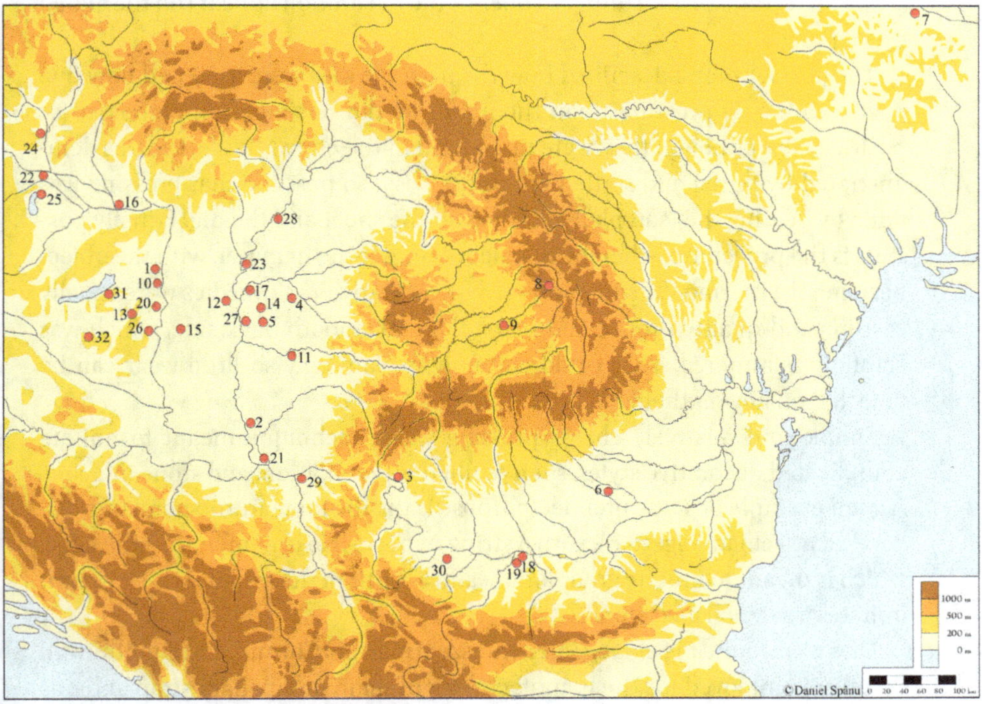

FIGURE 51 **Metal dies: the Carpathian Basin and the Dniestrian-Danube area.** 1. Adony (Hungary); 2. Aradac-Mečka (Serbia); 3. Banat (Danube Gorges area); 4. Békéscsaba-Nagyrét (Hungary); 5. Békéssámson (Hungary); 6. Bucharest-Tei (Bucharest); 7. Cherkasy, district (Ukraine); 8. Corund (Harghita co.); 9. Dumbrăveni (Sibiu co.); 10. Dunapentele (Dunaújváros, Hungary); 11. Felnac (Arad co.); 12. Gátér (Hungary); 13. Gyönk-Vásártéri út (Hungary); 14. Kardoskút (Békés co., Hungary); 15. Kiskunhalas, subdistrict (Hungary); 16. Komárno IV (Slovakia); 17. Kunszentmárton (Hungary); 18. Oescus (Gigen, Gulyantsi co., Bulgaria); 19. Oescus (Staroseltsi, Gulyantsi co., Bulgaria); 20. Paks-Gyapa (Hungary); 21. Pančevo (Serbia); 22. Petronell-Carnuntum (Austria); 23. Rákóczifalva-Kastélydomb (Hungary); 24. Ringelsdorf (Austria); 25. Seewinkel (?) (Austria); 26. Szekszárd-Palánk (Hungary); 27. Szentes (Hungary); 28. Tiszafüred-Majoros (Hungary); 29. Viminacium (Stari Kostolac, Serbia); 30. Vratsa (Bulgaria); 31. Zamárdi-Rétiföldek-dűlő (Hungary); 32. Zselickislak (Hungary)

engraved. Then beat the (silver) plate until it is so thin that it can be pressed and as long as you want and clean it with (wood) charcoal powder and a cloth, then polish it with scraped chalk. If it is ready, put the die on the anvil with the engraving upwards, place the silver stripe over it and a thick stripe of lead over it and beat hard with the hammer so that the lead over the silver foil gets stamped in the engraving and all its lines be well embossed. (…) This work is also done with the copper plate, the same way beaten, cleaned, gilded and polished. The iron die is placed so that the golden part is underneath, and the lead stripe on top and beaten until the lines of the decoration appear (on the gilded copper plate)."[3]

The jeweler monk described how the negative dies were used and how one needed to apply pressure upon them, but he did not mention embossed or positive dies, although they were often used in the early Middle Ages, as demonstrated by burial and settlement finds. It is also possible that pressing was done by beating the lead plate placed over the sheet and the die. Equally possible is the procedure, whereby the die was under the hammer, with the object between the die and the soft, protective sheet. Early medieval dies were usually cast in good-quality bronze and had a flat and smooth back side, which was carefully hammered. That could certainly explain why so little wear can be detected on any on them.[4]

Simple and relatively cheap, pressing was a technique meant to imitate complicated decorative styles, such as filigree, granulation, and stone inlaying. A good example of such intended purpose is the die for teardrop pendants discovered at Felnac (Fig. 38.8), with a string of pearl-like ornaments on the edge, which is meant to imitate granulation, and a motif in the middle which in turn imitates a set, polished stone.[5]

Dies were found in Felnac, Gátér, Kunszentmárton, Corund, and Dumbrăveni that were employed for the manufacturing of main or auxiliary strap ends, as well as for belt mounts and belt hole reinforcements. Such belts could also serve for suspending weapons at the waist or for horse gear. The vast majority of belt fittings discovered in Avar-age cemeteries in the Carpathian Basin are made by pressing. There are even good matches between known dies and belt fittings. For example, the belt mounts found in the warrior grave at Sânpetru German (Arad County) were most likely made with the corresponding dies found on the nearby site at Felnac.[6] A somewhat more distant parallel may be established between a brass mount with pressed ornament imitating granulation, which was found in Botoșana in a sunken-floored building together with a bronze coin struck for Emperor Justinian, has good analogies in Avar-age burial assemblages in Hungary and Transylvania. Another mount with a similar decoration is known from Bârlălești (Vaslui County).[7]

3 Brepohl, *Theophilus*, 230.
4 Bühler, "Untersuchungen," 434.
5 Garam, *Funde*, 38.
6 Egon Dörner, "Mormânt din epoca avară la Sânpetru German [Grave from the Avar epoch in Sânpetru German]," *Studii și Cercetări de Istorie Veche* 9, no. 2 (1962), 427, fig. 4.2.
7 Teodor, "Elemente și influențe bizantine," 107, fig. 6.3 – Botoșana, fig. 6.4; 110.

The discovery at Costești (Iași County) confirms that earrings could also be produced by pressing and that bone molds could also be used for pressing copper and silver foils. The sheets were pressed with a conical tool made of bone as well, with which one would lightly press to obtain the intended decoration.[8] Others have recently suggested that the earrings with star-shaped pendants were produced by "lost wax" casting, even though it is also possible that the Costești dies were employed in the production of jewelry by the pressing technique.[9]

2 Casting in Molds and Casting by the "Lost Wax" Method

On the hearth, in the fire made with charcoal, the metal was molten in crucibles, then let to settle and finally cast. The fire was lit with flint steels, such as found in the grave with tools from Aradac-Mečka, and was air-forced by means of bellows. Tubular tuyere fragments have been found in the graves with tools from Kunszentmárton[10] and Kisújszállás.[11] After the melting temperature was reached, the liquid metal was cast from crucibles into molds. In order to handle the crucibles, open-jaw tongs[12] were used, like those found at Band (Fig. 35.2).

The casting of finished items and semi-finished products was made in one- and two-valve molds made of stone or clay. On the surface of stone molds either the entire shape or only parts of the object to be cast were carved.

For casting dress accessories, metals with low melting temperatures were employed, such as tin and lead, in addition to metals with higher melting temperature, such as copper and silver. For a good cast, the mold had to be heated up to 50–100°C below the melting temperature of the metal to be cast. However, repeated heating of the stone shape could lead to breakage. Molds could be used only two or three times for metals with high melting temperatures and about five times for those with low melting temperatures.[13] Spectral analyses on stone molds from northern Germany and Poland have showed that ornaments of lead-tin alloy were cast in stone molds, while metals and alloys

8 Teodor, *Meșteșugurile*, 33.
9 Szmoniewski, "Production," 121–122.
10 Wolters, "Goldschmied," 367; Rácz, *Die Goldschmiedegräber*, 107.
11 Rácz, *Die Goldschmiedegräber*, 107.
12 Wolters, "Goldschmied," 373.
13 Volker Schmidt, "Die Gußtechnik im Schmuckhandwerk bei den Westslawen," *Zeitschrift für Archäologie* 28 (1994), 107–108.

with high melting temperature, such as bronze, brass, and silver, were cast in clay molds.[14]

Direct casting consisted of impressing in the clay the desired shape or pattern, by means of a model, thus obtaining two molds, and then wrapping them both in clay. A casting tube and an air vent were added to the clay package. After the metal cooled off, the clay package was broken, so that the valve could be used again.[15] Some objects still have traces of the valve on the back, with the other side in need of processing. Sometimes, after casting, the object received additional ornament by means of an engraver or a fine chisel.[16]

The valves could also be obtained by impressing a finished product (an object), not a model into the clay.[17] The bronze and lead models may also be used as "customer samples." There was in fact no mass production of dress accessories in the early Middle Ages. Hundreds of bow fibulae are known from the 6th- and 7th-century Western Europe, but few, if any identical pieces.[18] This is also true for bow fibulae found in Romania: except for a pair of fibulae from grave 3 in Gâmbaș (Alba County), no identical fibulae have so far been found.[19] This is explained by the fact that craftsmen had several molds in the workshop to show them to their customers, but also by the fact that they made molds upon commission.[20] The absence of identical fibulae is an indication that each piece was produced on demand, probably to be used only once, on a particular occasion.[21]

Jewelry may have also been made by means of the so-called "lost wax" method. Several archaeological experiments have been carried out in various European countries to replicate the sequences and results of that method. In Sweden, for example, lost-wax casting was done with tools made after those used in the 5th to 7th century in Ribe (Denmark), Helgö and Birka (Sweden). The objects were carved in wax, then packed in clay mixed with fine sand and crushed wooden charcoal or plant fibers, so that it would not to be destroyed upon drying. Bronze was melted in a crucible made of clay mixed with sand; when casting, the metal had a temperature of 1100–1140 centigrades, the fire being air-forced with bellows. After 15–20 minutes the metal melted, and at the same time the mold temperature reached 500–700 centigrades. The

14 Schmidt, "Die Gußtechnik," 120.
15 Aufleger, "Metallarbeiten," 621.
16 Bühler, "Untersuchungen," 439–440.
17 Teodor, *Meșteșugurile*, 29; Aufleger, "Metallarbeiten," 620.
18 Roth, *Kunst*, 46–47.
19 Horedt, *Contribuții*, 79, fig. 15. 8–9.
20 Amrein, Binder, "Mit Hammer und Zange," 364.
21 Curta, "Neither Gothic, nor Slavic," 69.

crucible was handled with small pliers, its content poured into the mold held in the other hand with another pair of pliers. The mold was opened after 15 minutes, when the metal cooled off and hardened. Casting imperfections were then chiseled and filed.[22]

Experimental archeology demonstrated that the "lost wax" method was quite effective, since within 30 minutes, no less than 60 wax patterns could be made for an object decorated on only one side.[23] This method provides great casting accuracy, which also implies skill. Direct casting is more primitive, while casting with the "lost wax" method is more complex. The two technologies coexisted, but the latter was more often used, because it was more advantageous to produce small dress accessories.[24] Experimental archaeology was also instrumental in understanding how bronze belt fittings were made by means of the lost-wax technique in the Carpathian Basin during the 8th century.[25] One of the conclusions drawn from the experiment was that in order to produce just one belt fitting, the entire technological process could take four to five days, and required skill and a high degree of specialization of the craftsman.[26]

Stone molds, especially for small pieces, could only be used to make wax patterns, and not to cast metal directly. True, traces of molten metal have been found on the mold for casting crosses found in Bucharest-Străulești-Lunca (Fig. 13.4), but that is a clay, not a stone mold.

Stone molds for casting jewelry, especially pendants and earrings, are known from the Balkan provinces of the Empire, including Scythia Minor. The mold from Tropeum Traiani (Adamclisi)[27] (Fig. 49.5), Aegyssus (Tulcea)[28]

22 Anders Söderberg, "Vikingerbronze, Blowing New Life in Ancient and Early Medievalkraft. Introduction." Available at http://web.comhem.se/vikingbronze/casting.htm. Accessed December 16, 2005.

23 Anders Söderberg, "Scandinavian Iron Age and Early Medieval ceramic molds – lost wax or not or both?" In *Proceedings of the 1st International Workshop. Experimental and Educational aspects on Bronze Metallurgy, Wilhelminaoord 18–22 October 1999*, eds. Caroline Tulp, Nigel Meeks and Roeland Paardekooper (Leiden: Vereniging voor Archeologische Experimenten en Educatie, 2001), pp. 15–16.

24 Söderberg, "Scandinavian Iron Age," 23.

25 Gergely Szenthe, "Meister und ihre Kunden. Herstellung und Verbreitung gegossener Bronzegegenstände im spätawarenzeitlichen Karpatenbecken," *Archaeologiai Értesítő* 137 (2012), 58–62.

26 Szenthe, "Meister," 69.

27 Barnea et al., *Tropaeum Traiani*, 218. fig. 169.10.14.

28 Andrei Opaiț, "Aegyssus '76 – Raport preliminar [Aegyssus '76 – Preliminary report]," *Pontica* 10 (1977), fig. 7.

(Fig. 49.6), Capidava[29] (Fig. 49.3–4), and Argamum (Jurilovca)[30] (Fig. 49.1) demonstrate that the lost-wax technique was also used inside the Empire. This may be explained in terms of the need to produce quickly a relatively large number of similar objects. That this was not a technology restricted to the border districts results from the stone mold found in the workshops at Justiniana Prima (Caričin Grad) and used for making small crosses, buckles and belt plates.[31]

Casts of fibulae with bent stem, buckles and keys have been found in the fortress of Theodora (Drobeta Turnu Severin), where a workshop may have operated.[32] Some have advanced the idea that the casts were brought to Drobeta Turnu Severin from somewhere else to be finished (decorated and assembled) on the site. To be sure, no traces of metalworking have been found at Drobeta, despite intensive archaeological excavations. But the same is true for other forts in the Balkans, which have no such workshops. The keys in the casts from Drobeta have good analogies in Dobrudja, the Crimea, southern Greece, and Constantinople. Also noteworthy is the fact that the highest density of finds of fibulae with bent stem is in the northeastern part of the Balkan Peninsula, which strongly suggests that the semi-finished products found in Drobeta came from there as well.[33] However, because of a lead model from Singidunum (Belgrade) and a mold for fibulae with bent stem from Caričin Grad, others have argued that the local production in Drobeta was quite possible.[34] The problem, of course, is that no molds have been found together with the semi-finished products, so the existence of a workshop is questionable. Be as it may, finds of molds and casts seem to suggest that the lost-wax technique

29 Zizi Covacef, "Accesorii vestimentare de toaletă şi podoabe descoperite în sectorul estic al cetăţii Capidava [Garment accessories and jewelry discovered in the eastern sector of the city of Capidava]," *Pontica* 28–29 (1995–1996), 113, 115; fig. VII/3–4.

30 Oanţă-Marghitu, "Argamum," pl. I.4.

31 Vujadin Ivanišević, "Metal Workshops of Caričin Grad (Justiniana Prima)," in *Lebenswelten zwischen Archäologie und Geschichte. Festschrift für Falko Daim zu seinem 65. Geburtstag*, eds. Jörg Drauschke, Ewald Kislinger, Karin Kühtreiber, Thomas Kühtreiber, Gabriele Scharrer-Liška and Tivadar Vida (Mainz: Verlag des Römisch-Germanischen Zentralmuseums, 2018), pp. 713–714.

32 Adrian Bejan, "Un atelier metalurgic din sec. VI e.n. de la Drobeta Turnu Severin [A metallurgical workshop from the 6th century AD from Drobeta Turnu Severin]," *Acta Musei Napocensis* 13 (1976), 257–259; 270, fig. 1.a–d; 271, fig. 1.a–e.

33 Florin Curta, Andrei Gândilă, "Too Much Typology, Too Little History: A Critical Approach to the Classification and Interpretation of Cast Fibulae with Bent Stem," *Archaeologia Bulgarica* 10, no. 3 (2011), 64–65.

34 Ivanišević, "Metal Workshops," p. 719.

spread to the barbarian world in the Middle and Lower Danube region from the Byzantine Empire.

Among dress accessories that appear in settlements and cemeteries, there are also cast bow. Local craftsmen were definitely capable of producing them, as demonstrated by finds of models such as those from the Clisura Dunării, Felnac, and Bucharest-Tei.[35] Some insist that such models for fibulae, earrings, and buckles were of Byzantine origin, even though the actual products followed the creative skills of the craftsman.[36] According to others, some bow fibulae from the Middle Dnieper region, Romania and the Western Balkans area are imitations of fibulae produced in Mazuria.[37] The stone mold found in Bernashivka (Ukraine) illustrates the production of bow fibulae by the lost-wax method, which means that different methods may have been used for the production of the same category of dress accessories[38] (Fig. 47.1). At any rate, molds discovered on the present-day territory of Romania prove the existence of the local production, the fibulae being cast in clay valves using both models and the lost-wax method.

The fibulae of the Gâmbaș type (Werner I C type) are said to have been produced by the Slavs in the region between the Middle and the Lower Danube, but they are of Roman-Byzantine influence,[39] as the scrollwork decoration appears on earlier fibulae from Crimea.[40] Some believe that the miniature fibulae of the Bucharest-Tei (Werner I D type) and Suceava-Piatra Frecăței

---

35 Ekaterina A. Shablavina, Bartlomiej S. Szmoniewski, "The Forming Model of the Kertch Type Finger-Shaped Fibula," *Sprawozdania Archeologiczne* 58 (2006), 521–522. Others claim that those were not models, but "customer samples" or purposefully unfinished items that were meant to replace symbolically the true fibulae in mortuary contexts (Florin Curta, "Some remarks on bow fibulae of Werner's class I C," *Slavia Antiqua* 49 (2008), 67; Curta, "Werner's Class I C," 70).

36 Aurelian Petre, "Fibulele „digitate" de la Histria (II) ["Bow" fibulae from Histria (II)]," *Studii și Cercetări de Istorie Veche* 16, no. 2 (1965), 280.

37 Curta, *The Making of the Slavs*, 254.

38 Curta, *The Making of the Slavs*, 271. The use of the "lost wax" method to create knobbed fibulae was also experimented in Russia. The clay paste used to cover the wax pattern contained 40–60% smashed sherds and sand. It was let dry and then fired up to 800–900°C temperate, the wax got melted and a "negative" of the fibula was obtained and then the melted metal was cast therein; after cooling, the clay cover was broken. See Curta, "'Slavic' Bow Fibulae," 29.

39 Maria Comșa, "Unele considerații cu privire la originea și apartenența etnică a complexelor cu fibule „digitate" de tip Gâmbaș-Coșoveni [Some considerations regarding the origin and ethnicity of the complexes with "bow" fibulae of the Gâmbaș-Coșoveni type]," *Apulum* 11 (1973), 264, 266, 270.

40 Florin Curta, "Some remarks on bow fibulae of Werner's class I C." *Slavia Antiqua* 49 (2008), 49.

(Werner I H type) groups were created by the local craftsmen in the Balkan region, as indicated by the model found in Bucharest-Tei.[41] It is also believed that the elaborate fibulae, such as that from Coşovenii de Jos, were made in Byzantine workshops and later taken to the lands north of the Danube.[42] Others claim that the Coşovenii de Jos fibula combining barbarian and Byzantine elements, was the product of a Byzantine craftsman who worked in the barbarian world, somewhere in southern Romania.[43]

According to other opinions, no workshops producing bow fibulae are known from the Balkan provinces of the Empire, and among the 100 graves found in Piatra Frecăvei, in only one has a pair of bow fibulae have been found, a clear indication that they were not of Byzantine origin. Such fibulae must have been made in workshops in the Crimea, and brought to the Lower Danube by Antes, either during plundering expeditions or as traded goods.[44]

I believe that models for bow fibulae show without any doubt that such fibulae were produced locally in the land by the Middle and Lower Danube. Bow fibulae were dress accessories, but also badges of elevated social status. Some have used grave finds, particularly dress accessories (including fibulae), to reconstruct the "national" costumes of past Germanic and Slavic populations. But fibulae are less an ethnic, and more a social status marker.[45] Moreover, influences from different cultural milieus mixed in the making of those dress accessories, which were most likely commissioned by wearers. Because of that, it is very unlikely that bow fibulae were ethnic markers. At any rate, "Slavic" bow fibulae appear in territories that were most certainly not inhabited by Slavs. As a matter of fact, some have advanced the idea that those fibulae were not "Slavic" *per se*. Instead, access to such dress accessories and their manipulation may have been a strategy to gain admission into a group of people known to the Byzantine authors as "Slavs."[46]

Several other dress accessories, such as bronze and iron belt buckles, were equally produced by casting into molds. In the lands north the Danube, buckles cast together with their plates have been discovered in cemeteries and

41 Dan Gh. Teodor, "Piese vestimentare bizantine din secolele VI–VIII în spaţiul carpato-dunăreamo-pontic. A. Catarame cu placa fixă [Byzantine garments from the 6th–8th centuries in the Carpathian-Danube-Pontic area. A. Fixed plate buckles]." *Arheologia Moldovei* 14 (1991), 127.

42 Aurelian Petre, "Fibulele 'digitate' de la Histria (I) ["Bow" fibulae from Histria (I)]," *Studii şi Cercetări de Istorie Veche* 16, no. 1 (1965), 90.

43 Comşa, "Socio-economic organization," 195.

44 Comşa, "Socio-economic organization," 189, 191.

45 Curta, "Neither Gothic, nor Slavic," 46.

46 Curta, *The Making of the Slavs*, 110.

stray finds. Most of those of the Sucidava, Pápa, Salona-Histria, and Syracuse types are undoubtedly of Byzantine origin.[47] But there are also locally produced imitations, such as that found in cemetery 3 at Bratei,[48] that combine the Salona-Histria and the Pápa types.[49] Locally produced iron buckles were also found in the cemetery excavated in Iclod (Cluj County), which is dated to the 7th century.[50] Such buckles are known from other cemetery sites as well: Bistrița,[51] Bratei,[52] Morești,[53] Noșlac,[54] Band,[55] and Târgu Mureș.[56]

Different types of earrings were also produced by casting,[57] such as the bronze earring found in Horodiștea (Botoșani County).[58] Their local production in the lands north of the river Danube results from finds of molds such as found in Costești (Fig. 45.1a–b), Dichiseni (Fig. 44.2a–b), or Lozna-Strătеni (Fig. 48.1.18). Moreover, molds are known for decorative parts of different types of earrings: Lozna-Strătеni (Fig. 29.1.15), Traian (Neamț County; Fig. 23.2), Moțca (Fig. 2.2), Davideni (Fig. 22.11), Dodești (Fig. 15.9), Bucharest-Străulești-Măicănești (Fig. 13.5), Bucharest-Soldat Ghivan (Fig. 13.6.5), and Budureasca (Fig. 8.1, Fig. 9.1–4).

---

47 Teodor, "Piese vestimentare," 117.

48 Syna Uenze, "Die Schnallen mit Riemenschlaufe aus dem 6. und 7. Jahrh." *Bayerische Vorgeschichtsblätter* 31, no. 1–2 (1966), 151, fig. 5.34; Bârzu, *Ein gepidisches Denkmal aus Siebenbürgen*, 280, pl. 2.6.6.

49 Teodor, "Piese vestimentare," 119.

50 Hica-Cîmpeanu, "Un grup de morminte din secolul al VII-lea e.n. la Iclod (jud. Cluj) [A group of tombs from the 7th century AD at Iclod (Cluj County)]," 287–295, 289, fig. 2.2.5–7.

51 Gaiu, "Le cimetière gépide," 117, fig. 2.1. T 3, T 14; 119, fig. 3, T 35, T 40, T 46; 120, fig. 4. T 48.

52 Bârzu, "Gepidische Funde," fig. 1.6; in cemetery 3 of Bratei iron belt buckles were found, entire and in fragmentary condition, in most graves: cf. Bârzu, *Ein gepidisches Denkmal*, 171–271 – description of the inventory and 279–329 – plates 1–51.

53 Horedt, *Morești*, 186–187.

54 Rusu, "The Prefeudal cemetery," 279.

55 Kovács, "A mezőbándi ásatások," 280, fig. 11. 1, 4; 287, fig. 15.1/2, 7; 296, fig. 19.10; 305, fig. 27.3; 305, fig. 29.3; 312; fig. 33. 1; 344, fig. 64; 346, fig. 66.6; 360; fig. 81.1–3.

56 István Kovács, "A marosvásárhelyi őskori telep, skytha-és népvándorláskori temető (Station préhistorique de Marosvásárhely, cimétiere de l'epoque scythe et de la migration des peuples) [Prehistoric station of Marosvásárhely/Târgu Mureș, cemetery of the Scythian era and the migration of peoples]," *Dolgozatok Cluj* 6, 1915, 278–296.

57 Comșa, "Quelques données concernant les rapports des territoires nord-danubiens avec Byzance," 383; Victor Teodorescu, "Boucles d'oreille de l'époque romano-byzantine d'aprés les moules d'orfèvre trouvés au nord du Danube en Roumanie," in *Actes du XIV-e Congrès international des études byzantines. Résumés. Communications*, eds. Mihai Berza and Eugen Stănescu (Bucharest: Editura Academiei RSR, 1971), pp. 157–158; Teodor, "Cercei," 187–206, with the entire bibliography.

58 Teodor, "Elemente și influențe bizantine," 109–110.

3 Granulation and Filigree

Granulation and filigree were refined and highly developed techniques, in which the metal was assembled without soldering, were used. The application of grains or wire to the metal support was done either by heating or by attachment by means of a special type of flux.[59] The granulation technique involved the use of gold grains on a base of the same material, without soldering. The operation proceeded as follows: fine gold plates were cut into small particles and placed in layers of wooden charcoal dust in a heated crucible until the particles acquired a globular shape and mixed with the dust thus lowering the melting point. Then, the grains were passed through a large sieve, washed and brushed with malachite powder and some kind of glue. After the grains were glued, the object to be decorated was heated again. Thanks to coal, a low melting point could be obtained. The technique was similar in the case of filigree, except that instead of grains, wire was used.[60]

On the present-day territory of Romania, several dress accessories have been found that were ornamented in those techniques: earrings with granulated bead pendants from Sânpetru German (Arad County),[61] grave 141 at Band,[62] Turda (Cluj county),[63] earrings decorated with granulations from Noșlac,[64] Coșovenii de Jos,[65] and Maglavit (Dolj County),[66] earrings with pyramid-shaped pendants decorated with granulations from an unknown location in Transylvania.[67]

Gold objects decorated with granulation have also been found in the eastern part of the Tisza Plain, at Gyula (Hungary): an iron bracelet plated with gold with rumpet-shaped ends decorated with granulation, three golden, semiglobular mounts with granulated edges, and a golden buckle with granulated ornament.[68]

---

59 Harhoiu, Gora, *Aurul*, 68.

60 Roth, *Kunst*, 56–57.

61 Dörner, "Mormânt," 427, fig. 4.4.

62 István Kovács, "A mezőbándi ásatások," 346, fig. 66.4.

63 Radu Harhoiu, "Quellenlage und Forschungsstand der Frühgeschichte Siebenbürgens im 6.–7. Jahrhundert," *Dacia Nouvelle Série* 43–45 (1999–2001), 117, pl. II.7b.

64 Rusu, "The Prefeudal cemetery," fig. 2.1–4.

65 Nestor, Nicolăescu-Plopșor, "Die völkerwanderungszeitlichen Schatz Negrescu," 34, pl. 8.

66 Octavian Toropu, *Romanitatea târzie și stră-românii în Dacia traiană sud-carpatică* (Craiova: Editura Scrisul Românesc, 1976), 138; pl. 17.1.1.

67 Harhoiu, "Quellenlage," 117, pl. II.8.

68 Items were found in a tomb discovered at the beginning of the 20th century, which also contained one *solidus* issued by Justinian I (between 537–542) and a golden belt prong, nowadays lost. Cf.: Daniela Tănase, "Piese de aur din epoca migrațiilor în colecția

4 Silver and *Niello* Inlaying

The *niello* technique involved the simultaneous melting of two mixtures. In a crucible, lead and sulfur were melted, in another one silver and copper. The lead-sulfur mixture was then poured over the silver-copper alloy, with the resulting blend heated and mixed well with a wooden stick, before being poured into another crucible with walls treated with sulfur and borax. After further heating and mixing with a broom, the alloy was poured into a container of water. Because of the water, the mixture cooled off, small chunks formed, which were then sprinkled and left to dry out. With a chisel or punch, the model was carved into the metal, and with a goose feather pipe grooves were filled with the *niello* powder. Those grooves were sulfur blown or sprinkled, before the object to be decorated was heated to melt the powder and was finally polished.[69] The black color of the silver-copper powder stood in a visually pleasant contrast to the gold- or silver-plated base.

The silver inlaying was done by cutting grooves into the iron plate by means of a chisel and an engraver. In those grooves, silver or brass wires, stripes or plates were then inserted with a hammer, before the entire surface was polished to obtain a flat surface.[70] The inlaying technique, which first appeared in prehistory, became very popular in the Merovingian period, specifically in the late 6th and in the 7th century. Dress accessories decorated with damascened (silver inlay) ornament have been found not only in Merovingian Gaul, but also in the Carpathian Basin, particularly in burial assemblages associated with male graves.[71] The specimens in the Carpathian Basin are of a notably different, often lower quality. The ornament consists of simple ribbons or the interlaced motif, on which the inlaying forms stripes finely crossed without reaching the ribbon contour line.[72]

Muzeului Banatului Timişoara [Gold pieces from the Migration Period in the collection of the Banat Museum Timişoara]," in *Între stepă şi imperiu. Studii în onoarea lui Radu Harhoiu*, eds. Andrei Măgureanu and Erwin Gáll (Bucharest: Editura Renaissance, 2010), 141–147.

69 Roth, *Kunst*, 54; Amrein, Binder, "Mit Hammer und Zange," 364.

70 Amrein, Binder, "Mit Hammer und Zange," 364; Aufleger, "Metallarbeiten und Metallverarbeitung," 625.

71 Max Martin, "Tauschierte Gürtelgarnituren und -beschläge des frühen Mittelalters im Karpatenbecken und ihre Träger," in *Ethnische und kulturelle Verhältnisse an der mittleren Donau vom 6. bis zum 11. Jahrhundert*, eds. Darina Bialeková and Jozef Zábojník (Bratislava: Veda, 1996), 63.

72 Max Martin, "Zu den tauschierten Gürtelgarnituren und Gürtelteilen der Männergräber von Kölked-Feketekapu A," in Attila Kiss, *Das awarenzeitliche gepidische Gräberfeld von*

The presence of such belt fittings, which are different from those in the Merovingian area in both decoration and technique, implies the existence of local workshops. None, however, has so far been found. The study of the belt fittings from the cemetery A excavated in Kölked-Feketekapu demonstrated that, unlike the Merovingian belt sets, those in the Carpathian Basin had three, not four components.[73] Belt sets with damascened decoration like those from Kölked Feketekapu A have also been found in Környe[74] and Szekszárd-Bogyszló Street (Hungary),[75] as well as Unirea (Alba County). Two assemblages on the latter site are particularly interesting in that respect. In grave 12, there was a fragment of a damascened belt mount with small silver rivets, while the fragment from grave 13 had an interlaced ornament.[76] It is possible that the belt fittings from Unirea were produced somewhere in Transdanubia (western Hungary), that is in a region with the most finds of damascened belt fittings. At any rate, the only such fittings known from Transylvania are those from Unirea.

5 Gilding

For hot gilding of bronze and silver items, a special mix of eight parts mercury and one part gold was used. The mixture was initially heated in a crucible and then poured into another crucible filled with water. After the evaporation of water, a mass of powder thus formed. The gilded object was brushed with a liquid mixture with three parts tartrate, one part salt, and four parts mercury and water. The amalgam was spread onto the object using a copper pin. The object was then heated to about 100 centigrades, and the layer uniformly spread further with a brush.[77]

Kölked-Feketekapu A (Innsbruck: Universitätsverlag Wagner, 1996), 348; Martin, "Tauschierte Gürtelgarnituren und -beschläge des frühen Mittelalters," 69.

73 Martin, "Zu den tauschierten Gürtelgarnituren," 346.

74 Ágnes Salamon, István Erdélyi, *Das völkerwanderungszeitliche Gräberfeld von Környe*, (Budapest: Akadémiai Kiadó, 1971) 46; pl. 2. 36–39; p. 9, 1–3; pl. 11. 16–19, 32–38; pl. 15. 25–27 (tombs 18, 66, 70, 77 and 97).

75 Gyula Rosner, "Ethnische Probleme im 8.–9. in Südostpannonien," in *Rapports du IIIe Congrés International d'Archaéologie Slave, Bratislava, 7–14 septembre 1975*, vol. 1, ed. Bohuslav Chropovský (Bratislava: Vydavatel'stvo Slovenskej Akadémie Vied, 1979), 672, fig. 1.7.

76 Márton Roska, "Das gepidische Gräberfeld von Vereșmort (Marosveresmart)," *Germania* 18 (1934), 123; fig. 3.4, fig. 4.2–3.

77 Roth, *Kunst*, 54; Amrein, Binder, "Mit Hammer und Zange," 365; Aufleger, "Metallarbeiten und Metall-verarbeitung," 628.

Theophilus Presbyter describes the preparation of the gold and silver amalgam as following: "When you smashed all the gold you want to cement, put a weight of 8 *denarii* on the balance and carefully weigh as much mercury, then stretch it over gold and rub it until it turns white. Take a small crucible where gold and silver are melted, and which must be thicker than the usual ones, and keep it on fire until it gets hotter. Take a thin, hook-shaped iron rod, which at one end has a handle and the other end is globular and also put it in the fire. When both are hot, take the crucible with the pliers and pour the mercury together with the gold in a wide and dry bowl and with the hot hook stretch and smash quickly, then pour water immediately. After the water is poured, take the gold in the left hand and wash it carefully and try with your finger if it is well crushed and if so, pour it on a clean linen towel and shake it up and down until water evaporates. (...) In the same way silver gets cleaned, finely smashed and mixed with mercury, because in the heated crucible it cannot be smashed with the hot iron hook. They can be mixed if there are five parts of mercury and the six parts of pure silver."[78]

Gilded artifacts have been found on several sites in Romania, but the most impressive are those decorated with the dentil ornament most typical for Animal Style II, e.g., the belt buckle found with the adult skeleton in grave 264 in Bratei 3, or the luxury fibula from Coșovenii de Jos.

6 Stones and Glass Inserts

The stone inserts were very popular in the 6th and 7th centuries, in the Italian Peninsula, in Merovingian Gaul, as well as in the Byzantine Empire. The cloisonné, or the technique of setting precious stones in cell works, was done in the following way: on a precious metal base plate, metal stripes were attached so to create a cell-work, and the cells were filled with a mixture of quartz sand and calcite or egg-white, which covered the gold or silver foil. The cells were filled with semiprecious stones – mostly red almandines or garnets – which had been cut to size, and the upper edges of the cells were then hammered with a wide hammer against the stones to prevent them from falling. The technique called cabochon involved setting rounded, polished semiprecious stones, gems, or pearls into detached, isolated cells.[79] Jewelers in the Carpathian Basin, as

78 Brepohl, *Theophilus*, 111.

79 Aufleger, "Metallarbeiten," 626–628.

well as in Byzantium (including the northern Black Sea region) also used beeswax for putty.[80]

Most artifacts decorated in the cloisonné technique and found in the lands north of the Alps came from the Mediterranean region, but the existence of local workshops cannot be excluded.[81] Such artifacts were also found on the present-day territory of Romania, but none of them was produced locally. For example, a golden ring discovered in grave 39 at Band was decorated in the cloisonné technique. Its semicircular and diamond-shaped cells were filled with glass, the surface of which did not rise above the cell.[82] Where was this ring made? It is likely that it has been brought from Transdanubia, because it shows great similarity with artifacts from Keszthely (County Zala, Hungary). At least one workshop working in cloisonné may have been located there, which combined the influences of several cultures (Merovingian, Byzantine, and Avar).[83] It has been long noted that during the Avar age, ancient Roman gems were recycled and incorporated into finger rings produced especially in the Keszthely region. A golden ring from Alba Iulia, with a cabochon of a dark-green, agate stone surrounded by granulated ornament, may also be dated to the Avar age.[84]

A gilt silver (?) buckle with a plate decorated in cloisonné of green glass settings was found in the western part of cemetery 3 at Bratei. It has been dated to the first half of the 6th century on the basis of analogies from Hungary and Italy.[85] Gilt silver buckles with eagle-headed plates, which were cast in the "lost wax" method, decorated in *niello*, but also with cloisonné or cabochon settings, are known from other sites in Transylvania – Cipău (Mureș County) and Fundătura (Cluj County) – as well as in the Serbian Banat (Kovin).[86] The manufacture of such buckles involved high technical skills, specifically in the cutting and polishing of precious and semi-precious stones. They could not have been possibly made in the barbarian world, but most likely in urban workshops in Byzantium, such as those in the northern Black Sea area (Bosporus/

80 Orsolya Heinrich-Tamáska, *Die Stein- und Glasinkrustationskunst des 6. und 7. Jahrhunderts im Karpatenbecken* (Budapest: Magyar Nemzeti Múzeum, 2006), 73, 80.

81 Roth, *Kunst*, 57; Amrein, Binder, "Mit Hammer und Zange," 366.

82 Kovács, "A mezőbándi ásatások," 409–410.

83 Heinrich-Tamáska, *Die Stein- und Glasinkrustationskunst*, 69–73.

84 Heinrich-Tamáska, *Die Stein- und Glasinkrustationskunst*, 59, 95; Garam, *Funde bizantinischer Herkunft in der Awarenzeit*, 303, pl. 52.3.

85 Bârzu, "Gepidische Funde," 212; fig. 2.3; 214.

86 Mircea Rusu, "Pontische Gürtelschnallen mit Adlerkopf (VI.–VII. u. Z)," *Dacia Nouvelle Série* 3 (1959), 486–491; 523.

Kerch and Chersonesus/Simferopol), which remained active well into the 7th century.[87] Finally, blue glass settings decorate the gilt silver fibula from Coşovenii de Jos, particularly the eyes of the bird heads.[88]

87 Rusu, "Pontische Gürtelschnallen," 514–515.

88 Nestor, Nicolăescu-Plopşor, "Die völkerwanderungszeitlichen Schatz Negrescu," 34.

CHAPTER 6

The Tools

Metalworking tools found in settlements and graves offer a unique glimpse into the activity of craftsmen and goldsmiths. Fewer tools have been found in settlements than in burial assemblages, and the latter are also the most interesting, because of variety.

Several categories of tools, such as pliers, hammers and chisels, are common in shape and size to most historical ages.[1] Others, such as the molds and the dies, reflect change and fashion, especially when they can be relatively well dated by means of comparison with finished products.

1 Pliers

Blacksmith's tongs: Band (Fig. 35.1), Moreşti (Fig. 2.1); Jeweler's pliers: Band (Fig. 35.2), Budureasca 4 (Fig. 8.7)

Pliers represent one of the tool categories most often found graves, but rarely on settlement sites. The early medieval specimens were different from those of the Late Iron (La Tène) age because of longer handles, rounded or elongated jaws, and straight-ended handles. In that respect, early medieval pliers are similar to those of Roman origin.[2] Moreover, they are different from 5th-century pliers with onion-shaped jaws, such as found in grave B of the cemetery 1 in Bratei, or in grave 2 of the Csongrád-Kenderfőldek graveyard. Nonetheless, the specimen from grave A of the latter cemetery has elongated jaws, much like pliers from 6th- to 7th-century assemblages.

Iron pliers were used in various operations: forging, casting, or holding clay crucibles in which metal was melted. Long-arm pliers (as long as 11 inches long) were making fine jewelry, while tools with even longer arms (27 to 40 inches) were employed by blacksmiths tools. The various shapes of the jaws indicate adaptability to various operations: some were arched, with straight and smooth tips, for working metal sheet; others had pointed and parallel

1 Sebastian Brather, *Ethnische Interpretationen in der frühgeschichtlichen Archäologie. Geschichte, Grundlagen und Alternativen* (Berlin/New York: Walter de Gruyter, 2004), 362.

2 Henning, "Schmiedegräber," 69.

© DANIELA TĂNASE, 2021 | DOI:10.1163/9789004436930_008

tips and were used in the ironworks, to hold blooms and large pieces of metal about to be forged.[3]

The small pliers found in grave 10 at Band (less than 9 inches long), could have been used to handle small ornaments, but also for making armor and helmet components, such as rivets. Equally small was the pair of pliers, a fragment of which was discovered in Budureasca 4. That too must have been a jeweler's tool.

By contrast, larger tongs for blacksmithing are known from grave 10 in Band and from Moreşti. They are 18 and 12 inches long, respectively. Tongs as long as that, and similar to those in Band and Moreşti have been found in cemetery B in Kölked Feketekapu (17.5 inches long),[4] Aradac-Mečka (about 14 inches long),[5] Poysdorf (Austria),[6] Dittigheim (Germany),[7] Kisújszállás (Hungary),[8] Schönebeck (Germany)[9] and Hérouvillette (France).[10]

2 Hammers

Band (Fig. 35.12–13), Budureasca 4 and 9 (Fig. 10.2.1–2)

Hammers of various shapes and sizes are relatively common among grave goods, but rarely found on settlement sites. Indispensable in metalworking, the hammer was used in smithing operations such as forging, hammering, riveting, as well as auxiliary tool in goldsmithing, for example, for driving engraving tools or pressing metal sheets on dies. It was also used in decorative techniques with no loss of material, such as decorative motifs by "pushing," but also in working the surface of pieces laid out on a lead, resin, pitch, or leather support. In the latter case, only small hammers were used.[11]

What made a hammer "small" or "large" ("heavy")? Scholars regard hammers that are between 4 and 5.5 inches long, with square or round heads, as heavy hammers used by blacksmiths. By contrast, hammers that are smaller

---

3 Müller-Wille, "Der frühmittelalterliche Schmied," 153, 156.

4 Kiss, *Das awarenzeitliche Gräberfeld*, 2: 39, pl. 25.1.

5 Nagy, "Nekropola kol Aradaca," 72, pl. V.3.

6 Beninger, "Der Langobardenfriedhof," 187, pl. 6.1.

7 Amrein, Binder, "Mit Hammer und Zange," 361, 400b.

8 Rácz, "Avar kori ötvös-és kovácsszerszámok," 79, fig. 13.5.

9 Berthold Schmidt, *Die späte Völkerwanderungszeit in Mitteldeutschland. Katalog (Nord- und Ostteil)*, (Veröffentlichungen des Landesmuseums für Vorgeschichte in Halle), 29 (Berlin: Veb Deutscher Verlag der Wissenschaften, 1975), 199, pl. 11.4 c.

10 Decaens et al., *Un nouveau cimetière*, 115, fig. 19.B2.

11 Bühler, "Untersuchungen," 431.

than that and have flared heads "pushing" hammers (*Treibhammer*) meant to process sheet metal.[12] A small hammer (no longer than 2.7 inches) was found in grave 10 of the cemetery in Band (Fig. 35.12). It is believed that that hammer was used to created relief patterns and burnished surfaces in the *au repoussé* technique, or globular surfaces.[13] In the same grave, a larger, about 6-inch-long hammer with a rectangular head was found (Fig. 35.13). This was a blacksmith tool.

Two rectangular hammers are known from Budureasca 9, one straight, the other with a slightly flared head. The former was 5.1 inches long, while the latter was a fragment, but still 4.7 inches long (Fig. 10.2.1). Another hammer fragment was found in the same settlement. These heavy hammers were used for forging, crushing iron ore, and for breaking the bloom extracted from the smelting furnace.[14]

Hammers like those from Band are known from many graves with tools found in Europe: Kölked Feketekapu B,[15] Kisújszállás,[16] Dittingheim,[17] Poysdorf,[18] Beckum,[19] Hérouvillette,[20] and Vestly.[21] Judging by this evidence, hammers were frequently deposited in graves together with other tools, particularly pliers.

3 Anvils

Band (Fig. 35.15–16), Budureasca 4 (Fig. 8.8)

Anvils are quite rare among 6th- to 7th-century finds, and appear mainly in graves with tools. Those anvils are between 2 and 6 inches tall, in the shape of prism or an inverted cone, ending with a pin that was inserted into a wooden stand. Some specimens have a horn-shaped side bevel. This tool was used for hammering, bending, and pushing, or for making nails, as well as for refined goldsmithing work.[22]

12 Müller-Wille, "Der frühmittelalterliche Schmied," 153.
13 Bühler, "Untersuchungen," 432.
14 Miclea, Florescu, *Strămoşii românilor*, 212. 818.
15 Kiss, *Das awarenzeitliche Gräberfeld in Kölked-Feketekapu B*, 2: 39, pl. 25.7–8, 10.
16 Rácz, "Avar kori ötvös-és kovácsszerszámok," 75, fig. 8.4.
17 Amrein, Binder, "Mit Hammer und Zange an Esse und Amboss," 361, 400b.
18 Beninger, "Der Langobardenfriedhof von Poysdorf," 187, pl. 6.9.
19 Capelle, *Das Gräberfeld Beckum I*, pl. 27.65.c.
20 Decaens et al., *Un nouveau cimetière*, 114, fig. 18.B1a–d.
21 Magnus, Mollerop, Sjovold, "Migration Period Graves," N3, 5 (4).22.
22 Müller-Wille, "Der frühmittelalterliche Schmied," 151.

Two anvils were found in grave 10 at Band. One of them is 4 inches tall, in the shape of an inverted, truncated pyramid, with a lateral bevel. The other one is 2.4 inches tall, cone-shaped, with a mushroom head. István Kovács believed that to be a chisel, not an anvil, but it is more likely that the tool was in fact used for refined goldsmithing work.

There are no anvils among settlement sites, with the exception of a small anvil from Budureasca 4,[23] which was used by a jeweler. Similarly small anvils for goldsmithing are known from the early 6th-century grave from Brno,[24] the early 7th-century grave in Kunszentmárton, as well as graves discovered in Kisújszállás and Csákberény-Orondpuszta.[25] Such anvils are also known from Poysdorf,[26] Schönebeck,[27] and Vestly.[28] The closest analogy for the Band anvil is the specimen from Brno.

By contrast, the closest analogy to the anvil found in Budureasca 4 is the specimen discovered in the fortified settlement at Runden Berg near Urach (Germany).[29] On the other hand, the Budureasca anvil looks very much like the anvil-shaped pendant on the golden chain with tool miniature replicas from Şimleul Silvaniei, which is dated to the 5th century.[30]

4 Drills

Band (Fig. 35.14), Davideni (Fig. 22.1.3), Dodești (Fig. 15.5)

Among tools used in metalworking, the drills played a key role. Those tools are quite rare among 6th- and 7th-century finds: one in Davideni, and another Dodești. An entire set of drills of various sizes, however, was found in a jeweler's box deposited in grave 10 at Band (Fig. 35.3–7): some smaller than 2 inches, others were as long as 2.2 inches.

Of outstanding significance is the mechanical, wheel-driven steel drill discovered in Band (Fig. 35.14). Its preserved part is 5.5 inches long, with a wheel

23 Teodorescu, Peneş, "Matricea de incidență," 46, fig. 21.9. The authors only presented the illustration without giving details of the discovery conditions.

24 Werner, "Waage," 24.

25 Rácz, "Avar kori ötvös-és kovácsszerszámok," 77, fig. 10.3; 96, table 2.

26 Beninger, "Der Langobardenfriedhof," 187, pl. 6.8.

27 Schmidt, *Die späte Völkerwanderungszeit*, 199, pl. 11.4f.

28 Magnus, Mollerop, Sjovold, "Migration Period Graves," N3, 5 (4).17.

29 Amrein, Binder, "Mit Hammer und Zange," 362, fig. 402.

30 Torsten Capelle, *Die Miniaturkette von Szilágysomlyó (Şimleul Silvaniei)* (Universitätsforschungen zur prähistorischen Archäologie) 22 (Bonn: Habelt, 1994), 49–50. A replica of a "pushing" hammer may also be found among those pendants.

of less than 2 inches in diameter. The upper part of the shaft is broken, which makes it impossible to know the exact shape of the tool. At the center of the shaft there is a drive-wheel made of two joined bronze discs with upward and downward curved edges, respectively; the space between them is filled with lead. The rotation movement of the drill was imparted by a bow, and the tool could function vertically or horizontally, as the lead weight acted as a flywheel.[31]

Although the number of drill finds in early medieval Europe is quite large, only two mechanical drills have so far been discovered, that from Band and that from Vestly.[32] A lead wheel was also found from the grave with tools in Brno.[33]

Mechanical drills were a novelty in the early medieval world, the result of the combination of Germanic-Celtic technical traditions, and the advanced Roman technology.[34] Some believe that mechanical drills were wood- and bone-working tools, perhaps because of the concave tip of the tool that suggests materials softer than metal for drilling.[35] However, the use of mechanical drills for metalworking cannot be ruled out, since the bits were made of steel and the drive wheel could impart a high speed that was sufficient for piercing the metal sheet.[36]

5 Wire-Drawing Plate (or Nail-Making Tool)

Band (Fig. 35.8)

Wire was made by twisting on a rotary die or by drawing through a metal plate with holes of different diameters.

A 4-inch-long tool was found in grave 10 at Band that appears to have been used exactly for that purpose (Fig. 35.8). Its shape resembles a rectangular hammer, with a sharp head, and five holes of different diameters in the hollow part of the tool.

A tool of probably similar purpose, but simpler make, was discovered in grave 80 of cemetery B in Kölked-Feketekapu. That tool is a rectangular iron plate, bent at a right angle longitudinally, and with 21 holes arranged in

31 Kovács, "A mezőbándi ásatások," 294.
32 Magnus, Mollerop, Sjovold, "Migration Period Graves," 1966, N 3, 5 (4).19.
33 Daim, Mehofer, Tobias, "Die langobardischen Schmiedegräber," 206.
34 Henning, "Schmiedegräber," 74.
35 Rácz, *Die Goldschmiedegräber*, 127.
36 Olteanu, "Quelques remarques," 47; Olteanu, *Societatea*, 130.

three rows.[37] No traces of wear or metal oxides have been found during examinations under the microscope, so the conclusion was drawn that this must have been the plate of a wool comb. Such combs have iron, wooden, or bone pins.[38] What would a wool comb have to do with blacksmith and carpenter tools? It is quite possible that the tool in question was employed for drawing wire, given that the holes are of different sizes and the plate is bent in a L-shaped form, most likely in order to be attached to a handle.

The next parallel is also much later, as it was found at Staraia Ladoga (Russia), and dated to the second half of 8th century. Unlike the Band tool with its five holes, the specimen in Staraia Ladoga has 78 holes.[39] While no alternative interpretations have been advanced for the tool found in Staraia Ladoga, that from Band is sometimes interpreted as a draw-plate,[40] and other times as a tool for making iron nails.[41] One of the main arguments in favor of the latter interpretation is the small number of holes at the bottom of the hollow part of the tool, which – the theory goes – is ideal for forming the nail heads. Similar tools are known from the Viking age, e.g., the tools from the 9th-century graves with tools from Skredtveit and Bygaland (Norway).[42] In both cases, the nail-making tools were found together with pliers, hammers, files, chisels, in other words in toolkits comparable to that in Band. Such parallels suggest that the technology involving the use of those tools remained basically the same between the 7th century and the Viking Age, and in various parts of the European continent.

In my opinion, the multifunctionality of this tool is quite possible. The fact that this tool could be used for nails does not exclude its use as a draw-plate, especially since the holes are very different in diameter. With this tool it was possible to make wire of different diameters, suitable in various assembling operations in smithing and armor-making.

37 Kiss, *Das awarenzeitliche Gräberfeld*, 2: 39, pl. 25.11.

38 Rácz, *Die Goldschmiedegräber*, 128–129.

39 Wolters, "Goldschmied," 370, fig. 39; 371.

40 Henning, "Schmiedegräber," 74.

41 Capelle, *Die Miniaturkette*, 21.

42 Müller-Wille, "Der frühmittelalterliche Schmied," 157, fig. 11; Müller-Wille, "Der Schmied," 257, fig. 22; 258, fig. 23.

6 Tools for Making Nails and Rivets

Band (Fig. 35.11)

Among the tools found in grave 10 at Band, there was also a tool for making cone-headed rivets[43] and wide-headed nails (Fig. 35.11). The tool is shaped like a hammer, with a well polish, acorn-like appendage at one end, in the center of which there is an oval hole. The appendage is split longitudinally. At the other end of the hammer there are traces of rust, an indication that an iron bar was at some point attached in that place, possibly to hold a piece, that would make the use of the tool easier. The smith worked the flat-headed nails already made, passing them through the cone-like appendage and then forging them. Alternatively, he could use the tool to strike against it with a hammer in order to form the head of a rivet or of a nail, and make it hemispherical. A large number of rivets were uncovered in the same grave at Band, which actually fit very well into the tool's appendage.[44] It is quite possible that the rivets made with this tool were for armor or dress accessories. As a matter of fact, the helmet discovered in the same grave has riveted plates. No similar tool is so far known from any early medieval site. A nail-making tool was found in Kunszentmárton, but it is rectangular in shape, resembles a hammer, and has three holes in the middle.[45]

7 Files

Dodești (Fig. 15.5)

Files were used to remove the traces left by the working tools, for smoothing the surface of the metal by means of grinding and polishing, as well as for sharpening the tools.

Those massive steel tools had different shapes and variable thickness, with round, semicircular, square, or triangular cross-sections. Making files was described as follows by Theophilus Presbyter: "after the tip was formed with a hammer, chisel or a knife, it (the file) was smeared with old pork lard, wrapped with strips of goatskin and tied with linen string. Then it was enveloped with well-kneaded clay, without covering the handle. After it has dried, it was put

43 Wolters, "Goldschmied," 370, fig. 2; 371.

44 Kovács, "A mezőbándi ásatások," 402.

45 Rácz, *Die Goldschmiedegräber*, 112, fig. 26.4.

into the fire and blown strongly until the skin burned. The peeling clay envelope was quickly removed, and it (the file) was put into the water, then it was pulled out and dried in the fire."[46]

A sharp-pointed file with round section (which could also be used as a drill) was discovered in a sunken-floored building of the settlement site excavated in Dodești. The building may have been a jeweler's workshop, as indicated by the small chisel, the ladle, and two stone molds found there.[47] No other files are known from Romania, and none was found among the tools deposited in grave 10 in Band. Similar tools, however, are known from graves with tools discovered in Aradac-Mečka,[48] Brno,[49] Kisújszállás,[50] Poysdorf,[51] and Jutas,[52] as well as on such West European sites as Dittigheim,[53] Schönebeck,[54] and Hérouvillette.[55] The closest analogies for the Dodești file are the specimens from grave 166 in Jutas – 9.4, 6.7, and 6.2 inches long.[56]

8 Engraving Tools

Budureasca 3 (Fig. 11.1.1), Budureasca 4 (Fig. 8.14), Budureasca 5 (Fig. 10.1.2), Băleni (Fig. 12.1.1–3), Davideni (Fig. 20.8–9, Fig. 21.12–13, Fig. 22.1.1–2), Ștefan cel Mare-Gutinaș (Fig. 23.1.1)

The engraving tools (Fig. 10.1.2, Fig. 8.14, Fig. 20.9), knives (Fig. 11.1.1) or burins (Fig. 22.1.1) were similar to chisels. Unlike them, however, engraving tools had sharp ends for cutting the lines of the decorative motifs or for burnishing the surface (Fig. 32.1.2). Such tools were used by applying hand pressure onto the metal surface.[57] Engraving was used to decorate only massive, cast objects, as artifacts made of thin metal sheet could be easily pierced.[58]

46 Brepohl, *Theophilus*, 81.
47 Teodor, *Continuitatea*, 25; 29. fig. 1–3, 10–11; 30, fig. 7. 1–3.
48 Nagy, "Nekropola kol Aradaca," 72, pl. V.5.
49 Daim, Mehofer, Tobias, "Die langobardischen Schmiedegräber," 217, fig. 14.
50 Rácz, "Avar kori ötvös-és kovácsszerszámok," 82, fig. 16. 5–6.
51 Beninger, "Der Langobardenfriedhof," 187, pl. 6.2.
52 Rhé, Fettich, *Jutas und Öskü*, pl.IV.16–18.
53 Amrein, Binder, "Mit Hammer und Zange," 361, fig. 400 b.
54 Schmidt, *Die späte Völkerwanderungszeit*, 199, pl. 11.4.e.
55 Decaens et al., *Un nouveau cimetière*, 117, fig. 7a–7b.
56 Rhé, Fettich, *Jutas und Öskü*, 32. Among the tools deposited in grave 166 in Jutas, there was also a drill similar to that found in Dodești in a different assemblage.
57 Bühler, "Untersuchungen," 434–435.
58 Aufleger, "Metallarbeiten," 625.

Like the chisels, the engraving tools had to be made of harder metal, with reinforced tips, while the body had to be soft and elastic. According to Theophilus Presbyter "the engraving tools were strengthened by the following method: after the piece was straightened and set into a handle, the tip was put into the fire until it became bright red and then pulled out and immersed in water."[59]

The engraving tools discovered in Romania have round, square or rectangular cross-section, and are between 2.3 and 4.7 inches long. For most specimens, however, the size is unknown due to faulty publication. In the Carpathian Basin, engraving tools have also been found in graves with tools, such as those discovered in Kölked-Feketekapu B[60] and Kunszentmárton.[61]

9 Chisels

Davideni, Dodești (Fig. 15.1), Band (Fig. 35.9–10), Budureasca 3, Budureasca 4 (Fig. 8.10, 12), Băleni (Fig. 12.1.2), Izvoare-Bahna, Botoșana (Fig. 12.2)

Employed primarily by jewelers interested in creating recesses to be filled with *niello* or stone settings, or in relief carving, chisels were always used together with hammers.[62] Chisels were also used for carving fine details, especially in relief, and were thus different from pointed and sharper engraving tools which were used only for ornamental lines.[63]

Some cut thicker plates and metal bars, others, of smaller size, were used for piercing. Irrespective of size, such tools needed to be made of harder metal; even if the tool had to be soft and elastic, the tip was strengthened (Fig. 15.1).[64]

Chisels have been found in workshops such as those from Dodești and Budureasca 3, but also in simple settlement assemblages in Davideni, Budureasca 4, Băleni, Izvoare-Bahna, Botoșana, Lozna-Strătеni, as well as in the 7th century in Dulceanca 4.[65] There were two chisels in the grave with tools from Band (Fig. 35.9–10) – one slightly concave with beveled tip, the other with a thinner and sharper tip. Chisels have also been found in other graves with

59 Brepohl, *Theophilus*, 71.

60 Kiss, *Das awarenzeitliche Gräberfeld*, 2: 39, pl. 25. 4.

61 Rácz, *Die Goldschmiedegräber*, 178; pl. 69.6. Another engraving tool is known from the Viking-Age grave with tools from Vestly (Magnus, Mollerop, Sjovold, "Migration Period Graves," N 3, 5 (4).20).

62 Bühler, "Untersuchungen," 434–435.

63 Bühler, "Untersuchungen," 440.

64 Bühler, "Untersuchungen," 436–437.

65 Dolinescu-Ferche, "Habitats," 153; 157; 171.

tools: grave 80 in Kölked-Feketekapu B,[66] grave 10 in Hérouvillette,[67] grave 166 of Jutas,[68] Neuwied,[69] and Vestly.[70]

10 Punches

Davideni (Fig. 22.1.2), Budureasca 4, Budureasca 5 (Fig. 10.1.2)

Punches were made of steel, with a pointed tip and a rounded end, and served for making dotted-line decorations and for burnishing surfaces, as well as for polishing. The rounded tip could also be used to make relief molding on the back of the sheet, a variation of the *au repoussé* technique.[71]

On some early medieval ornaments, very fine sketching lines tracing the decoration to be engraved are still visible, and have been drawn with very sharp needle-punches.[72]

Several punches, varying in length between 4.4 and 5 inches, have been found in Davideni, as well as in Budureasca 4 and 5. Such tools are also known from graves with tools (Hérouvillette,[73] Kunszentmárton,[74] and Neuwied).[75]

11 Mandrels

Budureasca 4 (Fig. 8.6), Davideni (Fig. 21.13), Lozna-Strâteni

Mandrels are cylindrical or conical rods designed to hold together, to release, to move a piece, to perforate or to enlarge holes, and some even have pins for fastening. Two borers, each slightly longer than 3 inches, have been found in association with engraving tools in two houses of the Davideni settlement. In addition, in house 36 there was also a stone mold and a crucible, all of which suggests that that was the workshop of a jeweler (Fig. 21.13).[76] Borerers were

66 Kiss, *Das awarenzeitliche Gräberfeld*, 2: 39, pl. 25.3,5.
67 Rhé, Fettich, *Jutas und Öskü*, pl. IV.19.
68 Rhé, Fettich, *Jutas und Öskü*, pl. IV.20.
69 Böhner, "Ein fränkisches Goldschmiedegrab," 115, fig. 2.4, 5, 7.
70 Magnus, Mollerop, Sjovold, "Migration Period Graves," N 3, 5 (4).21.
71 Bühler, "Untersuchungen," 431–432.
72 Bühler, "Untersuchungen," 437.
73 Decaens et al., *Un nouveau cimetière*, 116, fig. 20.12a, 12b.
74 Rácz, *Die Goldschmiedegräber*, 178; pl. 69.26.
75 Böhner, "Ein fränkisches Goldschmiedegrab," 115, fig. 2.3.
76 Mitrea, *Așezarea de la Davideni*, 320, fig. 60.2–3; 321, fig. 61.10.

also found in Budureasca 4 (Fig. 8.6). In workshop 7 of the Lozna-Străteni settlement, a borer with square cross-section was found together with a chisel, a mold and a ladle, all of which were most likely used for the production of dress accessories.[77]

12 Tweezers

Bucharest – Soldat Ghivan Street (Fig. 13.6.2)

Jeweler tweezers have been found in house 10 of the settlement site excavated on Soldat Ghivan Street in Bucharest together with a stone mold and a ladle (Fig. 13.6.2).[78]

The tweezers were no doubt used to handle small, hot objects or to fasten together small parts of the ornament. No similar tools are so far known. However, a pair of tweezers appear among the tool pendants of the 5th-century golden chain from Şimleul Silvaniei, along with the miniature replica of a ladle.[79]

13 Bone Dies

The manufacture of dress accessories also involved bone dies. They were found in Costeşti (Iaşi County) together with fragments of bronze and silver sheet, as well as a conical bone tool that was most likely used to press the sheets into the die (Fig. 45.3).[80] The shape and decoration of the artifacts were carved into the dies: appliqués, pendants, and belt mounts.

One of the dies has a trapezoidal shape and is carved on both sides (Fig. 45.1a–b). On one of them (Fig. 45.1a) there are two star-shaped earrings with a crescent-shaped pendant, then a square probably used for making appliqués, as well as several incised lines that seem to sketch an arrow or a spear head. On the other side (Fig. 45.1b), there is a rectangular plaque with interlaced border, decorated with the scale motif (some of the scales on the edge are marked inside with small round hollows); then a rounded negative, used to make semispherical appliqués or earring beads, as well as two diamond shapes

77 Teodor, *Un centru*, 18.
78 Victor Teodorescu, "Centre meşteşugăreşti," 77; 81, fig. 3.4.
79 Capelle, *Die Miniaturkette*, 56–57.
80 Teodor, "Elemente şi influenţe bizantine," 106.

with double border and concentric circles in the middle, perhaps parts of appliqués or pendants.

The second die is rectangular, with one broken end (Fig. 45.2a–b). On one side (Fig. 45.2a) a square is carved, with a "twisted ribbon" motif on the margins and three human silhouettes in the middle, all of the same size, sporting beards and long, probably priestly garments. To the top right of the die is the stylized silhouette of a deer, turning its head with antlers backwards. The other side of the die (Fig. 45.2b) has a circular appliqué with four concentric circles, as well as a rectangle decorated with geometrical motifs: horizontal and vertical lines form rectangles, with concentric arcs in the corners and in the center.

The third die is a parallelepiped, with carvings on its four long faces, for earring pearls, appliqués, and belt buckle decorations (Fig. 44.1a–d). On one side there are four round and one rectangular appliqué with a border and a line in the middle, which divides concentric circles, arranged three on each side (Fig. 44.1a). The second side has three round and one oval carvings, as well as two incised concentric circles located between the round carvings, in the upper area (Fig. 44.1b). The third side has three round and one square carving (Fig. 44.1c), while the fourth side has three carvings, one oval and two hemispherical (Fig. 44.1d).

The small cone-shaped object of bone found together with the die, has one elongated tip and a rounded end. This may well have been a tool for pressing metal sheets into the carvings, as a metal hammer would quickly destroy the bone dies (Fig. 45.3).

Bone dies are rare, and only two other specimens are known, one for strap ends from Zimne, the other for circular mounts from Pastyrs'ke (both sites in Ukraine)[81] (see Fig. 50).

Much of the discussion about the Costești dies concerns the three human figures. These have been interpreted as representations of the Church Fathers, St. John Chrysostom, St. Gregory of Nazianz and St. Basil the Great, and in that respect the mount with such an image must have decorated a reliquary box made of organic materials, or some miniature icon.[82]

This interpretation gains more substance when one compares the die with an almost identical human figure on a silver-plated appliqué from Poland.[83] That appliqué is most likely part of a reliquary. Several gilded, copper-alloy appliqués have been found at Bojná I (Slovakia) which show the scene of the Ascension and may be dated to the 9th century. The appliqués have portraits

81 Szmoniewski, "Production," 121.

82 Szmoniewski, "Production," 123.

83 Teodor, *Romanitatea*, 32.

of Christ, the Virgin Mary, St. Peter, and a few angels. Those appliqués may have decorated the altar table, the pulpit, or a reliquary box.[84] Their iconography is without any doubt of Byzantine origin, even though they have Latin inscriptions. Perhaps most important for the purpose of the book are the striking similarities with the Costești mold in terms of the conventional representation of saints.

The deer appearing on the same side of that die from Costești is, on the other hand, an old Christian iconographic motif employed as allegory of the soul in search of God, as indicated by many frescoes and mosaics of Byzantine churches.[85]

14 Metal Patterns

During the second half of 6th century and the 7th century, the dominant technique for the production of gold, silver and bronze dress accessories was by pressing metal sheets into or onto dies.

This was both inexpensive and very simple. All known dies are made of massive billon or bronze, and had a smooth backside. The bronze dies were made of very good material. Many show very little wear, most likely because craftsmen carefully hammered the dies on their back,[86] while the other side was placed over the metal sheet, itself sitting on a soft support of wax, pitch, lead, leather, or resin.

Dies had the ornament in relief (embossed) or carved.[87] Dies are a good indication of changing fashions and techniques. While in the early 6th century casting was preferred, during the last third of that century and throughout the seventh century, pressing became prevalent. Only casting molds have been found in the Germanic world, while dies predominated in the Avar environment. Models of a S-shaped and a bow fibula decorated with chip carving have

84 Mechthild Schulze-Dörrlamm, "Zur Interpretation der vergoldeten Kupferblechreliefs aus dem grossmährischen Burgwall Bojná I (Slowakei)." In *Zwischen Byzanz und der Steppe. Archäologische und historische Studien. Festschrift für Csanád Bálint zum 70. Geburtstag*, eds. Ádám Bollók, Gergely Csiky and Tivadar Vida (Budapest: Institute of Archaeology, Research Centre for the Humanities, Hungarian Academy of Sciences, 2016), 521–529, 532.

85 Szmoniewski, "Production," 123.

86 Bühler, "Untersuchungen," 434.

87 Capelle, Vierck, "Modeln," 43.

been found in Poysdorf in a grave with tools.[88] Those models were used for obtaining half-finished blanks.[89]

14.1 *Imprinting Models*

The process of manufacturing fibulae with the help of imprinting models consists in pressing the model into a block of soft clay, with the molten metal then poured into the clay imprint acting as a casting mold.

14.1.1. A bronze model for bow fibulae with five round knobs representing stylized flower buds; the head plate has a border of dashed lines outlining a volute, and the fibula bow has two incised vertical lines. The footplate, which is only fragmentary preserved, has two smooth buttons and two vertical lines framed by a border of horizontal notched dashes (Fig. 37.2.2). The die was discovered in a grave on Felnac. It was initially claimed to be a die used to press sheet metal,[90] but since no pressed fibulae have been found, and all of them are cast, it soon became clear that it was in fact an imprinting model for casting fibulae.[91] Dan Gh. Teodor established that this model belongs to his Desa-Felnac-Vârtoape type.[92]

14.1.2. Billon model, for type bow fibulae of Werner's class I D: miniature bow fibulae with semicircular headplate, which has five round knobs, and a border made by a line that surrounds three recesses. The bow had two incised lines (Fig. 11.2.2). The footplate has the shape of a diamond, flanked by four stylized bird heads, its center marked by stylized tulip with an incised line inside (shaped as a horizontal S) and with a round appendage at the end and two profiled lines at the base. The model is a stray find from Tei, a neighborhood on the northeastern part of Bucharest.[93]

14.1.3. Billon model for bow fibulae of the Werner's class I C: bow fibula with seven round knobs on a profiled ring; the headplate has a geometric decoration that consists of curved lines intersected by straight lines, and the border is made up of two profiled lines (Fig. 42.2a–c). The bow has four straight, vertical lines, the footplate is flanked by four bird heads arranged in pairs on either side; the end of the footplate is oval with two tear-shaped holes. The tip of the footplate is broken.

---

88 Werner, *Die Langobarden*, 7.

89 Daim, Mehofer, Tobias, "Die langobardischen Schmiedegräber," 205.

90 Hampel, *Altertümer*, vol. 3: 748.

91 Teodorescu, "Centre meşteşugăreşti," 74, 79–80.

92 Dan Gh. Teodor, "Fibules byzantines des Ve - VIIe siècles dans l'espace carpato-danubiano-pontique," *Études byzantines et post-byzantines* 3 (1997), 89, fig. 9.5.

93 Teodorescu, "Centre meșteșugărești," 74. The model was initially believed to be a fibula.

The model was probably discovered along the left bank of the Danube in southern Banat, between the Nera valley and the Gura Văii. The artifact was part of the collection of Imre Pongrácz, the commander of the Honvéd garrison who controlled the passage through the Orșova harbor customs during the last third of the 19th century. The collector had drawings made of all pieces in his collection, which is how the original artifact may be reconstructed. Its appendix, now missing, had a human mask, and must have fall after the fibula was bought by the Timișoara Museum.[94]

Initially published as a fibula, the artifact was classified as a specimen of Gâmbaș-type of fibulae.[95] Dan Gh. Teodor first noted that that was in fact an imprinting model for casting bow fibulae.[96]

There is a striking resemblance between the human-mask appendix of the model and that of the splendid fibula from Coșovenii de Jos. However, in general lines, the model is much more similar to the pair of fibulae from Gâmbaș, as it has a much simplified shape and decoration, unlike specimens of Coșoveni-Vețel type with more elaborate forms and ornamentation. The ornamentation is similar not only to that of the pair of fibulae from grave III in Gâmbaș, but also of the fibula fragment from Horga (Vaslui County), or of the fibula with 5 knobs from an inhumation grave discovered in Săcuieni (Bihor County).[97]

14.1.4. Bronze imprinting model, discovered in Felnac, which used to produce animal-shaped fibulae (?):[98] it is a moving animal with its head turned to the right (Fig. 38.15). The creature has a bushy tail, but has no mane or no antlers. This is perhaps a young animal, a foal or a doe, or perhaps a dog (?). However, dogs are not common in the art of steppe nomads, whereas deer, boars, hawks, dragons, and lions are preferred,[99] while in the art of Late Antiquity birds, deer, lions, and horses are the commonest, with the latter being especially preferred during the 6th and 7th centuries.[100] Thus, it is very likely that this model represents a foal in movement, especially as there are lines on the body that may

---

94 Tănase, Mare, "Piese de port," 206, pl. VIII.

95 Nestor, Nicolăescu-Plopșor, "Die völkerwanderungszeitlichen Schatz Negrescu," pl. 9.2; Joachim Werner, "Slawische Bügelfibeln des 7. Jahrhunderts," in *Festschrift zum 75. Geburstag von Paul Reinecke am 25 September 1947*, eds. Gustav Behrens and Joachim Werner (Mainz: E. Schneider Verlag, 1950), p. 153.

96 Teodor, "Fibules," 78.

97 Nicolae Chidioșan, Zoltán Nánássy, "Un mormânt din perioada prefeudală descoperit la Săcuieni [A tomb from the pre-feudal period discovered in Săcuieni]," *Acta Musei Napocensis* 5 (1968), 518, fig. 2.

98 Rácz, *Die Goldschmiedegräber*, 89.

99 Fettich, *Das awarenzeitliche Kunstgewerbe*, 39–41.

100 Rácz, *Die Goldschmiedegräber*, 89.

suggest the harness. Analogies suggest a Byzantine origin for this type of representation, perhaps a product of a workshop in the Balkan Peninsula.[101]

14.2 *Pressing Dies with Incised Decoration*

14.2.1 Dies for Belt Fittings

Dies of this category served for strap ends, as well as double-shield, shield-shaped, and "U"-shaped belt mounts.

14.2.1.1 *Felnac-Type Dies (Fig. 37.2.3–10)*

There are three distinct dies discovered in Felnac:

a) 1. Bronze die for strap ends, with three incised lines in the upper part, two curved lines at the bottom; with two concentric circles in the center, flanked by two dashes and circles grouped by three (Fig. 37.2.4).

b) 1. Bronze dies for the belt chape, decorated as follows: two dashes followed by two circles and then three semicircles arranged in a row, in the upper part, in the middle, a group of three circles and an overlapping one, which seem to represent a flower; in the lower part is a dot flanked by two commas. The pattern is preserved broken in two.

I have elsewhere wrongly claimed that there was also a die for casting strap ends with Felnac-type decoration.[102] In reality, there is only one die broken into two pieces.[103]

2. Bronze die for secondary strap ends, decorated with three dashes in the upper area, followed by two circles, with three semicircles below; the circles are grouped in the central area in a way similar to the previous pieces, in the lower part a dot flanked by two commas (Fig. 37.2.9).

3. Bronze die for double-shield shaped mounts; a circle is incised in the upper half, the lower half is decorated with a row of three semicircles followed by four circles arranged in the shape of a flower (Fig. 37.2.7).

4. Bronze die for shield-shaped mounts; a row of three semicircles is incised in the upper half, the central area is decorated with four overlapped circles arranged in the shape of a flower (Fig. 37.2.10).

c) 1. Bronze die for belt mounts, in the upper part with a dot flanked by two horizontal lines, followed by two groups of overlapping circles in the shape of a flower, surrounded by three points and separated by dots and commas

---

101 Rácz, *Die Goldschmiedegräber*, 90.

102 Tănase, "Câteva observații," 237, 260, pl. V.4; Daniela Tănase, *Prelucrarea metalelor în lumea barbară la Dunărea Mijlocie și Inferioară în sec. VI–VII* [Metal processing in the barbarian world in the Middle and Lower Danube in the 6th–7th centuries] (Timișoara: Editura Excelsior Art, 2010), 122, 362, pl. XXII.2.3.

103 László Dömötör, "Ujabb lemezsajtoló bronzmintár Fönlakról," 65, fig. 16.

arranged in the shape of a accolade; the lower part is decorated by a dot flanked by two commas (Fig. 37.2.5).

2. Bronze die for shield-shaped mounts; in the upper part with a dot flanked by two horizontal lines, four tangent small circles in the central area (with a fifth in the center, overlapped by the others, forming a flower); the lower part is decorated by a dot flanked by two commas (Fig. 37.2.6).

The group of belt fittings named after the site on which those dies have been found, the Felnac-type decoration is also found on dies discovered in 2013 in an Early Avar age grave in Békéssámson (Hungary),[104] as well as in Stari Kostolac (ancient Viminacium, in Serbia).[105] Moreover, the same decoration appears on two dies for double shield and shield-shaped belt mounts, accidentally found somewhere in the region of Cherkasy in Right Bank Ukraine. The dies are believed to have been made in some Byzantine workshop in the Crimea.[106]

14.2.1.2 *Akalan-Type Dies Decorated with Palmettes*

1. Bronze die for strap ends, decorated with two palmettes flanking a rosette composed of radial lines inscribed in a circle (Fig. 38.1).

This artifact is now lost.

2. Bronze die for secondary strap ends; the upper part is decorated with a dot flanked by two double lines, while the palmette, which occupies almost the entire surface of the piece, is framed by dot-comma motifs (Fig. 38.2).

3. Bronze die for double shield-shaped mounts, each shield is decorated with a palmette surrounded by dots and commas (Fig. 38.4).

4. Bronze die for shield-shaped mounts, the shield is decorated with a palmette surrounded by dots and commas (Fig. 38.3).

5. Bronze die for the hole reinforcement mount; its upper part is straight-edged, the lower part is a concave, decorated with a palmette framed by lines and commas (Fig. 38.5).

This type of decoration does not appear on any other dies in the Carpathian Basin, but may be found on belt fittings. A die with palmettes is known from Ukraine.[107]

---

104 Rácz, "Ein frühmittelalterlicher Pressmodelfund," 177.

105 *Die Welt von Byzanz. Europas östliches Erbe. Glanz, Krisen und Fortleben einer tausendjährigen Kultur*, (Schriftenreihe der Archäologischen Staatssammlung) 4, ed. Ludwig Wamser (Stuttgart: Theiss Verlag, 2004), 283, no. 470.

106 Rácz, "Ein frühmittelalterlicher Pressmodelfund," 176, fig. 1.1–2; 179.

107 Rácz, *Die Goldschmiedegräber*, 35, 202.

14.2.2 Dies for Earring Pendants, Strap Ends and Belt Mounts

14.2.2.1 *Martynivka-Type Dies*

Bronze die for strap end decorated with dots and curved lines that appear to depict a human mask and an animal head; discovered in Felnac (Fig. 38.6). This piece has been lost.

This type of decoration is found on a strap end discovered in a burial assemblage of cemetery 3 in Bratei.[108] The Martynivka-type decoration also appears on dies for belt fittings and strap ends that were discovered in Adony (Hungary),[109] grave 1 in Kunszentmárton,[110] and graves 569 and 1623 in Zamárdi-Rétiföldek (Hungary).[111]

14.2.2.2 *Tarnaméra-Type Pattern*

Bronze die for strap end, the decoration of which consists of double lines in a half circle, grouped by two, inside of which are droplets arranged in a triangle; the edges of the pattern are arched; discovered in Felnac (Fig. 38.7).

Similar dies have also been discovered in Adony[112] and in grave 202 in Szekszárd-Palánk (Hungary).[113]

14.2.2.3 *Pančevo-Type Dies*

Bronze die for double-shield-shaped belt mount, discovered in Corund (Harghita County), decorated with a pearl border that frames a field of woven schematic ribbons (Fig. 38.2.2). Another die with the same motif is known from Pančevo (Serbia).[114] A variation of this type of decoration is also found on dies for belt mounts found in Gátér (Hungary).[115]

This piece is nowadays lost.

14.2.2.4 *Animal Style II Die with Dentil Decoration*

1. Bronze die for strap end, discovered in Felnac. The decoration is represented by two strings of braided ribbons representing stylized animals, with claws accentuated by the sawtooth decoration (Fig. 40.1).

---

108 Bârzu, *Ein gepidisches Denkmal*, 112; 280, pl. 2.G.6.8.

109 Garam, *Funde*, 342, pl. 91.5; 343, pl. 92.9; 346, pl. 95.3.

110 Csallány, *A Kunszentmártoni avarkori ötvösir*, pl. I.10–12, 21.

111 Rácz, *Die Goldschmiedegräber*, 197–198; pl. 75.2–6.

112 Garam, *Funde*, 356, pl. 105.7.

113 Rácz, *Die Goldschmiedegräber*, 194; pl. 75.9.

114 Csallány, *A Kunszentmártoni avarkori ötvösir*, 19, pl. VII, 7.

115 Kada, "Gátéri (Kun-Kisszállási) temető," 369, fig. 11. 3–4.

A die for belt mounts, decorated in Animal Style II with dentil decoration ("Zahnschnitt") was discovered in Kunszentmárton.[116] Further dies of the same decorative style are known from Adony[117] and an unknown location in southern Transdanubia (Hungary), which is now preserved in the Szekszárd museum.[118]

14.2.2.5 *Die for Earring Pendants and Hemispherical Appliqués*

Bronze die, discovered in Felnac, in the shape of a slightly concave stick, with two cavities for semispherical appliqués, one whole and the other fragmentary (but larger than the other) – (Fig. 39.11).

Most likely, this die was used to make bead pendants for earrings, and not just for belt or harness mount. Similar dies are known from Kunszentmárton.[119]

14.2.2.6 *Die for Rectangular Appliqués*

Bronze die, discovered in Felnac, rectangular in shape, decorated with a pearl border and concentric circles in the corners and in the center (Fig. 38.10).

14.2.2.7 *Die for Rectangular Appliqués with Arched Edges*

Bronze die, discovered in Felnac, rectangular in shape, with arched edges, three arches on one side, three on the other, decorated with lines forming loops with circles and droplets inside (Fig. 38.12). Such appliqués could also be used as headdress pieces.[120]

14.2.2.8 *Dies for Animal-Shaped Appliqués*

Several dies found in Felnac were used to make animal-shaped appliqués, such as two lions with open mouths (Fig. 38.16–17). The dies have a good analogy in Pregradnaia Stanica on the Urup (Russia), in the Caucasus region. The silver appliqué found there, however, was cast, not pressed, and, according to Csanád Bálint, it shows a lion in a typically Byzantine manner.[121] The similarity between the Felnac dies and that appliqué is striking, in terms of both the body position of the animal and the representation of the mane and the open jaws. Another die was found in a cemetery excavated in Kamunta (Russia) in

116 Csallány, *A Kunszentmártoni avarkori ötvösir*, pl. I.18.

117 Rácz, *Die Goldschmiedegräber*, 66, 68–69; pl. 2.1–2.

118 Rácz, *Die Goldschmiedegräber*, 68; pl. 78.7.

119 Rácz, *Die Goldschmiedegräber*, 84; pl. 47.4; pl. 48, 2. 4. 6–7.

120 Rácz, *Die Goldschmiedegräber*, 89.

121 Csanád Bálint, *Die Archäologie der Steppe*, ed. Falko Daim, (Vienna/Cologne: Böhlau Verlag, 1989), 27, 28. fig. 6.2.

the northern Caucasus region.[122] A third die showing a lion is known from a hoard discovered in Kuzebaevo (Russia), on the Kama River, and attributed to a craftsman from Central Asia.[123]

The Felnac die showing a lion with its head turned to the right was lost, only the left-looking lion is still preserved (Fig. 38.17).

Lion-shaped appliqués produced with such dies seem to have been used to adorn the saddle.[124] However, an almost identical image of a lion appears on a buckle plate discovered in Suuk-Su (Crimea, Ukraine), which suggests a common origin.[125]

14.2.3 Dies for Strap Ends and Harness Appliqués

14.2.3.1 *Die with Geometrical Decoration*

Bronze die for strap end, with a "twisted rope," notched border framing a field of plaited ribbons, discovered in Felnac (Fig. 40.2). This is a variation of the type of geometric decoration found on some dies for strap ends and belt mounts discovered in Kunszentmárton.[126]

This piece is nowadays lost.

Silver strap ends for the harness, identical to the Felnac die, have been found in grave 55 of the cemetery excavated in Budapest-Csepel-Háros.[127]

14.2.3.2 *Animal Style II Die with Dentil Decoration*

1. Bronze die, discovered in Felnac, for a belt or harness appliqué, cross-shaped, consisting of four circles, with a semispherical cavity, enclosing a diamond-shaped field in which smaller diamonds are carved. The diamond border is decorated with a dentil motif (Fig. 39.1).

This piece is nowadays lost.

2. Bronze die, found in Felnac, used to make trefoil-shaped appliqués for the harness; three of the arms are circular and outline a diamond-shaped field, while the fourth arm is rectangular (Fig. 40.8). The whole surface of the die is

122 Rácz, *Die Goldschmiedegräber*, 79.

123 T. I. Ostanina, O. M. Kanunnikova, V. P. Stepanov, A. B. Nikitin, *Kuzebaevskiĭ klad iuvelira VII v. kak istoricheskiĭ istochnik* [The 7th century jeweler's treasure from Kuzebaevo as a historical source] (Izhevsk: Izdatel'stvo "Udmurtiia", 2011), 174, fig. 7.5.

124 Pentru o discuție detaliată în legătură cu acest tip de reprezentare: Rácz, *Die Goldschmiedegräber*, 77–80.

125 Rácz, *Die Goldschmiedegräber*, 78, fig. 21.5; p. 79.

126 Csallány, *A Kunszentmártoni avarkori ötvösir*, pl. I, 14, 20, pl. II.20.

127 Margit Nagy, *Awarenzeitliche Gräberfelder im Stadtgebiet von Budapest*, 2 vols. (Budapest: Magyar Nemzeti Múzeum 1998), 1: 163; 2: 119, pl. 111.55.9, 11.

carved with braided ribbons decorated in Animal Style II, on which the dentil decoration appears.

14.3 *Pressing Dies with Embossed Decoration*

14.3.1 Dies for Pendants

14.3.1.1 *Die for Tear-Shaped Pendants*

Bronze die, found in Felnac, for making teardrop-shaped pendants with pearl border; the central area is provided with a setting for semi-precious or precious stones, in the same shape as the pendant (Fig. 38.8).

14.3.1.2 *Die for Seashell-Shaped Pendants*

Bronze die, found in Felnac, for making seashell-shaped pendants (Fig. 38.9). It is worth mentioning that such seashell-shaped pendants are sometimes found in female burials of the Carpathian Basin.

14.3.2 Dies for Strap Ends and Belt Mounts

14.3.2.1 *Die for a Belt Mount with Monogram and Cross Pattern*

Bronze die for a belt mount, found in Dumbrăveni (Sibiu County) (Fig. 37.1). The decoration consists of a pearl border that frames arches surrounding a cross with a diamond at its center, perhaps a monogram. This is a simple variant of the Byzantine golden belt mount with monogram and cross.[128]

14.3.2.2 *Die for Circular Mounts*

1. Bronze die, discovered in Felnac, in the shape of a flattened, truncated cone, used to make circular belt mounts (Fig. 38.13).

2. Bronze die, discovered in Felnac, in the shape of a flattened, truncated cone, used to make circular belt mounts. This is a little larger than the other dies for circular mounts, and may have been lost (Fig. 38.14).

The existence of two separate dies is based on the drawings published by József Hampel,[129] as well as the photographs published by Nándor Fettich.[130]

14.3.2.3 *Die for Pearl-Dotted Mounts*

Bronze die, discovered in Felnac, used to make pearl-dotted mounts for decorating belts or harness straps; if bent, it could have been used only as a border

128 Garam, *Funde*, 153.

129 Hampel, "Emlékek és leletek," 119, fig. 9.

130 Fettich, *Das awarenzeitliche Kunstgewerbe*, pl. V.15–16; Rácz, *Die Goldschmiedegräber*, 156. I have myself long believed in the existence of two dies, but discussed only the one that was not lost (Tănase, "Câteva observații," 257, pl. II.8; Tănase, *Prelucrarea*, 273; 363, pl. XXIII.13).

for a piece of perishable material or even metal. The pattern is rectangular, with irregular edges; half of its surface is smooth, the other half bear three hemispherical, one next to the other (Fig. 39.10).

14.3.2.4 *Die for Butterfly-Shaped Mounts*

Bronze die, found in Felnac; the shape resembles a butterfly, but the decoration, composed of geometric shapes, circles, triangles and a rectangle, suggests a stylized owl head (Fig. 38.11). This type of mount may have also been used as a headdress piece.[131]

14.3.3 Dies for Harness Mounts

14.3.3.1 *Dies for Semispherical Mounts*

These bronze dies, discovered in Felnac, were used to produce smooth semi-globular mounts for harness (Fig. 39.8–9).

Such mounts were found in grave 58 of the cemetery excavated in Mokrin (Serbia), in the Banat, not far from the Serbian-Romanian border, within a short distance from Felnac.[132]

14.3.3.2 *Die for Pearl-Dotted, Rectangular Mounts*

1. Bronze die, discovered in Felnac, used to produce square-shaped mounts with arched edges and pearls border, which frame both the piece and the geometric shapes that make up the decoration – a diamond-shaped field within four semicircles that seem to be petals of a flower – (Fig. 39.3).

The decoration of this die appears on mounts of the harness from the grave with horse skeleton (grave 34) found in Tiszavasvári–Kashalom-dűlő (Hungary).[133]

2. Bronze die, discovered in Felnac, used to produce square-shaped mounts with arched edges, that seem to be petals of a flower. The petals are made of flat semicircles that surround a diamond-shaped field bordered with pearls. The piece is broken into two, probably by those who discovered it (Fig. 39.2).

---

131 Rácz, *Die Goldschmiedegräber*, 89.

132 Aleksandar Ranisavljev, *Ranosrednovekovna nekropola kod Mokrina* [An Early Medieval Necropolis near Mokrin] (Belgrade: Srpsko Arheološko Društvo, 2007), pl. XX.14–33.

133 Gábor Lőrinczy, Zsófia Rácz, "Szabolcs-Szatmár-Bereg megye avar sírleletei II. Tiszavasvári–Kashalom-dűlő kora avar kori temetkezései [Avarian finds from Szabolcs-Szatmár-Bereg County II. Early Avarian graves from Tiszavasvári–Kashalom-dűlő]," *A Nyíregyházi Jósa András Múzeum Évkönyvei* 56 (2014), 213–214, table X.

Harness mounts decorated in the style of the Felnac die were discovered Mokrin (Serbia) in graves 19 and 69,[134] and in grave 34 of the cemetery excavated in Tiszavasvári–Kashalom-dűlő (Hungary).[135]

14.3.3.3 *Dies for Rosette-Shaped Mounts*

Three dies from Felnac have a round button each, surrounded by an array of pearls, with hatches on the edges that suggest the petals of a flower.

Two of those pieces are preserved (Fig. 39.4–5), another has meanwhile been lost (Fig. 39.6).

A similarly decorated die is known from Kunszentmárton.[136]

The fourth bronze die found in Felnac has a round button surrounded by an array of pearls; the border is formed by volutes, probably stylized acanthus leaves, while the edge of the piece is smooth (Fig. 39.7). This type of rosette is similar to the die found in Gátér;[137] the only difference is that the center button is surrounded by dashes, not pearls, while the edge is hatched. A die for rosettes of the same type of decoration was discovered in the grave "B" of Rákóczifalva-Kastélydomb cemetery (Hungary);[138] however, unlike the Felnac die, that has a smooth surface with hatched edges.

Rosette-shaped bronze mounts, decorated in a manner similar to that of the Felnac die (Fig. 39.7) are known from Mokrin (Serbia).[139]

14.3.3.4 *Die for Trefoil-Shaped Mounts*

Bronze die, found in Corund (Harghita County), consisting of three circles and a rectangle, the center of each has a button surrounded by overlapping arched lines. Between the three circles and the rectangle there are two intersecting ribbons forming the letter "X" (Fig. 38.2.1).

The piece is nowadays lost.

14.3.3.5 *Die for Trefoil-Shaped, Tasseled Mount*

1. The bronze die for trefoil-shaped mounts, discovered in Felnac, has three petals decorated with hatching that surround a flower located in the center of the piece; the fourth end of the pattern is rectangular and has three rows of grooves representing the tassels (Fig. 40.4).

---

134 Ranisavljev, *Ranosrednovekovna nekropola*, pl. VIII.5–6; pl. XXXI.7–23.

135 Lőrinczy, Rácz, "Szabolcs-Szatmár-Bereg megye avar sírleletei II," 165, fig. 5.

136 Csallány, *A Kunszentmártoni avarkori ötvösir*, pl. II.14.

137 Kada, "Gátéri (Kun-Kisszállási) temető," 369, fig. 11. 1.

138 Rácz, *Die Goldschmiedegräber*, pl. 70.3.

139 Ranisavljev, *Ranosrednovekovna nekropola kod Mokrina*, 81, fig. 37.

A similar die, but with less decoration, is known from Gátér.[140]

2. Bronze die, discovered in Felnac, with the three semi-spherical petals surrounding a fourth hemisphere; all are flat. The fourth end of the piece is rectangular, with two oval, vertical cavities, in which beads are stacked, and with edge hatching that imitate tassels (Fig. 40.5).

An almost identical die was discovered in Kunszentmárton.[141] The only difference is the absence of oval cavities, while the hatches are not straight, but curved at their ends.

14.3.3.6 *Die for Rectangular, Tasseled Mounts*

1. Bronze, rectangular die, discovered in Felnac, ornamented with a network of diamonds that have small circles in their centers; at one end the piece has grooves that imitate tassels (Fig. 40.7).

2. Bronze, rectangular die, discovered in Felnac, flat, at one end has grooves that imitate tassels (Fig. 40.6).

This piece is identical to a die discovered in Kunszentmárton.[142]

14.3.3.7 *Die for Flat Strap Ends*

Bronze die, uncovered in Felnac, without decoration, but with a smooth surface. This die was used to make strap ends for the harness, although it could not be ruled out that it may also have been used to produce strap ends for the belt (Fig. 40.3).

A die of this type was also discovered in the grave "B" of the Rákóczifalva-Kastélydomb (Hungary) cemetery.[143]

15 Ladles

Melting and casting were not possible without the use of instruments allowing the liquid metal to be poured into crucibles or molds. Clay ladles, who sometimes have traces of the molten metal on the inside, as well as metal ladles, possibly used for the same purpose, are known especially from settlement sites.

---

140 Kada, "Gátéri (Kun-Kisszállási) temető," 369, fig. 11. 2.

141 Csallány, *A Kunszentmártoni avarkori ötvösir*, pl. II.2.

142 Csallány, *A Kunszentmártoni avarkori ötvösir*, pl. II.1.

143 Rácz, *Die Goldschmiedegräber*, pl. 70.2.

15.1 *Metal Ladles*

A round, spoon-shaped tool, similar to a frying pan, was found in Bucharest-Tei (Fig. 11.2.3). Even if the piece has no traces of molten metal, it may well have been designed as a casting tool. Another metal spoon was found in Dulceanca, but the excavator did not believe it to be a metalworking instrument. In Târgşor (Prahova County),[144] a tongue-shaped iron tool was found, which had traces of lead, a clear indication of its use in metalworking. The shape of the Târgşor tool is similar to that of the spoon-shaped pendant on the gold chain from the Şimleul Silvaniei 1 hoard. That narrow spoon is believed to have been used for melting glass.[145] Since the traces on the Târgşor instrument are of lead, it must have been used for melting lead.

15.2 *Clay Ladles*

Clay ladles have round or oval bowls, sometimes with pourer spout, as well as thick, flattened or round, but hollow shafts, often with traces of molten metal. A ladle with pourer spout is known from Lazuri (Satu Mare County; Fig. 4.2), while that from Bratei 2 has an oval bowl (Fig. 3.11).[146] Oval bowls may also be recognized on the ladles found in Botoşana (Fig. 17.1.4), Izvoare-Bahna (Fig. 7.4.6), Bucharest-Dămăroaia and Bucharest-Soldat Ghivan Nicolae Street (Fig. 13.6.3), as well as Gropşani (Fig. 7.4.5) and Govora (Fig. 7.1). By contrast, the bowl of the ladles from Davideni (Fig. 22.9), Dodeşti (Fig. 15.8), Lozna-Străteni (Fig. 29.1.17), Dulceanca IV (Fig. 14.2.13), and Budureasca 4 (Fig. 8.2) is round and shallow.

It is worth mentioning that the Dodeşti ladle was found along with some tools and copper-alloy sheet suggesting the local production of cast jewelry.[147] The ladles from Lozna-Străteni were also associated with clay crucibles, as well as clay and stone molds.[148] Metalworking tools were also found in the assemblage from Bucharest-Soldat Ghivan Nicolae Street which included a ladle.[149] Many clay ladles, both whole and fragmentary have been found in Dulceanca IV, and they had traces of slag and intense heating.[150] Although no other indications exist, this cluster of ladle finds strongly an intense metalworking activity.

144 Victor Teodorescu, "Centre meşteşugăreşti," 85, fig. 6.4.

145 Capelle, *Die Miniaturkette*, 57.

146 Zaharia, "La station nº 2 de Bratei," 302.

147 Teodor, *Continuitatea*, 24–25.

148 Workshop house no. 7: Teodor, *Un centru*, 18; workshop house no. 27: Teodor, *Un centru*, 28–29; dwelling no. 37: Teodor, *Un centru*, 33–34.

149 Dolinescu-Ferche, Constantiniu, "Un établissement," 293.

150 Dolinescu-Ferche, "Habitats," 167, fig. 31.8; 168, fig. 32.27; 169, fig. 33. 13, 31.

It is worth mentioning that the ladles with pourer spout from Lazuri and Bratei are similar to that from Bernashivka (Ukraine). Conversely, the ladles with oval bowls Poian, Bucharest-Soldat Ghivan Nicolae Street and Budureasca have good analogies in Cracow-Nowa Huta (Poland), Kadaň (Czech Republic), and Zimne (Ukraine).[151]

16 Crucibles

Commonly found in settlements, but also in graves, clay crucibles are conical, bag-shaped, globular cups, sometimes in the shape of truncated cones, but always of relatively small size (no more than four inches high). Such vessels for pouring molten metal were handled either directly by hand or with pliers.

That the vessels were employed in obtaining alloys and amalgams for jewelry results from the analysis of occasional traces of metal, such as those of silver and lead on the crucible found in a grave in Schönebeck (Germany).[152] Chemical analyses of ladles dated to the 8th century and found in Bohemia resulted in similar conclusions. For example, the ladle found in Věrovany was used to cast tin and lead, while that found in Pavlov was employed for melting bronze and gold. Moreover, a piece of lead with traces of gold was found in Pavlov, still preserving the shape of the ladle's bowl.[153]

16.1 *Cup-Shaped Crucibles*

There were crucibles in Botoșana as well (Fig. 12.3.2), one in the shape of a truncated cone with a profiled bottom. The crucible from Budureasca 4 is a small vessel with slightly flared lip, most likely used to pour molten metal.[154] Cup-shaped crucibles (bitronconical, conical, cylindrical, flat-bottomed or with profiled stems) have also been found in Suceava-Șipot (Fig. 18.1.1; Fig. 19.2.8, Fig. 19.2.8–9)[155] and Lozna-Străteni (Fig. 24.3; Fig. 26.2.14, Fig. 27.2.15; Fig. 28.1.15–16; Fig. 29.1.16).[156]

---

151 Ewa Kubica-Kabacińska, Bartlomiej Szymon Szmoniewski, "Shank Ladle from an Early Medieval Settlement in Kraków-Nowa Huta-Mogila, Site 1." *Materiały Archeologiczne Nowej Huty* 23 (2002), 76, fig. 2; 77, fig. 3.1–3.

152 Schmidt, *Die späte Völkerwanderungszeit*, 199, pl. 11.4b.

153 Jelinková, Šrein, Šťastný, "Doklady," pp. 69–89.

154 Teodorescu, Peneș, "Matricea de incidență," 46, fig. 21.17.

155 Teodor, *Așezarea medievală*, 124, fig. 32.2, 4–7.

156 Teodor, *Un centru*, 125, fig. 42.3–6, 9–10, 12–13.

16.2 *Round-Rimmed Crucibles with Rounded Bottoms*

Round-rimmed crucibles with convex bottoms were discovered in Bucharest-Casa Armatei (Fig. 13.2), Budureasca 9,[157] Botoşana (Fig. 12.3.2), and Lozna-Strătenі (Fig. 26.1.10, Fig. 27.1.1).[158] Fragments of similar crucibles are also known from Târgşor.[159]

Such crucibles have good analogies elsewhere in Europe, for example in Ditzingen (Germany),[160] as well as in two graves with tools from Wallerstädten[161] and Neuwied,[162] both dated to the 7th century.

16.3 *Crucibles with Trefoil-Shaped Openings and Rounded Bottoms*

Such crucibles were discovered in Bucharest-Băneasa (Fig. 13.1) and Sărata Monteoru (Fig. 6.4).

The Băneasa crucible, in the form of a bowl with a trefoil-shaped mouth, is only a little more than an inch long, but its mouts is two times larger.[163] Another crucible of the same type is known from Bucharest-Tei.[164] By contrast, the Sărata Monteoru crucibles are much taller (over two inches). A round-bottomed crucible with trefoil-shaped mouth was discovered in Budureasca 4.[165]

16.4 *Crucibles with Rounded Bottoms and Pouring Spouts*

A round bottomed crucible, similar to type 16.2, was found in Băleni (Dâmboviţa County), but its opening has a pouring spout (Fig. 12.1.7). Also included in this category is a rounded bottom crucible with triangular opening with rounded corners, one of which may have served as pouring spout (Fig. 28.2.1). That crucible was discovered in Lozna-Strătenі.[166]

Crucibles used by jewelers were typically small, with relatively thin walls. Traces of, silver, lead, and copper are commonly found inside.[167] So far, no crucible with metal traces is so far known from Romania. There can be no doubt that the crucibles from Budureasca, Bucharest-Băneasa, and Sărata Monteoru

---

157 Teodorescu, Peneş, "Matricea de incidenţă," 46, fig. 21.20.

158 Teodor, *Un centru*, 125, fig. 42.1.

159 Teodorescu, "Centre meşteşugăreşti," 75, footnote 11.

160 Helmut Roth, "Beobachtungen an merowingerzeitlichen Gußtiegeln," *Frühmittelalterliche Studien* 11 (1979), 87, fig. 1.1.

161 Shnellenkamp 1932, 63–67.

162 Böhner, "Ein fränkisches Goldschmiedegrab aus dem Neuwieder Becken." *Reinische Vorzeit in Wort und Bild* 2 (1939), 113.

163 Constantiniu, "Elemente romano-bizantine," 673.

164 Teodorescu, "Centre meşteşugăreşti," 96.

165 Teodorescu, Peneş 1984, "Matricea de incidenţă," 46, fig. 21.18.

166 Teodor, *Un centru*, 125, fig. 42.14.

167 Roth, "Beobachtungen," 85–87.

were jeweler's tools, but the same is also true for the other finds, especially for those discovered in dwellings that may have at the same time been workshops. As a matter of fact, most crucibles known from Romania are settlement finds. Only the crucibles from Sărata Monteoru are cemetery finds, as all eight of them, poorly fired, have been discovered in the cremation grave 14/1952.[168] The crucibles may have been deposited with the bones of a craftsman who employed such pieces in his everyday work.

The deposition of crucibles in graves is known from other parts of Europe as well. For example, crucibles have been found in graves with tools in Neuwied, Schönebeck and Wallerstädten, but also in cemeteries attributed to the Balts and to the Finns in Russia.

17 Clay Molds

Clay molds were used to cast metal pieces after an imprinting die, or even the object to be copied, was pressed into the lump of clay. In those clay forms, which thus became molds, the desired pieces were then cast,[169] although because of the drying of the clay form the resulting cast was typically smaller than the original.

17.1 *Molds for Earrings, Beads and Mounts*

The brick-red mold discovered in Bucharest-Tei is a circular concavity with spiralic lines around it, stylized acanthus leaves, and a bead-like appendage in the shape of a melon pip (Fig. 23.2.1). Dimensions: 6.1×4.1–3.4×2.1 cm.

Initially, that mold was interpreted as used for casting earring pendants.[170] In reality, it served for casting two types of pieces, namely beads and circular mounts for the harness, since the decoration of the stylized acanthus leaves appears only on harness decorations.[171]

A clay mold with the negative of a crescent-shaped earring was discovered in Lozna-Străteni (Fig. 29.1.18).[172] Three other fragmentary molds of clay are known from the same site and were used for casting beads and wires (Fig. 25.10;

---

168 Nestor et al., "Şantierul Sărata-Monteoru," 85, fig. 16.

169 Teodor, *Meşteşugurile*, 31.

170 Teodorescu, "Centre meşteşugăreşti," 80, 87, 95.

171 Margit Nagy, "Ornamenta Avarica I. Az avar kori ornamentika geometrikus elemei [Geometric elements of Avar Period ornamentation]," *A Móra Ferenc Múzeum Évkönyve, Studia Archaeologica* 4 (1998), 390.

172 Teodor, *Meşteşugurile*, 31; Teodor, "Tipare," 164–165, 172, fig. 7.1–2, 6–7; Teodor, *Un centru*, 124, fig. 41.1.

Fig. 26.1.11; Fig. 27.3.6; Fig. 29.1.15). Finally a clay mold served for casting tubular beads as well as rectangular mounts (?) (Fig. 26.2.13).[173]

A clay mold for making triangular pendants for earrings or necklaces (?) was discovered in Traian (Neamţ County; Fig. 23.2).[174] The closest analogy is a stone mold for casting bell-shaped pendants that was found in house 36 of Bernashivka, a site dated to the 6th century[175] (Fig. 47.8). The pendants produced with the Traian mold are similar to pyramidal pendants with granulated ornament, which are typical for early Byzantine earrings. Such earrings were widely imitated inside the Carpathian Basin during the late 6th and early 7th century, and have been found in Avar-age burial.[176] In other words, the triangular pendant on the Traian mold may well have been an imitation of an imitation.

A clay mold for conical mounts has been found in Budureasca 4 (Fig. 8.1), and has good analogies made of stone in D'yakovo (Russia)[177] and Bernashivka[178] (Fig. 47.2).

17.2 *Mold for Pendants*

The ceramic mold from Străulești-Lunca (Bucharest) was used for making crosses with equal arms, slightly widened at the ends, with a smooth surface. The mold had three runners (Fig. 13.4)[179] and was quite worn, which suggests repeated use.[180] Dimensions: 4.8×2.7×1.5 cm.

173 Teodor, *Un centru*, 124, fig. 41.3.

174 Hânceanu, "Două piese," 131, pl. 2.1–2.

175 Vynokur, "Ein Goldschmiede-Fundkomplex," 226 (end of the 5th century–beginning of the 6th century); Michel Kazanski, *Les Slaves. Les origines (Ier - VIIe siècle après J.-C.)* (Paris: Éd. Errance, 1999), 94 (end of the 6th century).

176 Garam, *Funde*, 261, pl. 10.8–9; Ranisavljev, *Ranosrednovekovna nekropola*, 93, fig. 62–64; Csilla Balogh, "Az avar kori gúlacsüngős fülbevalók [The Avar period pyramidal earrings pendants]," *Kuny Domokos Múzeum Közleményei* 20 (2014), 149, pl. 4.

177 Nikolaj Aleksandrovich Krenke, E. Iu. Tavlintseva, "Liteĭnye formy D'iakova gorodishcha [The stone molds from D'yakovo city]," *Rossijskaia Arkheologiia* 4 (2002), 97, fig. 7/4.

178 Ion S. Vynokur, *Slov'ianski iuveliry Podnistrov'ia. Za materialai doslidzhen Bernashivskoho kompleksu serediny I tys.n.e.* [Slavic Jewels of the Dniester. According to the research of the Bernashivskoho complex in the middle of the 1st millennium AD] (Oium: Kamyanets Podil'sky, 1997), 63, fig. 21; 94, fig. 41.

179 Victor Teodorescu, "Centre meșteșugărești," 95.

180 Constantiniu, "Elemente romano-bizantine," 675.

18 Stone Molds

Limestone, sandstone and marl were used for making molds used to cast dress accessories: earrings, pendants, mounts, and buckles. Only settlement finds are known so far in Romania, but stone molds have been found in burial assemblages, such as the Avar-age graves in Vác-Kavicsbánya (Fig. 49.8) and Szeged-Bilisics (Fig. 49.7), both in Hungary (see subchapter XII.2 and Fig. 50).

Although some molds were used for several types of ornaments, a typology may be obtained by looking at the most important pattern on each mold (Fig. 52). [**insert fig. 52 here**]

18.1 *Molds for Earring Accessories*

Molds for casting earring components such as granular, filiform, flower-shaped and horseshoe-shaped pendants are known from several settlements excavated in Moldavia and Walachia. It is possible that some of those pendants were worn on necklaces, while cast beads and wires were minute details of jewelry ornamentation.

18.1.1. A bivalve mold of marl, discovered in Ştefan cel Mare-Gutinaş has on one side omega-shaped fastener eyelets and rosette-shaped ornaments, and beaded wires on the other side (Fig. 23.1.2). An iron omega-shaped fastener eyelet, similar to that obtained with the Ştefan cel Mare-Gutinaş mold is known from grave 8 of the cemetery excavated at 12, Pusztadombi Street in Budapest.[181]

18.1.1.1. On one side of the mold made of fine white limestone and discovered in Bucharest-Soldat Ghivan Nicolae Street there are rosettes, a pattern with two loops, and another of filiform shape with a knot. On the other side, there are just four simple filiform elements (Fig. 13.6.5).

18.1.1.2. The stone mold discovered in Coroteni (Vrancea County) was used for casting circular and rosette-shaped earring accessories. The mold has four runners (Fig. 5.4).

18.1.1.3. The stone mold found in Dolheştii Mari (Suceava County) was used to cast rosette-shaped elements, as well as beads (Fig. 44.3).

18.1.1.4. The fragmentary, marl mold from Davideni was employed for casting wires and diamonds with beads in the upper and the lower parts. The mold has a runner on its upper side (Fig. 22.1.4).

18.1.1.5. The mold made of green, soft stone that was found in Dodeşti has three cavities for beads, one runner at the top, while the lower part is broken (Fig. 15.9).

181 Nagy, *Awarenzeitliche Gräberfelder*, 1: 27; 2: 40, pl. 32.8.2.

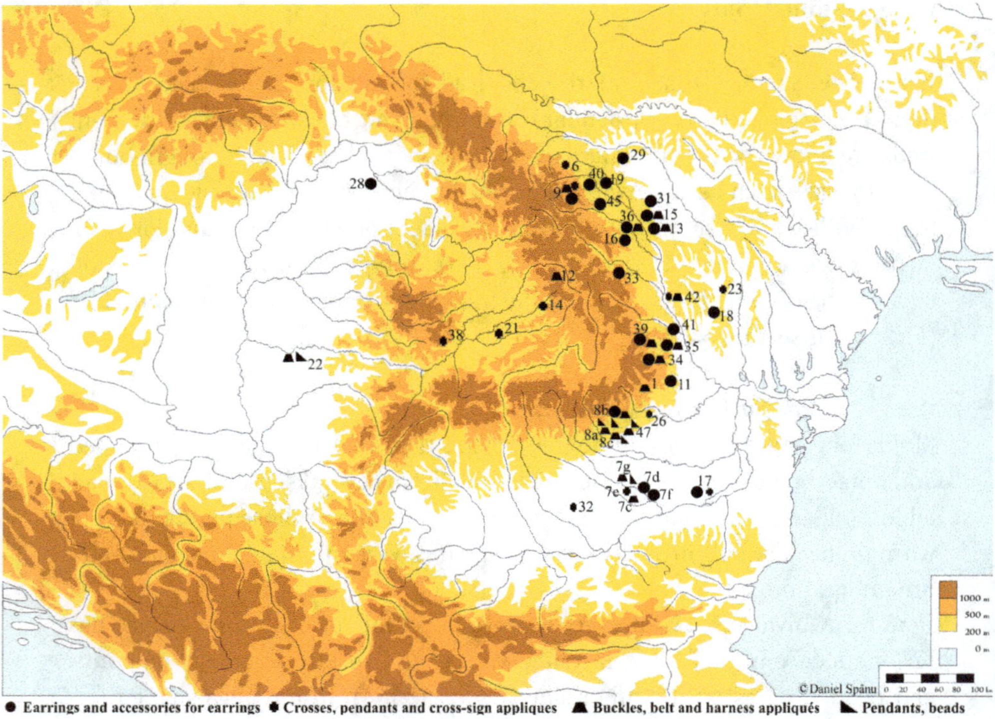

FIGURE 52 **Types of pieces made with molds and dies** (for numbering see Fig. 1) – **a. earrings and accessories for earrings:** Bucharest-str. Soldat Ghivan no. 10 (Bucharest); Bucharest-Străulești-Măicănești (Bucharest); Coroteni (Slobozia Bradului commune, Vrancea co.); Costești (Iași co.); Cucuteni (Iași co.); Davideni (Neamț co.); Dichiseni (Călărași co.); Dodești (Vaslui co.); Dolheștii Mari (Suceava co.); Lozna (Dersca commune, Botoșani co.); Moțca (Iași co.); Onești (Bacău co.); Poienița (Vrancea co.); Răcoasa (Vrancea co.); Rădeni (Păstrăveni commune, Neamț co.); Soveja (Vrancea co.); Ștefan cel Mare (Gutinaș village, Ștefan cel Mare commune, Bacău co.); Traian (Neamț co.) – **b. crosses, pendants and cross-sign appliqués:** Botoșana (Suceava co.); Bucharest-Străulești-Lunca (Bucharest); Cacica (Suceava co.); Cristuru Secuiesc (Harghita co.); Dichiseni (Călărași co.); Dumbrăveni (Sibiu co.); Giurcani (Vaslui co.); Izvorul Dulce (Merei commune, Buzău co.); Olteni (Dobrogostea village, Olteni commune, Teleorman co.); Sânmiclăuș (Șona commune, Alba co.); Traian (Bacău co.) – **c. buckles, belt and harness appliqués:** Aldeni (Buzău co.); Bucharest-Dămăroaia (Bucharest); Budureasca 3 (Prahova co.); Budureasca 5 (Prahova co.); Cacica (Suceava co.); Corund (Harghita co.); Costești (Arad co.); Cucuteni (Iași co.); Felnac (Arad co.); Poienița (Vrancea co.); Răcoasa (Vrancea co.); Rădeni (Păstrăveni commune, Neamț co.); Soveja (Vrancea co.); Traian (Bacău co.); Vadu Săpat (Prahova co.) – **d. pendants, beads**: Bucharest-Tei (Bucharest); Budureasca 3 (Prahova co.); Budureasca 4 (Prahova co.); Felnac (Arad co.); Vadu Săpat (Prahova co.)

18.1.1.6. The stone mold found in a refuse pit (G. T./1967) in Budureasca 4 was used to cast wires with bead-shaped endings (on one side), as well as ornaments with two loops each (on the other side). The mold has runners at both ends (Fig. 9.4).

18.1.1.7. The mold made of fine, fissile sandstone, and discovered in Străulești-Măicănești (Bucharest) was used for casting ornaments with beads (Fig. 13.5). The mold was found in a house dated to the 4th century on the basis of the associated, ceramic assemblage. However, the striking analogy with the Budureasca mold has encouraged Victor Teodorescu to re-date the mold (and the house) to the 6th century. At any rate, the mold is monovalve (one face destroyed in the past) and with two runners at each end.[182]

18.1.1.8. The mold discovered in Moțca (Iași County) is bivalve, of rectangular shape. On one side there are two grooved loops, from which two channels are drawn to a runner, the other face has a disc, and a row of three beads with notched edges. The left-hand bead is marked with a small channel, the right one has a dash outwards, and the left one has a large channel (Fig. 2.2).

18.1.2. A stone mold discovered in Budureasca 4 was used to cast ornaments with beaded triangular pendants, as well as ornaments with three loops at the end of each of which there are beaded rectangular pendants (Fig. 9.1).

18.1.2.1. A sandstone, bivalve mold was discovered in Cristuru Secuiesc (Harghita County), and was used to cast beaded "bells" and cross-shaped pendants with attachment rings. The mold has runners on both ends (Fig. 5.1).

18.1.3. A stone mold from Budureasca 4, has carvings for four little flowers, a horseshoe-shaped ornament with attachment ring, and another separate ring (Fig. 9.2).

18.2 *Molds for Casting Cross-Shaped Pendants and Mounts*

Molds for cross-shaped pendants are known from settlement sites in Transylvania, Moldavia, and Walachia.

18.2.1.1. A stone mold discovered in Botoșana has a carved, equal-armed cross on one side, with two runners. On the other side, there are only beads, and on the third side, there is a channel with two beads (Fig. 17.2.2).

18.2.1.2. The mold found in Olteni (Teleorman County) is made of light-brown, fine sandstone. It has been broken in the past. One face is carved with the shape of an earring, consisting of two loops and a group of six small, conical hollows, used for casting the beads. The other face bears the carving of a cross with the vertical arm slightly longer than the horizontal one; the surface of the cross is ornamented with two or three strings of slightly embossed

182 Victor Teodorescu, "Centre meșteșugărești," 95.

squares, separated by thin lines; in the middle, the cross has a round recess that was meant to receive precious stones or glass.[183] Both faces are provided with runners (Fig. 2.3).

18.2.1.3. The mold from Cacica (Suceava County) is bivalve, with three rectangular mounts decorated with notches on one face, and two crosses with equal, trapezoidal arms (Fig. 5.3). The mold was initially dated between the 16th and the 18th century,[184] but similar crosses are known from Central and Eastern Europe, all of which have been dated to the 7th century. This, of course, may also be the date for the notched mounts and the other appliqués cast with this mold.[185]

18.2.2. A brick-red stone mold discovered in Giurcani (Vaslui County) was used to cast crosses with equal, trapezoidal arms; it has a top runner and an incised line along the length of the mold face, possibly used to cast some metal wire (Fig. 7.2).

18.2.3. The mold discovered in Izvorul Dulce (Buzău County) is made of limestone. On one face a cross was carved, with equal arms and an attachment ring. On the ring arm there is an "X", on the opposite arm two triangles, two horizontal lines and a row of vertical dashes, and on the left and the right arms there are three points arranged in the shape of a triangle. The mold has three runners (Fig. 7.2).

18.2.4. A bivalve mold was discovered in Dichiseni. One face is carved with simple patterns for crosses, the other face with two crosses that seem attached to an earring lunule and a rectangular mount. A cross is inscribed in a circular appliqué with a notched ornament, perhaps an earring disc. On the same side there is a round pendant ornamented with curved lines, two square mounts with notched lines and a triangular ornamented with round holes (Fig. 44.2).

18.3 *Molds for Pendants*

18.3.1 Mold for Triangular Pendants

Stone mold discovered in the sunken-floored building 5 in Budureasca 3, with three circles arranged in the shape of a triangle, linked by a notched line; three beads are inscribed within the triangle; the mold has a large runner (Fig. 11.1.2). Good analogies for this mold are known from a metal mold found in Gigen (ancient Oescus, in Bulgaria), in Adamclisi (ancient Tropaeum Traiani,

183 Preda, "Tipar," 513–514.

184 Mugur Andronic, "Evoluția habitatului uman în bazinul hidrografic Soloneț din paleolitic până la sfârșitul secolului al XVIII-lea [The evolution of the human habitat in the Soloneț river basin from the Paleolithic to the end of the 18th century]," *Suceava. Anuarul Muzeului Național al Bucovinei* 22–23 (1995–1996) (1997), 65.

185 Măgureanu, Ciupercă, "The 6th–8th Centuries Metallurgical Activity," 296–297.

Romania),[186] in Bernashivka (Ukraine),[187] and in Ladoga (Russia).[188] Of all those finds, the mold from Adamclisi may be dated with some precision to the late 6th and early 7th century, on the basis of the finds associated with the latest stratigraphic level on the site (VI A).[189]

18.3.2 Molds for Beads in the Shape of Melon Pips, and for Pendants

The stone mold discovered in Budureasca 4 was used to make round beads with three incisions, in the shape of melon pips, probably used as components of some other ornaments (Fig. 9.3).

The stone mold from Vadu Săpat (Fig. 43.2) is rectangular, carved with the pattern of a pendant made of three melon-pip beads with a small button at the top. Beads of that could also be made with the clay mold from Bucharest-Tei, which seems to point to a regionally preferred type of ornament in the central part of Walachia.

18.3.3 Mold for Casting Pendants

The fragmentary mold discovered in the sunken-floored house 6 in Budureasca 3 is rectangular, and made of soft, gray-yellowish stone. The mold is carved with a pattern depicting a shape similar to a wavy blade dagger. It was probably used to make pendants, perhaps also amulets (Fig. 11.1.4). The mold has one runner.

18.4 *Molds for Belt Buckles and Mounts*

18.4.1. The stone, monovalve single-runner mold, discovered in Bucharest-Dămăroaia, has on one side the pattern of an oval buckle with rectangular plate, with open work decoration. The mold has a lateral runner (Fig. 13.3). Stone molds for similar belt buckles but also for mounts were discovered in Bernashivka[190] (Fig. 47.3).

18.4.2. The stone mold from Traian was used to make rectangular mounts decorated with spiral twisted fronds, and crosses with the rounded arm ends, ornamented with concentric circles inside. Concentric circles complement also the decoration of the fronds that have the ends finished with two acanthus

186 Barnea et al., *Tropaeum Traiani*, 218, fig. 169.10.14.

187 Vynokur, "Ein Goldschmiede-Fundkomplex," 217, fig. 6.1.

188 Olga A. Shcheglova, "Svintsovo-olobiannye ukrasheniia VIII–X vv. na severo-zapade vostochnoĭ Evropy [Lead-tin genre jewelry 8th–10th centuries in the northwest of Eastern Europe]," in *Ladoga i ee sosedi v epokhi srednevekov'ja*, ed. Anatolii N. Kirpichnikov (Sankt-Petersburg: Institut istorii material'noi kul'tury RAN, 2002), fig. 2/16.

189 Barnea et al., *Tropaeum Traiani*, 191, no. 10.14, fig. 169.

190 Vynokur, *Slov'ianski iuveliry*, 54, fig. 16; 81, fig. 33.

leaves each. The mold has a runner on its upper part, and two holes, possibly to be mounted onto a base (Fig. 23.3).

18.4.3.1. The sandstone, bivalve mold discovered in Rădeni (Neamţ County), has on one side three carved rosettes and a circular mount decorated with concentric circles, as well as two rectangular mounts and a fragment of a third, also rectangular. All patterns are decorated with notched lines, just like those on the Soveja mold (see below). On the other face there are two mounts, a rectangular one, ornamented with notches, just like the others, and a square one decorated with three intersecting lines (Fig. 6.1).

18.4.3.2. On one side of the bivalve stone mold discovered in Soveja (Vrancea County) there is a disk circumscribing nine beads arranged in the shape of a flower, and two rectangular mounts that have borders of notched lines that frame rectangular fields decorated with lines. The other side is carved with a rosette, a disk with a round hollow in the middle, a rectangular appliqué similar to the ones on the first face, as well as a mount in the shape of an oak leaf decorated with notched lines depicting the veins (Fig. 6.3).

18.4.3.3. The bivalve stone mold from Poieniţa (Vrancea County) has on one side two rectangular mounts, and on the other a circular mount with a rosette-like decoration, a rectangular mount, with one end outlined by two parallel lines, inscribed in a rectangle, as well as two less identifiable patterns: a stylized flower and four beads bordered by an arched line (Fig. 2.5).

18.4.3.4. The stone, bivalve mold from Răcoasa has a rectangular mount on one side, has a notched double decoration that encloses a rectangle in which three squares are inscribed, and a mount in the shape of a flower with four petals with the beaded border both in the middle and on each petal, on which a central bead is placed. On the other side there is a small circular channel; this might have been used to make open rings used as links for pendants or earrings. The mold has one runner (Fig. 2.6).

18.4.3.5. The monovalve, stone mold from Aldeni (Buzău County), on which are embossed patterns for pressing metal sheets, which could also be used as imprinting die for clay casting molds. On the mold two rectangular appliqués are carved, with notched borders, as well as two rosettes (Fig. 42.1).

18.4.3.6. The stone, bivalve mold from Cucuteni has on one side two rectangular mounts with notched borders framing rectangular fields decorated with incisions, a triangular mount decorated with triangular notches on the border and in the middle, as well as two rosettes inscribed in a circle. On the second face there are three rectangular mounts of the same type as those on the opposite side, as well as an ornamental figure with notched lines, consisting of two rosettes flanking an ovoid shape with pointed ends (Fig. 5.5).

18.4.3.7. A rectangular mold made of soft, gray-yellowish stone was found in the sunken-floored building 5 in Budureasca 5, and on it a filiform notched ornament was carved, with a pin at the end that reaches up to the runners (Fig. 10.1.1). The mold was used to cast wires for jewelry or for tubular beads and has a good analogy in a late 7th- and early 8th-century burial assemblage from Vác-Kavicsbánya.[191] A fragmentary mold for casting triple wires was also found in Zimne (Ukraine) and dated to the 6th–7th century.[192]

18.4.3.8. A bivalve mold made of flint and discovered in Vadu Săpat is carved on one side with patterns for rectangular belt mounts, with edges of notches and beads, decorated with volutes and geometric motifs, as well as for hemispherical mounts and for melon-pip pendants. On the other side there are carved patterns for rectangular mounts, with beaded edges, decorated with notches, for rosette-shaped mounts with geometrical and beaded decoration, as well as for heart-shaped mounts with beaded borders (Fig. 43.2).[193] Similar rosette-shaped mounts were made with the molds discovered in Lummelunda, Salem, and Igelsta in Sweden,[194] Saetrang in Norway,[195] and Gutenstein in Germany.[196] Those rosettes with bead crowns were fashionable in the 7th century.[197]

18.5 *Patterns Preserved in Fragmentary Form*

There are several settlement finds of fragmentary stone molds. The fragments are too small for the identification of the patterns. That is the case of the mold from Lozna-Străteni (Fig. 29.2), which is rectangular and has two orifices, one cylindrical and the other spherical, on both polished surfaces, intended for the casting ornaments of quite small size.[198] Difficult to assess are also the mold finds from Dulceanca I (Fig. 14.1.15, 20), Dodești (Fig. 15.10), and Șirna (Fig. 6.5.1–2). The finds of Davideni (Fig. 20.10), Onești (Bacău County; Fig. 2.4), and Botoșana (Fig. 12.4.4) may have been used for making beads for earrings or filiform ornaments (see one of the molds from Davideni, Fig. 21.11).

191 Tettamanti, *Das awarenzeitliche Gräberfeld*, 32, pl. 5, pl. 39.

192 Viktor Vitol'dovič Aulich, *Zimnivs'ke gorodishche – slov'jans'ka pam'jatka VI–VII st. n. e. v. Zachidnij Volynii* [Zimne settlement – Slavic monument 6th–7th AD in the Volyn region]. (Kiev: Naukova dumka, 1972), 74, no. 2, pl. XV/1.

193 Măgureanu, Ciupercă, "The 6th–8th Centuries Metallurgical Activity," 311, fig. 3.

194 Capelle, Vierck, "Modeln," 49, fig. 3.1–2, 5.

195 Capelle, Vierck, "Modeln," 49, fig. 3.3.

196 Capelle, Vierck, "Modeln," 49, fig. 3.4.

197 Capelle, Vierck, "Modeln," 48.

198 Teodor, "Elemente și influențe bizantine," 101.

CHAPTER 7

The Ornamentation of the Dies and of Contemporaneous Dress Accessories

In burial and settlement assemblages in the Carpathian Basin and in the regions to the east and to the south from the Carpathian Mountains, archaeologists have found dress accessories undoubtedly of Byzantine origin, but also local products. The latter are often the result of blending several ornamental styles of Byzantine and Germanic origin with those most typical for the steppe lands of Eastern Europe. In fact, a clear-cut classification of ornamental styles and decorative motifs in those regions during the 6th and 7th centuries is very difficult, precisely because of that mixture.

Dies were most likely made in the Empire, even when their decorative motifs are not of Byzantine origin. By contrast, stone, clay or bone molds are of undoubtedly local production, in that they were made by craftsmen outside the Empire, whether or not the craftsmen themselves were Byzantine. The stone mold found in Adamclisi (ancient Tropaeum Traiani, Constanța County) served for the production of dress accessories most typical for the forest-steppe region, and not for Byzantium. It is therefore quite possible that the mold in question was made in, and brought from the Middle Dnieper region.[1]

1 Ornamental Styles and Motifs of Byzantine Origin

The ornamental composition as well as the decorative motifs on many dress accessories discovered in the lands north of the Danube are of Byzantine origin, the result of a clear and constant influence of the Byzantine civilization upon *barbaricum*. Most conspicuous among motifs of undoubtedly Byzantine origin are palmettes, the dot-comma motif, geometric motifs, monograms in the form of rosettes, braids, concentric circles or circle-with-dot motifs – all in various combinations that have invited a typological approach.

1 Bartłomiej Sz. Szmoniewski, "Un moule d'orfèvre de la période romano-byzantine découvert à la cité de Tropaeum Traiani (Adamclisi, dép. Constanța)," *Pontica* 50 (2017), 280–287.

© DANIELA TĂNASE, 2021 | DOI:10.1163/9789004436930_009

1.1 *Concentric Circles and the Circle-with-Dot Motif*

Were widely used in the late Roman and Byzantine metalwork, particularly during the 6th and 7th centuries.[2] They also appear quite frequently in the barbarian world between the 5th and the 7th century, both on metal and on bone artifacts. This particular ornament appears on bronze and silver, articulated strap ends with punched decoration of concentric circles and half-circles, such as found in graves 8 and 59 in Band.[3] The same decoration appears on the belt mounts from graves 29 and 59 of that same cemetery.[4] Another mount with a similar, punched ornament was found in the contemporaneous assemblage associated with grave 27 from the cemetery excavated in Noşlac.[5] Punched was also the ornament of the belt mount and its counter-plate found in grave 17 of that same cemetery.[6]

1.2 *The Dot-Comma Motif*

Appears on artifacts of the Felnac type, dies and dress accessories, on which the motif is combined with rows of triangles framing circles arranged in a triangle like a flower with three petals (Fig. 37.3–10). All belt fittings – strap ends and belt mounts – are decorated with the dot-comma motif, as documented by many finds from western Hungary – grave 15 in Keszthely-Fenékpuszta,[7] grave 647 in Kölked-Feketekapu A,[8] and grave 696 in Budakalász-Dunapart.[9]

It is worth mentioning that artifacts decorated in such a manner are also known from the southeastern part of the Tisza Plain: the bronze dies from Felnac tomb and the silver belt fittings from the nearby sites at Klárafalva-Deszk[10] and Sânpetru German.[11] Grave 85 in Aradac-Mečka produced two strap ends, two double-shield belt mounts, and nine other belt mounts with the same decoration.[12] A bronze, shield-shaped belt mount decorated with the

2 Teodor, "Piese vestimentare," 132.

3 Kovács, "A mezőbándi ásatások," 280, fig. 11.3; 327, fig. 45.1.

4 Kovács, "A mezőbándi ásatások," 311 and 327, figs. 30.5 and 45.2–4.

5 Rusu, "The Prefeudal cemetery," 272, fig. 2.9.

6 Rusu, "The Prefeudal cemetery," 272, fig. 2.39. a–c.

7 Garam, *Funde*, 117.

8 Attila Kiss, *Das awarenzeitliche gepidische Gräberfeld von Kölked-Feketekapu A* (Innsbruck: Universitäts-verlag Wagner, 1996), 165–166.

9 Tivadar Vida, Adrien Pásztor, "Der beschlagverzierte Gürtel der Awaren am Beispiel des Inventars von Budakalász-Dunapart, Ungarn, Grab 696," in *Reitervölker aus dem Osten. Hunnen + Awaren. Ausstellungskatalog*, ed. Falko Daim (Eisenstadt: Amt der Burgenländischen Landesregierung, 1996), pp. 344–345.

10 Garam, *Funde*, 117.

11 Dörner, "Mormânt," 427, fig. 4.2; 429.

12 Nagy, "Nekropola kol Aradaca," 89, pl. XXII. 17–19; 90, pl. XXIII. 2–6, 8–12.

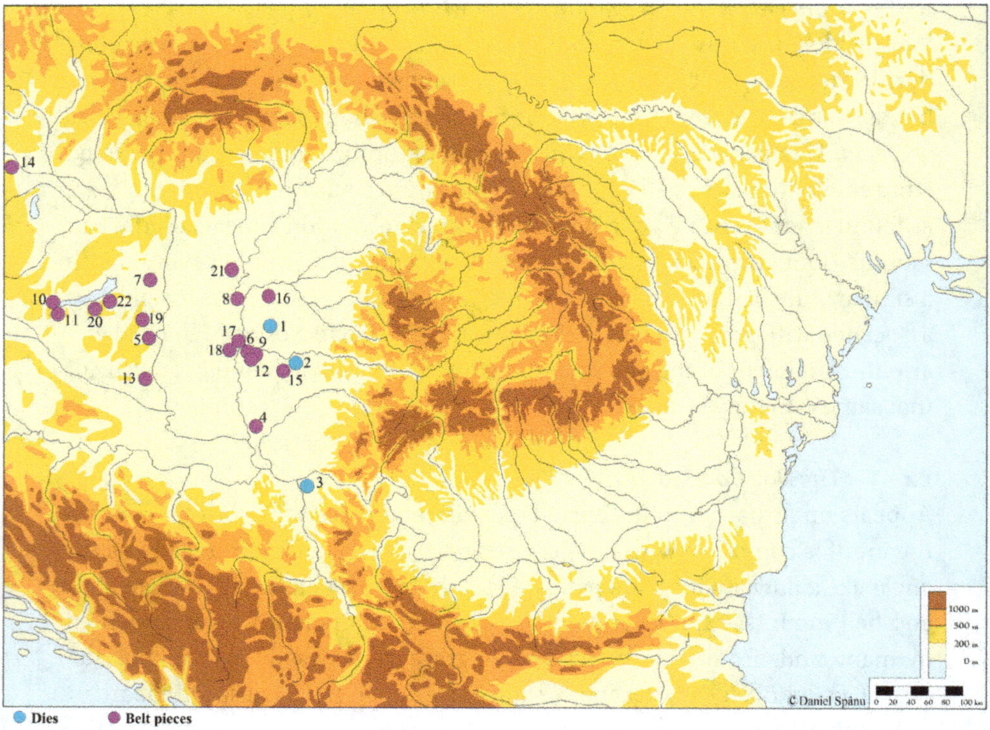

FIGURE 53 **Pieces with Felnac type motif in the Middle Danube region – a. dies:** 1. Békéssámson (Hungary); 2. Felnac (Arad co., Romania); 3. Viminacium (Stari Kostolac, Serbia) – **b. belt pieces:** 4. Aradac-Mečka (Serbia); 5. Cikó (Hungary); 6. Deszk-Ambrus (Hungary); 7. Dunapentele (Hungary); 8. Felgyő (Hungary); 9. Ferencszállás (Hungary); 10. Gyenesdiás-Algyenes (Hungary); 11. Keszthely-Fenékpuszta (Hungary); 12. Klárafalva (Hungary); 13. Kölked Feketekapu A (Hungary); 14. Linz-Zizlau (Austria); 15. Sânpetru German (Arad co., Romania); 16. Szarvas (Hungary); 17. Szeged-Királyhalom (Hungary); 18. Szeged-Kundomb (Hungary); 19. Szekszárd-Bogyiszlói út (Hungary); 20. Szigliget (Hungary); 21. Tiszavárkony (Hungary); 22. Zamárdi (Hungary)

dot-comma motif was discovered in grave 686 of the cemetery excavated in Szekszárd-Bogyiszló Street.[13] The mapping of those finds outlines a possible distribution area for the products of the goldsmith buried in Felnac (Fig. 53).

Moreover, artifacts with very similar, if not identical decoration have been found in the Crimea. One belt mount with dot-comma decoration

13 Gyula Rosner, *Das awarenzeitliche Gräberfeld in Szekszárd-Bogyszlói Straße* (Budapest: Magyar Nemzeti Múzeum, 1999), 86, 211, pl. 45. 686.1.

ornamentation is known from Suuk-Su (Fig. 37.6),[14] another pearl decoration from Eski-Kermen (Fig. 39.2).[15] In both Eski-Kermen[16] and Sakharna Golivka[17] strap ends of the so-called Martynivka type have been found that are similar to the Felnac die (Fig. 38.6). This, in my opinion, is sufficient proof that those decorative motifs originated in Byzantium, most likely in the urban environment of the northern Black Sea region. A recent discovery from Ukraine substantiates that conclusion. Two bronze dies decorated like those in Felnac have been found in the Cherkasy district of the Middle Dnieper region. They are both of Byzantine production and most likely came to the area from the Crimea.[18]

The "dot-comma" motif appears also on the belt fittings of the Tarnaméra type, which are characterized by deep lines surrounding the drop-shaped grooves. On strap ends of Tarnaméra type there is a rosette in the middle, an imitation of the monogram of Jesus Christ.[19] In that respect, there is a great deal of similarity between the Felnac die and the belt strap found in Szárazd (Hungary).[20] The difference between the two is that what looks like drops on the die appears as "dot-comma" ornament on the strap end.

The "dot-comma" motif, combined with "tamga" signs of eastern origin, also appears on the belt fittings of the Martynivka type from sites within a large swathe of land between the Caucasus region and northern Italy.[21] For its Byzantine origin speak also artifacts with trimmed decoration, which is rare in the regions inhabited by the Avars, but quite common in Byzantium.[22] To be sure, belt fittings decorated with the "dot-comma" motif can hardly be attributed to any specific ethnic group, but clearly reflect an international fashion.[23] Within the Carpathian Basin, the Martynivka decoration appears on

14 Aleksandr I. Ajbabin, "Khronologiia mogil'nikov Kryma pozdnerimskogo i rannesrednekovogo vremeni [Chronology of the tombs from Crimea from the Late Roman and Early Middle Ages]," *Materialy po arheologii i etnografii Tavrii* 1 (1990), fig. 51.36.

15 Ajbabin "Khronologiia," fig. 53.10.

16 Ajbabin "Khronologiia," fig. 43.35.

17 Ajbabin "Khronologiia," fig. 51.46.

18 Rácz, "Ein frühmittelalterlicher Pressmodelfund," 176, fig. 1.1–2; 179.

19 Garam, *Funde*, 141.

20 Garam, *Funde*, 356, pl. 105. 6.

21 Garam, *Funde*, 127.

22 Péter Somogyi, "Typologie, Chronologie und Herkunft der Maskenbeschläge. Zu den archäologischen Hinterlassenschaften osteuropäischer Reiterhirten aus der pontischen Steppe im 6. Jahrhundert," *Archaeologia Austriaca* 71 (1987), 121–154.

23 Csanád Bálint, "Kontakte zwischen Iran, Byzanz und der Steppe. Das Grab von Üc Tepe (Sow. Azerbajdzan) und der beschlagverzierten Gürtel im 6. und 7. Jahrhundert," in *Awarenforschungen. Archaeologia Austriaca Monographien 1 – Studien zur Archäologie der Awaren* 4, ed. Falko Daim (Vienna: Institut für Ur- und Frühgeschichte der Universität Wien, 1992), p. 408.

the die for strap ends found in Felnac, as well as on dies for belt fittings from Adony and Kunszentmárton.[24] Despite the existence of such dies, the number of finds in lands controlled by the Avars is relatively small, much smaller than in northern Italy.[25] Where present, such belt fittings with the Martynivka decoration appear in graves of armed men, and are typically used at decorating straps meant for the suspension of weapons.[26] That is also true for the strap end from grave 6 in Bratei 3, which also produced a leaf-shaped and two three-edged arrow heads, two iron buckles, a flint steel, and a purse buckle of the Pápa type.[27]

1.3 *The Central, Rosette Motif*

The Avar goldsmiths adopted many Byzantine symbols, such as the central, rosette motif, which appears on strap ends. The motif is believed by some to be a stylized human mask, and by others to be the monogram of Christ. The motif appears also on sword scabbard mounts, and may have an apotropaic role, namely to protect the owner of the weapon. During the Avar age, images of human heads appear rarely on such artifacts as rings, sword scabbard mounts, or female dress accessories.[28]

Belt fittings such as found in Pančevo have a pearl framework, the inner field being divided and decorated with braided ribbons, with an additional rosette motif in the middle.[29] It is important to note that the central rosette motif never appears together with the dot-comma motif.[30] Artifacts with the central rosette motif appear primarily in the region of the Middle Tisza, most likely in connection with the activity of a goldsmith located (and later buried) in Gátér. A few similar artifacts, however, are known from Transdanubia.[31] Moreover, the die for double-shield belt mounts with the central rosette motif, which was found in Corund is a member of the same group of artifacts. The braids on the Corund dies are stylized, but the string of pearls clearly observable, as is the division of the inner field. A somewhat more stylized ornamentation appears

24 Garam, *Funde*, 341, pl. 90.7; 342, pl. 91. 5, 6; 343, pl. 92.9.
25 Garam, *Funde*, 128.
26 Garam, *Funde*, 130.
27 Bârzu, *Ein gepidisches Denkmal*, 172–173; 280, pl. 2.G6.
28 Margit Nagy, "Ornamenta Avarica II. A fonatornamentika [The braided band ornamentation]," *A Móra Ferenc Múzeum Évkönyve, Studia Archaeologica* 5 (1999), 304–305.
29 Garam, *Funde*, 134–135.
30 Garam, *Funde*, 146.
31 Garam, *Funde*, 148.

on a belt mount from grave 58 in Győr-Téglavető, on a strap end from grave 264 in Jászapáti, and on the die from Pančevo mold.[32]

1.4 *The Palmette Motif*

Was used especially during the Early Avar age, when it appears in two variants. One of them is known as the Akalan-type palmette, which looks like a tree with the leaves opened into several fields and the middle leaf longer than the others. The other variant is known as the Ozora-type ornament and consists of small palmettes. Most artifacts decorated with the palmette motif have a pearl frame, with the inner field ornamented with the "dot-comma" motif.[33] Palmettes of the Akalan type appear on the Felnac dies (Fig. 38.1–5), on belt fittings from grave 84 in Aradac-Mečka, grave 259 in Kölked Feketekapu A, and from Mezőkomárom, Szeged, and Csengád (Hungary).[34] The Felnac dies demonstrate that strap ends had a central rosette motif, much like contemporaneous strap ends in Byzantium.[35] The oldest artifacts decorated with the palmette motif are those of Transdanubia and the southern part of the Tisza Plain, while the most recent appear in the Middle Tisza region.[36]

1.5 *The Star Motif*

Of equally Byzantine inspiration is the earring with star-shaped pendant, often decorated by means of granulation or filigree.[37] Cast earrings of that type appear also in *barbaricum*, but with an ornament of pseudo-granulation, as in Gâmbaş and Bratei 3.[38] Some have advanced the idea that those earrings were made either in the Middle Danube region, or in the Crimea.[39] But molds found in Romania show that lunular earrings with star-shaped pendants and granulated ornament were manufactured locally. Star-shaped pendants were cast with the mold from Ştefan cel Mare-Gutinaş (Fig. 23.1.2), Moţca (Fig. 2.2), and Dolheştii Mari (Fig. 44.3), in imitation of pendants with filigree

32 Garam, *Funde*, 360, pl. 109.1; 361, pl. 110.1–2.
33 Garam, *Funde*, 133.
34 Garam, *Funde*, 134; pl. 98.1–3, 4, 8; pl. 100.5.
35 Garam, *Funde*, 135.
36 Garam, *Funde*, 135, 137.
37 Dan Gh. Teodor, "Cercei cu pandantiv stelat din secolele VI–VIII d.Hr. în spaţiul carpato-dunăreano-pontic," Arheologia Moldovei 18 (1995), 191.
38 Comşa, "Quelques données concernant les rapports des territoires nord-danubiens avec Byzance," 379; Bârzu, *Ein gepidisches Denkmal aus Siebenbürgen*, 297, pl. 19.G.109.1; 309, pl. 31.G.183.1–2.
39 Comşa, "Quelques données," 387–388.

decoration such as those of the earrings discovered in Bratei,[40] Coșovenii de Jos,[41] and Sărata Monteoru.[42] Pendants such as cast with the mold from Soveja (Fig. 6.3) decorated the earrings from Noșlac, Moigrad, but also the earring die from Costești.[43] The granulated ornament was welded onto these pendants. Molds for casting granules have been found in Botoșana (Fig. 17.2.2), Olteni (Fig. 2.3), Dodești (Fig. 15.9), Budureasca 4 (Fig. 8.1, Fig. 9.1–2, 4), and Străulești-Măicănești (Fig. 13.5). Pendants in the form of a rosette with floral decoration, which may have originated in the northern Black Sea area, appear on the molds from Soveja (Fig. 6.3), Rădeni (Fig. 6.1), Poienița (Fig. 6.5), Cucuteni (Fig. 5.5), and Bucharest-Soldat Ghivan Nicolae Street (Fig. 13.6.5). Moreover, the rosettes on the Soveja, Rădeni, and Cucuteni molds resemble the figures on the models from the Biskupija hoard (Croatia).[44] Pendants similar to those discovered in Walachia and Moldavia appear on the stone molds from Bernashivka[45] (Fig. 47.4–6), on the stone molds from Seliște (Fig. 48.9), Dănceni (Fig. 48.4–5) and on the clay mold from Seliște (Fig. 48.8).

A flower-shaped pendant, similar to that on an earring found in Copăcești (Vrancea County),[46] was made with the die found in the nearby site at Răcoasa (Fig. 2.6), which is similar to another model from the Biskupija hoard.[47]

Floral applications similar to those on the mold from Budureasca 4 (Fig. 9.2) appear also on the mold from Aldeni (Fig. 42.1), which may have been used to manufacture both appliqués and earring pendants.

1.6 *The Cross Motif*

Crosses appear on dies (Dumbrăveni), as well as on molds meant to cast belt fitting (Traian), earring pendants (Cristuru Secuiesc, Dichiseni). A good number of molds, however, were used to produce pectoral crosses (Botoșana,

---

40 Ligia Bârzu, *Continuitatea creației materiale și spirituale a poporului român pe teritoriul fostei Dacii* [Continuity of the material and spiritual creation of the Romanian people in the former Dacian territory] (Bucharest: Editura Academiei Republicii Socialiste România, 1979), 66, fig. 13/1–2.

41 Nestor, Nicolăescu-Plopșor, "Die völkerwanderungszeitlichen Schatz Negrescu," pl. 8.

42 Teodor, "Cercei," 199, fig. 2.5–6.

43 Teodor, "Cercei," 201, fig. 4. 5–6, 9, 11 (Noșlac), 13, 15 (Costești), 16–17 (Moigrad).

44 Teodor, "Cercei," 205, fig. 8.

45 Vynokur, *Slov'ianski iuveliry*, 64–65, fig. 22–23; 68–69, fig. 24–25; 71, fig. 26; 73–75, fig. 27–29; 81, fig. 33; 85–87, fig. 35–37; 89, fig. 38; 91, fig. 39.

46 Anton Paragină, "Un cercel de proveniență bizantină descoperit în localitatea Copăcești, comuna Ruginești, județul Vrancea [An earring of Byzantine origin discovered in Copăcești, Ruginești commune, Vrancea county]," *Studii și Cercetări de Istorie Veche și Arheologie* 33, no. 1 (1982), 139, fig. 1.

47 Teodor, "Cercei," 205, fig. 8.

Cacica, Davideni, Giurcani, Izvorul Dulce, Olteni, Sânmiclăuș, Bucharest-Străulești-Lunca).[48] The cross on the Dumbrăveni die the cross is braided and framed by a pearl border and by arcades. In the middle, the cross has a diamond framed by "dot-comma" ornaments. This decorative arrangement is similar to those on a small cross and on belt fittings from Sirmium (Sremska Mitrovica, in Serbia), as well as from sites in Turkey and in Syria. The latter are the closest analogies, which suggest that the Dumbrăveni die came from some workshop in the eastern Mediterranean region.[49] By contrast, the stone and clay molds were undoubtedly made by local craftsmen in the lands north of the river Danube. The stone molds were used to cast Maltese crosses, an ornament most typical for the 6th and early 7th centuries. Maltese crosses have equal, trapezoidal arms. Pectoral crosses of that type have been found in Bratei 3,[50] Davideni,[51] and Rashkov (northern Bukovina, Ukraine). Two other stray finds of such crosses are known from Ruginoasa (Iași County) and Valea Voievozilor (Dâmbovița County).[52] Maltese-type crosses have also been found in the region of the Iron Gates segment of the Danube, as well as in the Carpathian Basin, along the Tisza, and to the west from the Middle Danube.[53] An interesting discovery is also the clay mold for casting crosses with equal arms, composed of four granules, which was found in the settlement of Hansca (Republic of Moldova)[54] (Fig. 48.7).

48 Andrei Măgureanu, "Identitate religioasă la nord de Dunăre. Creștinismul [Religious identity north of the Danube. The Christianity]," *Studii și Cercetări de Istorie Veche și Arheologie* 68, no. 1–4 (2017), 44, 47 questions the idea that the molds found in Cristuru Secuiesc, Davideni and Budureasca 4 were employed for the production of pectoral crosses. Instead, they were most likely used to cast diamond- or staff-shaped pendants.

49 Rácz, *Die Goldschmiedegräber*, 30, fig. 11.1–5; p. 32.

50 Bârzu, *Ein gepidisches Denkmal*, 292, pl. 14.G.76.3; 317, pl. 39.G.237.1–2.

51 Mitrea, *Așezarea de la Davideni*, 147, 327, fig. 67.2.

52 Alexandru Madgearu, "Semnificația purtării crucilor pectorale descoperite la nord de Dunăre în secolele VI–VII [The significance of wearing the pectoral crosses discovered north of the Danube in the 6th–7th centuries]," *Arheologia Moldovei* 30 (2007), 137.

53 Florin Curta, "Before Cyril and Methodius: Christianity and Barbarians beyond the Sixth- and Seventh-Century Danube Frontier," in *East Central and Eastern Europe in the Early Middle Age*, ed. Florin Curta (Ann Arbor: University of Michigan Press 2005), 216, fig. 8.8; Csilla Balogh, "A Byzantine gold cross in an Avar Period grave from southeastern Hungary," in *Lebenswelten zwischen Archäologie und Geschichte. Festschrift für Falko Daim zu seinem 65. Geburtstag*, eds. Jörg Drauschke, Ewald Kislinger, Karin Kühtreiber, Thomas Kühtreiber, Gabriele Scharrer-Liška and Tivadar Vida (Mainz: Verlag des Römisch-Germanischen Zentralmuseums, 2018), 32, fig. 5.12. A clay mold for Maltese cross and *lunula* form pendant has been discovered in Jász-Nagykun-Szolnok co., Hungary (Fig. 48.6): Rácz, *Die Goldschmiedegräber*, 199; pl. 80.2.

54 Teodor, "Tipare," 164, 173, fig. 8.2.

The molds from Izvorul Dulce (dated to the 5th century without any archaeological context[55]) and Giurcani (dated to the 6th to 7th century[56]) were used to cast Latin crosses. Such crosses – all dated to the 6th and 7th centuries – are known from Bratei 3,[57] Băleni-Români and Moigrad (Sălaj County).[58] A lead cross of the Latin type was discovered in a 6th- to 7th-century settlement site in Traian (Neamţ County).[59] Latin crosses appear also in the Carpathian Basin, near the mouth of the Mureş River into the Tisza, and in Transdanubia.[60]

There is a striking similarity between the cross and granular ornaments to be cast with two molds found in Cristuru Secuiesc and Argamum (Capul Dolojman, Dobrudja, Romania).[61] As the latter site is located within the Roman province of Scythia Minor, this is another indication of the close ties of the Empire and *barbaricum*, involving the movement of goods, people, and technological know-how.[62] To be sure, stone molds for casting Maltese crosses are also known from the Balkan provinces of the Empire. One such mold has been found in the early Byzantine hillfort at Golemanovo Kale near Sadovec (northern Bulgaria)[63] (Fig. 49.2). Crosses cast with that mold must have been very similar to those cast with the molds found in Botoşana and Olteni. Moreover, the Golemanovo Kale mold has a rosette motif that is similar to that on the molds from Ştefan cel Mare-Gutinaş, Soveja, and Rădeni, a clear indication of the direction of the imitation process. Two other stone molds from unknown locations in the eastern Mediterranean region are now in the collection of the Benaki Museum in Athens (Greece). One of them was used to cast crosses of the Latin type, but also mounts, circular pendants, and a lunular earring.[64] All those ornaments are similar to those cast with the molds found in Rădeni, Poieniţa and Ştefan cel Mare-Gutinaş. The second stone mold from the Benaki Museum was used to cast Maltese crosses with slightly arched arms, each having a medallion at the end.[65] Such crosses have so far not been found in the lands north of the river Danube.

55 Madgearu, "Semnificaţia," 134.
56 Teodor, "Tipare," 164.
57 Bârzu, *Ein gepidisches Denkmal aus Siebenbürgen*, 315, pl. 37.G.219.9.
58 Madgearu, "Semnificaţia," 137.
59 Hânceanu, "Două piese," 124–125; 132, pl. 3.1–2.
60 Curta, "Before Cyril and Methodius," 210, fig. 8.2; Balogh, "A Byzantine gold cross," 25–32.
61 Oanţă-Marghitu, "Argamum," pl. I.4.
62 Oanţă-Marghitu, "Argamum," 361.
63 Oanţă-Marghitu, "Argamum," pl. III.7.
64 Isabella Baldini Lippolis, *L'oreficeria nell'impero di Constantinopoli tra IV e VII secolo* (Bari: Edipuglia, 1999), 43; 44, fig. 17.
65 Baldini Lippolis, *L'oreficeria*, 123, fig. 56.

2 Ornamental Styles and Decorative Motifs of Germanic Origin

For the decoration of dress accessories, Germanic goldsmiths used during the 5th and 6th centuries a repertoire of late antique inspiration – meanders, symmetrical acanthus sprouts, "step-like" meanders, notches, and spirals.[66] However, the characteristic feature of the metalwork produced in those parts of Europe believed to have been inhabited by people speaking Germanic languages is the animal style, which was based on the representation of animals in the form of braided ribbons. Ever since Bernhard Salin, archaeologists distinguish between animal style I, with realistic depictions of animals or animal parts, and animal style II, in which the animal body parts are replaced by stylized ribbons.[67] Much has been written on the origin of the animal style – Celtic, nomadic (with influences from Iran), or Hellenistic.[68] Whatever its origin, the style is regarded as typical for the Germanic view of the world.[69] While no examples of animal style I are so far known from Romania, a rectangular silver belt mount from grave 74 in Band is clearly ornamented in animal style II.[70]

The most important element of animal style II, directly borrowed from Mediterranean art, is the interlaced motif.[71] The appearance of braided ornamentation in the Germanic art, and therefore of the animal style II, has been interpreted in terms of the Christianization of the Germanic people, as the result of the influence upon Germanic craftsmen of decorative motifs most

66 Nagy, "Ornamenta Avarica I," 389.

67 For a comprehensive discussion of the animal style development in the Germanic world, see Bernhard Salin, *Die altgermanische Tierornamentik. Typologische Studie über germanische Metallgegenstände aus dem IV. bis IX. Jahrhundert nebst einer Studie über irische Ornamentik* (Stockholm: K. L. Becksmans Buchdruckerei, 1904), 175–321. For a brief survey of the main differences between Animal Style I and Animal Style II, largely based on finds from the Carpathian Basin, see Orsolya Heinrich-Tamáska, "Zur Bestimmung Salins Tierstil I und II an zwei Beispielen aus der Umgebung von Keszthely," in *Germanen am Plattensee. Ausstellung des Balatoni Múzeums Keszthely im Museum für Frühgeschichte des Landes Niederösterreich, Schloss Traismauer, vom 6. April bis 1. November 2002*, ed. Robert Müller (Traismauer: Amt der Niederösterreichischen Landesregierung, 2002), pp. 36–39.

68 Others claim that the Germanic animal style drew inspiration from the animal style of the Scythians, especially in respect to such motifs as the running deer or stylized heads of birds of prey (Fettich, *Das awarenzeitliche Kunstgewerbe*, 38). Günter Haseloff has convincingly demonstrated that Animal Style I originates in the Roman ornamental repertoire, particularly that of metalwork decorated with chip carving (*Kerbschnitt*). Equally important were the representations of human faces or masks in the Late Roman art [Günther Haseloff, *Die germanische Tierornamentik der Völkerwanderungszeit. Studien zu Salin's Stil I* (Berlin/New York: Walter de Gruyter, 1981), 5–16)].

69 Bóna, *Der Anbruch*, 52.

70 Kovács, "A mezőbándi ásatások," 332, fig. 51.1.

71 Haseloff, *Die germanische Tierornamentik der Völkerwanderungszeit*, 609–614.

typical for illuminations produced in monastic *scriptoria*.[72] For a long while, scholars believed that the interlaced motif appears on dress accessories attributed to the Lombards only after their migration to Italy in 568. However, the braided ornament was in use in the Carpathian Basin shortly after the middle of the 6th century. Because the motif is of late antique origin, the explanation offered for this phenomenon is that workshops working in the late Roman tradition continued to exist in Transdanubia, and they influenced the Lombard craftsmen, who took with them that tradition to Italy.[73] The only piece of evidence that the interlaced motif reached even the eastern parts of the Carpathian Basin is the articulated strap end discovered in grave 8 in Unirea (Alba County).[74]

During the Early Avar age, geometric ornaments were used in frieze arrangements, combined with the interlaced motif. In addition, those frieze arrangements included other motifs that had previously been used by goldsmiths in the Carpathian Basin.[75] Stylized volutes inspired by the acanthus sprouts motif appear primarily on harness ornaments.[76] Such ornaments were most likely cast with the clay mold found in Bucharest-Tei (Fig. 11.2.1). Another frequently employed motif was the spiral. During the Early Avar age the motif took the form of circles connected by an oblique line. The motif was rendered in a variety of techniques: inlaying in cells, openwork wire, notching, punching, pressing, and casting.[77] The spiral motif appears on bow fibulae, such as those produced with the forming model found in Bucharest-Tei (Fig. 11.2.2). Notches imitating silver inlays and stylized spirals appear on the Felnac forming model for bow fibulae as well (Fig. 37.2.2). The same is true for the forming model found in the Banat (Fig. 42.2a–c), as well as for all bow fibulae of that same (Gâmbaș) type.

Early Avar-age jewelers also employed the motif of the "row of diamonds," the origin of which is believed to be the Germanic *Keilstich* notches. The "row of diamonds" appears on a relatively large number of cast or pressed dress

72 Birgit Arrhenius, "Einige christliche Paraphrasen aus dem 6. Jahrhundert," in *Zum Problem der Deutung frühmittelalterlicher Bildinhalte. Akten des 1. Internationalen Kolloquiums in Marburg a. d. Lahn, 15. bis 19. Februar 1983*, ed. (Sigmaringen: Jan Thorbecke Verlag, 1986), pp. 129–151.

73 Nagy, "Ornamenta Avarica I," 394.

74 Roska, "Das gepidische Gräberfeld," fig. 8.

75 Nagy, "Ornamenta Avarica I," 389.

76 Nagy, "Ornamenta Avarica I," 390.

77 Nagy, "Ornamenta Avarica I," 390.

accessories, and was made either by engraving or by punching.[78] For example, the motif appears on the die for strap ends from Felnac (Fig. 37.7).

Bird heads, another motif commonly used in the Germanic art, are believed to have been inspired by the art of the nomads. As the birds in question are eagles, it is more likely that the motif originated in the Greco-Roman art, even though birds of prey were viewed by nomads as messengers of the gods, royal attributes, and symbols of resurrection.[79] Eagle heads are particularly conspicuous on a certain group of silver and bronze belt buckles dated to the first half of the 6th century. Later, during the second half of the 6th and in the early 7th century, bird heads also appear on bow fibulae.

3 Animal Style II with Dentil Ornamentation

The animal style II with dentil ornamentation has long been viewed as typical for late 6th- and 7th-century goldsmithing in the Carpathian Basin. As it appears primarily on Avar-age artifacts, the style was also interpreted as a variant of the Germanic animal style II, under the assumption that Avar craftsmen simply added the dentil ornament to the repertoire of the style characterized by the interlaced motif.[80] Others believed that the Avar animal style II originated in workshops in Transdanubia, primarily in Keszthely.[81] At any rate, the style was popular in the Carpathian Basin for more than 50 years,[82] with the latest testimonies being dated to the late 7th century.[83] The representations of animal style II can be divided into two groups: beaked heads and clawed legs; ribbon compositions in which the details of the animal heads can no longer be recognized. Scholars believe that the first group is the earliest, with braided ribbons gradually replacing animal parts.[84] Thus both groups are dated to the first half of the 7th century, although only the second group continued into the second half of that century.[85]

---

78 Nagy, "Ornamenta Avarica I," 391.

79 Rusu, "Pontische Gürtelschnallen," 508–509.

80 Fettich, *Das awarenzeitliche Kunstgewerbe*, 42–43.

81 Andreas Alföldi, *Der Untergang der Römerherrschaft in Pannonien* (Berlin/Leipzig: W. de Gruyter & Co., 1926), 36–38.

82 Martin, "Tauschierte Gürtelgarnituren," 72.

83 Martin, "Tauschierte Gürtelgarnituren," 69–73.

84 Fettich, *Das awarenzeitliche Kunstgewerbe*, 55.

85 István Bóna, "Langobard fibulák ékszerek. Avar kori 2. Stilus. Avar-langobard kapcsolatok [Langobard fibulae jewelry. Avar period 2. Style. Avar-langobard contacts]," in *Hunok-Gepidák-Langobardok*, ed. István Bóna (Szeged: Balassi Kiadó, 1993), 150–153.

The dentil ornament is not purely geometric, for, according to some scholars, it originates in the representation of claws going back to the Scythian art of southern Russia.[86] Others believe that the dentil ornament was an imitation of the crested element of the Germanic animal style I.[87] A third group of scholars argue that the dentil ornament is a typically Avar-age, cheap imitation of the *niello* decoration.[88] However, the animal style II decoration with dentil ornament appears only on a few artifacts – pins, finger rings, and other dress accessories, which are believed to be characteristic for the "Germanic", but not for the "Avar" dress.[89] This is further substantiated by the presence of such artifacts in what Romanian archaeologists believe to be the late Gepidic milieu – the pin in grave 18 at Noşlac,[90] the gold ring in grave 34 at Band,[91] as well as the gilded bronze buckle plate from grave 264 at Bratei 3.[92] Animal style II decoration with the dentil ornament also appears on the dies for belt mounts from Adony, Felnac, and Kunszentmárton, as well as on a strap end for harness from Cikó, which seems to have been produced with the die found in Felnac (Fig. 39.1).[93] Another strap end with a decoration similar to that on the Felnac die was found in grave 16 at Aradac-Mečka.[94] In short, it is likely that the Felnac die was used for the production of strap ends found on other sites.

An interesting case is that of the gold ring from grave 39 at Band, on which two pairs of animals were engraved flanking a *cloisonné* style ornament of iridescent glass paste. The representation of the animals is geometrical, a characteristic of animal style II with dentil ornament; only parts of the animals' limbs are sketched. The closest analogy to this ring is the silver ring from Keszthely (Hungary), which, unlike that of Band, has no *cloisonné* ornament.[95]

86 Fettich, *Das awarenzeitliche Kunstgewerbe*, 54–55.

87 Günther Haseloff, "Germanische und östliche Tierornamentik im Donauraum," in *Frankfurter Beiträge zur Mittelalter-Archäologie II, Schriften des Frankfurter Museum für Vor- und Frühgeschichte 12*, 27–47. Bonn: Schnell & Steiner 1990.

88 Nagy, "Ornamenta Avarica II," 305.

89 Martin, "Tauschierte Gürtelgarnituren," 69–70.

90 Rusu, "The Prefeudal cemetery," 272, fig. 2.18.

91 Kovács, "A mezőbándi ásatások," 316, fig. 35.5.

92 Miclea, Florescu, *Strămoşii românilor*, fig. 830; Bârzu, *Ein gepidisches Denkmal*, 322, pl. 44, G.264.1.

93 Ilona Kovrig, "Adatok az avar megszállás kérdéséhez [Data to the question of the Avar occupation]," *Archaeologiai Értesitő* 82 (1955), 33, fig. 3.1.

94 Nagy, "Nekropola kol Aradaca," 71, pl. IV.1.

95 Fettich, *Das awarenzeitliche Kunstgewerbe*, 47–48, pl. I.15.

Animal style II with dentil ornament also appears on the luxury bow fibulae from Coșovenii de Jos.[96] The interlaced motif with the dentil ornament on that fibula is very similar to that on the belt mount from grave 16 at Aradac-Mečka, which is dated to the first half of the 7th century. Nonetheless, the Coșovenii de Jos fibula must be dated to the second half of the 7th century, because of the associated earrings, which have analogies in the Priseaca hoard that are coin-dated to the reign of Emperor Constantine IV (668–685).[97] Some have advanced the idea that the Coșovenii de Jos fibula was in fact produced by a Byzantine craftsman working on commission for some barbarian chieftain in southern Walachia, in eastern or southeastern Pannonia, or somewhere to the northwest from the former province of Dalmatia. Others believe that the artifact was produced in Byzantium and reached *barbaricum* as a gift.[98] It is important to note the role of the Germanic (Lombard and Gepid) goldsmiths in transmitting the decorative repertoire to those working in the Carpathian Basin after its occupation by the Avars. Of particular significance in this respect is the damascened (silver inlay) decoration of belt fittings (a decorative technique most popular in the Merovingian milieu) and the animal style II with the dentil ornament. Craftsmen working in that tradition must have also influenced the manufacturing of the Coșovenii de Jos fibula, which displays another favorite motif of the Germanic art – pairs of bird heads.[99] Whether or not the fibula is a Byzantine product, the Byzantine and barbarian elements were mixed quite often on artifacts most certainly produced in the Carpathian Basin.[100]

As a matter of fact, the Coșovenii de Jos fibula was probably made in *barbaricum*, most likely in Transdanubia, where the animal style II with dentil ornamentation first emerged.[101]

96 Florin Curta, "On the dating of the 'Vețel-Coșoveni' group of curved fibulae," *Ephemeris Napocensis* 4 (1994), 234–239; Curta, *The Making of the Slavs*, 249.

97 Florin Curta, "Female Dress and 'Slavic' Bow Fibulae in Greece," *Hesperia* 74 (2005), 108, 114, 117.

98 Petre, "Fibulele 'digitate'," 90; Comșa, "Quelques données," 287; Comșa, "Socio-economic organization," 195.

99 Rusu, "Pontische Gürtelschnallen," 508.

100 Harhoiu, "Quellenlage," 120, 145.

101 It is worth mentioning that with the exception of the Coșovenii de Jos fibula, most artifacts displaying the animal style II with dentil ornament are from the lands to the west of the Middle Danube (Orsolya Heinrich-Tamáska, "Megjegyzések a kora avarkori ötvösmüvészethez a fogazással díszített leletek kapcsán [Remarks on the goldsmithing technique of the early Avar Period using the example of the dentil decorated finds]," *A Móra Ferenc Múzeum Évkönyve, Studia Archaeologica* 8 (2002), 269). It is from Transdanubia that such

4 Ornamental Styles and Motifs from the Forest-Steppe Zone of Eastern Europe

Archaeologists believe that a number of ornaments most typical for the Avar age have an East European origin: animal-shaped appliqués, rosette-shaped harness mounts, the clover leaf motif, semiglobular appliqués with smooth surface, and mounts with tasseled decoration.[102] Some have noted that nomads had no interest in the realistic representation of the surrounding nature, since the animals most familiar to them (horses, fowl, wild birds, or fish) were not represented. Instead, animals such as lions or fantastic creatures are the most common in the art of the nomads.[103] Of particular interest in this respect are the dies found in Felnac that show lions (Fig. 38.15–16). Appliqués with similar images of lions are known from the Martynivka hoard[104] and from Pregradnaia Stanica in the Caucasus region.[105] Dies or casting models in the form of lions are also known from the Biskupija[106] and Velestino (Greece) hoards,[107] as well as from Kamunta in the northern Caucasus region.[108] The origin of this type of animal representation must be sought in the world of the steppe,[109] even though similar images appear in Byzantium as well.

Smooth globular appliqués similar to those produced with the dies in Felnac (Fig. 39.8–9) are known from grave 85 at Aradac-Mečka.[110] Grave 7 of that same cemetery produced a strap end very similar to those produced with another die from Felnac (Fig. 40.3).[111] Globular appliqués have also been found in an inhumation grave at Sânnicolau Mare (Timiș county).[112] Smooth

---

artifacts reached the lands farther to the east (Heinrich-Tamáska, "Megjegyzések," 281, fig. 7; 282, fig. 8).

102 Fettich, *Das awarenzeitliche Kunstgewerbe*, 41, 58.

103 Fettich, *Das awarenzeitliche Kunstgewerbe*, 41.

104 Bálint, *Die Archäologie der Steppe*, 89, fig. 37.17–18.

105 Bálint, *Die Archäologie der Steppe*, 27, 28, fig. 6.2.

106 Teodor, "Cercei," 205, fig. 8.

107 Rácz, *Die Goldschmiedegräber*, p. 78, fig. 21.4.

108 Rácz, *Die Goldschmiedegräber*, p. 79.

109 Szmoniewski, "Two worlds," 291.

110 Nagy, "Nekropola kol Aradaca," 90, pl. XXIII. 15a, 16b.

111 Nagy, "Nekropola kol Aradaca," 69, pl. II.4.

112 Florin Medeleț, "O descoperire de factură avară la Sânnicolau Mare (jud. Timiș) [A discovery relating to Avar Period in Sânnicolau Mare (Timiș County)]," *Analele Banatului Serie Nouă* 6 (1998), 316, pl. I.1–6.

semiglobular appliqués are known from several burial assemblages on the territory of present-day Budapest: grave 1 on Szőlő Street,[113] graves 39 and 55 at Csepel-Háros,[114] and grave 8 at Vöröskereszt.[115]

Grave 44 (a horse burial) in Band produced rosette-shaped mounts for the harness very similar to those made with two dies found in Felnac (Fig. 39.4–5).[116] Similar bronze and lead rosettes are known from graves 40, 52, and 73 in Budapest-Csepel-Háros[117] and from Szebény 2,[118] all dated to the first half of the 7th century.

Cross-shaped mounts with tasseled ornament, such as on another die from Felnac (Fig. 40.5) have been found on sites in Budapest – grave 1 on Szőlő Street,[119] grave 39 in Budapest-Csepel-Háros,[120] and grave 8 at Vöröskereszt.[121]

It is worth mentioning in this context that except the exceptionally rich, 7th-century assemblages in Malo Pereshchepyne and Hlodosy (Ukraine), the Early Avar-age, silver rosette-shaped appliqués for the harness have no analogies outside the Carpathian Basin.[122]

Among dress accessories, the origin of which may be in the forest-steppe zone of Eastern Europe, of particular significance are tubular beads, ribbed appliqués (or bars), and trapezoidal pendants. All three categories of artifacts were produced with molds such as found in Budureasca 5, Bernashivka, and Vác-Kavicsbánya. The clay mold from Traian may have also been used to cast trapezoidal pendants. Tubular beads, ribbed appliqués, and trapezoidal

113 Nagy, *Awarenzeitliche Gräberfelder*, 2: 46, pl. 38, 41–43, 45–46, 47–49.

114 Nagy, *Awarenzeitliche Gräberfelder*, grave 39: 1: 155 and 163; 2: 115, pl. 107.39.10–11 and 119, pl. 111.55.9, 11.

115 Nagy, *Awarenzeitliche Gräberfelder*, 1: 193; 2: 139, pl. 121.8.21, 22–45.

116 Kovács, "A mezőbándi ásatások," 321, fig. 39. 2, 4–5.

117 Nagy, *Awarenzeitliche Gräberfelder*, grave 40: 1: 156; 2: 116, pl. 108, 40.11. Grave 52: 1: 161; 2: 118, pl. 110, 52.20. Grave 73: 1: 169; 2: 12, pl. 114.15.

118 Éva Garam, "The Szebény I–III Cemetery," in *Avar Finds in the Hungarian National Museum. Cemeteries of the Avar Period (567–827) in Hungary* 1, ed. Ilona Kovrig (Budapest: Akadémiai Kiadó, 1975), 75, fig. 24, grave 9.5; 108.

119 Nagy, *Awarenzeitliche Gräberfelder*, 2: 46, pl. 38. 41–43, 45–46, 47–49.

120 Nagy, *Awarenzeitliche Gräberfelder*, grave 39: 1: 155; 2: 115, pl. 107, 39.10–11.

121 Nagy, *Awarenzeitliche Gräberfelder*, 1: 193; 2: 139, pl. 131.8.21, 22–45.

122 Curta, *The Making of the Slavs*, 205, note 33.

pendants are female dress accessories most typical for 7th-century assemblages in the Middle Dnieper region.[123]

123 Ya. V. Volodarets-Urbanovych, "Pronizki epokhi rann'ogo seredn'ovichchia zi slov'ians'kikh pam'iatok pivdnia Skhidnoi Evropy [Bronze tubular beads of early medieval Slavic antiquities]," *Arkheologiia i Davnia istoriia Ukraini* 13, no. 2 (2014), 45; Ya. V. Volodarets-Urbanovych, "Pronizki epokhi rann'ogo seredn'ovichchia zi slov'ians' kikh pam'iatok pivdnia Skhidnoi Evropy [Bronze tubular beads of early medieval Slavic antiquities from the South of Eastern Europe sites]," in *Starozhitnosti Livoberezhnogo Podniprov'ia* (2014), 39. For the typology of tubular beads and striated bars, see Volodarets-Urbanovych, "Pronizki epokhi rann'ogo seredn'ovichchia," in *Arkheologiia i Davnia istoriia Ukraini* 13.

CHAPTER 8

The Cultural and Chronological Framework of the Tool Finds

1 Graves with Tools

1.1 *Band*

Grave 10 from Band is part of a cemetery attributed to the late "Germanic" (Merovingian) milieu and dated between the last third of the 6th and the mid-7th century. An important element for the chronology of the cemetery is the finger-ring from grave 34, which is decorated in animal style II with dentil ornament, a style most typical for the late 6th and the early 7th century.[1] The grave was robbed, and many more chronologically sensitive artifacts may have been among the grave goods. Located on the edge of the excavated cemetery, the burial assemblage may be dated like those in the neighboring graves, some of which contain horse bones and grave goods dated between 600 and 630.[2] In my opinion, grave 10 is probably to be dated to ca. 600, because so many artifacts in that assemblage (including complex tools, such as the mechanically-driven drill) have analogies in 6th-century assemblages.[3] Most prominent among them is the grave with tools from Hérouvillette, in which, like in Band, a tool box was placed at the feet of the body to be buried. Particularly important in this context is the presence in the burial assemblage at Hérouvillette of Merovingian coins struck in the mid-6th century as well as of an axe dated to the first half of the 6th century.[4]

More graves with tools dated to the 6th century are known from Central Europe. The grave found in Brno was dated to the first decades of the 6th century.[5] Of a similar date is the grave with tools from Poysdorf,[6] while

1 Fettich, *Das awarenzeitliche Kunstgewerbe*, 51.

2 Kiss, *Das awarenzeitliche Gräberfeld*, 265. For horse burials in early medieval cemeteries in Transylvania, see Alpár Dobos, "Az erdélyi soros temetők lovastemetkezései [The horse burials of the row-grave cemeteries from Transylvania]," in *Erdély és kapcsolatai a kora népvándorlás korában*, ed. Zsolt Körösfői (Székelykeresztúr: Molnár István Múzeum, 2010–2011), pp. 397–398.

3 Magnus, Mollerop, Sjovold, "Migration Period Graves," N 3, 5 (2).

4 Decaens et al., *Un nouveau cimetière*, 91.

5 Jaroslav Tejral, *Grundzüge der Völkerwanderungszeit in Mähren* (Prague: Academia, 1976), 81–82.

6 Beninger, "Der Langobardenfriedhof," 179; for the date, see Capelle 1971, 51.

© DANIELA TĂNASE, 2021 | DOI:10.1163/9789004436930_010

only a general date within the 6th century can be established for the grave in Schönebeck (Germany).[7] All those examples suggest that the deposition of tools in graves was a specifically "Germanic" custom. If so, then the Band grave is an indication of the survival of Gepids under Avar rule. However, graves with tools have also been found in the western part of the Carpathian Basin. For example, grave 80 in Kölked Feketekapu B is dated to the Early Avar age (ca. 570 to ca. 630),[8] while grave 323 and 369 at Csákberény-Orondpuszta can only be dated broadly within the 7th century.[9] Only arrow heads, bow reinforcement plates, and armor plates have been found in the two assemblages in Csákberény-Orondpuszta, and none of those artifacts can narrow down the chronology. Unlike, Csákberény-Orondpuszta and Kölked Feketekapu B, there were no arrow heads in the Band grave, only a spear head. A spear head was associated with tools in the Kunszentmárton grave, which was dated to the 7th century. Both the spear head and the helmet suggest that the man was buried in grave 10 at Band according to the "Germanic" traditions pertaining to weapon burials. He may well have been a Gepid craftsman, but some have tried to give him a local or Byzantine identity, in an attempt to make him a member of the native, Romance-speaking population.[10] He was even believed to be an itinerant craftsman from Byzantium working on commission for barbarian patrons.[11]

In short, the grave with tools from Band is best understood against the background of "Germanic" traditions and of the late Gepid culture. Its date can be established with sufficient certainty around the year 600 or in the early 7th century.

1.2 *Felnac*

Felnac is commonly dated to the first third of 7th century.[12] The main argument in favor of that date is the similarity between some of the dies from Felnac and the golden belt mounts from the Akalan hoard. The most recent, "closing" coins in that hoard are two *solidi* struck for Emperor Heraclius between 616 and 629,

---

7 Schmidt, *Die späte Völkerwanderungszeit*, 30 and 205, pl. 17.2a.

8 Kiss, *Das awarenzeitliche Gräberfeld*, 1: 345.

9 Rácz, *Die Goldschmiedegräber*, 6; 149–151; 166, fig. 5–8. In fact, the grave may well be of a mid-7th-century date.

10 Gepid craftsman: Kovács, "A mezőbándi ásatások," 429; Werner, "Waage." Native or Byzantine: Teodor, "Elemente și influențe bizantine," 106; Teodor, *Romanitatea*, 32–33, 37.

11 Teodor, *Meșteșugurile*, 31, 33.

12 István Bóna, "Avar lovassír Iváncsáról [Grave of an Avar Horseman at Iváncsa]," *Archaeologiai Értesitő* 97 (1970), 262; Uwe Fiedler, "Die Gürtelbesatzstücke von Akalan, ihre Funktion und kulturelle Stellung," *Izvestiia na Arkheologičeskiia Institut* 38 (1994), 31; Curta, *The Making of the Slavs*, 264.

and a *hexagram* minted in the name of the same emperor at some point between 615 and 625.[13] The hoard was most likely buried during the Avar siege of Constantinople (626).[14] Similar mounts are also known from a horseman grave discovered in Sânpetru German (Arad County). The assemblage in that grave is coin-dated with a light-weight *solidus* struck for Emperor between 615 and 625.[15] The association in those two assemblages of belt fittings similar to the Felnac dies with gold coins minted at some point between 615 and 625 strongly suggests a date of ca. 630 for the grave with tools from Felnac.[16] To narrow down even further the date of the dies found in that grave, one must take into consideration the chronology of particular decorative motifs on the dies. The Martynivka-type decoration (Fig. 38.6), for example, is dated shortly before and shortly after 600,[17] while the palm-frond decoration (Fig. 38.1–5) appears throughout the 7th century.[18] Finally, the Tarnaméra-type motif (Fig. 38.7) is most typical for the second third and the middle of the 7th century.[19] Belt mounts like the dies in Felnac (Fig. 37.3–10) were in fashion in the first third of the 7th century.[20] To the same chronological interval point the specimens discovered in Transdanubia. Those found in grave 8 at Keszthelyi-Fenékpuszta were associated with a gold piece stamped with the obverse of a coin struck for Emperor Maurice.[21] The mounts in grave 132 of the cemetery excavated in Linz-Zizlau (Austria) were found together with half of a *hexagram* struck for Heraclius ca. 630.[22]

The ritual of including bronze dies in the grave goods was also certified in several other male graves in the Tisza Plain at Aradac, Békéssámson, Gátér,

13 Fiedler, "Die Gürtelbesatzstücke," 31.

14 Morrison, Popović, Ivanišević, *Les trésors monétaires byzantins des Balkans et d'Asie Mineure (491–713)*, 117.

15 Bóna, "Avar lovassír Iváncsáról," 262; Péter Somogyi, *Byzantinische Fundmünzen der Awarenzeit*, (Monographien zur Frühgeschichte und Mittelalterarchäologie) 5 (Innsbruck: Universitätsverlag Wagner, 1997), 77.

16 Curta, *The Making of the Slavs*, 264.

17 Garam, *Funde*, 129–130.

18 Garam, *Funde*, 135.

19 Garam, *Funde*, 146.

20 Garam, *Funde*, 119.

21 István Bóna, "Ein Vierteljahrhundert der Völkerwanderungszeitforschung in Ungarn," *Acta Archaeologica Academiae Scientiarum Hungaricae* (1971), 297; Somogyi, *Byzantinische Fundmünzen*, 50.

22 Hertha Ladenbauer Orel, *Linz-Zizlau. Das baierische Gräberfeld an der Traunmündung* (Linz: Anton Schroll & Co., 1960), 56; Wolfgang R. O. Hahn, "Die Fundmünzen des 5.–9. Jahrhunderts in Österreich und den unmittelbar angrenzenden Gebieten," in *Die Geburt Mitteleuropas. Geschichte Österreichs vor seiner Entstehung 378–907*, ed. Herwig Wolfram (Vienna: Verlag der österreichischen Akademie der Wissenschaften, 1987), p. 459.

Kunszentmárton, and Rákóczifalva-Kastélydomb, as well as in a female grave in Tiszafüred. The Kunszentmárton dies were used to manufacture belt fittings dated to the first half of the 7th century, despite being associated with 6th-century Byzantine *exagia*.[23] Buckles of the Pápa type cannot be dated earlier than 600 or later than 630.[24] By contrast, the dies found in Gátér were used to make belt and harness mounts that could be dated to the third quarter of the 7th century.[25] The Tiszafüred die may be dated to the middle or the last third of the 7th century.[26] Several other dies for belt mounts are dated to the first three decades (Aradac and Békéssámson) or the second half of the 7th century (Rákóczifalva-Kastélydomb).[27] The deposition of dies in graves is, therefore, restricted to the 7th century, the golden age of die-pressing as the main technique for jewelry manufacture.[28]

Some Romanian scholars believe that the craftsman buried in Felnac was an Avar,[29] others that he was either a Byzantine or a local craftsman.[30] Much like in the case of Band, later opinions tend to make him an itinerant craftsman from Byzantium working for barbarian patrons,[31] or a native craftsman working with an ornamental repertoire brought from and techniques learned in Byzantium.[32] Needless to say, there is no evidence to support either one of those claims. But the idea that the craftsman was of Byzantine origin is based primarily upon the assumption that the dies themselves are of Byzantine origin.[33] In my opinion, the fact that the ornamental style of the dies, or the dies themselves were made in Byzantium has absolutely nothing to do with the ethnic identity of the craftsman, whatever that may be.

While the Costești molds have been linked to a refugee from Byzantium at the time of the Iconoclastic Controversy,[34] nothing of that sort may be presumed

23 Csallány, *A Kunszentmártoni avarkori ötvösir*, 54.
24 Garam, *Funde*, 111.
25 Rácz, *Die Goldschmiedegräber*, p. 157.
26 Garam, *Funde*, 41.
27 Rácz, *Die Goldschmiedegräber*, p. 192.
28 The stamping technique appears in the Carpathian Basin as early as the 7th century AD: Rácz, *Die Goldschmiedegräber*, 93.
29 Kurt Horedt, "Das Awarenproblem," 104, 116; *Istoria României* [Romanian History], 4 vols., vol. 1: eds. Petre Constantinescu-Iași, Emil Condurachi, Constantin Daicoviciu (Bucharest: Editura Republicii Populare Române, 1960), 1: 716, fg. 179. 1–6; Tănase, "Câteva observații," 245–246.
30 Teodor, "Elemente și influențe bizantine," 106; Teodor, *Romanitatea*, pp. 32–33 and 37.
31 Teodor, *Meșteșugurile*, 31, 33.
32 Mărghitan, *Banatul*, 60–61; Olteanu, *Societatea*, 130.
33 For a brief overview of those opinions, see Rácz, *Die Goldschmiedegräber*, 22–23.
34 Szmoniewski, "Production," 129.

for the Felnac dies. During the first third of the 7th century, there was a continuing military pressure upon the Byzantine lands in the Balkans, and the political and military situation was too volatile for an itinerant craftsman from Byzantium to travel safely to the Avar Qaganate. There is nothing in Felnac that could remotely suggest that the craftsman in question was Christian or could have produced reliquaries or icons. It is also hard to believe that a Byzantine craftsman would have been buried together with a horse or parts of a horse body. Although burials are known from the lands north of the Danube that could be interpreted as Christian, graves with tools are not among them.[35]

That the grave in Felnac contained a horse skeleton (or bones) reminds one of the grave with tools from Kunszentmárton. In both cases, the burial custom is most typical for steppe nomads. The Avar warriors were buried with weapons and horses, and with richly decorated harness sets. Horse sacrifice at burial is clearly documented, as it is the burial of the entire body of the dead horse or only of parts thereof.[36] New discoveries, such as the three graves with horses from the cemetery excavated in Makó-Mikócsa-halom (Hungary), in a short distance from Felnac (see the map from the Fig. 2), confirm the association between the deposition of horses and the presence of tools in burial assemblages.[37]

It is likely that the two dies from Corund and Dumbrăveni were initially part of burial assemblages as well. That idea has already been advanced by Kurt Horedt, who first pointed out analogies in Avar-age assemblages.[38] While the Corund die used to produce Pančevo-type, double-shield belt mounts is dated to the last two thirds of the 7th century,[39] the die from Dumbrăveni, used to make for strap ends decorated with cross and geometric motifs, may be dated to the first half of the 7th century.[40]

1.3 *Sărata Monteoru*

The cremation cemetery at Sărata Monteoru includes a grave in which eight clay crucibles with round bottom and trefoil openings were deposited. The crucibles are similar to that found in the Bucharest-Bvneasa settlement. The idea has been put forward, according to which the grave in question was that of a jeweler, given that finds of dress accessories such as those from Sărata

35 László, *Steppenvölker*, 84.
36 Pohl, *Die Awaren*, 188, 203.
37 Rácz, *Die Goldschmiedegräber*, 191; Balogh, "Karpat havzasi'nda bir avar," 111–112, 117–120.
38 Horedt, *Contribuţii*, 70.
39 Garam, *Funde*, 148.
40 Rácz, *Die Goldschmiedegräber*, 31.

Monteoru are also known from Budureasca.[41] The only tools known so far in the region of the Middle and Lower Danube as associated with cremation, not inhumations graves are those from the Pókaszepetk (Hungary). A cremation grave of that biritual cemetery produced a scale with weights and Roman coins, most likely used as bullion. The grave was dated to the late 6th or to the first third of the 7th century, and attributed to a Slav merchant.[42] However, the idea of tool deposition was otherwise not associated in the Carpathian Basin cremations. Other than Sărata Monteoru and Pókaszepetk, no other such assemblages are known from the entire territory known to have been inhabited by Slavs in the early Middle Ages.

Some believe that clay crucibles were typically deposited in graves of Slavic women.[43] But that is true for the Balts, not the Slavs, and the graves in question are inhumations, not cremations.[44] Some inhumation graves dated to the 6th and 7th century in those areas of Eastern Europe that are believed to have been inhabited by Balts and Finns indeed contain tools such as clay crucibles, clay spoons, and molds. Moreover, such graves are typically of females, either teenagers and adults. Some have drawn the conclusion that in those communities, jewelry casting was practiced by women, not men.[45] The deposition of casting tools in female graves continued among the Finno-Ugrian peoples of the forest belt of Eastern Europe between the 9th and the 12th century, particularly in inhumations of biritual cemeteries of the Mari people in the Middle Volga region.[46] The Sărata Monteoru assemblage is therefore unique, and quite surprising. To be sure, the cremation cemetery discovered at Sărata Monteoru has been attributed to a Slav population.[47] Although some burial assemblages may be dated to the late 6th century,[48] most graves are likely of a 7th-century

---

41 Comșa, "Socio-economic organization," 186, 188.

42 Sós, "Frühmittelalterliche Brandbestattung," 426, 428.

43 Capelle, Vierck, "Modeln," 77.

44 The first to note that difference was Boris A. Rybakov, *Remeslo Drevneĭ Rusi* [The craft of ancient Russia] (Moskow: Izdatel'stvo Akademiia Nauk SSSR, 1948). I owe a debt of gratitude to Bartłomiej Sz. Szmonievski, who clarified for me this particular historiographic aspect.

45 Golubeva, "Devochki-Liteĭshchitsy," 32.

46 Nikitina, Efremova, "Pogrebal'nyĭ obriad," 146–165.

47 Ion Nestor, "Slavii pe teritoriul RPR în lumina documentelor arheologice [Slavs on the territory of the RPR in the light of archaeological documents]," *Studii și Cercetări de Istorie Veche* 10, no. 1 (1959), 51.

48 Ion Nestor, "Câteva considerații cu privire la cea mai veche locuire a slavilor pe teritoriul R.P.R. [Some considerations regarding the oldest habitation of the Slavs on the territory of R.P.R.]," in *Omagiu lui P. Constantinescu-Iași*, ed. Emil Condurachi (Bucharest: Editura Academiei Republicii Populare Române, 1965), p. 149.

date.[49] Because of the presence of wheel-made pottery, Ion Nestor attributed the cemetery to the so-called Ipotești-Cândești culture, which in turn was attributed to the local, Romance-speaking population.[50] More than a half-a-century after its excavation, the cemetery in Sărata Monteoru is still unpublished, with only a few, disparate finds known so far. For the moment, the only reason for attributing the grave with crucibles to a Slavic population is that the Slavs practiced cremation during the 6th and 7th centuries. If that date may be accepted for the grave itself, then it is important to note that the deposition of tools in graves was not restricted to the Germanic milieu. Exactly how a custom associated with populations practicing inhumation was adopted by another population practicing cremation remains unknown. However, it cannot be excluded that the cremating "Slavs" learned about tool deposition in graves from the local population.

2 Settlements

Only a small number of the tool finds have been found on settlement sites in assemblages that could help refine their chronology. Even if the archaeological context is known, its description is not sufficiently detailed. More often than not, the artifacts come from the filling of the settlement features, which they therefore post-date.[51] However, even though few tools come from well-dated contexts, they have been used to narrow down the chronology on the sites on which they have been found. This led to unwarranted assumptions about the time during which the tools were in use.

---

49 Ion Nestor, "L'établissement des Slaves en Roumanie à la lumière de quelques découvertes archéologiques récentes," *Dacia Nouvelle Série* 5 (1961), 437. It is quite possible that burial in Sărata Monteoru already began in the 5th century, as suggested by the fibula found in grave 1502, the analogies for which have been dated to the late 4th and first half of the 5th century [Uwe Fiedler, *Studien zu Gräberfeldern des 6. bis 9. Jahrhunderts an der unteren Donau* (Bonn: Rudolf Habelt, 1992), 82, 83 fig. 11/7].

50 Ion Nestor, "Continuitate în istoria formării poporului român. Reflecții pe marginea noilor date arheologice [Continuity in the history of the formation of the Romanian people. Reflections on the new archaeological data]," *Magazin Istoric* 3 (1969), 7; Ion Nestor, "Problèmes concernant les rapports entre les Slavs et la population autochtone en Roumanie," in *I Międzynarodowy Kongres archeologii slowianskiej. Warsawa, 14–18 IX 1965*, ed. Witold Hensel (Wroclaw/Warsaw/Cracow: Wydawnictwo Polskiej Akademii nauk, 1970), pp. 174–176.

51 Ciupercă, Măgureanu, "Unele observații," 151.

2.1 *Moldavia*

Settlements in Moldavia are commonly described as having two occupation phases. The first covers the last decades of the 5th and the first half of the 6th century, and has often been attributed to ever-present population speaking a Romance language (the presumed ancestors of the modern Romanians). The later occupation phase begins in the mid-6th century and covers much of the following century as well.[52] Most sites excavated in Moldavia have both occupation phases. A few that have only one phase are of a later date, and continued well in the 8th century (e.g., Lozna-Străteni).

One of the sites for which the idea of two consecutive phases has first been advanced is Botoşana.[53] Most casting implements from that site – molds, crucibles, ladles – have been attributed to the second occupation phase. Of a similar date are two other settlement sites excavated in Dolheştii Mari and Suceava-Şipot.[54] The dating of the latter site is secured by the find of a cast fibula with bent stem and of a so-called "Slavic" bow fibula.[55]

The settlement excavated in Lozna-Străteni was dated between the last quarter of the 7th and the late 8th century.[56] A cemetery was also found in Lozna-Străteni, with pit cremations. The cemetery was apparently in use at the same time as the occupation of the settlement.[57]

Unlike Botoşana, many of the metalworking tools found in Davideni have been attributed to the early phase of occupation dated to second half of the 5th and the first half of the 6th century, possibly up to 560–565.[58] The date of engravers and molds has thus been established on the basis of associated fibulae with bent stem, which are (wrongly) believed to be a late 5th or early 6th-century date.[59] Only two engravers have been attributed to the second occupation phase, which the excavator has dated between the second half of the

---

52 Teodor, "Unele probleme," 299–300; Mitrea, "Regiunea centrală," 98–100.

53 Teodor, *Civilizaţia romanică*, 63–65, 71–72.

54 Teodor, *Ceramica*, 73–75; Teodor, *Aşezarea medievală*, 53.

55 Teodor, *Aşezarea medievală*, 51–52. The fibula with bent stem found outside all known assemblages on the site may be dated to the late 6th century, on the basis of its analogies (Curta, Gândilă, "Too Much Typology," 67–71). The "Slavic" bow fibula found in house 2 has been dated to the year 600, or shortly before that (Curta, "Werner's class I H," 70).

56 Teodor, Mitrea, "Cercetări arheologice," 289–290; Teodor, *Un centru*, 74.

57 Teodor, "Slavii," 235; Dan Gh. Teodor, "Necropola medievală timpurie de incineraţie de la Lozna-Botoşani [Early medieval cremation necropolis from Lozna-Botoşani]," *Arheologia Moldovei* 35 (2012), 257.

58 Mitrea, *Aşezarea de la Davideni*, 132.

59 Mitrea, *Aşezarea de la Davideni*, 138–139, 142–143. This fibula may be dated to the second half of the 6th or to the early 7th century (Florin Curta, Andrei Gândilă, "Sixth-century fibulae with bent stem," *Peuce* 11 (2013), 125, 133, 173, fig. 29).

6th century and the late 7th century.[60] In my opinion, the second occupation phase at Davideni did not extend beyond the mid-7th century, as indicated by the "Slavic" bow fibulae found in assemblages attributed to that phase.[61] The same chronology was established for the settlements excavated in Ştefan cel Mare-Gutinaş[62] and Izvoare-Bahna.[63] A short occupation phase dated to the 6th and 7th century was postulated for Dodeşti.[64] This may well correspond to the second phase of occupation on most other sites dated between the late 6th century and the mid-7th century.

The molds from Cucuteni,[65] Poieniţa, Răcoasa, Rădeni, Coroteni,[66] and Traian (Neamţ co.)[67] have all been dated to the 6th and 7th century. Only the Rădeni mold is also believed to be of a 5th- or early 6th-century date.[68] By contrast, there seems to be no doubt that the bone molds from Costeşti are of a later 7th-century date.[69] Some have even dated them to the first half of the 8th century under the assumption that the craftsman employing the molds was a refugee from the Empire fleeing the persecutions of iconoclastic emperors. However, it is more likely that the molds have a 7th-century date.[70] The same is true for the molds from Cucuteni, Rădeni, Soveja, Poieniţa, Răcoasa, which are all stylistically similar, their ornamental motifs being quite common for the Avar age. Nonetheless, some have advanced the idea that the Soveja mold may be dated to the 7th century, and the others to the first half of the 8th century, a situation which reminds one of the discussion around the molds from Costeşti.[71] Based on such things as the rosette or lunular earring carvings, the molds from Aldeni and Dichiseni may also be dated to the second half of 7th century, much like the stone mold from Vác-Kavicsbánya.[72]

Advocates of the idea that settlement sites in Moldavia have two occupation phases typically attribute the first phase to the local, Romance-speaking population under the influence of the early Byzantine civilization, and the

60 Mitrea, *Aşezarea de la Davideni*, 157.
61 Mitrea, *Aşezarea de la Davideni*, 160–165.
62 Mitrea, Eminovici, Momanu, "Aşezarea," 231; Mitrea, *Aşezarea medievală*, 92–93.
63 Mitrea, *Aşezarea din secolele VI–IX*, 101–102.
64 Teodor, *Continuitatea*, 32.
65 Boghian, "Un moule," 118.
66 Bobi, "Contribuţii," 107, 112–113.
67 Hânceanu, "Două piese," 124.
68 Mitrea, "Regiunea centrală," 108.
69 Teodor, "Elemente şi influenţe bizantine," 101–102; 106; 107, fig. 6/12.
70 Szmoniewski, "Production," 129–130.
71 Szmoniewski, "Production," 127.
72 Tettamanti, *Das awarenzeitliche Gräberfeld*, 32; 133, pl. 5. grave 140.8.

second phase to the early Slavs.[73] The first phase has even been turned into an archaeological culture called Costişa-Botoşana-Hansca, which is believed to be authentically "native" with no "foreign" admixture.[74] Only in the second half of the 6th century does the material culture evidence appear that may signal newcomers, the Sclavenes and the Antes. Shortly before and after 600, northern Moldavia is believed to have been largely Slavic.[75]

The S(c)lav(ene)s, who are supposed to be identified archaeologically by means of the handmade pottery of the Korchak type, lived in the densely forested areas of Moldavia and the eastern Walachia, and even crossed the Eastern Carpathians into southeastern Transylvania. By contrast, the Antes used the supposedly typical Pen'kivka pottery, and lived in the forest-steppe region of southeastern Moldavia and eastern Walachia.[76] According to such theories, coming from their *Urheimat* in the north, the Slavs – Sclavenes and Antes – reached the Lower Danube during the reign of Justinian, and settled in southeastern Walachia. From southern Moldavia, they entered the southeastern part of Transylvania through the Oituz Pass, and from Walachia they moved to the west of the river Olt.[77]

However, some have recently disputed the idea that the Antes were Slavs. Instead, they are believed to have been a conglomerate of nomadic, seminomadic, or even settled populations, which included Alans, "Huns" (Cutrigurs, Utigurs, and Bulgars), and small group of Slavs. That, at least, is the interpretation of a passage in Procopius of Caesarea in which the Sclavenes and the Antes are described as living a "hard and unrefined life" and as preserving "the Hunnic character in all its simplicity."[78]

2.2 *Walachia and Oltenia*

Much like in Moldavia, settlements in Walachia are commonly regarded as having two occupation phases, one lasting until the mid-6th century and largely corresponding to the economic revival of the Empire between the reigns of Anastasius and Justinian, and to an increased influence of the Roman civilization in the lands north of the river Danube. By contrast, the second phase, which begins after the middle of the 6th century and continues well into the

73 Mitrea, *Aşezarea de la Davideni*, 205–206.

74 Teodor, *Civilizaţia romanică*, 63–73; Teodor, *Aşezarea medievală*, 53.

75 Teodor, *Ceramica*, 74–75.

76 Dan Gh. Teodor, "Unele consideraţii privind originea şi cultura anţilor," *Arheologia Moldovei* 16 (1993), 207.

77 Comşa, "Socio-economic," 171.

78 Procopius of Caesarea, *Wars* VII 14.28, 409; Teodor, "Unele consideraţii," 209; Teodor, "Slavii," 224, 225, note 12.

last third of the 7th century, was marked by the political and military preeminence of nomads – the Cutrigurs up to 559, and then the Avars until 626. Sites in southern Romania, however, display a number of common features dated between the second half of the 6th and the first decade of the 7th century. There is a clear increase in the number of sites, hoards and isolated finds of coins, which coincide in time with larger and better organized raids of the Slavs under their own chieftains. In other words, that was a period of political and social, as well as cultural change.[79] Most finds from this period come from northern, northeastern and southwestern Walachia.

Several settlements have been excavated on the territory of present-day Bucharest. That on the Soldat Ghivan Nicolae Street was dated to the second half or the last quarter of the 6th century.[80] The sites at Străulești-Măicănești and Străulești-Lunca – probably parts of one and the same settlement – were initially dated to the 6th century, perhaps also the early 7th century.[81] However, coins struck for Emperor Justinian and found on the site suggest a date in the middle or third quarter of the 6th century.[82] It is worth mentioning that in Străulești-Lunca the 6th-century settlement overlaps a 3rd-century settlement, a situation otherwise documented elsewhere in Walachia as well.[83]

Another cluster of settlements is located in the sub-Carpathian area of the Prahova and Buzău counties – Budureasca, Târgșor, Șirna, Aldeni, and Izvorul Dulce.

Budureasca was a valley protected by hills, with several settlements located very close to each other, and attributed to the very beginning of the Ipotești-Cândești culture, another archaeological culture of the "native" population.[84] However, a recent study of the Budureasca molds advanced a much broader dating between the late 6th and the early 8th century.[85] The beginning of the occupation on the settlement site in Târgșor is dated to the second half of 5th century or ca. 500.[86] Șirna was initially dated between the 5th and the 7th century.[87] Only later were two occupation phases distinguished – one in the 5th and first half of the 6th century, the other between the second

79 Curta, *The Making of the Slavs*, 246.

80 Dolinescu-Ferche, Constantiniu, "Un établissement," 324.

81 Teodor, *Ceramica*, 119–120.

82 Constantiniu, "Săpăturile de la Străulești-Măicănești," 189.

83 Constantiniu, "Așezarea autohtonă prefeudală de la Băneasa (La Stejar)," 80; Teodor, *Ceramica*, 121.

84 Teodor, *Ceramica*, 137–138.

85 Măgureanu, Ciupercă, "The 6th–8th Centuries Metallurgical Activity," 301.

86 Teodor, *Ceramica*, 140.

87 Olteanu, Teodorescu, Neagu, "Rezultatul," 417–419; Olteanu, Neagu, "Rezultatele," 385.

half of the 6th century and the late 7th century. Smelting furnaces slag, a ladle and stone molds are known from the first, more smelting furnaces and a chisel from the second occupation phase.[88] Comparing the later occupation phase at Şirna with the evidence from Dulceanca it appears that there was an intensification of ironworking activities in the late 6th and during the early 7th century, when some inhabitants of both settlements may have been specialist smelters.

Dulceanca is the most important settlement in another cluster of the Burdea Plain (Teleorman County). Dulceanca I is dated to the 6th century.[89] More recently, Dulceanca IV was dated, largely on the basis of ceramics, to the second decade of 6th century, followed by Dulceanca II in the third decade of the 6th century, and Dulceanca I from 560 to the end of the century, and Dulceanca III as of a 7th- but also 8th-century date.[90]

Excavations on a much smaller scale from Oltenia (Little Walachia) revealed other settlements at Craiova, Doba, Făcăi, Găneasa, Gropşani, Insula Banului, Izvorul Frumos, and Băbeni-Olteţ.[91] All those settlements are dated to the 6th, as well as at the early 7th century.[92] The settlement excavated in Gropşani was published in more detail and is dated to the first half of the 6th century.[93] A portion of another settlement has been excavated Craiova-Fântâna Obedeanu. Its beginnings may be dated to the late 5th century, but the main phase of occupation is clearly of a 6th-century date.[94]

As already mentioned, the material culture of the local population in Walachia has been dubbed the "Ipoteşti-Cândeşti-Ciurel culture," the chronology of which covers the entire period between the last third of the 5th century and the late 7th century. Advocates of that culture maintain that it had typically Romance features enhanced through contact with the Balkan provinces of the Empire. Because of that, the Slavs quickly adapted themselves to the much superior, local environment, which led to a Daco-Roman-Slavic synthesis – the very basis for the emergence of the Romanian language.[95]

Others, however, have maintained that the Ipoteşti-Cândeşti-Ciurel culture was "invented" by Romanian archaeologists to illustrate the life of the Romanian

88 Olteanu, Grigore, Nicolae, *Comunitatea sătească*, 42–50.

89 Dolinescu-Ferche, *Aşezări*, 126, 127, note 57.

90 Teodor, *Ceramica*, 105–106.

91 Zaharia, "La station nº 2 de Bratei," 316.

92 Teodor, *Ceramica*, 145–151.

93 Popilian, Nica, *Gropşani*, 123.

94 Gheorghe Popilian, Marin Nica, "Aşezarea prefeudală de la Craiova (Fântâna Obedeanu) [Pre-feudal settlement from Craiova (Obedeanu Fountain)]," *Drobeta* 15 (2005), 148.

95 Victor Teodorescu, "Despre cultura Ipoteşti-Cîndeşti," 496, 498–499; Teodor, "Elemente şi influenţe bizantine," 97; Comşa, "Socio-economic organization," 172.

civilization before the arrival of the "savage Slavs."[96] Still others claim that the label obscures the existence of two separate cultures. The Ciurel culture is characterized by clay ovens carved into the sides of house pits, usually with clay rolls inside or around it. The pottery is typically wheel-made, with shapes similar to those of the Roman pottery in the Balkans. The Cândești culture, by contrast, has stone ovens placed in the corners of the sunken-floored buildings, often opposite to the entrance, and without clay rolls. Metal, bone and antler artifacts are more often found on Ciurel- than in Cândești-type settlement sites. Moreover, the name Ipotești for this culture is inadequate, as only halves of two sunken-floored houses have been excavated on the eponymous site.[97] Others dismissed the idea of two different cultures, as the difference in heating installations could easily be explained by means of environmental conditions.[98] Be as it may, there seems to be general agreement that as early as the second half of the 6th century, the material culture of communities in Romania (Walachia and Moldavia), Moldova and southwestern Ukraine began to change. The archaeological features and artifacts point to a regional style. The economy of those communities was agrarian and based on the cultivation of cereals. Clay pans, which appear in great numbers in settlement sites, bespeak the consumption of flatbread, possibly of ritual significance, as such vessels are typically found in houses with a relative abundance of goods and which are located in the central area of the settlements.[99] This was the period during which clay or stone ovens appeared in houses, the pottery came to the decorated with finger impressions or notches on the lit, and the local production of so-called "Slavic" bow fibulae began. The communal activity took place in the central area of the settlement, around which there was a great concentration of clay pans, but also tools. This was, perhaps, the arena of ceremonies of significance for the communal identity.[100]

Much has been written about the ethnicity of the craftsmen. Stone molds are believed to have been used (only) by Byzantines or the natives (Romance-speaking population), while clay molds could be used both by natives and

96 Curta, *The Making of the Slavs*, 231.

97 Petre Diaconu, "Problemele necropolelor de la Dunărea de Jos din sec. VI–IX în viziunea lui Uwe Fiedler [The problems of the necropolis of the Lower Danube from the 6th–9th centuries in the vision of Uwe Fiedler]," in *Recenzii și discuții arheologice* by Petre Diaconu, vol. 1 (Călărași: S. C. Caro Trading '94 S.R.L., 1994), 132.

98 Stanciu, *Locuirea*, 101, note 709.

99 Florin Curta, "Social identity on the platter. Clay pans in sixth to seventh century ceramic assemblages," in *Entangled Identities and Otherness in Late Antique and Early Medieval Europe*, eds. Jorge López Quiroga, Michel Kazanski and Vujadin Ivanišević (Oxford: BAR Publishing, 2017), pp. 139–140, pp. 142–143.

100 Curta, *The Making of the Slavs*, 309.

by "foreign" (Slav) craftsmen, who thus adopted and adapted the Byzantine ornaments.[101] There is absolutely no evidential basis for such claims, for clay and stone molds were used concurrently. This is definitely the case of the settlement from Budureasca 4 and Șirna, in which both stone and clay molds were found. Others claimed that the existence of local, Romance-speaking craftsmen does not exclude the possibility of itinerant craftsmen from Byzantium. The latter worked on commission and spread the Byzantine fashions among both the native Dacoromans, and the Slavs.[102] At the same time, the local population used more primitive technologies, such as smelting "bog iron" in clay pots and special pits, a procedure adopted from the early Slavs. The archaeological evidence for such technologies, therefore, is no necessary indication of the existence of the Slavs.[103]

2.3 *Transylvania*

There are two kinds of settlement sites in Transylvania and the (north) western regions of present-day Romania, which have produced evidence of metalworking. Morești (Mureș County) has been attributed to the Gepids. The settlements of the so-called Lazuri-Pișcolt group in the northwest (Lazuri, Tășnad, Peleș, Zalău, Culciu Mare[104]), as well as those in Central and Southeastern Transylvania (Poian, Cernat, Ghidfalău, Sfântu Gheorghe, Bezid, Șimonești, Cristuru Secuiesc, and Filiaș[105]), which are very similar to settlement sites in Moldavia, have been attributed to the Slavs. In the middle of Transylvania, the settlement at site no. 2 in Bratei, which has been attributed to the Romance-speaking population, but which existed during and after the Gepid rule over Transylvania, poses problems of ethnic attribution. The material culture in the settlement is not different from that of cemetery no. 3 in Bratei, which has been attributed to the Gepids,[106] while finds related to ironworking (a ladle and iron slag) remind one of similar finds from Poian and Lazuri. Moreover, the settlement site in Bratei 2 has two occupation phases, one dated between the mid-6th and the first half of 7th century, and the other between the first half of the 7th and the beginning of 8th century.[107] Some have attributed the changes in the local society and material culture to the Slavic

101 Comșa, "Socio-economic organization," 189.
102 Teodor, *Meșteșugurile*, 105.
103 Teodor, "Slavii," 231.
104 Stanciu, "Așezarea," 161–163; Stanciu, *Locuirea*, 107.
105 Ioan Stanciu, "The Problem of the Earliest Slavs in Intra-Carpathian Romania (Transylvania and the North-West Vicinity)," *Slovenská archeológia* 61, no. 2 (2013), 338–349.
106 Bârzu, *Ein gepidisches Denkmal*, 146–148.
107 Zaharia, "La station n° 2 de Bratei," 329.

newcomers, although the same scholars insist that the Daco-Roman traditions prevailed and the Slavs were eventually assimilated.[108] For example, at Cristuru Secuiesc (Harghita County) both settlement features have been found, which have parallels in Moldavia, and a small, Gepid cemetery.[109] A process of acculturation between late Gepids and Slavs seems to have taken place at Cristuru Secuiesc during the second half of the 7th century. To be sure, the settlement was dated between the 6th and the 8th century, and the presence of the mold was interpreted as indicating the presence of a native, Christian population, not of the Slavs, who were converted to Christianity at a later time.[110] However, the Slavs are said to have entered southeastern Transylvania during the last third of the 6th century, and to have moved into the central part of the region only in the mid-7th century.[111]

One of the few sites clearly attributed to the Slavs is Lazuri (Satu Mare County). The settlement excavated there has been dated to the second half of 6th century and the first decades of 7th century.[112] That site is located in northwestern Romania, an area where the Slavic penetration appears to be somewhat earlier.

Finds related to metalworking are known from the settlements of Morești and Sânmiclăuș (Alba County), both dated between the second half of the 5th and the first half of the 6th century. While the Germanic character of both settlement and the cemetery discovered in Morești has not been disputed by anybody,[113] the situation at Sânmiclăuș is less clear.[114]

The chronology of the sites in Transylvania is based on cemetery sites and, to a lesser extent, on finds from settlements. The archaeology of the so-called "row grave cemeteries" in Transylvania is divided into four chronological groups, three of which concern the 6th and 7th centuries: group II, from 450 to 525; III, from 525 to 575; and IV, from ca. 600 to ca. 680. All archaeological features in those groups (both in cemeteries and in settlements) have been attributed to the Gepids.[115] The only debatable question was whether the Gepids survived under Avar rule, and whether any link may as a consequence be established between group III and IV. In other words, some maintained that

108 Zaharia, "La station nº 2 de Bratei," 330–331.

109 Harhoiu, "Quellenlage," 151.

110 Székely, "Eléments byzantins," 357–358.

111 Stanciu, "The Problem," 361.

112 Stanciu, "Așezarea," 161–163.

113 Horedt, *Morești*, 204–207.

114 Rustoiu, "Habitatul," 46, 53.

115 Kurt Horedt, *Siebenbürgen im Frühmittelalter* (Bonn: Dr. Rudolf Habelt GMBH, 1986), 22–46.

the Gepid settlements in Transylvania ceased to exist between 567–575, the population of group IV appearing after a while from elsewhere, following the Avars establishing control over Transylvania.[116] A 25-year long gap between groups III and IV has no support in the archaeological evidence. Moreover, following the occupation of the Carpathian Basin by the Avars, those coming to Transylvania in great numbers were Gepids under Avar rule, not Avars.[117] The acculturation process of the Gepids is also illustrated by cemetery finds of a later date.[118]

During the first three quarters of the 6th century, Transylvania was dominated by the, Gepid kingdom, after that by the qagan of the Avars. It is only in recent years that an approach from that particular perspective has been introduced to the interpretation of the archaeological data.[119] Over the last decades or so, scholars have highlighted the idea of the continuity of the Romance-speaking population and of its ability to assimilate other populations with which it has interacted. According to such views, before the immigration of the Slavs, Transylvania was inhabited by several groups of Gepids, who clustered in several small regions. Those groups were, in fact, military garrisons controlling the local, Romance-speaking population, which supplied

116 Horedt, "Die östliche Reihengräberkreis in Siebenbürgen," 251–268; Kurt Horedt, "Gepiden in Siebenbürgen-Gepiden an der Theiss. Eine Einwendung," *Acta Archaeologica Hungarica* 33, no. 1–4 (1981), 380; Kurt Horedt, "Germanen und Romanen in Siebenbürgen. Bemerkungen zu einer Besprechung," *Zeitschrift für Siebenbürgische Landeskunde* 77 (1983), 175; Horedt, *Siebenbürgen*, 31, 35–36. According to Horedt, Transylvania was not inhabited by anyone for 25 years.

117 István Bóna, "Gepiden in Siebenbürgen-Gepiden an der Theiss," *Acta Archaeologica Academiae Scientiarum Hungaricae* 31 (1979), 41–46; Attila Kiss, "Das Gräberfeld und die Siedlung der awarenzeitlichen germanischen Bevölkerung von Kölked," *Folia archaeologica* 30 (1979), 185–191; István Bóna, *Der Anbruch des Mittelalters*, 30; Radu Harhoiu, "Romanici și migratori în Dacia transilvană în secolele IV–VII [Romance-speaking population and migrators in the Transylvanian Dacia in the 4th–7th centuries]," *Memoriile secțiilor științifice (seria 4)* 12 (1987), 127 & sq.; Attila Kiss, "Das Weiterleben der Gepiden in der Awarenzeit," in *Die Völker Südosteuropa im 6. bis 8. Jahrhundert*, ed. Bernhard Hänsel, Südosteuropa Jahrbuch 17 (Berlin: Selbstverlag der Südosteuropa-Gesellschaft München und des Seminars für Ur- und Frühgeschichte der Freien Universität Berlin, 1987), pp. 210–214; Attila Kiss, "Germanen im awarenzeitlichen Karpatenbecken," in *Awarenforschungen. Archaeologia Austriaca Monographien 1 – Studien zur Archäologie der Awaren* 4, ed. Falko Daim (Vienna: Institut für Ur- und Frühgeschichte der Universität Wien, 1992), p. 49.

118 Harhoiu, "Quellenlage," 148.

119 Harhoiu, "Quellenlage," 132–149; Florin Curta, "Considerații privind conceptul de caracter etnic (etnicitate) în arheologia contemporană [Some remarks on the concept of ethnicity in contemporary archaeology]," *Arheologia Medievală* 4 (2002), 24.

them with provisions, including craft products. Those groups also oversaw the exploitation of salt and ore mines.[120]

3 The Issue of Ethnicity

For a long time in European archaeology, archaeological cultures were equated to ethnic groups.[121] In more recent studies, ethnicity is regarded as a social and cultural construct involving a certain way of manipulating material culture and of creating by such means an emblematic style. At the same time, ethnicity is also a function of power relations because both the emblematic style and the traditions gain significance in the context of changing power relations, when the representation of group identity is required.[122] However, ethnicity cannot be understood without the manipulation of material culture.[123] Thus, it may be possible to distinguish archaeologically between populations with particular characteristic features in terms of cultural behavior. A correct examination of the archaeological record and a critical analysis of the literary sources can also support the identification of ethnicity.[124]

Looking at the archaeological record the perspective of power structures in a given region means to find the historical context against which an emblematic style makes sense. Archaeological sources cannot tell what was the name a given population gave to itself. Only written sources can contribute to the understanding of that part of the problem, although in Late Antiquity (as well as later) many of them employed Empire. Moreover, ethnic groups in Late Antiquity were not defined on the basis of either language or culture, but according to their military and political significance.[125] Therefore, even the picture drawn in the written sources is far from clear, both for the "natives" in a given region, and for groups that came into being through the merging of several populations. An episode in the second book of the *Miracles of St. Demetrius*, written in the late 7th century, can illustrate the point. The unknown author

---

120 D. Gh. Teodor, "Autohtoni și slavi în spațiul carpato-dunăreano-pontic în secolele VII–VIII d. Hr. [Natives and Slavs in the Carpathian-Danube-Pontic space in the 7th–8th centuries AD]," in *Spațiul carpato-dunăreano-pontic în mileniul marilor migrații*, collections of studies written by Dan Gh. Teodor (Buzău: Alpha MDN, 2003), 421–422.

121 Brather, *Ethnische Interpretationen*, 319; Curta, "Considerații," 15.

122 Curta, "Considerații," 23–24; Florin Curta, "Ethnic Identity and Archaeology," in *Encyclopedia of Global Archaeology*, ed. Claire Smith (New York: Springer Reference, 2014), 2508–2509.

123 Curta, "Ethnic Identity," 2509.

124 Stanciu, *Locuirea*, 92.

125 Curta, *The Making of the Slavs*, 347.

of Book II describes how the Avars forcefully moved Roman prisoners from the Balkan provinces of the Empire to their lands in Pannonia. There, the descendants of those captives joined with Bulgars, Avars and other peoples, to form a new, quite large population, in which respect for tradition and love for the Roman people and customs seem to have been kept alive. After more than 60 years, a new ethnicity thus has emerged, and those belonging to that ethnic group wanted to be free. Even the qagan of the Avars regarded this as a separate ethnic group, for according to the Avar custom, the group received a ruler on its own in the person of a certain Kuver.[126] Many of Kuver's Christian subjects turned upon Thessalonica to take possession of the city and to establish there a great kingdom. One of its chiefs, Mavros, knew Greek, Slav(ic), Latin, and the language of the Bulgars.[127] A similarly complex identity is that of a Christian Gepid in the entourage of the Sclavene king Musokios. The Gepid also knew the Avar language.[128]

Byzantine writers were not interested in giving proper, accurate names to the populations in the lands north of the river Danube. They called them Scythians or Huns hundreds of years after those peoples had disappeared from history, and they generously extended the name of a contemporary population to other groups that were more or less geographically distant. "Sclavene," in the Byzantine sources, was a generic ("umbrella"-) name for various groups who lived across the border, in "Sclavini." As such, the name designated a heterogeneous conglomerate of ethnicities on the northern frontier of the Empire, reducing it to a single ethnicity. In that respect, the "Sclavinian" ethnicity is regarded as a Byzantine invention.[129]

Archaeologists have long established a number of analogies for finds in Moldavia and Walachia. Many of those analogies are from Slavic countries farther to the north or to the east, which made it possible to attribute certain categories of finds to the early Slavs.[130] However, it is impossible to apply that attribution to finds from Moldavia and Walachia, as there is no complete overlap between ethnicity and material culture.[131] Others have advanced the idea

126 Pohl, *Die Awaren*, 217; Harhoiu, "Quellenlage," 149.

127 Pohl, *Die Awaren*, 279.

128 Theophylact Simocatta, *History* VI 8.12–13, 9.1–10.

129 Curta, *The Making of the Slavs*, 118–119.

130 Andrei Măgureanu, Bartłomiej Sz. Szmoniewski, "Domestic dwellings in Moldavia and Wallachia in the initial phases of the Early Middle Ages," *Acta Archaeologica Carpathica* 38, (2003), 131.

131 Ion Nestor, "Formarea poporului român [Formation of the Romanian people]," in *Istoria poporului român*, ed. Andrei Oțetea (Bucharest: Editura Științifică, 1970), 103–104, 107. On the complexity of cultural assignation, see Stanciu, *Locuirea*, 93–110.

of an ethnically neutral term – the "post-Roman" archaeological culture[132] – as a better way to describe the ethno-cultural conglomerate in the making of the 6th-century northern frontier of Byzantium. Most Romanian scholars hold it as incontrovertible truth that during the 6th and 7th century, the present territory of Romania was inhabited by a Romance-speaking population, who coexisted with various other populations, which it gradually assimilated. The material culture of that population is the so-called Costișa-Botoșana-Hansca culture in Moldavia, the Ipotești-Cândești-Ciurel culture in Walachia, and Bratei-Biharea-Țaga culture in Transylvania. The argument has been forward that those three cultures are parts of a single cultural entity, for which some employ the term of Ipotești-Cândești-Filiaș-Botoșana culture.[133]

The molds for the production of pectoral crosses unmistakably point to a Christian population. Identical crosses were popular on contemporaneous sites in the central and western Balkans, and molds for making crosses were also found in several early Byzantine hillforts.[134] The presence of Christian symbols in the lands to the east and to the south from the Carpathian Mountains may be the indication of a slow inflow of Romance-speaking population from the Balkans.[135] According to the written sources, there were certainly prisoners of war and refugees from the Empire who lived among, and together with the Slavs and the Antes in the lands north of the Danube River. Prisoners of war could be ransomed, but were allowed to stay among their former masters, if they so chose.[136] Those remaining soon became so integrated into the native society that they appear as traitors to the Roman troops raiding the Sclavene territories in what is now southern Romania.[137] All of this shows a continuous movement of people from one bank of the river Danube to the other. As many must have been Christian, it is not difficult to imagine that they brought with them objects with Christian symbolism.

There are no indications, however, of any organized Christian community: there are no signs of conversion, and no churches. Objects with clearly Christian symbolism cannot therefore be associated with presumed missions to barbarians. They instead illustrate the manner in which barbarian elites employed objects of Roman origin for *imitatio imperii*. That crosses were primarily worn by women is perhaps an indication that such objects were viewed as

132 Teodor, *Ceramica*, 69.

133 Zaharia, "La station n° 2 de Bratei," 320.

134 Curta, *The Making of the Slavs*, 294.

135 Diaconu, "Problemele necropolelor," 132.

136 *Strategikon* XI 4.4, ed. Sophia Gyphtopoulou (Thessaloniki: Stamoulis, 2016). Others preferred to return to their homes in the Empire (*Strategikon* XI 4.31).

137 *Strategikon* XI 4.31.

symbols of religious identity for those who placed in God the hopes of them being one day ransomed and escaping from barbarian captivity.[138]

In Transylvania, such finds may also be associated to the Gepids, who were Arian Christians.[139] Despite the absence of any evidence of organized communities (such as those attested at about the same time in Hungary, at Keszthely, or in the mountains of Slovenia), it is quite possible that there were Christians in Transylvania.[140] Of particular concern in this respect are the crosses incised on pots found both in Transylvania and outside the Carpathian Mountains. Such pots could hardly be associated either with elites or with social prestige.[141]

A clear association between Christian symbols and the survival of a Romance-speaking population is also well documented in the western parts of the Carpathian Basin. A Christian population lived around an ecclesiastical center with a basilica in Keszthely (Zala County, in Hungary) and buried its dead with dress accessories bearing Christian scenes or symbols specific to the Mediterranean world.[142]

Therefore, one cannot exclude that the Christian artifacts may be used to mark ethnic boundaries. Refugees from Byzantium could have certainly used Christianity to mark the difference between themselves and the barbarians surrounding them. The same may be true for the many prisoners taken by Sclavenes during their numerous raids into the Empire, and then allowed to live among barbarians in the lands north of the river Danube.

Be as it may, many pieces of jewelry and dress accessories are imitations of products from the Empire. Not only the final product was imitated, but also the know-how. Stone molds, for example, were employed for casting on many hill-fort sites in the northern and northeastern Balkans, for example at Aegyssus

---

138 Curta, "Before Cyril and Methodius," 188–189; Curta, "Werner's Class I C," 110; Măgureanu, "Identitate religioasă," 39–41.

139 Ioan Stanciu, "Cross-shaped signs on 6th and 7th centuries pottery," in *Studia Romana et Mediævalia Europænsia Miscellanea in honorem annos LXXXV peragentis professoris emeriti Dan Gh. Teodor oblate*, eds. Dan Aparaschivei and George Bilavschi (Bucharest/Brăila: Editura Academiei Române, Muzeul Brăilei "Carol" Editura Istros, 2018), pp. 321–324; p. 351, fig. 11.

140 Florin Curta, "New remarks on Christianity beyond the 6th and early 7th century frontier of the Roman Empire," in *Keszthely-Fenékpuszta im Kontext spätantiker Kontinuitätsforschung zwischen Noricum und Moesia*, ed. Orsolya Heinrich-Tamáska (Budapest-Leipzig-Keszthely-Rahden: Verlag Marie Leidorf, 2011), p. 313.

141 Stanciu, "Cross-shaped signs," 319; 342, fig. 1a.

142 Tivadar Vida, "'They Asked to be Settled in Pannonia …' A Study on Integration and Acculturation – the Case of the Avars," in *Between Byzantium and the Steppe. Archaeological and Historical Studies in Honour of Csanád Bálint on the Occasion of his 70th Birthday*, eds. Ádám Bollók, Gergely Csiky and Tivadar Vida (Budapest: Institute of Archaeology, Research Centre for the Humanities, Hungarian Academy of Sciences, 2016), pp. 260–261.

(Tulcea), Argamum or Tropaeum Traiani in the province of Scythia Minor. The same is true of bronze dies for pressing metal sheets, which have been discovered in Oescus[143] (Fig. 48.2–3), Vratsa[144] (Fig. 48.1), Adalia,[145] Carthage,[146] in the Crimea,[147] in Constantinople,[148] and in Syria.[149] This is probably why some authors maintain that the first, authentically Byzantine products were brought to the lands north of the Danube by itinerant Byzantine merchants, after which they began to be produced by Byzantine techniques, such as mold casting.

Elsewhere, the blending of Byzantine and barbarian technological traditions is even more apparent. At the Bosporus and Chersonesus, in the Crimea, stone molds for casting bow fibulae have been found, along with metal dies for pressing metal sheets, not unlike those in the Tisza Plain.[150] That dies so similar to each other have been found in the Middle Danube region and in the Crimea has led some to the conclusion that Gepid craftsmen took refuge in the northern Black Sea area after the fall of the Gepid kingdom. They must have opened shop in the Byzantine cities of the Crimea, and began working on the basis of a mixture of their own decorative techniques and the techniques and styles most typical to early Byzantium.[151]

Leaving aside the debates surrounding the ethnic identity of the inhabitants of the 6th- to 7th-century settlements in Walachia and Moldavia, I have noted that metalworking instruments appear primarily in the second occupation phase, dated between the late 6th and the 7th century. This is a period during which, although the region north of the Lower Danube was under the military control of the Avars, the Avar culture as well as the culture of the people living in Walachia and Moldavia were under considerable Byzantine influence. This

143 Daskalov, Dimitrov, "On a Production," 69. fig. 1–2, 74.

144 Daskalov, Dimitrov, "On a Production," 69, fig. 1.3, 74.

145 Werner, "Zur Verbreitung," pl. 7.

146 Helmut Roth, "Almandinhandel und -verbreitung im Bereich des Mittelmeeres," *Beiträge zur allgemeine und vergleichende Archäologie* 2 (1980), 330, fig. 7/2.

147 Măgureanu, Ciupercă, "The 6th–8th Centuries Metallurgical Activity," 297.

148 Marvin C. Ross, *Catalogue of the Byzantine and early Medieval Antiquities in the Dumbarton Oaks Collection, 2, Jewelry, Enamels and Art of the Migration Period* (Washington D.C. 1965), 57, no. 66.

149 Etienne Coche de la Ferté, *L'antiquité chrétienne au Musée du Louvre* (Paris: Éditions de l'Oeil, 1958), 100, no. 31, fig. 38.

150 Aleksandr I. Ajbabin, "La fabrication des garnitures de ceintures et des fibules à Chersonèse, au Bosphore Cimmérien et dans la Gothie de Crimée aux VIe - VIIIe siècles," in *Outils d'orfèvres des temps anciens*, ed. Christiane Eulère (Saint-Germain-en-Laye: Société des Amis du Musée des Antiquités Nationales et du Château de Saint-Germain-en-Laye, 1993), p. 167, fig. 8. 1–4, 6.

151 Ajbabin, "La fabrication," pp. 165–166.

is further substantiated by the use of molds to produce dress accessories of essentially Byzantine origin – certain types of earrings, belt fittings, and pectoral crosses. Such dress accessories may be found in contemporaneous Avar or late Gepid cemeteries.

At the same time, however, there are clear influences of the "barbarian," know-how, as in the use of indoor smelting furnaces and clay pots for smelting iron. Equally "barbarian" is the preference of pressing dies for the production of dress accessories, both in the Banat and in Transylvania during the Avar age. Such dies have not so far been discovered either in Moldavia or in Walachia, where the commonest technology for the production of similar dress accessories was mold casting.

CHAPTER 9

Metalworking Craft and the Social Status of Blacksmiths and Goldsmiths

1 Metalworking and the Craftsmen's Way of Life

Plotting tool finds on a map of East Central and Eastern Europe it becomes evident that east and south of the Carpathian Mountains, most tools have been found on settlement sites. To the west from those mountains, however, tools were typically found in graves. While the settlements in the forest and forest-steppe zone of Eastern Europe suggest a sedentary population, many tools have been found in burial assemblages attributed either to a population of the nomadic origin (Avars) or to populations under their rule. What tools and technologies were chosen may well have been a function of the general mode of living – sedentary or nomadic. That mode of life was in turn closely related to the political and military power. The Avars were in fact a warrior elite, who was in almost permanent contact, both violent and peaceful with the Byzantine civilization. It was through them that contacts with that civilization were facilitated and the transfer of technological know-how and fashions made possible. This phenomenon is documented even at a greater distance from the Empire, at Kuzebaevo, on the Kama River. The hoard of a craftsman that was found there includes a number of pressing dies for dress accessories of undoubtedly Byzantine origin.[1] The attraction that the Empire represented for barbarians is largely responsible for the large-scale process of imitation behind the production of 6th- to 7th-century jewelry in East Central and Eastern Europe.

Scholars believe that until the late 7th century, the Avars maintained a nomadic form of life, their economy being largely based on pastoralism, with few and temporary settlements.[2] The mobility of the Avars must be responsible for this mobility of the craftsmen, who moved around as necessary, following their patrons. On the other hand, a sedentary population is clearly documented in the western parts of the lands controlled by the Avars, in Transdanubia. That

---

1 T. I. Ostanina, "Klad iuvelira iz d. Kuzebaevo Udmurtskoi Respubliki [The jeweller's hoard from Kuzebaevo]." *Finno-ugrica* 10 (2007), 125–127; Ostanina, Kanunnikova, Stepanov, Nikitin, *Kuzebaevskiĭ klad*, 170, fig. 3.1–10; 171, fig. 4.1–6, 9.

2 Vida, "They Asked to be Settled in Pannonia …," p. 253.

© DANIELA TĂNASE, 2021 | DOI:10.1163/9789004436930_011

population maintained contacts with the Merovingian world, even though the favorite metalworking technique was still die pressing. This technological choice may well have been a function of the strong ties the population in Transdanubia maintained with the Empire.

In the lands north of the Lower Danube, the warrior elite was smaller[3] and most likely subordinated, if only temporarily, to the qagan of the Avars.[4] The communities over which that elite exercised its authority lived in permanent, rural settlements, in which not only agriculture and animal husbandry were practiced, but also ironworking. The local smelters used surfaces ores in the vicinity of their settlements.

The exploitation of surface ores has been documented in the Carpathian Basin at Zamárdi, on the southern shore of Lake Balaton. Archaeologists found there an ironworking center dated between the 7th and the 9th century, the golden age of which seems to have been in the 8th century. The quality of the iron produced by smelting at Zamárdi was mediocre by the standards of the time.[5] As no evidence exists of such a center for the 6th and 7th centuries, one can only conclude the high-quality weapons and pieces of the military equipment found in the Carpathian Basin were produced in Byzantium or Central Asia.[6] While die pressing was preferred in the Carpathian Basin, mold casting, a technology requiring less skill, was popular in the regions to the east and south of the Carpathian Mountains (Fig. 54). In both cases, the technology chosen was meant to imitate more sophisticated decorative techniques typical for artifacts of Byzantine origin – granulation, filigree, stone and glass inlay.

To date, no less than 31 settlement sites have been found in Romania, which can be dated to the 6th and 7th century and have produced tools. Ten of them are located in Moldavia (Botoșana, Coroteni, Davideni, Dodești, Izvoare Bahna, Lozna-Străteni, Ștefan cel Mare-Gutinaș, Suceava-Șipot, Traian, and Udești), 16 in Walachia (Băleni-Români, Bucharest-Băneasa, Bucharest-Casa Armatei, Bucharest-Dămăroaia, Bucharest-Soldat Ghivan Nicolae Street, Bucharest-

3 Andrei Măgureanu, "Expresivitatea așezărilor în discuția despre identitatea elitelor (sec. VI–VII) [Settlement's expressiveness related to the identity of elites (6th–7th)]," *Studii și Cercetări de Istorie Veche și Arheologie* 66, no. 3–4 (2015), 265–267.

4 Vida, "They Asked to be Settled in Pannonia …," p. 256.

5 Gallina, "Avar kori vaskohászati és települési centrum," 179–188; Török, Kovács, Gallina, "Iron metallurgy," 229–237.

6 Florin Curta, "The earliest Avar-Age Stirrups, or "The Stirrup Controversy" Revisited," in *The Other Europe in the Middle Ages. Avars, Bulgars, Khazars, and Cumans. East Central and Eastern Europe in the Middle Ages 450–450*, vol. 2, ed. Florin Curta (Leiden/Boston; Brill, 2008), pp. 308–319; Vida, "They Asked to be Settled in Pannonia …," p. 256, see also the note 32.

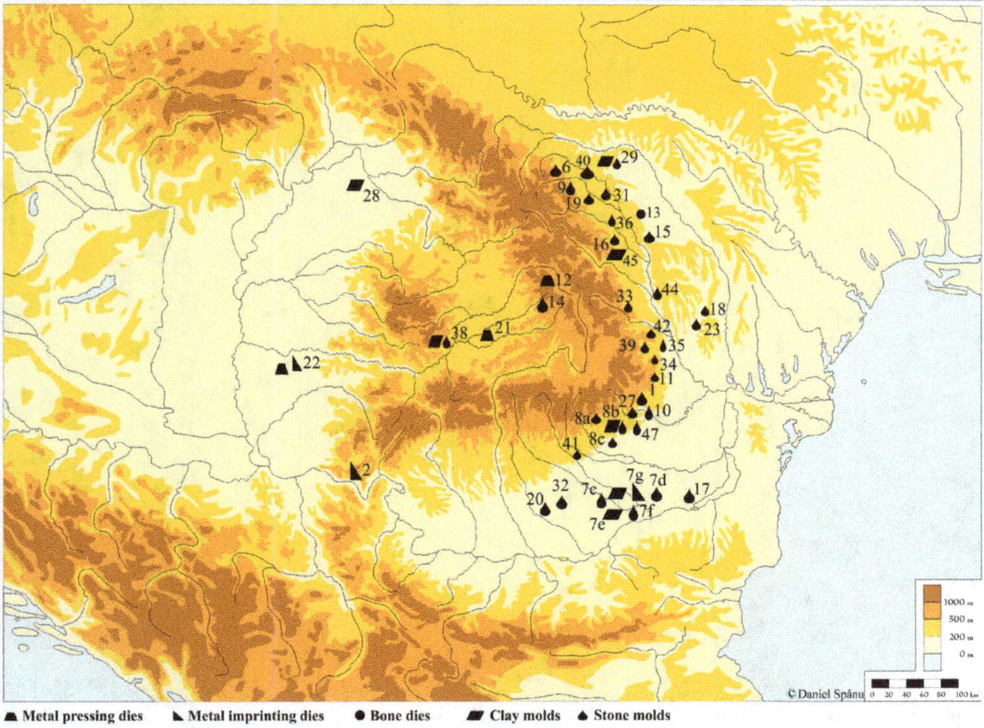

FIGURE 54 **Dies and molds from the current territory of Romania** (for numbering see Fig. 1) – **a. metal pressing dies:** Corund (Harghita co.); Dumbrăveni (Sibiu co.); Felnac (Arad co.) – **b. metal imprinting dies:** Banat (Danube Gorges area); Bicharest-Tei (Bucharest); Felnac (Arad co.) – **c. bone dies:** Costești (Iași co.) – **d. clay molds:** Bucharest-Străulești-Lunca; Bucharest-Tei; Budureasca 4 (Prahova co.); Lazuri (Satu Mare co.); Lozna (Dersca commune, Botoșani co.); Sânmiclăuș (Șona commune, Alba co.); Șirna (Prahova co.); Traian (Neamț co.) – **e. stone molds:** Aldeni (Buzău); Botoșana (Suceava co.); Bucharest-Dămăroaia (Bucharest); Bucharest-str. Soldat Ghivan no. 10 (Bucharest); Bucharest-Străulești-Măicănești (Bucharest); Budureasca 3 (Prahova co.); Budureasca 4 (Prahova co.); Budureasca 5 (Prahova co.); Cacica (Suceava co.); Cândești (Buzău co.); Coroteni (Slobozia Bradului commune, Vrancea co.); Cristuru Secuiesc (Harghita co.); Cucuteni (Iași co.); Davideni (Neamț co.); Dichiseni (Călărași co.); Dodești (Vaslui co.); Dolheștii Mari (Suceava co.); Dulceanca (Teleorman co.); Giurcani (Vaslui co.); Izvorul Dulce (Merei commune, Buzău co.); Lozna, com. Dersca (Botoșani co.); Moțca (Iași co.); Olteni (Dobrogostea village, Olteni commune, Teleorman co.); Onești (Bacău co.); Poienița (Vrancea co.); Răcoasa (Vrancea co.); Rădeni (Păstrăveni commune, Neamț co.); Sânmiclăuș (Șona commune, Alba co.); Soveja (Vrancea co.); Șirna (Prahova co.); Ștefan cel Mare (Bacău co.); Traian = Parincea (Bacău co.); Vadu Săpat (Prahova co.)

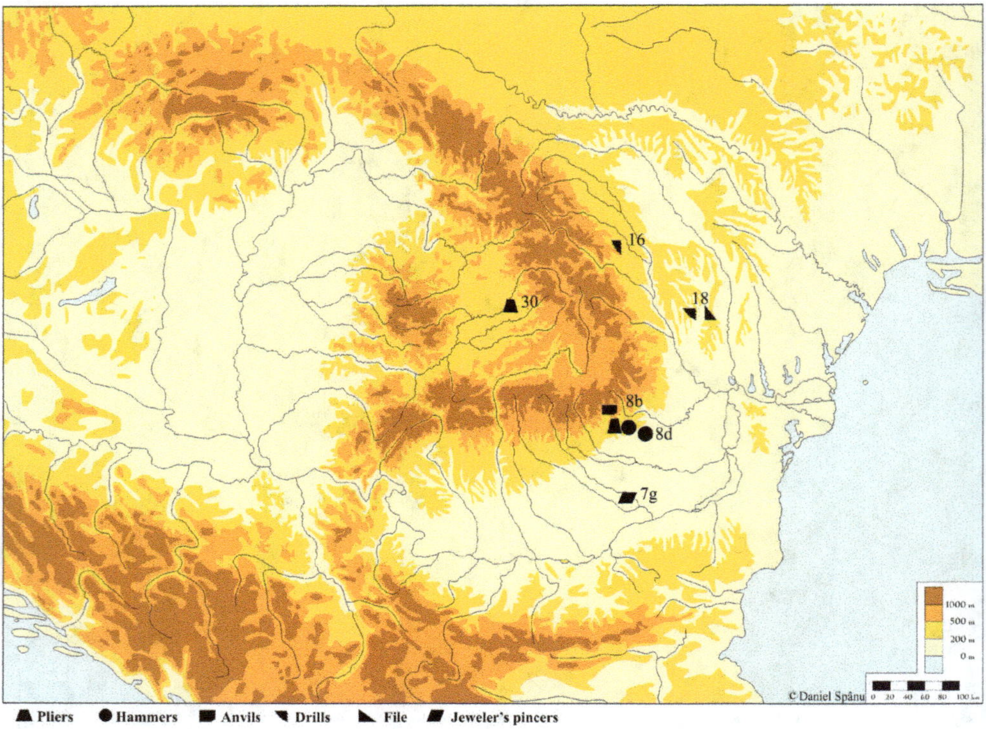

FIGURE 55 **Tools in the settlements** (for numbering see Fig. 1) – **a. pliers:** Budureasca 4 (Prahova co.); Morești (Mureș co.) – **b. hammers:** Budureasca 4 (Prahova co.); Budureasca 9 (Prahova co.) – **c. anvils:** Budureasca 4 (Prahova co.) – **d. drills:** Davideni (Neamț co.); Dodești (Vaslui co.) – **e. file:** Dodești (Vaslui co.) – **f. jeweler's pincers:** Bucharest – str. Soldat Ghivan no. 10 (Bucharest)

Străulești Lunca, Bucharest-Străulești Măicănești, Bucharest-Tei, Budureasca 3–5 and 9, Dulceanca I–IV, Gropșani Șirna, and Târgșor), and five in Transylvania (Bratei 2, Cristuru Secuiesc, Lazuri, Morești, and Sânmiclăuș). That there are visibly more finds outside than inside the Carpathian Arc is simply the result of the current state of research (Fig. 55–56). It is important to note that no settlement features are known from Hungary that could be interpreted as workshops,[7] as tool finds are exclusively from graves. Irrespective of the region of Romania in which they were found, casting tools are basically the same – crucibles, ladles, and molds. There are comparatively fewer engraving tools or chisels, and those that have been found may necessarily been involved in metalworking,[8] especially when not associated with other jewelry-making tools.

7 Rácz, *Die Goldschmiedegräber*, 107.
8 Ciupercă, Măgureanu, "Unele observații," 151.

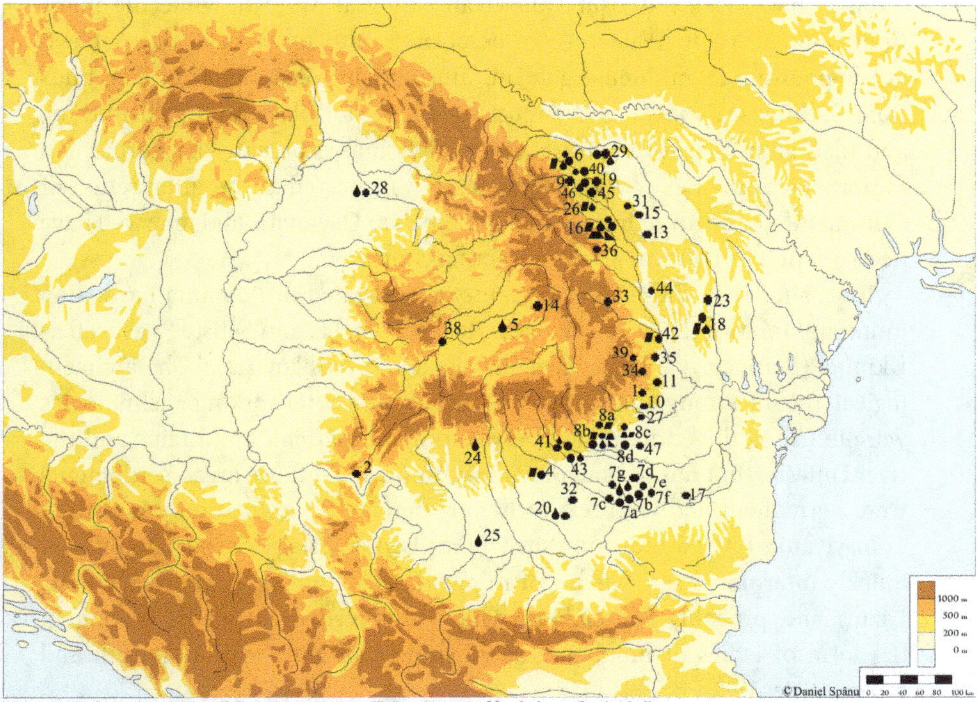

FIGURE 56 **Tools in the settlements** (for numbering see Fig. 1) – **a. engravers, chisels:** Băleni-Români (Dâmbovița co.); Botoșana (Suceava co.); Budureasca 3 (Prahova co.); Budureasca 4 (Prahova co.); Budureasca 5 (Prahova co.); Davideni (Neamț co.); Dodești (Vaslui co.); Izvoare-Bahna (Neamț co.); Lozna (Botoșani co.); Ștefan cel Mare (Bacău co.) – **b. punches:** Budureasca 4 (Prahova co.); Budureasca 5 (Prahova co.); Davideni (Neamț co.) – **c. mandrels:** Budureasca 4 (Prahova co.); Davideni (Neamț co.) – **d. casting ladles:** Bratei (Sibiu co.); Botoșana (Suceava); Bucharest-str. Soldat Ghivan no. 10 (Bucharest); Bucharest-Tei (Bucharest); Budureasca 4 (Prahova co.); Davideni (Neamț co.); Dodești (Vaslui co.); Dulceanca (Teleorman co.); Govora (Vâlcea co.); Gropșani (Dolj); Izvoare-Bahna (Neamț co.); Lazuri (Satu Mare co.); Lozna (Botoșani co.); Șirna (Prahova co.); Târgșor (Prahova co.) – **e. crucibles:** Băleni-Români (Dâmbovița co.); Botoșana (Suceava co.); Bucharest-Băneasa (Bucharest); Bucharest-Casa Armatei (Bucharest); Bucharest-Tei (Bucharest); Budureasca 4 (Prahova co.); Budureasca 9 (Prahova co.); Davideni (Neamț co.); Lozna (Botoșani co.); Șirna (Prahova co.); Târgșor (Prahova co.) – **f. molds and dies:** Aldeni (Buzău co.); Banat (Danube Gorges area); Botoșana (co.); Bucharest-Dămăroaia (Bucharest); Bucharest-str. Soldat Ghivan no. 10 (Bucharest); Bucharest-Străulești-Lunca (Bucharest); Bucharest-Străulești-Măicănești (Bucharest); Bucharest-Tei (Bucharest); Budureasca 3 (Prahova co.); Budureasca 4 (Prahova co.); Budureasca 5 (Prahova co.); Cacica (Suceava co.); Cândești (Buzău co.); Coroteni (Slobozia Bradului commune, Vrancea co.); Costești (Iași co.); Cristuru Secuiesc (Harghita co.); Cucuteni (Iași co.); Davideni (Neamț co.); Dichiseni (Călărași co.); Dodești (Vaslui co.); Dolheștii Mari (Suceava co.); Dulceanca (Teleorman co.); Giurcani (Vaslui co.); Izvorul Dulce (Merei commune, Buzău co.); Lazuri (Satu Mare co.); Lozna (Botoșani co.); Moțca (Iași co.); Olteni (Teleorman); Onești (Bacău co.); Poienița (Vrancea co.); Răcoasa (Vrancea co.); Rădeni (Păstrăveni commune, Neamț co.); Sânmiclăuș (Șona commune, Alba co.); Soveja (Vrancea co.); Șirna (Prahova co.); Ștefan cel Mare (Bacău co.); Traian (Bacău co.); Traian (Neamț co.); Vadu Săpat (Prahova co.)

Pliers have been found in Transylvania only at Moreşti, while the pliers from Budureasca in Walachia are associated with other categories of evidence pointing to an intense goldsmithing activity. As a matter of fact, finds from Budureasca appear as the most significant for black- and goldsmithing and blacksmithing in the entire region of Romania outside the Carpathian Mountains. Some believe that Budureasca was located at the intersection of cultural influences from Byzantium and the Avar Qaganate, and may well have been a center of political power attracting craftsmen.[9]

Tools similar to those from settlements excavated in Romania have been found in Moldova (Dănceni, Hansca, Hucea, Ivancea, and Selişte[10]) as well as Ukraine (Bernashivka, Luka-Kavetchinskaia and Rashkov III).[11] The archaeological record strongly suggests that the same metalworking technologies were in use in the entire region between the Carpathian Mountains and the river Dniester, but not so much in Transylvania. In all those areas, settlements were permanent and with relatively long periods of occupation. Moreşti, in Transylvania, is the 6th-century site where pliers and slag have been found and quickly interpreted as evidence of ironworking.[12] Bratei 2, Cristuru Secuiesc, Lazuri and probably Sânmiclăuş, which produced evidence of casting in the form of ladles or molds are dated somewhat later, to the late 6th and 7th centuries.

Neither the number, nor the variety of tools found in settlements match those of toolkits found in graves. Most prominent in this respect are the blacksmith kit from Band, the (possibly incomplete) jeweler kit from Felnac and the craftsman toolkits found in Avar-age graves in the Middle Danube region (Aradac-Mečka, Csákberény-Orondpuszta, Gátér, Jutas, Kisújszállás-Nagykert, Klárafalva B, Kölked-Feketekapu B, and Kunszentmárton). Burial finds, therefore, include a wide variety of both blacksmith (pliers, anvils, hammers of various sizes, metal sheet clippers, files, dies, die-stocks, and chisels), and goldsmith tools (dies, engraving tools, and small-size anvils).

There are great similarities between the tools found in Band, on one hand, and those from Kölked-Feketekapu B, Kunszentmárton, Kisújszállás, Jutas, and Csákberény-Orondpuszta, on the other hand. However, there are good analogies in more distant finds such as Brno (Czech Republic) or Vestly (Norway). However, the tool kit Band has so far no analogies in the lands to the east and to the south from the Carpathian Mountains.

---

9 Ciupercă, Măgureanu, "Unele observaţii," 151–152.

10 Corman, *Contribuţii*, 57, 59.

11 Vynokur, *Slov'ianski iuveliry*, 46–99; Corman, *Contribuţii*, 57, 59.

12 Horedt, *Moreşti*, 150.

Similarly, the dies from Felnac kit have many parallels in the Middle Danube region. The only analogy in the lands to the south (east) is the forming model for a bow fibula from Bucharest-Tei. Dies for the production of jewelry and dress accessories are the most relevant indicator of how technological choices reflect different patterns of cultural behavior, as well as long-distance contacts. So far no dies have yet been found in the lands to the east and south of the Carpathian Mountains (which were closest to the Empire), which could be used for pressing. Instead, stone and clay molds for direct or "lost-wax" casting unmistakably show a different technological choice. To be sure, casting molds have also been found in Transylvania (Cristuru Secuiesc, Lazuri, and Sânmiclăuş) and Hungary (Szeged-Bilisics and Vác-Kavicsbánya). The latter were typically found in female graves, which may be an indication of cultural contacts with the areas in which casting was the technology of choice. In other words, it is possible that the women buried in those graves either were from the lands to the east or to the south of the Carpathian Mountains, or had some kind of contacts with them.

Metal dies have been found primarily in graves of men buried together with horse bones according to nomadic rituals. Numerous dies have been found in isolated graves (Felnac – 44) or in small cemeteries in the Tisza Plain (Kunszentmárton – 41). Isolated graves or small cemeteries seem to be typical for the nomads of the Early Avar age (shortly before and after AD 600).[13] It is also in the Tisza Plain, but in the very large, early 7th-century cemetery at Gátér that eight more dies were found.[14] They were associated with arrowheads, which points to possibly Avar origin of those buried there. Comparatively fewer dies have been found in graves of both men and women in Transdanubia (Gyönk-Vásártéri út, Szekszárd-Palánk, Zamardi, Zselickislak) (see Chapter XII.2). Such finds suggest that dies for pressing were not used only by "Avars," but by the "Germanic" (and possibly Romance-speaking) population under their control as well. This was because during the first half of the 7th century, the deposition of dies in graves had become a burial custom most typical for the entire Avar Qaganate.

Even though the metal dies are of Byzantine origin, since they are high-quality products, and their ornaments are distinctly Byzantine, that is no basis for claiming that the craftsmen buried with them had come from the Empire. The burial customs implied in those cases have nothing in common with those in use in Byzantium. Unlike stone molds, metal dies were probably used for high-quality jewelry. Those imitations of Byzantine jewelry were made for

---

13 Vida, "They Asked to be Settled in Pannonia …," pp. 253–254.

14 Rácz, *Die Goldschmiedegräber*, 156–157.

people who wanted to imitate the lifestyle of the imperial aristocracy. There are no indications of such lofty aspirations among the elites in the lands to the south and east of the Carpathian Mountains. Moreover, stone molds appear inside the Avar Qaganate at a comparatively later date (second half of the 7th century), at a time when the social position of the old elites inside the qaganate was seriously challenged.[15] The civil war of the 630s was accompanied by the shrinking of the Avar sphere of military control in the lands north of the river Danube and north of the Black Sea.[16] Moreover, direct contact with Byzantium was now interrupted because of the Bulgar settlement in the Balkans. Although ties with Byzantium continued via Italy, they were sporadic, and the *solidi* struck for Emperor Constantine IV were the last Byzantine coins to reach in significant numbers.[17]

Those were the circumstances in which, with no significant contact with the Byzantine world, the Avar elite changed. During the 8th century, ornaments became less spectacular than in the previous period. More importantly, they were made by casting, usually of bronze, sometimes gilded.[18]

2 Craftsmen's Mobility

Unlike Western Europe, where there are both written and iconographic sources pertaining to the activity of craftsmen,[19] the only such sources for Central

---

15 Vida, "They Asked to be Settled in Pannonia ...," pp. 261–265. For the phenomenon of sedentarization, as mirrored in burial customs, such as those identified through the excavation of the Vác-Kavicsbánya cemetery, see Gergely Szenthe, "Kulturális összeolvadás a 'középavar korban'. A Vác-Kavicsbányai temető [Cultural fusion in the 'Middle Avar Period'. The cemetery of Vác-Kavicsbánya]," *Archaeologiai Értesítő* 139 (2014), 99–125.

16 Pohl, *Die Awaren*, 255, 274.

17 Péter Somogyi, *Byzantinische Fundmünzen der Awarenzeit in ihrem europäischen Umfeld* (Budapest: Eötvös Loránd University, Institute of Archaeological Sciences, 2014), 65–86.

18 Gergely Szenthe, "Material culture patterning as the source of the Avar power network, 8th century AD," in *Hadak útján. A népvándorláskori fiatal kutatóinak XXVI. konferenciája. Gazdaság – kereskedelem – kézművesség*, eds. Zsófia Rácz, István Koncz and Bence Gulyás (Budapest: Institute of Archaeological Sciences, 2018), pp. 291–314.

19 For examples of implements in monastic workshops and in settlements in Western Europe, see Aufleger, "Metallarbeiten," 620; Henning, "Handel," 972; Ursula Koch, "Handwerker in der alamannischen Höhensiedlung auf dem Runden Berg bei Urach," *Archäologisches Korrespondenzblatt* 14 (1984), 99–100. Iconographic sources: Aufleger, "Metallarbeiten," 621, fig. 475 (the bone box of Auzun, dated ca. 700); Roth, *Kunst und Handwerk*, 64 (the Utrecht Psalter, 816–835); Amrein, Binder, "Mit Hammer und Zange," 360, fig. 399 (the Stuttgart Psalter, 820–835); Karl Hauck, "Wielands Hort. Die sozialgeschichzliche Stellung des Schmiedes in frühen Bildprogrammen nach und vor dem

and Eastern Europe are archeological: tools from settlements and graves, products, and smelting furnaces.

Within the Carpathian Basin, the existence of active jewelers results from the use of the silver inlaying technique, finds of tools (chisels and punches) in graves (Kölked-Feketekapu B, Kunszentmárton, and Jutas), as well as a certain type of belt fitting on which braided ribbons are represented using small inlaying lines that do not touch the contour line of the piece. Such ribbons set crosswise decorated artifacts discovered in Transdanubia, in the Tisza region, and in Transylvania.[20] This decoration, which appears only inside the Carpathian Basin, demonstrates the existence of craftsmen capable of working in the inlaying technique. Most likely, those craftsmen were located in the western part of the Carpathian Basin, where both the Roman legacy and the Byzantine influence were stronger.

Another indication of the craftsmen specialized in specific ornamental patterns is the emergence, during the last third of the 6th century, of the animal style II with a dentil ornamentation, which is found mostly on artifacts discovered in the Carpathian Basin. The appearance of the animal style II with dentil ornamentation is most likely the result of Germanic population moving away from the decorative styles favored by the Avar elite and inspired by Byzantium, and, at the same time, establishing ties with the Merovingian culture.[21]

In Romania, the activity of local jewelers is documented archeologically in settlements excavated in Bucharest-Soldat Ghivan Nicolae Street, Străulești or Bucharest-Tei, Davideni, Dodești, Botoșana, at Budureasca 3–5 and 9, as well as at Lazuri, Sânmiclăuș and Cristuru Secuiesc. In all those cases, ornaments were made in a more rudimentary manner and on a smaller scale, for members of the local community. However, the distribution of certain types of molds with certain decorative styles may well indicate itinerant craftsmen. In fact, some dress accessories appearing on molds found in settlements seem to be imitations of belt fittings of Avar origin, or earrings and pendants of Byzantine origin. Paradoxically, this is in fact truer for finds from Moldavia and northeastern Walachia, more than for those from Transylvania.

Religionswechsel," *Antikvarist Arkiv* 64 (1977), 14–16 (the sculpture of Ardre, 8th century). See also Tănase, *Prelucrarea*, 194; Daniela Tănase, "Despre artizanii metalelor în izvoare scrise din zorii Evului Mediu [About metal craftsmen in written sources from the Early Middle Ages]," *Analele Banatului Serie Nouă* 18 (2010), 115–121.

20 Martin, "Zu den tauschierten Gürtelgarnituren," 348.

21 Vida, "They Asked to be Settled in Pannonia ...," 260.

There is of course the possibility that the craftsmen active in the barbarian lands were themselves Byzantine, and had come to those lands as captives, refugees, or willingly, in search for patrons.[22]

Itinerary craftsmen carrying their own toolboxes relied on materials provided by their patrons.[23] In fact, plotting on the map various types of pieces produced by those craftsmen, one can see not a radial distribution from some fixed workshop, but an itinerary, much like in the case of coins produced by mints.[24] The itinerary of the traveling craftsmen from the Avar Qaganate, along the rivers Tisza, Criș and Mureș, may be traced by means of finds of within a 60–80 km radius from graves with dies.[25] For example, that the goldsmith of Felnac was itinerant results from finds of belt fittings decorated with one of the dies found in the grave. Such finds appear within a relatively limited area around the confluence of the Mureș and the Tisza rivers. Belt fittings with a so-called Felnac-type decoration (Fig. 36.2.3–10) have been found in Deszk, Klárafalva, Szeged,[26] Ferencszállás, Szarvas, Tiszavárkony,[27] Felgyő,[28] Aradac,[29] and Sânpetru German[30] (Fig. 53). The same is true for the distribution of artifacts decorated with the dies found in Gátér. The Gátér goldsmith seems to have been more active within his own area than those of Felnac and Kunszentmárton, since many more artifacts decorated with the dies found in his grave have been found in the Tisza Plain.[31]

There is of course the possibility that instead of the jeweler, it was the mold that "traveled," while the distribution of belt fittings may also be explained in

22 Ciupercă, Măgureanu, "Unele observații," 152.

23 Werner, "Zur Verbreitung," 70; Brather, *Ethnische Interpretationen*, 409. This is true not only for *barbaricum*, but for the Byzantine Empire as well. In all known cases, jewelers worked using the client's material, cf. Arnold Hugh Martin Jones, *The Later Roman Empire, 284–602: A Social, Economic and Administrative Survey* (Oxford: Basil Blackwell, 1964), 653.

24 Werner, *Die Langobarden*, 316.

25 Rácz, *Die Goldschmiedegräber*, 96–97.

26 Garam, *Funde*, 117; pl. 81.3–4, pl. 82. 3–4.

27 Rácz, *Die Goldschmiedegräber*, 41 – map no. 4, and 202.

28 Csilla Balogh, "A Felgyő, Ürmös-tanyai avar kori temető [The Avar Cemetery at Felgyő, Ürmös-tanya]," in Csilla Balogh, Klára P. Fischl, *Felgyő, Ürmös-tanya. Bronzkori és avar kori leletek László Gyula felgyői ásatásának anyagából* (Szeged: Móra Ferenc Múzeum, 2010), 219, fig. 88, 6–19.

29 Nagy, "Nekropola kol Aradaca," 90, pl. XXIII.3–11.

30 Dörner, "Mormânt," 423–433.

31 Garam, *Funde*, 157.

terms of exchange or mobility related to marriage alliances.[32] Nonetheless, the existence of itinerant craftsmen remains the most likely explanation for the distribution of belt fittings decorated in the same manner. Some believe that Byzantine traveling craftsmen may have brought with them semi-finished products from Constantinople, the center of jewelry production during the 6th and 7th centuries. Those products were then finished according to the wishes of the customers in the regions to which they traveled.[33] However, the presence of Byzantine molds does not necessarily imply the existence of traveling craftsmen from the Empire, as the molds could travel without the craftsmen, being procured from workshops urban markets in the Balkan provinces of the Byzantine Empire.[34] A great concentration of Byzantine artifacts may be observed in the western part of the Carpathian Basin, on the territory of the former province of Pannonia. This is also the area with a great number of belt fittings matching dies found in craftsmen's tombs.[35] It is of course possible to interpret this cluster of finds as indicating Byzantine craftsmen who arrived in the area either voluntarily or as captives from Avar raids into the Empire.

Dies for belt fittings may have also been made in the Crimea, which was located next to the steppe lands of Eastern Europe. The dies found in the Middle Dnieper region came probably from Crimea and they served for the production of simple strap ends, belt mounts with Felnac-type decoration, and rosette-, lion-, and bird-shaped horse tack mounts.[36]

While the presence of itinerant craftsmen from Byzantium can not be ruled out, it is nonetheless unlikely that they played any significant role in barbarian regions north of the river Danube or within the Carpathian Basin. In both areas, there must have been many sufficiently skilled craftsmen, some of whom can be identified archaeologically by means of graves with tools, such as found in Felnac and Band and probably linked to the finds of dies Corund and Dumbrăveni. Those may have been itinerant craftsmen, but nothing suggests that they were from Byzantium. Moreover, traces of the activity of jewelers and blacksmiths have been also found in settlements, such as Bratei, Sânmiclăuş, Lazuri, Poian and Cristuru Secuiesc. That graves with tools were

32 Werner, "Zur Verbreitung," 71; fig. 3, map showing the spread of a type of knobbed fibula, and particularly the area of considerable density of such items as well as four eccentric points; 74; 78.

33 Turčan, "Hroby," 489.

34 Werner, "Zur Verbreitung," 74.

35 Rácz, *Die Goldschmiedegräber*, p. 95.

36 Rácz, "Ein frühmittelalterlicher Pressmodelfund," 176, fig. 1.1–8, 177–179.

found along the axis of the river Mureș may not be an accident, since that was the most important artery of communication and transportation (of salt for example) in early medieval Transylvania. Similarly, graves with tools appear in the Carpathian Basin along the Tisza and the Danube rivers, which strongly suggests that in the 6th and 7th centuries, the main communication arteries were the rivers.

While within the Carpathian Basin, (traveling) craftsmen may be identified by means of the graves with tools, outside the Carpathian Mountains, the situation is different. In Walachia and Moldavia, jeweler tools, especially molds, are found in settlements or around them. The only exception is a cremation grave that may have been of a jeweler traveling up the Buzău valley before dying and being buried in Sărata Monteoru.[37] The molds found in Walachia and Moldavia served for casting belt fittings and earrings. Even if the archaeological context remains unknown for some molds, their distribution and great similarities in terms of shape and decoration suggest that they may have actually been used by itinerant craftsmen.[38] On the other hand, the activity of those traveling craftsmen was made possible by patrons with sufficient economic and political power.[39] As a matter of fact, it is precisely around AD 600 that a number of barbarian chieftains appear in the written sources as ruling over Walachia and southern Moldavia.

However, the concomitant presence in those regions of smelting furnaces, all of them being settlement finds, is a clear indication of stable craftsmen, if not also workshops. There are even settlements specialized in ironworking, which may have served a larger area, as they most certainly did not produce only to meet their own needs. In this regard, the finds from Șirna and Dulceanca IV are the most illustrative, followed by those from Lozna-Străteni, Ștefan cel Mare-Gutinaș and Davideni. Where available, the metallographic analyses have shown that the source of iron were surface deposits next to the respective settlement. To judge by the existing evidence, both smelting and blacksmithing were performed by the same craftsmen.[40]

37 Comșa, "Socio-economic organization," 186.

38 Măgureanu, "Observații," 176.

39 Măgureanu, "Observații," 180–181.

40 Ștefan Olteanu, Constantin Șerban, *Meșteșugurile din Țara Românească și Moldova în evul mediu* [Crafts from Walachia and Moldavia in the Middle Ages] (Bucharest: Editura Academiei Republicii Socialiste România, 1969), 11–13; Mitrea, "Dovezi arheologice privind prelucrarea metalelor," 13.

3 Sketching Regional Styles – a Traveling Sign?

The issue of the craftsmen's mobility may also be gauged on the basis of certain types of dress accessories and jewelry. For example, the so-called "Slavic" bow fibulae were female dress accessories, worn by women as a symbol of their social status.[41] Four regions in East Central and Eastern Europe have produced such fibulae: Mazuria (northeastern Poland and the Kaliningrad region of Russia), the Middle Dnieper region, the Crimea, and the valley of the Middle and Lower Danube river. Similarities between specimens found in those respective areas have been rightly interpreted as a sign of long-distance contacts and exchange between elites.[42]

The largest number of specimens, however, are from the Middle and Lower Danube region, where molds have also been found for their production. There is so far no one-to-one correspondence between molds and actual fibulae, and the absence of exact replicas point to variations due to the craftsmen's technical skills, as well as the taste of those individuals for whom they worked. Moreover, the discovery of Helgö (Sweden), where a large amount of fragments clay molds used for different parts of the fibula (as opposed to the entire) is particularly significant in this respect.[43] In other words, the Helgö finds shows that bow fibulae could be produced in stationary workshops, by craftsmen working for distant customers. Another argument in favor of the idea of stable (as opposed to itinerary) craftsmen is the discovery of the Bernashivka stone molds. They clearly show the local production of dress accessories and parts thereof by means of the "lost wax," which is in direct contradiction to the idea of traveling craftsmen working with forming models made of bronze or of lead.[44] Nonetheless, forming models for bow fibulae, such as those from Felnac, Bucharest-Tei, and an unknown location in the Banat are similar to fibulae found at a considerable distance, which is after all an argument in favor of traveling craftsmen. It is therefore possible that local and traveling craftsmen coexisted in time.

41 Florin Curta, "*Slavic* Bow Fibulae? Werner's class I D revisited," *Acta Archaeologica Hungarica* 57 (2006), 461–462; Curta, "A contribution," 99–100.

42 Curta, "'Slavic' Bow Fibulae," 20–28; 58–59.

43 Curta, "Werner's class I H," 65–66. Those parts were made by means of direct, and not "lost wax" casting [Kristina Lamm, "Helgö as a goldsmiths' workshop in Migration Period Sweden," in *Goldsmith Mysteries Archaeological, pictorial and documentary evidence from the 1st millennium AD in northern Europe*, eds. Alexandra Pesch and Ruth Blankenfeldt (Neumünster: Wachholtz Verlag 2012), p. 148].

44 Curta, "Female Dress," 124–125.

Earrings and other dress accessories were also cast. Mapping molds for the casting of similar items reveals the regions where such accessories and ornaments were popular. For example, rectangular appliqués decorated with notches appear on the molds from Soveja, Răcoasa, Rădeni, Poienița, and Cucuteni, all very similar to each other. Slightly different ornaments occur on the molds from Aldeni and Vadu-Săpat. Two regions thus stand out in terms of the regional style described by such ornaments, central and southern Moldavia, as well as northeastern of Walachia.[45] The same is true for floral appliqués, such as cast with the molds from Aldeni, Vadu Săpat, and Budureasca 4, and for floral appliqués engraved in a circle, possibly used as earrings disc-like pendants, such as cast with the molds from Soveja, Rădeni, and Poienița, all in the Vrancea County. Rectangular appliqués also appear outside the regional style areas mentioned above, at Cacica (Suceava County) and Dichiseni (Călărași County), but they are much simpler than the others.

A watermelon seed-shaped pendant on the mold from Vadu Săpat (Fig. 43.2) is identical with the bead (or pendant) on the mold from Bucharest-Tei. Similar beads, but without the central button, appear on the mold from Budureasca 4 (Fig. 9.3). Moreover, a silver pendant identical to the watermelon seed-shaped pendant on the Vadu Săpat mold has been found in Maglavit (Dolj County),[46] but that has been interpreted as an indication of Balkan origin of this type of jewelry, and not as the product of an itinerant craftsman working in Walachia.[47] An imitation of such a pendant, obtained by casting, was also found in Șirna,[48] that is not far from Vadu Săpat. Judging by the existing evidence, one may conclude that pieces of jewelry brought from the Balkans were rapidly imitated by local craftsmen in central Walachia.

Much more distant similarities between the dies for harness mounts with volute decoration found in Felnac and Gátér, on one hand, the appliqués produced with the mold from Bucharest-Tei are more difficult to explain. Moreover, the die for rectangular appliqués from Felnac has an ornament of concentric circles, which is almost identical to the ornament on the molds from Costești, Rădeni, and Cucuteni. There are also similarities between the heart-shaped appliqué on the Vadu Săpat mold and the dies for tear-shaped pendants from Felnac.[49] As far as earring parts, they appear on sites located at considerable

45 Teodor, "Tipare," 166, fig. 1. Map showing the spread of molds in the 6th–11th centuries, pointing out first of all the concentration of molds in certain areas, a fact that might indicate the area of certain centers of power.

46 Toropu, *Romanitatea*, 138, pl. 17.1.5.

47 Măgureanu, "Observații," 180.

48 Olteanu, Grigore, Nicolae, *Comunitatea sătească*, 56, 92, fig. 20/5.

49 Măgureanu, Ciupercă, "The 6th–8th Centuries Metallurgical Activity," 298.

distance from each other, which suggests that they were not part of a regional style. This is definitely the case of the rosettes on the molds from Dolheştii Mari, Moţca, Ştefan cel Mare-Gutinaş, Coroteni, Soveja, and Bucharest-Soldat Ghivan Nicolae Street.

Settlements excavated in Moldavia and Walachia, as well as in the central part of Transylvania have produced molds for pectoral crosses with equal arms (of the Malta type) and appliqués with Christian iconography. Several artifacts with Christian symbolism are known from all three regions, but in Transylvania they also appear in burial assemblages.[50] The presence of Christians among barbarians in the lands north of the river Danube is documented in the written sources,[51] but scholars are reluctant to attribute those artifacts to them. As a matter of fact, Christian symbols could have been adopted by pagan elites simply as a form of *imitatio imperii*, without any necessary understanding of the religious precepts.[52] In other words, those objects were adopted and imitated, because they were displayed at the same time by the Byzantine military and religious elite.[53] The production of such artifacts with Christian symbolism may be dated only after the middle of the 6th century, and they have been found in archaeological assemblages that could be related, one way or another, to local elites.[54] However, most pectoral crosses and medallions with cross-shaped ornament are made of bronze, not of precious metals. That is why other scholars believe that instead of symbols of power adopted by local elites, those artifacts expressed the religious identity of the Romance-speaking, relatively poorer population that lived among pagan barbarians.[55] Few scholars have noticed that pectoral crosses are also a female dress accessory, and may therefore be associated to female prisoners from the Balkan provinces of the Empire who have been brought to the barbarian lands. As such, the pectoral crosses were a sign of Christian identity. Instead of *imitatio*, they were an expression of the *desiderium imperii*, namely of the hope that one day those women would return to the Christian Empire.[56]

---

50 Madgearu, "Semnificaţia," 133–135; Bârzu, *Ein gepidisches Denkmal*, 79, fig. 46. 76, 237, 219-typ 14d1–d3; 106, fig. 58.81-typ 16a.2b.7.

51 Florin Curta, "Limes and Cross: the Religious Dimension of the Sixth-Century Danube Frontier of the early Byzantine Empire," *Starinar* 51 (2001), 63–64.

52 Curta, "Limes and Cross," 64–67; Curta, "Before Cyril and Methodius," 188.

53 Curta, "Before Cyril and Methodius," 185–186.

54 Curta, "Before Cyril and Methodius," 191.

55 Madgearu, "Semnificaţia," 132.

56 Florin Curta, "New remarks on Christianity beyond the 6th and early 7th century frontier of the Roman Empire," in *Keszthely-Fenékpuszta im Kontext spätantiker Kontinuitätsforschung zwischen Noricum und Moesia*, ed. Orsolya Heinrich-Tamáska (Budapest/Leipzig/Keszthely/Rahden: Verlag Marie Leidorf, 2011), p. 310.

Be as it may, the pectoral crosses clearly point to a population of Christians in the lands north of the river Danube. Those may have been people brought forcefully (as captives) from the Balkan provinces of the Empire, or refugees from those provinces. The molds reveal one of the ways in which Christians could obtain the symbolic objects of their religion while away from the Empire. That Christianity was not restricted to the Romance-speaking population results from the mention in the written source of Christian (Arian?) Gepids living side by side with the local population of Sclavenes.[57]

Molds for casting dress accessories and ornaments strongly suggest the existence of regional styles of clothing perhaps linked to the representation of social status. If so, then power centers must have existed in Moldavia and Walachia, in which imitation of Byzantine ornaments was not fundamentally different from that clearly attested for Avar elites in the Carpathian Basin. Traveling or sedentary craftsmen simply responded to the demand of local elites for dress accessories of Byzantine inspiration. In other words, responsible for the regional styles were not the craftsmen, but the elites who favored the emblematic style of the local populations for many other reasons than simply fashion. The existence of regional styles of clothing has little, if anything to do with the mobility of the craftsmen, even though the spread of those fashions may well have been facilitated by itinerant craftsmen.

Power centers are also known for the 6th and 7th centuries from western (Little) Walachia, but only from hoards and stray finds.[58] No archeological evi-

57 Theophylact Simocatta, *History* VI 8.12–9.6: "And so the brigadier Alexander encircled the place and tried to consign the barbarians to fire, but the flame languished and grew feeble because of the damp conditions, and Alexander's attack was inglorious. Now there was with the barbarians a Gepid, who had once long before been of the Christian religion. This man deserted to the Romans and also pointed out the means of entry ... But the Gepid described everything and revealed events in detail, saying that the prisoners were subjects of Musocius, who was called rex in the barbarian tongue, that this Musocius was encamped thirty parasangs away, that he had also heard about the misfortunes which had recently befallen Ardagastus ... Therefore the Gepid came to Musocius, and asked to be provided by him with a number of canoes, so that he could ferry across those involved in Ardagastus' misfortunes. And so Musocius, regarding as a godsend the plan woven against him by deceit, provided canoes to that the Gepid could save Ardagastus' followers."

58 Andrei Măgureanu, "About power in the sixth–seventh century in the extra-Carpathian area," in *Potestas et communitas. Interdisziplinäre Beiträge zu Wesen und Darstellung von Herrschaftsverhältnissen im Mittelalter ostlich der Elbe/Interdisciplinary Studies of the Constitution and Demonstration of Power Relations in the Middle Ages East of the Elbe*, eds. Aleksander Paroń, Sébastien Rossignol, Bartłomiej Sz. Szmoniewski and Grischa Vercamer (Wrocław/Warsaw: Instytut Archaeologii i Etnologii Polskiej Akademii Nauk and Deutches Historiches Institut Warschau, 2010), pp. 80–84, with the entire bibliography.

dence related to the making of jewelry (molds or any other types of tools) is known from that region, except a ladle from the settlement site excavated in Gropșani (Fig. 7.4.5) and another one from Govora (Fig. 7.1). It is possible that unlike the rest of the territory in southern and eastern Romania, most dress accessories and ornaments from western Walachia were either of Byzantine or Avar origin (e.g., the luxury fibula from Coșovenii de Jos, decorated in animal style II with the dentil ornament).

4 Who Were the Craftsmen?

So far three graves with tools are known from the territory of present-day Romania, one from the Germanic (Gepid) milieu in Transylvania (Band), another from the Avar milieu (Felnac), and a third from the Slavic milieu (Sărata Monteoru). Those assemblages bespeak the special position reserved for craftsmen in three different, but contemporaneous societies.

The ritual deposition of tools in graves is already documented in the 6th-century Germanic milieu of Central Europe, particularly at Brno and Poysdorf. The custom survived well into the Avar age, both in Transdanubia and in Transylvania, and was apparently adopted by Avars as well. But who were the people buried with tools?

In the lands along the Middle and Lower Danube river, there can be no discussion of the free status of craftsmen, because the social structure was fundamentally different from that of the contemporaneous societies in Western Europe. Moreover, the phenomenon of *imitatio imperii* did not translate into the elaboration of lawcodes following the Roman model.[59]

59 On crafts in written sources see Amrein, Binder, "Mit Hammer und Zange," 363; Driehaus, "Zum Problem," 402; Decaens et al., *Un nouveau cimetière*, 88; Jean-Paul Morel, "Artizanul [The Artisan]," in *Omul roman*, coordinated by Andrea Giardina, translated into Romanian by Dragoș Cojocaru (Iași: Polirom 2001), p. 196, p. 200; Henri Pirenne, *Mahomed și Carol cel Mare* [Muhammad and Carol the Great] (Bucharest: Editura Meridiane, 1996), 30; Enrico Zanini, "Artisans and Traders in the Early Byzantine City: Exploring the Limits of Archaeological Evidence," in *Social and Political Life in Late Antiquity*, eds. William Bowden, Adam Gutteridge and Carlos Machado (Leiden/Boston: Brill, 2006), p. 375. On members of the elite who were concerned with metal processing, see Aufleger, "Metallarbeiten," 620; Wolters, "Goldschmied," 366; Vierck, "Werke des Eligius," 2: 310; Enrico Castelnuovo, "Artistul [The Artist]," in *Omul medieval*, coordinated by Jacques Le Goff, translated into Romanian by Ingrid Ilinca and Dragoș Cojocaru (Iași: Editura Polirom, 1999), p. 200. On legally free craftsmen in Western Europe and objects with the name of the goldsmiths, see Roth, *Kunst*, 41; Driehaus, "Zum Problem merowingerzeitlicher Goldschmiede," 396; Henning, "Handel," 799–800.

On the other hand, in nomadic societies, blacksmiths and jewelers had a privileged position, were well armed and were buried with their horses and tools, a fact revealed by the archaeological finds in the Carpathian Basin. Blacksmiths had a particularly elevated social position in most steppe societies, so much so that some believe the word "qagan" to derive from Kava, the name of the blacksmith of Iranian mythology. The great appreciation of blacksmiths may be explained in terms of the development of metallurgy, which was necessary both for military and for economic superiority.[60] Mastering fire and the ability to transform matter, the mysterious character of the smith's work, involving professional secrets, placed him in the company of wizards and magicians, which explains the key role that blacksmiths play in a series of legends about civilizing heroes and mythical kings, founders of dynasties.[61] The Norse literature glorifies blacksmiths for having superior powers, as in the case of Wayland the Smith.[62] The skills of the craftsmen were attributed to supernatural powers, the only way to explain the ability of those people to fashion weapons as well as ornaments of surprising beauty and detail.

That early medieval world black- and goldsmiths were free and had an elevated social status is often illustrated archaeologically with graves with tools such as those from Poysdorf and Brno,[63] Hérouvillette, Vestly, and Hovgärdsberg Vendel. The same applies to similar finds from the Carpathian Basin: Aradac-Mečka, Band, Kölked Feketekapu "B", Csákberény-Orondpuszta, Felnac, Jutas, Kisújszállás, and Kunszentmárton (Fig. 57). The presence of weapons in some of those assemblages suggests that craftsmen were members of the elite, a suggestion substantiated by such finds as the helmet from Band or the armor plates from Csákberény-Orondpuszta, Kölked Feketekapu B, and Kunszentmarton. Weapons, on the other side, have been used by archaeologists as an indicator of free status, since only freemen had access to weapon and the right to bear them.[64] This is also true for steppe peoples. Avar warriors

60 Pohl, *Die Awaren*, 194.

61 Mircea Eliade, *Făurari și alchimiști* [The Forge and the Crucible] (Bucharest: Humanitas, 1996), 78–109; Daim, Mehofer, Tobias, "Die langobardischen Schmiedegräber," 203.

62 Decaens et al., *Un nouveau cimetière*, 89; Hauck, "Wielands Hort," 5–7; Amrein, Binder, "Mit Hammer und Zange," 360.

63 Wilfried Menghin, *Die Langobarden. Archäologie und Geschichte* (Stuttgart: Theiss, 1985), 68–69.

64 Werner, "Zur Verbreitung," 68. For a discussion of weapons in graves with tools from the Carpathian Basin, see Daniela Tănase, "Gräber mit Goldschmiede- und Schmiedewerkzeugen aus der Awarenzeit. Zeichen der Macht oder Beweis für die Ausübung des Handwerks," in *Potestas et communitas. Interdisziplinäre Beiträge zu Wesen und Darstellung von Herrschaftsverhältnissen im Mittelalter ostlich der Elbe/Interdisciplinary Studies of the Constitution and Demonstration of Power Relations in the Middle Ages East of the*

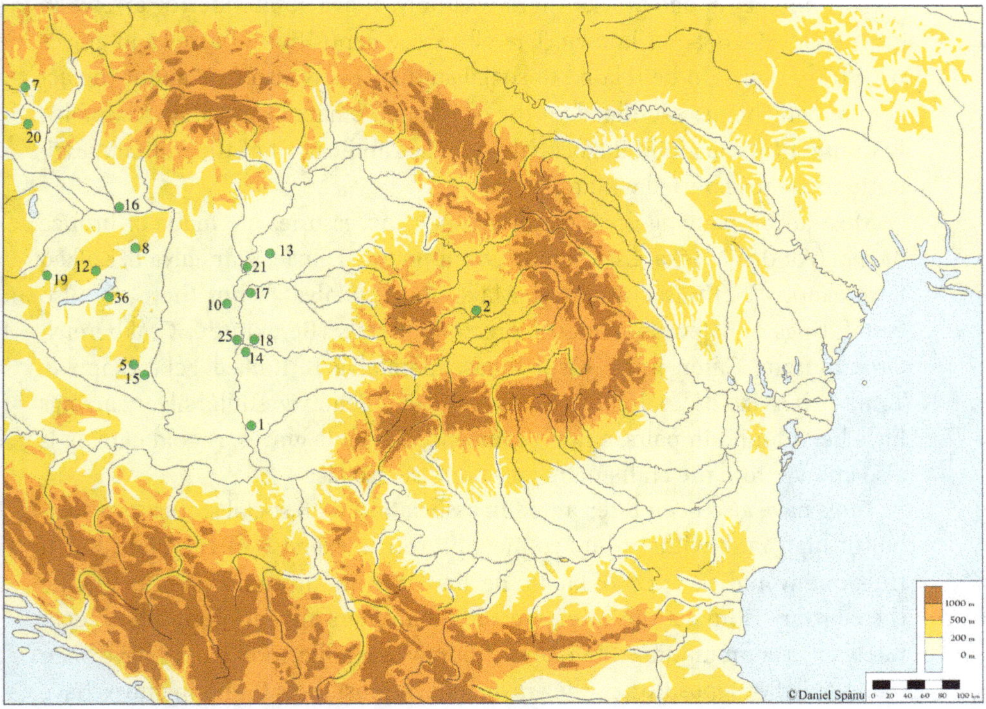

FIGURE 57 **Tombs with tools and weapons at the Middle Danube area** (for numbering see Fig. 30): Aradac-Mečka (Serbia); Band (Mureş co., Romania); Bóly (Hungary); Brno (Czech Republic); Csákberény-Orondpuszta (Hungary); Gátér (Hungary); Jutas (Hungary); Kisújszállás-Nagykert (Hungary); Klárafalva B (Hungary); Kölked-Feketekapu B (Hungary); Komárno (Slovakia); Kunszentmárton (Hungary); Makó (Hungary); Pókaszepetk (Hungary); Poysdorf (Austria); Rákóczifalva-Kastélydomb (Hungary); Szeged-Kiskundorozsma (Hungary); Zamárdi (Hungary)

were buried together with their stallions, richly decorated harness, as well as swords and arrowheads (the number of which indicated social rank). Two dozen arrowheads have been found in the princely graves of Kunbábony and Bócsa. "Six arrows" (Alti-ok, Alzeco) was the honorary title of a Bulgar leader expelled from the qaganate at the end of the civil war in the 630s.[65] Seven arrows were found in grave 369 of Csákberény-Orondpuszta, six at Jutas, five at Klárafalva B,[66] four at Kölked-Feketekapu B, two at Gátér and Kunszentmárton

Elbe, eds. Aleksander Paroń, Sébastien Rossignol, Bartłomiej Sz. Szmoniewski and Grischa Vercamer (Wrocław/Warszawa: Instytut Archaeologii i Etnologii Polskiej Akademii Nauk and Deutches Historiches Institut Warschau, 2010), pp. 221–223, fig. 3 and table III.

65 Pohl, *Die Awaren*, 184, 188.

66 Balogh, "Martinovka-típusú övgarnitúra," 267.

each, while at Aradac-Mečka there was only one. The number of arrows in grave 61 at Makó is not known. Therefore, the deposition of arrows in graves with tools seems to be related to social status. This is also true about the accompanying horses sacrificed for the occasion (Felnac, Kisújszállás, Klárafalva B, Kunszentmárton, and Rákóczifalva), a clear indication of the military attributions of those buried with tools.

Most accompanying dress (primarily belt) accessories are made of bronze or iron (Aradac-Mečka, Csákberény-Orondpuszta, Felnac, Klárafalva B, Kölked Feketekapu "B", Kunszentmárton, Makó, Rákóczyfalva),[67] but there are also belt fittings and jewels made of precious metals (Berekfürdő, Csákberény-Orondpuszta, Gátér, Jutas, Kisújszállás, Klárafalva B, Kölked Feketekapu B, Tolna-Fehérvize-dűlő). In both Gátér and Tolna-Fehérvize-dűlő, silver earrings have been found in pairs, a rare occurrence for male graves. A gold earring is also known from the craftsman's grave in Kisújszállás.

Tools have also been interpreted in association with social status, as a symbol of high rank without any connection to the exercise of the craft. But if true, one would except tool kits to be similar, without much variation. Quite the contrary is in fact the case, pliers and hammers appear more often, separately or in combinations.[68] Second, if purely symbolic, tools would have been made only for deposition in the grave. In fact, most tools found in graves have clear traces of wear indicating that they had been used in metalworking prior to their deposition in graves. They are therefore relevant to the study of early medieval crafts, and not of symbols of high rank. If only high-ranking persons who had craftsmen working for them were buried with tools, then all graves of the elite should contain (some) tools. Nonetheless, many continue to believe that tools are badges of social status and power.[69] To be sure, the number of tools deposited in graves varies greatly. Some graves in row-grave cemeteries have only a few tools, others have toolkits.[70] But the highest number of tools is in isolated burials.[71] There are also graves with one tool each, which probably symbolizing, as *pars pro toto*, the practice of blacksmithing or jewelry making.

67 For dress accessories in graves with tools, see Tănase, "Gräber," pp. 219–221 and fig. 2 and table II.

68 For the structure of the toolkit in the craftsmen's tombs of the Carpathian basin, see Tănase, "Gräber," pp. 215–218 and fig. 1 and table I.

69 Rácz, "Sind Goldschmiede in den „Goldschmiedegräber" der Awarenzeit bestattet?" 362, notes 4 and 5; Zsófia Rácz, "Metallhandwerkszeug aus den Gräbern 323 und 369," in Gyula László, *Das awarenzeitliche Gräberfeld in Csákberény-Orondpuszta* (Budapest: Magyar Nemzeti Múzeum, 2015), 209, note 668.

70 Rácz, "Sind Goldschmiede in den „Goldschmiedegräber" der Awarenzeit bestattet?" 367, 369.

71 Rácz, "Sind Goldschmiede in den „Goldschmiedegräber" der Awarenzeit bestattet?" 372.

Alongside tools, semi-finished products or raw materials were deposited as well, which suggests that there was no selection of artifacts as symbols of power, but rather as markers of activity and the ability to manufacture tools or weapons, without any direct connection to social status.[72]

Since metal dies discovered in graves of the Tisza Plain have little to no signs of wear, nor have many pieces of decoration been discovered, scholars used to believe that those dies were not related to craftsmanship, but they were rather part of a ritual highlighting social rank. It is however possible that the jewelers together with dies were active only for a short period prior to death.[73] On the other hand, this may simply be the state of research. In recent years, several harness mounts have been published that are similar in shape and decoration to the dies from Felnac and Kunszentmárton.[74]

Another implement that may be regarded as associated with social rank is the scale. Two-arm scales, the so-called *libera*, have been found together with Byzantine weights (*exagia*) in graves with tools Kunszentmárton,[75] Jutas,[76] and Pókaszepetk.[77] No currency existed in the Avar Qaganate that could be compared to that in Merovingian Gaul. Instead, Byzantine coins were deposited in graves. The redistribution of gold and silver coins received from Byzantium was restricted to a small group of people at the top of the social hierarchy. The presence of weights is also related to Byzantine coins, for in Byzantium they were used to verify the purity of gold coins. For example, the bronze weight found in Jutas weighed as much as six *solidi*, i.e., 28.57 g, while the glass *exagia* and bronze weights from Kunszentmárton served for verifying the purity of *tremisses* and *solidi*. There were imitations of Byzantine coins inside the Avar Qaganate, the role of which was exclusively funerary (i.e., they were produced to be deposited in graves). Indeed, although it is quite clear that the Avars were familiar with the Byzantine coins, they did not use them as means of exchange.[78] Balances and weights produced in the Empire were also found inside the Carpathian Basin. Unlike the Empire, where they were used to verify

72 Rácz, "Sind Goldschmiede in den „Goldschmiedegräber" der Awarenzeit bestattet?" 379.

73 Garam, *Funde*, 157.

74 For instance: Lőrinczy, Rácz, *Die Goldschmiedegräber*, pp. 213–214; Csilla Balogh, "Orta Tisa Bölgesi'nde Doğu Avrupa Bozkır Kökenli Göçebe Bir Topluluğa Ait Mezarlık 'Makó, Mikócsa-Halom, Macaristan' [A cemetery belonging to a nomad community of Eastern Europe Steppe origin in the Middle Tisza Region "Makó, Mikócsa-Halom, Hungary"]," *Art Sanat* 7 (2017), 67, fig. 6.2–3.

75 Csallány, *A Kunszentmártoni avarkori ötvösir*, 51–52.

76 Rhé, Fettich, *Jutas und Öskü*, 32.

77 Sós, "Frühmittelalterliche Brandbestattung mit Feinwaage in Pókaszepetk," 425, fig. 2; 427.

78 Florin Curta, "Remarks on the economic and funerary uses of imitations of Early Byzantine coins," *Byzantion* 89 (2019), 177–208.

the purity of the golden coins, inside the Avar Qaganate, such instruments served a much more practical purpose, namely to weigh the metal to be melted and turned into jewels. This strongly suggests that the scales found in Avar-age graves were deposited there as tools, and not as symbol of power.[79]

Were the tools deposited in graves used at all before that? There has been no examination of the tools from Band such as done for those found in Brno and Poysdorf. The metallographic analyses of the tools in the latter two assemblages revealed not only the techniques employed to make those tools, but also the fact that they had been used intensively for metalworking. Some of them still had minuscule particles from processed precious metal or fine traces from various metalworking operations in which they were employed.[80] Judging by the parallels between Poysdorf and Brno, on one hand, and Band, on the other, it is therefore likely that the tools deposited in those graves were not signs of social rank, but true craftsman implements.

The toolkit found in Band includes a wide variety of implements, primarily related to blacksmithing: die-stock and a tool for riveting, anvil, but also pliers, hammers, drills, chisels, and files. The blacksmith was also working in metal casting, as indicated by the chunks of casts iron and the pieces of slag discovered with the tools. Fragments from a silver mirror were also found, which probably constituted the raw material used to make ornamental pieces, which suggests that the blacksmith was also jeweler. Could he also have been responsible for the production of the helmet, or was that brought from elsewhere (i.e., the Empire)? The existence, among grave goods of rivets for attaching metal plates, of tools presumably used to produce nails (or rivets), and of hammers for working metal sheets strongly suggest that if not directly responsible for the production of the helmet, the Band craftsman could have certainly repaired such a helmet. However, the deposition of the helmet in the grave could hardly be interpreted as a sample of the craftsman's skill, and must rather be associated with the martial posture and the elevated social status of the man buried in Band.[81] The toolkit in Band includes a number of unique tools, such as the mechanical drill, the analogy for which is dated to the pre-Viking age (Vestly). Equally unique are the die-stock (or nail-making tool, with much simpler analogies in Kölked Feketekapu B, as well as in Viking-age Scandinavia) and the riveting tool. In my opinion, the great variety of tools in the Band toolbox is a strong argument in favor of the idea that he was a craftsman, and not just a member of the local elite, whose status was symbolically represented through

79 Werner, "Waage," 25–26.

80 Daim, Mehofer, Tobias, "Die langobardischen Schmiedegräber," 211–214.

81 Menghin, *Die Langobarden*, 69.

the deposition of the toolkit. No such toolkits have been found in many graves of the upper echelon of the early medieval society in the Carpathian Basin. Moreover, similar finds are known from very distant areas with completely different cultural makeups, such as the Merovingian assemblage in Hérouvillette and the pre-Viking age assemblage in Vestly. Moreover, the ritual deposition of dies in graves, which is only documented in the Carpathian Basin, may well be a regional adaptation of the general custom of depositing tools in graves of craftsmen.

That similar toolkits appear in culturally different assemblages at a considerable distance from each other is not the result of trade, but of the similar skills involved in early medieval black- and goldsmithing. In other words, whether in Merovingian Gaul, Avar-age Carpathian Basin, or Viking-age Scandinavia, craftsmen worked in essentially the same way and employed the same kinds of tools.[82] Inside the Carpathian Basin, a direct link between grave goods and the profession or occupation of the buried individual has been established in other cases as well. For example, graves with scales have been attributed to merchants, as in grave 373 of Kölked Feketekapu A.[83] A craftsman working with bone and antler is believed to have been buried in grave 61 at Makó, because of the associated tools.[84] To be sure, the mechanical drill found in grave 10 at Band could have just as well been used for processing wood or bone,[85] and not just metals. Several other graves from the same cemetery produced evidence of leather- (grave 11)[86] or wood-working tools (squint chisels, drills, and punches, such as found in graves 12, 13, 20, and 23).[87] None of those graves, however, contained weapons or dress accessories similar to those found in graves of metalworkers. This clearly indicated the importance of that craft in contemporaneous society, and the special social status of blacksmiths and goldsmiths. The deposition of tools in graves of metalworkers is a mirror of the appreciation they actually enjoyed during their lifetime in their respective communities. In other words, if symbolizing the social status of the metalworkers, the tools deposited in graves did so because they were first associated with their skills as craftsmen. That is why the ritual deposition of tools cannot be seen primarily as a way to mark elite social status, for no symbols of social power

82 Daim, Mehofer, Tobias, "Die langobardischen Schmiedegräber," 203.
83 Kiss, *Das awarenzeitliche gepidische Gräberfeld von Kölked-Feketekapu A*, 103; fig. 16, pl. 73.
84 Balogh, "Karpat havzasi'nda bir avar," 109.
85 Rácz, *Die Goldschmiedegräber*, 128.
86 Kovács, "A mezőbándi ásatások," 296, fig. 19. 5–6, 12; 403, 428.
87 Kovács, "A mezőbándi ásatások," 403, 428.

and no heirlooms have so far been found in any grave with tools.[88] That does not of course exclude the possibility of some of the blacksmiths (such as buried in Band, Kisújszállás, or Kölked Feketekapu B) and goldsmiths (such as that buried in Kunszentmárton) being members of the elite.[89] That was clearly the case in Merovingian Francia, as demonstrated by the gold- and blacksmithing skills of King Chilperic I and Bishop Eligius.[90] But there is no archaeological evidence in the Carpathian Basin for placing those black- and goldsmiths on a par with the Avar elite, the graves of which are substantially different. The same applies to the cremation burial in Sărata Monteoru, which produced eight vessels interpreted as crucibles, on the basis of their similarity with a crucible from the contemporaneous settlement excavated in Bucharest-Băneasa. Together with those crucibles, small fragments of a knife have been found. Although knives appear more often in male burials, they have also been found in female graves. That, therefore, is no indication of the gender of the jeweler buried in Sărata Monteoru. If he was a man, he does not seem to have been a member of the elite, since there were no weapons deposited in his grave, although weapon deposition is archaeologically documented for cremation burials, for example in Pókaszepetk. It is difficult to draw firm conclusions from the existing evidence, because of the possibility that the funeral ritual at Sărata Monteoru operating with different conceptual categories than those pertaining to the Carpathian Basin.

Judging from the evidence from the latter region, particularly the anthropological sexing of the skeletons from Aradac-Mečka, Csákberény-Orondpuszta, Kölked Feketekapu B, and Szekszárd-Tószegi-dűlő, metalworking was a male activity.[91] By contrast, elsewhere in Eastern Europe, the evidence suggests that women were also involved in jewelry making. In the central and eastern parts of European Russia, casting implements have been regularly found in graves of young and adult women, which has led to the conclusion that in those

88 For artifacts symbolizing high social status (gold bracelets, torcs, scepters, vessels, luxury belt fittings), see Attila Kiss, "Tanulmányok a kora avar kori Kunbábonyi vezérsírról [Studies on the Early Avar cemetery from Kunbábonyi]," *A Móra Ferenc Múzeum Évkönyve, Studia Archaeologica* 1 (1995), 146–147. Nor are there any artifacts related to consumption of special foods, such as the silver spoons or strainers found in Avar-age female burials (Bendeguz Tobias, "Die awarenzeitlichen Sieblöffel im Karpatenbecken," *Communicationes Archaeologicae Hungaricae* (2001), 177).

89 István Bóna, "Die Geschichte der Awaren im Lichte der Archäologischen Quellen," in *Popoli delle Steppe: Unni, Avari, Ungari*, vol. 2, Settimane di studio del Centro italiano di studi sull'alto medievo 35 (Spoleto: Presso la Sede del Centro, 1988), 448.

90 Aufleger, "Metallarbeiten," 620; Vierck, "Werke des Eligius," vol. 2: 310.

91 Zsófia Rácz, "Sind Goldschmiede in den „Goldschmiedegräber" der Awarenzeit bestattet?" 377–378.

societies, women were jewelers.[92] Molds and ingots appear in female graves attributed to the Finnish Mari population of Russia without interruption from the 6th century to the 11th century.[93] Tools have been discovered in female graves in Western Europe as well. An anvil was found in a woman's grave dated to the early 6th century in Westheim (Germany).[94] At Burton-upon-Humber (England),[95] a 7th-century female grave produced a scale and a die for making bracteates. Such assemblages have been interpreted either symbolically or as indications that women occasionally engaged in metalworking.[96] Inside the Carpathian Basin, dies have also been found with female graves dated to the 7th century at Gyönk, Szekszárd-Palánk, Tiszafüred (Hungary), as well as in 8th century female burials, such as excavated in Komárno IV (Slovakia). Since dies are also known from contemporaneous male graves (grave III in Aradac, Békéssámson, graves 1623 and 1999 in Zamárdi), sometimes in association with pliers (Rákóczifalva), the deposition of dies in female graves may be an indication that women engaged in metalworking as well. To be sure, all stone molds known from the Carpathian Basin have also been found in female graves dated to the 7th and 8th centuries (Szeged-Bilisics and Vác-Kavicsbánya).[97] The remarkable similarity between those assemblages with stone molds and those from the forest zone of central Russia suggests that the women in question may have come from afar or that their burial followed exotic customs from distant lands. Be as it may, there can be no doubt that the women in question engaged in metalworking.[98]

Although the evidence is sufficient, no studies have so far been dedicated to female smelters and jewelers from the Carpathian Basin. Whether the craftsmen active in settlements from Walachia and Moldavia were women or men is impossible to tell.

The ritual deposition of tools in graves came to an end in the Carpathian Basin at some point in the late 7th century. During the Late Avar age, besides the stone mold from the female grave in Komárno IV, the deposition of

92 Golubeva, "Devochki-Liteĭshchitsy," 31.

93 Nikitina, Efremova, "Pogrebal'nyĭ obriad," 149–150.

94 Capelle, *Die Miniaturkette*, 62–63.

95 Capelle, Vierck, "Modeln," 71.

96 Capelle, Vierck, "Modeln," 77.

97 Dezső Csallány, "Az Átokháza-bilisicsi avarkori sírleletek [The Avar Age Tombs from Bilisics-Átokháza]," *A Móra Ferenc Múzeum Évkönyve* (1957), 113; Nándor Fettich, "Symbolischer Gürtel aus der Awarenzeit (Fund von Bilisics)," *A Móra Ferenc Múzeum Évkönyve* 1 (1963), 66–70; Tettamanti, *Das awarenzeitliche Gräberfeld*, 32, 121, pl. v.8.

98 Burial of women together with casting implements has been also interpreted as a magic ritual for the protection of the house or of the clan (Nikitina, Efremova, "Pogrebal'nyĭ obriad," 160–162).

hammers, pliers, and axes is occasionally attested in a few graves (a female grave in Komárno IX, and male graves in Szeged-Kiskundorozsma-Hármashatár, Sajópetri-Hosszúrét, and Szentes-Kaján, all three in Hungary).[99] After ca. 800, metalworking tools were rather deposited in hoards alongside agricultural tools and weapons.[100]

99 Rácz, *Die Goldschmiedegräber*, 170, 193 and 195; Vályi, "Das Detail," 223, 226, fig. 3.10.

100 For the detailed discussion of hoards of iron implements, see Curta, "Blacksmiths."

CHAPTER 10

Conclusions

Metalworking involved ore extraction, smelting, and processing. Judging by the existing evidence, there was no distinction in the 6th and 7th centuries between smelters, blacksmiths, and jewelers. Easier to spot archaeologically at first glance are goldsmiths because of their tools. But even they seem to have been quite capable of performing the job of blacksmiths, much like blacksmiths could produce jewelry as well. At any rate, metalworking played a very important role in early medieval societies, and practicians were highly appreciated in their respective communities, as revealed, among other things, by mortuary assemblages.

The first graves with tools were found in the 19th century, but they did not stir any interest per se. The number of discoveries pertaining to craft activities increased considerably throughout the 20th century, and archaeologists became very interested in the topic. The existence of workshops, the social condition and mobility of craftsmen, the iron ore sources and smelting procedures, the techniques of jewelry production – all of that attracted the attention of such prominent scholars as Nándor Fettich, Dezső Csallány, Éva Garam, Zsófia Rácz (Hungary), Joachim Werner, C. Driehaus, Michael Müller-Wille, Hans Roth, C. von Carnap-Bornheim, Falko Daim, Joachim Henning (Germany), Birgit Arrhenius, Hayo Vierck (Sweden), Bartłomiej Szmoniewski (Poland), and Ion S. Vynokur (Ukraine). Among all of them, Joachim Werner had the greatest contribution, as he first drew attention to 5th to 7th century toolkits. As early as 1954, he compiled the first list of graves with tools and tackled the problem of the social status of craftsmen, and of their role in the community. Werner was particularly interested in the significance of depositing tools in graves, and believed that blacksmiths and goldsmiths were freemen, itinerant craftsmen. That line of thought was then followed by Michael Müller-Wille, Birgit Arrhenius (with special reference to Scandinavia), Vladimir Turčan, and Joachim Henning. A different approach was that of J. Driehaus and Hans Roth, who assumed that early medieval blacksmiths and goldsmiths were of servile condition and worked at the order of their lords.

The advent, particularly in recent decades, of metallographic and chemical analyses, as well as trasological studies have shifted the emphasis from craftsmen to their tools and products (other tools, weapons, or dress accessories). Some have also tackled the problem of raw materials, specifically the source of the metal (Birgit Bühler, Anders Söderberg, Falko Daim, Mathias Mehofer,

© DANIELA TĂNASE, 2021 | DOI:10.1163/9789004436930_012

and Bendeguz Tobias). In Romania, the emphasis was primarily on the analysis of iron slags from settlements, the composition of which reveals the exploitation of the local deposits. The iron obtained from those deposits was a rather poor quality, indicating both that the smelting technology was rudimentary and that in order to produce tools and weapons, one needed a considerable amount of forging (Eugen Stoicovici and Ștefan Olteanu).

Many finds pertaining to metalworking were meanwhile wrongly dated, with little, if any attention to processing techniques on short chronological segments. Black- and goldsmithing, as well as the socio-economic network involved in such activities were only rarely and superficially discussed when relevant finds were published (Dan Gh. Teodor, Ioan Mitrea, Ștefan Olteanu, Victor Teodorescu, Suzana Dolinescu-Ferche, and Margareta Constantiniu). Scholars seem to have been rather interested in the ethnic identity of the craftsmen, almost invariably believed to be native, from among the Romance-speaking population, and in close contact with the Byzantine civilization. Only recently have possible influences from the Avar Qaganate been brought to the fore in relation to finds from southeastern Romania (Andrei Măgureanu).

Such technological contacts redirected the research towards metalworking within a relatively short time span (6th and 7th centuries), but over a relatively large area in the valley of the Middle and Lower Danube River. This was a period of dramatic transformations, which is traditionally viewed as the beginning of the Middle Ages in Central and Eastern Europe, marked by the disappearance of the Germanic kingdoms of the Lombards and the Gepids and the rise of new power structures associated with the steppe nomads (the Avar and the Bulgar Qaganates). Those changes significantly altered cultural relations with the neighboring Byzantine Empire.

The careful study of the archaeological sources suggests that during the 6th and 7th centuries, certain metalworking techniques ornamental patterns were preferred over others, just certain mortuary practices were chosen to highlight the position of blacksmiths and goldsmiths in local communities.

In the lands to the south and east from the Carpathian Mountains now in Romania, and the neighboring territories to the east, smelting was done by rather rudimentary means the preferred technology for jewelry production was casting. Meanwhile, in the Carpathian Basin, smelting was rather rare, and the main technology for jewelry production was die pressing. Ironworking was clearly an economically more prominent activity outside than inside the Carpathian Basin. While the smelting furnaces discovered in Șirna indicate that ironworking on that site has started in earnest in the early 6th century, the first clear evidence of activity on the Zamárdi site in Hungary cannot be dated before 600, and was most likely of a late 7th or early 8th-century date. In that respect, Zamárdi is a mirror image of the site excavated at Lozna-Străteni, which is dated to the same time.

Both inside and outside the Carpathian Mountains, jewelry produced by different methods imitated personal and dress accessories from the Byzantine Empire, even if the imitation was somewhat closer to Byzantine prototypes in the Carpathian Basin than in Moldavia or Walachia. From the map distribution of molds and jewelry tools, a preference for certain types of ornaments may be distinguished at regional level. In other words, technological choices overlapped regional styles. In turn, such styles and the cluster of finds related to jewelry production may indicate power centers, such as those of central Transylvania, southeastern Walachia, the sub-Carpathian region of Moldavia, and the Moldavian Plateau (see Fig. 49).

Tools deposited in craftsmen's graves seem to have been selected with the idea in mind of illustrating craft activities. Thus, pliers and hammers were meant to be the most representative tools of the blacksmith, just like swords, lances, bows and arrows were for warriors. Graves with tools but without weapons are simply a way to distinguish craftsmen who were also warriors from those who were not (possibly apprentices or assistants). Tools deposited in graves represent the entire array of metalworking activities – blacksmithing, bronze casting, weapon making, and goldsmithing. Craftsmen produced not only jewelry and weapons, but also household tools and utensils. Such artifacts have been found in both settlements and graves: flint steels, iron buckles, knives.

It is therefore clear that metalworkers played an important economic and military role, for they made tools, weapons, and pieces of military equipment. It is also worth noting that craftsmen did not necessarily belong to any particular social group. Some of them were perhaps members of the elite, other were not. Irrespective of their social position, their talent and skill were greatly appreciated in the community.

The most important finds from present-day Romania that can shed some light on metalworking are the graves with tools from Band and Felnac, to which one may add the crucibles found in a cremation grave from Sărata Monteoru. Various tools have also been found on no less than 44 sites, most of them settlements, which can be linked to metalworking: stone molds, crucibles and ladles, pliers, anvils, engraving tools, punches, and chisels. While in Transylvania and the Banat most tools have been found in burial assemblages, outside the Carpathian Mountains the only such example is the grave from Sărata Monteoru. This may well be the result of the current state of research, but the ritual depositing of tools has not been so far documented in the lands to the east and southeast from the Carpathian Basin.

Craftsmen procured metal from different sources. Gold came in relatively large quantities to the Carpathian Basin in the form of tribute payments from Constantinople or as ransom for prisoners, as well as gifts (vessels, ornaments, harness items, or weapons plated with gold and silver). Bronze objects from the ruins of the Roman cities were recycled, and so were various objects obtained from Byzantium; there is no indication of an exploitation of copper and tin deposits. The only metal obtained from the local, surface ores was iron. Smelting was widely practiced in Walachia and Moldavia, with fewer traces of such activity so far found in central and northwestern Transylvania. The typical smelting furnace had a side vent, much like furnaces of earlier periods. However, two new, but quite primitive smelting technologies are documented archaeologically – in pits and in clay pots.

Craftsmen employed a variety of tools. Some prove the blacksmith's skill, such as the mechanical drill from Band. The variety of tools bespeaks the technological variety – casting, forging, beating, drawing, riveting, die pressing, mold casting, engraving, punching, gilding, *niello*, silver inlaying, and precious stones inlaying. Out of this panoply of techniques, two stand out in relation to jewelry production: casting and pressing, the latter being preferred in the Carpathian Basin. Mold casting was preferred in the lands to the east and to the south from the Carpathian Mountains, although it was also used on a smaller scale in the Carpathian Basin. Conversely, no dies for pressing have been so far discovered in the regions to the south and to the east of the Carpathian Mountains. As for decorative styles, they are a reflection of influences from several directions – Byzantium, the steppe world and the Merovingian milieu of Central Europe. Due to the many connections between different civilizations, new decorative styles emerged, such as the animal style II with the dentil decoration, which is typical for the Carpathian Basin.

It is important to note the many, more or less distant analogies for most artifacts from the present-day territory of Romania, which suggests that 6th- to 7th-century finds of tools and metal artifacts were not ethnically specific. Instead, such analogies illustrate contacts between cultural areas and the corresponding populations, which were also reflected in the archaeological evidence pertaining to metalworking, as well as in the shape and ornamentation of the personal and dress accessories.

Perhaps the way of life, sedentary or nomadic, as well as the desire of barbarian elites to imitate as close as possible the lifestyle of the Byzantine elites may be responsible for the particular technological choices in matters of jewelry production. On the other hand, the jewels themselves displayed specific emblematic style that were particular to specific elites of subject or allied populations associated with Avar power. The choice of casting as the preferred technology in Walachia and Moldavia may therefore be set in contrast with a more diversified panoply of technologies in Transylvania, a region closer to the heart of the Avar Qaganate.

The presence of dies and of tools of superior quality, many with good analogies in Western Europe and in Byzantium, illustrate the ties between Transylvania and the rest of the Carpathian Basin. It is only during the last third of the 7th century that influences from outside the Carpathian Mountains began to prevail in Transylvania, as illustrated by an increasing number of molds for casting. This change may well be associated with the interruption of contacts with Byzantium through the settlement of the Bulgars in the Balkans and the rise of early medieval Bulgaria.

The exact ethnicity of the goldsmiths (Gepid, Avar, Slavic, Byzantine, or native, Romance-speaking) remains a matter of speculation. However, analogies for the ritual deposition of tools in graves such as that in Band leave no room for doubt – the practice is of Germanic origin. Similarly, the presence of horse bones in Felnac suggests Avar mortuary practices, and the use of cremation in Sărata Monteoru is commonly linked to a Slavic population. Much more difficult, if not impossible is to "read" ethnicity in tools found in settlements, as it is to establish whether the craftsmen who employed them were sedentary or traveling. An exercise in futility, the considerable efforts made to establish the ethnicity of the craftsmen in 6th- to 7th-century settlements in Moldavia and Walachia obscure the fact that many of them worked in technological traditions of Byzantine inspiration. The idea of itinerant craftsmen, on the other hand, does not exclude the participation of native metalworkers. On the contrary, goldsmiths may have remained for a relatively long time in the same place, and they may have been both (long-term) sedentary and (short-term) traveling within relatively restricted areas. Some of them were perhaps members of the elite, others rose to social prominence through their skills. At any rate, those skills, and especially the ability to transform matter (molten into solid metals) using fire guaranteed a special status in local communities: those were people in contact with, if not also control of mysterious powers. That commanded respect and appreciation, which most clearly translated into mortuary practices as well.

While craftsmen in the Carpathian Basin traveled together with their toolkits to work upon request, the presence of toolkits accompanying itinerant craftsmen is harder to identify in Moldavia and Walachia, because of the lack of evidence from burial assemblages. However, other factors, such as the great similarity of tools (mold) and products (dress accessories) suggest the existence of itinerant craftsmen. None of them worked in special facilities as the only "workshops" known so far are not different from regular dwellings except in terms of associated tools. Such evidence may also be interpreted as pointing to the possibility that at least some of those metalworkers were women. It is likely that sedentary and itinerant craftsmen coexisted both in the regions outside the Carpathian Mountains, and in the Carpathian Basin. It goes without saying that the mobility of the craftsmen was a function of access to raw materials and the availability of patrons. In that respect, much more may be expected from advanced, comparative studies of stylistic variation in jewelry within and among different regions.

Despite the insistence of Romanian archaeologists on the unity of the material culture on the territory of present-day Romania, including those aspects pertaining to metalworking, there is a clear contrast between the inter- and the trans-Carpathian territories. While dies for pressing are preferred in Transylvania and the Banat, as well as farther west in the Tisza Plain, stone molds for casting appear primarily in Moldavia and Walachia, as well as farther to the east and northeast on the territories of present-day Ukraine and the Republic of Moldova. Smelting is so far more prominent outside than inside the Carpathian Mountains, and the only 6th- and 7th-century ironworking centers known from Romania are all from Walachia (Șirna, Budureasca, Dulceanca IV) and Moldavia (Lozna-Strătеni). Despite different technological options, all those regions share a great concern with imitating Byzantine fashions. The Byzantine influence is also the element that makes comparison possible between the lands along the lower and those along the middle course of the Danube. On a both technological and ideological level, the Byzantine influence is indeed the background against which the early medieval history of the barbarian world north of the Empire may be understood.

CHAPTER 11

Catalogue of Finds from Romania

1 Aldeni (Buzău Co.) (Fig. 42.1)

1. Discovery place: –
2. Discovery conditions: by chance, by pupils of the local school
3. Year of discovery: –
4. Context of discovery:
Context literature: Victor Teodorescu, "Centre meşteşugăreşti din sec. V/VI–VII. e. n. în Bucharest," 91, note 47.
5. Item category: mold for pressing (Fig. 42.1)
6. Description: One-face mold, on which two rectangular appliqués are carved in relief, with notched frame, in the middle it has a row of three squares bordered by another notched frame, and one rosette-shaped appliqué with a central button and the petals are represented by six circles. Dimensions: 17×10.6×2.4 cm
7. Material: stone
8. Absolute dating: 7th century
9a. Preserving place: Buzău County Museum
9b. Literature: Victor Teodorescu, "Centre meşteşugăreşti," 91 and fig. 7/3,3 a–b; Andrei Măgureanu, Bogdan Ciupercă, "Discuţii despre tiparul de la Aldeni, jud. Buzău [Discussions about the Aldeni pattern, Buzău County]," in *Arheologia mileniului I p. chr. Dunărea de jos între antichitate şi evul mediu* 6, Ploieşti, forthcoming.

2 Banat? (Fig. 42.2a–c)

1. Discovery place: Danube Gorges area
2. Discovery conditions: by chance; the item was part of the collection of Imre Pongrácz, the commander of the Honvéd garrison in the port Orşova during the last third of the 19th century.
3. Year of discovery: –
4. Context of discovery:
Context literature: –

© DANIELA TĂNASE, 2021 | DOI:10.1163/9789004436930_013

5. Item category: pressing mold (Fig. 42.2a–c)
6. Description: forming model for bow fibulae of Werner's type I C with seven round buttons with a profiled ring base, the end plate has a geometric decoration consisting of curved lines intersected by straight lines, and the frame is made up of two profiled lines. The neck has four profiled, vertical lines, the foot plate is flanked by four bird heads arranged in twos on one side and the other, has an oval shape and two tear-shaped holes at the end being broken. The lost part was an appendage in the form of a human mask that had the well-defined features and hairstyle. Dimensions: L: 7.9 cm, w: 4.6 cm end plate and 1.2 cm at the foot.
7. Material: potin
8. Absolute dating: 7th century
9a. Preserving place: Banat National Museum, in Timișoara, inv. no. 2134.
9b. Literature: Nestor, Nicolăescu-Plopșor, "Die völkerwanderungszeitlichen Schatz Negrescu," plate 9.2, 37; Teodor, "Fibules," 78, 88, fig. 8.3. Tănase, Mare, "Piese de port," 190, 203, pl. V.4.

3 Band/Bandu de Câmpie/Mezőbánd/Bandorf (Mureș Co.) (Fig. 31–36)

1. Discovery place: "Cetatea Surpăturii" at 2.5 km from the locality. Inhumation cemetery, excavated in 1906–1907, with 179 inhumation graves, all robbed. The skeletons follow a W-E orientation, pits are simple; pottery is found in almost every assemblage, together with household items, tools and weapons. There are also E-W-oriented graves, as well as tombs where the deceased was buried with the horse.
2. Discovery conditions: systematic archeological excavations; tomb no. 10, W-E oriented, 250×100 cm, depth of 50 cm. The bones were disturbed by the robbery of the tomb long ago. At the eastern end of the tomb, near the ankle of the deceased, a set of tools placed in a wooden box was found, as evidenced by the fragments of iron armor with pieces of wood. Other inventory items:
- costume pieces: iron buckles, iron belt tongues, iron belt plates with bronze rivets
- weapons: dagger, pieces of spear heads
- military equipment: helmet
- usual tools: sharpened stone, clay spindle whorl
- other items: finished items, head nails, discards, cast iron pieces, slag, fragments of metal items, among which fragments of a silver mirror.

3. Year of discovery: 1906
4. Context of discovery: iron helmet, items of bronze belt: oval buckles with oval plates, small square belt plates, all with large rives, buckle pin. Context literature: Kovács, "A mezőbándi ásatások," 398–402.

5.1. Item category: smithing tongs (Fig. 35.1, Fig. 36.1)
6.1. Description: smithing tongs with long arms and oval buckle, with unequal ends, close to each other. Dimensions: L: 45.5 cm
7.1. Material: iron

5.2. Item category: jewelry pliers (Fig. 35.2, Fig. 36.2)
6.2. Description: jewelry pliers with short arms, unequal and oval buckle, with unequal ends, distanced one from the other. Dimensions: L: 22.5 cm
7.2. Material: iron

5.3. Item category: smithing hammer (Fig. 35.13, Fig. 36.13a–b)
6.3. Description: smithing hammer, with oval fitting hole, with one of the ends rectangular and the other slightly rounded. Dimensions: L: 15 cm.
7.3. Material: iron

5.4. Item category: jewelry hammer (Fig. 35.12, Fig. 36.12)
6.4. Description: jewelry hammer, with oval fitting hole, with one of the ends slightly rounded, and the other end straight, with bent head; of small dimensions: L: 7 cm.
7.4. Material: iron

5.5. Item category: anvil (Fig. 35.16, Fig. 36.14)
6.5. Description: anvil of trapezoid shape, with the large base of the trapeze in the upper part, where it has a blunt area on a side. Dimensions: H: 10.5 cm, w: 2.4–10 cm.
7.5. Material: iron

5.6. Item category: draw plate (Fig. 35.8, Fig. 36.11)
6.6. Description: the tool has the shape of a small rectangular hammer, with one pointed end, notched on the inside; in the notch there are five orifices of various dimensions. Dimensions: L: 10.5 cm.
7.6. Material: iron

5.7. Item category: rivet-making tool (Fig. 35.11)
6.7. Description: the tool has the shape of a small hammer, with one of the ends provided with an appendage having the shape of a truncated cone, similar to the acorn hull, well polished, and in the middle, it has an oval orifice. The appendage has been longitudinally split. Dimensions: L: 3.5 cm, w: 1.9 cm.
7.7. Material: iron

5.8. Item category: mechanically driven drill (Fig. 35.14, Fig. 36.9)
6.8. Description: steel iron drill with driving wheel, mechanically driven. The preserved part is 15 cm long, and the wheel has a 4 cm diameter. The cylindric axis is broken in the upper part, while at the lower end the perforating end is preserved. Approximately in the middle of the axis, there is the driving wheel formed of two bronze disks with upwards and downwards curved sides, and the approximately 2 cm-space between them is filled up with lead. Dimensions: L: 14.5 cm, disk diameter: 4–4.5 cm.
7.8. Material: iron

5.9. Item category: drills (Fig. 35.5–7, Fig. 36.5–7)
6.9. Description: three fragments of bars with twisted lower part and pointed head, that initially served as drills. Dimensions: Fig. 17.5: L: 5.4 cm; Fig. 17.6: L: 4.8 cm; Fig. 17.7: L: 5.6 cm.
7.9. Material: iron

5.10. Item category: drill (Fig. 35.3)
6.10. Description: iron stick which has twisted lower part and pointed head. Dimensions: L: 5.4 cm.
7.10. Material: iron

5.11. Item category: chisel (Fig. 35.9, Fig. 36.3)
6.11. Description: iron stick, with straight blunt upper part, and in the lower part it has the pointed head. Dimensions: L: 15 cm.
7.11. Material: iron

5.12. Item category: jewelry anvil (Fig. 35.15, Fig. 36.8)
6.12. Description: short conical rod, with the head blunted as if it was a mushroom, and the tip is pointed. Dimensions: H: 6.2 cm
7.12. Material: iron

5.13. Item category: chisel (Fig. 35.10, Fig. 36.10)
6.13. Description: flat rod, at one end pointed, at the other blunt, possibly it was broken. I. Kovács claims it would be a drill, but according to us it is rather a chisel. Dimensions: L: 11 cm.
7.13. Material: iron

8. Absolute dating: the last thirds of the 6th century and the first half of the 7th century

9a. Preserving place: National History Museum of Transylvania in Cluj-Napoca

9b. Literature: Kovács, "A mezőbándi ásatások," 284–296; 294, fig. 16.1–18; 398–403.

4 Băleni-Români (Dâmbovița Co.) (Fig. 12.1)

1. Discovery place: on the "Plantation"
2.1. Discovery conditions: systematic researches, settlement
3.1. Year of discovery: –
4.1. Context of discovery:
Context literature: –

5.1. Item category: small knife for engraving (Fig. 12.1.1)
6.1. Description: engraver in the form of a small knife with a pointed tip. Dimensions: no data on the size of the artifact.
7.1. Material: iron

5.2. Item category: chisel (Fig. 12.1.2)
6.2. Description: chisel, with one flat end, and with a pointed tip at the other end. Dimensions: no data on the size of the artifact.
7.2. Material: iron

5.3. Item category: chisel (Fig. 12.1.3)
6.3. Description: chisel with one flat end, and with a pointed tip at the other end. Dimensions: no data on the size of the artifact.
7.3. Material: iron

2.2. Discovery conditions: dwelling no. 28, around the furnace and on the floor
3.2. Year of discovery: 1979
4.2. Context of discovery: ceramicware of Praga type, rectangular bronze buckle with small oval plate.
Context literature: Muscă, Muscă, "Săpăturile arheologice de la Băleni-Români," 425–426; 428, fig. 8.

5.2. Item category: crucible (Fig. 12.1.7)
6.2. Description: quasi-cylindrical vessel, the oval mouth has a pouring beak, the bottom is rounded. Also a fragment from another crucible was found. Dimensions: no data on the size of the artifact.
7.2. Material: clay
8. Absolute dating: end of the 6th century–beginning of the 7th century
9a. Preserving place: "Curtea Domnească" National Museum Complex of Târgoviște
9b. Literature: Miclea, Florescu, *Strămoșii românilor*, fig. 819; 212; Muscă, Muscă, "Săpăturile arheologice," 428, fig. 8.

5 Botoșana (Suceava Co.) (Fig. 12.2–4, Fig. 17)

1. Discovery place: south-east end of the hill named "La Cruci", located in the eastern side of the commune, limited to the north-east by Brook Pietrosul, to the south and south-east by Brook Botoșanei and to the west by Brook Jghiaburi.

2.1. Discovery conditions: systematic excavations, dwelling no. 18 **(Fig. 12.3)**, among demolished hearth pieces, between the oven and the northern side of the dwelling.
3.1. Year of discovery: 1967
4.1. Context of discovery: wheel-made ceramicware, hand-made ceramicware.
Context literature: Teodor, *Civilizația romanică*, 10; 15; 35; 99, fig. 20.6.
5.1. Item category: crucible (Fig. 12.3.2)
6.1. Description: tumbler-shaped vessel, with round mouth, prominent body, the bottom is ring-shaped. Dimensions: no data on the size of the artifact.
7.1. Material: clay

2.2. Discovery conditions: systematic excavations, settlement-dwelling no. 20 (Fig. 17.1.1–6), discovered in trench LXXV, among the spread stones of the oven, towards the eastern side of the dwelling
3.2. Year of discovery: 1968
4.2. Context of discovery: bronze coin, issued during the time of Justinian I; wheel-made ceramicware: jars; hand-made ceramicware: jars and trays; clay crucible.
Context literature: Teodor, *Civilizația romanică*, 10; 15; 37; 129, fig. 30.2; 99, fig. 20.2; 132, fig. 33,5, 136, 37.5; 140, 41.3–4; 147, 48.1; 99, 20.4–5.
5.2.1. Item category: metal casting spoon (Fig. 17.1.4)
6.2.1. Description: dipper-spoon, fragmentary, oval dipper, with tubular handle of average length. Dimensions: no data on the size of the artifact.
7.2.1. Material: clay
5.2.2. Item category: crucible (Fig. 17.1.3)
6.2.2. Description: cylindric vessel, the round mouth is broken, it has rounded bottom.
7.2.2. Material: clay

2.3. Discovery conditions: settlement, systematic excavations, in dwelling no. 25 (Fig. 12.2), on stones fallen from the oven.
3.3. Year of discovery: 1971
4.3. Context of discovery: hand-made and wheel-made potsherds from pot jars, biconical clay spindle whorl.
Context literature: Teodor, *Civilizația romanică*, 10; 15; 39–40; 99, fig. 20.3.
5.3. Item category: mold (Fig. 12.4.4)
6.3. Description: fragment of mold made of grayish-blackish rock, on which there are engraved two circles placed on an incised line. Dimensions: 3.6×2.4 cm.
7.3. Material: stone

2.4. Discovery conditions: systematic excavations, dwelling no. 27 (Fig. 17.2), situated in trench XCIV, in the filling of the dwelling
3.4. Year of discovery: 1972
4.4. Context of discovery: –
Context literature: Teodor, *Civilizația romanică*, 10; 15; 41; 99, fig. 20.1.
5.4. Item category: mold (Fig. 17.2.2)
6.4. Description: mold of marl, preserved in fragmentary condition, of rectangular shape; on one of the faces there is carved a cross with equal arms, flared at the ends, at the end of one of the arms there is an intake, at the end of one of them there is an intake and at the end of the opposite arm there is a straight incised line, there are also two small incised circles for casting grains (or affixing orifices?); on another face there are also two circles for casting grains, and on the third face there is an incised line which has in the middle two small circles. Dimensions: 5.9×4.2 cm
7.4. Material: stone.
9a. Museum of the History of Moldova Iași, inv. no. 23771.9b.

2.5. Discovery conditions: systematic excavations, isolated (Fig. 12.2)
5.6. Item category: chisel (Fig. 12.2)
6.6. Description: blade-shaped chisel, of rectangular cross-section, with one flat end and at the other end it has a more pointed tip. Dimensions: no data on the size of the artifact.
7.6. Material: iron

8. Absolute dating: the second half of the 6th century–first half of the 7th century

9a. Preserving place: "Bucovina" Museum Complex of Suceava, Museum of the History of Moldova Iași
Literature: Teodor, *Civilizația romanică,* 35, 37, 40–41, 99, fig. 20.1–6; Teodor, *Meșteșugurile*, 136, fig. 22.1.

6 Bratei/Pretau/Baráthely (Sibiu Co.) (Fig. 3)

1. Discovery place: "la Zăvoi", on the left bank of river Târnava Mare
2. Discovery conditions: systematic researches, settlement no. 2, dwelling no. 1.
3. Year of discovery: 1964
4. Context of discovery: fast wheel-made pottery, ovoid and biconical pots, some vessels ornamented with waved lines; hand-made ceramic-ware, among which a potsherd of a vessel ornamented on the shoulder with an incised waved line.
Context literature: Zaharia, "La station n° 2 de Bratei," 301–302; 345, fig. 9. 1–7, 17; 356, fig. 20.8.
5. Item category: metal casting spoon (Fig. 3.11)
6. Description: ovoid dipper-spoon with pointed ends, which served as pouring beaks, provided with tubular handle. Dimensions: L: 7.5 cm, w: 5.5 cm.
7. Material: clay
8. Absolute dating: 6th–7th century
9a. Preserving place: National Museum Bruckenthal in Sibiu
9b. Literature: Zaharia, "La station n° 2 de Bratei," 301–302; 356, fig. 20.8.

7 Bucharest

7 a *Băneasa (Fig. 13.1)*

1. Discovery place: Băneasa, "La Stejar"
2. Discovery conditions: systematically researched settlement; the crucible was discovered in the oven of a dwelling no. 20
3. Year of discovery: –
4. Context of discovery: hand- and wheel-made pottery
Context literature: –
5. Item category: crucible (Fig. 13.1)
6. Description: vessel bowl-shaped, trefoil-like mouth and rounded bottom, its walls show traces of melted bronze. Dimensions: H: 3.5 cm, width: 6.2 cm.

7. Material: clay
8. Absolute dating: 6th century
9a. Preserving place: Museum of the City of Bucharest
9b. Literature: Constantiniu, "Șantierul arheologic," 95; Constantiniu, "Elemente romano-bizantine," 674, fig. 5.1.

7 b *Casa Armatei (Fig. 13.2)*
1. Discovery place: Army House
2. Discovery conditions: –
3. Year of discovery: –
4. Context of discovery: –
Context literature: –
5. Item category: crucible (Fig. 13.2)
6. Description: crucible with round mouth, quasi-cylindrical body and rounded bottom. Dimensions: H: 5.5 cm.
7. Material: clay
8. Absolute dating: 6th century
9a. Preserving place: Museum of the City of Bucharest
9b. Literature: *București I. Rezultatele săpăturilor arheologice și ale cercetărilor istorice din anul 1953* [Bucharest I. The results of the archeological excavations and of the historical research from the year 1953] (Bucharest: Editura Academia Republicii Populare Romîne, 1954), 248, fig. 40.8.

7 c *Dămăroaia (Fig. 13.3)*
1. Discovery place: Dămăroaia
2. Discovery conditions: –
3. Year of discovery: –
4. Context of discovery: –
Context literature: –
5.1. Item category: mold (Fig. 13.3)
6.1. Description: mold of pentagonal shape, one-faced, on it there is engraved a buckle with the oval link and the embedding orifice of the trapezoid spike, brokenthrough; it has a side intake. Dimensions: no data on the size of the artifact.
7.1. Material: stone
5.2. Item category: metal casting spoon (without illustration)
6.2. Description: dipper-spoon. Dimensions: no data on the size of the artifact.
7.1. Material: clay

8. Absolute dating: 6th century
9a. Preserving place: Museum of the City of Bucharest
9b. Literature: Morintz, Rosetti, "Din cele mai vechi timpuri," 11–47, pl. XXXI, 12.

7 d *10, Soldat Ghivan Str. (Fig. 13.6)*
1. Discovery place: 10, Soldat Ghivan Nicolae str., on the bank of lake Fundeni along the Colentina creek
2. Discovery conditions: systematic researches, sunken house (marked no. 10), where a jeweler's workshop functioned.
3. Year of discovery: 1962
4. Context of discovery: buckle with the pin of the type *Schlaufenriemenzunge*, arrow head with three edges, leaf-shaped, stone mold with matrices for earrings, clay spoon for casting metal.
Context literature: Teodorescu, "Centre meșteșugărești," 77; 81, fig. 3.4, fig. 3.1–3, 5; Dolinescu-Ferche, Constantiniu, "Un établissement," 320; 321, fig. 17.16.
5.1. Item category: jeweler's pincers (Fig. 13.6.2)
6.1. Description: pincers made of an iron blade, bent, it has unequal ends. Dimensions: L: 3.3 cm.
7.1. Material: iron
5.2. Item category: metal casting spoon (Fig. 13.6.3)
6.2. Description: oval dipper-spoon, with short tubular collet, for embedding the wooden handle. It was shaped out of a higher quality paste, it shows a yellowish hue with darker traces. Dimensions: L: 6.5 cm.
7.2. Material: clay
5.3. Item category: mold (Fig. 13.6.5)
6.3. Description: mold of fine limestone, of whitish hue, of rectangular shape, two-faced, with a groove; on one of the faces it has rosette dies, two links and one thread-shaped element with a grain at the end, and on the opposite face four simple thread-shaped elements. Dimensions: 6.3×3.5×1.4–1.8 cm
7. Material: stone
8. Absolute dating: last third of the 6th century
9a. Preserving place: Museum of the City of Bucharest
9b. Literature: Teodorescu, "Centre meșteșugărești," 81, fig. 3,1,4; 94; Dolinescu-Ferche, Constantiniu, "Un établissement," 307–311; 321, fig. 17.16; 322, fig. 18.13; 323, fig. 19.1.

7 e *Străulești-Lunca (Fig. 13.4)*

1. Discovery place: Străulești-Lunca
2. Discovery conditions: settlement
3. Year of discovery: –
4. Context of discovery:

Context literature: –

5. Item category: mold (Fig. 13.4)

6. Description: mold of blackish hue, of rectangular shape, on which an equal arm cross is represented, with the ends slightly widened. On the sides the notching is more obvious, and in the center of the cross there is a notched point. The cross is provided with a link for being attached to the necklace. The mold has three grooves. The wear degree of the item is rather high considering the repeated use, and on the right side, a deep scratch is probably due to the pointed instrument used to try to detach the cross from the mold after the metal gets cold. Dimensions: 4.8×2.7×1.5 cm.

7. Material: clay

8. Absolute dating: 6th century

9a. Preserving place: Museum of the City of Bucharest

9b. Literature: Constantiniu, "Elemente romano-bizantine," 674, Fig. 5.3.

7 f *Străulești-Măicănești (Fig. 13.5)*

1. Discovery place: Străulești-Măicănești – settlement I
2. Discovery conditions: settlement, in the filling of house 9 (dated to the 4th century)
3. Year of discovery: 1961
4. Context of discovery: wheel-made pottery, both coarse and fine fabric (the latter with burnished ornament), fragments of amphorae, handmade pottery

Context literature: Constantiniu, "Săpăturile de la Străulești-Măicănești," 157–161.

5. Item category: mold (Fig. 13.5)

6. Description: mold of rectangular shape, of fine splittable gritstone, with limestone content, of light coffee brown hue, on which there are placed on opposite directions two bunches with grains at their ends. The mold is one-faced (one of the faces was destroyed in the old times) and bipolar (with two grooves at each pole). The mold was used at casting grains, that were further needed to create the ornamentation of jewelry items with grain details or ornaments. Dimensions: 5.8×4×1 cm.

7. Material: stone
8. Absolute dating: 6th century
9a. Preserving place: Museum of the City of Bucharest
9b. Literature: Constantiniu, "Săpăturile," 161, fig. 72.

7 g *Tei (Fig. 11.2)*
1. Discovery place: settlement
2. Discovery conditions: systematic researches
3. Year of discovery: 1930–1933
4. Context of discovery: prongs of the *Schlaufenriemenzunge* type, clay mold for earrings or rosette-appliqués and pearls, impressing mold for knobbed fibulae.
Context literature: Victor Teodorescu, "Centre meșteșugărești," 74, nota 3; 82, fig. 4. 2–3.

5.1. Item category: imprinting mold (Fig. 11.2.2)
6.1. Description: mold for miniatural knobbed fibulae with semicircular end plate, which has five round buttons and one frame made of a line which encloses three notches, and the curved neck has two incised lines. The plate on the foot is rhomboid, flanked by four stylized, in the center there is the stylized representation of a tulip which has inside a lying S-shaped line, and at the end one round appendix with two profiled lines at the basis. Dimensions: L: 3.2 cm.
7.1. Material: potin

5.2. Item category: metal casting spoon (Fig. 11.2.3)
6.2. Description: dipper-spoon for casting melted metal, of almost round shape, with the tail of which only a part has been preserved. Dimensions: dipper: 10 × 8.5 cm, tail: L: 3.7 cm.
7.2. Material: iron

5.3. Item category: crucible (without illustration)
6.3. Description: vessel bowl-shaped, trefoil-like mouth and rounded bottom. Dimensions: no data on the size of the artifact.
7.3. Material: clay

5.4. Item category: mold (Fig. 11.2.1)
6.4. Description: mold of reddish hue, which was used at making semi-globular appliqués and beads: the appliqué is disk-shaped, with a round button in the center surrounded by stylized acanthus leaves. The bead is of the *melon seed* type and is situated near the disk. Dimensions: 6.1×4.1–3.4×2.1 cm.
7.4. Material: fired clay

8. Absolute dating: 6th–7th centuries
9a. Preserving place: Museum of the City of Bucharest
9b. Literature: Rosetti, "*Din preistoria Bucureștilor I, Civilizația tip București. Die Bukarester Kultur* [From the prehistory of Bucharest I, the civilization Bucharest type]," Bucharest: Editura Tipografia Curții Regale, 1936, pl. IX, fig. 49; Teodorescu, "Centre meșteșugărești," 82, fig. 4, 1, 4–5; 95–96.

8 Budureasca, Vadu Săpat Village, Fântânele Commune (Prahova Co.)

8 a *Budureasca 3 (Fig. 11.1)*

1. Discovery place: "La Greci" or "La stupina C.A.P. Vadu"
2. Discovery conditions: systematic researches, settlement
3. Year of discovery: 1964
4. Context of discovery: bilateral bone comb, bracelet with one pointed end and the other thickened, hand-made ceramicware whose paste contains smashed sherds (pots, pans), querns, fragments of metal vessel.
Context literature: Măgureanu, Ciupercă, "The 6th–8th Centuries Metallurgical Activity," 293.

5.1. Item category: small knife for engraving (Fig. 11.1.1)
6.1. Description: tiny thine knife with pointed and slightly curved head. Dimensions: L: 7.7 cm.
7.1. Material: iron

5.2. Item category: engraver (without illustration)
6.2. Description: wide bar, obliquely cut at one end and which has a pointed end, while the other is rounded, it has the shaped of a small knife. Dimensions: no data on the size of the artifact.
7.2. Material: iron

5.3. Item category: mold (Fig. 11.1.2), house 6
6.3. Description: mold made of fine stone, with limestone content, of rectangular shape, on which three notched circles were created, being placed so to form a triangle, linked between them by a notched line. Notches seem to be imitations of the braid. Inside the triangle there are three circles. The mold has a large groove and two round orifices for embedding. Dimensions: L: 5 cm, w: 2.2 cm, thickness: 1.4 cm.
7.3. Material: stone
9a. Romania's National History Museum of Bucharest, inv. no. 106660

5.4. Item category: mold (Fig. 11.1.3), house 6

6.4. Description: mold of rectangular shape, fragmentary condition, of soft rock, grayish-yellowish, on which a shape similar to a dagger with sinusoid blade is represented. It might have been used for creating pendants, possibly also used as amulets. The mold has a groove. Dimensions: L: 4.2 cm, w: 2.2 cm, thickness: 1.1 cm.
7.4. Material: stone
9a. History and Archeology Museum of Prahova County Ploiești, inv. no. 19365

5.5. Item category: mold (Fig. 11.1.4), house 6
6.5. Description: mold of trapezoid shape, of soft rock, grayish-yellowish of hue, with a trapezoid groove which communicates with a semispheric representation, used for creating semispheric appliqués. Dimensions: L: 2.5 cm, w: 2.3 cm, thickness: 0.7 cm.
7.5. Material: stone
9a. History and Archeology Museum of Prahova County Ploiești, inv. no. 19364

5.6. Item category: waste item
6.6. Description: metal sheet fragments with obvious traces of battering
7.6. Material: copper
8. Absolute dating: 6th–7th centuries
9a. Preserving place: History and Archeology Museum of Prahova County Ploiești
9b. Literature: Teodorescu, "Centre meșteșugărești," 85. fig. 6.1; Miclea, Florescu, *Strămoșii românilor*, fig. 819; 212; Teodorescu, Peneș, "Matricea de incidență," 11–50; 45, fig. 21. 1; Măgureanu, Ciupercă, "The 6th–8th Centuries Metallurgical Activity," 304; 315, fig. 7.

8 b ***Budureasca 4 (Fig. 8.1–14, Fig. 9.1–4)***
1. Discovery place: "Puțul Tătarului" or "Puțul Mare"
2. Discovery conditions: systematic excavations, settlement
3. Year of discovery: –
4. Context of discovery:
Context literature: –

5.1. Item category: jewelry pliers (Fig. 8.7)
6.1. Description: Fragment of jewelry pliers, a fragment of the grabbing curl was preserved, it is oval, with equal, pointed ends, straightly cut on the interior. Dimensions: no data on the size of the artifact.
7.1. Material: iron

5.2. Item category: jeweler anvil (Fig. 8.8)
6.2. Description: small jeweler anvil, almost 4 cm high, of rectangular shape, provided with a pin. Dimensions: H: 4 cm.
7.2. Material: iron

5.3. Item category: bolt (Fig. 8.13)
6.3. Description: wrought iron rod with one of the ends pointed and the other rounded, of cylindrical shape. Dimensions: L: 6 cm.

5.4. Item category: bolt (Fig. 8.6)
6.4. Description: wrought iron stick with one of the ends square, slightly blunt, and the other pointed, fastened in a disk, only the pointed head being free as it was to be embedded into a support. Dimensions: no data on the size of the artifact.
7.4. Material: iron

5.5. Item category: bolt (without illustration)
6.5. Description: rod wrought iron with one of the ends pointed and the other blunt.
7.5. Material: iron

5.6. Item category: engraver (Fig. 8.14)
6.6. Description: wide bar with pointed head at both ends. Dimensions: L: 12.8 cm.
7.6. Material: iron

5.7. Item category: engraver (without illustration)
6.7. Description: metal rod cu un end pointed and another one rounded. Dimensions: no data on the size of the artifact.
7.7. Material: iron

5.8. Item category: engraver (Fig. 8.11)
6.8. Description: slender bar with pointed head at both ends. Dimensions: L: 7 cm.
7.8. Material: iron

5.9. Item category: engraver (Fig. 8.9)
6.9. Description: slender bar with pointed head at both ends. Dimensions: L: 6.9 cm.
7.9. Material: iron

5.10. Item category: engraver (without illustration)
6.10. Description: wide bar, stretched out towards the ends with pointed heads. Dimensions: no data on the size of the artifact.
7.10. Material: iron

5.11. Item category: engraver (without illustration)
6.11. Description: metal rod with one end thinner and pointed. Dimensions: no data on the size of the artifact.
7.11. Material: iron
5.12. Item category: small knife for engraving (Fig. 8.10)
6.12. Description: small knife for engraving, with pointed head at both ends. Dimensions: L: 7.1 cm.
7.12. Material: iron
5.13. Item category: punch-engraver (without illustration)
6.13. Description: metal rod, straight, with one curved end and the other almost straight, but it is possible that a pointed head got broken. Dimensions: no data on the size of the artifact.
7.13. Material: iron
5.14. Item category: punch-engraver (Fig. 8.12)
6.14. Description: metal rod, slightly curved, with one straight end and the other more pointed. Dimensions: L: 13.8 cm.
7.14. Material: iron
5.15. Item category: chisel (without illustration)
6.15. Description: blade-shaped chisel, with one pointed end, and the other slightly blunt and pointed. Dimensions: no data on the size of the artifact.
7.15. Material: iron
5.16. Item category: chisel (without illustration)
6.16. Description: blade-shaped chisel, slightly curved, with one straight end, and the other slightly blunt and pointed. Dimensions: no data on the size of the artifact.
7.16. Material: iron
5.17. Item category: metal casting spoon (Fig. 8.2)
6.17. Description: oval dipper-spoon, preserved as fragments, provided with a tubular collet, for embedding the wooden tail. Dimensions: L: 6.5 cm.
7.17. Material: clay
5.18. Item category: crucible (without illustration)
6.18. Description: pot-shaped vessel, of small dimensions, with slightly flared rim, flat bottom. Dimensions: no data on the size of the artifact.
7.18. Material: clay
5.19. Item category: crucible (without illustration)
6.19. Description: bowl-shaped vessel, trefoil-like mouth and rounded bottom, on its walls it has traces of melted bronze. Dimensions: no data on the size of the artifact.
7.19. Material: clay

5.20. Item category: crucible (Fig. 8.3)

6.20. Description: vessel of rectangular shape, with flat bottom. Dimensions: H: 4.5 cm.

7.20. Material: clay

5.21. Item category: crucible (Fig. 8.4)

6.21. Description: vessel of ovoid shape, with flat bottom. Dimensions: H: 2 cm.

7.21. Material: clay

5.22. Item category: crucible (Fig. 7.5)

6.22. Description: fragment of pear-shaped vessel, with umbo-shaped bottom, the rim is broken. Dimensions: H: 4 cm.

7.22. Material: clay

5.23. Item category: mold (Fig. 8.1)

6.23. Description: mold of hue brownish, with traces of firing, with a groove. On the mold three grains are represented and also a circular shape for conical appliqués. Dimensions: L: 4,9 cm, w: 2,1 cm, thickness: 0,9 cm.

7.23. Material: clay

9a. History and Archeology Museum of Prahova County Ploiești, inv. no. 20118

5.24. Item category: ingot (without illustration)

6.24. Description:

7.24. Material: lead

5.25. Item category: ingot (without illustration)

6.25. Description:

7.25. Material: bronze

2.26. Discovery conditions: systematic excavations, settlement, pit A/1965, G. T./1967

3.26. Year of discovery: 1965, 1967

4.26. Context of discovery: –

Context literature: Măgureanu, Ciupercă, "The 6th–8th Centuries Metallurgical Activity," 293–294.

5.26. 1. Item category: mold, pit A/1965 (Fig. 9.1)

6.26. 1. Description: gritstone mold, of grayish-yellowish hue, of rectangular shape, with two broken corners and three perforations for embedding the third mold, it has cones for casting at both ends. On the mold, dies for earring and pendant accessories are carved and grouped at the end of two bunches of threads oppositely laid: one thread has two grains, one to the point and one towards the end, the other four threads have links provided with grain pendants, one stick-shaped and three triangled-shaped, of which two have a link at the end. The other bunch is formed of six threads which have grains and one U-shaped ornament at their ends. Dimensions: L: 9.4 cm, w: 5.9 cm, thickness: 2.8 cm.

7.26.1. Material: stone

9a. Romania's National History Museum of Bucharest, inv. no. 106661

5.26.2. Item category: mold, pit G. T./1967 (Fig. 9.4)

6.26.2. Description: mold of soft rock, of rectangular shape, on which a bunch of threads with grains at the ends are carved, and at the opposite end there is a bunch of threads forming two curls with grains at the ends; it has grooves on both poles. Dimensions: L: 7.7 cm, w: 5 cm, thickness: 2.2 cm.

7.26. 2. Material: stone

9a. Romania's National History Museum of Bucharest, inv. no. 106689

5.26.3. Item category: mold, pit A/1965 (Fig. 9.2)

6.26.3. Description: mold of rectangular shape, of fine rock, with limestone content, of yellowish and grayish hue; it shows traces of firing. On the mold there are carved dies for the appliqués or earring accessories, four have the shape of a six-petal flower, one has a horseshoe-shape, with grain ends and connecting link. On the mold there are also represented four small grains and one small link. Dimensions: L: 6.5 cm, w: 4.4 cm, thickness: 2–2.3 cm.

7.26.3. Material: stone

9a. Preserving place: History and Archeology Museum of Prahova County Ploiești, inv. no. 19387

5.26.4. Item category: mold, G. T./1967 (Fig. 9.3)

6.26.4. Description: mold two-faced, fragmentary condition, of soft rock, whitish, probably limestone, on which there are carved four dies for the creation of pearls of the *melon seed* type. On the back there is a small line which also continues in the groove.

Dimensions: L: 6.1 cm, w: 6.2 cm, thickness: 2.1–2.2 cm.

7.26.4. Material: stone

9a. History and Archeology Museum of Prahova County Ploiești, inv. no. 19342

8. Absolute dating: 6th–7th centuries–beginning of the 8th century

9a. Preserving place: History and Archeology Museum of Prahova County Ploiești and Romania's National History Museum of Bucharest

9b. Literature: Teodorescu, "Centre meşteşugăreşti," 85, fig. 6.1, 3, 5–13; Teodorescu, Peneş, "Matricea de incidenţă," 11–50; 45, fig. 21.6; Miclea, Florescu, *Strămoşii românilor*, fig. 82; 212; Măgureanu, Ciupercă, "The 6th–8th Centuries Metallurgical Activity," 302–305; 312, fig. 4; 313, fig. 5; 315, fig. 6; 316, fig. 8, cat. no. 5.

8 c *Budureasca 5 (Fig. 10.1.1–2)*

1. Discovery place: "Onceşti"

2.1. Discovery conditions: systematic excavations, settlement, sunken house no. 5

3.1. Year of discovery: 1973

4.1. Context of discovery:

Context literature: Măgureanu, Ciupercă, "The 6th–8th Centuries Metallurgical Activity," 294.

5.1. Item category; mold (Fig. 10.1.1)

6.1. Description: Mold of rectangular shape, of soft rock, grayish-yellowish, with a large groove. On the mold a thread-shaped small groovy stick is carved. The small stick has a peduncle which crosses the groove. Possibly this item was a clothing ornament or maybe a tool, a file, for the finishing of some jewelry, and the peduncle might have been used to embed it in a wooden handle. Dimensions: L: 9.9 cm, w: 3–3.2 cm, thickness: 1.7–2 cm.

7.1. Material: stone

9a. History and Archeology Museum of Prahova County Ploieşti, inv. no. 23789

2.2. Discovery conditions: systematic excavations

3.2. Year of discovery: –

4.2. Context of discovery: –

5.2.1. Item category: engraver (without illustration)

6.2. 1. Description: slender bar with pointed head at both ends. Dimensions: no data on the size of the artifact.

7.2. 1. Material: iron

5.2.2. Item category: punch-engraver (Fig. 10.1.2)

6.2.2. Description: metal rod, slightly curved, with one thinner pointed end and the other thickened, slightly pointed. Dimensions: L: 6.6 cm.

7.2.2. Material: iron

8. Absolute dating: 6th century

9a. Preserving place: History and Archeology Museum of Prahova County Ploieşti

9b. Literature: Miclea, Florescu, *Strămoșii românilor*, fig. 819; 212; Teodorescu, Peneș, "Matricea de incidență," 11–50; 45, fig. 21. 15; Măgureanu, Ciupercă, "The 6th–8th Centuries Metallurgical Activity," 303; 316, fig. 8, cat. no. 3.

8 d ***Budureasca 9 (Fig. 10.2.1–2)***

1. Discovery place: "La puțul lui Burciu"
2. Discovery conditions: systematic researches, settlement
3. Year of discovery: –
4. Context of discovery:

Context literature: –

5.1. Item category: hammer-sledge (Fig. 10.2.2)

6.1. Description: Fragment of hammer with cylindrical body, straight at one of the ends, at the other end slightly flared and profiled, with oval embedding orifice, placed at one of the ends. Dimensions: L: 12.1 cm, w: 6 cm.

7.1. Material: iron

5.2. Item category: hammer-sledge (Fig. 10.2.1)

6.2. Description: paralelipipedic hammer, almost square cross-, with oval fitting hole, placed at one of the ends: The hammer is straight at one of the ends, and at the other end it is slightly flared and profiled. Dimensions: L: 13.1 cm, w: 6.4 cm

7.2. Material: iron

5.3. Item category: hammer (without illustration)

6.3. Description: Fragment of hammer of rectangular shape. Dimensions: no data on the size of the artifact.

7.3. Material: iron

5.4. Item category: crucible (without illustration)

6.4. Description: vessel with round mouth and rounded bottom, almost conical. Dimensions: no data on the size of the artifact.

7.4. Material: clay

8. Absolute dating: 6th–7th centuries

9a. Preserving place: History and Archeology Museum of Prahova County Ploiești

9b. Literature: Miclea, Florescu, *Strămoșii românilor*, fig. 818; 212; Teodorescu, Peneș, "Matricea de incidență," 11–50; 46, fig. 21. 18.

9 Cacica/Kaczyka (Suceava Co.) (Fig. 5.3)

1. Discovery place: "Călugărița"
2. Discovery conditions: by chance
3. Year of discovery: –
4. Context of discovery:
Context literature: Andronic, "Evoluția habitatului uman în bazinul hidrografic Soloneț," 64–65, fig. VII.3.
5. Item category: mold (Fig. 5.3)
6. Description: mold of pentagonal shape, two-faced; on one side there are carved three rectangular appliqués with notched edges and two grains, and on the other side there are two crosses with equal, trapezoidal arms with notched edges. Dimensions: 3.8×3.6 cm.
7. Material: stone
8. Absolute dating: 7th century
9a. Preserving place: "Bucovina" Museum Complex of Suceava County
9b. Literature: Andronic, "Evoluția," 65; 178, pl. VII.3.

10 Cândești (Buzău Co.)

1. Discovery place: –
2. Discovery conditions: systematic excavations V. Teodorescu
3. Year of discovery: –
4. Context of discovery:
Context literature: Teodor, "Elemente și influențe bizantine," 102, note 18.
5. Item category: mold
6. Description: mold for casting jewelry items.
7. Material: stone
8. Absolute dating: 6th–7th centuries
9a. Preserving place: Museum of Buzău County
9b. Literature: Teodor, "Elemente și influențe bizantine," 102, note 18.

11 Coroteni, Slobozia Bradului Com. (Vrancea Co.) (Fig. 5.4)

1. Discovery place: "Sediul CAP"
2. Discovery conditions: salvage excavation, settlement, near dwelling-sunken house no. 2, with stone furnace

3. Year of discovery: 1977–1980
4. Context of discovery: –
Context literature: Bobi, "Contribuţii la repertoriul arheologic al judeţului Vrancea," 107, 112; fig. 16–19; fig. 20.1–2; fig. 21–24; 138, fig. 25.6.

5. Item category: mold (Fig. 5.4)
6. Description: mold on which small circles and rosettes for earrings were carved; it has four grooves. Dimensions: 6.2×5.8 cm.
7. Material: stone
8a. Absolute dating: 6th–7th centuries
9a. Preserving place: Museum of Vrancea in Focşani
9b. Literature: Bobi, "Contribuţii," 107; 112; 138, fig. 25.6; Teodor, "Tipare," 163, 167, fig. 2.6.

12 Corund/Korond (Harghita Co.) (Fig. 5.2.1–2)

1. Discovery place: –
2. Discovery conditions: isolated
3. Year of discovery: –
4. Context of discovery:
Context literature: Horedt, *Contribuţii*, 69–70; 75. 6–7; 88; 95.

5.1. Item category: mold for double shield-shaped plates (Fig. 5.2.2)
6.1. Description: mold for double shield-shaped belt plates, ornamented with a pearled frame that contains braided schematized ribbons. Dimensions: no data on the size of the artifact.
7. 1. Material: bronze

5.2. Item category: mold for harness plates (Fig. 5.2.1)
6.2. Description: trefoiled mold, composed of three circles and a rectangle, which have each in the central part one button surrounded by overlapped arched lines. Between the three circles and rectangle there are two crossed ribbons forming an "X". Dimensions: no data on the size of the artifact.
7.2. Material: bronze
8. Absolute dating: end of the first half of the 7th century
9a. Preserving place: once they were preserved in the Sfântu Gheorghe Museum, nowadays they are lost.
9b. Literature: Horedt, *Contribuţii*, 75, fig. 13.6–7; 95; Garam, *Funde*, 390, pl. 139.9; Rácz, *Die Goldschmiedegräber*, 149; pl. 78.6.

13 Costești, Town of Târgu Frumos (Iași Co.) (Fig. 44.1, Fig. 45)

1. Discovery place: within the territory of the commune
2. Discovery conditions: found by chance, together with three other molds and a conical tool for pressing, as well as copper and silver sheets
3. Year of discovery: 1960
4. Context of discovery: –
Context literature: Teodor, "Elemente și influențe bizantine," 102–105, fig. 3–5; 106.

5.1. Item category: mold (Fig. 45.1a–b)
6.1. Description: mold of trapezoid shape, engraved on both faces. On one of the faces (Fig. 45.1a) there are represented two starred earrings with halfmoon-shaped plate, then a square probably used for appliqués, and also several incised lines which seem to sketch an arrow head or a spear point. On the other face (Fig. 45.1b), a rectangular plaque with a laced border, decorated with the fish scale motif is engraved, some of the scales on the edge of the item have small round cavities inside, then a round negative, used to make hemispherical appliqués for earrings as well as two diamonds with double border and in the middle with concentric circles that could be used to make pendants. Dimensions: 8,9×10.7 cm

5.2. Item category: mold (Fig. 45.2a–b)
6.2. Description: mold of rectangular shape, broken at one of the ends. On one of the faces (Fig. 45.2a), a square plate is incised, with an anthropomorphic decoration representing three personages of the same size, wearing beard and clerical garments, the drawing being surrounded by a laced border. On the top right of the mold, the stylized silhouette of a two small horned deer is engraved, with the head turned to the back. On the other face, a circular appliqué representing four concentric circles, as well as a rectangular plate decorated with geometrical motifs, are drawn: horizontal and vertical lines form rectangles, and concentric circles are arranged in the corners and in the middle (Fig. 45.2b). Dimensions: 8.2×5.5 cm.

5.3. Item category: mold (Fig. 44.1a–d)
6.3. Description: mold of parallelepiped shape, on the four surfaces negatives for earrings, appliqués, belt buttons are dug. On the first face there are four round negatives of different dimensions and a rectangular appliqué with a border and a line in the middle, which divides concentric circles, arranged three on each side (Fig. 44.1a). The second face has three round cavities of various dimensions and an oval one, as well as

two incised concentric circles located between the upper round cavities (Fig. 44.1b). The third face has three round cavities of different dimensions and a square cavity (Fig. 44.1c), and the fourth face has three cavities, one oval and two round (Fig. 44.1d). Dimensions: 12.6×5.3 cm.

5.4. Item category: tool for pressing (Fig. 44.2)

6.4. Description: conical item of small dimensions, with non-ornamented surfaces, having one of the ends extended and rounded, used as instrument for pressing metal sheets on molds. Dimensions: 8.5 cm.

7. Material: bone

8. Absolute dating: 7th–8th centuries

9a. Preserving place: private collection of physician I. Diaconescu in Fălticeni (Suceava co.)

9b. Literature: Teodor, "Elemente și influențe bizantine," 102; 103, fig. 3; 104, fig. 4; 105, fig. 5; Teodor, *Romanitatea*, fig. 11; Teodor, *Meșteșugurile*, 131, fig. 17; Szmoniewski, "Production," 113; 114, fig. 2; 115, 116, fig. 3.

14 Cristuru Secuiesc/Székelykeresztúr/Kreuz (Harghita Co.) (Fig. 5.1)

1. Discovery place: near the town, in the place named "Valea Pârâului Cetății"

2. Discovery conditions: systematic excavations, settlement, near the hearth of dwelling no. 4.

3. Year of discovery: 1969

4. Context of discovery: ceramic material

Context literature: Székely, "Eléments byzantins dans la civilization matérielle," 357.

5. Item category: mold (Fig. 5.1)

6. Description: two-faced gritstone mold, of rectangular shape, with orifices on the border for the embedment of the valves. At two centimeters from the lower end is an incised straight line which crosses the extremity of two small "bells" formed of grains and incised lines. On the same face there are two small rhombs and a small cross formed of grains, each having a link, and at the base of the small cross there is a small ring. On the other face of the mold are three x shapes, each consisting of two granular triangles. On both sides of these three x there are two grains larger than those forming the small triangular groups. It has grooves at both poles. Dimensions: L: 7 cm, w: 4,4 cm, thickness: 1,5 cm.

7. Material: stone, gritstone

8. Absolute dating: 7th–8th centuries
9a. Preserving place: History Museum of Sfântu Gheorghe
9b. Literature: Székely, "Eléments byzantins," 353; 354, fig. 1.3; Székely, "Săpăturile," 222; 223, fig. 3.4.

15 Cucuteni (Iași Co.) (Fig. 5.5)

1. Discovery place: "Grădina lui Mihai Gh. Ioan", situated in the southwest part of the settlement, 200 m west of Cucuteni Brook, in the southern part of the settlement, in the place named "Mazilie"
2. Discovery conditions: by chance by villager Gheorghe Agavriloaie
3. Year of discovery: 1985
4. Context of discovery: sherds of jars, created with the fast potter's wheel, of brown-reddish hue, made of paste with pebble.
Context literature: Boghian, "Un moule," 115.
5. Item category: mold (Fig. 5.5)
6. Description: two-faced mold, of grayish hue, pentagonal shape, engraved cavities for whole parts or different parts of ornaments or clothing accessories: appliqués, buttons, simple pearls and laced ones. On one of the faces are carved two rectangular appliqués with a notched border that frame a rectangle crest, a triangular appliqué ornamented with triangular notches in the middle and on the border, two rosettes engraved in a circle. On the second face, there are three rectangular plaques of the same type as those on the first face, as well as an ornamented figure with a notched line, consisting of two rosettes that frame an ovoid shape with the pointed ends. Dimensions: L: 10.5 cm, maximal width: 8.8 cm, minimal width: 5.5 cm.
7. Material: gritstone
8. Absolute dating: 6th–7th centuries
9a. Preserving place: Museum of Târgu Frumos
9b. Literature: Boghian, "Un moule," 115–118; 122, fig. 2.1; Teodor, "Tipare," 164, 169, fig. 4.5.

16 Davideni, Țibucani Com. (Neamț Co.) (Fig. 20–22)

1. Discovery place: "La izvoare-Spiești" to the right of the road Davideni-Păstrăveni-Târgu Neamț, on the 12–15 m terrace on the right bank of River Moldova.

2.1. Discovery conditions: dwelling no. 33/between trenches LIII and LIV. (Fig. 20)

3.1. Year of discovery: 1988

4.1. Context of discovery: hand-made ceramicware: pot jars, trays, crucibles (?); wheel-made ceramicware: pot jars and food storage vessels; biconical clay spindle whorls, iron knife, engraver, stone mold.

Context literature: Mitrea, *Așezarea de la Davideni*, 71–72; 321, fig. 61.5; 325, fig. 65.5; 356, fig. 95. 3–4; 362, fig. 101.2, 12, 15, 22; 363, fig. 102, 3, 5–8.

5.1.1. Item category: chisel (Fig. 20.9)

6.1. 1. Description: chisel of square cross-section, slightly rounded at both ends. Dimensions: L: 7 cm.

7.1. 1. Material: iron

5.1.2. Item category: mold (Fig. 20.10)

6.1.2. Description: fragmented two-faced mold, on one face two small lines are engraved, and on the other side three circles of various dimensions are engraved for carving the grains used as jewelry accessories. Dimensions: 5.6×5 cm.

7.1.2. Material: stone

2.2. Discovery conditions: dwelling no. 35/trench LIV.

3.2. Year of discovery: 1988

4.2. Context of discovery: hand-made ceramicware: trays, pot jars of hue grayish, one with notched rim; wheel-made ceramicware, jars, ornamented with straight lines, and also with wavy lines; two iron knives, iron engraver, bone handle and horn handle for the knife.

Context literature: Mitrea, *Așezarea de la Davideni*, 73–74; 320. fig. 60.2; 322. 3,7; 362, fig. 101. 13, 16; 363, fig. 102. 4, 11; 365, fig. 104. 2–3, 5–6, 8; 373, fig. 112. 11–12.

5.2. Item category: mandrel/dorn (without illustration)

6.2. Description: cylindrical rod, both its ends are suddenly ended. Dimensions: L: 12 cm.

7.2. Material: iron

2.3. Discovery conditions: dwelling no. 36/trench LIV (Fig. 21).

3.3. Year of discovery: 1988

4.3. Context of discovery: hand-made ceramicware: trays of brickish hue, pot jars of grayish hue, some have an alveoli-shaped burunele au buza alveolată; wheel-made ceramicware, jars, food storage vessel,

ornamented with straight lines, but also with wavy lines; biconical spindle whorl, stone mold, engraver iron, clay crucible.
Context literature: Mitrea, *Așezarea de la Davideni*, 75–76; 321. fig. 61.9–10; 325. fig. 65.4; 365. fig. 104. 9, 12, 14, 17–18; 366, fig. 105. 1–4, 6–7; 368, fig. 107. 1–4, 7–11; 370, fig. 109.4; 371, fig. 110.2, 4–7, 13–14; 372, fig. 111.7; 373, fig. 3, 13; 374, fig. 113.1,6; 375, fig. 114.7, 13.

5.3.1. Item category: bolt (Fig. 21.13)
6.3.1. Description: cylindrical rod, with one end thinner and slightly pointed and the other end straight. Dimensions: L: 8.7 cm.
7.3.1. Material: iron

5.3.2. Item category: chisel (Fig. 21.12)
6.3.2. Description: chisel of square cross-section, at one end slightly pointed, at the other rounded. Dimensions: L: 6.3 cm.
7.3.2. Material: iron

5.3.3. Item category: mold (Fig. 21.11)
6.3.3. Description: fragmentary one-faced mold, on which are engraved lines laid so that they resemble a fish skeleton. Dimensions: 5.5×4 cm.
7.3.3. Material: stone

2.4. Discovery conditions: dwelling no. 37/trench LIV.
3.4. Year of discovery: 1988
4.4. Context of discovery: hand-made ceramicware, raw paste, jar type vessels, trays; wheel-made ceramicware, ornamented on the shoulder with straight or wavy folds.
Context literature: Mitrea, *Așezarea de la Davideni*, 76–78; 320, fig. 60.4, 366, fig. 105.8; 368, fig. 107. 6, 12, 14.373, fig. 112. 5, 8.

5.4. Item category: chisel (without illustration)
6.4. Description: chisel of round cross-section, with pointed ends on both sides. Dimensions: L: 8 cm.
7.4. Material: iron

2.5. Discovery conditions: dwelling no. 39/trench LVII
3.5. Year of discovery: 1989
4.5. Context of discovery: hand-made pottery: trays, jars; two sherds of wheel-made ceramicware, made of sandy paste; iron lighter with inner curved ends, rhomboid arrow head, iron knife, clay conical spindle whorl.
Context literature: Mitrea, *Așezarea de la Davideni*, 79–80; 322, fig. 62. 14; 323, fig. 63. 8; 324, fig. 64. 9; 368, fig. 107. 5, 13; 369, fig. 108. 1, 4; 370, fig. 109. 2, 5; 371, fig. 110. 1; 372, fig. 111. 3, 8, 13.

5.5. Item category: chisel (without illustration)
6.5. Description: rectangular chisel, with a blunt end. Dimensions: L: 8.5 cm.
7.5. Material: iron

2.6. Discovery conditions: dwelling no. 69/trench LXXIX.
3.6. Year of discovery: 1995
4.6. Context of discovery: hand-made ceramicware: trays, jars, some ornamented with notches on the rim; wheel-made ceramicware, jars, sandy or ragged paste, some have inner ribs; two bone piercers and bone needle.
Context literature: Mitrea, *Așezarea de la Davideni*, 111–113; 386, fig. 125. 3, 9–10, 12–13, 15; 387, fig. 126. 1, 4–6, 10–11; 389, fig. 128. 5–6, 9–10; 390, fig. 129.3.

5.6. Item category: punch (without illustration)
6.6. Description: metal rod of round cross-section, one pointed end, bent, at the other end, of rectangular cross-section, the end is straight, the point is straight and pointed. The item is considered by the author as engraver, but in our opinion it rather looks like a punch. Dimensions: L: 11.2 cm.
7.6. Material: iron

2.7. Discovery conditions: dwelling no. 72/trench LXXXII
3.7. Year of discovery: 1997
4.7. Context of discovery: iron fibula with wrapped stem and turned underneath, wide body and on the foot there are several signs looking like alphabet signs; hand-made ceramicware: trays and pot jars, wheel-made ceramicware: sherds of a food storage vessels of grayish hue made of cement paste.
Context literature: Mitrea, *Așezarea de la Davideni*, 117–119; 326, fig. 66.3; 392, fig. 131. 1–2, 4–5, 7; 393, fig. 132. 9, 12–13; 395, fig. 134. 6, 8, 13.

5.7. Item category: engraver (without illustration)
6.7. Description: blade of rectangular cross-section, similar to a small knife, it has a more pointed end. Dimensions: L: 4 cm.
7.7. Material: iron

2.8. Discovery conditions: dwelling no. 74/trench LXXXIII
3.8. Year of discovery: 1997
4.8. Context of discovery: hand-made ceramicware, raw paste, jars, vessels without rim also occur, the mouth being drawn to the inside, straightly

cut, and trays; small sherds of wheel-made vessels. Other items, with no precise dating: fragment of thickle, a knife, two biconical spindle whorls. Context literature: Mitrea, *Așezarea de la Davideni,* 120–121; 321, fig. 61.6; 389, fig. 128. 3; 392, fig. 131. 14–15; 393, fig. 132. 5.

5.8. Item category: engraver (without illustration)

6.8. Description: chisel of round cross-section, with one end rounded and the other straight, it has a slit, possibly the item was broken. Dimensions: L: 6 cm.

7.8. Material: iron

2.9. Discovery conditions: dwelling no. 75, identified in trench LXXXIV (Pl. XVIII.2)

3.9. Year of discovery: 1997

4.9. Context of discovery: iron fibula with the stem turned underneath; hand-made ceramicware: jars and trays; wheel-made ceramicware: jars ornamented with stripes of folds on the shoulder or facetted lines or horizontal, irregular lines; fragments of small amphorae.

Context literature: Mitrea, *Așezarea de la Davideni,* 121–122; 326, fig. 66.6; 335, fig. 74.5; 389, fig. 128. 7–8, 11, 13–14; 391, fig. 130. 2–5, 8, 14; 393, fig. 132. 8.

5.9. Item category: metal casting spoon (Fig. 22.2.3)

6.9. Description: dipper-spoon of ovoid shape, with tubular handle, made out of a more dense paste. Both the dipper and the collet are broken. Dimensions: L: 6.5 cm, w: 4.5. cm.

7.9. Material: clay

2.10. Discovery conditions: trench S I, in the excavated earth, near a bronze fibula and an iron knife.

3.10. Year of discovery: 1970

4.10. Context of discovery: Mitrea, *Așezarea de la Davideni,* 128; 326, fig. 66.2.

5.10. Item category: mold (Fig. 22.1.4)

6.10. Description: mold of rectangular shape, fragmentary condition, made of marl, on it there are three bunches of two threads (grooves for the pouring of the metal), at the end of which there are rhombs with grains in the upper part and in the lower part, with a groove in the upper part. On the broken mold one can notice a part of the arm of a small cross. The grains and the rhombs were used to create jewelry items, most probably earrings. Dimensions: 4.9×3.2 cm.

7.10. Material: stone

2.11. Discovery conditions: trench XXXI
3.11. Year of discovery: 1977
4.11. Context of discovery: –
Context literature: Mitrea, *Așezarea de la Davideni*, 129; 321,f. 61.2. The item is considered an engraver, but in our view it is rather a drill.
5.11. Item category: drill (Fig. 22.1.3)
6.11. Description: fragment of rod with twisted end and pointed head. Dimensions: L: 4.3 cm.
7.11. Material: iron

2.12. Discovery conditions: trench LIV, on the 5th–7th century tredding level. It is worth pointing out that it is in this trench that dwellings nos. 35, 36 and 37 were found, with tools inside them, which might be connected with these complexes, the author does not specify this aspect.
3.12. Year of discovery: 1988
4.12. Context of discovery:
Context literature: Mitrea, *Așezarea de la Davideni*, 130; 320, fig. 60.3.
5.12. Item category: punch (Fig. 22.1.2)
6.12. Description: metal rod of rectangular cross-section with one pointed head, slightly bent and the other bent. The item is considered by the author as a bolt, but in our opinion it is rather a punch. Dimensions: L: 10.5 cm.
7.12. Material: iron

2.13. Discovery conditions: trench LVIII
3.13. Year of discovery: 1989
4.13. Context of discovery:
Context literature: Mitrea, *Așezarea de la Davideni*, 130; 321, fig. 61.8.
5.13. Item category: engraver (Fig. 22.1.1)
6.13. Description: engraving needle of square cross-section, with one very pointed head. Dimensions: L: 8.4 cm.
7.13. Material: iron
8. Absolute dating: 6th–7th centuries
9a. Preserving place: Museum Complex of Neamț County, Piatra Neamț
9b. Literature: Mitrea, "Regiunea centrală," 107; pl. XLVI.3; Mitrea, *Așezarea de la Davideni*, 71–72; 74; 76; 78; 80; 113; 119; 121; 128–130; 320, fig. 60.1–4; 321, fig.61.2–6, 8–10; 325, fig. 1, 4–5; 335, fig. 74.5.

17 Dichiseni (Călărași Co.) (Fig. 44.2a–b)

1. Discovery place: –
2. Discovery conditions: –
3. Year of discovery: –
4. Context of discovery:
Context literature: –
5. Item category: mold (Fig. 44.2a–b)
6. Description: two-faced mold, of rectangular shape, on one face negatives are carved for simple crosses, on the other side, there are carved a lunule for the earrings and a rectangular appliqué and a discoid appliqué with the notched edge in which a cross is contained, perhaps a disk for earrings or a medallion. On the same face there were also carved a round pendant ornamented with notched lines, two square appliqués, decorated also with notched lines and a triangular appliqué ornamented with round notches. Dimensions: 10.2×8.5 cm.
7. Material: stone
8. Absolute dating: 6th–7th centuries
9a. Preserving place: The Lower Danube Museum Călărași, inv. no. 14412.
9b. Literature: *Două milenii*, 34. Fig. 33.

18 Dodești, Viișoara Com. (Vaslui Co.) (Fig. 15–16)

1. Discovery place: "Șipot"
2. Discovery conditions: systematic researches, settlement, dwelling no. 4 of the sunken house type, in trench S VII in Șipot I sector.
3. Year of discovery: 1973
4. Context of the discovery: potsherds from a Roman-Byzantine amphora, potsherds from hand-made vessels, stone molds, two chisels, two horn piercers, spindle whorl ornamented by notches.
Context literature: Teodor, *Continuitatea*, 24; 29, fig. 6. 10–11; 30, fig. 7.1–3.
5.1. tem category: file-drill (Fig. 15.5)
6.1. Description: fragment of a round file, of which the folds are still preserved, it has a pointed head, being also used as a drill. Dimensions: L: 4.5 cm
7.1. Material: iron
5.2. Item category: chisel (Fig. 15.2)

6.2. Description: chisel of round cross-section, at one end rounded, at the other broken. Dimensions: no data on the size of the artifact.
7.2. Material: iron

5.3. Item category: chisel (Fig. 15.1)
6.3. Description: chisel of rectangular cross-section, at one end rounded, at the other it has a more pointed end. Dimensions: no data on the size of the artifact.
7.3. Material: iron

5.4. Item category: metal casting spoon (Fig. 15.8)
6.4. Description: dipper-spoon, of round shape, with chippy rim, provided with a handle, which is broken. Dimensions: L: 8.1 cm
7.4. Material: clay

5.5. Item category: mold (Fig. 15.9)
6.5. Description: mold of rectangular shape, made of soft greenish hue stone, on which three grains are carved; it has a groove in the upper part; in the lower part it is broken. Grains were used for making the earrings. Dimensions: 5.4×3.9 cm
7.5. Material: stone

5.6. Item category: mold (Fig. 15.10)
6.6. Description: gritstone mold, of irregular parallelepiped shape, on which a small circle is engraved with a groove and fine lines; in the middle there is a small indentation. Dimensions: 9,5×6.1 cm.
7.6. Material: stone
8. Absolute dating: 6th–7th centuries
9a. Preserving place: "Ștefan cel Mare" County Museum of Vaslui
9b. Literature: Teodor, *Continuitatea*, 24–25; 29, Fig. 6.1–3, 10–11; 30, Fig. 7.1–3.

19 Dolheștii Mari, Dolhești Com. (Suceava Co.) (Fig. 44.3)

1. Discovery place: –
2. Discovery conditions: by chance
3. Year of discovery: 1970
4. Context of discovery:
Context literature: Teodor, "Tipare," 164.

5. Item category: mold (Fig. 44.3)
6. Description: marl mold, on which a rosette and three grains forming a vertical line are carved. Dimensions: 4.9×3 cm.

7. Material: stone
8. Absolute dating: 6th–7th centuries
9a. Preserving place: Institute of Archeology in Iași
9b. Literature: Teodor, *Meșteșugurile*, 130, fig. 16.2; 163; Teodor, "Tipare," 164; 168, fig. 3.5.

20 Dulceanca (Teleorman Co.) (Fig. 14)

1. Discovery place: lower terrace near the confluence of River Vedea to Brook Burdea.
2.1. Discovery conditions: systematic researches, settlement of Dulceanca IV, sunken house no. 13.
3.1. Year of discovery: –
4.1. Context of discovery: potsherds, slag pieces
Context literature: Dolinescu-Ferche, "Habitats," 155, 167, fig. 31. 1–10.
5.1. Item category: metal casting spoon (without illustration)
6.1. Description: fragment of tubular handle, from a dipper-spoon, with traces of spongious melted slag and strong firing traces. Dimensions: L: 6 cm.
7.1. Material: clay

2.2. Discovery conditions: systematic researches, settlement of Dulceanca IV, sunken house no. 23.
3.2. Year of discovery: –
4.2. Context of discovery: potsherds, slag pieces, fragment of iron knife
Context literature: Dolinescu-Ferche, "Habitats," 157, 167, fig. 31. 11–49.
5.2. Item category: metal casting spoon (without illustration)
6.2. Description: fragment of tubular handle, from a dipper-spoon, with traces of spongious melted slag and strong firing traces. Dimensions: L: 4.6 cm.
7.2. Material: clay

2.3. Discovery conditions: systematic researches, settlement of Dulceanca IV, sunken house no. 27 (Fig. 35.2.1–15).
3.3. Year of discovery: –
4.3. Context of discovery: potsherds, slag pieces, fragment of a knife, iron arrow heads.
Context literature: Dolinescu-Ferche, "Habitats," 157, 169, fig. 33.1–15.

5.3. Item category: metal casting spoon (Fig. 14.2.13)
6.3. Description: dipper-spoon, round, broken, provided with a tubular collet in which the wooden tail was inserted; it has traces of spongious melted slag and strong firing traces. Dimensions: L: 12.3 cm.
7.3. Material: clay

2.4. Discovery conditions: systematic researches, settlement of Dulceanca IV, sunken house no. 25.
3.4. Year of discovery: –
4.4. Context of discovery: potsherds, slag pieces, fragment of a knife, iron arrow heads.
Context literature: Dolinescu-Ferche, "Habitats," 157, 168, fig. 32. 15–27.

5.4. Item category: metal casting spoon (without illustration)
6.4. Description: dipper-spoon, round, broken, provided with a tubular collet in which the wooden tail was inserted; it has traces of spongious melted slag and strong firing traces. Dimensions: L: 5 cm.
7.4. Material: clay

2.5. Discovery conditions: systematic researches, settlement of Dulceanca III, pit B.
3.5. Year of discovery: –
4.5. Context of discovery: potsherds, slag pieces
Context literature: Dolinescu-Ferche, "Habitats," 158, 169, fig. 33. 25–33.

5.5. Item category: metal casting spoon (without illustration)
6.5. Description: dipper-spoon, round, broken, provided with a tubular collet in which the wooden tail was inserted; it has traces of spongious melted slag and strong firing traces. Dimensions: L: 8.3 cm.
7.5. Material: clay
8a.1–5. Absolute dating: 7th century

2.6. Discovery conditions: systematic researches, settlement of Dulceanca I, sunken house no. 2 (Fig. 14.1)
3.7. Year of discovery: 1968
4.6. Context of discovery: hand-made potsherds, some of them ornamented with wavy lines framed by horizontal lines; wheel-made potsherds, of brick-red hue, ornamented with incised wavy or straight lines, some of them grooved; fragment of an amphora, wattle and daub, clay tray, clay spindle whorl, two molds, bronze needles.
Context literature: Dolinescu-Ferche, *Așezări*, 83–90, 96, fig. 104–106.

5.6.1. Item category: mold (Fig. 14.1.20)

6.6. 1. Description: fragment of a whitish stone mold (?), with a perfectly round shape, of which a deepened line starts, like a ray. Dimensions: L: 3.8 cm, w: 3.30 cm.

7.6. 1. Material: stone

5.6.2. Item category: mold (Fig. 14.1.15)

6.6.2. Description: fragment of a reddish stone mold, which is of a very vivid red at the end where is the slot in which metal was cast; it is formed of two concentric circles deepened at different degrees; it was broken in the old times and reused as whetstone. Dimensions: L: 5.7 cm, w: 2.3 cm.

7.6.2. Material: stone

8.6. Absolute dating: 6th century

9a. Preserving place: History Museum in Alexandria

9b. Literature: Dolinescu-Ferche, *Așezări*, 87, 90, 96, fig. 106.4; Dolinescu-Ferche, "Habitats," 157–158; 169, fig. 33.13, 31.

21 Dumbrăveni/Elisabethstadt/Erzsébetváros (Sibiu Co.) (Fig. 37.1)

1. Discovery place: –

2. Discovery conditions: isolated

3. Year of discovery: The mold was sold to the Hungarian National Museum of Budapest in 1914 by Armenian tradesman Rustuni Szerkis.

4. Context of discovery:

Context literature: Horedt, *Contribuții*, 69–70; 75. 8; 88; 95.

5. Item category: mold for belt plate (Fig. 37.1)

6. Description: mold for main belt prong, the ornamentation consists in a pearl frame bordering arcades that surround a cross having a rhomb in its center, probably a monogram. Dimensions: 5×3.8 cm.

7. Material: bronze

8a. Absolute dating: end of the first half of the 7th century

9a. Preserving place: Hungarian National Museum of Budapest

9b. Literature: Fettich, *Das awarenzeitliche Kunstgewerbe*, pl. VII.3; Horedt, *Contribuții*, 75, fig. 13.8; 95; Garam, *Funde*, 390, pl. 139.2; Rácz, *Die Goldschmiedegräber*, 152.

22 Felnac/Fönlak (Arad Co.) (Fig. 37.2.1–10–41)

1. Discovery place: on a limited surface, situated on a lot of land which River Mureș would not flood any more, being drained off, and where a gravel quarry was located. In the neighborhood, there was a heap with a ditch where ruins of several buildings could be seen.
2. Discovery conditions: by chance, while workers were quarrying out stone, they found human bones mixed with horse bones. The following items were gathered:
- one bronze belt appliqué
- 44 bronze molds

3. Year of discovery: 1899
4. Context of discovery: bronze belt appliqué, having the shape of a Malta cross (eight-pointed cross)
Context literature: Dömötör, "Ujabb lemezsajtoló bronzmintár Fönlakról," 62; 63, fig. 5; 64–65.

5.1. Item category: impressing mold (Fig. 37.2, Fig. 41.1–1a)
6.1. Description: impressing mold for casting knobbed fibulae with five round buttons which suggest stylized sthoos; the end plate has a frame made of notched lines bordering a coil, and the neck of the fibula has two vertical incised lines. The foot plate, preserved in fragmentary condition, has two smooth buttons and two vertical lines bordered by a frame made of notched horizontal lines. Dimensions: L: 3.5 cm, w: 3.1 cm, end plate and 2.2 cm, foot plate.
7.1. Material: bronze
9a.1. Preserving place: Romania's National History Museum of Bucharest, inv. no. 72646.

5.2. Item category: mold for main buckle pin (Fig. 37.2.4)
6.2. Description: mold for main buckle pin with three incised lines in the upper part, two curved lines (commas) in the lower part, and in the center there are two concentric circles flanked by two small lines and circles grouped in threes. Dimensions: L: 8 cm, w: 2.5 cm, thickness: 0.5 cm.
7.2. Material: bronze
9a.2. Preserving place: Hungarian National Museum of Budapest, inv. no. 201/1899.2.

5.3. Item category: mold for main buckle pin (Fig. 37.2.3, 8, Fig. 41.5–5a)
6.3. Description: mold for main buckle pin, broken in two parts, on which are represented: in the upper part two small lines followed by two circles and then three half-circles forming a row, in the middle with three small

circles grouped and one on top, which seem to suggest a flower, and in the lower part there is a dot flanked by two commas. Reconstructed dimensions: L: 7.2 cm, w: 3 cm, thickness: 0.4 cm

7.3. Material: bronze

9a.3. Preserving place: Romania's National History Museum of Bucharest, inv. no. 72639 (Fig. 37.2.3, Fig. 41.5–5a)

Hungarian National Museum of Budapest, inv. no. 201/1899.4 (Fig. 37.2.8).

5.4. Item category: mold for main buckle pin (Fig. 37.2.5)

6.4. Description: mold for main buckle pin, in the upper part with a dot flanked by two horizontal lines, followed by two groups of overlapped circles, forming a flower, surrounded by three dots and separated by dots and commas laid so to form an accolade, and in the lower part a dot flanked by two commas were represented. Dimensions: L: 6.2 cm, w: 2.7 cm, thickness: 0.5 cm.

7.4. Material: bronze

9a.4. Preserving place: Hungarian National Museum of Budapest, inv. no. 201/1899.2.

5.5. Item category: mold for secondary buckle pin (Fig. 37.2.7)

6.5. Description: mold for secondary buckle pin, in the upper part there are represented three small lines, followed by two circles under which there is a row of three half-circles, in the middle, the circles are grouped like in the case of the previous items, and in the lower part there is a dot flanked by two commas. Dimensions: L: 5.2 cm, w: 3.2 cm, thickness: 0.5 cm.

7.5. Material: bronze

9a. 6. Preserving place: Hungarian National Museum of Budapest, inv. no. 201/1899.6.

5.6. Item category: mold for belt plate having the shape of double shield (Fig. 37.2.9)

6.6. Description: mold for belt plate having the shape of double shield, in the upper half a circle was incised, and in the lower part a row of three half-circles followed by four small circles forming a flower. Dimensions: L: 4.7 cm, w: 3 cm, thickness: 0.4 cm.

7.6. Material: bronze

9a.6. Preserving place: Hungarian National Museum of Budapest, inv. no. 201/1899.3.

5.7. Item category: mold for belt plate (Fig. 37.2.10, Fig. 41.3–3a)

6.7. Description: mold for shield-shaped belt plate, having in the upper part a row of three half-circles, and in the middle with four small

overlapped circles forming a flower. Dimensions: L: 3.2 cm, w: 3.1 cm, thickness: 0.5 cm.
7.7. Material: bronze
9a.7. Preserving place: Romania's National History Museum of Bucharest, inv. no. 72638.

5.8. Item category: mold for secondary buckle pin (Fig. 37.2.6)
6.8. Description: mold for shield-shaped belt plate, having in the upper part a point flanked by two small straight lines, having in the center four small tangent circles and an overlapped circle in the middle forming a flower, and in the lower part, a point flanked by two commas. Dimensions: L: 2.9 cm, w: 2.8 cm, thickness: 0.5 cm.
7.8. Material: bronze
9a.8. Preserving place: Hungarian National Museum of Budapest, inv. no. 201/1899.5.

5.9. Item category: mold for main buckle pin (Fig. 38.1)
6.9. Description: mold for main buckle pin, decorated with two palmettes flanking a rosette composed of ray lines contained within a circle.
7.9. Material: bronze
9a.9. Nowadays, the item is lost.

5.10. Item category: mold for secondary buckle pin (Fig. 38.2)
6.10. Description: mold for secondary buckle pin, in the upper part it has a dot flanked by two double lines, and the palmette which occupies almost the entire surface of the item is flanked by the "dot-comma" motif. Dimensions: L: 3 cm, w: 2.2 cm, thickness: 0.4 cm.
7.10. Material: bronze
9a.10. Preserving place: Hungarian National Museum of Budapest, inv. no. 72/1899.9.

5.11. Item category: mold for belt plate (Fig. 38.4, Fig. 41.4–4a)
6.11. Description: mold for belt plate having the shape of double shield, on each shield being represented a palmette surrounded by dots and commas. Dimensions: L: 4.4 cm, w: 2.4 cm, thickness: 0.4 cm.
7.11. Material: bronze
9a.11. Preserving place: Romania's National History Museum of Bucharest, inv. no. 72643.

5.12. Item category: mold for belt plate (Fig. 38.3)
6.12. Description: mold for shield-shaped belt plate, on which there is a palmette surrounded by dots and commas. Dimensions: L: 2.5 cm, w: 2.8 cm, thickness: 0.4 cm.
7.12. Material: bronze

9a.12. Preserving place: Hungarian National Museum of Budapest, inv. no. 72./1899.8.

5.13. Item category: mold for belt plate (Fig. 38.5, Fig. 41.2–2a)

6.13. Description: mold for plate delimiting the edge of the belt, *Lochschützer*, in the upper part it has a straight edge, and in the lower part it is concave, decorated with a palmette framed by lines and commas. Dimensions: L: 2.6 cm, w: 2.3 cm, thickness: 0.3 cm.

7.13. Material: bronze

9a.13. Preserving place: Romania's National History Museum of Bucharest, inv. no. 72641.

5.14. Item category: mold for main buckle pin (Fig. 38.6)

6.14. Description: mold for buckle pin ornamented with dots, commas, signs of the tamga type, which seem to suggest a human mask and an animal head.

7.14. Material: bronze

9a.14. Nowadays, the item is lost.

5.15. Item category: mold for main buckle pin (Fig. 38.7, Fig. 41.6)

6.15. Description: mold for buckle pin with an ornamentation formed of double lines in half-circle grouped in twos and inside them with drops arranged so to form triangles. Edges of the mold are arched. Dimensions: L: 3.5 cm, w: 1.7 cm, thickness: 0.4 cm.

7.15. Material: bronze

9a.15. Preserving place: Museum Complex of Arad, inv. no. 1832.

5.16. Item category: mold for pendants (Fig. 38.8)

6.16. Description: mold for pendants in the shape of "tear" with pearl border, and inside it has a slot for precious or semi-precious stones, having the same shape as the pendant. Dimensions: L: 2.2 cm, w: 1.6 cm, thickness: 0.5 cm.

7.16. Material: bronze

9a.16. Preserving place: Hungarian National Museum of Budapest, inv. no. 205/1899.20.

5.17. Item category: mold for pendants (Fig. 38.9)

6.17. Description: mold for pendants having the shape of sea shell. Dimensions: L: 1.9 cm, min. w: 1.6 cm, max. w.: 2.1 cm, thickness: 0.4 cm.

7.17. Material: bronze

9a.17. Preserving place: Hungarian National Museum of Budapest, inv. no. 205/1899.19.

5.18. Item category: mold for belt appliqués (Fig. 39.1)
6.18. Description: mold for cross-shaped belt appliqués, composed of four circles with a round notch in the middle, which frames a rhomb in which several smaller rhombs are contained. The rhomb has a frame with teethed ornamentation.
7.18. Material: bronze
9a.18. Nowadays, the item is lost.
5.19. Item category: mold for belt appliqués (Fig. 38.13)
6.19. Description: mold in the shape of a flat truncated cone, which was used at creating round belt appliqués. Dimensions: L: 1 cm, w: 0.3 cm, thickness: 0.4 cm.
7.19. Material: bronze
9a.19. Preserving place: Hungarian National Museum of Budapest, inv. no. 205/1899.24.
5.20. Item category: mold for belt appliqués (Fig. 38.14)
6.20. Description: mold in the shape of a flat truncated cone, which was used at creating round belt appliqués.
7.20. Material: bronze
9a.19. Preserving place: Hungarian National Museum of Budapest, inv. no. 205/1899.25.
5.21. Item category: mold for belt appliqués (Fig. 39.11)
6.21. Description: mold in the shape of a stick with slightly concave edges, of which two shapes for creating semiglobular appliqués, one whole and the other fragmentary, but of larger dimensions than the previous one. Dimensions: L: 6.8 cm, w: 3 cm, thickness: 1.2 cm.
7.21. Material: bronze
9a.21. Preserving place: Hungarian National Museum of Budapest, inv. no. 205/1899.1.
5.22. Item category: mold for belt appliqués (Fig. 39.10)
6.22. Description: mold used at creating pearled appliqués which could ornament belt or harness stripes, but if bent, it could be used only as a frame for an item made of perishable material or even of metal. The mold is rectangular, with irregular edges, half is even, and the other half has three half-spheres stuck one to the other. Dimensions: L: 3.8 cm, w: 0.8 cm, thickness: 0.4 cm.
7.22. Material: bronze
9a.22. Preserving place: Hungarian National Museum of Budapest, inv. no. 205/1899.27.

5.23. Item category: mold for belt appliqués (Fig. 38.10)
6.23. Description: mold having a quadrilateral shape, ornamented with a pearl frame and with concentric circles placed both in the corners and in the center. Dimensions: L: 1.5 cm, w: 1.3 cm, thickness: 0.2 cm.
7.23. Material: bronze
9a.23. Preserving place: Hungarian National Museum of Budapest, inv. no. 205/1899.23.

5.24. Item category: mold for belt appliqués (Fig. 38.12)
6.24. Description: mold of rectangular shape, with arched edges, with three arcades on one side, three on the other side, decorated with lines forming curls inside which there are small circles and "drops". Dimensions: L: 1.8 cm, w: 1.3 cm, thickness: 0.2 cm.
7.24. Material: bronze
9a.24. Preserving place: Hungarian National Museum of Budapest, inv. no. 205/1899.22.

5.25. Item category: mold for belt appliqués (Fig. 38.11)
6.25. Description: mold with a butterfly-like shape, but with the ornamentation made of geometric shapes, small circles, triangles and a quadrilateral shape, rather suggesting a stylized owl head. Dimensions: L: 2.4 cm, w: 2, thickness: 0.3 cm.
7.25. Material: bronze
9a.25. Preserving place: Hungarian National Museum of Budapest, inv. no. 205/1899.21.

5.26. Item category: impressing mold for zoomorphic fibulas (Fig. 38.15)
6.26. Description: mold for animal-shaped belt appliqués (deer or horse, dog?), to the right, with the neck, paws and upper thigh decorated with crosswise placed double lines.
7.26. Material: bronze
9a.26. Nowadays, the item is lost.

5.27. Item category: mold for saddle aplice (Fig. 38.16)
6.27. Description: mold for belt appliqués having the shape of a lion, to the right, in aggressive position, with wide opened mouth, the crest is in relief, it has fine grooves, and so have the paws.
7.27. Material: bronze
9a.27. Nowadays, the item is lost.

5.28. Item category: mold for saddle aplice (Fig. 38.17)
6.28. Description: mold for belt appliqués having the shape of a lion, to the left, in aggressive position, with wide opened mouth, the crest is in relief, it has fine grooves, and so have the paws.

Dimensions: L: 6.8 cm, w. max: 4.1, cm, thickness: 0.4 cm.
7.28. Material: bronze
9a.28. Preserving place: Hungarian National Museum of Budapest, inv. no. 205/1899.25.

5.29. Item category: mold for prongs (Fig. 40.2)
6.29. Description: mold for buckle pin with a simple notched frame, imitating a lace and which border to braided ribbons.
7.29. Material: bronze
9a.29. Nowadays, the item is lost.

5.30. Item category: mold for harness prongs (Fig. 40.1, Fig. 41.8–8a)
6.30. Description: mold for buckle pin, the ornamentation consists of two rows of braided ribbons representing stylized animals, whose claws are pointed out by the teethed ornamentation. Dimensions: L: 4.8 cm, w: 2.2 cm, thickness: 0.4 cm.
7.30. Material: bronze
9a.30. Romania's National History Museum of Bucharest, inv. no. 72642.

5.31. Item category: mold for harness appliqués (Fig. 39.3)
6.31. Description: mold in relief, of a square shape, with arched edges and pearl frame, bordering both the item and the geometric shapes that compose the ornamentation, a rhomb delimited by four half-circles, which seem to be the petals of a flower. Dimensions: L: 2.3 cm, w: 2.2 cm.
7.31. Material: bronze
9a.31. Preserving place: Hungarian National Museum of Budapest, inv. no. 205/1899.16.

5.32. Item category: mold for harness appliqués (Fig. 39.2)
6.32. Description: fragment of a mold in relief, of a square shape, with arched edges which seem to be the petals of a flower, petals formed of smooth half-circles which delimit a rhomb with pearl contour. Dimensions: L: 1.9 cm, w: 1 cm.
7.32. Material: bronze
9a.32. Preserving place: Hungarian National Museum of Budapest, inv. no. 205/1899.17.

5.33–34. Item category: molds for harness appliqués (Fig. 39.8–9)
6.33–34. Description: molds of semiglobular shape, smooth, without ornamentation, for harness appliqués. Dimensions: L: 2.5 cm, w: 1.3 cm (Fig. 38.8) and L: 2.6 cm, w: 1.5 cm (Fig. 38.9).
7.33–34. Material: bronze
9a.33–34. Preserving place: Hungarian National Museum of Budapest, inv. no. 205/1899.11 (Fig. 39.8), inv. no. 205/1899. 12. (Fig. 39.9).

5.35. Item category: mold for harness appliqués (Fig. 39.4)
6.35. Description: mold in relief, having the shape of a rosette, with a round button in its center, surrounded by a row of pearls, and on the side there are notches suggesting petals. Dimensions: D: 2.5 cm, H: 1.8 cm.
7.35. Material: bronze
9a.35. Muzeu: Hungarian National Museum of Budapest, inv. no. 205/1899.13.

5.36. Item category: mold for harness appliqués (Fig. 39.6)
6.36. Description: mold in relief, having the shape of a rosette, with a round button in its center, surrounded by a row of pearls, and on the side there are notches suggesting petals.
7.36. Material: bronze
9a.36. Nowadays, the item is lost.

5.37. Item category: mold for harness appliqués (Fig. 39.5)
6.37. Description: mold in relief, having the shape of a rosette, with a round button in its center, surrounded by a row of pearls, and on the side there are notches suggesting petals. D: 1.9 cm, H: 0.7 cm.
7.37. Material: bronze
9a.37. Preserving place: Hungarian National Museum of Budapest, inv. no. 205/1899.14.

5.38. Item category: mold for harness appliqués (Fig. 39.7)
6.38. Description: mold having the shape of a rosette, with a round button in its center, surrounded by a row of pearls, the frame is formed of coils, probably stylized accanth leaves, and the edge is smooth. Dimensions: D: 2.1 cm, H: 0.8 cm.
7.38. Material: bronze
9a.38. Preserving place: Hungarian National Museum of Budapest, inv. no. 205/1899.15.

5.39. Item category: mold for harness appliqués (Fig. 40.4)
6.39. Description: mold having a trefoiled shape, with the three petals ornamented with notches that surround a flower placed in the center of the item, the fourth end of the item is rectangular and has three rows of grooves representing the tufts. Dimensions: L: 3.3 cm, w. max.: 2.8 cm, w. min.: 1 cm.
7.39. Material: bronze
9a.39. Preserving place: Hungarian National Museum of Budapest, inv. no. 205/1899.18.

5.40. Item category: mold for harness appliqués (Fig. 40.5, Fig. 41.9–9a)
6.40. Description: mold having a trefoiled shape, with the three petals forming a half-sphere, that surround a fourth half-sphere; they are all

smooth. The fourth end of the item is rectangular and has two oval vertical notches, in which are the row-forming pearls, and on the sides there are the notches that imitate the tufts. Dimensions: L: 4.9 cm, w. max.: 4 cm, w. min.: 1.4 cm.

7.40. Material: bronze

9a.40. Preserving place: Romania's National History Museum in Bucharest, inv. no. 72640.

5.41. Item category: mold for harness appliqués (Fig. 40.8)

6.41. Description: mold used at creating trefoiled harness appliqués, three of the arms have the shape of circles bordering a rhomb, while the fourth arm has a rectangular shape. On the entire surface of the mold there are incised braided ribbons, in the animal style II, with dentil ornamentation. Dimensions: L: 7.2 cm, w. min.: 2 cm, w. max.: 4.8 cm, thickness: 0.3 cm.

7.41. Material: bronze

9a.41. Preserving place: Hungarian National Museum of Budapest, inv. no. 205/1899.10.

5.42. Item category: mold for harness appliqués (Fig. 40.7)

6.42. Description: rectangular mold, ornamented with a network of rhombs which contain small circles, and on one of the ends it has grooves imitating the tufts.

Dimensions: L: 6.4 cm, w: 2.5 cm, thickness: 0.6 cm.

7.42. Material: bronze

9a.42. Preserving place: Hungarian National Museum of Budapest, inv. no. 205/1899.7.

5.43. Item category: mold for harness appliqués (Fig. 40.6, Fig. 41.10–10a)

6.43. Description: mold of rectangular shape, smooth, with one grooved end, representing an imitation of tufts. Dimensions: L: 5.9 cm, w: 2 cm, thickness: 0.5–0.8 cm.

7.43. Material: bronze

9a.43. Preserving place: Romania's National History Museum in Bucharest, inv. no. 72645.

5.44. Item category: mold for harness prongs (Fig. 40.3, Fig. 41.7–7a)

6.44. Description: mold with smooth surface, without ornamentation. Dimensions: L: 2.5 cm, w: 2.8 cm, thickness: 0.4 cm.

7.44. Material: bronze

9a.44. Preserving place: Romania's National History Museum of Bucharest, inv. no. 72644.

8a. Absolute dating: first third of the 7th century

9b. Literature: Hampel, "Emlékek és leletek," 117–118; 119, pl. I.1–15; 120; 121, pl. II.1–11; 122; Dömötör 1901, 62; 63, fig. 1–12; 64; 65, fig. 13–16; Fettich, *Das awarenzeitliche Kunstgewerbe*, 1926, pl. IV.1–21; pl. V.1–23; Garam, *Funde*, 388, pl. 137; Mărghitan, *Banatul*, 43–49; Tănase, "Câteva observații," 237–239; 256, pl. I.1–9; 240, pl. II.1–10; 258, pl. III.1–8; 259, pl. IV.1–9; 260, pl. V.1–11; Rácz, *Die Goldschmiedegräber*, 152–156; pl. 9–19.

23 Giurcani, Găgești Com. (Vaslui Co.) (Fig. 7.2)

1. Discovery place: –
2. Discovery conditions: by chance, surface researches
3. Year of discovery: 1993–1994
4. Context of discovery:
Context literature: Teodor, "Tipare," 164.
5. Item category: mold (Fig. 7.2)
6. Description: Mold made of brick red hue, used at casting small crosses of the so-called Malta type (eight-pointed); it has a groove in the upper part and an incised line along the length of the mold, it was possibly used as well for casting metal threads. Also another mold made of stone for casting crosses was found. Dimensions: L: 8.4 cm, w: 3.9 cm.
7. Material: stone
8. Absolute dating: 6th–7th centuries
9a. Preserving place: collector Rotaru Marin
9b. Literature: *Două milenii*, 35, fig. 38; Teodor, "Tipare," 164; 173, fig. 8.1.

24 Govora, Mihăiești Com. (Vâlcea Co.) (Fig. 7.1)

1. Discovery place: "Huidu II"
2. Discovery conditions: trial excavation
3. Year of discovery: 1984
4. Context of discovery:
Context literature: Terteci, "Despre cultura Ipotești-Cândești," 104; 107.
5. Item category: ladle (Fig. 7.1)
6. Description: oval bowl, tubular handle. Dimensions: L: 7.3 cm, w: 6.1-tail, w: 6.5 cm – dipper.
7. Material: clay
8. Absolute dating: 6th century–7th century

9a. Preserving place: "Gh. Petre-Govora" Archaeology and Religious Art Museum, Băile Govora
9b. Literature: Terteci, "Despre cultura Ipotești-Cândești," 107.

25 Gropșani (Dolj Co.) (Fig. 7.4)

1. Discovery place: settlement, sector "Gura Gurgotei"
2. Discovery conditions: systematic researches; dwelling no. 13, with a horseshoe-shaped clay oven.
3. Year of discovery: 1976
4. Context of discovery: fragments of wheel-made ceramicware from pot jars, without ornamentation, only on a sherd there are fine incised lines; hand-made ceramicware, pot jars and trays; wattle and daub. The archaeological materials were grouped in the furnace or in its immediate vicinity.
Context literature: Popilian, Nica, *Gropșani*, 28–29; 172, Fig. 20, loc. 13.1–5 (13.5: spoon)
5. Item category: metal casting spoon (Fig. 7.4.5)
6. Description: dipper-spoon of oval shape, with tubular handle; out of the dipper a piece close to the handle has been preserved. Dimensions: no data on the size of the artifact. The scale of the drawing is wrong.
7. Material: clay
8. Absolute dating: 6th century
9a. Preserving place: Museum of Oltenia in Craiova
9b. Literature: Popilian, Nica, *Gropșani*, 28; 172, Fig. 20. loc. 13.5.

26 Izvoare-Bahna (Neamț Co.) (Fig. 7.5)

1. Discovery place: "La pod la Hărmănești"
2. Discovery conditions: systematic researches, settlement, trench S XLIV
3. Year of discovery: 1977
4. Context of discovery:
Context literature: Mitrea, "Așezarea prefeudală de la Izvoare-Bahna," 215; fig. 9.11; Mitrea, "Regiunea centrală a Moldovei," pl. XLVIII.4. Mitrea, *Așezarea din secolele VI–IX*, 142, fig. 26. 10; 171, fig. 55. 10, 12?.

5.1. Item category: chisel (without illustration)
6.1. Description: stick of rectangular cross-section, with one end pointed and the other blunt with a splitting towards the end. Dimensions: no data on the size of the artifact.
7.1. Material: iron

5.2. Item category: chisel (without illustration)
6.2. Description: blade-shaped stick similar to a knife, with one narrower end, then the blade gets slightly wider and then narrower again towards the pointed head. Dimensions: no data on the size of the artifact.
7.2. Material: iron

5.3. Item category: chisel (without illustration)
6.3. Description: stick of rectangular cross-section, with one end pointed and the other blunt with a splitting towards the end. Dimensions: no data on the size of the artifact.
7.3. Material: iron

2.4. Discovery conditions: dwelling no. 28/case of trench LXXXIX, in the filling earth, clot to the floor
3.4. Year of discovery: 1983
4.4. Context of discovery: potsherds from hand-made pot jars and trays, biconical clay spindle whorl; fragment of silver earring of the type with star pendant (?).
Context literature: Mitrea, *Așezarea din secolele VI–IX*, 37–38; 141, fig. 25. 1 (earring), fig. 25.7 (spoon).

5.4. Item category: metal casting spoon (Fig. 7.5.6)
6.4. Description: dipper-spoon of round shape, provided with short tubular handle; it is 10.7 cm long and its diameter is of 11.5 cm. By the embedment orifice there were found the carbonized remains of the handle, consisting in charcoal stripes of ca. 30 cm length.
7.4. Material: clay
8. Absolute dating: 6th–7th centuries
9a. Preserving place: Museum Complex of Neamț County, Piatra Neamț
9b. Literature: Mitrea, "Așezarea prefeudală," 215; fig. 9.11; Mitrea, "Regiunea centrală," pl. XLVIII.4; Mitrea, *Așezarea din secolele VI–IX*, 141, fig. 25.7; 142, fig. 26.10; 171, fig. 55.10, 12.

27 Izvorul Dulce, Merei Com. (Buzău Co.) (Fig. 7.3)

1. Discovery place: –
2. Discovery conditions: –
3. Year of discovery: –
4. Context of discovery:
Context literature: –

5. Item category: mold (Fig. 7.3)
6. Description: mold made of limestone, used at casting small crosses and jewelry items. The two-faced, quadrilateral valve, was provided with a metal casting cone at the upper end of both faces. In the die of one of the two faces of the mold jewelry items with pseudo-granular elements (probably earrings) were cast, and on the opposite face there was a die for crosses of the Latin type, provided with a small ear and having the body ornamented with crossed lines (in the shape of letter X) and small grains forming pseudo-pearls. Dimensions: L: 5.3 cm, w: 4.5 cm.
7. Material: stone
8. Absolute dating: 5th–6th centuries
9a. Preserving place: History and Archeology Museum, Ploiești.
9b. Literature: Miclea, Florescu, *Strămoșii românilor*, fig. 760; 209; 760.

28 Lazuri/Lázári/Neuschlag (Satu Mare Co.) (Fig. 4)

1. Discovery place: "Lubi tag", at 2 km N-W from the center of the commune and 250 m to the right of the road Lazuri-Peleș (Peleșu Mare).
2.1. Discovery conditions: systematic researches, settlement; in the filling earth of dwelling no. 1a, trench I.
3.1. Year of discovery: 1977
4.1. Context of discovery: potsherds of brown hue resulting from handmade pots out of raw paste, mixed with smashed shards; wattle and daub, and clay cakes, iron ingot.
Context literature: Stanciu, "Așezarea," 156–157; 166–168; 216, pl. V. 8: 217, pl. VI. 6–8; 219, pl. VIII.1.

5.1. Item category: metal casting spoon (Fig. 4.2)
6.1. Description: spoon of ovoid shape, on one side it has a pouring beak and it also has a short, tubular handle collet. The spoon was shaped out of raw compact paste, mixed with few smashed shards, and inside the cup there are traces of secondary firing. Dimensions: L: 8.5 cm.

7.1. Material: clay

2.2. Discovery conditions: systematic researches, settlement
3.1. Year of discovery: –
4.1. Context of discovery: –
Context literature: Stanciu, "Așezarea," 157.

5.2. Item category: mold (Fig. 4.1)
6.2. Description: mold of rectangular shape, with two grooves situated on the same side, and on which a place for grain casting is represented. Dimensions: 7.5×6 cm.
7.2. Material: clay
8a. Absolute dating: the second half of the 6th century
9a. Preserving place: Satu Mare County Museum
9b. Literature: Stanciu, "Așezarea," 157; 216, pl. v.8; Stanciu, *Locuirea*, 631, pl. 22.8.

29 Lozna, Dersca Com. (Botoșani Co.) (Fig. 24–29)

Lozna-*Dorohoi* = Lozna-*Strâteni*

1. Discovery place: "La Ocoale", southeastern part of the commune, on one of the terraces situated near Brook Turbărie
2.1. Discovery conditions: settlement, systematic researches, in oven no. 2, situated near dwelling no. 3
3.1. Year of discovery: 1963
4.1. Context of discovery: small beads of bronze
Context literature: Teodor, Mitrea, "Cercetări arheologice," 279–291; Teodor, *Un centru*, 36; 123, fig. 40/6.

5.1. Item category: mold (Fig. 29.2)
6.1. Description: marl mold, of rectangular shape, it shows on the two polished surfaces two orifices, one cylindrical and another one spherical probably meant for casting some jewelry items as seem to indicate its small dimensions. Dimensions: 3.3×2.6 cm.
7. 1. Material: stone

2.2. Discovery conditions: settlement, systematic researches, trench I, in the workshop-dwelling no. 6
3.2. Year of discovery: 1979

4.2. Context of discovery: stone furnace and fragments of hand-made pot jars and bowls with thick walls, with traces of iron oxides, partly slagged. In the filling of the dwelling numerous iron ingots were found, weighing about 50–60 kg, a small iron bolt, several clay crucibles in fragmentary condition; two spindle whorls, a clay bead, two piercing instruments made of bone, hand-made and wheel-made potsherds.
Context literature: Teodor, *Un centru*, 17–18; 125, fig. 42/8.

5.2. Item category: blowing tube for introducing air (Fig. 24.4)
6.2. Description: cylindrical tube, preserved in fragmentary condition, one end is obliquely cut, with profiled edge, and the other end is flared and thickened. Dimensions: L: 4.6 cm.
7. 2. Material: clay

5.3. Item category: crucible (Fig. 24.3)
6.3. Description: rectangular crucible with flat bottom and the slightly rounded body in the upper part; the rim is straight. Dimensions: H: 3 cm.
7. 3. Material: clay

2.4. Discovery conditions: settlement, systematic researches, trench I, in the workshop-dwelling no. 7
3.4. Year of discovery: 1979
4.4. Context of discovery: two clay furnaces used at iron ore reduction were found as well as potsherds resulting from thick wall vessels, partly slagged, and also iron ingots weighing 50–60 kg. Among the furnace remains inside the dwelling there were found a chisel, an iron bolt, several clay crucibles, whole and fragmentary, one clay spoon for metal casting. In the same context there were also found iron items (hooks, links, knife blades, whole or fragmentary), one bronze link, 18 clay spindle whorls, one white loam spindle whorl, piercing tools made of bone, potsherds from wheel-made pot jars and potsherds from hand-made bowls, pot jars and pans.
Context literature: Teodor, "Tipare," 164, 172, fig. 7.6; Teodor, *Un centru*, 18; 118, fig. 35/11, 15; 123, fig. 40/1; 124, fig. 41/2; 125, fig. 42/2.

5.4. Item category: mold (Fig. 25.10)
6.4. Description: fragmentary mold, on which grains are represented. Dimensions: 5.5×4.2 cm
7.4. Material: clay

5.5. Item category: metal casting spoon (Fig. 25.11)
6.5. Description: spoon with conical dipper, preserved in fragmentary condition; the ear is broken. Dimensions: L: 4 cm.
7.5. Material: clay

5.6. Item category: chisel (Fig. 25.8)
6.6. Description: chisel of rectangular cross-section, with one flat end and slightly curved, at the other end. In the middle there is an arched portion. Dimensions: L: 6 cm.
7.6. Material: iron
5.7. Item category: dorn (Fig. 25.7)
6.7. Description: Dorn of square cross-section, with one straight, profiled end, while the other end has a half-circle shape. Dimensions: L: 3.5 cm.
7.7. Material: iron

2.8. Discovery conditions: settlement, systematic researches, trench I, dwelling no. 8
3.8. Year of discovery: 1979
4.8. Context of discovery: among the hearth remains and the furnace vault, there was found one fragmentary clay mold and whole and fragmentary clay crucibles. Apart from these, also iron items were found (knife blade, piercing tool, belt buckle, hook, chain), one fragment of a glass tumbler, many whole and fragmentary bone tools, four clay spindle whorls; wheel-made potsherds and hand-made potsherds from pot jars and pans. This dwelling is supposedly a bone processing workshop.
Context literature: Teodor, "Tipare," 164, 172, fig. 7.1; Teodor, *Un centru*, 18–19; 123, fig. 40/3; 124, fig. 41/8; 125, fig. 42/1.
5.8. Item category: mold (Fig. 26.1.11)
6.8. Description: fragmentary mold, on which grains are represented and an appliqué having the shape of a flower composed of four round grains. There are also several lines that seem to sketch the contour of a rectangular buckle. Dimensions: 6.6×6.1 cm
7.8. Material: clay
5.9. Item category: crucible (Fig. 26.1.10)
6.9. Description: crucible of cylindrical shape, the rim is straight and the bottom is slightly rounded. Dimensions: H: 5 cm.
7.9. Material: clay

2.10. Discovery conditions: settlement, systematic researches, trench II, in the dwelling-workshop no. 10, with stone furnace
3.10. Year of discovery: 1980
4.10. Context of discovery: inside the dwelling there were found: one fragment of a clay mold and two clay crucibles, fragmentary iron items (knife blades, axe blades, flint, tweezers (?)), nine clay spindle whorls, piercing

instruments made of bone, wheel-made and hand-made potsherds. Also a large hand-made clay vessel was found. It has thick walls and the bottom is provided with an orifice, probably at the reduction of the ore in the bog.
Context literature: Teodor, *Un centru*, 19–20; 123, fig. 40/5, 11; 124, fig. 41/3; 125, fig. 42/6.

5.10. Item category: mold (Fig. 26.2.13)
6.10. Description: fragmentary mold, on which an item of rectangular shape is represented, narrower, probably a tubular bead (?) or an appliqué (?). Dimensions: 7.2×6.7 cm.
7.10. Material: clay

5.11. Item category: crucible (Fig. 26.2.14)
6.11. Description: biconical crucible, with straight rim and flat and slightly profiled bottom. Dimensions: H: 3.2 cm.
7.11. Material: clay

2.12. Discovery conditions: settlement, systematic researches, trench VI, dwelling no. 12, stone furnace
3.12. Year of discovery: 1980
4.12. Context of discovery: a fragment of crucible was found, together with iron objects (knife blades, belt buckle), piercing instruments made of bone, clay zoomorphic figurine (?), wheel-made and hand-made potsherds, the latter ones from pot jars and pans.
Context literature: Teodor, *Un centru*, 21; 125, fig. 42/13.

5.12. Item category: crucible (Fig. 27.1.1)
6.12. Description: crucible preserved in fragmentary condition, with straight walls and slightly arched rim. Dimensions: H: 4.7 cm.
7.12. Material: clay

2.13. Discovery conditions: settlement, systematic researches, trench XVI, dwelling no. 17, with stone furnace
3.13. Year of discovery: 1981
4.13. Context of discovery: there were found a bolt and a clay crucible, together with iron objects (knife blades, axe blade, spear point, three edged-arrow, belt buckle), bone items (piercing instruments, hook, whistle, pipe, ankle bone), two clay spindle whorls, remains of deer antlers in various processing phases, wheel-made and hand-made potsherds (pot jars, pans).
Context literature: Teodor, *Un centru*, 23; 118, fig. 35/4; 125, fig. 42/9.

5.13. Item category: bolt (27.2.15)
6.13. Description: bolt of circular cross-section, at one end it is wider and rounded, at the other end it is narrower and slightly rounded. Dimensions: L: 5.4 cm.
7.13. Material: iron
5.14. Item category: crucible (Fig. 27.2.16)
6.14. Description: conical crucible, with slightly rounded rim and flat bottom. Dimensions: H: 3.4 cm.
7.14. Material: clay

2.15. Discovery conditions: settlement, systematic researches, trench XXXIX, dwelling no. 21, with stone furnace
3.15. Year of discovery: 1983
4.15. Context of discovery: two clay crucibles, together with iron objects (knife blades, arrow head, appliqué), a glass bead, piercing instruments made of bone, a piece of a deer antler with processing traces, wheel-made and hand-made potsherds (pot jars, pans).
Context literature: Teodor, *Un centru*, 25–26; 123, fig. 40/10; 125, fig. 42/3, 10.
5.15. Item category: crucible (Fig. 28.1.15)
6.15. Description: crucible of which only the flat bottom has been preserved. Dimensions: H: 1.8 cm.
7.15. Material: clay
5.16. Item category: crucible (Fig. 28.1.16)
6.16. Description: crucible with slightly flared rim to the outside, slightly rounded body, flat bottom. Dimensions: H: 4.5 cm.
7.16. Material: clay

2.17. Discovery conditions: settlement, systematic researches, trench XXXIX, dwelling-workshop no. 27, with stone furnace
3.17. Year of discovery: 1985
4.17. Context of discovery: two clay crucibles and a metal casting spoon made of clay, together with iron knife blades, clay spindle whorls, hand-made potsherds, pieces of iron slag and bronze scrap parts.
Context literature: Teodor, *Un centru*, 28–29; 123, fig. 40/12; 125, fig. 42/5, 7, 14.
5.17. Item category: crucible (Fig. 28.2.1)
6.17. Description: crucible of cylindrical shape, with rounded bottom and triangular mouth; the rim is straight. Dimensions: H: 5.6 cm.
7.17. Material: clay

5.18. Item category: crucible (Fig. 28.2.3)

6.18. Description: tumble-shaped crucible, preserved in fragmentary condition: the bottom is flat, profiled and the body is slightly rounded. Dimensions: H: 2.7 cm.

7.18. Material: clay

5.19. Item category: metal casting spoon (Fig. 28.2.2)

6.19. Description: spoon with round dipper, preserved in fragmentary condition and with massive handle, broken. Dimensions: L: 4.1 cm.

7.19. Material: clay

2.20. Discovery conditions: settlement, systematic researches, dwelling no. 28 with stone furnace.

3.20. Year of discovery: 1985.

4.20. Context of discovery: iron objects (knife blade, hook), fragment of glass tumbler, piercing instruments made of bone, three clay spindle whorls, hand-made potsherds

Context literature: Teodor, "Tipare," 164, 172, fig. 7.7; Teodor, *Un centru*, 29; 124, fig. 41/4.

5.20. Item category: mold (Fig. 27.3.6)

6.20. Description: fragmentary mold, on which several lines are represented. Dimensions: 8×7.6 cm.

7.20. Material: clay

2.21. Discovery conditions: settlement, systematic researches, trench XLVI, dwelling no. 37, with stone furnace

3.21. Year of discovery: 1986

4.21. Context of discovery: there were found four fragmentary clay molds, a clay spoon for casting metal, three fragmentary clay crucibles, together with knife blades, bronze twisted bracelet, clay and white loam spindle whorls, piercing instrument made of bone, an ankle bone ornamented with a cross, four clay cakes, wheel-made and hand-made potsherds.

Context literature: Teodor, "Tipare," 164, 172, fig. 7.2; Teodor, *Un centru*, 33–34; 123, fig. 40/2, 4, 7, 9; 124, fig. 41/1, 5, 7, 9; 125, fig. 42/11–12.

5.21. Item category: mold (Fig. 29.1.18)

6.21. Description: fragmentary mold, on which the lunular plate of an earring is represented. The plate has three notched frames, which imitate the lace, it had rounded ends, strongly in relief, and an ear for allowing its attachment. Dimensions: 6.1×4 cm

7.21. Material: clay

5.22. Item category: mold? (Fig. 29.1.8)
6.22. Description: fragmentary mold, of oval shape, with the rim turned towards the interior. Dimensions: L: 4.4 cm, w: 2.3 cm.
7.22. Material: clay
5.23. Item category: mold? (Fig. 29.1.11)
6.23. Description: fragmentary mold, of semi-cylindrical shape, with the rim turned towards the interior. Dimensions: L: 5 cm, w: 3.8 cm.
7.23. Material: clay
5.24. Item category: mold (Fig. 29.1.15)
6.24. Description: fragmentary mold, on which are represented grains of various sizes. Dimensions: 6.1×4.8 cm.
7.24. Material: clay
5.25. Item category: crucible (Fig. 29.1.16)
6.25. Description: conical crucible, preserved in fragmentary condition. The bottom is flat and the wall has a slightly arching towards the upper part. Dimensions: H: 3.7 cm.
7.25. Material: clay
5.25. Item category: metal casting spoon (Fig. 29.1.17)
6.25. Description: spoon with round dipper, preserved in fragmentary condition, with short handle, of round shape. Dimensions: L: 5 cm.
7.25. Material: clay

2.26. Discovery conditions: settlement, systematic researches, extending from trench I, pit workshop A, of circular shape.
3.26. Year of discovery: 1980
4.26. Context of discovery: pieces of iron slag, scrap pieces (small grains) of bronze; three hand-made potsherds, iron items (knife, a puncher, an arrow head with three wings), a clay spindle whorl, a fragment of deer antler with processing traces.
Context literature: Teodor, *Un centru*, 35–36.
5.26. Item category: crucible (without illustration)
6.26. Description: –
7.26. Material: clay

8. Absolute dating: the second half of the 7th century–8th century
9a. Preserving place: History Museum of Botoșani, Institute of Archeology in Iași
9b. Literature: Teodor, Mitrea, "Cercetări arheologice," 279–291; Teodor, "Elemente și influențe bizantine," 101; Teodor, *Meșteșugurile*, 31; Teodor,

"Tipare," 164–165; 172, Fig. 7.1–2, 6–7; Teodor, *Un centru*; 17–21; 23; 26; 29; 34; 123, fig. 40.1–12; 124, fig. 41.1–9; 125, fig. 42.1–14.

30 Morești/Malomfalva/Mühlendorf, Ungheni Com. (Mureș Co.) (Fig. 2.1)

1. Discovery place: Morești-*Podei*, settlement situated in the western part of the village on a terrace highland.
2. Discovery conditions: the pincers were discovered during archeological excavations, by chance, by a peasant, at about 30 cm depth, rather close to the investigated area
3. Year of discovery: 1954
4. Context of discovery: in the area where the pincers were discovered, there is a 6th century settlement, in which dwellings with pottery inventory were discovered, including here polished and stamped ceramicware. Context literature: Horedt, *Morești*, 101–150.
5. Item category: smithing tongs (Fig. 2.1)
6. Description: ironsmith pincers with average-sized arms, oval buckle with relatively close, unequal, pointed ends. Dimensions: L: 30.5 cm
7. Material: iron
8. Absolute dating: 6th century
9a. Preserving place: History Museum in Târgu Mureș
9b. Literature: Horedt, *Morești*, 150; pl. 43.1.

31 Moțca (Iași Co.) (Fig. 2.2)

1. Discovery place: within the perimeter of the City Hall
2. Discovery conditions: by chance, with the occasion of the excavations for the foundations
3. Year of discovery: –
4. Context of discovery: potsherds
Context literature: Teodor, Descoperiri arheologice și numismatice la est de Carpați în secolele V–XI d. H. (Contribuții la continuitatea daco-romană și veche românească [Archaeological and numismatic discoveries east of the Carpathians in the 5th–11th centuries AD (Contributions to the Dacian-Roman and Old Romanian continuity)]) (Bucharest: Muzeul Național de Istorie a României, 1997), 119.

5. Item category: mold (Fig. 2.2)
6. Description: two-faced mold, of rectangular shape, on one face 2 links were sculpted with grooved edges and from there start two ducts leading to a groove, while on the other face a disk was engraved, on the interior having a round button surrounded by two notched links, three grains with notched edges, forming a row, the left grain having towards the exterior a small groove, the one in the right side has a tiny line towards the exterior, and the one in the left has a large groove. The dies were used at casting earring accessories. Dimensions: 5.3×3.4 cm.
7. Material: stone
8. Absolute dating: 7th century
9a. Preserving place: Collection of the Primary and Secondary School of din Moţca
9b. Literature: Chirică, Tanasachi, *Repertoriul arheologic al Judeţului Iaşi*, 1: 255, fig. 12/12; Teodor, *Descoperiri*, 119, no. 464; Teodor, "Tipare," 165; 167, fig. 2.5.

32 Olteni, Dobrogostea Village, Olteni Com. (Teleorman Co.) (Fig. 2.3)

1. Discovery place: southern part of Dobrogostea village, east of the Alexandria-Piteşti road
2. Discovery conditions: archeological excavations, in the filling earth of a trench meant to find out by testing the limits of the necropolis of the Sântana de Mureş-Cerniahov type.
3. Year of discovery: 1960
4. Context of discovery: –
Context literature: –
5. Item category: (Fig. 2.3)
6. Description: fragmentary mold made from a fine gritstone of light brownish hue, two-faced, broken at one end already in ancient times. On one side there appears the shape of a two-ring earring and a group of six small conical notches, designed for casting the grains. On the other side, there is a cross with vertical arms slightly longer than the horizontal ones, the surface of the cross is ornamented with two or three rows of squares slightly in relief, separated by thin lines, in the middle of the cross there is a round recess which after casting became a prominence in which precious stones or glass beads might have been embedded. Both sides have a groove. Dimensions: L: 4.8 cm, w: 4.5 cm, H: 3.1 cm.

7. Material: stone
8. Absolute dating: 6th century
9a. Preserving place: Romania's National History Museum of Bucharest, inv. no. 18348
9b. Literature: Preda, "Tipar," 513, 514, fig. 1.6.

33 Onești (Bacău Co.) (Fig. 2.4)

1. Discovery place: southern part of the town
2. Discovery conditions: surface researches
3. Year of discovery: 1959
4. Context of discovery: potsherds
Context literature: Teodor, "Tipare," 165.
5. Item category: mold (Fig. 2.4)
6. Description: mold made of gritstone, of rectangular shape, in fragmentary condition, on which two small circles are engraved, together with a straight crosswise line on which are perpendicularly placed four small parallel lines. On one of the lateral faces a small circle is engraved. Dimensions: 9.1×3.2 cm
7. Material: stone
8. Absolute dating: 6th–7th centuries
9a. Preserving place: –
9b. Literature: Teodor, *Meșteșugurile*, 130, fig. 16.9; Teodor, "Tipare," 165; 168, fig. 3.7.

34 Poienița, Năruja Com. (Vrancea Co.) (Fig. 2.5)

1. Discovery place: –
2. Discovery conditions: by chance
3. Year of discovery: 1963
4. Context of discovery: Teodor, "Tipare," 165.
Context literature: –
5. Item category: mold (Fig. 2.5)
6. Description: marl mold, two-faced, on one side there are two engraved rectangular appliqués, and on the other side there is a round appliqué with an ornament suggesting a rosette, a rectangular appliqué, bordered at one end by two parallel lines, contained into a rectangle, and also two

more difficult to identify figures: a stylized flower and four grains bordered by an arched line. Dimensions: 4.6×3.4 cm
7. Material: stone
8. Absolute dating: 6th–7th centuries
9a. Preserving place: Museum of Vrancea in Focșani
9b. Literature: Teodorescu, "Centre meșteșugărești," 91; Teodor, "Tipare," 165; 169, fig. 4.2.

35 Răcoasa (Vrancea Co.) (Fig. 2.6)

1. Discovery place: –
2. Discovery conditions: surface researches
3. Year of discovery: 1979–1980
4. Context of discovery: –
Context literature: Teodor, "Tipare," 165.
5. Item category: mold (Fig. 2.6)
6. Description: gritstone mold, two-faced, on one face a rectangular appliqué with double notched ornament has been engraved. It frames a rectangle that contains three squares and an appliqué shaped like a flower with four petals with pearl contour both in the center and on each petal, where one grain is placed in the center. On the other face, a groove is dug, delimiting a disk, and its role might have been the one of creating open-end links which could have served as pendant hangers or earrings. Dimensions: 8×4.7 cm.
7. Material: stone
8. Absolute dating: 6th–7th centuries
9a. Preserving place: Museum of Vrancea in Focșani
9b. Literature: Bobi, "Contribuții," 107; 140, fig. 27.5; Teodor, "Tipare," 165, 169, fig. 4.4.

36 Rădeni, Păstrăveni Com. (Neamț Co.) (Fig. 6.1)

1. Discovery place: settlement
2. Discovery conditions: by chance, cercetare de suprafață
3. Year of discovery: 1979
4. Context of discovery: potsherds of 6th–7th centuries

Context literature: Mitrea, "Influențe bizantine în cultura materială," 151, note 18; Teodor, "Tipare," 165.

5. Item category: mold (Fig. 6.1)

6. Description: mold made of gritstone, two-faced, on one face there are three carved rosettes and a round appliqué ornamented with concentric circles, as well as two rectangular appliqués and a fragment of a third one; on all appliqués there are notched lines. On the other face, there are two engraved appliqués, one rectangular, ornamented with notches, just like the others, while the other one is square and contains three intersecting lines. Dimensions: 7×4.6 cm.

7. Material: stone

8. Absolute dating: 6th–7th centuries

9a. Preserving place: –

9b. Literature: Mitrea, "Influențe bizantine," 153, fig. 4.3; Teodor, "Tipare," 165; 169, fig. 4.3.

37 Sărata Monteoru (Buzău Co.) (Fig. 6.4)

1. Discovery place: very close to "Cetăţuia", on the Col that connects it to Poiana Scorușului

2. Discovery conditions: incineration cemetery, in tomb no. 14, over the bundle of bones and mixed among them were found eight small ceramic tumblers, placed between the bones, partly with the point up and partly laid down. None contained burned bones; several other small fragments of an iron knife blade were found.

3. Year of discovery: 1952

4. Context of discovery: some small fragments of an iron knife blade.

Context literature: Nestor et al., "Șantierul Sărata-Monteoru," 84–85, fig. 16.

5. Item category: crucible (Fig. 6.4)

6. Description: vessel of conical-pyramidal shape, with three-lobed mouth and rounded bottom, poorly fired. Dimensions: H: 5.6 cm.

7. Material: clay

8. Absolute dating: 7th century

9a. Preserving place: History Museum of Buzău

9b. Literature: Nestor et al., "Șantierul Sărata-Monteoru," 84, 85, fig. 16.

38 Sânmiclăuş/Bethlenszentmiklós/Klosdorf bei Kleinkopisch, Şona Com. (Alba Co.) (Fig. 6.2)

1. Discovery place: point "Răstoci"
2. Discovery conditions: settlement, systematic excavations.
3. Year of discovery: 1974
4. Context of discovery: the idea that the mold was found together with a coin struck for King Stephen III (1162–1172) on the floor of a house is false.
Context literature: Anghel, Blăjan, "Săpăturile," 286; Dănilă, "Consideraţii," 735–736; Dănilă, "Tipare," 560; Velter, *Transilvania*, 458.

5.1. Item category: mold (Fig. 6.2)
6.1. Description: two-face mold, fragmented, made of red-fired clay, with traces of yellow-green enamel on both sides; on one side there is a representation of a small cross with equal arms, with a slot for stone in the middle, as well as two grains; on the other side there is an earring and a fibula/buckle and earring. Dimensions: 5.5×5.3×1 cm.
7.1. Material: clay

5.2. Item category: die (without illustration)
6.2. Description: –
7.2. Material: stone

5.3. Item category: die (without illustration)
6.3. Description: –
7.3. Material: fired clay
8. Absolute dating: 6th century
9a. Preserving place: The National Museum of the Union Alba Iulia
9b. Literature: Anghel, Blăjan, "Săpăturile," 286; Dănilă, "Consideraţii," 735–736; 1–742; Dănilă, "Tipare," 560; Velter, *Transilvania*, 458; Rustoiu, "Habitatul," 63.

39 Soveja (Vrancea Co.) (Fig. 6.3)

1. Discovery place: area of Dragomirna canton
2. Discovery conditions: by chance
3. Year of discovery: 1950–1953
4. Context of discovery: –
Context literature: Teodor, "Tipare," 165.

5. Item category: mold (Fig. 6.3)
6. Description: mold of soft marl, of yellow-brown hue, two-faced, a disk is carved on one face and inside it there are nine grains arranged in the shape of a flower, two rectangular appliqués which have a border consisting of notched lines that frame a rectangle in which there are marked a straight line (1) or broken line (2). On the other face there are a rosette, a disk with a round hollow in the middle, a rectangular appliqué similar to the one on the first face, and an appliqué having the shape of an oak leaf decorated with notched lines symbolizing the ribs. Dimensions: 7×5 cm.
7. Material: stone
8. Absolute dating: 6th–7th centuries
9a. Preserving place: –
9b. Literature: Teodor, *Meșteșugurile*, 130, Fig. 16.7; Teodor, "Tipare," 165;169, Fig. 4.1.

40 **Suceava-*Șipot* (Suceava Co.) (Fig. 18–19)**

1. Discovery place: in the eastern part of the city of Suceava, on the place named Șipot, located at circa 300–400 m in front of the highland where there are the ruins of the *Princely Fortress*.
2.1. Discovery conditions: settlement, systematic archeological researches, trench XV, in dwelling no. 8, with clay hearth surrounded by river stones.
3.1. Year of discovery: 1961
4.1. Context of discovery: potsherds of wheel-made and hand-made ceramicware, a clay spindle whorl, an iron knife blade, a piercing tool made of deer antler.
Context literature: Teodor, *Așezarea medievală*, 17; 124, fig. 32/4.
5.1. Item category: crucible (Fig. 18.1.1)
6.1. Description: crucible preserved in fragmentary condition, only the lower part thereof; the bottom is flat, profiled and slightly curved walls. Dimensions: H: 2.4 cm.
7.1. Material: clay

2.2. Discovery conditions: settlement, systematic archeological researches, trench X dwelling no. 15, near the clay and stone hearth
3.2. Year of discovery: 1962

4.2. Context of discovery: potsherds of hand-made ceramicware and several fragmentary items: two iron knife blades, appliqué (?) of a bronze sheet

Context literature: Teodor, *Așezarea medievală timpurie de la Suceava-Şipot*, 20; 124, fig. 32/7–8.

5.2. Item category: mold (Fig. 18.2.7)

6.2. Description: rectangular mold, broken in the old times, on which a large grain and two small grains were carved; there are also two grooves. Dimensions: 6.4×4.4 cm.

7.2. Material: stone

5.3. Item category: crucible (Fig. 18.2.8)

6.3. Description: crucible of biconical shape, preserved in fragmentary condition. The bottom is flat, profiled. Dimensions: H: 5.5 cm.

7.3. Material: clay

2.4. Discovery conditions: settlement, systematic archeological researches, trench XXII, in dwelling no. 16, with wall-recessed oven and a clay and stone hearth.

3.4. Year of discovery: 1963

4.4. Context of discovery: potsherds of wheel-made and hand-made ceramicware (clay pans).

Context literature: Teodor, *Așezarea medievală*, 21; 124, fig. 32/2.

5.4. Item category: crucible (Fig. 19.1.2)

6.4. Description: crucible of cylindric shape, with flat bottom; the rim is broken. Dimensions: H: 5.5 cm.

7.4. Material: clay

2.5. Discovery conditions: settlement, systematic archeological researches, trench XXII, in dwelling no. 19, with clay and stone hearth

3.5. Year of discovery: 1963

4.5. Context of discovery: quern stones, potsherds of hand-made ceramicware, a fragment of an iron knife, a piercing instrument made of bone, a biconical clay spindle whorl and a stone ball.

Context literature: Teodor, *Așezarea medievală*, 22; 124, fig. 32/5–6.

5.5. Item category: crucible (Fig. 19.2.9)

6.5. Description: conical crucible, with flat bottom and a median profiled element, decorated with a zigzag line; the rim is broken. Dimensions: H: 4.7 cm.

7.5. Material: clay

5.6. Item category: crucible (Fig. 19.2.8)
6.6. Description: crucible preserved in fragmentary condition, only the lower part thereof; the bottom is flat, slightly profiled and with slightly flared walls. Dimensions: H: 2.2 cm.
7.6. Material: clay
8. Absolute dating: 6th–7th centuries
9a. Preserving place: –
9b. Literature: Teodor, *Așezarea medievală*, 17; 20–22; 124, fig. 32/4–8.

41 Șirna (Prahova Co.) (Fig. 6.5)

1. Discovery place: promontory "Fântâna lui Hârțu"
2.1. Discovery conditions: settlement, systematic researches, dwelling no. 19, trench VI
3.1. Year of discovery: –
4.1. Context of discovery: –
Context literature: Olteanu, Grigore, Nicolae, *Comunitatea sătească*, 43; 176, fig. 23, 4.
5.1. Item category: mold (Fig. 6.5.1)
6.1. Description: fragmentary mold on which two sinuous lines are noticed. Dimensions: L: 4.3 cm, w: 3.4 cm.
7.1. Material: clay

2.2. Discovery conditions: settlement, systematic researches, dwelling no. 19, trench VI
3.2. Year of discovery: –
4.2. Context of discovery: –
Context literature: Olteanu, Grigore, Nicolae, *Comunitatea sătească*, 43; 176, fig. 23, 5.
5.2. Item category: mold (Fig. 6.5.2)
6.2. Description: fragmentary mold on which two sinuous lines are noticed. On one of the sides it has an orifice. Dimensions: L: 4.8 cm, w: 4.1 cm.
7.2. Material: stone

2.3. Discovery conditions: settlement, systematic researches, dwelling no. 61, trench XIX
3.3. Year of discovery: –

4.3. Context of discovery: potsherds of wheel-made and hand-made ceramicware, of rough paste, of brick-red hue, wheel-made clay spindle whorl.
Context literature: Olteanu, Grigore, Nicolae, *Comunitatea sătească*, 46; 187, fig. 34, 1.

5.3. Item category: spoon (Fig. 6.5.4)
6.3. Description: fragment of clay spoon with dipper of rectangular shape, the handle is broken. Dimensions: no data on the size of the artifact.
7.3. Material: clay

2.4. Discovery conditions: –
3.4. Year of discovery: –
4.4. Context of discovery: –
Context literature: Olteanu, Grigore, Nicolae, *Comunitatea sătească*, 187, fig. 34.1.

5.4. Item category: crucible (Fig. 6.5.3)
6.4. Description: crucible of ovoid shape, with flowing beak. Dimensions: no data on the size of the artifact.
7.4. Material: clay

2.5. Discovery conditions: settlement, systematic researches, pit in trench IX
3.5. Year of discovery: –
4.5. Context of discovery: potsherds
Context literature: Olteanu, Grigore, Nicolae, *Comunitatea sătească*, 46; 174, fig. 21, 2.

5.5. Item category: chisel (without illustration)
6.5. Description: chisel with collet. Dimensions: L: 3.5 cm, w: 2–2.5 cm.
7.5. Material: iron
8. Absolute dating: 6th century
9a. Preserving place: History Museum in Ploiești
9b. Literature: Olteanu, Grigore, Nicolae, *Comunitatea sătească*, 176, fig. 23.4–5; 187, fig. 34.4.

42 Ştefan cel Mare, Sat Gutinaş, Com. Ştefan cel Mare (Bacău Co.) (Fig. 23.1)

1. Discovery place: "La Selişte", a lot of land on a ca. 60–70 m high terrace, to the right of River Trotuş, delimited by brook Rădeana to the southeast
2.1. Discovery conditions: systematic excavations, dwelling no. 2, partly uncovered
3.1. Year of discovery: 1977
4.1. Context of discovery: –
Context literature: Mitrea, "Regiunea centrală," 108; Mitrea, *Aşezarea medievală*, 77.
5.1. Item category: mold (Fig. 23.1.2)
6.1. Description: two-faced marl mold, on one face small ears and rosette-shaped ornaments were carved, and on the other side, threads with grains. The cast items were used at creating jewelry items, first of all earrings. Dimensions: 8.2×4.7 cm.
7.1. Material: stone

2.2. Discovery conditions: systematic excavations, settlement, trench 4, dwelling no. 5 with stone furnace, clay furnace for ore reduction
3.2. Year of discovery: 1985
4.2. Context of discovery: hand-made ceramicware of the jar and tray types, wheel-made ceramicware of the jar type, several potsherds of cement paste, from a brick-red food storage vessel with wide rim, ornamented with wide grooves.
Context literature: Mitrea, Eminovici, Momanu, "Aşezarea," 224–225; fig. 13.6; fig. 17.2; Mitrea, *Aşezarea medievală*, 45–46; 171, fig. 50/1.
5.2. Item category: engraving needle (Fig. 23.1.1)
6.2. Description: engraving needle, thin, slightly curved, at one end it is straight at the other pointed. Dimensions: L: 1.5 cm.
7.2. Material: iron

2.3. Discovery conditions: systematic excavations, settlement, trench 8, dwelling no. 8 with stone oven, in the filling earth at the level of the bolders dislocated therefrom.
3.3. Year of discovery: 1987.
4.3. Context of discovery: hand-made ceramicware of the jar type, wheel-made ceramicware, two biconical spindle whorls.
Context literature: Mitrea, *Aşezarea medievală*, 51; 171, fig. 50/7.

5.3. Item category: chisel (Fig. 23.1.3)
6.3. Description: chisel, with one flat end and the other pointed. Dimensions: L: 19.5 cm.
7.3. Material: iron

2.4. Discovery conditions: systematic excavations, settlement, trench 24, dwelling no. 18 – in front of the mouth of the stone oven.
3.4. Year of discovery: 1990.
4.4. Context of discovery: hand-made ceramicware, a biconical spindle whorl.
Context literature: Mitrea, *Așezarea medievală*, 63.
5.4. Item category: engraver (without illustration)
6.4. Description: very rusted engraver. Dimensions: no data on the size of the artifact.
7.4. Material: iron

8. Absolute dating: 6th–7th centuries
9a. Preserving place: History Museum of Bacău
9b. Literature: Mitrea, "Regiunea centrală," 108; pl. XLVI.1; Mitrea, Eminovici, Momanu, "Așezarea," 224–225; fig. 13.6; fig. 17.2; 260, fig. 17.2; Mitrea, *Așezarea medievală*, 45–46; 51; 63; 77; 169, fig. 48.2; 170, fig. 49.2; 171, fig. 50/1, 7.

43 Târgșor (Prahova Co.) (without Illustration)

1. Discovery place: –
2. Discovery conditions: systematic researches, settlement
3. Year of discovery: –
4. Context of discovery: –
Context literature: Victor Teodorescu, "Centre meșteșugărești," 85, fig. 6.4.
5.1. Item category: tongue-shaped instrument
6.1. Description: tongue-shaped instrument, lead stained, which was used at casting the melted metal. Dimensions: no data on the size of the artifact.
7.1. Material: iron
5.2. Item category: crucible
6.2. Description: quasi-cylindrical crucible, with round mouth and ovoid bottom. Dimensions: no data on the size of the artifact.

7.2. Material: clay
8. Absolute dating: 6th–7th centuries
9a. Preserving place: History Museum in Ploiești
9b. Literature: Victor Teodorescu, "Centre meșteșugărești," 75, nota 11; 85, fig. 6.4.

44 Traian = Parincea (Bacău Co.) (Fig. 23.3)

1. Discovery place: –
2. Discovery conditions: field research M. Florescu, V. Căpitanu
3. Year of discovery: 1961
4. Context of discovery:
Context literature: Teodor, "Elemente și influențe bizanține," 101, nota 11.
5. Item category: mold (Fig. 23.3)
6. Description: marl mold, which was used at the creation of a rectangular appliqué with the décor composed of twisted spiraled sprouts and a cross with rounded arm ends, ornamented to the interior with concentric circles. Concentric circles also complement the decoration of the sprout having the ends finished with two accanth leaves; in the upper part it has a groove and two holes, possibly for fixing the item to a support. The presence of two lateral cylindrical orifices and of a groove at the top of the item shows that initially the mold was composed of two valves. Dimensions: 9×7.3×4.6 cm.
7. Material: stone
8. Absolute dating: 6th–7th centuries
9a. Preserving place: History Museum of Bacău
9b. Literature: Teodor, "Elemente și influențe bizantine," 101; 107, fig. 6.12.

45 Traian (Neamț Co.) (Fig. 23.2)

1. Discovery place: Săbăoani
2. Discovery conditions: archeological excavations
3. Year of discovery: 1998
4. Context of discovery: in dwelling no. 14
Context literature: Hânceanu, "Două piese din secolele VI–VII p. Chr.," 123.

5. Item category: mold (Fig. 23.2)
6. Description: mold made of clay mixed and smashed shells, which was used at creating triangular pendants (?) with links in the lower part, most probably for earrings. The mold is preserved in fragmentary condition. Dimensions: L: 5.5 cm, w: 4.2 cm.
7. Material: clay
8. Absolute dating: 6th–7th centuries
9a. Preserving place: History Museum in Roman
9b. Literature: Hânceanu, "Două piese," 2015, 124, 131, pl. 2.

46 Udești (Suceava County) (Fig. 43.1)

1. Place of discovery:
2. Conditions of discovery: systematic research, settlement
3. Year of the discovery: 1976
4. Context of the discovery: in a large dwelling where three golden Byzantine coins (*solidi*) issued by Phocas, Heraclius and Heraclius with Heraclius Constantin were found; animal bones.
Context literature: Monica Dejan, "Tezaurul cu monede bizantine de la Udești, jud. Suceava [The Byzantine coin hoard from Udești, Suceava county]," in *Aurul și argintul antic al României. Catalog de expoziție*, ed. Rodica Oanță-Marghitu (Bucharest: Muzeul Național de Istorie a României, 2013), 660; Monica Dejan, *Elemente răsăritene în ținuturile extracarpatice (secolele VI–X)* [Eastern elements in the extra-Carpathian lands (6th–10th centuries)] (Suceava: Editura Karl A. Romstorfer, 2015), 78, Fig. 2.

5.1. Item category: metal casting spoon (Fig. 43.1.1)
6.1. Description: ovoid spoon, on one side it has a beak for casting and it also has a tubular plug, preserved in fragmentary condition. Dimensions: L: 5.8 cm, w: 5.1 cm, H: 3.7 cm.
7.1. Material: clay

5.2. Item category: crucible (Fig. 43.1.2)
6.2. Description: fragment of crucible, of rectangular shape, it has flat bottom. Dimensions: L: 6.6 cm, w: 3.3 cm, H: 4.5 cm.
7.2. Material: clay

8. Absolute dating: 6th–7th centuries
9a. Preserving place: Bucovina Museum Suceava
9b. Literature: Dejan, "Tezaurul," 660–661; Dejan, *Elemente*, 78, Fig. 2; 283.

47 Vadu Săpat, Fântânele Com. (Prahova Co.) (Fig. 43.2)

1. Discovery place: pe teritoriul comunei
2. Discovery conditions: by chance, by Moise Nicolae Dan
3. Year of discovery: 1981
4. Context of discovery:
Context literature: –
5. Item category: mold (Fig. 43.2)
6. Description: two-faced flintstone mold, on one face a rectangular belt plate is incised, composed of a trapezoidal part with notched edges, ornamented with a star, in the center there are openwork coils, and in the end part there is a U-shaped plate, with a central button and pearl edges, with geometric ornamentation. On the same face there is a round, half-globular appliqué that was carved, together with a pendant composed of three pearls of the *melon seed* type, attached to a link. On the other face, a rectangular appliqué was carved out, with pearl edges, decorated with notches, as well as three rosette-shaped appliqués, with geometric and pearl ornamentation, and a heart-shaped appliqué, with pearl frames. Dimensions: L: 12.5 cm, w: 4.6 cm, thickness: 2.1 cm.
7. Material: stone
8. Absolute dating: 7th century
9a. Preserving place: History Museum of Prahova County Ploiești, inv. no. 23788.
9b. Literature: Măgureanu, Ciupercă, "The 6th–8th Centuries Metallurgical Activity," 301–302; 311, fig. 3.

CHAPTER 12

Finds from Central and Eastern Europe

1 Dies and Molds from Central and Eastern Europe

1.1 *Bronze Dies for Pressing and Impressing Bronze Dies*

1.1.1. Adony (Fejér co.), Hungary

No details are known on the discovery context, the items were part of the collection of the noble family Zichy.

12 dies for making head ornamenting plates (diadem), belt items (main buckle pin, secondary buckle pin, U-shaped and T-shaped plates).

Lit.: József Hampel, "Nemzeti Muzeum régiségosztályának gyarapodása 1880 julius, augusztus, szeptember, oktober, november [Augmentation of the Antiquities Department of the National Museum, July, August, September, October, November, 1880]," *Archaeologiai Értesitő* 14 (1881), 348, pl. XLIII.1–4, 6–13; Fettich, *Das awarenzeitliche Kunstgewerbe*, pl. VI.1–7, 9–13; Rácz, *Die Goldschmiedegräber*, 143–144.

1.1.2. Békéscsaba-Nagyrét (Békés co.), Hungary

Random discovery, in the field, on the surface of the ground.

Copper die, of rectangular shape, with rounded ends, with positive and negative models represented on it. On one face, there is a palmette ornamentation (helmet point?). On the other face the die has four decorative motifs: a palmette, a rosette, a bearded man's head (belt plates) and an astragal-cylinder (earring ornament?).

Lit.: Rácz, *Die Goldschmiedegräber*, 147–148; pl. 79.2.

1.1.3. Bucharest-Tei, Romania – see catalogue no. 7g

1.1.4. Cherkasy District, Ukraine

Discovery made with the metal detector by an amateur. Items were found at a small depth.

Eight bronze dies for creating belt and harness items: buckle pin, appliqués with ornamentation of the Felnac type (2), rosette-shaped appliqués (2), lion-shaped appliqués (1) and raptor bird-shaped (2).

Lit.: Rácz, "Ein frühmittelalterlicher Pressmodelfund," 176, Fig. 1.1–8.

1.1.5. Corund (Harghita co.), Romania – See Catalogue No. 12

1.1.6. Dumbrăveni (Sibiu co.), Romania – See Catalogue No. 21

1.1.7. Dunapentele (Dunaújváros) (Fejér co.), Hungary

Random discovery

Bronze die for prongs

© DANIELA TĂNASE, 2021 | DOI:10.1163/9789004436930_014

Lit.: Rácz, *Die Goldschmiedegräber*, 152; pl. 75.11.

1.1.8. Kardoskút (Békés co.), Hungary

Stray find.

Bronze die for belt buckles with shield-shaped plates.

Lit.: Zsófia Rácz, Zoltán May, "Öntőminta pajzsos testű csat készítéséhez [Mold for making a shielded buckle]," in *Mozaikok Orosháza és vidéke múltjából 19. Fémek a földből*, 1 (Orosháza: Orosháza Város Önkormányzat Nagy Gyula Területi Múzeuma, 2018), 50, fig. 24.

1.1.9. Kiskunhalas, Subdistrict (Bács-Kiskun co.), Hungary

Discovery on the surface of the ground.

Palmette-shaped bronze die.

Lit.: Fettich, *Das awarenzeitliche Kunstgewerbe*, 33, pl. VII, 6; Rácz, *Die Goldschmiedegräber*, 161.

1.1.10. Oescus (Gigen, Gulyantsi co.), Bulgaria – Metal Die

Lit.: Daskalov, Dimitrov, "On a Production," 69, fig. 1.1, 74.

1.1.11. Oescus (Staroseltsi, Gulyantsi co.), Bulgaria – Metal Die

Lit.: Daskalov, Dimitrov, "On a Production," 69, fig. 1.2, 74.

1.1.12. Paks-Gyapa, The Archaeological Site 15 (Tolna co.), Hungary

Random discovery – field research

Bronze die for pressing/casting anthropomorphic appliqués

Lit.: Zsófia Rácz, "Emberalakos kistárgyak az avar korból," 409; pl. 79.1.

1.1.13. Pančevo (South Banat), Serbia

Discovery in the area of a brick factory, whose owner had an antiques collection. After his death which took place in 1924, his collection which contained items from the Avars's epoch, human and horse bones, was sold to the Hungarian National Museum of Budapest.

It is possible that the bronze die for pressing main prongs was found in a tomb.

Bronze die for pressing main prongs with a rosette in the median part of the item

Lit.: Csallány, *A Kunszentmártoni avarkori ötvösir*, 19, pl. VII.7; Vinski, "O nalazima," 22, pl. IV, 13; Rácz, *Die Goldschmiedegräber*, 171.

1.1.14. Petronell-Carnuntum (Near Bruck An Der Leitha), Austria

It was part of a private collection, no details are known about the discovery.

Bronze die for pressing shield-shaped belt plates, with *Zahnschnitt* ornamentation

Lit.: Rácz, *Die Goldschmiedegräber*, 191–192.

1.1.15. Ringelsdorf (Gänserndorf co.), Austria

It was part of a private collection.

Bronze die for pressing rosette-shaped appliqués

Lit.: Rácz, *Die Goldschmiedegräber*, 193.

1.1.16. Seewinkel (?) (Neusiedlersee co., Burgenland), Austria
Bronze die for pressing double shield-shaped belt plates
Lit.: Rácz, *Die Goldschmiedegräber*, 193.
1.1.17. Szentes (Csongrád co.), Hungary
Random discovery
Bronze die for pressing rosette-shaped belt plates for harness
Lit.: Csallány, *A Kunszentmártoni avarkori ötvösir*, 19, pl. VII.8; Rácz, *Die Goldschmiedegräber*, 195.
1.1.18. Hungary (6), Austria (1), Serbia (4), without known discovery place.
11 bronze dies for creating by pressing prongs and belt plates
Lit.: Rácz, *Die Goldschmiedegräber*, p. 193.
1.1.19. Vratsa (Vratsa co.), Bulgaria – metal die
Lit.: Daskalov, Dimitrov, "On a Production," 69, fig. 1.3, 74.
1.1.20. Viminacium (Stari Kostolac, Braničevo co.), Serbia – metal die for double-shield belt plate, with ornamentation of the Felnac type
Lit.: *Die Welt von Byzanz*, 283, Cat. no. 470.

1.2 *Stone Molds*

1.2.1. Aegyssus (Tulcea, Tulcea co.), Romania – one stone mold
Lit.: Opaiţ, "Aegyssus '76 – Raport preliminar," 310; fig. 6; Miclea, Florescu, *Strămoşii românilor*, fig. 620; 170.
1.2.2. Aldeni (Buzău co.), Romania – stone mold – see catalogue no. 1
1.2.3. Argamum (Jurilovca, Tulcea co.), Romania – stone mold
Lit.: Oanţă-Marghitu, "Argamum," 355–356; pl. I.4.
1.2.4. Bernashivka (Mohyliv-podil'ský co.), Ukraine – stone molds: two of limestone, eight of gritstone, four of marl, two of rock with limestone content, 31 of stone.
Lit.: Vynokur, *Slov'ianski iuveliry*, 54–97.
1.2.5. Botoşana (Suceava co.), Romania – two stone molds – see catalogue no. 5
1.2.6. Bucharest-Dămăroaia, Romania – stone mold – see catalogue no. 7c
1.2.7. Bucharest-Soldat Ghivan no. 10, Romania – stone mold – see catalogue no. 7d
1.2.8. Bucharest-Străuleşti-Măicăneşti, Romania – stone mold – see catalogue no. 7f
1.2.9. Budureasca 3 (Prahova co.), Romania – 3 stone molds – see catalogue no. 8a
1.2.10. Budureasca 4 (Prahova co.), Romania – 3 stone molds – see catalogue no. 8b
1.2.11. Budureasca 5 (Prahova co.), Romania – stone mold – see catalogue no. 8c

1.2.12. Cacica (Suceava co.), Romania – stone mold – see catalogue no. 9
1.2.13. Capidava (Constanța co.), Romania – two stone molds
Lit.: Covacef, "Accesorii," 112, plate VII.3–4; 113.
1.2.14. Cândești (Buzău co.), Romania – stone mold – see catalogue no. 10
1.2.15. Coroteni (Vrancea co.), Romania – stone mold – see catalogue no. 11
1.2.16. Cristuru Secuiesc (Harghita co.), Romania – stone mold – see catalogue no. 14
1.2.17. Cucuteni (Iași co.), Romania – stone mold – see catalogue no. 15
1.2.18. Davideni (Neamț co.), Romania – three stone molds – see catalogue no. 16
1.2.19. Dănceni (Ialoveni co.), Republic of Moldova – stone molds
Lit.: Teodor, "Tipare," 164, 167, fig. 2.7–8.
1.2.20. Dichiseni (Călărași co.), Romania – stone mold – see catalogue no. 17
1.2.21. Dodești (Vaslui co.), Romania – stone molds – see catalogue no. 16
1.2.22. Dolheștii Mari (Suceava co.), Romania – stone mold – see catalogue no. 19
1.2.23. Dulceanca I (Teleorman co.), Romania – stone molds – see catalogue no. 20
1.2.24. Giurcani (Vaslui co.), Romania – stone mold – see catalogue no. 23
1.2.25. Golemanovo Kale, Bulgaria – stone mold
Lit.: Oanță-Marghitu, "Argamum," pl. III.7.
1.2.26. Izvorul Dulce (Buzău co.), Romania – stone mold – see catalogue no. 27
1.2.27. Lozna (Botoșani co.), Romania – stone mold – see catalogue no. 29
1.2.28. Moțca (Iași co.), Romania – stone mold – see catalogue no. 31
1.2.29. Olteni (Teleorman co.), Romania – stone mold – see catalogue no. 32
1.2.30. Onești (Bacău co.), Romania – stone mold – see catalogue no. 33
1.2.31. Poienița (Vrancea co.), Romania – stone mold – see catalogue no. 34
1.2.32. Răcoasa (Vrancea co.), Romania – stone mold – see catalogue no. 35
1.2.33. Rădeni (Neamț co.), Romania – stone mold – see catalogue no. 36
1.2.34. Sânmiclăuș (Alba co.), Romania – stone mold – see catalogue no. 38
1.2.35. Seliște-Orhei (Orhei co.), Republic of Moldova – stone mold
Lit.: Teodor, "Tipare," 165, 167, fig. 2.3.
1.2.36. Soveja (Vrancea co.), Romania – stone mold – see catalogue no. 39
1.2.37. Suceava-Șipot (Suceava co.), Romania – stone mold – see catalogue no. 40
1.2.38. Șirna (Prahova co.), Romania – stone mold – see catalogue no. 41
1.2.39. Ștefan cel Mare (Bacău co.), Romania – stone mold – see catalogue no. 42
1.2.40. Traian (Bacău co.), Romania – stone mold – see catalogue no. 44

1.2.41. Tropaeum Traiani (Adamclisi, Constanța co.), Romania – stone mold
Lit.: Barnea et al., *Tropaeum Traiani*, 218, fig. 169.10.14.
1.2.42. Vadu Săpat (Prahova co.), Romania – stone mold – see catalogue no. 47

1.3 *Clay Molds*

1.3.1. Bucharest-Străulești-Lunca, Romania – clay mold – see catalogue no. 7e
1.3.2. Bucharest-Tei, Romania – clay mold – see catalogue no. 7g
1.3.3. Budureasca 4 (Prahova co.), Romania: 1. clay mold – see catalogue no. 8b
1.3.4. Hansca (Ialoveni co.), Republic of Moldova – clay mold
Lit.: Teodor, "Tipare," 164, 173, fig. 8.2.
1.3.5. Jász-Nagykun-Szolnok co., Hungary – clay mold
Lit.: Rácz, *Die Goldschmiedegräber*, 199; pl. 80.2.
1.3.6. Lazuri (Satu Mare co.), Romania – clay mold – see catalogue no. 28
1.3.7. Lozna (Botoșani co.), Romania – 4 clay molds – see catalogue no. 29
1.3.8. Sânmiclăuș (Alba co.), Romania – stone mold – see catalogue no. 38
1.3.9. Seliște-Orhei (Orhei co.), Republic of Moldova – clay mold
Lit.: Teodor, "Tipare," 165, 172, fig. 7.3.
1.3.10. Șirna (Prahova co.), Romania – clay mold – see catalogue no. 41
1.3.11. Traian (Neamț co.), Romania – clay mold – see catalogue no. 45

1.4 *Bone Dies*

1.4.1. Costești (Iași co.), Romania – three bone dies – see catalogue no. 13
1.4.2. Pastyrs'ke (Smila co., Cherkasy region), Ukraine – bone die for perforated hemispherical appliqués
Lit.: Szmoniewski, "Production," 121.
1.4.3. Zimne (Volodimir-Podil's'kij co., Volins'ka region), Ukraine – bone die for belt tongue
Lit.: Szmoniewski, "Production," 121.

2 Graves with Implements/Tools in Central and Eastern Europe

2.1. Aradac-Mečka (near Zrenjanin, Central Banat), Serbia – end of 6th century–first third of the 7th century
Tomb 18, inhumation
Inventory:
Costume and jewelry items: glass beads, fragment of a glass bracelet, iron buckles.
implements: 1. knife, flint, flintstone

2. pincers, file, metal sheet clippers, whetstone, bronze chump
weapons: arrow head
coins: two bronze coins from Constantine II (317–340)

Lit.: Nagy, "Nekropola kol Aradaca," 45–102.

2.2. Aradac-Mečka
Tomb III, inhumation
Inventory:
costume and jewelry items: bronze belt plates, bronze and iron buckles
implements: 1. knife, flint and flintstone
2. metal die, raw material
weapons: axe

Lit.: Nagy, "Nekropola kol Aradaca," 45–102.

2.3. Band/Bandu de Câmpie (Mureș co.), Romania – see catalogue no. 3 (Fig. 31–36).

2.4. Békéssámson (Békés County), Hungary – first half of the 7th century
Inhumation tomb
Inventory:
1. implements: bronze mold for belt appliqués with ornamentation of the Felnac type

Lit.: Rácz, "Ein frühmittelalterlicher Pressmodelfund," 177, note 4.

2.5. Berekfürdő – Tsz-major (Jász-Nagykun-Szolnok co.), (Hungary) – the second half of the 7th century
Tomb 12 – inhumation
Inventory:
costume and jewelry items: silver belt items: buckle pin, plates, lyre-shaped iron belt buckle, trapezoidal iron belt buckle
implements: 1. knife
2. pincers, fragments of iron implements?

Lit.: Rácz, *Die Goldschmiedegräber*, 148.

2.6. Bóly – Sziebert puszta A (Baranya co.), Hungary – 7th century
Tomb 3 – inhumation, a knight's tomb
Inventory:
costume and jewelry items: bronze and iron buckles, silver plates, bronze prongs

implements: 1. knife
2. hammer
weapons: three arrow heads
harness items: saddle ladder, bit, belt buckle
animal offerings: cow skull, horse skeleton
coins: illegible Byzantine coin

Lit.: Henning, "Schmiedegräber," 81; Rácz, *Die Goldschmiedegräber*, 148.

2.7. Bratislava-Záhorská Bystrica, Lokvy pri Morave, Slovakia – the second half of the 7th century–8th century
Tomb 215: inhumation
Inventory:
costume and jewelry items: helmet point
implements: hammer, anvil

Lit.: L'udmila Kraskovská, *Slovansko-avarské pohrebísko pri Záhorskej Bystrici* (Bratislava: Vyd. Osveta, 1972), 41, fig. 43, 2–4; Rácz, *Die Goldschmiedegräber*, 148.

2.8. Csákberény-Orondpuszta, Meránföld (Fejér co.), Hungary – 7th century
Tomb 323 – inhumation; disturbed tomb
Inventory:
costume and jewelry items: bronze link, iron link, fragmentary bronze plates from leather bag, fragments of iron plates
implements: hammer, pincers
weapons: bow

Lit.: Henning, "Schmiedegräber," 81; Rácz, *Die Goldschmiedegräber*, 149–150; Gyula László, *Das Awarenzeitliche Gräberfeld in Csákberény-Orondpuszta*, with contributions from Gergely Csiky, Kinga Éry, Gábor Fancsalszky, Gyula Fülöp, Adrien Pásztor, Zsófia Rácz, József Szentpéteri, Tivadar Vida, István Vörös, István Koncz, Péter Skriba, Gergely Szenthe (Budapest: Magyar Nemzeti Múzeum 2015), 77; 271, pl. 28.323.1–6.

2.9. Csákberény-Orondpuszta
Tomb 369 – inhumation; disturbed tomb
Inventory:
implements: 1. two knives, flintstone
2. pincers, hammer, anvil, metal casting spoon, whetstone
weapons: fragment of breastplate, seven arrowheads

fragments of iron, bronze and silver belt plates and also from various cloth and wooden items attached to the belt.

Lit.: Henning, "Schmiedegräber," 81; Rácz, *Die Goldschmiedegräber*, 150–152; László, *Das Awarenzeitliche Gräberfeld*, 77; 212, fig. 53–54; 285.

2.10. Felnac (Arad co.), Romania, first third of the 7th century, see catalogue no. 22 (Fig. 37.2.1–10–Fig. 41).

2.11. Gátér-Vasútállomás (Bács-Kiskun co.), Hungary – first third of the 7th century; the items were destroyed during World War II.
Tomb 11, inhumation
Inventory:
costume and jewelry items: globular silver earring, bronze buckles, silver belt plates
implements: 1. knife, flint
2. hammer, eight metal dies, chisel, two preformed items
weapons: two arrowheads with three edges
bronze plates and iron link from items that would be attached to the belt

Lit.: Kada, "Gátéri (Kun-Kisszállási) temető," 360–384; Rácz, *Die Goldschmiedegräber*, 156–158.

2.12. Gyönk-Vásártéri út (Tolna co.), Hungary
Tomb 267 – inhumation, a woman's tomb
Inventory:
costume and jewelry items: belt buckle iron
implements: 1. knife
2. bronze die for T-shaped belt plates

Lit.: Rácz, *Die Goldschmiedegräber*, 158.

2.13. Jutas (Veszprém co.), Hungary – beginning of the 7th century
Tomb 166, inhumation
Inventory:
jewelry and costume items: lead plated silver belt plates
implements: balance with two weights: a bronze one and a glass one, pincers, clippers for metal sheet, saw, three files, borer, chisel, item used at soldering, bronze globe – mold, knife, piece of red chalk or piece of tar, fragments of bronze items, bronze link.
weapons: three edged-arrow heads

Lit.: Rhé, Fettich, *Jutas und Öskü*, 32; IV.12–20, VIII.1–13; Rácz, *Die Goldschmiedegräber*, 159–161.

2.14. Kisújszállás-Nagykert (Jász-Nagykun-Szolnok co.), Hungary – beginning of the 7th century
Tomb – inhumation
Inventory:
jewelry and costume items: a gold earring with globular pendant, three perforated eagle claws, Neolithic beads and fragments of chopped deer antlers worn as amulets, iron buckles, bronze items (two links, rod, belt buckle pin and stripe).
implements: 1. knife, bone puncher/polisher
2. pincers, hammer, anvil, metal sheet clippers, two files, chisel, bronze pipe for bellows, bronze engraver, fragments of iron and bronze implements, pieces from the casting of a copper alloy, half-globular mold (?) made of stone with limestone content for pressing plates, presat plăcuțe, half-globular items made of stone and bone, whetstone, stone with traces of rust, stone with firing traces.
weapons: sword, spear point, harness items: bit, pair of pear-shaped saddle ladder with long ears, pear-shaped saddle ladder with short ears.
vessels: clay vessel in which Neolithic stone axes and chisels were deposited

Lit.: Rácz, *Die Goldschmiedegräber*, 161–164.

2.15. Klárafalva B (Csongrád co.), Hungary – 7th century
Tomb 60, inhumation, a knight's tomb
Inventory:
jewelry and costume items: bone pendant, silver and bronze belt plates, iron buckles, bronze chain, bone and bronze hanger
implements: knife, flint with flintstone, hammer; metal sheet clippers, raw material, iron spoon for metal casting, borer, fragment of implement (file?), fragments of bronze and iron items, ponce stone
weapons: dagger, five three-edged arrow heads, bone plates from a bow
animal offerings: horse skeleton

Lit.: Balogh, "Martinovka-típusú övgarnitúra," 241–303; Rácz, *Die Goldschmiedegräber*, 164–166.

2.16. Kölked-Feketekapu B (Baranya co.), Hungary – mid of the 7th century
Tomb 80, inhumation
Inventory:

costume and jewelry items: earring of silver wire, silver plate decorated in animal style II with Zahnschnitt, oval bronze belt buckle, iron belt buckle with plate, iron prongs with cells
weapons: three edged-arrow heads, spear point, fragments of breastplate
implements: 1. knife, flint with flintstone, harpon
2. three hammers, large pincers, two fragments of pincers, three chisels, a punch, a tool for drawing the wire, raw material: bronze Roman coins, fragments of bronze Roman items: statuettes, vessels, a piece of a bronze stick with hammering traces
coins: bronze Roman coin

> **Lit.:** Kiss, *Das awarenzeitliche Gräberfeld in Kölked-Feketekapu B*, 1: 25–26, 2: 38–41, pl. 24–27; Rácz, *Die Goldschmiedegräber*, 166–170.

2.17. Kölked-Feketekapu B – the second half of the 7th century
Tomb 204, inhumation
implements: 1. knife
2. hammer.

> **Lit.:** Kiss, *Das awarenzeitliche Gräberfeld in Kölked-Feketekapu B*, 2: 91, pl. 54.

2.18. Komárno IV – J. Váradiho street (Komárno co.) – Slovakia – 8th century
Tomb 23 – inhumation, a woman's tomb, burial with horse
Inventory:
costume and jewelry items: gold earrings, bronze buckle, iron buckle
coins: two bronze coins – Constantin the Great (306–337)
implements: 1. three knives with wooden sheath
2. two bronze dies for pressing for leaf-shaped appliqués, fragment of melted bronze
weapons: harness items: bit, two saddle ladder
animal offering: cow bones
vessels: clay vessel, iron plates from (wooden) bucket

> **Lit.**: Zlata Čilinska, "Dve pohrebiská z 8.–9. storočia v Komárne [Two necropolises from the 8th–9th centuries in Komárno]," *Slovenská Archeologia* 30, no. 2 (1982), 354–355, 380, pl. IX.1–26; Henning, "Schmiedegräber," 81; Rácz, *Die Goldschmiedegräber*, 170.

2.19. Komárno IX – Lodenica I. (shipyard) – 8th century
Tomb 98 – inhumation, a woman's tomb
implements: 1. knife
2. hammer

animal offering: cow bones
vessels: clay vessel, iron plates from (wooden) bucket

Lit.: Alexander Trugly, "Gräberfeld aus der Zeit des awarischen Reiches bei der Schiffswerft in Komárno II," *Slovenská Archeológia* 41, no. 2 (1993), 193; 238, pl. I.14; Rácz, *Die Goldschmiedegräber*, 170.

2.20. Kunszentmárton (Jász-Nagykun-Szolnok co.), Hungary – first half of the 7th century
Tomb 1, inhumation, a rider's tomb; coffin brackets
Inventory:
costume and jewelry items: bronze buckle pin, belt buckle for bag of the Pápa type
implements: 1. knife, whetstone, flint and flintstone
2. glass and bronze balance and weights, including Byzantine equivalent weights for gold coins (*solidus*), silver coins (*semissis*) and bronze coins (*tremissis*), 41 bronze dies for pressing belt and harness items, a lead and iron alloy piece with a mold for casting rosettes, hammer, pincers, anvil, two metal sheet clippers, implement for drawing metal wire, punch, engraving stylet, lead stand for shaping items, bronze blowing pipe for bellows, fragmentary iron implements, whetstones, finished and preformed items (bronze belt and harness plates, silver stripe, bronze rivet), raw material (fragments of silver, bronze, lead, copper items), iron slag.
weapons: breastplate, sword, spear, fragments of iron arrowheads.
vase: small copper tray, fragments of glass tumbler
animal offering: horse bones

Lit.: Csallány, *A Kunszentmártoni avarkori ötvösir*, 5–17; pl. I–VII; Rácz, *Die Goldschmiedegräber*, 171–191; pl. 43–69.

2.21. Makó-Mikócsa-halom (Csongrád co.), Hungary
Three inhumation tombs
They all have in their inventory: implements, weapons, horse skeletons
Unpublished – two of them

Lit.: Rácz, *Die Goldschmiedegräber*, 191.

2.22. Makó-Mikócsa-halom
Tomb no. 61, inhumation, a knight's tomb – end of the 6th century–beginning of the 7th century
The pit has a niche.
Inventory:
jewelry and costume items: metal items for belt and shoes

implements for processing bone, horn and metals: two hammers, two adzes, a file, an iron saw, a knife for bone shaping, a hand drill, an instrument with two teeth, an iron crucible, raw material: processed horn and bone
weapons: sword, arrow heads
harness items: saddle ladder, harness appliqués
animal offering: horse skeleton; animal bones

Lit.: Balogh, "Karpat havzasi'nda bir avar," 111–112, 117–120.

2.23. Pókaszepetk (Zala co.), Hungary, 7th century
Tomb 360, incineration
Inventory:
jewelry and costume items: amber bead, fragment of oval iron belt buckle, fragment of square iron belt buckle, belt buckle for a bag, cast in bronze, of the Pápa type
implements: balance with bronze weights, glass exagium, dark green "glass weight", raw material: **coins:** bronze coin, 1st century AD (Domitianus, BMC 268), small bronze Roman coin of the 4th century AD, two perforated bronze Roman coins, of the 4th century
implements and tools: wooden box with silver plate, flintstone
weapons: two spear points
diverse: two pieces of bronze wire, bucată de ciob de sticlă roman, of hue verde-deschis

Lit.: Sós, "Frühmittelalterliche Brandbestattung," 424–430.

2.24. Rákóczifalva-Kastélydomb (Jász-Nagykun-Szolnok co.), Hungary – the second half of the 7th century
Tomb "B" – inhumation, a knight's tomb
implements: four bronze dies for pressing, pincers
weapons: sword, bit, saddle ladder
vessels: clay vessel
other items: bronze and iron items with uncertain functionality

Lit.: Rácz, *Die Goldschmiedegräber*, 192–193; pl. 70.

2.25. Sajópetri-Hosszúrét (Borsod-Abaúj-Zemplén co.) Hungary – 8th century
Inhumation tomb
implements: hammer

Lit.: Rácz, *Die Goldschmiedegräber*, 193.

2.26. Sărata Monteoru (Buzău co.), Romania – 7th century, see catalogue no. 37 (Fig. 6.4).

2.27. Szeged-Bilisics (Csongrád co.), Hungary – end of 7th century–8th century
Tomb 1 – inhumation, a woman's tomb
jewelry and costume items: bronze bracelets
implements: stone mold for casting various types of earrings and beads

Lit.: Csallány, "Az Átokháza-bilisicsi avarkori sírleletek," 113; Fettich, "Symbolischer Gürtel," 66, 67 fig. 2, 68; *Awaren in Europa. Schätze eines asiatisches Reitervolkes 6.–8. Jh.* Ausstellungskatalog, ed. Walter Meier-Arendt (Frankfurt am Main 1985), 65, cat. no. XVII, 9 fig. 61.

2.28. Szeged-Kiskundorozsma-Hármashatár (Csongrád co.), Hungary – 7th–8th centuries
Tomb 4 – inhumation
jewelry and costume items: helical iron belt plate
implements: 1. knife
2. pliers
weapons: two arrow heads
animal offering: cow bones

Lit.: Vályi, "Das Detail," 212. 256, fig. 3, 10–13, 15–16; Rácz, *Die Goldschmiedegräber*, 193–194.

2.29. Székkutas-Kápolnadűlő (Békés co.), Hungary – 7th–8th centuries
Tomb 349 – inhumation
jewelry and costume items: two buckles iron
implements: 1. knife
2. hammer
Lit.: Rácz, *Die Goldschmiedegräber*, 194; pl. 74.2.

2.30. Szekszárd-Palánk (Tolna co.), Hungary – 7th century
Tomb 202 –inhumation, a woman's tomb
implements: bronze die for pressing double shield-shaped plates with ornamentation of the Tarnamera type

Lit.: Rácz, *Die Goldschmiedegräber*, 194; pl. 75.9.

2.31. Szekszárd-Tószegi-dűlő (Tolna co.), Hungary – end of the 6th century–beginning of the 7th century
Tomb 967 – inhumation; plundered tomb
jewelry and costume items: silver earring, bronze belt plate
implements: 1. flintstone
2. two files, bronze crucible
vessels: clay vessel

Lit.: Ódor, Rácz, "Szerszámmellékletes sír a Szekszárd-Tószegi-dűlőiavar temetőből," 245–246, 253–255; Rácz, *Die Goldschmiedegräber*, 194–195.

2.32. Szentes-Kaján (Csongrád co.), Hungary – 8th century
Tomb 159 – inhumation
jewelry and costume items: cast, openwork belt fitting, decorated with sprouts
implements: fighting hammer/axe?
Lit.: Rácz, *Die Goldschmiedegräber*, 195.

2.33. Tiszafüred-Majoros (Jász-Nagykun-Szolnok co.), Hungary – 7th century
Tomb 28 – inhumation, a woman's tomb
jewelry and costume items: gold earrings
implements: 1. knife, iron stilus
2. bronze die for pressing bird-shaped earring pendants, raw material?: Roman fibula, bronze chain
Lit.: Éva Garam, *Das awarenzeitliche Gräberfeld von Tiszafüred. Cemeteries of the Avar Period (567–827) in Hungary 3* (Budapest: Akadémiai Kiadó, 1995), 11, pl. 60; Rácz, *Die Goldschmiedegräber*, 196.

2.34. Tolna (Mözs)-Fehérvize-dűlő, (com. Tolna), Hungary – 7th century
Tomb 69 – inhumation, coffin traces
jewelry and costume items: silver earrings, iron belt buckle
tools: bronze tweezers
implements: 1. knife, spindle whorl
2. pincers, hammer, metal sheet clippers, engraver
Lit.: Rácz, *Die Goldschmiedegräber*, 196.

2.35. Üllő-Disznójárás (Pest co.), Hungary – 8th century
Tomb 142 – inhumation
jewelry and costume items: cast bronze belt fitting
implements: fighting hammer/axe?
Lit.: Rácz, *Die Goldschmiedegräber*, 196.

2.36. Vác-Kavicsbánya (Pest co.), Hungary – beginning of the 7th century–half or end of the 8th century
Tomb 140, a woman's tomb, inhumation
costume and jewelry items: bone comb, a large bead made of glass paste, three pieces of a cylindrical arched silver item, an arched silver plate, decorated with rows of dots, silver ring with bezel

implements: stone mold for casting lunules and stripes with horizontal lines
containers: hand-made ceramic vessel, of brown hue, whose paste was mixed with silicates (flintstone).

Lit.: Tettamanti, *Das awarenzeitliche Gräberfeld*, 32, 121, pl. V; Rácz, *Die Goldschmiedegräber*, 196–197; pl. 81.

2.37. Vrbas – brick factory (Južna Bačka co.), Serbia – 8th century
Tomb 118 – inhumation
costume and jewelry items: iron belt buckle
implements: 1. knife, flintstone
2. fighting hammer/axe?

Lit.: Sandor Nagy, "Nekropola iz ranog sredneg veka u ciglani "Polet" u Vrbasu [Necropolis from the early Middle Ages in the "Polet" brick factory in Vrbas]," *Rad Vojvođanskih Muzeja* 20 (1971), 208, 240, pl. XXIII.118.9; Rácz, *Die Goldschmiedegräber*, 197.

2.38. Zalakomár-Lesvári-dűlő (Zala co.), Hungary – 8th century
Tomb – inhumation
implements: hammer

Lit.: Rácz, *Die Goldschmiedegräber*, 197.

2.39. Zamárdi-Rétiföldek-dűlő (Somogy co.), Hungary – 7th century
Tomb 250/a – inhumation
costume and jewelry items: bronze pendant, rosette-shaped appliqué for belt
implements: 1. flint and flintstone
2. file, raw material (fragments of bronze and iron items)
weapons: eight three-edged arrowheads

Lit.: Bárdos, Garam, *Das awarenzeitliche Gräberfeld*, 43, pl. 31; Rácz, *Die Goldschmiedegräber*, 197.

2.40. Zamárdi-Rétiföldek-dűlő
Tomb 569 – inhumation, an adolescent's tomb
implements: 1. knife
2. bronze die for secondary preset prongs, with ornamentation of the Martynivka type

Lit.: Bárdos, Garam, *Das awarenzeitliche Gräberfeld*, 84, pl. 73, 1; Rácz, *Die Goldschmiedegräber*, 197.

2.41. Zamárdi-Rétiföldek-dűlő
Tomb 661 – inhumation, a child's tomb
implements: 1. knife, four clay spindle whorls
2. file (?)
vessels: bronze stripe of a wooden bucket
other items: iron stripe, iron link

Lit.: Bárdos, Garam, *Das awarenzeitliche Gräberfeld*, 95, pl. 84.11; Rácz, *Die Goldschmiedegräber*, 197–198.

2.42. Zamárdi-Rétiföldek-dűlő
Tomb 825 – inhumation, a child's tomb
implements: 1. knife, four clay spindle whorls
2. file (?)
vessels: bronze stripe of a wooden bucket
other items: iron stripe, iron link

Lit.: Bárdos, Garam, *Das awarenzeitliche Gräberfeld*, 95, pl. 84.11; Rácz, *Die Goldschmiedegräber*, 197.

2.43. Zamárdi-Rétiföldek-dűlő
Tomb 1623 – inhumation, a man's tomb
implements: three bronze dies for pressing belt and harness plates with ornamentation of the Martynivka type and half-moon shaped plate with floral ornamentation.
weapons: bag for arrowheads

Lit.: Rácz, *Die Goldschmiedegräber*, 198.

2.44. Zamárdi-Rétiföldek-dűlő
Tomb 1999 – inhumation
implements: 1. flintstone
2. bronze die for pressing shield-shaped belt plates, raw material (?) – bronze bar and chain link

Lit.: Rácz, *Die Goldschmiedegräber*, 198.

2.45. Zselickislak (Somogy co.), Hungary
Balatoni Múzeum, Keszthely
Inhumation? tomb, a woman's? tomb
costume and jewelry items: hair rings made of silver wire, necklace and bronze globular pendant, bronze finger ring
implements: bronze die for pressing/casting round belt plates or clips, decorated with sprouts and flanked by a pearl frame.

Lit.: Rácz, *Die Goldschmiedegräber*, 198–199.

Bibliography

Primary Sources

Codex Iustinianus, ed. by Paul Krüger, *Corpus Iuris Civilis*, 2, Berlin: Weidmann, 1892.

Eginhard, *The Life of Charlemagne*, edited and translated by Arthur James Grant. In Parentheses Publications. Medieval Latin Series. (Cambridge/Ontario 1999).

Jordanes, *Getica*, ed. by Theodor Mommsen. Berlin: Weidmann, 1882; translated by Charles C. Mierow. Princeton: Princeton University Press, 1915.

Menander the Guardsman, *History*, edited and translated by Roger C. Blockley. Liverpool: F. Cairns, 1985.

Priscus of Panion, in *The Fragmentary Classicising Historians of the Late Roman Empire. Eunapius, Olympiodorus, Priscus and Malchus*, ed. Roger C. Blockely, vol. 2. Liverpool: F. Cairns, 1983.

Procopius of Caesarea, *Wars*, ed. Jakob Haury. 5 vols. (Cambridge: Harvard University Press, 1914–1928); translated by H. B. Dewing and Anthony Kaldellis. Indianapolis/ Cambridge: Hackett, 2014.

Strategikon, ed. Sophia Gyphtopoulou. Thessaloniki: Stamoulis, 2016; translated by George T. Dennis. Philadelphia: University of Pennsylvania Press, 1984.

Themistius, *Orations*, eds. Heinrich Schenkl and Glanville Downey. Leipzig: Teubner, 1965–1974.

Theophylact Simocatta, *History*, eds. Carl de Boor and Peter Wirth. Stuttgart: B. G. Teubner, 1972.

Scientific Literature

Ajbabin, Aleksandr I. "Khronologiia mogil'nikov Kryma pozdnerimskogo i rannesred-nekovogo vremeni [Chronology of the tombs from Crimea from the Late Roman and Early Middle Ages]." *Materialy po arheologii i etnografii Tavrii* 1 (1990): 5–86.

Ajbabin, Aleksandr I. "La fabrication des garnitures de ceintures et des fibules à Chersonèse, au Bosphore Cimmérien et dans la Gothie de Crimée aux VIe - VIIIe siècles." In *Outils d' orfèvres des temps anciens*, ed. Christiane Eulère, 163–70. Saint-Germain-en-Laye: Société des Amis du Musée des Antiquités Nationales et du Château de Saint-Germain-en-Laye, 1993.

Alföldi, Andreas. *Der Untergang der Römerherrschaft in Pannonien*. Berlin/Leipzig: W. de Gruyter & Co., 1926.

Amrein, Heidi, Binder, Eugen. "Mit Hammer und Zange an Esse und Amboss: Metallgewinnung und Schmiedekunst im frühen Mittelalter." In *Die Alamannen*, ed. Karlheinz Fuchs, 359–370. Stuttgart: Theiss, 1997.

Andronic, Mugur. "Evoluţia habitatului uman în bazinul hidrografic Soloneţ din paleolitic până la sfârşitul secolului al XVIII-lea [The evolution of the human habitat in the Soloneţ river basin from the Paleolithic to the end of the 18th century]." *Suceava. Anuarul Muzeului Naţional al Bucovinei* 22–23 (1995–1996) (1997): 13–186.

Angelova, Stefka, Penčev, Vladimir. "Un trésor d'argent de Silistra." *Archaeologiia* 31, no. 2 (1990): 38–43.

Anghel, Gheorghe, Blăjan, Mihai. "Săpăturile arheologice de la Sânmiclăuş (com Şona, jud. Alba-1974) [The archaeological excavations from Sânmiclăuş (comm. Şona, Alba county-1974)]." *Apulum* 15 (1977): 283–307.

Anghel, Gheorghe, Blăjan, Mihai. "Săpăturile arheologice de la Sînmiclăuş-'Gruişor', comuna Şona, judeţul Alba, 1978 [The archaeological excavations from Sînmiclăuş-'Gruişor', Şona commune, Alba county, 1978]." *Materiale şi Cercetări Arheologice* 13 (1979): 281–284.

Arrhenius, Birgit. "Ein Goldschmiedgrab von Hovgardsberg Vendel, Uppland, Schweden." *Frühmittelalterliche Studien* 13 (1979): 393–414.

Arrhenius, Birgit. "Einige christliche Paraphrasen aus dem 6. Jahrhundert." In *Zum Problem der Deutung frühmittelalterlicher Bildinhalte. Akten des 1. Internationalen Kolloquiums in Marburg a. d. Lahn, 15. bis 19. Februar 1983*, ed. Helmuth Roth, 129–151. Sigmaringen: Jan Thorbecke Verlag, 1986.

Aufleger, Michaela. "Metallarbeiten und Metallverarbeitung." In *Die Franken wegbereiter Europas. Vor 1500 Jahren: König Chlodwig und seine Erben [Ausstellungskatalog]*, 618–628. Mainz: Verlag Philipp von Zabern, 1996.

Aulich, Viktor Vitol'dovič. *Zimnivs'ke gorodishche – slov'jans'ka pam'jatka VI–VII st. n. e. v. Zachidnij Volynii* [Zimne settlement – Slavic monument 6th–7th AD in the Volyn region], Kiev: Naukova dumka, 1972.

Awaren in Europa. Schätze eines asiatisches Reitervolkes 6.–8. Jh. Ausstellungskatalog, ed. Walter Meier-Arendt, Frankfurt am Main, 1985.

Baldini Lippolis, Isabella. *L'oreficeria nell'impero di Constantinopoli tra IV e VII secolo.* Bari: Edipuglia, 1999.

Bálint, Csanád. *Die Archäologie der Steppe*, ed. Falko Daim, Vienna/Cologne: Böhlau Verlag, 1989.

Bálint, Csanád. "Kontakte zwischen Iran, Byzanz und der Steppe. Das Grab von Üc Tepe (Sow. Azerbajdzan) und der beschlagverzierten Gürtel im 6. und 7. Jahrhundert." In *Awarenforschungen. Archaeologia Austriaca Monographien 1 – Studien zur Archäologie der Awaren* 4, ed. Falko Daim, 309–496. Vienna: Institut für Ur- und Frühgeschichte der Universität Wien, 1992.

Bálint, Csanád. "Über den Schatz von Nagyszentmiklós-kurze Übersicht." In *Gold der Awaren. Der Goldschatz von Nagyszentmiklós*, ed. Tibor Kovács and Éva Garam, 57–80. Budapest: Magyar Nemzeti Múzeum. Helikon kiadó, 2002.

Balogh, Csilla. "Martinovka-Típusú övgarnitúra kecelről. A Kárpát-medencei maszkos veretek tipokronológiája [Martinovka-Type belt set from Kecel. Tipochronology of the Carpathian Basin mask fittings]." *A Móra Ferenc Múzeum Évkönyve, Studia Archaeologica* 10 (2004): 241–303.

Balogh, Csilla. "A Felgyő, Ürmös-tanyai avar kori temető [The Avar Cemetery at Felgyő, Ürmös-tanya]." In Csilla Balogh, Klára P. Fischl, *Felgyő, Ürmös-tanya. Bronzkori és avar kori leletek László Gyula felgyői ásatásának*, 185–381. Szeged: Móra Ferenc Múzeum, 2010.

Balogh, Csilla. "Az avar kori gúlacsüngős fülbevalók [The Avar period pyramidal earrings pendants]." *Kuny Domokos Múzeum Közleményei* 20 (2014): 91–157.

Balogh, Csilla. "Karpat havzasi'nda bir avar yay ustasinin mezar kalintilari eski türklerde bileşik (kompozit) yay yapimina ilişkin arkeolojik bulgular [The Grave of an Avar Bowyer in the Carpathian Basin]." *Art Sanat* 6 (2016): 109–120.

Balogh, Csilla. "Orta Tisa Bölgesi'nde Doğu Avrupa Bozkır Kökenli Göçebe Bir Topluluğa Ait Mezarlık "Makó, Mikócsa-Halom, Macaristan" [A cemetery belonging to a nomad community of Eastern Europe Steppe origin in the Middle Tisza Region "Makó, Mikócsa-Halom, Hungary"]." *Art Sanat* 7 (2017): 53–70.

Bárdos, Edith, Garam, Éva. *Das awarenzeitliche Gräberfeld in Zamárdi-Rétiföldek*, vol. 1. (Monumenta Avarorum) 9. Budapest: Magyar Nemzeti Múzeum, 2009.

Barnea, Alexandru. "Voies de communication au Bas-Danube aux IVe - VIe s. ap. J. C." *Études Byzantines et post-byzantines* 3 (1997): 29–42.

Barnea, Ion et al. *Tropaeum Traiani. Cetatea* [Tropaeum Traiani. Fortress]. vol. 1, Bucharest: Editura Academiei Republicii Socialiste România, 1979.

Barnea, Alexandru, Bercea, Sorin. "Neuf bronzes paléochrétiens." In *The Antique Bronzes: Typology, Chronology, Authenticity. The Acta of the 16th International Congress of Antiqua Bronzes Bucharest May 26th–31st 2003*, ed. Crişan Muşeţeanu, 43–47. Bucharest: Editura Cetatea de Scaun, 2004.

Băcueţ-Crişan, Dan. "Despre cuptorul de olar din perioada medievală timpurie descoperit la Sighişoara "Dealul Viilor" -sector Necropolă (jud. Mureş). Observaţii privind tehnica de modelare a ceramicii şi cronologia. Comparaţii cu olăria medievală timpurie modelată la roata rapidă din spaţiul nord-vestic al României [About the early medieval pottery kiln discovered in Sighişoara "Dealul Viilor"- Necropolă Sector (Mureş County). Observations on chronology and the pottery modelling technology. Comparisons with the early medieval pottery made on the fast turning potters' wheel in the north-western part of Romania]." In *Locuirea medievală timpurie din*

Transilvania și vecinătăți, Orbis mediaevalis 1, eds. Florin Mărginean, Ioan Stanciu, Dan Băcueț-Crișan, 189–209. Cluj-Napoca: Editura Mega, 2017.

Bârzu, Ligia. *Continuitatea populației autohtone în Transilvania în secolele IV–V (Cimitirul 1 de la Bratei)* [Continuity of the native population in Transylvania in the 4th–5th centuries (Cemetery 1 from Bratei)]. Bucharest: Editura Academiei Republicii Socialiste România, 1973.

Bârzu, Ligia. *Continuitatea creației materiale și spirituale a poporului român pe teritoriul fostei Dacii* [Continuity of the material and spiritual creation of the Romanian people in the former Dacian territory]. Bucharest: Editura Academiei Republicii Socialiste România, 1979.

Bârzu, Ligia. *La continuité de la création matérielle et spirituelle du peuple roumain sur le territoire de l'ancienne Dacie*. Bucharest: Editura Academiei Republicii Socialiste România, 1980.

Bârzu, Ligia. "Gepidische Funde von Bratei." *Dacia Nouvelle Série* 36 (1992): 211–214.

Bârzu, Ligia. "La station nº 1 de Bratei, dép. De Sibiu (IVe - VIIe siècles)." *Dacia Nouvelle Série* 38–39 (1994–1995): 239–295.

Bârzu, Ligia. *Ein gepidisches Denkmal aus Siebenbürgen. Das Gräberfeld Nr. 3 von Bratei*, ed. Radu Harhoiu, with contributions from Eugenia Zaharia and Radu Harhoiu (Archaeologia Romanica) 4. Cluj-Napoca: Editura Accent, 2010.

Bejan, Adrian. "Un atelier metalurgic din sec. VI e.n. de la Drobeta Turnu Severin [A metallurgical workshop from the 6th century AD from Drobeta Turnu Severin]." *Acta Musei Napocensis* 13 (1976): 257–268.

Beninger, Eduard. "Der Langobardenfriedhof von Poysdorf, Niederösterreich." *Archaeologia Austriaca* 40 (1966): 167–187.

Bobi, Victor. "Contribuții la repertoriul arheologic al județului Vrancea (Dovezi ale continuității de locuire, sec. II–VII e.n.) [Contributions to the archaeological repertoire of Vrancea county (Proofs of continuity of habitation, 2nd–7th centuries AD)]." *Vrancea. Studii și comunicări* 4 (1981): 97–140.

Boghian, Dumitru. "Un moule en pierre des VIe - VIIe siècles découvert á Cucuteni (Dép. de Iași)." *Studia Antiqua et Archaeologica* 6 (1999): 115–124.

Böhner, Kurt. "Ein fränkisches Goldschmiedegrab aus dem Neuwieder Becken." *Reinische Vorzeit in Wort und Bild* 2 (1939): 113–119.

Bóna, István. "Avar lovassír Iváncsáról [Grave of an Avar Horseman at Iváncsa]." *Archaeologiai Értesitő* 97 (1970): 243–263.

Bóna, István. "Ein Vierteljahrhundert der Völkerwanderungszeitforschung in Ungarn." *Acta Archaeologica Academiae Scientiarum Hungaricae* (1971): 265–336.

Bóna, István. *Der Anbruch des Mittelalters. Gepiden und Longobarden im Karpatenbekken*. Budapest: Corvina Verlag, 1976.

Bóna, István. "Gepiden in Siebenbürgen-Gepiden an der Theiss." *Acta Archaeologica Academiae Scientiarum Hungaricae* 31 (1979): 9–50.

Bóna, István. "Die Geschichte der Awaren im Lichte der Archäologischen Quellen." In *Popoli delle Steppe: Unni, Avari, Ungari*, vol. 2, Settimane di studio del Centro italiano di studi sull'alto medievo 35. Spoleto: Presso la Sede del Centro, 1988: 437–463.

Bóna, István. "Langobard fibulák ékszerek. Avar kori 2. Stilus. Avar-langobard kapcsolatok [Langobard fibulae jewelry. Avar period 2. Style. Avar-langobard contacts]." In *Hunok-Gepidák-Langobardok*, ed. István Bóna, 135–141, 151–153, 153–155. Szeged: Balassi Kiadó, 1993.

Bonfante, Giuliano. *Studii Române* [Romanian Studies]. translated by Mariana Adameşteanu. Bucharest: Saeculum I. O., 2001.

Brather, Sebastian. *Ethnische Interpretationen in der frühgeschichtlichen Archäologie. Geschichte, Grundlagen und Alternativen.* Berlin/New York: Walter de Gruyter, 2004.

Brepohl, Erhard. *Theophilus Presbyter und die mittelalterliche Goldschmiedekunst.* Vienna/Cologne/Graz: Böhlaus Verlag, 1987.

Bucureşti I. Rezultatele săpăturilor arheologice şi ale cercetărilor istorice din anul 1953 [Bucharest I. The results of the archeological excavations and of the historical research from the year 1953]. Bucharest: Editura Academia Republicii Populare Romîne, 1954.

Bühler, Birgit. "Untersuchungen zu Guß, Oberflächenbearbeitung und Vergoldung an frühmittelalterlichen Bunt- und Edelmetallgegenständen." *Archaeologia Austriaca* 82–83 (1998–1999): 429–478.

Butnariu, Viorel M. "Răspândirea monedelor bizantine din secolele VI–VII în teritoriile carpato-dunărene [The spread of Byzantine coins from the 6th–7th centuries in the Carpathian-Danube territories]." *Buletinul Societăţii Numismatice Române* 78–79 (1983–1985) (1986): 199–235.

Butoi, Mihai. "Un tezaur de monede şi obiecte de podoabă din secolul al VII-lea descoperit în comuna Priseaca-Slatina [A treasure of coins and jewelry from the 7th century discovered in the village of Priseaca-Slatina]." *Studii şi comunicări. Istorie-Ştiinţele Naturii – Muzeul din Piteşti* 1 (1968): 97–104.

Canache, Adrian, Curta, Florin. "Depozite de unelte şi arme medievale timpurii de pe teritoriul României [Deposits of early medieval tools and weapons on the territory of Romania]." *Mousaios* 4, no. 1 (1994): 179–221.

Capelle, Torsten, Vierck, Hayo. "Modeln der Merowinger- und Wikingerzeit." *Frühmittelalterliche Studien* 5 (1971): 42–100.

Capelle, Torsten. *Das Gräberfeld Beckum I.* Münster-Westfalen: Aschendorff, 1979.

Capelle, Torsten. *Die Miniaturkette von Szilágysomlyó (Şimleul Silvaniei).* (Universitätsforschungen zur prähistorischen Archäologie) 22. Bonn: Habelt, 1994.

von Carnap-Bornheim, Claus. "The Social Position of the Germanic Goldsmith A.D. 0–500." In *Roman Gold and the Development of the Early Germanic Kingdom. KVHAA Konferenser 51*, ed. Bente Magnus, 263–278. Stockholm: Almqvist & Wiksell International, 2001.

Castelnuovo, Enrico. "Artistul [The Artist]." In *Omul medieval*, coordinated by Jacques Le Goff, translated into Romanian by Ingrid Ilinca and Dragoş Cojocaru, 193–222. Iaşi: Editura Polirom, 1999.

Căpitanu, Viorel. "Tezaurul de monede bizantine descoperit la Horgeşti (jud. Bacău) [The Byzantine coins hoard discovered in Horgeşti (Bacău county)]." Carpica 4 (1971): 253–269.

Chidioşan, Nicolae, Nánássy, Zoltán. "Un mormânt din perioada prefeudală descoperit la Săcuieni [A tomb from the pre-feudal period discovered in Săcuieni]." *Acta Musei Napocensis* 5 (1968): 517–520.

Chirică, Vasile, Tanasachi, Marcel. *Repertoriul arheologic al Judeţului Iaşi* [The archaeological repertoire of Iaşi County]. 2 vols., Iaşi: Institutul de Istorie şi Arheologie "A. D. Xenopol", 1985.

Čilinska, Zlata. "Dve pohrebiská z 8.–9. storočia v Komárne [Two necropolises from the 8th–9th centuries in Komárno]." *Slovenská Archeologia* 30, no. 2 (1982): 347–393.

Ciugudean, Horia, Moga, Vasile, Ciobanu, Radu, Drîmbărean, Matei, Dragotă, Aurel, Gligor, Adrian, Inel, Constantin, Cauuet, Béatrice, Rico, Christian, Ancel, Bruno. "Roşia Montană, jud. Alba (Alburnus Maior) [Roşia Montană, Alba County (Alburnus Maior)]." In *Cronica cercetărilor arheologice din România (campania 2000)*, eds. Mircea Victor Angelescu, Corina Borş and Irina Oberländer-Târnoveanu, 209–213. Bucharest: cIMeC Institutul de Memorie Culturală, 2001.

Ciupercă, Bogdan, Măgureanu, Andrei. "Unele observaţii asupra problemei tiparelor din secolele V–VII descoperite în spaţiul extra-carpatic [Regarding the problem of the 6th–7th century mould finds in the extra-Carpathian area]." *Buletinul Muzeului Judeţean Teleorman. Seria Arheologie* 1 (2009): 149–157.

Coche de la Ferté, Etienne. *L'antiquité chrétienne au Musée du Louvre*. Paris: Éditions de l'Oeil, 1958.

Coman, Ghenuţă. "Contribuţii la cunoaşterea fondului etnic al civilizaţiei secolelor V–XII în jumătatea sudică a Moldovei [Contributions to the knowledge of the ethnic background of the civilization of the 5th–12th centuries in the southern half of Moldavia]." *Carpica* 11 (1979): 178–192.

Comşa, Maria. "Quelques données concernant les rapports des territoires nord-danubiens avec Byzance aux VIe - VIIIe siècles (Pendants d'oreille en forme d'étoile)." *Revue des Études Sud-Est Européennes* 9, no. 3 (1971): 377–390.

Comşa, Maria. "Unele consideraţii cu privire la originea şi apartenenţa etnică a complexelor cu fibule 'digitate' de tip Gâmbaş-Coşoveni [Some considerations regarding the origin and ethnicity of the complexes with "bow" fibulae of the Gâmbaş-Coşoveni type]." *Apulum* 11 (1973): 259–272.

Comşa, Maria. "Socio-economic organization of the Daco-Romanic and Slav populations on the Lower Danube during the 6th–8th centuries." In *Relations between the autochthonous population and the migratory populations on the territory of Romania*, eds. Miron Constantinescu, Ştefan Pascu and Petre Diaconu, 171–200. Bucharest: Editura Academiei Republicii Socialiste România, 1975.

Comşa, Maria. "Bemerkungen über die Beziehungen zwischen den Awaren und Slawen im 6.–7. Jahrhundert." In *Interaktionen der mitteleuropäischen Slawen und anderen Ethnika im 6.–10. Jahrhundert. Symposium Nove Vozokany 3.–7. Oktober 1983*, ed. Bohuslav Chropovský, 63–74. Nitra, 1984.

Constantinescu, Eugen-Marius. *Memoria pământului dintre Carpaţi şi Dunăre. Nord-estul Munteniei şi sud-vestul Moldovei în veacurile IV–XI d. Hr.* [The memory of the land between the Carpathians and Danube. Northeast of Muntenia and south-west of Moldavia in the 4th–11th centuries AD]. Bucharest: Editura Fiat Lux, 1999.

Constantiniu, Margareta. "Aşezarea autohtonă prefeudală de la Băneasa (La Stejar) [The Pre-feudal autochthonous settlement from Băneasa (La Stejar)]." *Cercetări Arheologice în Bucureşti* 2 (1965): 77–98.

Constantiniu, Margareta. "Săpăturile de la Străuleşti-Măicăneşti. Aşezarea prefeudală I. Aşezarea prefeudală II [The excavations from Străuleşti-Măicăneşti. Pre-feudal settlement I. Pre-feudal settlement II]." *Cercetări Arheologice în Bucureşti* 2 (1965): 140–189.

Constantiniu, Margareta. "Elemente romano-bizantine în cultura materială a populaţiei autohtone din partea centrală a Munteniei în secolele VI–VII e.n. [Romano-Byzantine elements in the material culture of the native population from the central part of Muntenia in the 6th–7th centuries AD]." *Studii şi Cercetări de Istorie Veche* 17, no. 4 (1966): 665–678.

Corman, Igor. *Contribuţii la istoria spaţiului pruto-nistrian în epoca evului mediu timpuriu (sec. V–VII d. Chr.)* [Contributions to the history of the Pruto-Dniester area in the early Middle Ages (5th–7th century AD)]. Chişinău: Cartdidact, 1998.

Covacef, Zizi. "Accesorii vestimentare de toaletă şi podoabe descoperite în sectorul estic al cetăţii Capidava [Garment accessories and jewelry discovered in the eastern sector of the city of Capidava]." *Pontica* 28–29 (1995–1996): 95–120.

Crăciun, Cristina. "Roşia Montană, jud. Alba (Alburnus Maior) [Roşia Montană, Alba County (Alburnus Maior)]." In *Cronica cercetărilor arheologice din România (campania 2000)*, eds. Mircea Victor Angelescu, Corina Borş and Irina Oberländer-Târnoveanu, 213–214. Bucharest: cIMeC Institutul de Memorie Culturală, 2001.

Csallány, Dezső. *A Kunszentmártoni avarkori ötvösir (Goldschmiedgrab aus der Awarenzeit von Kunszentmárton Ungarn)* [The grave of a goldsmith from the avars time at Kunszentmárton]. Szentes, 1933.

Csallány, Dezső. "Az Átokháza-bilisicsi avarkori sírleletek [The Avar Age Tombs from Bilisics-Átokháza]." *A Móra Ferenc Múzeum Évkönyve* (1957): 109–132.

Curta, Florin. "On the dating of the 'Veţel-Coşoveni' group of curved fibulae." *Ephemeris Napocensis* 4 (1994): 233–265.

Curta, Florin. "Invasion or inflation? Sixth- to seventh-century Byzantine coin hoards in Eastern and Southeastern Europe." *Annali dell'Istituto Italiano di Numismatica* 43 (1996): 65–224.

Curta, Florin. "Blacksmiths, Warriors and Tournaments of Value: Dating and Interpreting Early Medieval Hoards of Iron Implements in Eastern Europe." *Ephemeris Napocensis* 7 (1997): 211–268.

Curta, Florin. *The Making of the Slavs. History and Archaeology of the Lower Danube Region, c. 500–700*. Cambridge: Cambridge University Press, 2001.

Curta, Florin. "Limes and Cross: the Religious Dimension of the Sixth-Century Danube Frontier of the early Byzantine Empire." *Starinar* 51 (2001): 45–70.

Curta, Florin. "Consideraţii privind conceptul de caracter etnic (etnicitate) în arheologia contemporană [Some remarks on the concept of ethnicity in contemporary archaeology]." *Arheologia Medievală* 4 (2002): 5–26.

Curta, Florin. "Werner's class I H of 'Slavic' bow fibulae revisited." *Archaeologia Bulgarica* 8, no. 1 (2004): 59–78.

Curta, Florin. "Byzantium in Dark-Age Greece (the numismatic evidence in its Balkan context)." *Byzantine and Modern Greek Studies* 29, no. 2 (2005): 113–146.

Curta, Florin. "Female Dress and 'Slavic' Bow Fibulae in Greece." *Hesperia* 74 (2005): 101–146.

Curta, Florin. "Before Cyril and Methodius: Christianity and Barbarians beyond the Sixth- and Seventh-Century Danube Frontier." In *East Central and Eastern Europe in the Early Middle Age*, ed. Florin Curta, 181–219. Ann Arbor: University of Michigan Press, 2005.

Curta, Florin. "*Slavic* Bow Fibulae? Werner's class I D revisited." *Acta Archaeologica Hungarica* 57 (2006): 423–474.

Curta, Florin. "A contribution to the study of bow fibulae of Werner's class I G." *Arheologia Moldovei* 29 (2006): 93–124.

Curta, Florin. "Some remarks on bow fibulae of Werner's class I C." *Slavia Antiqua* 49 (2008): 45–98.

Curta, Florin. "The earliest Avar-Age Stirrups, or "The Stirrup Controversy" Revisited." In *The Other Europe in the Middle Ages. Avars, Bulgars, Khazars, and Cumans. East Central and Eastern Europe in the Middle Ages 450–450*, vol. 2, ed. Florin Curta, 297–325. Leiden-Boston: Brill, 2008.

Curta, Florin. "Neither Gothic, nor Slavic: bow fibulae of Werner's class II B." *Archaeologia Austriaca* 93 (2009): 45–77.

Curta, Florin. "Werner's Class I C: Erratum Corrigendum Cum Commentars." *Ephemeris Napocensis* XXI (2011): 63–110.

Curta, Florin. "New remarks on Christianity beyond the 6th and early 7th century frontier of the Roman Empire." In *Keszthely-Fenékpuszta im Kontext spätantiker Kontinuitätsforschung zwischen Noricum und Moesia*, ed. Orsolya Heinrich-Tamáska, 303–321. Budapest/Leipzig/Keszthely/Rahden: Verlag Marie Leidorf, 2011.

Curta, Florin. "'Slavic' Bow Fibulae: Twenty Years of Research." *Bericht der Römisch-Germanischen Komission* 93 (2012): 1–108.

Curta, Florin. "Ethnic Identity and Archaeology." In *Encyclopedia of Global Archaeology*, ed. Claire Smith, 2507–2514. New York: Springer Reference, 2014.

Curta, Florin. "Amphorae and seals: the "sub-Byzantine" Avars and the *quaestura exercitus*." In *Zwischen Byzanz und der Steppe. Archäologische und historische Studien. Festschrift für Csanád Bálint zum 70. Geburtstag*, eds. Ádám Bollók, Gergely Csiky and Tivadar Vida, 307–334. Budapest: Institute of Archaeology, Research Centre for the Humanities, Hungarian Academy of Sciences, 2016.

Curta, Florin. "Coins, Forts and Commercial Exchanges in the Sixth and Early Seventh-Century Balkans." *Oxford Journal of Archaeology* 36 (2017): 439–454.

Curta, Florin. "Social identity on the platter. Clay pans in sixth to seventh century ceramic assemblages." In *Entangled Identities and Otherness in Late Antique and Early Medieval Europe*, eds. Jorge López Quiroga, Michel Kazanski and Vujadin Ivanišević, 132–177. Oxford: BAR Publishing, 2017.

Curta, Florin. "Remarks on the economic and funerary uses of imitations of Early Byzantine coins." *Byzantion* 89 (2019): 177–208.

Curta, Florin, Gândilă, Andrei. "Too Much Typology, Too Little History: A Critical Approach to the Classification and Interpretation of Cast Fibulae with Bent Stem." *Archaeologia Bulgarica* 10, no. 3 (2011): 51–81.

Curta, Florin, Gândilă, Andrei. "Hoards and hoarding patterns in the early Byzantine Balkans." *Dumbarton Oaks Papers* 65–66 (2011–2012): 45–111.

Curta, Florin, Gândilă, Andrei. "Sixth-century fibulae with bent stem." *Peuce* 11 (2013): 101–176.

Daim, Falko, Mehofer, Mathias, Tobias, Bendeguz. "Die langobardischen Schmiedegräber aus Poysdorf und Brno. Fragen, Methoden, erste Ergebnisse." In *Die Langobarden. Herrschaft und Identität, Forschungen zur Geschichte des Mittelalters*, ed. Falko Daim and Peter Erhart, 201–224. Wien: Verlag der Österreichischen Akademie der Wissenschaften, 2005.

Damian, Paul et al. "Roșia Montană, jud. Alba (Alburnus Maior) [Roșia Montană, Alba County (Alburnus Maior)]." In *Cronica cercetărilor arheologice din România (campania 2003)*, eds. Mircea Victor Angelescu, Irina Oberländer-Târnoveanu, Florela

Vasilescu, Carmen Bem, Paula Jercan and Irina Nicolae, 262–280. Bucharest: cIMeC Institutul de Memorie Culturală, 2004.

Damian, Paul et al. "Roşia Montană, jud. Alba (Alburnus Maior) [Roşia Montană, Alba County (Alburnus Maior)]." In *Cronica cercetărilor arheologice din România (campania 2004)*, eds. Mircea Victor Angelescu, Irina Oberländer-Târnoveanu and Florela Vasilescu, 297–316. Bucharest: cIMeC Institutul de Memorie Culturală, 2005.

Damian, Paul et al. "Roșia Montană, jud. Alba (Alburnus Maior) [Roșia Montană, Alba County (Alburnus Maior)]." In *Cronica cercetărilor arheologice din România (campania 2005)*, eds. Mircea Victor Angelescu and Florela Vasilescu, 292–301. Bucharest: cIMeC Institutul de Memorie Culturală, 2006.

Daskalov, Metodi, Dimitrov, Dimitar J. "On a Production in the 6th–7th Centuries in the Bulgarian Lands." *Arheologiia* 42, no. 3–4 (2001): 69–74.

Dănilă, Nicolae. "Consideraţii asupra noilor materiale arheologice paleocreştine din Transilvania [Considerations on the new paleo-Christian archaeological materials from Transylvania]." *Biserica Ortodoxă Română* 100, no. 7–8 (1982): 731–742.

Dănilă, Nicolae. "Tipare pentru turnat cruci, din secolele IV–VI, descoperite pe teritoriul României [Patterns for the casting of crosses, from the 4th–6th centuries, discovered on the territory of Romania]." *Biserica Ortodoxă Română* 101, no. 7–8 (1983): 557–561.

Decaens, Jean et al. *Un nouveau cimetière du haut moyen âge en Normandie: Hérouvillette*. Caen: Centre de Recherches Archéologiques Médiévales, 1971.

Dejan, Monica. "Tezaurul cu monede bizantine de la Udeşti, jud. Suceava [The Byzantine coin hoard from Udeşti, Suceava county]." In *Aurul şi argintul antic al României. Catalog de expoziţie*, ed. Rodica Oanţă-Marghitu, 660–661. Bucharest: Muzeul Naţional de Istorie a României, 2013.

Dejan, Monica. *Elemente răsăritene în ţinuturile extracarpatice (secolele VI–X)* [Eastern elements in the extra-Carpathian lands (6th–10th centuries)]. Suceava: Editura Karl A. Romstorfer, 2015.

Dengate, James A. "Coin hoards from the Gymnasium area at Corinth." *Hesperia* 50 (1981): 153–175.

Dergacev, Valentin, Larina, Olga, Postică, Gheorghe. "Raskopki 1980 g. na mnogoslojnom poselenii Dančeny I [Excavations of 1980 at the multilayer settlement Dančeny I]." *Archeologičeskie issledovanija v Moldavii* 1979–1980 (1983): 112–136.

Diaconu, Petre. "Problemele necropolelor de la Dunărea de Jos din sec. VI–IX în viziunea lui Uwe Fiedler [The problems of the necropolis of the Lower Danube from the 6th–9th centuries in the vision of Uwe Fiedler]." In *Recenzii şi discuţii arheologice*, by Petre Diaconu, vol. 1, 121–135. Călăraşi: S. C. Caro Trading '94 S.R.L., 1994.

Die Welt von Byzanz. Europas östliches Erbe. Glanz, Krisen und Fortleben einer tausendjährigen Kultur, (Schriftenreihe der Archäologischen Staatssammlung) 4, ed. Ludwig Wamser, Stuttgart: Theiss Verlag, 2004.

Distelberger, Anton. *Österreichs Awarinnen. Frauen aus Gräbern des 7. und 8. Jahrhunderts*. St. Pölten: Niederösterreichischer Institut für Landeskunde, 2004.

Dobos, Alpár. "Az erdélyi soros temetők lovastemetkezései [The horse burials of the row-grave cemeteries from Transylvania]." In *Erdély és kapcsolatai a kora népvándorlás korában*, ed. Zsolt Körösfői, 377–403. Székelykeresztúr: Molnár István Múzeum, 2010–2011.

Dolinescu-Ferche, Suzana. *Aşezări din secolele III şi VI e. n. în sud-vestul Munteniei. Cercetările de la Dulceanca (jud. Teleorman)* [Settlements from the 3rd and 6th centuries AD in the southwest of Muntenia. Researches from Dulceanca (Teleorman county)]. Bucharest: Editura Academiei Republicii Socialiste România, 1974.

Dolinescu-Ferche, Suzana. "Ciurel, habitat des VIe - VIIe siècles de notre ère." *Dacia Nouvelle Série* 23 (1979): 179–230.

Dolinescu-Ferche, Suzana, Constantiniu, Margareta. "Un établissement du VIe siècle a Bucarest. Decouvertes de la rue Soldat Ghivan N." *Dacia Nouvelle Série* 25 (1981): 289–330.

Dolinescu-Ferche, Suzana. "Contributions archéologique sur la continuité daco-romaine. Dulceanca, deuxiéme habitat de VIe siècle de n.è." *Dacia Nouvelle Série* 30, no. 1–2 (1986): 121–154.

Dolinescu-Ferche, Suzana. "Habitats des VIe et VIIe siècle de notre ère à Dulceanca IV." *Dacia Nouvelle Série* 36 (1992): 125–178.

Dömötör, László. "Ujabb lemezsajtoló bronzmintár Fónlakról [Newer bronze dies from Fónlak]." *Archaeologiai Ért*esitő 21 (1901): 62–66.

Dörner, Egon. "Mormânt din epoca avară la Sânpetru German [Grave from the Avar epoch in Sânpetru German]." *Studii şi Cercetări de Istorie Veche* 9, no. 2 (1962): 423–433.

Două milenii de creştinism/Deux millénaires de christianisme (Exhibition catalog), ed. Mircea Mamalaucă. Bârlad: Muzeul Vasile Pârvan, 2000.

Driehaus, Jürgen. "Zum Problem merowingerzeitlicher Goldschmiede." *Nachrichten der Akademie der Wissenschaften in Göttingen phil.-hist. Klasse* 7 (1972): 389–406.

Eliade, Mircea. *Făurari şi alchimişti* [The Forge and the Crucible]. Bucharest: Humanitas, 1996.

Entwistle, Chris. "The Early Byzantine weights from Kunszentmárton, Hungary." *Acta Archaeologica Academiae Scientiarum Hungaricae* 67 (2016): 287–300.

Fettich, Nándor. *Das awarenzeitliche Kunstgewerbe in Ungarn*, (Archaeologia Hungarica) 1. Budapest, 1926.

Fettich, Nándor. "Symbolischer Gürtel aus der Awarenzeit (Fund von Bilisics)." *A Móra Ferenc Múzeum Évkönyve* 1 (1963): 61–88.

Fiedler, Uwe. *Studien zu Gräberfeldern des 6. bis 9. Jahrhunderts an der unteren Donau*. Bonn: Rudolf Habelt, 1992.

Fiedler, Uwe. "Die Gürtelbesatzstücke von Akalan, ihre Funktion und kulturelle Stellung." *Izvestiia na Arkheologičeskiia Institut* 38 (1994): 31–47.

Fülöp, Gyula. "Die awarenzeitliche Fürstenfunde von Igar." *Acta Archaeologica Academiae Scientiarum Hungaricae* 40 (1988): 151–190.

Gaiu, Corneliu. "Așezarea prefeudală de la Șirioara, com. Șieu-Odorhei, jud. Bistrița Năsăud [Pre-feudal settlement from Șirioara, Șieu-Odorhei commune, Bistrița Năsăud county]." *Marisia* 13–14 (1983–1984): 59–64.

Gaiu, Corneliu. "Le cimetière gépide de Bistrița." *Dacia Nouvelle Série* 36 (1992): 115–124.

Gallina, Zsolt. "Avar kori vaskohászati és települési centrum Zamárdiban [Avar Iron and Metallurgical Center in Zamárdi]." In *A Barbaricum ösvényein ... A 2005-ben Kecskeméten tartott tudományos konferencia előadásai*, eds. Agnés Somogyvári, György V. Székely and Valéria Kulcsár, 179–198. Kecskemét: Bács-Kiskun Megyei Önkormányzat Katona József Múzeum, 2011.

Gallina, Zsolt, Hornok, Péter. "Avar kori vaskohászati centrum Zamárdiban (Magyarország, Somogy megye) [Avar Iron Metallurgical Center in Zamárdi (Hungary, Somogy County)]." In *Bányászati, kohászati és földtani konferencia. Sepsiszentgyörgy, 2006, április 6–9*, 161–170. Cluj-Napoca: Erdélyi Magyar Múszaki Tudományos Társaság, 2006.

Gallina, Zsolt, Hornok, Péter. "Vorbericht über die archäologischeUntersuchung eines awarischen Eisenverhüttungszentrums in der Gemeinde Zamárdi, Komitat Somogy (Ungarn)." In *Arts and Crafts in Medieval Rural Environment: 22nd–29th September 2005*, edited by Jan Klápště and Petr Sommer, 71–81. Turnhout: Brepols, 2007.

Garam, Éva. "The Szebény I–III Cemetery." In *Avar Finds in the Hungarian National Museum. Cemeteries of the Avar Period (567–827) in Hungary* 1, ed. I. Ilona Kovrig, 49–120. Budapest: Akadémiai Kiadó, 1975.

Garam, Éva. *Das awarenzeitliche Gräberfeld von Tiszafüred. Cemeteries of the Avar Period (567–827) in Hungary 3*. Budapest: Akadémiai Kiadó, 1995.

Garam, Éva. *Funde bizantinischer Herkunft in der Awarenzeit vom Ende des 6. Bis zum Ende des 7. Jahrhunderts.* (Monumenta Avarorum) 5. Budapest: Magyar Nemzeti Múzeum, 2001.

Garam, Éva. "Die Verbindung awarenzeitlicher Fürsten- und Gemeinvolk- Grabfunde mit dem Schatz von Nagyszentmiklós." In *Gold der Awaren. Der Goldschatz von Nagyszentmiklós*, eds. Tibor Kovács and Éva Garam, 81–111. Budapest: Magyar Nemzeti Múzeum. Helikon kiadó, 2002.

Gândilă, Andrei. "Face value or bullion value? Early Byzantine coins beyond the Lower Danube border." In *Byzantine Coins in Central Europe Between the 5th and 10th Century. Proceedings from the Conference Organized by the Polish Academy of Arts and Sciences and the Institute of Archaeology of the University of Rzeszów under the Patronage of Union Académique International (Programme No. 57 Moravia Magna), Kraków, 23–26 IV 2007*, ed. Marcin Wołoszyn, 449–471. Cracow: Institute of Archaeology University of Rzeszów, 2009.

Golubeva, Leonilla Anatol'evna. "Zhenshchiny-liteĭshchitsy (k istorii zhenskogo remeslennogo lit'ya u – finno-ugrov) [Female casters (on the history of female craft casting and Finno-Ugric peoples)]." *Sovetskaya Arkheologiya* 4 (1988): 75–88.

Golubeva, Leonilla Anatol'evna. "Devochki-Liteĭshchitsy [Maidens-Foundries]." In *Drevnosti Slavyan i Rusi*, ed. Boris A. Timoshchiuk, 31–34. Moskva: Nauka 1988.

Gömöri, János. "Frühmittelalterliche Eisenschmelzofen von Tarjanpuszta und Nemeskér." *Acta Archaeologica Academiae Scientiarum Hungaricae* 32 (1980): 317–43.

Gömöri, János. "Az avar kori és X–XI. századi vaskohaszát régészeti emlékei Somogy megyében [The archaeometallurgical sites of county Somogy in the Avar and early Árpád-period]." *Somogyi Múzeumok Közleményei* 14 (2000): 163–217.

Gömöri, János. "The legacy of 9th century craftsmen in the Carpathian Basin." In *The History of Handicraft in Hungary*, ed. János Szulovszky, 15–22. Budapest: Hungarian Chamber of Commerce and Industry, 2012.

Hahn, Wolfgang R. O. "Die Fundmünzen des 5.–9. Jahrhunderts in Österreich und den unmittelbar angrenzenden Gebieten." In *Die Geburt Mitteleuropas. Geschichte Österreichs vor seiner Entstehung 378–907*, ed. Herwig Wolfram, 453–464. Vienna: Verlag der österreichischen Akademie der Wissenschaften, 1987.

Hampel, József. "Nemzeti Muzeum régiségosztályának gyarapodása 1880 julius, augusztus, szeptember, oktober, november [Augmentation of the Antiquities Department of the National Museum, July, August, September, October, November, 1880]." *Archaeologiai Értesitő* 14 (1881): 340–350.

Hampel, József. "Emlékek és leletek. Újabb haza leletek az avar uralom korából [Relics and artifacts. Recent findings from the period of the avars's domination]." *Archaeologiai Értesitő* 20 (1900): 97–125.

Hampel, József. *Altertümer des frühen Mittelalters in Ungarn*. 3 vols, Braunschweig: Verlag Friedrich Vieweg und Sohn, 1905.

Harhoiu, Radu. "Romanici și migratori în Dacia transilvană în secolele IV–VII [Romance-speaking population and migrators in the Transylvanian Dacia in the 4th–7th centuries]." *Memoriile secțiilor științifice (seria 4)* 12 (1987): 137–149.

Harhoiu, Radu. "Semnificația tezaurelor din secolul al V-lea de pe teritoriul României [The significance of the hoards from the 5th century on the territory of Romania]." *Studii și Cercetări de Istorie Veche și Arheologie* 43, no. 4 (1992): 425–431.

Harhoiu Radu. *Die frühe Völkerwanderungszeit in Rumänien*. Bucharest: Editura Enciclopedică, 1998.

Harhoiu, Radu. "Quellenlage und Forschungsstand der Frühgeschichte Siebenbürgens im 6.–7. Jahrhundert." *Dacia Nouvelle Série* 43–45 (1999–2001): 97–158.

Harhoiu, Radu, Gora, Daniel. *Aurul migrațiilor. Das Gold der Völkerwanderungszeit.* Bucharest: Editura Enciclopedică, 2000.

Haseloff, Günther. *Die germanische Tierornamentik der Völkerwanderungszeit. Studien zu Salin's Stil I.* Berlin/New York: Walter de Gruyter, 1981.

Haseloff, Günther. "Germanische und östliche Tierornamentik im Donauraum." In *Frankfurter Beiträge zur Mittelalter-Archäologie 2 Schriften des Frankfurter Museum für Vor- und Frühgeschichte* 12, 27–47. Bonn: Schnell & Steiner, 1990.

Hauck, Karl. "Wielands Hort. Die sozialgeschichzliche Stellung des Schmiedes in frühen Bildprogrammen nach und vor dem Religionswechsel." *Antikvarist Arkiv* 64 (1977): 5–31.

Hânceanu, George Dan. "Două piese din secolele VI–VII p. Chr. descoperite la Traian (jud. Neamț) [Two pieces from the 6th–7th centuries AD discovered at Traian (Neamț County)]." *Mousaios* XX (2015): 123–132.

Heinrich-Tamáska, Orsolya. "Megjegyzések a kora avarkori ötvösmüvészethez a fogazással díszített leletek kapcsán [Remarks on the goldsmithing technique of the early Avar Period using the example of the dentil decorated finds]." *A Móra Ferenc Múzeum Évkönyve, Studia Archaeologica* 8 (2002): 245–282.

Heinrich-Tamáska, Orsolya. "Zur Bestimmung Salins Tierstil I und II an zwei Beispielen aus der Umgebung von Keszthely." In *Germanen am Plattensee. Ausstellung des Balatoni Múzeums Keszthely im Museum für Frühgeschichte des Landes Niederösterreich, Schloss Traismauer, vom 6. April bis 1. November 2002*, ed. Robert Müller, 36–39. Traismauer: Amt der Niederösterreichischen Landesregierung, 2002.

Heinrich-Tamáska, Orsolya. *Die Stein- und Glasinkrustationskunst des 6. und 7. Jahrhunderts im Karpatenbecken.* Budapest: Magyar Nemzeti Múzeum, 2006.

Heinrich-Tamáska, Orsolya. "Frühe 'Awarinnen' und späte "Germaninnen"? Bemerkungen zur Interpretation reicher Frauengräber der Frühawarenzeit." In *Weibliche Eliten in der Frühgeschichte. Internationale Tagung vom 13. bis zum 14. Juni 2008 im RGZM im Rahmen des Forschungschwerpunktes "Eliten"*, ed. Dieter Quast, 89–110. Mainz: Verlag des Römisch-Germanischen Zentralmuseums, 2011.

Henning, Joachim. "Schmiedegräber nördlich der Alpen. Germanisches Handwerk zwischen keltischer Tradition und römischen Einfluß." *Saalburg Jahrbuch* 46 (1991): 65–82.

Henning, Joachim. "Handel, Verkehrswege und Beförderungsmittel im Merowingerreich." In *Die Franken wegbereiter Europas. Vor 1500 Jahren: König Chlodwig und seine Erben [Ausstellungskatalog]*, 789–801. Mainz: Verlag Philipp von Zabern, 1996.

Hica-Cîmpeanu, Ioana. "Un grup de morminte din secolul al VII-lea e.n. la Iclod (jud. Cluj) [A group of tombs from the 7th century AD at Iclod (Cluj County)]." *Acta Musei Napocensis* 15 (1978): 287–294.

Hica-Cîmpeanu, Ioana, Mureşan, Alexe. "Un mormânt din secolul al VI-lea e.n. la Sighişoara [A tomb from the 6th century AD in Sighişoara]." *Marisia* 8 (1978): 761–763.

Horedt, Kurt. *Contribuţii la istoria Transilvaniei, sec. IV–XIII* [Contributions to the history of Transylvania, 4th–13th centuries]. Bucharest: Editura Academiei Republicii Populare Romîne, 1958.

Horedt, Kurt. "Das Awarenproblem in Rumänien." *Študijné Zvesti* 16 (1968): 103–120.

Horedt Kurt. "Die östliche Reihengräberkreis in Siebenbürgen." *Dacia Nouvelle Série* 21 (1977): 251–268.

Horedt, Kurt. *Moreşti, Grabungen in einer vor- und frügeschichtlichen Siedlung in Siebenbürgen*. Bucharest: Kriterion Verlag, 1979.

Horedt, Kurt. "Gepiden in Siebenbürgen-Gepiden an der Theiss. Eine Einwendung." *Acta Archaeologica Hungarica* 33, no. 1–4 (1981): 377–381.

Horedt, Kurt. *Siebenbürgen in spätrömischer Zeit*. Bucharest: Kriterion Verlag, 1982.

Horedt, Kurt. "Germanen und Romanen in Siebenbürgen. Bemerkungen zu einer Besprechung." *Zeitschrift für Siebenbürgische Landeskunde* 77 (1983): 168–176.

Horedt, Kurt. *Siebenbürgen im Frühmittelalter*. Bonn: Dr. Rudolf Habelt GMBH, 1986.

Horedt, Kurt, Székely, Zoltán, Molnár, Ştefan. "Săpăturile de la Porumbenii Mici (r. Odorhei) [The excavations from the Porumbenii Mici (Odorhei district)]." *Materiale şi Cercetări Arheologice* 8 (1962): 633–641.

Iaroslavschi, Eugen, Petrovszky, Richard. "Cuptoarele de redus minereul de fier de la Fizeş, jud. Caraş-Severin [Furnaces for the reduction of iron ore from Fizeş, Caraş-Severin county]." *Tibiscus* 3 (1974): 147–155.

Istoria Romåniei [Romanian History], 4 vols., vol. 1: eds. Petre Constantinescu-Iaşi, Emil Condurachi, Constantin Daicoviciu. Bucharest: Editura Republicii Populare Române, 1960.

Ivanišević, Vujadin. "Metal Workshops of Caričin Grad (Justiniana Prima)." In *Lebenswelten zwischen Archäologie und Geschichte. Festschrift für Falko Daim zu seinem 65. Geburtstag*, eds. Jörg Drauschke, Ewald Kislinger, Karin Kühtreiber, Thomas Kühtreiber, Gabriele Scharrer-Liška and Tivadar Vida, 711–723. Mainz: Verlag des Römisch-Germanischen Zentralmuseums, 2018.

Jelinková, Dagmar, Šrein, Vladimír, Šťastný, Martin. "Doklady slévačství neželezných kovů v kultuře s keramikou pražského typu na Moravě [Evidence of non-ferrous metal foundry in culture with Prague-type ceramics in Moravia]." In *Mezi raným a vrcholným středověkem. Pavlu Kouřilovi k šedesátým narozeninám přátelé, kolegové a žáci*, ed. Jiří Doležel and Martin Wihoda, 69–90. Brno: Archeologický ústav Akademie věd České Republiky, Brno, 2012.

Jones, Arnold Hugh Martin. *The Later Roman Empire, 284–602: A Social, Economic and Administrative Survey*. Oxford: Basil Blackwell, 1964.

Kada, Elek. "Gátéri (Kun-Kisszállási) temető a régibb középkorból [Gátéri (Kun-Kisszállás) cemetery from the early Middle Ages]." *Archaeologiai Értesitő* 25 (1905): 360–384.

Kazanski, Michel. *Les Slaves. Les origines (Ier - VIIe siècle après J.-C.)*. Paris: Éd. Errance, 1999.

Kiss, Attila. "Das Gräberfeld und die Siedlung der awarenzeitlichen germanischen Bevölkerung von Kölked." *Folia archaeologica* 30 (1979): 185–192.

Kiss, Attila. "Das Weiterleben der Gepiden in der Awarenzeit." In *Die Völker Südosteuropa im 6. bis 8. Jahrhundert*, ed. Bernhard Hänsel, Südosteuropa Jahrbuch 17, 203–218. Berlin: Selbstverlag der Südosteuropa-Gesellschaft München und des Seminars für Ur- und Frühgeschichte der Freien Universität Berlin, 1987.

Kiss, Attila. "Germanen im awarenzeitlichen Karpatenbecken." In *Awarenforschungen. Archaeologia Austriaca Monographien 1 – Studien zur Archäologie der Awaren* 4, ed. Falko Daim, 35–134. Vienna: Institut für Ur- und Frühgeschichte der Universität Wien, 1992.

Kiss, Attila. "Tanulmányok a kora avar kori Kunbábonyi vezérsírról." *A Móra Ferenc Múzeum Évkönyve, Studia Archaeologica* 1 (1995): 131–149.

Kiss, Attila. *Das awarenzeitliche gepidische Gräberfeld von Kölked-Feketekapu A*. Innsbruck: Universitätsverlag Wagner, 1996.

Kiss, Attila. *Das awarenzeitliche Gräberfeld in Kölked-Feketekapu B*. Budapest: Magyar Nemzeti Múzeum, 2001.

Koch, Ursula. "Handwerker in der alamannischen Höhensiedlung auf dem Runden Berg bei Urach." *Archäologisches Korrespondenzblatt* 14 (1984): 99–109.

Kovács, István. "A mezőbándi ásatások (Les fouilles de Mezöband) [The excavations at Mezöband]." *Dolgozatok Cluj* 4 (1913): 265–428.

Kovács, István. "A marosvásárhelyi őskori telep, skytha-és népvándorláskori temető (Station préhistorique de Marosvásárhely, cimétiere de l'epoque scythe et de la migration des peuples) [Prehistoric station of Marosvásárhely, cemetery of the Scythian era and the migration of peoples]." *Dolgozatok Cluj* 6 (1915): 226–325.

Kovrig, Ilona. "Adatok az avar megszállás kérdéséhez [Data to the question of the Avar occupation]." Archaeologiai Értesitő 82 (1955): 30–44.

Kraskovská, L'udmila. *Slovansko-avarské pohrebísko pri Záhorskej Bystrici*. Bratislava: Vyd. Osveta, 1972.

Krenke, Nikolaj Aleksandrovich, Tavlintseva, E. Iu. "Liteĭnye formy D'jakova gorodishcha [The stone molds from D'yakovo city]." *Rossijskaja Arheologija* 4 (2002): 90–110.

Kubica-Kabacińska, Ewa, Szmoniewski, Bartlomiej Szymon. "Shank Ladle from an early Medieval Settlement in Kraków-Nowa Huta-Mogila, Site 1." *Materiały Archeologiczne nowej huty* 23 (2002): 75–83.

Ladenbauer Orel, Hertha. *Linz-Zizlau. Das baierische Gräberfeld an der Traunmündung*. Linz: Anton Schroll & Co., 1960.

Lamm, Kristina. "Helgö as a goldsmiths' workshop in Migration Period Sweden." In *Goldsmith Mysteries Archaeological, pictorial and documentary evidence from the 1st millennium AD in northern Europe*, eds. Alexandra Pesch and Ruth Blankenfeldt, 143–155. Neumünster: Wachholtz Verlag, 2012.

La Salvia, Vasco. "Notes on early Medieval Ironmaking in Italy." In *Traditions and Innovations in the Early Medieval Iron Production*, ed. János Gömöri, 83–87. Sopron-Somogyfajsz: Dunaferr, 1999.

László, Gyula. *Steppenvölker und Germanen: Kunst der Völkerwanderungszeit*. Vienna-Munich: Anton Schroll, 1970.

László, Gyula. *Das Awarenzeitliche Gräberfeld in Csákberény-Orondpuszta*. With contributions from Gergely Csiky, Kinga Éry, Gábor Fancsalszky, Gyula Fülöp, Adrien Pásztor, Zsófia Rácz, József Szentpéteri, Tivadar Vida, István Vörös, István Koncz, Péter Skriba, Gergely Szenthe. Budapest: Magyar Nemzeti Múzeum, 2015.

László, János. "Ein Eisengerätfund vom Fundort Tatabánya-24." A Móra Ferenc Múzeum Évkönyvei: Studia Archaeologica 9 (2003): 165–169.

Lăzărescu-Ionescu et al., Lăzărescu-Ionescu, L., Rosetti, Dinu V., Ionescu, Gheorghe, Astagăi, Gheorghe, Teodoru, H. "Săpăturile arheologice din sectorul Curtea Veche [The archaeological excavations in the Curtea Veche sector]." In *Bucharest. Rezultatele săpăturilor arheologice și ale cercetărilor istorice din anul 1953*, 184–261. Bucharest: Editura Academiei Republicii Populare Române, 1954.

Lörinczy, Gábor, Rácz, Zsófia. "Szabolcs-Szatmár-Bereg megye avar sírleletei II. Tiszavasvári–Kashalom-dűlő kora avar kori temetkezései [Avarian finds from Szabolcs-Szatmár-Bereg County II. Early Avarian graves from Tiszavasvári–Kashalom-dűlő]." *A Nyíregyházi Jósa András Múzeum Évkönyvei* 56 (2014): 141–217.

Madgearu, Alexandru. "Despre cataramele de tip „Pápa" și unele probleme ale secolului al VII-lea [About "Pápa" type buckles and some problems of the 7th century]." *Studii și Cercetări de Istorie Veche și Arheologie* 44, no. 2 (1993): 171–184.

Madgearu, Alexandru. *Continuitate și discontinuitate culturală la Dunărea de Jos în secolele VII–VIII* [Cultural continuity and discontinuity at the Lower Danube in the 7th–8th centuries]. Bucharest: Editura Universității din București, 1997.

Madgearu, Alexandru. "Semnificația purtării crucilor pectorale descoperite la nord de Dunăre în secolele VI–VII [The significance of wearing the pectoral crosses discovered north of the Danube in the 6th–7th centuries]." *Arheologia Moldovei* 30 (2007): 129–136.

Magnus, Bente, Mollerop, Odmund, Sjovold, Thorleif. "Migration Period Graves." In *Inventaria Archaeologica. Norway*, ed. by Per Fett, 1 set. N 1. N.3. Bonn: Rudolf Habelt Verlag, 1966.

Martin, Max. "Zu den tauschierten Gürtelgarnituren und Gürtelteilen der Männergräber von Kölked-Feketekapu A." In Attila Kiss, *Das awarenzeitliche gepidische Gräberfeld von Kölked-Feketekapu A*, 345–361. Innsbruck: Universitätsverlag Wagner, 1996.

Martin, Max. "Tauschierte Gürtelgarnituren und -beschläge des frühen Mittelalters im Karpatenbecken und ihre Träger." In *Ethnische und kulturelle Verhältnisse an der mittleren Donau vom 6. bis zum 11. Jahrhundert*, eds. Darina Bialeková and Jozef Zábojník, 63–74. Bratislava: Veda, 1996.

Măgureanu, Andrei. "Observații privind semnificația unor descoperiri din spațiul extracarpatic (sec. VI–VII p. Chr.) [Remarks on the significance of some findings from the extra-Carpathian space (6th–7th AD)]." *Mousaios* 13 (2008): 173–190.

Măgureanu, Andrei. "About power in the sixth–seventh century in the extra-Carpathian area." In *Potestas et communitas. Interdisziplinäre Beiträge zu Wesen und Darstellung von Herrschaftsverhältnissen im Mittelalter ostlich der Elbe/Interdisciplinary Studies of the Constitution and Demonstration of Power Relations in the Middle Ages East of the Elbe*, eds. Aleksander Paroń, Sébastien Rossignol, Bartłomiej Sz. Szmoniewski and Grischa Vercamer, 73–86. Wrocław/Warsaw: Instytut Archaeologii i Etnologii Polskiej Akademii Nauk and Deutches Historiches Institut Warschau, 2010.

Măgureanu, Andrei. "Expresivitatea așezărilor în discuția despre identitatea elitelor (sec. VI–VII) [Settlement's expressiveness related to the identity of elites (6th–7th)]." *Studii și Cercetări de Istorie Veche și Arheologie* 66, no. 3–4 (2015): 265–285.

Măgureanu, Andrei. "Identitate religioasă la nord de Dunăre. Creștinismul [Religious identity north of the Danube. The Christianity]." *Studii și Cercetări de Istorie Veche și Arheologie* 68, no. 1–4 (2017): 31–70.

Măgureanu, Andrei, Ciupercă, Bogdan. "The 6th–8th Centuries Metallurgical Activity from Budureasca Valley. The Molds." *Acta Musei Napocensis* 41–42/I, 2004–2005 (2007): 291–318.

Măgureanu, Andrei, Ciupercă, Bogdan. "Discuții despre tiparul de la Aldeni, jud. Buzău [Discussions about the Aldeni pattern, Buzău County]." In *Arheologia mileniului I p. chr. Dunărea de jos între antichitate și evul mediu* 6, Ploiești, forthcoming.

Măgureanu, Andrei, Szmoniewski, Bartłomiej Sz. "Domestic dwellings in Moldavia and Wallachia in the initial phases of the Early Middle Ages." *Acta Archaeologica Carpathica* 38 (2003): 111–136.

Mărghitan, Liviu. *Banatul în lumina arheologiei* [The Banat in the light of archeology], vol. 3, Timișoara: Facla, 1985.

Medeleț, Florin. "O descoperire de factură avară la Sânnicolau Mare (jud. Timiș) [A discovery relating to Avar Period in Sânnicolau Mare (Timis County)]." *Analele Banatului Serie Nouă* 6 (1998): 307–316.

Menghin, Wilfried. *Die Langobarden. Archäologie und Geschichte*. Stuttgart: Theiss, 1985.

Miclea, Ion, Florescu, Radu. *Strămoșii românilor. Vestigii milenare de cultură și artă. Daco-romanii* [The ancestors of the Romanians. Millennial vestiges of culture and art. Daco-Romans]. vol. 2, Bucharest: Editura Meridiane, 1980.

Minasian, R. S. "Osobennosti ranneslavianskogo liteĭnogo i iuvelirnogo proizvodstva [Characteristics of the Slavic casting technology and jewelry production]." In *Drevnosti Podvin'ia: istoricheskiĭ aspekt. Po materialam kruglogo stola, posviashchennogo pamiati A. M. Mikliaeva (6–8 oktiabria 1999)*, ed. G. V. Vilinbakhov, B. S. Korotkevich, A. N. Mazurkevich and Iu. Iu. Piotrovskii, 206–211. Sankt Petersburg: Izdatel'stvo Gosudarstvennogo Ermitazha, 2003.

Mitrea, Bucur. "Date noi cu privire la secolul al VII-lea. Tezaurul de hexagrame bizantine de la Priseaca (jud. Olt) [New data on the seventh century. The Byzantine Hexagram Treasure from Priseaca (Olt County)]." *Studii și Cercetări de Numismatică* 6 (1975): 113–125.

Mitrea, Ion. "Așezarea prefeudală de la Izvoare-Bahna, contribuții la arheologia epocii de formare a poporului român [Pre-feudal settlement from Izvoare-Bahna, contributions to the archeology of the epoch of formation of the Romanian people]." *Carpica* 10 (1978): 205–252.

Mitrea, Ion. "Influențe bizantine în cultura materială și spirituală din regiunea sub-carpatică a Moldovei în secolele VI–IX [Byzantine influences in the material and spiritual culture of the sub-Carpathian region of Moldavia in the 6th–9th centuries]." *Studii și Cercetări de Istorie Veche* 30, no. 2 (1979): 145–161.

Mitrea, Ion. "Regiunea centrală a Moldovei dintre Carpați și Siret în secolele VI–IX [The central region of Moldavia between the Carpathians and Siret in the 6th–9th centuries]." *Carpica* 12 (1980): 55–190.

Mitrea, Ion. "Dovezi arheologice privind prelucrarea metalelor în secolele VI–IX, în regiunea subcarpatică a Moldovei [Archaeological evidence on the processing of metals in the 6th–9th centuries, in the sub-Carpathian region of Moldavia]." *Studii și Comunicări de Istorie a Civilizației Populare din România* 2 (1981): 13–18.

Mitrea, Ion. "Principalele rezultate ale cercetărilor arheologice din așezarea de la Davideni (sec. V – VII) [The main results of the archaeological researches from the Davideni settlement (5th–7th centuries)]." *MemAntiq* 6–8 (1974–1976) (1981): 65–92.

Mitrea, Ion. "Așezarea din secolele V–VII de la Davideni – Neamț. Cercetările arheologice din anii 1988–1991 [The settlement from the 5th–7th centuries from Davideni – Neamț. Archaeological researches from 1988 to 1991]." *Memoria Antiquitatis* 19 (1994): 279–332.

Mitrea, Ion. *Așezarea din secolele VI–IX de la Izvoare Bahna* [The settlement from the 6th–9th centuries from Izvoare Bahna]. Piatra Neamț: Editura Nona, 1998.

Mitrea, Ion. *Așezarea de la Davideni din secolele* v–viii [The settlement from Davideni from the 5th–8th centuries]. Piatra Neamț: Editura Constantin Matasă, 2001.

Mitrea, Ion. *Așezarea medievală timpurie de la Ștefan Cel Mare-Gutinaș, județul Bacău* [Early medieval settlement from Ștefan Cel Mare-Gutinaș, Bacău county]. Onești: Magic Print, 2015.

Mitrea, Ion, Eminovici, Constantin, Momanu, Vasile. "Așezarea din secolele v–vii de la Ștefan cel Mare, județul Bacău [The settlement from the 5th–7th centuries from Ștefan cel Mare, Bacău County]." *Carpica* 18–19 (1986–1987): 215–250.

Moldovanu, Dragoș. "Toponime de origine romană în Transilvania și în sud-vestul Moldovei. [Toponyms of Roman origin in Transylvania and the south-west of Moldavia]." *Anuar de Lingvistică și Istorie Literară* 49, no. 1 (2009–2010): 17–95.

Morel, Jean-Paul. "Artizanul [The Artisan]." In *Omul roman*, coordinated by Andrea Giardina, translated into Romanian by Dragoș Cojocaru, 195–222. Iași: Polirom, 2001.

Morintz, Sebastian, Rosetti, Dinu V. "Din cele mai vechi timpuri și până la formarea Bucureștiului [From the earliest times to the formation of Bucharest]." In *Bucureștii de odinioară*, 11–47. Bucharest: Editura Științifică, 1959.

Morrison, Cécile, Popović, Vladislav, Ivanišević, Vujadin. *Les trésors monétaires byzantins des Balkans et d'Asie Mineure (491–713)*. Paris: Lethielleux, 2006.

Muscă, Luciana, Muscă, Tiberiu I. "Săpăturile arheologice de la Băleni-Români, județul Dâmbovița [The archaeological excavations from Băleni-Români, Dâmbovița county]." *Materiale și Cercetări Arheologice* 14 (1980): 423–428.

Musteață, Sergiu. "Unele concretizări privind vasul de metal din tezaurul monetar de la Horgești, jud. Bacău, România [Some concretizations regarding the metal vessel from the monetary hoard from Horgești, Bacău County, Romania]." In *Arheologia între știință, politică și economia de piață*, ed. Sergiu Musteață, 99–127. Chișinău: Pontos, 2010.

Müller-Wille, Michael. "Der frühmittelalterliche Schmied im Spiegel skandinavischer Grabfunde." *Frühmittelalterliche Studien* 11 (1977): 127–201.

Müller-Wille, Michael. "Der Schmied im Spiegel archäologischer Quellen. Zur Aussage von Schmiedegräbern der Wikingerzeit." In: *Das Handwerk in vor- und frühgeschichtlicher Zeit. Bericht über die Kolloquien der Kommission für die Altertumskunde Mittel- u. Nordeuropas in den Jahren 1977–1980*. vol. 2 (Archäologische und Philologische Beiträge), eds. Herbert Jankuhn, Walter Janssen, Ruth Schmidt-Wiegand, Heinrich Tiefenbach, 216–260. Göttingen: Vandenhoeck & Ruprecht, 1983.

Nagy, Sandor. "Nekropola kod Aradaca iz ranog srednjeg veka [The Necropolis near Aradac from the Early Middle Ages]." *Rad Vojvodjanskih Muzeja* 8 (1959): 45–102.

Nagy, Sandor. "Nekropola iz ranog sredneg veka u ciglani "Polet" u Vrbasu [Necropolis from the early Middle Ages in the "Polet" brick factory in Vrbas]." *Rad Vojvođanskih Muzeja* 20 (1971): 187–268.

Nagy, Margit. "Ornamenta Avarica I. Az avar kori ornamentika geometrikus elemei [Geometric elements of Avar Period ornamentation]." *A Móra Ferenc Múzeum Évkönyve, Studia Archaeologica* 4 (1998): 377–459.

Nagy, Margit. *Awarenzeitliche Gräberfelder im Stadtgebiet von Budapest*, 2 vols. Budapest: Magyar Nemzeti Múzeum, 1998.

Nagy, Margit. "Ornamenta Avarica II. A fonatornamentika [The braided band ornamentation]." *A Móra Ferenc Múzeum Évkönyve, Studia Archaeologica* 5 (1999): 279–315.

Nedopako, Dmitrij. "Development of Iron-working in the Ukraine in the 1st Millennium AD." In *Traditions and Innovations in the Early Medieval Iron Production*, ed. János Gömöri, 77–82. Sopron-Somogyfajsz: Dunaferr, 1999.

Negru, Mircea, Bădescu, Alexandru, Cuculea-Sandu, Vasilica. *Militari-Câmpul Boja, an Archaeological Site on the Territory of Bucharest (Archaeological Investigations since 1958 up to 2005). VI. Settlements Dating from the 5th–7th Centuries*. Bucharest: Minerva Expres, 2009.

Nestor, Ion. "Slavii pe teritoriul RPR în lumina documentelor arheologice [Slavs on the territory of the RPR in the light of archaeological documents]." *Studii și Cercetări de Istorie Veche* 10, no. 1 (1959): 49–64.

Nestor, Ion. "L'établissement des Slaves en Roumanie à la lumière de quelques découvertes archéologiques récentes." *Dacia Nouvelle Série* 5 (1961): 429–448.

Nestor, Ion. "Câteva considerații cu privire la cea mai veche locuire a slavilor pe teritoriul R.P.R. [Some considerations regarding the oldest habitation of the Slavs on the territory of R.P.R.]." In *Omagiu lui P. Constantinescu-Iași*, ed. Emil Condurachi, 147–151. Bucharest: Editura Academiei Republicii Populare Române, 1965.

Nestor, Ion. "Continuitate în istoria formării poporului român. Reflecții pe marginea noilor date arheologice [Continuity in the history of the formation of the Romanian people. Reflections on the new archaeological data]." *Magazin Istoric* 3 (1969): 2–7, 24–37.

Nestor, Ion. "Problèmes concernant les rapports entre les Slavs et la population autochtone en Roumanie." In *I Międzynarodowy Kongres archeologii slowianskiej. Warsawa, 14–18 IX 1965*, ed. Witold Hensel, 174–176. Wroclaw/Warsaw/Cracow: Wydawnictwo Polskiej Akademii nauk, 1970.

Nestor, Ion. "Formarea poporului român [Formation of the Romanian people]." In *Istoria poporului român*, ed. Andrei Oțetea, 91–113. Bucharest: Editura Științifică, 1970.

Nestor, Ion et al. "Șantierul Sărata-Monteoru [The Sărata-Monteoru site]." *Studii și Cercetări de Istorie Veche* 4, no. 1–2 (1953): 69–89.

Nestor, Ion, Nicolăescu-Plopșor, Constantin. "Die völkerwanderungszeitlichen Schatz Negrescu." *Germania* 22 (1938): 33–41.

Nikitina, Tatiana B., Efremova, Diana Yu. "Pogrebal'nyĭ obriad kompleksov s liteĭnymi prinadlezhnostiami iz srednevekovykh mogil'nikov IX–XII vv. Vetluzhsko-Viatskogome zhdurech'ia [The funeral rite of complexes with molded tools from medieval sepulchers of IX–XII centuries of the Vetluga-Vyatka Interfluve]." *Povolzhskaia Arkheologiia* 2 (2012): 146–165.

Oanță-Marghitu, Rodica. "Argamum între Imperiul Roman târziu și „barbari". Obiectele mărunte ca ipostaze ale comunicării [Argamum between the late Roman Empire and "barbarians". Small objects as hypostases of communication]." In *Orgame/ Argamum. Supplementa 1. A la recherché d'une colonie. Actes du Colloque International 40 ans de recherche archéologique à Orgamè/Argamum, Bucarest-Tulcea-Jurilovca, 3–5 octobre 2005*, ed. Mihaela Mănucu-Adameșteanu, 345–374. Bucharest: Edition Agir, 2006.

Oberländer-Târnoveanu, Ernest. "La monnaie byzantine des VIe - VIIIe siècles au-delà de la frontière du Bas-Danube. Entre politique, économie et diffusion culturelle." *Histoire & Mesure* 17 (2002): 3–4, 155–196.

Ódor, János Gábor, Rácz, Zsófia. "Szerszámmellékletes sír a Szekszárd-Tószegi-dűlői avar temetőből [Tomb with tools from avar cemetery Szekszárd-Tószegi-dűlői]." *A Móra Ferenc Múzeum Évkönyve, Studia Archaeologica* 12 (2011): 245–255.

Olteanu, Ștefan. "Vechi preocupări de reducere a minereului de fier pe teritoriul orașului București [Old preoccupations about the reduction of iron ore in the territory of Bucharest]." *București* 9 (1972): 109–114.

Olteanu, Ștefan. "Quelques remarques sur les activités industrielles pratiquées dans le territoire de la Roumanie aux IVe - XIe siècles." *Slovenska Archeologia* 26 (1978): 46–50.

Olteanu, Ștefan. *Societatea carpato-danubiano-pontică în secolele IV–XI. Structuri demo-economice și social-politice* [The Carpathian-Danubian-Pontic society in the 4th–11th centuries. Demo-economic and social-political structures]. Bucharest: Editura Didactică și pedagogică R.A., 1997.

Olteanu, Ștefan, Șerban, Constantin. *Meșteșugurile din Țara Românească și Moldova în evul mediu* [Crafts from Walachia and Moldavia in the Middle Ages]. Bucharest: Editura Academiei Republicii Socialiste România, 1969.

Olteanu, Ștefan, Teodorescu, Victor, Neagu, Nina. "Rezultatul cercetărilor arheologice de la Șirna, cu privire la secolele III–XI [The result of the archaeological researches from Șirna regarding the 3rd–11th centuries]." *Materiale și Cercetări Arheologice* 14 (1980): 417–419.

Olteanu, Ștefan, Neagu, Nina, Șeclăman, Doina. "Tehnologia obținerii fierului din minereu și problema continuității istorice pe teritoriul României în mileniul I e. n. [The technology of obtaining iron from the ore and the problem of historical continuity on the territory of Romania in the 1st millennium AD]." *Studii și Comunicări de Istorie Veche și Arheologie* 32, no. 2 (1981): 217–232.

Olteanu, Ştefan, Neagu, Nina. "Rezultatele cercetărilor de la Şirna-Prahova [Results of research from Şirna-Prahova]." *Materiale şi Cercetări Arheologice* 15 (1983): 384–386.

Olteanu, Ştefan, Grigore, Nina, Nicolae, Victor. *Comunitatea sătească de la Şirna, judeţul Prahova (secolele II–X d. H.) în lumina izvoarelor arheologice* [The village community from Şirna, Prahova county (2nd–10th centuries AD) in the light of archaeological sources]. Bucharest: Editura Maşina de Scris, 2007.

Opaiţ, Andrei. "Aegyssus '76 – Raport preliminar [Aegyssus '76 – Preliminary report]." *Pontica* 10 (1977): 307–311.

Ostanina, T. I. "Klad iuvelira iz d. Kuzebaevo Udmurtskoi Respubliki [The jeweller's hoard from Kuzebaevo]." *Finno-ugrica* 10 (2007): 125–127.

Ostanina, T. I., Kanunnikova, O. M., Stepanov, V. P., Nikitin, A. B. *Kuzebaevskiĭ klad iuvelira VII v. kak istoricheskiĭ istochnik* [The 7th century jeweler's treasure from Kuzebaevsk as a historical source]. Izhevsk: Izdatel'stvo "Udmurtiia", 2011.

Paliga, Sorin. "Etnicitatea mileniului I: studii de caz în drumul spre o analiză globală [Ethnicity in the 1st millennium CE: case studies towards a global analysis]." In *Arheologia mileniului I p. Chr.* 5, ed. Bogdan Ciupercă, 309–320. Brăila: Muzeul Brăilei "Carol I", Editura Istros, 2016.

Paliga, Sorin. "Terram uero, que est a fluuio morus usque ad Castrum Vrscia (Anonymus, Gesta Hungarorum, VI)." In *Arheovest IV/2. Interdisciplinaritate în Arheologie şi Istorie. In honorem Adrian Bejan*, eds. Dorel Micle, Andrei Stavilă, Cristian Oprean and Sorin Forţiu, 861–872. Szeged: JatePress Kiadó, 2016.

Panait, Panait I., Ştefănescu, Aristide. *Muzeul Curtea Veche. Palatul Voievodal* [The Curtea Veche Museum. Voivodal Palace]. Bucharest: Muzeul de Istorie a Municipiului Bucureşti, 1973.

Paragină, Anton. "Un cercel de provenienţă bizantină descoperit în localitatea Copăceşti, comuna Rugineşti, judeţul Vrancea [An earring of Byzantine origin discovered in Copăceşti, Rugineşti commune, Vrancea county]." *Studii şi Cercetări de Istorie Veche şi Arheologie* 33, no. 1 (1982): 138–139.

Párducz, Mihály. "Archäologische Beiträge zur Geschichte der Hunnenzeit in Ungarn." *Acta Archaeologica Academiae Scientiarum Hungaricae* 11 (1959): 309–398.

Petre, Aurelian. "Fibulele „digitate" de la Histria (I) ["Bow" fibulae from Histria (I)]." *Studii şi Cercetări de Istorie Veche* 16, no. 1 (1965): 67–96.

Petre, Aurelian. "Fibulele „digitate" de la Histria (II) ["Bow" fibulae from Histria (II)]." *Studii şi Cercetări de Istorie Veche* 16, no. 2 (1965): 275–289.

Pirenne, Henri. *Mahomed şi Carol cel Mare* [Muhammad and Carol the Great]. Bucharest: Editura Meridiane, 1996.

Pohl, Walter. *Die Awaren. Ein Steppenvolk im Mitteleuropa 567–822 n. Chr.* Munich: Verlag C. H. Beck, 1988.

Popilian, Gheorghe, Nica, Marin. *Gropşani. Monografie arheologică* [Gropşani. Archaeological monograph]. (Bibliotheca Thracologica) 24, Bucharest: Editura Semne, 1998.

Popilian, Gheorghe, Nica, Marin. "Aşezarea prefeudală de la Craiova (Fântâna Obedeanu) [Pre-feudal settlement from Craiova (Obedeanu Fountain)]." *Drobeta* 15 (2005): 148–165.

Preda, Constantin. "Tipar pentru bijutierii din secolul al VI-lea e. n., descoperit la Olteni (r. Videle, reg. Bucharest) [Pattern for jewelers from the 6th century AD discovered in Olteni (Videle district, Bucharest region)]." *Studii şi Cercetări de Istorie Veche* 18, no. 3 (1967): 513–520.

Preda, Constantin. "Circulaţia monedelor bizantine în regiunea carpato-dunăreană [The circulation of Byzantine coins in the Carpathian-Danube region]." *Studii şi Cercetări de Istorie Veche* 23, no. 3 (1972): 375–415.

Pribulová, Alena, Mihok, Ljubomir, Mácelová, Marta. "Forschung über die Herstellung und Verarbeitung von Eisen in der slawische Siedlung Sliač-Horné Zeme." In *Traditions and Innovations in the Early Medieval Iron Production*, ed. János Gömöri, 94–103. Sopron-Somogyfajsz: Dunaferr, 1999.

Protase, Dumitru. *Ţaga. Două aşezări din perioada finală a etnogenezei românilor (sec. IV–VI şi sec. VII–VIII)* [Ţaga. Two settlements from the final period of Romanians' ethnogenesis (4th–6th centuries and 7th–8th centuries)]. Cluj-Napoca: Nereamia Napocae, 2003.

Protase, Dumitru, Ţigărea, Ioan. "Şantierul arheologic Soporul de Câmpie [The Soporul de Câmpie archaeological site]." *Materiale şi Cercetări Arheologice* 6 (1959): 383–395.

Rácz, Zsófia. "Avar kori ötvös-és kovácsszerszámok [Avar age goldsmiths and blacksmiths]." In *A vasművesség évezredei a Kárpát-medencébeni*, eds. János Gömöri, János Szulovszky and Zoltán Nagy, 67–95. Szombathely, 2009.

Rácz, Zsófia. "Emberalakos kistárgyak az avar korból [Miniature human figures from the Avar era]." In: *Thesaurus Avarorum. Régészeti tanulmányok Garam Éva tiszteletére* [Archaeological Studies in Honour of Éva Garam], ed. Tivadar Vida, 409–436. Budapest, 2012.

Rácz, Zsófia. "Sind Goldschmiede in den „Goldschmiedegräber" der Awarenzeit bestattet?" In *Macht des Goldes, Gold der Macht. Herrschafts- und Jenseitsrepräsentation zwischen Antike und Frühmittelalter im mittleren Donauraum*, ed. Matthias Hardt and Orsolya Heinrich-Tamáska, 361–379. Weinstadt: Bernhard A. Greiner Verlag, 2013.

Rácz, Zsófia. *Die Goldschmiedegräber der Awarenzeit*. Mainz: Verlag des Römisch-Germanischen Zentralmuseums, 2014.

Rácz, Zsófia. "Metallhandwerkszeug aus den Gräbern 323 und 369." In Gyula László, *Das awarenzeitliche Gräberfeld in Csákberény-Orondpuszta*, 209–215. Budapest: Magyar Nemzeti Múzeum, 2015.

Rácz, Zsófia. "Ein frühmittelalterlicher Pressmodelfund aus dem Mittleren Dnjepr-Gebiet." In *Between Byzantium and the Steppe. Archaeological and Historical Studies in Honour of Csanád Bálint on the Occasion of His 70th Birthday*, ed. Ádám Bollók, Gergely Csiky and Tivadar Vida, 175–181. Budapest: Institute of Archaeology, Research Centre for the Humanities, Hungarian Academy of Sciences, 2016.

Rácz, Zsófia, May, Zoltán. "Öntőminta pajzsos testű csat készítéséhez [Mold for making a shielded buckle]." In *Mozaikok Orosháza és vidéke múltjából 19. Fémek a földből*, 1, 50–51. Orosháza: Orosháza Város Önkormányzat Nagy Gyula Területi Múzeuma, 2018.

Rafalovich, Isaak A. "K voprosu o vremeni poiavleniia pervykh politicheskikh obrazovaniĭ romanizirovannogo naseleniia na zemliakh k severu ot Dunaia [To the question of the time of the first political entities romanized population on earth north of the Danube]." In *Iugo-Vostochnaia Evropa v epokhu feodalizma* (*Reziume dokladov Kishinevskogo simpoziuma 1973 g.*), 33–41. Kishinev: Shtiintsa, 1973.

Ranisavljev, Aleksandar. *Ranosredčovekovna nekropola kod Mokrina* [An Early Medieval Necropolis near Mokrin]. Belgrade: Srpsko Arheološko Društvo, 2007.

Repertoriul arheologic al Mureşului Inferior. Judeţul Arad [The archaeological repertoire of the Lower Mureş. Arad County]. Timişoara: Editura Orizonturi Universitare, 1999.

Rhé, Gyula, Fettich, Nándor. *Jutas und Öskü*. Prag: Seminarium Kondakovianum, 1931.

Roman, Cristian-Aurel, Paki, Adela, Rusu-Bolindeţ, Viorica, Isacu, Adriana, Bota, Emilian, Bodea, Monica, Marcu, Felix, Tecar, Tiberiu. "Roşia Montană, jud. Alba (Alburnus Maior) [Roşia Montană, Alba County (Alburnus Maior)]." In *Cronica cercetărilor arheologice din România* (*campania 2001*), eds. Mircea Victor Angelescu, Corina Borş and Irina Oberländer-Târnoveanu, 257–261. Bucharest: cIMeC Institutul de Memorie Culturală, 2002.

Rosetti, Dinu V. *Din preistoria Bucureştilor 1, Civilizaţia tip Bucureşti. Die Bukarester Kultur*. Bucharest: Editura Tipografia Curtii Regale, 1936.

Roska, Márton. "Das gepidische Gräberfeld von Vereşmort (Marosveresmart)." *Germania* 18 (1934): 123–124.

Rosner, Gyula. "Ethnische Probleme im 8.–9. in Südostpannonien." In *Rapports du IIIe Congrés International d'Archaéologie Slave, Bratislava, 7–14 septembre 1975*, vol. 1, ed. Bohuslav Chropovský, 671–677. Bratislava: Vydavatel'stvo Slovenskej Akadémie Vied, 1979.

Rosner, Gyula. *Das awarenzeitliche Gräberfeld in Szekszárd-Bogyszlói Straße*. Budapest: Magyar Nemzeti Múzeum, 1999.

Ross, Marvin C. *Catalogue of the Byzantine and early Medieval Antiquities in the Dumbarton Oaks Collection, 2, Jewelry, Enamels and Art of the Migration Period*. Washington D.C., 1965.

Roth, Helmut. "Beobachtungen an merowingerzeitlichen Gußtiegeln." *Frühmittelalterliche Studien* 11 (1979): 85–91.

Roth, Helmut. "Almandinhandel und -verbreitung im Bereich des Mittelmeeres." *Beiträge zur allgemeine und vergleichende Archäologie* 2 (1980): 309–335.

Roth, Helmut. *Kunst und Handwerk im frühen Mittelalter*, Stuttgart: Konrad Theiss, 1986.

Rozmus, Dariusz, Szmoniewski, Bartlomiej Sz. "Early medieval lead processing in the slavic territories and the possible mention of trade in lead by Ibrāhīm Ibn Ya'qūb." *Peuce S.N.* 6 (2008): 323–330.

Rustoiu, Gabriel T. "Habitatul în Transilvania în a doua jumătate a secolului al V-lea și prima jumătate a secolului al VI-lea [The Habitat in Transylvania in the second half of the 5th century and the first half of the 6th century]." In *Relații interetnice în Transilvania (secolele VI–XIII)*, eds. Zeno Karl Pinter, Ioan Marian Țiplic and Maria Emilia Țiplic, 42–85. Bucharest: Editura Economică, 2005.

Rusu, Mircea. "Pontische Gürtelschnallen mit Adlerkopf (VI.–VII. u. Z)." *Dacia Nouvelle Série* 3 (1959): 485–523.

Rusu, Mircea. "The Prefeudal cemetery of Noșlac (VI–VII centuries)." *Dacia Nouvelle Série* 6 (1962): 269–292.

Rusu, Mircea. "Transilvania și Banatul în secolele VI–IX. [Transylvania and Banat in the 6th–9th centuries]." *Banatica* 4 (1976): 169–213.

Rybakov, Boris A. *Remeslo Drevneĭ Rusi* [The craft of ancient Russia]. Moskow: Izdatel'stvo Akademiia Nauk SSSR, 1948.

Salamon, Ágnes, Erdélyi, István. *Das völkerwanderungszeitliche Gräberfeld von Környe*. Budapest: Akadémiai Kiadó, 1971.

Salin, Bernhard. *Die altgermanische Tierornamentik. Typologische Studie über germanische Metallgegenstände aus dem IV. bis IX. Jahrhundert nebst einer Studie über irische Ornamentik*. Stockholm: K. L. Becksmans Buchdruckerei, 1904.

Sandu, Vasilica. "Cercetări arheologice în zona Lunca-Bârzești [Archaeological research in the Lunca-Bârzești area]." *Cercetări Arheologice în București* 4 (1992): 163–193.

Sandu, Vasilica. "Situl Străulești-Măicănești. Așezarea din secolele VI–VII d. Hr. Săpătura din anul 2000 [The Străulești-Măicănești site. The settlement from the 6th–7th centuries AD. The excavation of the year 2000]." *Revista de cercetări arheologice și numismatice* 2 (2016): 166–187.

Saramandu, Nicolae. "Despre coborârea aromânilor în sudul Peninsulei Balcanice. "Mărturia lui Kekaumenos" [On the migration of the Vlachs to the southern Balkans. The "testimony" of Kekeumenos]." *Studii și Cercetări Lingvistice* 48, no. 1–4 (1997): 407–417.

Saramandu, Nicolae. "À propos de l'origine du roumain (à partir de quelques ouvrages récentes)." *Revue des Études Sud-Est Européennes* 47, no. 1–4 (1999): 315–321.

Saramandu, Nicolae. "Originea românei și a dialectelor sale (observații critice pe marginea unor lucrări recente) [The origin of Romanian and its dialects (critical observations on recent works)]." *Philologica Jassyensia* 4, no. 2 (2008): 159–164.

Saramandu, Nicolae. "Atestări istorice ale continuității (secolele IV–VII) [Historical attestations of continuity (4th–7th centuries)]." *Studii și Cercetări Lingvistice* 59, no. 1 (2008): 219–227.

Saramandu, Nicolae. "În legătură cu teritoriul de formare a limbii române (perspectivă istorică) [In connection with the territory of the formation of the Romanian language (historical perspective)]." In *Lucrările celui de-al XIV-lea Simpozion Internațional de Dialectologie*, eds. Nicolae Mocanu, Dumitru Loșonți and Eugen Beltechi, 355–368. Cluj-Napoca: Argonaut Scriptor, 2012.

Saramandu, Nicolae. "Teritoriul și perioada de formare a limbii române. Originea dialectelor românești [The territory and the period of formation of the Romanian language. The origin of the Romanian dialects]." *Fonetică și Dialectologie* 35 (2016): 5–25.

Schmauder, Michael. *Oberschichtgräber und Verwahrfunde in Südosteuropa im 4. und 5. Jahrhundert*, (Archaeologia Romanica 3) 2 vols. Bucharest: Editura Academiei Române, 2002.

Schmidt, Berthold. *Die späte Völkerwanderungszeit in Mitteldeutschland. Katalog (Nord- und Ostteil)*. (Veröffentlichungen des Landesmuseums für Vorgeschichte in Halle), 29. Berlin: Veb Deutscher Verlag der Wissenschaften, 1975.

Schmidt, Volker. "Die Gußtechnik im Schmuckhandwerk bei den Westslawen." *Zeitschrift für Archäologie* 28 (1994): 107–121.

Schnellenkamp, Werner. "Ein Grabhügel bei Wallerstädten in Hessen-Starkenburg mit Bestattungen der Hallstatt-, Latène- und Merowingerzeit." *Mainzer Zeitschrift* 27 (1932): 59–74.

Schramm, Gottfried. *Ein Damm bricht. Die römische Donaugrenze und die Invasionen des 5.–7. Jahrhunderts im Lichte von Namen und Wörtern*. München: R. Oldenbourg Verlag, 1997.

Schulze-Dörrlamm, Mechthild. "Zur Interpretation der vergoldeten Kupferblechreliefs aus dem grossmährischen Burgwall Bojná I (Slowakei)." In *Zwischen Byzanz und der Steppe. Archäologische und historische Studien. Festschrift für Csanád Bálint zum 70. Geburtstag*, eds. Ádám Bollók, Gergely Csiky and Tivadar Vida, 519–536. Budapest: Institute of Archaeology, Research Centre for the Humanities, Hungarian Academy of Sciences, 2016.

Shablavina, Ekaterina A. "Vizual'no opredelyaemye osobennosti lit'ia metallcheskikh ukrasheni ĭ po voskovoĭ modeli Dneprovskogo Levoberezh'ia VII v. n. é. [The visual assessment of the technological details employed for the casting of metal artifacts in the lost-wax technique from the Dnieper Left Bank in the 7th century AD]." In *Drevnie remeslenniki Priural'ia. Materialy Vserossiiskoi nauchnoi konferencii, Izhevsk, 21–23 noiabria 2000 g.*, ed. V. I. Zav'ialov, 308–321. Izhevsk: Udmurtskii institut istorii, iazyka i literatury Ural'skogo Otdeleniia RAN, 2001.

Shablavina, Ekaterina A., Szmoniewski, Bartlomiej S. "The Forming Model of the Kertch Type Finger-Shaped Fibula." *Sprawozdania Archeologiczne* 58 (2006): 519–526.

Shcheglova, Olga A. "K voprosu o meste i vremeni formirovaniia traditsii izgotovleniia svintsovo-olovyannykh ukrahseniĭ v formochkakh "tipa Kamno-Ryuge" [Where and when did appear the tradition of producing tin-lead-alloy accessories in molds of the "Kamno-Ryuge" type?]." In *Migratsii i osedlost' ot Dunaia do Ladogi v I tysiacheletii khristianskoĭ éry: pamiatnye chteniia pamiati Anny Machinskoĭ. Staraia Ladoga, 21–22 dekabria 2000. Materialy k chteniiam*, eds. Dmitrii A. Machinskii and A. A. Selin, 46–55. Sankt Petersburg: Staroladozhskoi istoriko-arkhitekturnyi i arkheolo-gicheskii muzei-zapovednik, 2001.

Shcheglova, Olga A. "Svintsovo-olobiannye ukrasheniia VIII–X vv. na severo-zapade vostochnoĭ Evropy [Lead-tin genre jewelry 8th–10th centuries in the northwest of Eastern Europe]." In *Ladoga i ee sosedi v epohi srednevekov'ja*, ed. Anatolii N. Kirpichnikov, 134–150. Sankt-Petersburg: Institut istorii material'noi kul'tury RAN, 2002.

Shcheglova, Olga A. "Kompleks iuvelira iz Bernshevki na Dnestre i "antskie" klady Dneprovskogo Levoberezh'ia [The workshop of Bernashivka on the Dniester and the "Antian" hoards in Left-Bank Ukraine]." In *Vostochnoslavianskiĭ mir Dnepro-Donskogo mezhdurech'ia i kochevniki iuzhno-russkikh stepeĭ v épokhu rannego srednevekov'ia Materia-ly nauchnogo konferencii*, ed. A. Z. Vinnikov, 35–40. Voronezh: Istoki, 2008.

Söderberg, Anders. "Scandinavian Iron Age and Early Medieval ceramic molds – lost wax or not or both?" In *Proceedings of the 1st International Workshop. Experimental and Educational aspects on Bronze Metallurgy, Wilhelminaoord 18–22 October 1999*, eds. Caroline Tulp, Nigel Meeks and Roeland Paardekooper, 15–24. Leiden: Vereniging voor Archeologische Experimenten en Educatie, 2001.

Söderberg, Anders. 2005. Vikingerbronze, Blowing New Life in Ancient and Early Medievalkraft. Introduction. Available at http://web.comhem.se/vikingbronze/casting.htm. Accessed December 16, 2005.

Somogyi, Péter. "Typologie, Chronologie und Herkunft der Maskenbeschläge. Zu den archäologischen Hinterlassenschaften osteuropäischer Reiterhirten aus der pontischen Steppe im 6. Jahrhundert." *Archaeologia Austriaca* 71 (1987): 121–154.

Somogyi, Péter. *Byzantinische Fundmünzen der Awarenzeit*. (Monographien zur Frühgeschichte und Mittelalterarchäologie) 5. Innsbruck: Universitätsverlag Wagner, 1997.

Somogyi, Péter. "New remarks on the flow of Byzantine coins in Avaria and Walachia during the second half of the seventh century." In *The Other Europe in the Middle Ages. Avars, Bulgars, Khazars, and Cumans*, ed. Florin Curta, 83–149. Leiden/Boston: Brill, 2008.

Somogyi, Péter. *Byzantinische Fundmünzen der Awarenzeit in ihrem europäischen Umfeld*. Budapest: Eötvös Loránd University, Institute of Archaeological Sciences, 2014.

Sós, Ágnes Cs. "Frühmittelalterliche Brandbestattung mit Feinwaage in Pókaszepetk." *Slovenska Archeologia* 26, no. 2 (1978): 424–430.

Spânu, Daniel, Gáll, Erwin. "Cuptorul de olar din secolul al VIII-lea p.Chr. de la Sighișoara-Dealul Viilor [The pottery oven of the 8th century AD from Sighișoara-Dealul Viilor]." *Materiale și Cercetări Arheologice (Serie Nouă)* 12 (2016): 177–203.

Stanciu, Ioan. "Așezarea slavă timpurie de la Lazuri [Early Slavic settlement from Lazuri]." *Satu Mare. Studii și comunicări* 15–16 (1998–1999): 115–266.

Stanciu, Ioan. "Despre ceramica medievală de uz comun, lucrată la roata rapidă, în așezările de pe teritoriul României (secolele VIII–X) [About the medieval ceramics of common use, worked on the fast wheel, in the settlements on the territory of Romania (8th–10th centuries)]." *Arheologia Medievală* 3 (2000): 127–191.

Stanciu, Ioan. *Locuirea teritoriului nord-vestic al României între antichitatea târzie și perioada de început a epocii medievale timpurii (mijlocul sec. V–sec. VII timpuriu)* [The habitation of the north-western territory of Romania between the Late Antiquity and the beginning period of the Early Middle Ages (the middle of the 5th century–early 7th century)]. Cluj-Napoca: Editura Academia Română. Centrul de Studii Transilvane. Editura Mega, 2011.

Stanciu, Ioan. "The Problem of the Earliest Slavs in Intra-Carpathian Romania (Transylvania and the North-West Vicinity)." *Slovenská archeológia* 61, no. 2 (2013): 323–370.

Stanciu, Ioan. "Cross-shaped signs on 6th and 7th centuries pottery." In *Studia Romana et Mediævalia Europænsia Miscellanea in honorem annos LXXXV peragentis professoris emeriti Dan Gh. Teodor oblate*, eds. Dan Aparaschivei and George Bilavschi, 307–354. Bucharest/Brăila: Editura Academiei Române, Muzeul Brăilei "Carol" Editura Istros, 2018.

Stanciu, Ioan. *Așezarea de la Lazuri-Lubi Tag (jud. Satu Mare). Aspecte ale locuirii medievale timpurii în nord-vestul României* [The settlement in Lazuri-Lubi Tag (Satu

Mare County). Aspects of early medieval habitation in north-west Romania]. Cluj-Napoca: Editura Mega, 2019.

Stoicovici, Eugen. "Unele caracteristici ale zgurilor din atelierele metalurgice daco-romane și prefeudale." *Banatica* 7 (1983): 239–247.

Székely, Zoltán. "Săpăturile arheologice de la Porumbenii Mici [Archaeological excavations from Porumbenii Mici]." *Materiale și Cercetări Arheologice* 6 (1959): 523–530.

Székely, Zoltán. "Contribuții la cultura slavă în sec. VII–VIII în sud-estul Transilvaniei [Contributions to the Slavic culture in the 7th–8th centuries in southeastern Transylvania]." *Studii și Cercetări de Istorie Veche* 13, no. 1 (1962): 47–58.

Székely, Zoltán. "Săpăturile executate de Muzeul Sfântu Gheorghe [The excavations performed by the Sfântu Gheorghe Museum]." *Materiale și Cercetări Arheologice* 10 (1970): 219–229.

Székely, Zoltán. "Eléments byzantins dans la civilization matérielle des VIe - VIIIe siècles dans la Sud-Est de la Transylvanie." *Dacia Nouvelle Série* 15 (1971): 353–358.

Székely, Zoltán. "Săpăturile executate de Muzeul Sfântu Gheorghe." *Materiale și Cercetări Arheologice* 10 (1973): 219–229.

Székely, Zoltán. "Așezări din sec. VI.–IX p. Ch. în bazinul Oltului Superior [Settlements from the 6th–11th centuries AD in the Upper Olt basin]." *Studii și Cercetări de Istorie Veche și Arheologie* 43, no. 3 (1992): 245–306.

Székely, Zoltán. "Vestigiile unui cuptor de topit minereu de fier din secolul al IV-lea d. Ch. de la Sfântu-Gheorghe-Chilieni [The remains of an iron ore smelting furnace from the 4th century AD from Sfântu-Gheorghe-Chilieni]." *Acta Musei Napocensis* 31 (1994): 299–304.

Szenthe, Gergely. "Meister und ihre Kunden. Herstellung und Verbreitung gegossener Bronzegegenstände im spätawarenzeitlichen Karpatenbecken." *Archaeologiai Értesítő* 137 (2012): 57–75.

Szenthe, Gergely. "Kulturális összeolvadás a 'középavar korban'. A Vác-Kavicsbányai temető [Cultural fusion in the 'Middle Avar Period'. The cemetery of Vác-Kavicsbánya]." *Archaeologiai Értesítő* 139 (2014): 99–125.

Szenthe, Gergely. "Material culture patterning as the source of the Avar power network, 8th century AD." In *Hadak útján. A népvándorláskori fiatal kutatóinak XXVI. konferenciája. Gazdaság – kereskedelem – kézművesség*, eds. Zsófia Rácz, István Koncz and Bence Gulyás, 291–314. Budapest: Institute of Archaeological Sciences, 2018.

Szmoniewski, Bartłomiej Sz. "Production of early medieval ornaments made of non-ferrous metals. Dies from archaeological finds in north-east Romania." *Acta Archaeologica Carpathica* 37 (2002): 111–135.

Szmoniewski, Bartłomiej Sz. "Anthropozoomorfic brooches of the Dnepr Type in initial phases of the Early Middle Ages. The migration of a style-idea-object." In *Wedrówká rzeczy i jdei w średniowieczu, špotkania bytomskie, v. v*, ed. Sławomir Moździoch, 111–137. Wroclaw 2004.

Szmoniewski, Bartłomiej Sz. "The production of objects from non-ferrous metals in the area of Central and Eastern Europe, in the initial phases of the Early Middle Ages." *Revista Română de Studii Eurasiatice* 1 (2005): 107–120.

Szmoniewski, Bartłomiej Sz. "Two worlds, one hoard: what do metal finds from the forest-steppe belt speak about?" in *The Other Europe in the Middle Ages. Avars, Bulgars, Khazars and Cumans. East Central and Eastern Europe in the Middle Ages, 450–1450*, ed. Florin Curta and Roman Kovalev, vol. 2, 263–296. Leiden-Boston: Brill, 2008.

Szmoniewski, Bartłomiej Sz. "Byzantium and the Slavs in the light of goldsmiths' production." In *Intelligible Beauty. Recent Research into Byzantine Jewellery*, ed. Chris Entwistle and Nöel Adams, 161–172. London: British Museum Press, 2010.

Szmoniewski, Bartłomiej Sz. "Un moule d'orfèvre de la période romano-byzantine découvert à la cité de Tropaeum Traiani (Adamclisi, dép. Constanța)." *Pontica* 50 (2017): 279–305.

Tănase, Daniela. "Câteva observații cu privire la mormântul de orfevru din epoca avară descoperit la Felnac (jud. Arad) [Some observations on the goldsmith's tomb from the avars age discovered in Felnac (Arad county)]." *Analele Banatului Serie Nouă* 12–13 (2004–2005): 237–264.

Tănase, Daniela. *Prelucrarea metalelor în lumea barbară la Dunărea Mijlocie și Inferioară în sec. vi–vii* [Metal processing in the barbarian world in the Middle and Lower Danube in the 6th–7th centuries]. Timișoara: Editura Excelsior Art, 2010.

Tănase, Daniela. "Piese de aur din epoca migrațiilor în colecția Muzeului Banatului Timișoara [Gold pieces from the Migration Period in the collection of the Banat Museum Timișoara]." In *Între stepă și imperiu. Studii în onoarea lui Radu Harhoiu*, eds. Andrei Măgureanu and Erwin Gáll, 141–147. Bucharest: Editura Renaissance, 2010.

Tănase, Daniela. "Despre artizanii metalelor în izvoare scrise din zorii Evului Mediu [About metal craftsmen in written sources from the Early Middle Ages]." *Analele Banatului Serie Nouă* 18 (2010): 115–121.

Tănase, Daniela. "Gräber mit Goldschmiede- und Schmiedewerkzeugen aus der Awarenzeit. Zeichen der Macht oder Beweis für die Ausübung des Handwerks." In *Potestas et communitas. Interdisziplinäre Beiträge zu Wesen und Darstellung von Herrschaftsverhältnissen im Mittelalter ostlich der Elbe/Interdisciplinary Studies of the Constitution and Demonstration of Power Relations in the Middle Ages East of the Elbe*, eds. Aleksander Paroń, Sébastien Rossignol, Bartłomiej Sz. Szmoniewski and Grischa Vercamer, 213–225. Wrocław/Warsaw: Instytut Archaeologii i Etnologii Polskiej Akademii Nauk and Deutches Historiches Institut Warschau, 2010.

Tănase, Daniela, Mare, Mircea. "Piese de port și de podoabă din secolele III–VII în colecția Pongrácz. Catalog [Costume and adornment pieces from the 3rd–7th centuries in the Pongrácz collection. Catalog]." *Analele Banatului Serie Nouă* 9 (2001): 181–206.

Tejral, Jaroslav. *Grundzüge der Völkerwanderungszeit in Mähren*. Prague: Academia, 1976.

Teodor, Dan Gh. "Unele probleme privind evoluția culturii materiale din Moldova în secolele VI–X [Some problems regarding the evolution of material culture in Moldova in the 6th–10th centuries]." *Carpica* 2 (1969): 253–307.

Teodor, Dan Gh. "Elemente și influențe bizantine în Moldova în secolele V–XI [Byzantine elements and influences in Moldavia in the 5th–11th centuries]." *Studii și Cercetări de Istorie Veche* 21, no. 1 (1970): 97–128.

Teodor, Dan Gh. *Teritoriul est-carpatic în veacurile V–XI e. n., contribuții arheologice și istorice la problema formării poporului român* [The East-Carpathian territory in the 5th–11th centuries AD, archaeological and historical contributions to the problem of the formation of the Romanian people]. Iași: Editura Junimea, 1978.

Teodor, Dan Gh. "Cercetări în așezarea din secolele VII–VIII de la Lozna-Strătеni, Jud. Botoșani [Research in the settlement of the 7th–8th centuries from Lozna-Strătеni, Botoșani Co.]." *Materiale și Cercetări Arheologice* 14 (1980): 455–461.

Teodor, Dan Gh. *Romanitatea carpato-dunăreană și Bizanțul în veacurile V–XI* [Carpathian-Danube Romanity and Byzantium in the 5th–11th centuries]. Iași: Editura Junimea, 1981.

Teodor, Dan Gh. "Principalele rezultate ale cercetărilor arheologice de la Lozna-Strătеni, jud. Botoșani [The main results of the archaeological researches from Lozna-Strătеni, Botoșani county]." *Materiale și Cercetări Arheologice* 15 (1983): 452–455.

Teodor, Dan Gh. *Civilizația romanică la est de Carpați în sec. V–VII e. n. Așezarea de la Botoșana-Suceava* [Romance civilization east of the Carpathians in the 5th–7th centuries AD. The settlement from Botoșana-Suceava]. Bucharest: Editura Academiei Republicii Socialiste România, 1984.

Teodor, Dan Gh. *Continuitatea populației autohtone la est de Carpați în secolele VI–XI e. n. Așezările din secolele VI–XI e.n. de la Dodești-Vaslui* [Continuity of the autochthonous population to the east of the Carpathians in the 6th–11th centuries AD Settlements of the 6th–11th centuries from Dodești-Vaslui]. Iași: Editura Junimea, 1984.

Teodor, Dan Gh. *Creștinismul la est de Carpați, de la origini până în secolul al XIV-lea* [Christianity east of the Carpathians, from its origins to the fourteenth century]. Iași: Editura Mitropoliei Moldovei și Bucovinei, 1991.

Teodor, Dan Gh. "Piese vestimentare bizantine din secolele VI–VIII în spaţiul carpato-dunăreano-pontic. A. Catarame cu placa fixă [Byzantine garments from the 6th–8th centuries in the Carpathian-Danube-Pontic area. A. Fixed plate buckles]." *Arheologia Moldovei* 14 (1991): 117–138.

Teodor, Dan Gh. "Unele consideraţii privind originea şi cultura anţilor." *Arheologia Moldovei* 16 (1993): 205–213.

Teodor, Dan Gh. "Slavii la nordul Dunării de Jos în secolele VI–VII d. Hr. [The Slavs north of the Lower Danube in the 6th–7th centuries AD]." *Arheologia Moldovei* 17 (1994): 223–251.

Teodor, Dan Gh. "Cercei cu pandantiv stelat din secolele VI–VIII d.Hr. în spaţiul carpato-dunăreano-pontic." Arheologia Moldovei 18 (1995): 187–206.

Teodor, Dan Gh. *Meşteşugurile în secolele IV–XI* [Crafts to the north of the Lower Danube in the 4th–11th centuries]. Iaşi: Editura Helios, 1996.

Teodor, Dan Gh. "Fibules byzantines des Ve - VIIe siècles dans l'espace carpato-danubiano-pontique." *Études byzantines et post-byzantines* 3 (1997): 61–91.

Teodor, Dan Gh. *Descoperiri arheologice şi numismatice la est de Carpaţi în secolele V–XI d. H. (Contribuţii la continuitatea daco-romană şi veche românească)* [Archaeological and numismatic discoveries east of the Carpathians in the 5th–11th centuries AD (Contributions to the Dacian-Roman and Old Romanian continuity)]. Bucharest: Muzeul Naţional de Istorie a României, 1997.

Teodor, D. Gh. "Autohtoni şi slavi în spaţiul carpato-dunăreano-pontic în secolele VII–VIII d. Hr. [Natives and Slavs in the Carpathian-Danube-Pontic space in the 7th–8th centuries AD]." In *Spaţiul carpato-dunăreano-pontic în mileniul marilor migraţii*, collections of studies written by Dan Gh. Teodor, 421–426. Buzău: Alpha MDN, 2003.

Teodor, Dan Gh. "Tipare din secolele VI–XI d. Hr. în regiunile carpato-nistriene [Patterns from the 6th–11th centuries AD in the Carpathian-Dniestrian regions]." *Arheologia Moldovei* 28 (2005): 159–174.

Teodor, Dan Gh. *Un centru meşteşugăresc din evul mediu timpuriu. Cercetările arheologice de la Lozna-Botoşani* [A craft center from the Early Middle Ages. The archaeological research from Lozna-Botoşani]. Brăila: Editura Istros a Muzeului Brăilei, 2011.

Teodor, Dan Gh. "Necropola medievală timpurie de incineraţie de la Lozna-Botoşani [Early medieval cremation necropolis from Lozna-Botoşani]." *Arheologia Moldovei* 35 (2012): 253–269.

Teodor, Dan Gh. *Aşezarea medievală timpurie de la Suceava-Şipot* [Early medieval settlement from Suceava-Şipot]. Iaşi: Casa Editorială Demiurg Plus, 2013.

Teodor, Dan Gh., Mitrea, Ioan. "Cercetări arheologice în aşezarea prefeudală de la Lozna-Dorohoi [Archaeological research in the pre-feudal settlement of Lozna-Dorohoi]." *Arheologia Moldovei* 4 (1966): 279–291.

Teodor, Eugen S. Ceramica din Muntenia, de la sfârșitul veacului al V-lea până la mijlocul veacului al VII-lea [The pottery from Muntenia, from the end of the 5th century to the middle of the 7th century]. PhD dissertation, Universitatea "Alexandru Ioan Cuza" Iași, 2001. Available at http://www.esteo.ro/TTW/index_est.html. Accessed November 20, 2016.

Teodorescu, Victor. "Despre cultura Ipotești-Cîndești în lumina cercetărilor arheologice din nordul-estul Munteniei (regiunea Ploiești) [About the Ipotești-Cîndești culture in the light of archaeological researches in the north-east of Muntenia (Ploiești region)]." *Studii și Cercetări de Istorie Veche* 15, no. 4 (1964): 485–503.

Teodorescu, Victor. "Boucles d'oreille de l'époque romano-byzantine d'aprés les moules d'orfèvre trouvés au nord du Danube en Roumanie." In *Actes du XIV-e Congrès international des études byzantines. Résumés. Communications*, eds. Mihai Berza and Eugen Stănescu, 157–158. Bucharest: Editura Academiei RSR, 1971.

Teodorescu, Victor. "La civilisation Ipotești-Cîndești (V–VII-e s.)." In *Actes du VII-e Congrès international des sciences préhistoriques et protohistoriques, Prague 21–27 août 1966*, ed. Jan Filip, vol. 2, 1041–1044. Prague: Academia, 1971.

Teodorescu, Victor. "O nouă cultură arheologică recent precizată în țara noastră, cultura Ipotești-Cîndești (sec. V–VII) [A new archeological culture recently specified in our country, the Ipotești-Cîndești culture (5th–7th centuries)]." In *Sesiunea de comunicări științifice a muzeelor de istorie, dec. 1964*, vol. 2, 104–130. Bucharest, 1971.

Teodorescu, Victor. "Centre meșteșugărești din sec. V/VI–VII. e. n. în Bucharest [Craft centers from the 5/6th–7th century AD in Bucharest]." *Materiale de Istorie și Muzeografie* 9 (1972): 73–99.

Teodorescu, Victor, Peneș, Marinela. "Matricea de incidență a siturilor arheologice de la Budureasca (Budureasca 1–31) [The incidence matrix of the archaeological sites from Budureasca (Budureasca 1–31)]." *Anuarul Prahova* 1 (1984): 11–50.

Teodorescu, Victor, Dupoi, Vasile, Peneș, Marinela, Lichiardopol, Dan, Panait, Gheorghe. "Stațiunea arheologică Budureasca, jud. Prahova. Complexe daco-romane și străromânești [Budureasca archeological station, Prahova county. Daco-Roman and Ancestor Romanians complexes]." *Materiale și Cercetări Arheologice* 17 (1993): 365–387.

Teodorescu, Victor, Dupoi, Vasile, Peneș, Marinela, Panait, Gheorghe. "Budureasca, străveche și statornică vatră de civilizație la originile poporului român (Cercetările arheologice din anul 1983 privind complexele străromânești de tip Ipotești-Cândești, sec. V–VII e. n.) [Budureasca, ancient and steadfast hearth of civilization at the origins of the Romanian people (The archaeological researches from 1983 regarding the Ancestor Romanians complexes of type Ipotești-Cândești, 6th–7th centuries AD)]." *Mousaios* 5 (1999): 91–122.

Terteci, Carol. "Despre cultura Ipotești-Cândești în județul Vâlcea [About the culture Ipotești-Cândești in Vâlcea county]." *Buridava. Studii și Materiale* VIII (2010): 103–110.

Tettamanti, Sarolta. *Das awarenzeitliche Gräberfeld in Vác-Kavicshánya*. Budapest: Magyar Nemzeti Múzeum, 2000.

Tobias, Bendeguz. "Die awarenzeitlichen Sieblöffel im Karpatenbecken." *Communicationes Archaeologicae Hungaricae* (2001): 161–182.

Tobias, Bendeguz. Frühmittelalterliche Gräber mit Beigabe von Schmiedewerkzeugen. Einleitung. PhD dissertation: Wien 2008, 7–9. Unpublished: Available at https://www.academia.edu/24313533/B._Tobias_Frühmittelalterliche_Gräber_mit_Beigabe_von_Schmiedewerkzeugen_Diss._Universität_Wien_2008. Accessed November 11, 2017.

Tobias, Bendeguz. "Eliten und Schmiedegräber – Untersuchungen zu frühmittelalterlichen Gräbern mit Schmiedewerkzeugen im Rahmen des Eliteprojektes." In *Aufstieg und Untergang: Zwischenbilanz des Forschungsschwerpunktes "Studien zu Genese und Struktur von Eliten in vor-und frühgeschichtlichen Gesellschaften"*, ed. Markus Egg and Dieter Quast, 143–152. Mainz: Verlag des Römisch-Germanischen Zentralmuseums, 2009.

Toropu, Octavian. *Romanitatea târzie și stră-românii în Dacia traiană sud-carpatică*. Craiova: Editura Scrisul Românesc, 1976.

Tóth, Elvira H., Horváth, Attila. *Kunbábony. Das Grab eines Awarenkhagans*. Kecskemét, 1992.

Török, Béla, Kovács, Árpád, Gallina, Zsolt. "Iron metallurgy of the Pannonian Avars of the 7th–9th century based on excavations and material examinations." In *Archaeometallurgy in Europe* III. *Proceedings of the 3rd International Conference, Deutsches Bergbau-Museum, Bochum, June 29–July 1, 2011*, eds. Andreas Hauptmann and Diana Modarressi-Tehrani, 229–238. Bochum: Deutsches Bergbau-Museum, 2015.

Trugly, Alexander. "Gräberfeld aus der Zeit des awarischen Reiches bei der Schiffswerft in Komárno II." *Slovenská Archeológia* 41, no. 2 (1993): 191–307.

Turčan, Vladimir. "Hroby zlatníkov v 6.–7. Storočí v Karpatskej Kotline [Burials of Goldsmith of the 6th–7th centuries AD in the Carpathian Basin]." *Archeologickè rozbledy* 36 (1984): 481–489.

Uenze, Syna. "Die Schnallen mit Riemenschlaufe aus dem 6. und 7. Jahrh." *Bayerische Vorgeschichtsblätter* 31, no. 1–2 (1966): 142–186.

Ungureanu, Dan. "*Româna și dialectele italiene* [*Romanian and the Italian Dialects*]." Bucharest: Editura Acadèmiei Române, 2016.

Varsik, Vladimir. "Byzantinische Gürtelschnallen im mittleren und unteren Donauraum im 6. und 7. Jahrhundert." *Slovenská Archeológia* 11, no. 1 (1992): 77–108.

Vályi, Katalin. "Das Detail eines spätawarenzeitlichen Gräberfeldes in Szeged-Kiskundorozsma-Hármashatár." A Móra Ferenc Múzeum Évkönyve, Studia Archaeologica 9 (2003): 211–227.

Velter, Ana-Maria. *Transilvania în secolele V–XII. Interpretări istorico-politice și economice pe baza descoperirilor monetare din bazinul carpatic, secolele V–XII* [Transylvania in the 5th–12th centuries. Historical-political and economic interpretations based on the monetary discoveries in the Carpathian Basin, 5th–12th centuries]. Bucharest: Paideia, 2002.

Vida, Tivadar. "Conflict and coexistence: the local population of the Carpathian Basin under Avar rule (sixth to seventh century)." In *The Other Europe in the Middle Ages. Avars, Bulgars, Khazars and Cumans. East Central and Eastern Europe in the Middle Ages, 450–1450*, ed. Florin Curta and Roman Kovalev, 13–46. Leiden-Boston: Brill, 2008.

Vida, Tivadar. "'They Asked to be Settled in Pannonia ...' A Study on Integration and Acculturation – the Case of the Avars." In *Between Byzantium and the Steppe. Archaeological and Historical Studies in Honour of Csanád Bálint on the Occasion of his 70th Birthday*, eds. Ádám Bollók, Gergely Csiky and Tivadar Vida, 251–270. Budapest: Institute of Archaeology, Research Centre for the Humanities, Hungarian Academy of Sciences, 2016.

Vida, Tivadar. *Die frühbyzantinische Messingkanne mit Jagdszenen von Budakalász (Ungarn)*. Budapest: Institut für Archaeologie. Forschungzentrum für Humanwissenschaften Ungarische Akademie der Wissenschaften, 2017.

Vida, Tivadar, Pásztor, Adrien. "Der beschlagverzierte Gürtel der Awaren am Beispiel des Inventars von Budakalász-Dunapart, Ungarn, Grab 696." In *Reitervölker aus dem Osten. Hunnen + Awaren. Ausstellungskatalog*, ed. Falko Daim, 341–348. Eisenstadt: Amt der Burgenländischen Landesregierung, 1996.

Vierck, Hayo. "Werke des Eligius." In *Festschrift für Joachim Werner*, 2 vols., ed. Georg Kossack and Ulbert Günter, 309–378. Munich: C. H. Beck, 1974.

Vinski, Zdenko. "O nalazima 6. i 7. stoleća u jugoslaviji s posebnim obzirom na arheološku ostavštinu iz vremena prvog avarskoga kaganata [On the findings of the 6th and 7th centuries in Yugoslavia with special reference to the archeological heritage from the time of the first Avar kaganate]." *Opuscula Archaeologica/Radovi Arheološkog zavoda* 3 (1958): 13–67.

Voișian, Valentin, Țentea, Ovidiu, Cauuet, Béatrice et al. "Roșia Montană, jud. Alba (Alburnus Maior). Punct: Cârnic [Roșia Montană, Alba County (Alburnus Maior). Point: Cârnic]." In *Cronica cercetărilor arheologice din România (campania 2003)*, eds. Mircea Victor Angelescu, Irina Oberländer-Târnoveanu, Florela Vasilescu, Carmen Bem, Paula Jercan and Irina Nicolae, 283–288. Bucharest: cIMeC Institutul de Memorie Culturală, 2004.

Volodarets-Urbanovych, Ya. V. "Pronizki epokhi rann'ogo seredn'ovichchia zi slov'ians'kikh pam'iatok pivdnia Skhidnoi Evropy [Bronze tubular beads of early medieval Slavic antiquities]." *Arkheologiia i Davnia istoriia Ukraini* 13, no. 2 (2014): 37–49.

Volodarets-Urbanovych, Ya. V. "Pronizki epokhi rann'ogo seredn'ovichchia zi slov'ians' kikh pam'iatok pivdnia Skhidnoi Evropy [Bronze tubular beads of early medieval Slavic antiquities from the South of Eastern Europe sites]." In *Starozhitnosti Livoberezhnogo Podniprov'ia* (2014): 10–39.

Volodarets-Urbanovych, Ya. V. "Livarni formochki slov'ian rann'ogo seredn'ovichchia reinterpretatsiia znakhidok [Casting molds of the early medieval Slavs: a reinterpretation of finds]." *Arkheologiia i Davnia istoriia Ukraini* 22, no. 1 (2017): 331–346.

Vynokur, Ion S. *Slov'ianski iuveliry Podnistrov'ia. Za materialai doslidzhen Bernashivskoho kompleksu serediny I tys.n.e.* [Slavic Jewels of the Dniester. According to the research of the Bernashivskoho complex in the middle of the 1st millennium AD]. Oium: Kamyanets Podil'sky, 1997.

Vynokur, Ion S. "Ein Goldschmiede-Fundkomplex frühmittelalterlicher Slawen." *Archaeoslavica* 3 (1998): 209–226.

Werner, Joachim. "Slawische Bügelfibeln des 7. Jahrhunderts." In *Festschrift zum 75. Geburstag von Paul Reinecke am 25 September 1947*, eds. Gustav Behrens and Joachim Werner, 150–172. Mainz: E. Schneider Verlag, 1950.

Werner, Joachim. "Waage und Geld in der Merowingerzeit." *Sitzungsberichte der Bayerischen Akademie der Wissenschaften. Philosophisch-historische Klasse* (1) (1954): 3–40.

Werner, Joachim. *Die Langobarden in Pannonien. Beiträge zur Kenntniss der langobardischen Bodenfunde vor 568.* Munich: Verlag der Bayerischen Akademie der Wissenschaften, 1962.

Werner, Joachim. "Fernhandel und Naturwirtschaft im östlichen Merowingerreich nach archäologischen Zeugnissen." *Bericht der Reinisch-Germanischen Komission* 42 (1962): 307–346.

Werner, Joachim. "Zur Verbreitung frühgeschichtlicher Metallarbeiten (Werkstatt -Wanderhandwerk-Handel-Familienverbindung)." *Antikvarist arkiv* 38 (1970): 65–81.

Windisch, Rudolf. "Die frühesten Erwähnugen der Rumänen und ihrer Vorfahren in den antiken, bzyantinischen, mittelalterlichen und neuren Quellen." *Buletinul Bibliotecii Române: studii și documente românești* (Freiburg Breisgau) 8 (12) (1980–1981): 153–192.

Windisch, Rudolf. "Teza lui Robert Rösler – O sută de ani mai târziu [Robert Rösler's thesis – One hundred years later]," in *Logos Semantikos. Studia linguistica in honorem Eugenio Coseriu*, ed. Jürgen Trabant, volume 1, 405–415. Madrid/Berlin/New York: Editorial Gredos Madrid, Walter de Gruyter Berlin-New York, 1981.

Windisch, Rudolf. "Die Herkunft der Rumänen im Lichte der deutschen Forschung." *Vox Romanica* 41 (1982): 46–72.

Wolters, Jochem. "Goldschmied, Goldschmiedekunst." In *Reallexicon der germanischen Altertumskunde*, vol. 12, eds. Heinrich Beck, Heiko Steuer and Dieter Timpe, 362–386. Berlin-New York: Walter de Gruyter, 1998.

Zaharia, Eugenia. "La station n° 2 de Bratei, Dép. de Sibiu (VIe - VIIIe siècles)." *Dacia Nouvelle Série* 38–39 (1994–1995): 297–356.

Zanini, Enrico. "Artisans and Traders in the Early Byzantine City: Exploring the Limits of Archaeological Evidence." In *Social and Political Life in Late Antiquity*, eds. William Bowden, Adam Gutteridge and Carlos Machado, 373–411. Leiden/Boston: Brill, 2006.

Zdroba, Mircea, Barbu, Mircea. "Săpăturile arheologice de la Felnac și Vladimirescu (rapoarte preliminare) [The archaeological excavations from Felnac and Vladimirescu (preliminary reports)]." *Ziridava* 6 (1976): 47–56.

Index

www.ingramcontent.com/pod-product-compliance
Lightning Source LLC
LaVergne TN
LVHW010638300926
849161LV00005B/981

* 9 7 8 9 0 0 4 3 8 0 3 7 0 *